Modern American Prose

Fifteen Writers + 15

Modern American Prose

Third Edition

Fifteen Writers + 15

John Clifford
University of North Carolina, Wilmington

Robert DiYanni
Pace University, Pleasantville

McGraw-Hill, Inc.
New York St. Louis San Francisco Auckland Bogotá
Caracas Lisbon London Madrid Mexico City Milan
Montreal New Delhi San Juan Singapore
Sydney Tokyo Toronto

This book is printed on acid-free paper.

This book was developed by STEVEN PENSINGER, Inc.

MODERN AMERICAN PROSE
Fifteen Writers +15

Acknowledgments appear on pages 691–697, and on this page by reference.

10 11 12 13 14 15 DOC/DOC 0 9 8 7 6 5 4 3 2 1

ISBN 0-07-011396-3

This book was set in Baskerville by The Clarinda Company.
The editors were Steve Pensinger and John M. Morriss;
the production supervisor was Phil Galea.
The cover was designed by Karen K. Quigley.
Project supervision was done by The Clarinda Company.
R. R. Donnelley & Sons Company was printer and binder.

Library of Congress Cataloging-in-Publication Data

Modern American prose: fifteen writers + 15 / [edited by] John Clifford, Robert
    DiYanni.—3rd ed.
        p.   cm.
    ISBN 0-07-011396-3
    1. College readers.   2. English language—Rhetoric.   3. American prose
literature—20th century.   I. Clifford, John.   II. DiYanni, Robert.
PE1417.M57   1993
808'.0427—dc20   92-124

About the Editors

John Clifford is a professor of English at the University of North Carolina at Wilmington (UNCW) where he teaches literature, writing, and theory. In the summer he also teaches at the University of Pennsylvania's Graduate School of Education and at Northeastern University's Martha's Vineyard Institute. He taught high school English for ten years in Brooklyn, New York, and worked for four years in the writing program at Queens College, City University of New York, before moving to UNCW in 1978. He was a National Endowment for the Humanities Fellow at the University of Southern California, 1980–1981 in literature and literacy.

Professor Clifford studied literary theory with Louise Rosenblatt at New York University, and wrote his dissertation for his Ph.D. in 1977 on collaborative learning and composition. He has written articles and reviews on literary and writing theory for *College English, College Composition and Communication, English Journal, Journal of Advanced Composition, Rhetoric Review, Reader,* and others. Recent essays have appeared in *Contending with Words, The Right to Literacy, Literary Nonfiction, New Voices in Collaborative Learning,* and *Pedagogy is Politics.* He has edited a collection of essays on Louise Rosenblatt, *The Experience of Reading,* and has co-authored several other books, including *Writing, Reading, and Research* and *Constellations.* With John Schilb, he is currently editing a collection of essays, *Writing Theory and Critical Theory,* for the Modern Language Association.

Robert DiYanni is Professor of English and Director of Inter-disciplinary Studies at Pace University, Pleasantville, New York, where he teaches courses in literature, writing, and humanities. He has also taught at Queens College of the City University of New York, at New York University in the Graduate Rhetoric Program, and most recently in the Expository Writing Program at Harvard University. He received his B.A. from Rutgers University and his Ph.D. from the City University of New York, with interim study at the Johns Hopkins University.

Professor DiYanni has written articles and reviews on various aspects of literature, composition, and pedagogy. His books include *Literature, The Art of Reading, Prose Pieces, Women's Voices, Modern American Poets,* and most recently, *The McGraw-Hill Book of Poetry.* Current projects include a critical study of reader-response theory, a handbook, and an introduction to the humanities. Robert DiYanni resides in Bedford, New York, with his wife, Mary, and his children, Karen and Michael.

In memory of our fathers

Patrick J. Clifford (1905–1991)
Edward S. DiYanni (1921–1987)

Contents

SEVENTEEN
Other Voices

Thematic Table of Contents

History and Politics

Science and Technology

Work and Play

Race, Culture, and Society

The Natural World

Relationships

Personal Values

Writing and Language

Ignorance and Insight

Rhetorical Table of Contents

Persuasion

Preface

Modern American Prose: Fifteen Writers + 15 is based upon our conviction that reading and writing are reciprocal acts that
should be integrated rather than separated. Because reading and
writing stimulate and reinforce one another, we believe that the
best way to go about either is to ally it with the other. Associated
with this belief in the reciprocity of reading and writing is anoth
er: that in addition to their own writing, students can profit most
as readers and writers from reading essays that are accessible,
engaging, thought-provoking, and, above all, well crafted. In saying this we do not mean to deny that students learn to write primarily by writing, but rather to suggest that in learning to read
and respond critically to their own writing and to the writing of
others—both amateurs and professionals alike—students mature
as writers themselves.

The essayists whose works we anthologize are among the
best of contemporary American writers. Taken together they have
produced a diversified and substantial body of outstanding
nonfictional prose. Ranging widely in subject, style, structure, and
tone, their prose includes autobiographical and polemical essays,
observations and speculations, reminiscences and sketches, medi-
tations and expostulations, celebrations and attacks. Overall, our
selections from their works offer a balance of the flamboyant and
innovative with the restrained and classically lucid.

This third edition of *Modern American Prose* follows the principles that guided the first: to select as models for student writing
contemporary American essays from among our best prose stylists;
to offer multiple selections from the work of each writer. The
changes we have made in this edition increase the range and

scope of the text. We have replaced two writers from the second edition—Norman Mailer and Lillian Hellman—with Barry Lopez and Maxine Hong Kingston, each represented with four selections. In addition we have freshened the selections for all but a few of the other writers. Finally, we have added selections from fifteen other essays to increase the range and diversity of voices and visions represented.

Our aim in choosing selections for *Modern American Prose* has been to collect between the covers of one book some of the most distinctive nonfiction of the last fifty years, written by American writers who have something to say and know how to say it powerfully. It has been our experience that nonfictional prose in general and the essay in particular have been underrated as literature. Traditionally accorded secondary status behind the major genres of fiction, poetry, and drama, the essay has consistently been relegated to a literary limbo. But this has recently begun to change. Nonfictional prose has benefited from the revitalization of studies in rhetoric and composition as well as from the upsurge of scholarly work in linguistics and style. Also contributing to the belated recognition of the literary stature of nonfictional prose has been the rise of the new journalism. New journalistic experiments with the novel-as-history and with the nonfiction novel along with a general elevation in the significance of brute fact and sharply observed details of social and personal history have all contributed to the acceptability of the essay as a flexible instrument for recording reality and expressing the self.

By concentrating on fifteen writers, we have been able to include at least four essays by each. We have done this because we believe students can come closer to an understanding of an author's ideas, style, and tone by encountering more than one example of his or her work. Within the selections from a particular writer we have tried to offer variety of subject, purpose, tone, and length of essay. And we have included, for the most part, either complete essays, complete chapters, or self-contained sections of books. In addition, we have tried to show each writer working in the four rhetorical modes: narration, description, exposition, and argumentation. Sometimes these modes are kept fairly pure. Far more often, however, they are mixed in complex and interesting ways, as in Joan Didion's essay "On Going Home," which is reprinted along with an extended commentary in the Introduction.

To help students simultaneously become more critical readers and more confident writers, we have provided a thorough discussion of how to read and respond to essays (the Introduction).
In addition, following each essay selection is an extensive set of
questions designed to guide students through a careful reading—
or rereading—of the pieces, and to assist them in analyzing their
style, structure, and meaning. The group of questions headed
"Ideas" is meant to serve as a set of probes, a series of ways into
the author's main point or central idea. The questions on
"Organization," "Sentences," and "Words" invite students to look
closely at the writer's craft. Our "Suggestions for Writing" invite
students to learn to write by writing, with the essayists as exem-
plars and fellow writers. Some of these writing suggestions ask for
short, informal opinions, often as reactions to an author's ideas.
Other assignments ask for more considered assessments of style,
form, and meaning. Still others ask students to imitate effective
patterns of language and form, in phrase, sentence, paragraph,
essay. For a few essays we have avoided categorizing our questions
because we wanted to focus less on aspects of style than on what
the writers have to say about writing as craft and vocation.

Beyond these aids to reading and writing we have written, for
each writer, a headnote that subordinates biographical and biblio-
graphical information to focus on how and why each writes. In these
introductory headnotes we have explored different facets of the
writer's world: his or her writing habits, reasons for writing, methods
of composition, conceptions of intention, purpose, and design.
And in each we have commented briefly on the essays in that section.

Throughout *Modern American Prose* our intent has been to
help students read, understand, and imitate good writing in the
belief that, by providing students with guided practice in reading
and writing, we will help them increase both their competence
and their confidence. Through repeated acts of attention to their
own writing and to the writing of others, we expect students to
acquire a sense of the original meaning of "essay": a foray into
thought, an attempt to discover an idea, work out its implications,
and share it with others. And we hope further that our students
will come to see the essay as a way of both enriching their experience and discovering effective ways to communicate it.

John Clifford
Robert DiYanni

Editors' Acknowledgments

For assistance of varying kinds at different stages of our work we would like to thank our friends and colleagues who inspired, criticized, and sustained by listening carefully and giving good advice. Appreciation and thanks to Linnea Aycock, Cynthia Bathurst, Lil Brannon, Janet M. Ellerby, Janis Forman, Dennis Jarrett, Kathleen Kelly, Robert Lyons, Bill Naufftus, Steve Schmidt, Sally Sullivan, Karen Thomas, Myron Tuman, and Dick Veit, and to Wendy Gwathmey and Joyce Hollingsworth who did research, wrote drafts of questions, and gave expert advice at all stages of the third Edition. Thanks also to our reviewers Victoria Casana, Fred Crews, Richard Hootman, Paula Johnson, Dick Larson, and Don McQuade.

We have been fortunate in working with a knowledgeable and exacting professional staff at McGraw-Hill. We would like to thank especially Steve Pensinger and John Morriss. We also thank Carol Barnes and Pat Kolonosky, both of Kansas State University; Teresa M. Brown, University of Florida; Pat Hoy, Harvard University; Robert Lorenzi, Camden County College; Edward McCarthy, Harrisburg Area Community College; Robert G. Noreen, California State University at Northridge; David Schaafsma, Grand Valley State College; and Robert Seufert, MacMurray College.

Finally, we would like to thank our children, Christine and Pam Clifford, and Karen and Michael DiYanni, whose presence in our lives is a source of inspiration and joy.

John Clifford
Robert DiYanni

Modern American Prose

Fifteen Writers + 15

ONE

Introduction

1: READING ESSAYS

Common sense can often lead us astray. Most readers, for example, assume that the meaning of a story or essay is there, in the text. But that is only partially true. A writer certainly does have a theme in mind as he or she composes an essay, but equally important is what a competent reader brings to the work. The author's intention is only one of the three important ingredients in literary nonfiction. In a complete reading, the writer, the reader, and the text must all play their parts.

Critical reading, therefore, is a creative process, requiring active minds. The black marks on the white page have potential meaning, but they remain inert until readers bring the words to life in the reading process. That's not an exaggeration or a metaphor. Critical reading is not simply decoding from printed symbol to sound to meaning. It is, rather, an interaction or a transaction. What a particular reader gets from the page is a blend of that reader's experiences, ideas, and attitudes and the experiences, ideas, and attitudes the writer put in the text. Readers do not simply discover what is already there, like solving a puzzle. Instead, engaged readers use their familiarity with the conventions of writing as tools to make meaning. As readers, our previous experiences in the world, our present preoccupations and biases, our familiarity with the conventions of nonfiction, our knowledge of vocabulary, syntax, and organization join with a writer's intention at the crossroads of meaning. Although the

1

road has already been paved by the writer, only an active reader can give the journey significance.

An active response to a written text has long been considered an important dimension of the reading of literary texts, especially fictional ones. And although most college students think of essays as merely the packages that information comes in, we want to suggest that nonfiction texts, especially essays, require a similar kind of attentiveness and an equal degree of critical response. Even when the author's primary purpose is to convey information, as it is in many essays, the reader's contribution is also crucial. Reading involves two minds—the mind of the writer and the mind of the reader. And even though the writer isn't there to respond to your questions and criticisms or to your expressions of approval and disapproval, a real conversation can occur, as long as you respond honestly and fully.

Although some writing—the scientific prose in your biology text, for example—does try to minimize creative contributions, it still demands your participation. Whereas literature asks that you be an active reader, technical prose tries to keep you passively receptive to its purely informational or directional goal. Some scientific writers strive to be objective and detached through techniques such as omitting the use of "I," letting the subject of the sentence receive the action (via verbs in the passive voice), avoiding highly connotative words, and appealing primarily to logic. In technical writing, snappy, personal anecdotes, wide swings of feeling, and literary language are inappropriate.

Even so, if your background is inadequate on a particular subject, you will not make much sense of sophisticated scientific prose, regardless of how clearly and objectively it is written. Try reading a bridge or chess column without any practical experiences of those games: you will know the words, but because you do not bring enough background with you, you will not be able to read for meaning. If you can't bring the relevant knowledge to the reading, the content will be opaque. Of course, this need for background information is not limited just to reading. We all know people who think quality rock bands like Bruce Springsteen and the E Street Band and Pink Floyd all sound alike—noisy; while others think Bach, Mozart, and Beethoven all sound alike— classical. They can't "read" or hear the differences because they don't have the necessary knowledge and experience of the kind of music in question. The result is a blurring of distinctions, an oversimplifying and stereotyping of complex, individual forms of expression. Discrimination comes with experience. You rarely find what you don't even know exists: you see more when you know what to look for.

Although some of the essays in this collection deal with technical matters, they cannot be considered scientific writing. This may sound odd, but it isn't. The content of the essays is not the deciding factor. More telling is the way the ideas are presented. In distinguishing literary from scientific prose, an author's style, attitude, purpose, and organizational pattern are all more important than the essay's content, its facts. Lewis Thomas, for example, writes about DNA, symbiants, rhizobial bacteria, and death, with emotion and grace, in the most natural language. Perhaps Thomas's audience is crucial. He is not writing to fellow scientists, reporting on his latest research; he is writing to a much wider lay audience (of which you are a part). At times he tries to explain his deepest feelings about life and death, cells and computers; at times he tries to change your mind about the nature of man, hoping to share with you his awe at the complexity and wonder of our world. And he does all this with imagination and style. His aim is not exclusively to provide particular factual information; he wants instead to engage your intellect and imagination; he wants you to bring your own experiences to his essay so that reader and writer are both present, ready for an active conversation, an intellectual transaction. All the writers in this book offer an invitation to enter this kind of creative dialog, one that can lead to a literary experience. Because this conversation between reader and writer adds such an energizing dimension to the life of the mind, it is central to a vigorous university education.

In fact, many of the essays in this book *are* literature, and should be read as such. Although students generally know that poems, drama, and fiction are literature, they often assume that nonfiction is not. They figure that since literature involves the imaginative and the fanciful, nonfiction, especially essays, do not qualify as serious literature. This attitude, we believe, denies status to undeniably great works of imagination and literary art—works like Boswell's *Life of Samuel Johnson,* Gibbon's *Decline and Fall of the Roman Empire,* essays such as Swift's "A Modest Proposal" and Lamb's "A Dissertation on Roast Pig." Because these works don't fall under the canonized literary categories of poetry, drama, or fiction, they are accorded an inferior place as literary or belletristic works, but not literature.

Without pursuing the complex issue of just how "literature" ought to be defined, we want to suggest that works of nonfiction such as the essays included in this collection should be accorded the same status, granted the same respect, and read with the same care as a poem by Robert Frost or a story by Joyce Carol Oates. Like a Frost poem or an Oates story, many of the essays in this volume will reward repeated readings. They invite and gratify a considered and deliberate reading primarily because the authors gave as much attention to diction, voice, image, form, and theme as they gave to information.

The distinction between fiction and nonfiction raises one other problem: the puzzle of what is real, of what a fact is. Norman Mailer's book *The Executioner's Song* and some of his earlier work, including *Miami and the Siege of Chicago* and *The Armies of the Night,* are based on fact, on historical events, on real people. But they are also novelistic in technique. His books oscillate uneasily between fact and fiction, history and novel, objective reality and subjective response. As a result, there is considerable confusion about how to read them and what to label them.

The traditional division between factual and fictional discourse creates more problems than it solves. The notion that nonfiction mirrors reality while literature creates its own reality is oversimplified. Joan Didion has a relevant comment in her essay "On Keeping a Notebook": "Not only have I always had trouble distinguishing what happened and what merely might have happened, but I remain unconvinced that the distinction, for my purposes, matters." The essays in this anthology use language in such a way that they help readers give birth to a new creation. They are nonfiction, but they are also literature.

And literature, as we have said, demands more than your attention: it demands your active participation as well. Without you, these essays are merely texts; with your imaginative participation they become something more: literary experiences. And to do your part you don't have to be a highly skilled reader, knowledgeable about esoteric writing techniques and about a wide range of topics. Yet, there is no denying that these essays were written to be read by good readers. We expect that you are one of these good readers, or that in working through the essays, you will become one.

II: READING TECHNIQUES

To emphasize our point that literature requires active readers, we said that scientific writing tries to discourage imagination, to make the words point to specific objects in the world. That is true, in a way. It would be better, however, to think of prose as a continuum with imaginative literature on one end and pure scientific discourse on the other. The essays in this book would lie somewhere in between. Strangely enough, much will depend on your attitude and on the special reading you give each essay. One thing to observe as you read essays is how much the language differs from conventional practice. Poetry, for example, consciously calls attention to its language. Technical language, on the other hand, tries for anonymity, with attention focused only on the message. When you are trying to read instructions for defusing a bomb, for example, you want the language to be as clear as a pane of glass. Essays generally fall between the density and resonance of poetry and the clarity and directness of a set of directions, often containing something of each.

To get the most out of reading the nonfiction in this book, then, you will need to read each piece more than once. You will want to focus primarily on ideas the first time and then on organization and style, keeping in mind, however, that content and form are ultimately inseparable.

There are, nonetheless, different ways to read. You can, if you want, read the most lyrical of poems for information; or you can read a physics text for its syntax and structure. Here, we are asking for a synthesis, for a balanced reading, attending first to ideas, then to structure and syntax. To get a full reading, you will be called on to use your imagination and your analytical ability, or in a current formulation, to integrate the right and left sides of your brain, to blend intuition with logic.

Reading literature is not a one-shot event, it is a process that involves repetition and reflection. Meaning emerges out of the fog only after you read, reflect, reread, and reflect again. As with writing, few people get it right the first time, or even the second. If, as Thoreau noted, books should be read with the same care and deliberation with which they were written, then your investment of time in repeated readings of these essays will be essential for real understanding. This kind of investment of time and effort will also be a necessary first step toward literary competence and confidence. To gain that competence and to acquire that confidence, we suggest the following reading sequence:

1. Read the essay through in one sitting. When you finish, jot down some notes indicating what the piece was about, if only in a literal sense. This simple notemaking about the essay's subject and ideas should help you clarify what the piece is about. Be sure to notice your personal reactions, your subjective responses, to the events and the ideas of the essay. These seemingly random associations are part of the unique baggage each of us brings to reading. In reading an essay about death, for example, we can't ignore our preconceptions about suicide, nor can we forget our biases for or against rap when reading an article about popular music. Meaning exists, Kenneth Burke suggests, in the "margin of overlap between the writer's experience and the reader's." Don't try to deny that you are a person whose experiences and ideas are relevant. It is important that your gender, race, class, ethnicity, and so forth not be forgotten. Since the writer of the essay certainly didn't, neither should you.

The easiest way to bring these valuable associations to the surface is to write quickly for a few minutes, sketching your immediate feelings and thoughts in any order that occurs to you. Concentrate on getting down an honest, detailed response: if you were bored or confused, say so. But try to locate the source of the boredom or confusion. Finally, write one or two sentences about your impression of the author's point in this piece, that is, the theme or generalization that might cover or bind together most of the information the essay presents. Remember: depending on your experiences and attitudes, or even on your present mood, you will probably have different notions about what this general statement might be, especially after one reading.

2. Do your second reading, remembering that it will probably be different from the first: no two readings can be the same, especially since you will be integrating the memory of the first reading experience with this more informed second reading. This is the excitement and surprise of reading literary exposition: each encounter is unique, each reading unfolds new insights and new possibilities. As you read, try to fill in the gaps, to creatively participate in the literary experience. After this reading, jot down your reaction. Has the writer's focus now become clearer to you? What minor points are developed?

This is also the time to begin seeing how the parts of the essay work together. A crucial question in this regard is the rela- tion between the theme (or the purpose) and the material the author presents to support it. What is the relationship between the general and the specific, the abstract and the concrete? Another important consideration is whether the writer presents the main point in the introduction and then supports it in the body, or whether he or she builds up to the point, arranging facts, anecdotes, events, and arguments in such a way that the point is made forcefully in the conclusion. Ask yourself also about the major parts, and whether there are natural "blocks of discourse," that is, paragraphs that go together, that develop the same idea. Although it may sound strange to you, the purpose of taking an essay apart like this is to better understand how it was put togeth- er. An active reader first analyzes, then synthesizes.

3. At the end of your second reading, take note of the voice, the personality, you hear. It may be forceful and direct; it may be effacing and oblique. Sometimes you'll hear the same writer being alternately sarcastic and tender. Each time we write we need to decide anew what mask—or persona—will work best. Of course, the writer's ideas are important in determining tone, but equally crucial is how they are stated. Read groups of sentences out loud, slowly. Try to see how close the writing is to the rhythms of speech. Some writers, like Didion and Thomas, will seem clear and natural; others, like Baldwin and Eiseley, will seem elaborate, formal, and complex. Try to explain to yourself why this is so.

4. You are now ready for the third and best reading of all, the one that should clarify your impressions of the author's theme, persona, and arguments. You will also be more aware of why you are responding to certain ideas and images. If you focus primarily on one thing, and another reader focuses on something else, it doesn't mean one of you is wrong. Perhaps you are both responding openly to the rich possibilities of literature. If in dis- cussing your responses and in analyzing the craft of expository writing you find yourself differing from others in the class, you should look to the text to see if you can support your reading. If you think the text validates your minority view, it might be because your experiences, your attitudes, or your expectations dif- fer from those of your classmates. Fine. Literary critics have been arguing for hundreds of years over Hamlet's madness and

Macbeth's motives. As a dissenter, you are in the best of company. What is important is that you learn to engage intelligently in the process of analytical reading.

We will try to illustrate some ideas by looking at the following essay by Joan Didion. One editor of this book, John Clifford, then presents his response to the essay in order to illustrate one possible approach, one reading among many he might have chosen, depending on his audience and his purposes. A psychologist's first reaction would be quite different, as would that of a teenage reader from China, or an elderly woman from Italy. All readers are different simply because people are. That notion should give you confidence in responding. You shouldn't be looking for what the teacher wants or what critics see. Your ideas and experiences and your training as a reader will enable you to feel, think, and read with your own personal style. That's just as it should be in a university setting that encourages critical and speculative discussion.

Reading well, then, means reading on several levels. One teacher, Robert Scholes from Brown University, has a useful set of definitions about how to do this, how to give more dimension to your responses.

In *Reading,* suggests Professor Scholes, we decode and paraphrase, attempting a literal translation of the text. In the average college classroom there will be a rough agreement about what happens in most of the nonfiction in this text. There will be a general consensus, in such classrooms, about the subject of the essays and their general purpose. In *Interpretation* we move beyond "what's there" to what it means, to generalizations about society or human nature, to looking at events or details as standing for something else, something representative. In moving from reading to interpretation, there will be more differences of opinion, more individual responses. The more homogeneous the class, the more consensus. The more diverse the class, the less agreement about meaning. In *Criticism* we reach outside the text to the world. We take issue with the writer's ideas, his or her vision of right and wrong; we compare the social issues in the story or essay with the world we know; we may be angered by a character's racism or sexism; we may accuse the writer of oversimplifying leftist politics, or of unfairly stereotyping the military.

According to Scholes's formulation, in *reading* we create a text within a text; in *interpreting* we produce a text upon a text;

and in *criticism* we generate a text against a text. If you were reading directions for assembling a computer, *reading* would be primary. In reading a lyric poem, you might highlight *interpretation*, whereas in a realistic novel, *criticism* might be more important. Of course, all three are to be considered in reading most literature.

In the following essay, the *reading* is fairly simple, but the literary nature of Didion's piece encourages a range of *interpretations* and *criticism*. In the scientific essays of Lewis Thomas and Stephen Jay Gould, the *reading* is more difficult, but they still require some *interpretation* and *criticism*. See if you can unravel these three aspects of response in the notes that follow Didion's classic essay, "On Going Home."

On Going Home

---

1   I am home for my daughter's first birthday. By "home" I do not mean the house in Los Angeles where my husband and I and the baby live, but the place where my family is, in the Central Valley of California. It is a vital although troublesome distinction. My husband likes my family but is uneasy in their house, because once there I fall into their ways, which are difficult, oblique, deliberately inarticulate, not my husband's ways. We live in dusty houses ("D-U-S-T," he once wrote with his finger on surfaces all over the house, but no one noticed it) filled with mementos quite without value to him (what could the Canton dessert plates mean to him? how could he have known about the assay scales, why should he care if he did know?), and we appear to talk exclusively about people we know who have been committed to mental hospitals, about people we know who have been booked on drunk-driving charges, and about property, particularly about property, land, price per acre and C-2 zoning and assessments and freeway access. My brother does not understand my husband's inability to perceive the advantage in the rather common real-estate transaction known as "sale-leaseback," and my husband in turn does not understand why so many of the people he hears about in my father's house have recently been committed to mental hospitals or booked on drunk driving charges. Nor does he understand

that when we talk about sale-leasebacks and right-of-way condem-
nations we are talking in code about the things we like best, the
yellow fields and the cottonwoods and the rivers rising and falling
and the mountain roads closing when the heavy snow comes in.
We miss each other's points, have another drink and regard the
fire. My brother refers to my husband, in his presence, as "Joan's
husband." Marriage is the classic betrayal.

2   Or perhaps it is not any more. Sometimes I think that those
of us who are now in our thirties were born into the last generation to carry the burden of "home," to find in family life the
source of all tension and drama. I had by all objective accounts a
"normal" and a "happy" family situation, and yet I was almost thirty years old before I could talk to my family on the telephone
without crying after I had hung up. We did not fight. Nothing was
wrong. And yet some nameless anxiety colored the emotional
charges between me and the place that I came from. The question of whether or not you could go home again was a very real
part of the sentimental and largely literary baggage with which we
left home in the fifties; I suspect that it is irrelevant to the children born of the fragmentation after World War II. A few weeks
ago in a San Francisco bar I saw a pretty young girl on crystal take
off her clothes and dance for the cash prize in an "amateur-top-
less" contest. There was no particular sense of moment about this,
none of the effect of romantic degradation, of "dark journey," for
which my generation strived so assiduously. What sense could that
girl possibly make of, say, *Long Day's Journey into Night?* Who is
beside the point?

3   That I am trapped in this particular irrelevancy is never
more apparent to me than when I am home. Paralyzed by the
neurotic lassitude engendered by meeting one's past at every
turn, around every corner, inside every cupboard, I go aimlessly
from room to room. I decide to meet it head-on and clean out a
drawer, and I spread the contents on the bed. A bathing suit I
wore the summer I was seventeen. A letter of rejection from The
Nation, an aerial photograph of the site for a shopping center my
father did not build in 1954. Three teacups hand-painted with
cabbage roses and signed "E.M.," my grandmother's initials.
There is no final solution for letters of rejection from The Nation
and teacups hand-painted in 1900. Nor is there any answer to
snapshots of one's grandfather as a young man on skis, surveying
around Donner Pass in the year 1910. I smooth out the snapshot

and look into his face, and do and do not see my own. I close the drawer, and have another cup of coffee with my mother. We get along very well, veterans of a guerrilla war we never understood.

4   Days pass. I see no one. I come to dread my husband's evening call, not only because he is full of news of what by now seems to me our remote life in Los Angeles, people he has seen, letters which require attention, but because he asks what I have been doing, suggests uneasily that I get out, drive to San Francisco or Berkeley. Instead I drive across the river to a family graveyard. It has been vandalized since my last visit and the monuments are broken, overturned in the dry grass. Because I once saw a rattlesnake in the grass I stay in the car and listen to a country-and-Western station. Later I drive with my father to a ranch he has in the foothills. The man who runs his cattle on it asks us to the roundup, a week from Sunday, and although I know that I will be in Los Angeles I say, in the oblique way my family talks, that I will come. Once home I mention the broken monuments in the graveyard. My mother shrugs.

5   I go to visit my great-aunts. A few of them think now that I am my cousin, or their daughter who died young. We recall an anecdote about a relative last seen in 1948, and they ask if I still like living in New York City. I have lived in Los Angeles for three years, but I say that I do. The baby is offered a horehound drop, and I am slipped a dollar bill "to buy a treat." Questions trail off, answers are abandoned, the baby plays with the dust motes in a shaft of afternoon sun.

6   It is time for the baby's birthday party: a white cake, strawberry-marshmallow ice cream, a bottle of champagne saved from another party. In the evening, after she has gone to sleep, I kneel beside the crib and touch her face, where it is pressed against the slats, with mine. She is an open and trusting child, unprepared for and unaccustomed to the ambushes of family life, and perhaps it is just as well that I can offer her little of that life. I would like to give her more. I would like to promise her that she will grow up with a sense of her cousins and of rivers and of her great-grandmother's teacups, would like to pledge her a picnic on a river with fried chicken and her hair uncombed, would like to give her *home* for her birthday, but we live differently now and I can promise her nothing like that. I give her a xylophone and a sundress from Madeira, and promise to tell her a funny story.

III: A PERSONAL RESPONSE

1. Didion returns to her home in the Central Valley of California with her husband for her daughter's first birthday. Her husband's discomfort with her family makes Didion think marriage is a betrayal of family bonds. But then she wonders if young people today worry about "the burden of home" in the same way she did.

She wanders around her old home, poking into drawers, finding old clothes, letters, and snapshots. Her present home in Los Angeles now seems far away as she drives to family graves and visits great aunts who barely remember her. After the baby's party, she watches her child sleep and realizes that she will grow up with a different sense of home.

The following are my slightly edited notes written in response to "On Going Home," and in general accord with the sequence described earlier; they are not meant as a formal essay, merely the kind of notes you might write as you read. In a sense, they are writer-based, prepared not for readers but to help me understand my response to Didion's essay. I would have to do lots of rearranging and cutting to make these notes into a reader-based essay. Because I am trying to illustrate a technique I have tried to be detailed. Perhaps you will not want to do as much. And because I have different goals and a different reading background from you, you should not compare yours to mine, except to see how each of us follows the suggested steps.

The essay seems to be about the difference between Didion's sense of home now—as a grown woman—and her sense of it when she was a child. Is she talking about home as a place or as a point in time? Somehow I think she means both. I am wondering why she stayed for so long; her visits are probably infrequent. Her husband was uncomfortable in her house. I can understand that. Families seem to develop their own idiosyncratic ways of doing things, of relating to each other. I can understand his uneasiness: he couldn't bear all that real estate talk; neither could I.

I'm not sure what she means by marriage as the "classic betrayal." Perhaps she thinks her family felt rejected when she left home. But she takes that idea away in the second paragraph: "Perhaps it is not any more." I can see that time will be important here. This is probably an essay that comes to a resolution at the end Didion is giving me a record of her thinking; she is showing me how she arrived at her conclusion about the possibility of going home. Going home surely has a wider meaning than just physically returning. She says hers is the last generation to carry the burden of home. "Burden" is a strong word.

She claims she was normal but then talks about crying and about a nameless anxiety. Then she says it is different for those born of the "fragmentation after World War II." I guess that is the key to her concept of home. She seems to be focusing on the differences between the extended and the nuclear family. That's interesting for me, since I grew up in the forties and fifties during the break-up of the traditional family structure. My grandparents lived around the corner from me, and their nine children and their families all lived within ten city blocks. Their house was the center around which our lives revolved. Gradually, however, my aunts and uncles drifted off, first to the edges of the city and then to the growing suburbs of Long Island and New Jersey. And now, some thirty years later, we are scattered throughout the East, with a few grandchildren testing the exotic climes of Los Angeles and San Diego.

My grandmother's house was also a moral and cultural center. At holiday parties we had to ask her permission to play American music instead of traditional Irish ballads and dance music. So I can understand the poignancy of Didion's feeling that she was "beside the point," of feeling irrelevant. She had to struggle, as I did, to break away from the established moral and cultural traditions of an extended family. The topless girl, of course, never had those rules to begin with. And as I read this essay, I am thinking that my daughters, thousands of miles from my childhood neighborhood and decades from the conformity and pressure of a religious upbringing, will also never experience Didion's "dark journey." Their sense of morality will be mostly their own construction; they will have themselves to answer to, not to scores of relatives and to a tradition many centuries old.

As Didion walks through her former home, I also sense her mixed feelings of nostalgia and distance. I read the last sentence of the third paragraph several times: I'm not sure why she says "guerrilla war"; isn't that a contradiction of normal and happy? Perhaps not. But her not understanding makes sense. I don't think I ever understood the reasons for the disagreement, the points missed, the tension.

I am surprised that she dreads her husband's evening call. I would have thought she would be anticipating it, as an escape. Maybe her old ways are taking over again. When she visits her old aunts, I could not help but remember my last visit to my grandmother, then ninety-five: she thought I was several people, never me. And questions trailed off, answers were abandoned. Her description here seems very real.

In her conclusion she paints a vivid picture, one I've experienced many times: staring at my sleeping children, wondering about their future, their "possibilities," my hopes and dreams for them, and my fears about the world they will have to cope with. Will it be easier or harder? Didion's thoughts are clear: she wants for her daughter the myth of the happy extended family, a sense of roots and shared values, a connection to a rich cultural heritage, a sense of community, of belonging somewhere with people who accept and support your efforts. But realistically, she promises what she can: a xylophone, a sundress, and a story. I like that. She seems to be coming to grips with her break with the home she can never go back to. Instead of depression or anger, she thinks positively. She seems to be saying: "OK, things are not what they were or what they could be, but given the way I live now, this is the best I can do."

I am still wondering if she thinks her "home" in the Central Valley of California is worth going back to—back in the sense of becoming a part of an extended family, adopting its values, its idiosyncratic customs—or if she wants to go back in time to a simpler America, one with common purposes and dreams. Looking back to the first paragraph, I notice her description of her family's ways: "difficult, oblique, deliberately inarticulate." Then I remember the "nameless anxiety" of the second paragraph and the "guerrilla war" and "my mother shrugs." Finally, I looked at the third sentence in the last paragraph, especially the phrase "unprepared for and unaccustomed to the ambushes of family life, and perhaps it is just as well that I can offer her little of that life." All this certainly sounds negative, as if her daughter is better off without that home in the Central Valley. I am wondering why she didn't put a "Yet" before the next sentence: "I would like to give her more." More of what? Of the comforts and benefits of community? Surely Didion realizes that the positive feelings of belonging cannot be separated from the disadvantages of conformity.

2. After my second reading the focus does seem clearer. I think she is talking about accepting the present without attempting to recapture the past, a past that had a good many problems anyhow. I think she realizes that America has changed, that the old center—the extended family rooted for generations in the same place—is no more. New ways are replacing the old. But even if things fall apart, even if we cannot go home again, I do not sense pessimism or despair here. I sense rather a need to confront reality, to see what's possible. She is a realist; she does not offer false hope for a world that isn't (and perhaps wasn't).

Didion is not afraid to admit that her moral concerns are, in the modern world, irrelevant. She is not afraid to admit that she has ambiguous, contradictory feelings about her home: she longs for and flees from the "picnic on a river with fried chicken." After all, if the "young girl on crystal" taking off her clothes is the result of the atomization of modern life, then perhaps an alternative is to be hoped for. Somehow winning an amateur topless contest strung out on acid in front of tipsy strangers doesn't seem like much of a victory for freedom.

As I turn my attention to the organization, I notice that there are only six paragraphs. Didion begins concretely, with lots of specific details (dust, plates, real estate talk, people committed to mental hospitals) to suggest what she means by the first three sentences. This place is different from her home in Los Angeles. She is surely making this point, but indirectly. She lets her details do the work—or rather she invites you to make the connections, to work out the implications. She respects the reader's ability to do just that. I respond to that challenge positively; I know it will pay off.

The second paragraph picks up the last sentence of the first. Here, however, she is both more explicit and more abstract. She is, in a sense, thinking out loud about the links between her generation (those born in the 1930s) and their childhood homes. Her opening sentence clearly states the idea she wants to explore: she left a clearly defined home, and the young girl in the bar never had one. I assume she wants us to imagine that she's making a point about different generations, not just one or two people. She seems to be setting herself up as typical, as representative. This universality is, in fact, one of the touches of art that makes this essay literature. So she makes her point again by ending with a concrete and provocative image. Her concluding question is at this point rhetorical, since today she would have little of the old morality to rebel against. Again she weaves this last sentence into the pattern of the next paragraph. And again she supports this abstract topic sentence by poignantly detailing specific items from her past, a past that makes little sense to the present generation.

The next paragraph, however, is loosely tied to the previous one. The first three paragraphs form a block; the last three, another. She picks up the abandoned narrative again. She tells us about the dread and then gives us the details of her drive to the graveyard. Is this incident meant to suggest the present generation's lack of respect for death, for the past and its traditional values? I think so.

The fifth paragraph focuses on a specific visit to the edges of her family. The details here are rich and telling. It is clear that this is only a ritual visit: no real contact is made. Didion seems comfortable with specific details; she seems to shy away from the announced theme, the explicit point. That is one of the things I like about her work: I'm included; I'm asked to see the relation between the abandoned answers and her inability to go "home."

And finally her snapshot of the party. We have come back now to the essay's opening sentence. The details here are sharply drawn: crisp and appropriate. The final statement, the wrap-up, is, typically, given in concrete form. She cannot bear to say "this is what I meant." No, that would break the cooperative bond with the reader. She wants more; she wants creative involvement, a partner in her art. Perhaps I am going beyond what she calls for, but I think Didion is saying that we can give our children culture, style, grace and love, or whatever else the presents suggest to our imagination. These can create a new definition of home.

IV: CONCLUSION

The traditional essays usually written in college bear little resemblance to "On Going Home," at least when the editors of this anthology were in college in the sixties. We were usually asked, instead, to begin with an explicit thesis statement (or to lead up to it, placing it dramatically as the last sentence of the first paragraph). We were then asked to support that generalization with three paragraphs all beginning with clear topic sentences and providing detailed evidence for our thematic assertion. It is clear that Didion chose not to follow that mode; yet, we suspect that she wrote many of these traditional deductive essays at Berkeley in the fifties. Her choice, however, was not arbitrary; she selected a structure that would best fit her meaning. If a traditional five-paragraph theme were appropriate, she would not hesitate to use it.

Organization is not neutral. It suggests a writer's attitude toward his or her readers and material. If Didion had begun, as is typical in academic articles, with a strong thematic statement, such as "After World War II, the American family was transformed from a closely knit community to a mobile nuclear unit," she would then have developed and supported this thesis with evidence from sociology. She would have been the authority telling us something she knows. Didion, however, chose to begin with a specific incident from her own experience, which she hedges on throughout. She is suggesting that her abstract thinking is firmly rooted in her own experiences. She does not begin with a strong thesis because she doesn't feel that secure about it. She is exploring and wondering. She is also presenting us with a tentative persona, one who is willing to look at the topic with us. Only after she has illustrated her experiences of going home does she make her point about "we live differently now." And even then it is couched in concrete details, not in the usual abstractions that often refer only vaguely to a world the reader knows.

Didion's honest voice is reinforced by her unadorned style. There is little flowery or pompous diction here. Look at the opening sentences of each paragraph: simple, clear, declarative sentences. Notice how she varies the rhythm and length of her sentences in the first paragraph, ending with a crisp and powerful expression of her thought. Her vivid, stark prose suggests that she is trying not to delude herself or us with uncalled-for optimism or self-defeating pessimism. She is just trying to see clearly, to understand. Cluttered sentences would fog that understanding. That seems a realistic alternative to the sometimes artificial authority of the deductive essay.

There is, of course, no doubt that the generalization-support pattern is useful and necessary. You will find some fine examples of that form in this anthology. But Didion's essay demonstrates that a writer can also be forceful, focused, and informative by developing a structure that parallels her intention. Writers usually try to let their content and purpose determine their organization, not the other way around. This discussion of Didion's essay, and the questions in the text, are intended to turn your attention to two things: the essay as a finished product and crafted work, and the essay as an action and a process.

Fortunately, by being such an alert reader, you are also preparing yourself to be an attentive writer. It is no secret that one effective way to become a better writer is to read frequently. Since other writers are the most fertile resource for topics, forms, styles, and ideas, it makes sense to read them often. Professional writers regularly read other practitioners because they know it enriches their own prose. Consciously or not, writers imitate each other, modifying and experimenting as they borrow. It follows that your writing is more likely to improve if you read with a writer's eye, noting voice, style, and language, and studying the development of ideas, the movement between the general and the specific that informs all good writing.

Of course, the most obvious way to become a stronger writer is to write frequently. That's why we have questions and suggestions for writing after each piece in this anthology: so that you will blend your reading with regular writing. They do, after all, have a good deal in common. Both are processes, not static activities; both are ways to make meaning. Reading and writing are also recursive; we move forward but we are always going back to see what we've read or written so we can clarify, rearrange, reformulate, and reinterpret. We only gradually come to understand what we read or what we want to write. This essential act of revision is at the heart of both; without it your reading and writing run the risk of superficiality. By writing about your reading you not only clarify and discover what you think, you also learn how to control your own composing habits. And when your instructor, classmates, or friends read and comment on these responses, you become part of a literate environment where writers can flourish.

TWO

James Baldwin

(1924–1987)

James Baldwin was born in Harlem, the son of fundamentalist religious parents. Baldwin followed his father's vocation and became, at fourteen, a preacher. At seventeen he abandoned the ministry and devoted himself to the craft of writing. He had been writing all along, from early childhood, but this writing had been discouraged by his family in favor of the religion that overshadowed it.

Baldwin received institutional support in the form of fellowships to help sustain him while he wrote and published his first two novels: *Go Tell It on the Mountain* (1953) and *Giovanni's Room* (1956), both of which were written abroad. Sandwiched between these works was a collection of essays, *Notes of a Native Son* (1955), which many readers consider his finest work. More fiction and essays followed: *Nobody Knows My Name* (essays, 1961), *Another Country* (a novel, 1962), *The Fire Next Time* (a polemical essay, 1963), *Going to Meet the Man* (stories, 1965)—and more.

In his early essays, for which he has received considerable praise, Baldwin struggled to define himself—as an American, as a writer, and as a black. (And for Baldwin the three are inextricably intertwined.) In coming to terms with what was, for him, the most difficult thing in his life—the fact that he was born a Negro, "and was forced, therefore, to effect some kind of truce with this reality"—Baldwin revealed himself to be a passionate and eloquent writer. His most frequent subject has been the relations between the races, about which he notes sardonically, "the color of my skin makes me, automatically, an expert."

Baldwin has written of pain, of rage and bitterness, of persecution and paranoia, of identity and responsibility, of the relations between fathers and sons, and of the search for equanimity, understanding, and love. Regardless of title, occasion, and place of composition, his essays revolve around these subjects and often stress the importance of accepting and understanding one another, whatever our differences of race, sex, culture, religion, or intellectual disposition.

In "Autobiographical Notes" Baldwin explores the meaning and purpose of his vocation, which he describes simply as to be "a good writer," to get his work done. But the essay explores something more: the fact of Baldwin's blackness and its effect on both his life and his writing. Another essay that explores Baldwin's identity as a writer and as a black is "The Discovery of What It Means to Be an American," an essay whose title reveals a third dimension of Baldwin's identity—his American-ness. This last element of his identity Baldwin examines with thoroughness and acuity by developing a set of contrasts between the social and cultural contexts available to a writer in Europe and in America. In "Notes of a Native Son" Baldwin is more strictly autobiographical than in any of his other essays. This piece combines a reminiscence of his father with an account of the day of his father's funeral. And it includes as well a narrative of an unpleasant incident that brought home to Baldwin a painful social fact concerning his race and an important and even more painful personal revelation of his feelings toward white people. As one of Baldwin's most impressive attempts to explore problematic social issues through personal experience, "Notes of a Native Son" fulfills what Baldwin sees as one of the most important obligations of the writer: "to examine attitudes, to go beneath the surface, to tap the source."

In the prefatory essay to the collection *Notes of a Native Son,* Baldwin stressed the absolute priority of his personal experience for his writing. He put it this way: "One writes out of one thing only—one's own experience. . . . Everything depends on how relentlessly one forces from this experience the last drop, sweet or bitter, it can possibly give." That Baldwin's experience was bitter helped his writing as much as it hindered it. For he himself noted that "any writer . . . finds that the things which hurt him and the things which helped him cannot be divorced from each other." Baldwin's anguished experience thus was essential for his acute understanding of the hatred and bitterness in his own heart and of the bitter hatred at the heart of the racial antagonisms existing between many Americans.

Although Baldwin may have resigned from his religious ministry at seventeen, his writing, nonetheless, is strongly influenced by the style of pulpit oratory. It possesses the same strong emotional cast, a similar quality of exhortation, and a common vision of apocalypse. In its rhythm, in its imagery, and in its ethical imperatives, Baldwin's style reveals the influence of both the King James Bible and the storefront church—the two influences he specifically mentions as formative.

Preacher, polemicist, social critic, autobiographer, essayist—Baldwin brings together repeatedly, in deeply affecting ways, public issues and private agonies with relentless candor and inexorable logic. On the success of his best essays rest his fame and fate as a writer, on what he himself claims is the only real concern of the artist: "to recreate out of the disorder of life that order which is art."

Autobiographical Notes

ı   I was born in Harlem thirty-one years ago. I began plotting novels at about the time I learned to read. The story of my childhood is the usual bleak fantasy and we can dismiss it with the restrained observation that I certainly would not consider living it again. In those days my mother was given to the exasperating and mysterious habit of having babies. As they were born, I took them over with one hand and held a book with the other. The children probably suffered, though they have since been kind enough to deny it, and in this way I read *Uncle Tom's Cabin* and *A Tale of Two Cities* over and over and over again; in this way, in fact, I read just about everything I could get my hands on— except the Bible, probably because it was the only book I was encouraged to read. I must also confess that I wrote—a great

deal—and my first professional triumph, in any case, the first
effort of mine to be seen in print, occurred at the age of twelve or
thereabouts, when a short story I had written about the Spanish
revolution won some sort of prize in an extremely short-lived
church newspaper. I remember the story was censored by the lady
editor, though I don't remember why, and I was outraged.

2   Also wrote plays, and songs, for one of which I received a letter of congratulations from Mayor La Guardia, and poetry, about
which the less said, the better. My mother was delighted by all
these goings-on, but my father wasn't; he wanted me to be a
preacher. When I was fourteen I became a preacher, and when I
was seventeen I stopped. Very shortly thereafter I left home. For
God knows how long I struggled with the world of commerce and
industry—I guess they would say they struggled with *me*—and
when I was about twenty-one I had enough done of a novel to get
a Saxton Fellowship. When I was twenty-two the fellowship was
over, the novel turned out to be unsalable, and I started waiting
on tables in a Village restaurant and writing book reviews—mostly, as it turned out, about the Negro problem, concerning which
the color of my skin made me automatically an expert. Did another book, in company with photographer Theodore Pelatowski,
about the store-front churches in Harlem. This book met exactly
the same fate as my first—fellowship, but no sale. (It was a
Rosenwald Fellowship.) By the time I was twenty-four I had decided to stop reviewing books about the Negro problem—which, by
this time, was only slightly less horrible in print than it was in
life—and I packed my bags and went to France, where I finished,
God knows how, *Go Tell It on the Mountain*.

3   Any writer, I suppose, feels that the world into which he was
born is nothing less than a conspiracy against the cultivation of
his talent—which attitude certainly has a great deal to support it.
On the other hand, it is only because the world looks on his talent
with such a frightening indifference that the artist is compelled to
make his talent important. So that any writer, looking back over
even so short a span of time as I am here forced to assess, finds
that the things which hurt him and the things which helped him
cannot be divorced from each other; he could be helped in a certain way only because he was hurt in a certain way; and his help is
simply to be enabled to move from one conundrum to the next—
one is tempted to say that he moves from one disaster to the next.
When one begins looking for influences one finds them by the

score. I haven't thought much about my own, not enough anyway; I hazard that the King James Bible, the rhetoric of the storefront church, something ironic and violent and perpetually understated in Negro speech—and something of Dickens' love for bravura — have something to do with me today; but I wouldn't stake my life on it. Likewise, innumerable people have helped me in many ways; but finally, I suppose, the most difficult (and most reward-ing) thing in my life has been the fact that I was born a Negro and was forced, therefore, to effect some kind of truce with this reali-ty. (Truce, by the way, is the best one can hope for.)

4   One of the difficulties about being a Negro writer (and this is not special pleading, since I don't mean to suggest that he has it worse than anybody else) is that the Negro problem is written about so widely. The bookshelves groan under the weight of infor-mation, and everyone therefore considers himself informed. And this information, furthermore, operates usually (generally, popu-larly) to reinforce traditional attitudes. Of traditional attitudes there are only two—For or Against—and I, personally, find it difficult to say which attitude has caused me the most pain. I am speaking as a writer; from a social point of view I am perfectly aware that the change from ill-will to good-will, however motivat-ed, however imperfect, however expressed, is better than no change at all.

5   But it is part of the business of the writer—as I see it—to examine attitudes, to go beneath the surface, to tap the source. From this point of view the Negro problem is nearly inaccessible. It is not only written about so widely; it is written about so badly. It is quite possible to say that the price a Negro pays for becoming articulate is to find himself, at length, with nothing to be articu-late about. ("You taught me language," says Caliban to Prospero, "and my profit on't is I know how to curse.") Consider: the tremendous social activity that this problem generates imposes on whites and Negroes alike the necessity of looking forward, of working to bring about a better day. This is fine, it keeps the waters troubled; it is all, indeed, that has made possible the Negro's progress. Nevertheless, social affairs are not generally speaking the writer's prime concern, whether they ought to be or not; it is absolutely necessary that he establish between himself and these affairs a distance which will allow, at least, for clarity, so that before he can look forward in any meaningful sense, he must first be allowed to take a long look back. In the context of the

Negro problem neither whites nor blacks, for excellent reasons of their own, have the faintest desire to look back; but I think that the past is all that makes the present coherent, and further, that the past will remain horrible for exactly as long as we refuse to assess it honestly.

6   I know, in any case, that the most crucial time in my own development came when I was forced to recognize that I was a kind of bastard of the West; when I followed the line of my past I did not find myself in Europe but in Africa. And this meant that in some subtle way, in a really profound way, I brought to Shakespeare, Bach, Rembrandt, to the stones of Paris, to the cathedral at Chartres, and to the Empire State Building, a special attitude. These were not really my creations, they did not contain my history; I might search in them in vain forever for any reflection of myself. I was an interloper; this was not my heritage. At the same time I had no other heritage which I could possibly hope to use—I had certainly been unfitted for the jungle or the tribe. I would have to appropriate these white centuries, I would have to make them mine—I would have to accept my special attitude, my special place in this scheme—otherwise I would have no place in *any* scheme. What was the most difficult was the fact that I was forced to admit something I had always hidden from myself, which the American Negro has had to hide from himself as the price of his public progress; that I hated and feared white people. This did not mean that I loved black people; on the contrary, I despised them, possibly because they failed to produce Rembrandt. In effect, I hated and feared the world. And this meant, not only that I thus gave the world an altogether murderous power over me, but also that in such a self-destroying limbo I could never hope to write.

7   One writes out of one thing only—one's own experience. Everything depends on how relentlessly one forces from this experience the last drop, sweet or bitter, it can possibly give. This is the only real concern of the artist, to recreate out of the disorder of life that order which is art. The difficulty then, for me, of being a Negro writer was the fact that I was, in effect, prohibited from examining my own experience too closely by the tremendous demands and the very real dangers of my social situation.

8   I don't think the dilemma outlined above is uncommon. I do think, since writers work in the disastrously explicit medium of language, that it goes a little way towards explaining why, out of

the enormous resources of Negro speech and life, and despite the example of Negro music, prose written by Negroes has been generally speaking so pallid and so harsh. I have not written about being a Negro at such length because I expect that to be my only subject, but only because it was the gate I had to unlock before I could hope to write about anything else. I don't think that the Negro problem in America can be even discussed coherently without bearing in mind its context; its context being the history, traditions, customs, the moral assumptions and preoccupations of the country; in short, the general social fabric. Appearances to the contrary, no one in America escapes its effects and everyone in America bears some responsibility for it. I believe this the more firmly because it is the overwhelming tendency to speak of this problem as though it were a thing apart. But in the work of Faulkner, in the general attitude and certain specific passages in Robert Penn Warren, and, most significantly, in the advent of Ralph Ellison, one sees the beginnings—at least—of a more genuinely penetrating search. Mr. Ellison, by the way, is the first Negro novelist I have ever read to utilize in language, and brilliantly, some of the ambiguity and irony of Negro life.

9   About my interests: I don't know if I have any, unless the morbid desire to own a sixteen-millimeter camera and make experimental movies can be so classified. Otherwise, I love to eat and drink—it's my melancholy conviction that I've scarcely ever had enough to eat (this is because it's *impossible* to eat enough if you're worried about the next meal)—and I love to argue with people who do not disagree with me too profoundly, and I love to laugh. I do *not* like bohemia, or bohemians, I do not like people whose principal aim is pleasure, and I do not like people who are *earnest* about anything. I don't like people who like me because I'm a Negro; neither do I like people who find in the same accident grounds for contempt. I love America more than any other country in the world, and, exactly for this reason, I insist on the right to criticize her perpetually. I think all theories are suspect, that the finest principles may have to be modified, or may even be pulverized by the demands of life, and that one must find, therefore, one's own moral center and move through the world hoping that this center will guide one aright. I consider that I have many responsibilities, but none greater than this: to last, as Hemingway says, and get my work done.

10   I want to be an honest man and a good writer.

QUESTIONS

1. Baldwin, like many writers, says he read voraciously as a child. And he says also that he wrote a lot as well. Do you think there is any connection between these two facts? What is the relationship between reading and writing?

2. Does Baldwin seem honest in this brief overview of his life as a writer? Does he seem boastful? Modest? Paranoid? Cite specific sentences where you sense strongly his tone.

3. In paragraph 3 Baldwin discusses the effect of circumstance on a writer's talent. How, specifically, does he apply that point to his own situation? What is the single most important fact of his life—the fact that conditions, influences, and affects all others?

4. How do you explain this remark of Baldwin's: "I suppose the most difficult (and most rewarding) thing in my life has been the fact that I was born a Negro and was forced, therefore, to come to some kind of truce with reality. (Truce, by the way, is the best one can hope for.)" How does this statement tie in with his earlier statement that a writer "finds that the things which hurt him and the things which helped him cannot be divorced from each other"?

5. In paragraph 4 Baldwin makes a distinction between how the changes in the civil status of blacks affect him as a man and how they affect him as a writer. Why is or isn't this a valid and useful distinction?

6. What does Baldwin see as the business of the writer? Should a writer be more concerned with art and craft or with ideas and values, perhaps even with social change? Does Baldwin seem to stress one or the other? (See paragraphs 5 and 7.)

7. Baldwin states that "the past is all that makes the present coherent." From what you have learned about Baldwin in reading this essay, and perhaps others, how has this been true for him? Is it true for you? How?

8. Baldwin makes two complex and important points in paragraph 6. One concerns his attitude toward the cultural monuments of Western civilization. What is this point? Can it be extended to others besides blacks?

9. The second important point of paragraph 6 comes at the end, where Baldwin says he hated both white and black people. Why is this an important aspect of his experience?

10. In paragraph 8 Baldwin remarks: "I have not written about being a Negro at such length because I expect that to be my only subject, but only because it was the gate I had to unlock before I could write about anything else." Explain.

11   The last long paragraph of the essay (paragraph 9) contains a miscellany of things Baldwin does and does not like. Which do you think is the most important? Is there any relationship between this point and the final sentence of the essay: "I want to be an honest man and a good writer"?

12.   Reread the first sentence of each paragraph. What do these opening sentences reveal about the organization of "Autobiographical Notes"?

Suggestions for Writing

A.   Write your own "Autobiographical Notes," perhaps focusing on one central fact of your life such as your race, religion, ethnic background, special talents, place of birth. You could, if you wish, structure your essay as Baldwin structures his: facts in the opening and closing paragraphs, longer speculations and explanations in the middle.

B.   Write an essay discussing, exploring, examining one of the ideas raised in Baldwin's essay—perhaps hatred, the white world, or blackness.

The Discovery of What It Means to Be an American

1   "It is a complex fate to be an American," Henry James observed, and the principal discovery an American writer makes in Europe is just how complex this fate is. America's history, her aspirations, her peculiar triumphs, her even more peculiar defeats, and her position in the world—yesterday and today—are all so profoundly and stubbornly unique that the very word "America" remains a new almost completely undefined and extremely controversial proper noun. No one in the world seems to know exactly what it describes, not even we motley millions who call ourselves Americans.

2   I left America because I doubted my ability to survive the fury of the color problem here. (Sometimes I still do.) I wanted to prevent myself from becoming *merely* a Negro; or, even, merely a Negro writer. I wanted to find out in what way the *specialness* of my experience could be made to connect me with other people

instead of dividing me from them. (I was as isolated from Negroes
as I was from whites, which is what happens when a Negro begins,
at bottom, to believe what white people say about him.)

3   In my necessity to find the terms on which my experience
could be related to that of others, Negroes and whites, writers and
non-writers, I proved, to my astonishment, to be as American as
any Texas G.I. And I found my experience was shared by every
American writer I knew in Paris. Like me, they had been divorced
from their origins, and it turned out to make very little difference
that the origins of white Americans were European and mine
were African—they were no more at home in Europe than I was.

4   The fact that I was the son of a slave and they were the sons
of free men meant less, by the time we confronted each other on
European soil, than the fact that we were both searching for our
separate identities. When we had found these, we seemed to be
saying, why, then, we would no longer need to cling to the shame
and bitterness which had divided us so long.

5   It became terribly clear in Europe, as it never had been
here, that we knew more about each other than any European
ever could. And it also became clear that, no matter where our
fathers had been born, or what they had endured, the fact of
Europe had formed us both was part of our identity and part of
our inheritance.

6   I had been in Paris a couple of years before any of this
became clear to me. When it did, I, like many a writer before me
upon the discovery that his props have all been knocked out from
under him, suffered a species of breakdown and was carried off to
the mountains of Switzerland. There, in that absolutely alabaster
landscape, armed with two Bessie Smith records and a typewriter,
I began to try to recreate the life that I had first known as a child
and from which I had spent so many years in flight.

7   It was Bessie Smith, through her tone and her cadence, who
helped me to dig back to the way I myself must have spoken when
I was a pickaninny, and to remember the things I had heard and
seen and felt. I had buried them very deep. I had never listened to
Bessie Smith in America (in the same way that, for years, I would
not touch watermelon), but in Europe she helped to reconcile me
to being a "nigger."

8   I do not think that I could have made this reconciliation
here. Once I was able to accept my role—as distinguished, I must

say, from my "place"—in the extraordinary drama which is America, I was released from the illusion that I hated America.

9   The story of what can happen to an American Negro writer in Europe simply illustrates, in some relief, what can happen to any American writer there. It is not meant, of course, to imply that it happens to them all, for Europe can be very crippling, too; and, anyway, a writer, when he has made his first breakthrough, has simply won a crucial skirmish in a dangerous, unending and unpredictable battle. Still, the breakthrough is important, and the point is that an American writer, in order to achieve it, very often has to leave this country.

10   The American writer, in Europe, is released, first of all, from the necessity of apologizing for himself. It is not until he *is* released from the habit of flexing his muscles and proving that he is just a "regular guy" that he realizes how crippling this habit has been. It is not necessary for him, there, to pretend to be something he is not, for the artist does not encounter in Europe the same suspicion he encounters here. Whatever the Europeans may actually think of artists, they have killed enough of them off by now to know that they are as real—and as persistent—as rain, snow, taxes or businessmen.

11   Of course, the reason for Europe's comparative clarity concerning the different functions of men in society is that European society has always been divided into classes in a way that American society never has been. A European writer considers himself to be part of an old and honorable tradition—of intellectual activity, of letters—and his choice of a vocation does not cause him any uneasy wonder as to whether or not it will cost him all his friends. But this tradition does not exist in America.

12   On the contrary, we have a very deep-seated distrust of real intellectual effort (probably because we suspect that it will destroy, as I hope it does, that myth of America to which we cling so desperately). An American writer fights his way to one of the lowest rungs on the American social ladder by means of pure bull-headedness and an indescribable series of odd jobs. He probably *has* been a "regular fellow" for much of his adult life, and it is not easy for him to step out of that lukewarm bath.

13   We must, however, consider a rather serious paradox: though American society is more mobile than Europe's, it is easier to cut across social and occupational lines there than it is here. This has something to do, I think, with the problem of status in American life. Where everyone has status, it is also perfectly possi-

ble, after all, that no one has. It seems inevitable, in any case, that
a man may become uneasy as to just what his status is.

14   But Europeans have lived with the idea of status for a long
time. A man can be as proud of being a good waiter as of being a
good actor, and, in neither case, feel threatened. And this means
that the actor and the waiter can have a freer and more genuinely
friendly relationship in Europe than they are likely to have here.
The waiter does not feel, with obscure resentment, that the actor
has "made it," and the actor is not tormented by the fear that he
may find himself, tomorrow, once again a waiter.

15   This lack of what may roughly be called social paranoia causes
the American writer in Europe to feel—almost certainly for the first
time in his life—that he can reach out to everyone, that he is accessible to everyone and open to everything. This is an extraordinary
feeling. He feels, so to speak, his own weight, his own value.

16   It is as though he suddenly came out of a dark tunnel and
found himself beneath the open sky. And, in fact, in Paris, I
began to see the sky for what seemed to be the first time. It was
borne in on me—and it did not make me feel melancholy—that
this sky had been there before I was born and would be there
when I was dead. And it was up to me, therefore, to make of my
brief opportunity the most that could be made.

17   I was born in New York, but have lived only in pockets of it.
In Paris, I lived in all parts of the city—on the Right Bank and the
Left, among the bourgeoisie and among *les misérables,* and knew
all kinds of people, from pimps and prostitutes in Pigalle to
Egyptian bankers in Neuilly. This may sound extremely unprinci-
pled or even obscurely immoral: I found it healthy. I love to talk
to people, all kinds of people, and almost everyone, as I hope we
still know, loves a man who loves to listen.

18   This perceptual dealing with people very different from
myself caused a shattering in me of preconceptions I scarcely
knew I held. The writer is meeting in Europe people who are not
American, whose sense of reality is entirely different from his
own. They may love or hate or admire or fear or envy this country—they see it, in any case, from another point of view, and this
forces the writer to reconsider many things he had always taken
for granted. This reassessment, which can be very painful, is also
very valuable.

19   This freedom, like all freedom, has its dangers and its
responsibilities. One day it begins to be borne in on the writer,

and with great force, that he is living in Europe as an American. If he were living there as a European, he would be living on a different and far less attractive continent.

20   This crucial day may be the day on which an Algerian taxi-driver tells him how it feels to be an Algerian in Paris. It may be the day on which he passes a café terrace and catches a glimpse of the tense, intelligent and troubled face of Albert Camus. Or it may be the day on which someone asks him to explain Little Rock and he begins to feel that it would be simpler—and, corny as the words may sound, more honorable—to *go* to Little Rock than sit in Europe, on an American passport, trying to explain it.

21   This is a personal day, a terrible day, the day to which his entire sojourn has been tending. It is the day he realizes that there are no untroubled countries in this fearfully troubled world; that if he has been preparing himself for anything in Europe, he has been preparing himself—for America. In short, the freedom that the American writer finds in Europe brings him, full circle, back to himself, with the responsibility for his development where it always was: in his own hands.

22   Even the most incorrigible maverick has to be born somewhere. He may leave the group that produced him—he may be forced to—but nothing will efface his origins, the marks of which he carries with him everywhere. I think it is important to know this and even find it a matter for rejoicing, as the strongest people do, regardless of their station. On this acceptance, literally, the life of a writer depends.

23   The charge has often been made against American writers that they do not describe society, and have no interest in it. They only describe individuals in opposition to it, or isolated from it. Of course, what the American writer is describing is his own situation. But what is *Anna Karenina* describing if not the tragic fate of the isolated individual, at odds with her time and place?

24   The real difference is that Tolstoy was describing an old and dense society in which everything seemed—to the people in it, though not to Tolstoy—to be fixed forever. And the book is a masterpiece because Tolstoy was able to fathom, and make us see, the hidden laws which really governed this society and made Anna's doom inevitable.

25   American writers do not have a fixed society to describe. The only society they know is one in which nothing is fixed and in

which the individual must fight for his identity. This is a rich confusion, indeed, and it creates for the American writer unprecedented opportunities.

26   That the tensions of American life, as well as the possibilities, are tremendous is certainly not even a question. But these are
dealt with in contemporary literature mainly compulsively; that is,
the book is more likely to be a symptom of our tension than an
examination of it. The time has come, God knows, for us to examine ourselves, but we can only do this if we are willing to free ourselves of the myth of America and try to find out what is really
happening here.

27   Every society is really governed by hidden laws, by unspoken
but profound assumptions on the part of the people, and ours is
no exception. It is up to the American writer to find out what
these laws and assumptions are. In a society much given to smashing taboos without thereby managing to be liberated from them,
it will be no easy matter.

28   It is no wonder, in the meantime, that the American writer
keeps running off to Europe. He needs sustenance for his journey
and the best models he can find. Europe has what we do not have
yet, a sense of the mysterious and inexorable limits of life, a sense,
in a word, of tragedy. And we have what they sorely need: a new
sense of life's possibilities.

29   In this endeavor to wed the vision of the Old World with
that of the New, it is the writer, not the statesman, who is our
strongest arm. Though we do not wholly believe it yet, the interior
life is a real life, and the intangible dreams of people have a tangible effect on the world.

QUESTIONS

Ideas

1. Why is to be an American a "complex fate"? Why, particularly, was it
    a complex fate for Baldwin?

2. What does Baldwin suggest about origins—about what and where a
    person is born and how he is raised? Why does he mention Bessie
    Smith?

3. Throughout the second and third parts of this essay, Baldwin con-
    trasts Europe with America. What differences does he emphasize?
    And what are the reasons for and the focus of his contrasts?

4. How can living in another country help a writer—or any artist? (See especially paragraph 18.)

Organization

5. Why is the essay divided into three sections? What are the focus and emphasis of each?
6. How does Baldwin achieve coherence and continuity in this essay? Look closely at the first sentence of each paragraph of section two, for example. What words and phrases link the thought of each opening sentence to the idea of the paragraph before it? Look also at paragraph 20. Notice how Baldwin begins each sentence in that paragraph:

> This crucial day may be the day on which . . .
> It may be the day on which . . .
> Or it may be the day on which . . .

And then paragraph 21:

> This is a personal day, a terrible day, the day to which . . .
> It is the day . . .

Are these repetitions necessary? Helpful? Monotonous? Explain.

Sentences

7. Read paragraphs 11–15, noting particularly the length of Baldwin's sentences. In that five-paragraph stretch, do you find any consistency in the kind of sentence Baldwin uses or in how he begins and ends his paragraphs?
8. Baldwin uses balance and parallelism of syntax throughout the essay. Here are two brief examples:

> This reassessment, which can be very painful,
> is also   very valuable.

> This freedom, like all freedom, has its dangers
>   and its responsibilities.

In both of these simple sentences Baldwin interrupts the direct flow of syntax with interpolated phrases or clauses. These interruptions change the rhythm of the sentences, making them more emphatic. Analyze the repetitions, balances, and interruptions of the following two sequential sentences from paragraph 5:

> It became terribly clear in Europe,
>   as it never had been here,
>   that we knew more about each other than any
>   European ever could.

And it also became   clear   that,
     no matter where our fathers had been born,
    or   what   they   had endured,
    the fact of Europe had formed us both,
          was part of our identity
       and   part of our inheri-
      tance.

9. Baldwin varies the rhythm of his sentences and achieves emphasis and expansiveness by careful use of punctuation. Consider, for example, the commas in paragraphs 16-19. Read the sentences aloud, noting the pauses and the pacing. Try reading the same paragraphs as if the commas had been omitted.

10. Baldwin interrupts his sentences with the dash as well as with the comma. Consider the dashes in the following paragraphs: 1, 8, 10, 11, 15, 16, and 17. What kind of information is interpolated between the dashes? Can we remove the words between dashes, thus eliminating the internal punctuation of those sentences? In reading the sentences aloud, what tone of voice would you use and why?

11. In paragraphs 2 and 7, Baldwin could have used dashes or commas instead of parentheses. Try reading the sentences aloud, testing in turn parentheses, dashes, commas. What differences do you hear?

Words

12. Many words in the essay convey the meaning of division or separation. Reread paragraphs 2–12, marking off these words as well as those suggesting an opposite idea, that of unity or reconciliation.

13. In paragraph 9, Baldwin uses a central metaphor—that for the writer life is a battle. What specific words and phrases carry the comparison between life and war? What is the point of the paragraph overall, and how do the comparisons help to convey it?

14. How would you describe Baldwin's language in this essay? Is it formal, informal, serious, casual, heavy, or light? How, for example, would you classify the language of the following phrases: "the mysterious and inexorable limits of life" (28), "incorrigible maverick" (22), "obscure resentment" (14)? Is the essay written primarily in this style of language? In another?

15. Why does Baldwin use quotation marks around the following words: "nigger" (7), "place" (8), "regular guy" (10), "made it" (14)?

Suggestions for Writing

A. Write an essay explaining what it means to be an American, especially what it means to be a particular kind of American, such as a Jewish or Chinese American or an American traveling abroad. Try to focus on your identity as this particular kind of American—or upon the reactions of other people to you as a particular kind of American. Has it been a complex fate for you to be an American? Explain.

B. Write an essay in which you identify and define yourself as belonging to a particular social group or as being one of a particular type of people. You might explain what it means, for example, for you to be a musician, an athlete, a feminist, a science fiction fan, or a moviegoer.

C. In the last section of "The Discovery of What It Means to Be an American," and especially in paragraphs 22–27, Baldwin comments on the American writer and his relation to American society. Apply any one of Baldwin's remarks on this subject to a writer whose work you know (perhaps Baldwin's) and develop an essay either confirming or refuting Baldwin's assertion. You might take, for example, one of the following comments:

> The charge has often been made against American writers that they do not describe society, and have no interest in it. They only describe individuals in opposition to it, or isolated from it. (23)

> American writers do not have a fixed society to describe. The only society they know is one in which nothing is fixed and in which the individual must fight for his identity. (25)

> [The tensions of American life] are dealt with in contemporary literature mainly compulsively; that is, the book is more likely to be a symptom of our tension than an examination of it. (26)

If Black English Isn't a Language, Then Tell Me, What Is?

1   ST. PAUL DE VENCE, France—The argument concerning the use, or the status, or the reality, of black English is rooted in American history and has absolutely nothing to do with the question the argument supposes itself to be posing. The argument has nothing to do with language itself but with the *role* of language. Language, incontestably, reveals the speaker. Language, also, far more dubiously, is meant to define the other—and, in this case, the other is refusing to be defined by a language that has never been able to recognize him.

2   People evolve a language in order to describe and thus control their circumstances, or in order not to be submerged by a
reality that they cannot articulate. (And, if they cannot articulate
it, they *are* submerged.) A Frenchman living in Paris speaks a subtly and crucially different language from that of the man living in
Marseilles; neither sounds very much like a man living in Quebec;
and they would all have great difficulty in apprehending what the
man from Guadeloupe, or Martinique, is saying, to say nothing of
the man from Senegal—although the "common" language of all
these areas is French. But each has paid, and is paying, a different
price for this "common" language, in which, as it turns out, they
are not saying, and cannot be saying, the same things: They each
have very different realities to articulate, or control.

3   What joins all languages, and all men, is the necessity to confront life, in order, not inconceivably, to outwit death: The price
for this is the acceptance, and achievement, of one's temporal
identity. So that, for example, though it is not taught in the
schools (and this has the potential of becoming a political issue)
the south of France still clings to its ancient and musical Proven-
çal, which resists being described as a "dialect." And much of the
tension in the Basque countries, and in Wales, is due to the Basque
and Welsh determination not to allow their languages to be
destroyed. This determination also feeds the flames in Ireland for
among the many indignities the Irish have been forced to undergo at English hands is the English contempt for their language.

4   It goes without saying, then, that language is also a political
instrument, means, and proof of power. It is the most vivid and
crucial key to identity: It reveals the private identity, and connects
one with, or divorces one from, the larger, public, or communal
identity. There have been, and are, times, and places, when to
speak a certain language could be dangerous, even fatal. Or, one
may speak the same language, but in such a way that one's antecedents are revealed, or (one hopes) hidden. This is true in France,
and is absolutely true in England: The range (and reign) of ac-
cents on that damp little island make England coherent for the
English and totally incomprehensible for everyone else. To open
your mouth in England is (if I may use black English) to "put your
business in the street": You have confessed your parents, your youth,
your school, your salary, your self-esteem, and, alas, your future.

5   Now, I do not know what white Americans would sound like
if there had never been any black people in the United States, but
they would not sound the way they sound. *Jazz*, for example, is a

very specific sexual term, as in *jazz me, baby,* but white people purified it into the Jazz Age. *Sock it to me,* which means, roughly, the same thing, has been adopted by Nathaniel Hawthorne's descendants with no qualms or hesitations at all, along with *let it all hang out* and *right on! Beat to his socks,* which was once the black's most total and despairing image of poverty, was transformed into a thing called the Beat Generation, which phenomenon was, largely, composed of *uptight,* middle-class white people, imitating poverty, trying to *get down,* to get *with it,* doing their *thing,* doing their despairing best to be *funky,* which we, the blacks, never dreamed of doing—we *were* funky, baby, like *funk* was going out of style.

6   Now, no one can eat his cake, and have it, too, and it is late in the day to attempt to penalize black people for having created a language that permits the nation its only glimpse of reality, a language without which the nation would be even more *whipped* than it is.

7   I say that this present skirmish is rooted in American history, and it is. Black English is the creation of the black diaspora. Blacks came to the United States chained to each other, but from different tribes: Neither could speak the other's language. If two black people, at that bitter hour of the world's history, had been able to speak to each other, the institution of chattel slavery could never have lasted as long as it did. Subsequently, the slave was given, under the eye, and the gun, of his master, Congo Square, and the Bible—or, in other words, and under these conditions, the slave began the formation of the black church, and it is within this unprecedented tabernacle that black English began to be formed. This was not, merely, as in the European example, the adoption of a foreign tongue, but an alchemy that transformed ancient elements into a new language: *A language comes into existence by means of brutal necessity, and the rules of the language are dictated by what the language must convey.*

8   There was a moment, in time, and in this place, when my brother, or my mother, or my father, or my sister, had to convey to me, for example, the danger in which I was standing from the white man standing just behind me, and to convey this with a speed, and in a language, that the white man could not possibly understand, and that, indeed, he cannot understand, until today. He cannot afford to understand it. This understanding would reveal to him too much about himself, and smash that mirror before which he has been frozen for so long.

9   Now, if this passion, this skill, this (to quote Toni Morrison) "sheer intelligence," this incredible music, the mighty achievement of having brought a people utterly unknown to, or despised by "history"—to have brought this people to their present, troubled, troubling, and unassailable and unanswerable place—if this absolutely unprecedented journey does not indicate that black English is a language, I am curious to know what definition of language is to be trusted.

10   A people at the center of the Western world, and in the midst of so hostile a population, has not endured and transcended by means of what is patronizingly called a "dialect." We, the blacks, are in trouble, certainly, but we are not doomed, and we are not inarticulate because we are not compelled to defend a morality that we know to be a lie.

11   The brutal truth is that the bulk of the white people in America never had any interest in educating black people, except as this could serve white purposes. It is not the black child's language that is in question, it is not his language that is despised: It is his experience. A child cannot be taught by anyone who despises him, and a child cannot afford to be fooled. A child cannot be taught by anyone whose demand, essentially, is that the child repudiate his experience, and all that gives him sustenance, and enter a limbo in which he will no longer be black, and in which he knows that he can never become white. Black people have lost too many black children that way.

12   And, after all, finally, in a country with standards so untrustworthy, a country that makes heroes of so many criminal mediocrities, a country unable to face why so many of the non-white are in prison, or on the needle, or standing, futureless, in the streets—it may very well be that both the child, and his elder, have concluded that they have nothing whatever to learn from the people of a country that has managed to learn so little.

QUESTIONS

Ideas

1. What are the essential attributes or characteristics of a language (as opposed to a dialect) as Baldwin describes them? What, according to Baldwin, is the relation between language and reality?

2. What, according to Baldwin, are the functions of language? What does a language *do* for its speakers?

3. What are the purpose and point of the essay? Who is the intended or implied audience?

Organization

4. Baldwin begins with a reference to a previously articulated position —or at least a counterview—to the one he wishes to argue. He enters the debate in the middle of things rather than at the beginning. What does this approach suggest about the audience for whom Baldwin originally wrote this essay?

5. Outline the structure of the essay—its movement of thought from one paragraph to another. State in a single sentence the main thrust of each paragraph and examine the relationship of each paragraph to the ones before and after it.

Sentences

6. Single out two sentences you consider particularly effective and explain why they are effective.

7. Examine the sentences in which Baldwin expresses his ideas by punctuating with a colon. For each sentence explain the relationship between the information on the right and left sides of the colon. Consider a revision of each sentence to eliminate the colon and decide which version you prefer, and why.

Words

8. Examine the italicized words and phrases in paragraphs 5 and 6. What does Baldwin illustrate with these examples?

9. Consider the following adverbs from paragraphs 1–4. What would be gained or lost if each were omitted?

    absolutely, incontestably, dubiously (1);
    subtly, crucially, very (2);
    inconceivably (3);
    absolutely, totally (4).

Suggestions for Writing

A. Explain and illustrate from your own experience or from your reading how language, as Baldwin says in paragraph 4, "is a political instrument, means, and proof of power."

B.   Discuss Baldwin's idea that language is a key to identity—both per-
     sonal identity and social identity.

C.   Agree or disagree with Baldwin's comment that to open your mouth
     and speak is to confess "your parents, your youth, your school, your
     salary, your self-esteem, and alas, your future."

Notes of a Native Son

I

1   On the 29th of July, in 1943, my father died. On the
same day, a few hours later, his last child was born. Over a month
before this, while all our energies were concentrated in waiting
for these events, there had been, in Detroit, one of the bloodiest
race riots of the century. A few hours after my father's funeral,
while he lay in state in the undertaker's chapel, a race riot broke
out in Harlem. On the morning of the 3rd of August, we drove
my father to the graveyard through a wilderness of smashed plate
glass.

2   The day of my father's funeral had also been my nineteenth
birthday. As we drove him to the graveyard, the spoils of injustice,
anarchy, discontent, and hatred were all around us. It seemed to
me that God himself had devised, to mark my father's end, the
most sustained and brutally dissonant of codas. And it seemed to
me, too, that the violence which rose all about us as my father left
the world had been devised as a corrective for the pride of his
eldest son. I had declined to believe in that apocalypse which had
been central to my father's vision; very well, life seemed to be saying, here is something that will certainly pass for an apocalypse
until the real thing comes along. I had inclined to be contemptuous of my father for the conditions of his life, for the conditions
of our lives. When his life had ended I began to wonder about
that life and also, in a new way, to be apprehensive about my own.

3   I had not known my father very well. We had got on badly,
partly because we shared, in our different fashions, the vice of
stubborn pride. When he was dead I realized that I had hardly
ever spoken to him. When he had been dead a long time I began
to wish I had. It seems to be typical of life in America, where

opportunities, real and fancied, are thicker than anywhere else on
the globe, that the second generation has no time to talk to the
first. No one, including my father, seems to have known exactly
how old he was, but his mother had been born during slavery. He
was of the first generation of free men. He, along with thousands
of other Negroes, came North after 1919 and I was part of that
generation which had never seen the landscape of what Negroes
sometimes call the Old Country.

4   He had been born in New Orleans and had been a quite
young man there during the time that Louis Armstrong, a boy,
was running errands for the dives and honky-tonks of what was
always presented to me as one of the most wicked of cities—to this
day, whenever I think of New Orleans, I also helplessly think of
Sodom and Gomorrah. My father never mentioned Louis
Armstrong, except to forbid us to play his records; but there was a
picture of him on our wall for a long time. One of my father's
strong-willed female relatives had placed it there and forbade my
father to take it down. He never did, but he eventually maneuvered her out of the house and when, some years later, she was in
trouble and near death, he refused to do anything to help her.

5   He was, I think, very handsome. I gather this from photographs and from my own memories of him, dressed in his
Sunday best and on his way to preach a sermon somewhere, when
I was little. Handsome, proud, and ingrown, "like a toe-nail,"
somebody said. But he looked to me, as I grew older, like pictures
I had seen of African tribal chieftains: he really should have been
naked, with war-paint on and barbaric mementos, standing
among spears. He could be chilling in the pulpit and indescrib-
ably cruel in his personal life and he was certainly the most bitter
man I have ever met; yet it must be said that there was something
else in him, buried in him, which lent him his tremendous power
and, even, a rather crushing charm. It had something to do with
his blackness, I think—he was very black—with his blackness and
his beauty, and with the fact that he knew that he was black but
did not know that he was beautiful. He claimed to be proud of his
blackness but it had also been the cause of much humiliation and
it had fixed bleak boundaries to his life. He was not a young man
when we were growing up and he had already suffered many
kinds of ruin; in his outrageously demanding and protective way
he loved his children, who were black like him and menaced, like
him; and all these things sometimes showed in his face when he

tried, never to my knowledge with any success, to establish contact with any of us. When he took one of his children on his knee to play, the child always became fretful and began to cry; when he tried to help one of us with our homework the absolutely unabating tension which emanated from him caused our minds and our tongues to become paralyzed, so that he, scarcely knowing why, flew into a rage and the child, not knowing why, was punished. If it ever entered his head to bring a surprise home for his children, it was, almost unfailingly, the wrong surprise and even the big watermelons he often brought home on his back in the summertime led to the most appalling scenes. I do not remember, in all those years, that one of his children was ever glad to see him come home. From what I was able to gather of his early life, it seemed that this inability to establish contact with other people had always marked him and had been one of the things which had driven him out of New Orleans. There was something in him, therefore, groping and tentative, which was never expressed and which was buried with him. One saw it most clearly when he was facing new people and hoping to impress them. But he never did, not for long. We went from church to smaller and more improbable church, he found himself in less and less demand as a minister, and by the time he died none of his friends had come to see him for a long time. He had lived and died in an intolerable bitterness of spirit and it frightened me, as we drove him to the graveyard through those unquiet, ruined streets, to see how powerful and overflowing this bitterness could be and to realize that this bitterness now was mine.

6   When he died I had been away from home for a little over a year. In that year I had had time to become aware of the meaning of all my father's bitter warnings, had discovered the secret of his proudly pursed lips and rigid carriage: I had discovered the weight of white people in the world. I saw that this had been for my ancestors and now would be for me an awful thing to live with and that the bitterness which had helped to kill my father could also kill me.

7   He had been ill a long time—in the mind, as we now realized, reliving instances of his fantastic intransigence in the new light of his affliction and endeavoring to feel a sorrow for him which never, quite, came true. We had not known that he was being eaten up by paranoia, and the discovery that his cruelty, to our bodies and our minds, had been one of the symptoms of his

illness was not, then, enough to enable us to forgive him. The younger children felt, quite simply, relief that he would not be coming home anymore. My mother's observation that it was he, after all, who had kept them alive all these years meant nothing because the problems of keeping children alive are not real for children. The older children felt, with my father gone, that they could invite their friends to the house without fear that their friends would be insulted or, as had sometimes happened with me, being told that their friends were in league with the devil and intended to rob our family of everything we owned. (I didn't fail to wonder, and it made me hate him, what on earth we owned that anybody else would want.)

8   His illness was beyond all hope of healing before anyone realized that he was ill. He had always been so strange and had lived, like a prophet, in such unimaginably close communion with the Lord that his long silences which were punctuated by moans and hallelujahs and snatches of old songs while he sat at the living-room window never seemed odd to us. It was not until he refused to eat because, he said, his family was trying to poison him that my mother was forced to accept as a fact what had, until then, been only an unwilling suspicion. When he was committed, it was discovered that he had tuberculosis and, as it turned out, the disease of his mind allowed the disease of his body to destroy him. For the doctors could not force him to eat, either, and, though he was fed intravenously, it was clear from the beginning that there was no hope for him.

9   In my mind's eye I could see him, sitting at the window, locked up in his terrors; hating and fearing every living soul including his children who had betrayed him, too, by reaching towards the world which had despised him. There were nine of us. I began to wonder what it could have felt like for such a man to have had nine children whom he could barely feed. He used to make little jokes about our poverty, which never, of course, seemed very funny to us; they could not have seemed very funny to him, either, or else our all too feeble response to them would never have caused such rages. He spent great energy and achieved, to our chagrin, no small amount of success in keeping us away from the people who surrounded us, people who had all-night rent parties to which we listened when we should have been sleeping, people who cursed and drank and flashed razor blades on Lenox Avenue. He could not understand why, if they had so

much energy to spare, they could not use it to make their lives better. He treated almost everybody on our block with a most uncharitable asperity and neither they, nor, of course, their children were slow to reciprocate.

10   The only white people who came to our house were welfare workers and bill collectors. It was almost always my mother who dealt with them, for my father's temper, which was at the mercy of his pride, was never to be trusted. It was clear that he felt their very presence in his home to be a violation: this was conveyed by his carriage, almost ludicrously stiff, and by his voice, harsh and vindictively polite. When I was around nine or ten I wrote a play which was directed by a young, white schoolteacher, a woman, who then took an interest in me, and gave me books to read and, in order to corroborate my theatrical bent, decided to take me to see what she somewhat tactlessly referred to as "real" plays. Theatergoing was forbidden in our house, but, with the really cruel intuitiveness of a child, I suspected that the color of this woman's skin would carry the day for me. When, at school, she suggested taking me to the theater, I did not, as I might have done if she had been a Negro, find a way of discouraging her, but agreed that she should pick me up at my house one evening. I then, very cleverly, left all the rest to my mother, who suggested to my father, as I knew she would, that it would not be very nice to let such a kind woman make the trip for nothing. Also, since it was a schoolteacher, I imagine that my mother countered the idea of sin with the idea of "education," which word, even with my father, carried a kind of bitter weight.

11   Before the teacher came my father took me aside to ask *why* she was coming, what *interest* she could possibly have in our house, in a boy like me. I said I didn't know but I, too, suggested that it had something to do with education. And I understood that my father was waiting for me to say something—I didn't quite know what; perhaps that I wanted his protection against this teacher and her "education." I said none of these things and the teacher came and we went out. It was clear, during the brief interview in our living room, that my father was agreeing very much against his will and that he would have refused permission if he had dared. The fact that he did not dare caused me to despise him: I had no way of knowing that he was facing in that living room a wholly unprecedented and frightening situation.

12   Later, when my father had been laid off from his job, this woman became very important to us. She was really a very sweet and generous woman and went to a great deal of trouble to be of help to us, particularly during one awful winter. My mother called her by the highest name she knew. She said she was a "christian." My father could scarcely disagree but during the four or five years of our relatively close association he never trusted her and was always trying to surprise in her open, Midwestern face the genuine, cunningly hidden, and hideous motivation. In later years, particularly when it began to be clear that this "education" of mine was going to lead me to perdition, he became more explicit and warned me that my white friends in high school were not really my friends and that I would see, when I was older, how white people would do anything to keep a Negro down. Some of them could be nice, he admitted, but none of them were to be trusted and most of them were not even nice. The best thing was to have as little to do with them as possible. I did not feel this way and I was certain, in my innocence, that I never would.

13   But the year which preceded my father's death had made a great change in my life. I had been living in New Jersey, working in defense plants, working and living among southerners, white and black. I knew about the south, of course, and about how southerners treated Negroes and how they expected them to behave, but it had never entered my mind that anyone would look at me and expect *me* to behave that way. I learned in New Jersey that to be a Negro meant, precisely, that one was never looked at but was simply at the mercy of the reflexes the color of one's skin caused in other people. I acted in New Jersey as I had always acted, that is as though I thought a great deal of myself—I had to *act* that way—with results that were, simply, unbelievable. I had scarcely arrived before I had earned the enmity, which was extraordinarily ingenious, of all my superiors and nearly all my co-workers. In the beginning, to make matters worse, I simply did not know what was happening. I did not know what I had done, and I shortly began to wonder what *anyone* could possibly do, to bring about such unanimous, active, and unbearably vocal hostility. I knew about jim-crow but I had never experienced it. I went to the same self-service restaurant three times and stood with all the Princeton boys before the counter, waiting for a hamburger and coffee; it was always an extraordinarily long time before anything was set before me; but it was not until the fourth visit that I

learned that, in fact, nothing had ever been set before me: I had simply picked something up. Negroes were not served there, I was told, and they had been waiting for me to realize that I was always the only Negro present. Once I was told this, I determined to go there all the time. But now they were ready for me and, though some dreadful scenes were subsequently enacted in that restaurant, I never ate there again.

14   It was the same story all over New Jersey, in bars, bowling alleys, diners, places to live. I was always being forced to leave, silently, or with mutual imprecations. I very shortly became notorious and children giggled behind me when I passed and their elders whispered or shouted—they really believed that I was mad. And it did begin to work on my mind, of course; I began to be afraid to go anywhere and to compensate for this I went places to which I really should not have gone and where, God knows, I had no desire to be. My reputation in town naturally enhanced my reputation at work and my working day became one long series of acrobatics designed to keep me out of trouble. I cannot say that these acrobatics succeeded. It began to seem that the machinery of the organization I worked for was turning over, day and night, with but one aim: to eject me. I was fired once, and contrived, with the aid of a friend from New York, to get back on the payroll; was fired again, and bounced back again. It took a while to fire me for the third time, but the third time took. There were no loopholes anywhere. There was not even any way of getting back inside the gates.

15   That year in New Jersey lives in my mind as though it were the year during which, having an unsuspected predilection for it, I first contracted some dread, chronic disease, the unfailing symptom of which is a kind of blind fever, a pounding in the skull and fire in the bowels. Once this disease is contracted, one can never be really carefree again, for the fever, without an instant's warning, can recur at any moment. It can wreck more important things than race relations. There is not a Negro alive who does not have this rage in his blood—one has the choice, merely, of living with it consciously or surrendering to it. As for me, this fever has recurred in me, and does, and will until the day I die.

16   My last night in New Jersey, a white friend from New York took me to the nearest big town, Trenton, to go to the movies and have a few drinks. As it turned out, he also saved me from, at the very least, a violent whipping. Almost every detail of that night

stands out very clearly in my memory. I even remember the name of the movie we saw because its title impressed me as being so patly ironical. It was a movie about the German occupation of France, starring Maureen O'Hara and Charles Laughton and called *This Land Is Mine*. I remember the name of the diner we walked into when the movie ended: it was the "American Diner." When we walked in the counterman asked what we wanted and I remember answering with the casual sharpness which had become my habit: "We want a hamburger and a cup of coffee, what do you think we want?" I do not know why, after a year of such rebuffs, I so completely failed to anticipate his answer, which was, of course, "We don't serve Negroes here." This reply failed to discompose me, at least for the moment. I made some sardonic comment about the name of the diner and we walked out into the streets.

17   This was the time of what was called the "brown out," when the lights in all American cities were very dim. When we re-entered the streets something happened to me which had the force of an optical illusion, or a nightmare. The streets were very crowded and I was facing north. People were moving in every direction but it seemed to me, in that instant, that all of the people I could see, and many more than that, were moving toward me, against me, and that everyone was white. I remember how their faces gleamed. And I felt, like a physical sensation, a *click* at the nape of my neck as though some interior string connecting my head to my body had been cut. I began to walk. I heard my friend call after me, but I ignored him. Heaven only knows what was going on in his mind, but he had the good sense not to touch me—I don't know what would have happened if he had—and to keep me in sight. I don't know what was going on in my mind, either; I certainly had no conscious plan. I wanted to do something to crush these white faces, which were crushing me. I walked for perhaps a block or two until I came to an enormous, glittering, and fashionable restaurant in which I knew not even the intercession of the Virgin would cause me to be served. I pushed through the doors and took the first vacant seat I saw, at a table for two, and waited.

18   I do not know how long I waited and I rather wonder, until today, what I could possibly have looked like. Whatever I looked like, I frightened the waitress who shortly appeared, and the moment she appeared all of my fury flowed towards her. I hated

her for her white face, and for her great, astounded, frightened eyes. I felt that if she found a black man so frightening I would make her fright worthwhile.

19   She did not ask me what I wanted, but repeated, as though she had learned it somewhere, "We don't serve Negroes here." She did not say it with the blunt, derisive hostility to which I had grown so accustomed, but, rather, with a note of apology in her voice, and fear. This made me colder and more murderous than ever. I felt I had to do something with my hands. I wanted her to come close enough for me to get her neck between my hands.

20   So I pretended not to have understood her, hoping to draw her closer. And she did step a very short step closer, with her pencil poised incongruously over her pad, and repeated the formula: ". . . don't serve Negroes here."

21   Somehow, with the repetition of that phrase, which was already ringing in my head like a thousand bells of a nightmare, I realized that she would never come any closer and that I would have to strike from a distance. There was nothing on the table but an ordinary water-mug half full of water, and I picked this up and hurled it with all my strength at her. She ducked and it missed her and shattered against the mirror behind the bar. And, with that sound, my frozen blood abruptly thawed, I returned from wherever I had been, I *saw*, for the first time, the restaurant, the people with their mouths open, already, as it seemed to me, rising as one man, and I realized what I had done, and where I was, and I was frightened. I rose and began running for the door. A round, pot-bellied man grabbed me by the nape of the neck just as I reached the doors and began to beat me about the face. I kicked him and got loose and ran into the streets. My friend whispered, *"Run!"* and I ran.

22   My friend stayed outside the restaurant long enough to misdirect my pursuers and the police, who arrived, he told me, at once. I do not know what I said to him when he came to my room that night. I could not have said much. I felt, in the oddest, most awful way, that I had somehow betrayed him. I lived it over and over and over again, the way one relives an automobile accident after it has happened and one finds oneself alone and safe. I could not get over two facts, both equally difficult for the imagination to grasp, and one was that I could have been murdered. But the other was that I had been ready to commit murder. I saw nothing very clearly but I did see this: that my life, my *real* life, was

in danger, and not from anything other people might do but from the hatred I carried in my own heart.

II

23   I had returned home around the second week in June—in great haste because it seemed that my father's death and my mother's confinement were both but a matter of hours. In the case of my mother, it soon became clear that she had simply made a miscalculation. This had always been her tendency and I don't believe that a single one of us arrived in the world, or has since arrived anywhere else, on time. But none of us dawdled so intolerably about the business of being born as did my baby sister. We sometimes amused ourselves, during those endless, stifling weeks, by picturing the baby sitting within in the safe, warm dark, bitterly regretting the necessity of becoming a part of our chaos and stubbornly putting it off as long as possible. I understood her perfectly and congratulated her on showing such good sense so soon. Death, however, sat as purposefully at my father's bedside as life stirred within my mother's womb and it was harder to understand why he so lingered in that long shadow. It seemed that he had bent, and for a long time, too, all of his energies towards dying. Now death was ready for him but my father held back.

24   All of Harlem, indeed, seemed to be infected by waiting. I had never before known it to be so violently still. Racial tensions throughout this country were exacerbated during the early years of the war, partly because the labor market brought together hundreds of thousands of ill-prepared people and partly because Negro soldiers, regardless of where they were born, received their military training in the south. What happened in defense plants and army camps had repercussions, naturally, in every Negro ghetto. The situation in Harlem had grown bad enough for clergymen, policemen, educators, politicians, and social workers to assert in one breath that there was no "crime wave" and to offer, in the very next breath, suggestions as to how to combat it. These suggestions always seemed to involve playgrounds, despite the fact that racial skirmishes were occurring in the playgrounds, too. Playground or not, crime wave or not, the Harlem police force had been augmented in March, and the unrest grew—perhaps, in fact, partly as a result of the ghetto's instinctive hatred of police-

men. Perhaps the most revealing news item, out of the steady
parade of reports of muggings, stabbings, shootings, assaults, gang
wars, and accusations of police brutality is the item concerning six
Negro girls who set upon a white girl in the subway because, as
they all too accurately put it, she was stepping on their toes.
Indeed she was, all over the nation.

25   I had never before been so aware of policemen, on foot, on
horseback, on corners, everywhere, always two by two. Nor had I
ever been so aware of small knots of people. They were on stoops
and on corners and in doorways, and what was striking about
them, I think, was that they did not seem to be talking. Never,
when I passed these groups, did the usual sound of a curse or a
laugh ring out and neither did there seem to be any hum of gossip. There was certainly, on the other hand, occurring between
them communication extraordinarily intense. Another thing that
was striking was the unexpected diversity of the people who made
up these groups. Usually, for example, one would see a group of
sharpies standing on the street corner, jiving the passing chicks;
or a group of older men, usually, for some reason, in the vicinity
of a barber shop, discussing baseball scores, or the numbers or
making rather chilling observations about women they had
known. Women, in a general way, tended to be seen less often
together—unless they were church women, or very young girls, or
prostitutes met together for an unprofessional instant. But that
summer I saw the strangest combinations: large, respectable,
churchly matrons standing on the stoops or the corners with their
hair tied up, together with a girl in sleazy satin whose face bore
the marks of gin and the razor, or heavy-set, abrupt, no-nonsense
older men, in company with the most disreputable and fanatical
"race" men, or these same "race" men with the sharpies, or these
sharpies with the churchly women. Seventh Day Adventists and
Methodists and Spiritualists seemed to be hobnobbing with
Holyrollers and they were all, alike, entangled with the most
flagrant disbelievers; something heavy in their stance seemed to
indicate that they had all, incredibly, seen a common vision, and
on each face there seemed to be the same strange, bitter shadow.

26   The churchly women and the matter-of-fact, no-nonsense
men had children in the Army. The sleazy girls they talked to had
lovers there, the sharpies and the "race" men had friends and
brothers there. It would have demanded an unquestioning patrio-
tism, happily as uncommon in this country as it is undesirable, for

these people not to have been disturbed by the bitter letters they received, by the newspaper stories they read, not to have been enraged by the posters, then to be found all over New York, which described the Japanese as "yellow-bellied Japs." It was only the "race" men, to be sure, who spoke ceaselessly of being revenged— how this vengeance was to be exacted was not clear—for the indignities and dangers suffered by Negro boys in uniform; but everybody felt a directionless, hopeless bitterness, as well as that panic which can scarcely be suppressed when one knows that a human being one loves is beyond one's reach, and in danger. This helplessness and this gnawing uneasiness does something, at length, to even the toughest mind. Perhaps the best way to sum all this up is to say that the people I knew felt, mainly, a peculiar kind of relief when they knew that their boys were being shipped out of the south, to do battle overseas. It was, perhaps, like feeling that the most dangerous part of a dangerous journey had been passed and that now, even if death should come, it would come with honor and without the complicity of their countrymen. Such a death would be, in short, a fact with which one could hope to live.

27   It was on the 28th of July, which I believe was a Wednesday, that I visited my father for the first time during his illness and for the last time in his life. The moment I saw him I knew why I had put off this visit so long. I had told my mother that I did not want to see him because I hated him. But this was not true. It was only that I *had* hated him and I wanted to hold on to this hatred. I did not want to look on him as a ruin: it was not a ruin I had hated. I imagine that one of the reasons people cling to their hates so stubbornly is because they sense, once hate is gone, that they will be forced to deal with pain.

28   We traveled out to him, his older sister and myself, to what seemed to be the very end of a very Long Island. It was hot and dusty and we wrangled, my aunt and I, all the way out, over the fact that I had recently begun to smoke and, as she said, to give myself airs. But I knew that she wrangled with me because she could not bear to face the fact of her brother's dying. Neither could I endure the reality of her despair, her unstated bafflement as to what had happened to her brother's life, and her own. So we wrangled and I smoked and from time to time she fell into a heavy reverie. Covertly, I watched her face, which was the face of an old woman; it had fallen in, the eyes were sunken and lightless; soon she would be dying, too.

29   In my childhood—it had not been so long ago—I had thought her beautiful. She had been quick-witted and quick-moving and very generous with all the children and each of her visits had been an event. At one time one of my brothers and myself had thought of running away to live with her. Now she could no longer produce out of her handbag some unexpected and yet familiar delight. She made me feel pity and revulsion and fear. It was awful to realize that she no longer caused me to feel affection. The closer we came to the hospital the more querulous she became and at the same time, naturally, grew more dependent on me. Between pity and guilt and fear I began to feel that there was another me trapped in my skull like a jack-in-the-box who might escape my control at any moment and fill the air with screaming.

30   She began to cry the moment we entered the room and she saw him lying there, all shriveled and still, like a little black monkey. The great, gleaming apparatus which fed him and would have compelled him to be still even if he had been able to move brought to mind, not beneficence, but torture; the tubes entering his arm made me think of pictures I had seen when a child, of Gulliver, tied down by the pygmies on that island. My aunt wept and wept, there was a whistling sound in my father's throat; nothing was said; he could not speak. I wanted to take his hand, to say something. But I do not know what I could have said, even if he could have heard me. He was not really in that room with us, he had at last really embarked on his journey; and though my aunt told me that he said he was going to meet Jesus, I did not hear anything except that whistling in his throat. The doctor came back and we left, into that unbearable train again, and home. In the morning came the telegram saying that he was dead. Then the house was suddenly full of relatives, friends, hysteria, and confusion and I quickly left my mother and the children to the care of those impressive women, who, in Negro communities at least, automatically appear at times of bereavement armed with lotions, proverbs, and patience, and an ability to cook. I went downtown. By the time I returned, later the same day, my mother had been carried to the hospital and the baby had been born.

III

31   For my father's funeral I had nothing black to wear and this posed a nagging problem all day long. It was one of those

problems, simple, or impossible of solution, to which the mind insanely clings in order to avoid the mind's real trouble. I spent most of that day at the downtown apartment of a girl I knew, celebrating my birthday with whiskey and wondering what to wear that night. When planning a birthday celebration one naturally does not expect that it will be up against competition from a funeral and this girl had anticipated taking me out that night, for a big dinner and a night club afterwards. Sometime during the course of that long day we decided that we would go out anyway, when my father's funeral service was over. I imagine *I* decided it, since, as the funeral hour approached, it became clearer and clearer to me that I would not know what to do with myself when it was over. The girl, stifling her very lively concern as to the possible effects of the whiskey on one of my father's chief mourners, concentrated on being conciliatory and practically helpful. She found a black shirt for me somewhere and ironed it and, dressed in the darkest pants and jacket I owned, and slightly drunk, I made my way to my father's funeral.

32   The chapel was full, but not packed, and very quiet. There were, mainly, my father's relatives, and his children, and here and there I saw faces I had not seen since childhood, the faces of my father's one-time friends. They were very dark and solemn now, seeming somehow to suggest that they had known all along that something like this would happen. Chief among the mourners was my aunt, who had quarreled with my father all his life; by which I do not mean to suggest that her mourning was insincere or that she had not loved him. I suppose that she was one of the few people in the world who had, and their incessant quarreling proved precisely the strength of the tie that bound them. The only other person in the world, as far as I knew, whose relationship to my father rivaled my aunt's in depth was my mother, who was not there.

33   It seemed to me, of course, that it was a very long funeral. But it was, if anything, a rather shorter funeral than most, nor, since there were no overwhelming, uncontrollable expressions of grief, could it be called—if I dare to use the word—successful. The minister who preached my father's funeral sermon was one of the few my father had still been seeing as he neared his end. He presented to us in his sermon a man whom none of us had ever seen—a man thoughtful, patient, and forbearing, a Christian inspiration to all who knew him, and a model for his children. And no doubt the children, in their disturbed and guilty state,

were almost ready to believe this; he had been remote enough to be anything and, anyway, the shock of the incontrovertible, that it was really our father lying up there in that casket, prepared the mind for anything. His sister moaned and this grief-stricken moaning was taken as corroboration. The other faces held a dark, non-committal thoughtfulness. This was not the man they had known, but they had scarcely expected to be confronted with *him;* this was, in a sense deeper than questions of fact, the man they had not known, and the man they had not known may have been the real one. The real man, whoever he had been, had suffered and now he was dead: this was all that was sure and all that mattered now. Every man in the chapel hoped that when his hour came he, too, would be eulogized, which is to say forgiven, and that all of his lapses, greeds, errors, and strayings from the truth would be invested with coherence and looked upon with charity. This was perhaps the last thing human beings could give each other and it was what they demanded, after all, of the Lord. Only the Lord saw the midnight tears, only He was present when one of His children, moaning and wringing hands, paced up and down the room. When one slapped one's child in anger the recoil in the heart reverberated through heaven and became part of the pain of the universe. And when the children were hungry and sullen and distrustful and one watched them, daily, growing wilder, and further away, and running headlong into danger, it was the Lord who knew what the charged heart endured as the strap was laid to the backside; the Lord alone who knew what one *would* have said if one had had, like the Lord, the gift of the living word. It was the Lord who knew of the impossibility every parent in that room faced: how to prepare the child for the day when the child would be despised and how to *create* in the child—by what means?—a stronger antidote to this poison than one had found for oneself. The avenues, side streets, bars, billiard halls, hospitals, police stations, and even the playgrounds of Harlem—not to mention the houses of correction, the jails, and the morgue—testified to the potency of the poison while remaining silent as to the efficacy of whatever antidote, irresistibly raising the question of whether or not such an antidote existed; raising, which was worse, the question of whether or not an antidote was desirable; perhaps poison should be fought with poison. With these several schisms in the mind and with more terrors in the heart than could be named, it was better not to judge the man who had gone down under an impossible burden. It was better to remember: *Thou knowest this man's fall; but thou knowest not his wrassling.*

34   While the preacher talked and I watched the children—years of changing their diapers, scrubbing them, slapping them, taking them to school, and scolding them had had the perhaps inevitable result of making me love them, though I am not sure I knew this then—my mind was busily breaking out with a rash of disconnected impressions. Snatches of popular songs, indecent jokes, bits of books I had read, movie sequences, faces, voices, political issues—I thought I was going mad; all these impressions suspended, as it were, in the solution of the faint nausea produced in me by the heat and liquor. For a moment I had the impression that my alcoholic breath, inefficiently disguised with chewing gum, filled the entire chapel. Then someone began singing one of my father's favorite songs and, abruptly, I was with him, sitting on his knee, in the hot, enormous, crowded church which was the first church we attended. It was the Abyssinia Baptist Church on 138th Street. We had not gone there long. With this image, a host of others came. I had forgotten, in the rage of my growing up, how proud my father had been of me when I was little. Apparently, I had had a voice and my father had liked to show me off before the members of the church. I had forgotten what he had looked like when he was pleased but now I remembered that he had always been grinning with pleasure when my solos ended. I even remembered certain expressions on his face when he teased my mother—had he loved her? I would never know. And when had it all begun to change? For now it seemed that he had not always been cruel. I remembered being taken for a haircut and scraping my knee on the footrest of the barber's chair and I remembered my father's face as he soothed my crying and applied the stinging iodine. Then I remembered our fights, fights which had been of the worst possible kind because my technique had been silence.

35   I remembered the one time in all our life together when we had really spoken to each other.

36   It was on a Sunday and it must have been shortly before I left home. We were walking, just the two of us, in our usual silence, to or from church. I was in high school and had been doing a lot of writing and I was, at about this time, the editor of the high school magazine. But I had also been a Young Minister and had been preaching from the pulpit. Lately, I had been tak-

ing fewer engagements and preached as rarely as possible. It was said in the church, quite truthfully, that I was "cooling off."

37   My father asked me abruptly, "You'd rather write than preach, wouldn't you?"

38   I was astonished at his question—because it was a real question. I answered, "Yes."

39   That was all we said. It was awful to remember that that was all we had *ever* said.

40   The casket now was opened and mourners were being led up the aisle to look for the last time on the deceased. The assumption was that the family was too overcome with grief to be allowed to make this journey alone and I watched while my aunt was led to the casket and, muffled in black, and shaking, led back to her seat. I disapproved of forcing the children to look on their dead father, considering that the shock of his death, or, more truthfully, the shock of death as a reality, was already a little more than a child could bear, but my judgment in this matter had been overruled and there they were, bewildered and frightened and very small, being led, one by one, to the casket. But there is also something very gallant about children at such moments. It has something to do with their silence and gravity and with the fact that one cannot help them. Their legs, somehow, seem *exposed,* so that it is at once incredible and terribly clear that their legs are all they have to hold them up.

41   I had not wanted to go to the casket myself and I certainly had not wished to be led there, but there was no way of avoiding either of these forms. One of the deacons led me up and I looked on my father's face. I cannot say that it looked like him at all. His blackness had been equivocated by powder and there was no suggestion in that casket of what his power had or could have been. He was simply an old man dead, and it was hard to believe that he had ever given anyone either joy or pain. Yet, his life filled that room. Further up the avenue his wife was holding his newborn child. Life and death so close together, and love and hatred, and right and wrong, said something to me which I did not want to hear concerning man, concerning the life of man.

42   After the funeral, while I was downtown desperately celebrating my birthday, a Negro soldier, in the lobby of the Hotel Braddock, got into a fight with a white policeman over a Negro girl. Negro girls, white policemen, in or out of uniform, and Negro males—in or out of uniform—were part of the furniture of

the lobby of the Hotel Braddock and this was certainly not the first time such an incident had occurred. It was destined, however, to receive an unprecedented publicity, for the fight between the policeman and the soldier ended with the shooting of the soldier. Rumor, flowing immediately to the streets outside, stated that the soldier had been shot in the back, an instantaneous and revealing invention, and that the soldier had died protecting a Negro woman. The facts were somewhat different—for example, the soldier had not been shot in the back, and was not dead, and the girl seems to have been as dubious a symbol of womanhood as her white counterpart in Georgia usually is, but no one was interested in the facts. They preferred the invention because this invention expressed and corroborated their hates and fears so perfectly. It is just as well to remember that people are always doing this. Perhaps many of those legends, including Christianity, to which the world clings began their conquest of the world with just some such concerted surrender to distortion. The effect, in Harlem, of this particular legend was like the effect of a lit match in a tin of gasoline. The mob gathered before the doors of the Hotel Braddock simply began to swell and to spread in every direction, and Harlem exploded.

43   The mob did not cross the ghetto lines. It would have been easy, for example, to have gone over Morningside Park on the west side or to have crossed the Grand Central railroad tracks at 125th Street on the east side, to wreak havoc in white neighborhoods. The mob seems to have been mainly interested in something more potent and real than the white face, that is, in white power, and the principal damage done during the riot of the summer of 1943 was to white business establishments in Harlem. It might have been a far bloodier story, of course, if, at the hour the riot began, these establishments had still been open. From the Hotel Braddock the mob fanned out, east and west along 125th Street, and for the entire length of Lenox, Seventh, and Eighth avenues. Along each of these avenues, and along each major side street—116th, 125th, 135th, and so on—bars, stores, pawnshops, restaurants, even little luncheonettes had been smashed open and entered and looted—looted, it might be added, with more haste than efficiency. The shelves really looked as though a bomb had struck them. Cans of beans and soup and dog food, along with toilet paper, corn flakes, sardines and milk tumbled every which way, and abandoned cash registers and cases of beer leaned crazi-

ly out of the splintered windows and were strewn along the
avenues. Sheets, blankets, and clothing of every description
formed a kind of path, as though people had dropped them while
running. I truly had not realized that Harlem *had* so many stores
until I saw them all smashed open; the first time the word *wealth*
ever entered my mind in relation to Harlem was when I saw it
scattered in the streets. But one's first, incongruous impression of
plenty was countered immediately by an impression of waste.
None of this was doing anybody any good. It would have been better to have left the plate glass as it had been and the goods lying
in the stores.

44   It would have been better, but it would also have been intolerable, for Harlem had needed something to smash. To smash
something is the ghetto's chronic need. Most of the time it is the
members of the ghetto who smash each other, and themselves.
But as long as the ghetto walls are standing there will always come
a moment when these outlets do not work. That summer, for
example, it was not enough to get into a fight on Lenox Avenue,
or curse out one's cronies in the barber shops. If ever, indeed, the
violence which fills Harlem's churches, pool halls, and bars erupts
outward in a more direct fashion, Harlem and its citizens are likely to vanish in an apocalyptic flood. That this is not likely to happen is due to a great many reasons, most hidden and powerful
among them the Negro's real relation to the white American.
This relation prohibits, simply, anything as uncomplicated and
satisfactory as pure hatred. In order really to hate white people,
one has to blot so much out of the mind—and the heart—that
this hatred itself becomes an exhausting and self-destructive pose.
But this does not mean, on the other hand, that love comes easily:
the white world is too powerful, too complacent, too ready with
gratuitous humiliation, and, above all, too ignorant and too innocent for that. One is absolutely forced to make perpetual
qualifications and one's own reactions are always canceling each
other out. It is this, really, which has driven so many people mad,
both white and black. One is always in the position of having to
decide between amputation and gangrene. Amputation is swift
but time may prove that the amputation was not necessary—or
one may delay the amputation too long. Gangrene is slow, but it is
impossible to be sure that one is reading one's symptoms right.
The idea of going through life as a cripple is more than one can
bear, and equally unbearable is the risk of swelling up slowly, in

agony, with poison. And the trouble, finally, is that the risks are real even if the choices do not exist.

45   "But as for me and my house," my father had said, "we will serve the Lord." I wondered, as we drove him to his resting place, what this line had meant for him. I had heard him preach it many times. I had preached it once myself, proudly giving it an interpretation different from my father's. Now the whole thing came back to me, as though my father and I were on our way to Sunday school and I were memorizing the golden text: *And if it seem evil unto you to serve the Lord, choose you this day whom you will serve; whether the gods which your fathers served that were on the other side of the flood, or the gods of the Amorites, in whose land ye dwell: but as for me and my house, we will serve the Lord.* I suspected in these familiar lines a meaning which had never been there for me before. All of my father's texts and songs, which I had decided were meaningless, were arranged before me at his death like empty bottles, waiting to hold the meaning which life would give them for me. This was his legacy: nothing is ever escaped. That bleakly memorable morning I hated the unbelievable streets and the Negroes and whites who had, equally, made them that way. But I knew that it was folly, as my father would have said, this bitterness was folly. It was necessary to hold on to the things that mattered. The dead man mattered, the new life mattered; blackness and whiteness did not matter; to believe that they did was to acquiesce in one's own destruction. Hatred, which could destroy so much, never failed to destroy the man who hated and this was an immutable law.

46   It began to seem that one would have to hold in the mind forever two ideas which seemed to be in opposition. The first idea was acceptance, the acceptance, totally without rancor, of life as it is, and men as they are: in the light of this idea, it goes without saying that injustice is a commonplace. But this did not mean that one could be complacent, for the second idea was of equal power: that one must never, in one's own life, accept these injustices as commonplace but must fight them with all one's strength. This fight begins, however, in the heart and it now had been laid to my charge to keep my own heart free of hatred and despair. This intimation made my heart heavy and, now that my father was irrecoverable, I wished that he had been beside me so that I could have searched his face for the answers which only the future would give me now.

QUESTIONS

Ideas

1. In section I Baldwin describes his father and characterizes him.
    Where does this begin and end? What does Baldwin say about his
    father? What observations about his father does Baldwin make in
    section III, and how do they relate to his observations and descrip-
    tions of section I?

2. In the descriptions of his father, Baldwin also reveals things about
    himself, particularly, of course, about his relationship with his
    father. What kind of relationship was it? What is Baldwin's final
    assessment of his father—of his life and character?

3. We might say that Baldwin uses description and narration through-
    out the essay in the service of argumentation. What point does
    Baldwin make in narrating the restaurant incident? What point is
    made in the description of Harlem as he rides through in a car on
    the day of his father's funeral?

4. In the second paragraph of section II, Baldwin moves out in
    thought. Up to that point—in section I and in the first paragraph of
    section II—he has been describing his family. What new considera-
    tions are introduced, and how are they related to the facts and
    actions presented in section I?

5. Trace the sequence of ideas—and the pattern of cause and effect—
    through paragraphs 24, 25, and 26. What is Baldwin's point here?

6. What ironies of circumstance does Baldwin indicate in the first
    paragraph of section III? What other ironies do you detect in the
    essay?

7. What is the point of mentioning who attended the funeral?
    What does Baldwin mean when he suggests that his aunt was one
    of the few people in the world who had loved his father, and yet
    "their incessant quarreling proved precisely the strength of their
    tie"?

8. In paragraph 45 Baldwin brings together the personal and the
    social, the private and public, his father and Harlem. What conclu-
    sions does he draw about his relationship to his father and about
    the hatred and rage and bitterness that sparked the riots? Explain
    the final sentence of the paragraph: "Hatred, which could destroy
    so much, never failed to destroy the man who hated and this was an
    immutable law."

9. "Notes of a Native Son" ends with a pair of contradictory impulses,
    with two irreconcilable ideas. What are they, and how does Baldwin
    both emphasize them and tie them in with what has gone before?

Organization

10. The essay is divided into three major sections. Provide a title for each, explain the main point of each, and comment on the relation-ship among the three sections.

11. Take any one of the three sections and examine its structure. Explain how it begins, where it goes, and how it ends. Explain how each of its parts fits into the whole section and into the entire essay.

12. As you reread the first paragraph of section II, think back or look back to the opening of section I. What connections do you notice? Why does Baldwin begin section II this way? How does this opening tie in to the essay as a whole?

13. The third paragraph of section III (33) splits in half. In the first part Baldwin mentions that his father was eulogized, that the preacher's description of the man he and his brothers and sisters had known was strikingly different from the reality. Yet Baldwin finds comfort and meaning in this discrepancy. Why? In the second part of this paragraph Baldwin himself eulogizes his father—but not only his father. He presents an imaginative and sympathetic account of how his father and other men under similar pressures of prejudice, fear, insecurity, and bitterness must have felt and why they must be for-given this bitter hatred. Find the place where Baldwin shifts from one concern to the other. How, specifically, does he accomplish the shift?

14. How does Baldwin manage the shift from the preacher's sermon to happier memories of his childhood? (Consider paragraph 34.) Paragraphs 35–39 form a unit. What is the point of this highly con-densed segment, and why is it so brief?

Sentences

15. Baldwin ends many of his paragraphs with emphatic, vivid sen-tences. Read through the final sentences of all the paragraphs in section I in sequence. What do you notice?

16. What balances and parallels does Baldwin include in his opening sentences? How do the rhythm and the word order of the third and fourth sentences continue the rhythm and structure established in the first and second sentences? What is the effect of this structural and rhythmic patterning? For convenience, here are the first four sentences of the essay:

> On the 29th of July, in 1943, my father died. On the same day, a few hours later, his last child was born. Over a month before this, while all our energies were concentrated in waiting for these events, there had been, in Detroit, one of the bloodiest race riots of the century. A few hours after my father's funeral, while he lay

in state in the undertaker's chapel, a race riot broke out in Harlem. On the morning of the 3rd of August, we drove my father to the graveyard through a wilderness of smashed plate glass.

17.   In paragraph 2 of section I Baldwin again uses parallel sentences. Look especially at sentences 3 and 4 and at sentences 5 through 7. Read the sentences aloud, noting pacing and pauses.

18.   Reread one of Baldwin's paragraphs, mentally deleting all material between commas. What happens to the sound and the weight of the sentences?

19.   Here is one of Baldwin's paragraphs without punctuation. Punctuate it, then compare your version with those of other students and with Baldwin's punctuation. What differences in tone, rhythm, and emphasis do you notice?

My friend stayed outside the restaurant long enough to misdirect my pursuers and the police who arrived he told me at once I do not know what I said to him when he came to my room that night I could not have said much I felt in the oddest most awful way that I had somehow betrayed him I lived it over and over and over again the way one relives an automobile accident after it has happened and one finds oneself alone and safe I could not get over two facts both equally difficult for the imagination to grasp and one was that I could have been murdered but the other was that I had been ready to commit murder I saw nothing very clearly but I did see this that my life my real life was in danger and not from anything other people might do but from the hatred I carried in my own heart.

20.   In the third paragraph from the end of the essay, Baldwin uses two unusual sentence patterns: a sentence beginning with an infinitive; another sentence beginning with a nominalization:

infinitive: To smash something is the ghetto's chronic need.
nominalization: That this is not likely to happen is due to a great many reasons, most hidden and powerful among them the Negro's real relation to the white American.

In this paragraph also, Baldwin mixes and varies his sentences in length, form, and opening phrasing. Examine the paragraph from these standpoints.

21.   The final paragraph of the essay achieves coherence, continuity, and emphasis, mainly by careful repetition of words and phrases. Circle or underline the words and phrases that establish this coherence and continuity.

Words

22.   There are two vocabularies in "Notes of a Native Son": simple, common words; more formal and unusual longer words, usually of Latin

derivation. Read paragraphs 2 and 3, marking off words of each type. Then find a passage of five or six sentences where Baldwin blends the two kinds of diction What is the effect of the mixture?

23. In the narrative portions of the essay, especially in paragraphs 17, 21, and 22, Baldwin employs comparisons. What is the point of each?

24. Explain how Baldwin uses imagery—especially comparisons—to make his point in paragraphs 28, 29, 30, and 45.

25. Read the following passage, noting especially its sound effects of assonance, consonance, rhyme, and alliteration:

> He could be chilling in the pulpit and indescribably cruel in his personal life and he was certainly the most bitter man I have ever met; yet it must be said that there was something else in him, buried in him, which lent him his tremendous power and, even, a rather crushing charm. It had something to do with his blackness, I think—he was very black—with his blackness and beauty, and with the fact that he knew that he was black but did not know that he was beautiful. He claimed to be proud of his blackness but it had also been the cause of much humiliation and it had fixed bleak boundaries to his life.

26. In paragraph 43 Baldwin describes the effects of the looting. What comparisons does he use and how effective are they? In the next paragraph (44) he uses the language of disease to express the consequences for blacks of race relations in the United States. What psychological difference is Baldwin suggesting by means of describing the physical differences between gangrene and amputation?

Suggestions for Writing

A. Baldwin ends section I with a narrative account of an episode at a New Jersey restaurant. He begins this account with an idea and he ends it with one. Write an essay in which you describe something that happened to you, something that made you aware of yourself, or something that made you aware of a social, political, religious, or racial situation. Begin and end your account, as Baldwin does, with an idea.

B. Write your own "Notes of a Native Son or Daughter." Try to come to terms with your ethnic or racial heritage and with your place in relation to the society of which you are a part.

C. Describe one of your parents or relatives, examining your relationship with that person. Or compare your parents or two of your other relatives.

D. Reread the last paragraph of section I and of section III. Discuss the ideas in an essay.

E.   Write imitations of the sentences discussed in questions 15–21.

F.   Discuss the following poem by Stephen Crane in relation to what Baldwin says about himself in the final paragraph of section I.

A MAN FEARED

A man feared that he might find an assassin;
Another that he might find a victim.
One was more wise than the other.

THREE

Joan Didion

(1934–   )

Joan Didion writes to understand herself and her culture. For her, writing is a tool, a way to overcome the randomness of life and to create order and clarity. Writing can do that. It can help us give shape to experience. In fact, one cognitive skill that separates us from primitive cultures is our ability to create an identity, a special voice for ourself by writing down what we think about things.

If you lived in a traditional culture, your identity would be given to you. You would not think of shaping and interpreting your experience, and you would not even imagine that you could create new and important ways of looking at the world. In highly literate societies, however, writers do just that. Didion is often striving for greater self-knowledge through her essays. She does not accept what is given to her by the media, her parents, or school. She is exploring and searching for her own understanding of the world through language. In advanced societies, like ours, writing can be a powerful tool for knowing.

But Didion goes even further than that. She begins one of her essays, "The White Album" (after the famous 1968 Beatles double album), with this provocative sentence: "We tell ourselves stories in order to live." Isn't she implying that giving shape and meaning to our lives through writing is necessary and vital? When we see and read about events, we can impose a structure and significance on them through writing. As a result, we really begin to know them. This is what E. M. Forster meant when he said, "How do I know what I think until I see what I say?" Our experiences and ideas exist as shapeless, half-articulated thoughts and impressions until we impose order on them through writing. Didion continues: "We interpret what we see, select the most workable of the multiple choices. We live entirely, especially if we are writers, by the imposition of a narrative line upon disparate images, by the 'ideas' with which we have learned to freeze the shifting phantasmagoria which is our actual experience."

That sounds positive and encouraging. Writing, unlike speech, freezes our experiences and our ideas and helps us to see, to understand, to contemplate what we have written. Then we can look back and revise; we can get to the center of things, the heart of the matter. And in doing so, Didion refines and strengthens her voice and her sense of self.

Although Didion is a reporter, she is not strictly a journalist. In *The White Album,* for example, she gives us vivid and representative snapshots of life in the 1960s. But these are subjective reports, usually offered without commentary. She does not tie things together in neat bundles, and she is clearly not trying to be objective. She wants readers to fit the pieces together to form their own pictures, their own understanding, their own theme. She is a witness to important truths about our culture, but she does not usually present her findings explicitly. In "Salvador" and "Marrying Absurd" she makes her points by carefully selecting details and placing them in precisely the right place. The reader must do the rest.

Didion's prose style is also understated, almost indirect. She gives the impression of being in control, of withholding strong emotion. And she can be direct "without being trivial or colloquial." The following two sentences from "Goodbye to All That" are typical of her spare, elegant prose: "All I know is that it was very bad when I was twenty-eight. Everything that was said to me I seemed to have heard before, and I could no longer listen." The directness of these lines makes a promise to the reader. Didion is not hiding behind elaborately complex sentences or difficult vocabulary. Such clear, strong writing does not come naturally to anyone. Didion had to work at it, long and hard. Like all writers, regardless of ability or success, Didion worries about her ability to "get it right." Her solution is both simple and rigorous: revise, cut, rearrange, rework—again and again. The hard work pays off in the bite and authority of her exact prose.

Some of this concern for stylistic precision she learned as a student, from reading Hemingway:

> I learned a lot about how sentences worked. How a short sentence worked. How they worked in a paragraph. Where the commas worked. How every word had to matter. It made me excited about words. . . . When I was fifteen or sixteen I would type out his stories . . . I mean they're perfect sentences. Very direct sentences, smooth rivers, clear water over granite, no sinkholes.

After she graduated from the University of California, Berkeley, in 1956 with a degree in English, she wrote for such national magazines as *Mademoiselle, Saturday Evening Post,* and *Life.* Early in her career she worked on *Vogue*'s editorial staff. Later, she commented that she learned how verbs work from a senior editor there: "Every day I would go into her office with eight lines of copy or a caption or something. She would sit there and mark it up with a pencil and get very angry about extra words, about verbs not working. . . . In an eight-line caption everything had to work, every word, every comma."

She went on to publish a novel, *Run River,* in 1963. Then, after having spent about eight years in New York, she moved back to California, where she still lives with her husband, the novelist John Gregory Dunne. She wrote about the move: "We took an afternoon flight back to Los Angeles, and on the way home from the airport that night I could see the moon on the Pacific and smell jasmine all around and we both knew that there was no longer any point in keeping the apartment we still kept in New York." Although she continues to write interesting novels *(Play It As It Lays, The Book of Common Prayer,* and *Democracy),* she has received the most acclaim for her essay collections, *Slouching Towards Bethlehem* (1968), *The White Album* (1979), and *Salvador* (1983), a journalistic chronicle of the two weeks that she and her husband spent amidst the confusion of war-torn El Salvador in 1982. Supporters of the government did not like her account. It has been praised as "a withering indictment of American foreign policy." Most, however, agree that in this "surrealist docudrama" Didion is able to achieve what she seldom does in her fiction: "a consummate political artwork."

Her most recent nonfiction, *Miami* (1987), is also her most praised. She paints a complex portrait of the relationship between the Cuban exiles in Miami and the city's history, racial mix, and political drama. In the excerpt given here, Didion juxtaposes two cultures, one a city of old-fashioned Southern racial tension, the other a city of fast money on the edge of Latin America. Their confrontation is disturbing.

Probably because her family has lived in Sacramento for generations, Didion is concerned with traditional values in conflict with modern life-styles, with what we've lost and what we still have in America. She is afraid that "the children of the aerospace engineers" who "have never met a great-aunt" will "have lost the real past and gained a manufactured one, and there will be no way for them to know, no way at all." But even this nostalgia cannot withstand her passion for a deeper, more personal truth. She continues: "But perhaps it is presumptuous of me to assume that they will be missing something. Perhaps in retrospect this has been a story not about Sacramento at all, but about the things we lose and the promises we break as we grow older; perhaps I have been playing out unawares the Margaret in the poem:

> Margaret, are you grieving
> Over Goldengrove unleaving? . . .
> It is the blight man was born for,
> It is Margaret you mourn for.

There is no doubt that Didion often despairs about the fragmentation and banality of contemporary American life, but the clarity and energy of her writing suggest that she has found an antidote to inconclusiveness and plastic values.

Marrying Absurd

---

1   To be married in Las Vegas, Clark County, Nevada, a bride must swear that she is eighteen or has parental permission and a bridegroom that he is twenty-one or has parental permission. Someone must put up five dollars for the license. (On

Sundays and holidays, fifteen dollars. The Clark County Courthouse issues marriage licenses at any time of the day or night except between noon and one in the afternoon, between eight and nine in the evening, and between four and five in the morning.) Nothing else is required. The State of Nevada, alone among these United States, demands neither a premarital blood test nor a waiting period before or after the issuance of a marriage license. Driving in across the Mojave from Los Angeles, one sees the signs way out on the desert, looming up from that moonscape of rattlesnakes and mesquite, even before the Las Vegas lights appear like a mirage on the horizon: "GETTING MARRIED? Free License Information First Strip Exit." Perhaps the Las Vegas wedding industry achieved its peak operational efficiency between 9:00 p.m. and midnight of August 26, 1965, an otherwise unremarkable Thursday which happened to be, by Presidential order, the last day on which anyone could improve his draft status merely by getting married. One hundred and seventy-one couples were pronounced man and wife in the name of Clark County and the State of Nevada that night, sixty-seven of them by a single justice of the peace, Mr. James A. Brennan. Mr. Brennan did one wedding at the Dunes and the other sixty-six in his office, and charged each couple eight dollars. One bride lent her veil to six others. "I got it down from five to three minutes," Mr. Brennan said later of his feat. "I could've married them *en masse*, but they're people, not cattle. People expect more when they get married."

2   What people who get married in Las Vegas actually do expect—what, in the largest sense, their "expectations" are— strikes one as a curious and self-contradictory business. Las Vegas is the most extreme and allegorical of American settlements, bizarre and beautiful in its venality and in its devotion to immediate gratification, a place the tone of which is set by mobsters and call girls and ladies' room attendants with amyl nitrite poppers in their uniform pockets. Almost everyone notes that there is no "time" in Las Vegas, no night and no day and no past and no future (no Las Vegas casino, however, has taken the obliteration of the ordinary time sense quite so far as Harold's Club in Reno, which for a while issued, at odd intervals in the day and night, mimeographed "bulletins" carrying news from the world outside); neither is there any logical sense of where one is. One is standing on a highway in the middle of a vast hostile desert looking at an eighty-foot sign which blinks "STARDUST" or "CAESAR'S PALACE." Yes,

but what does that explain? This geographical implausibility reinforces the sense that what happens there has no connection with
"real" life; Nevada cities like Reno and Carson are ranch towns,
Western towns, places behind which there is some historical
imperative. But Las Vegas seems to exist only in the eye of the
beholder. All of which makes it an extraordinarily stimulating and
interesting place, but an odd one in which to want to wear a candlelight satin Priscilla of Boston wedding dress with Chantilly lace
insets, tapered sleeves and a detachable modified train.

3   And yet the Las Vegas wedding business seems to appeal to
precisely that impulse. "Sincere and Dignified Since 1954," one
wedding chapel advertises. There are nineteen such wedding
chapels in Las Vegas, intensely competitive, each offering better,
faster, and, by implication, more sincere services than the next:
Our Photos Best Anywhere, Your Wedding on A Phonograph
Record, Candlelight with Your Ceremony, Honeymoon
Accommodations, Free Transportation from Your Motel to
Courthouse to Chapel and Return to Motel, Religious or Civil
Ceremonies, Dressing Rooms, Flowers, Rings, Announcements,
Witnesses Available, and Ample Parking. All of these services, like
most others in Las Vegas (sauna baths, payroll-check cashing,
chinchilla coats for sale or rent), are offered twenty-four hours a
day, seven days a week, presumably on the premise that marriage,
like craps, is a game to be played when the table seems hot.

4   But what strikes one most about the Strip chapels, with their
wishing wells and stained-glass paper windows and their artificial
bouvardia, is that so much of their business is by no means a matter of simple convenience, of late-night liaisons between show
girls and baby Crosbys. Of course there is some of that. (One
night about eleven o'clock in Las Vegas I watched a bride in an
orange minidress and masses of flame-colored hair stumble from
a Strip chapel on the arm of her bridegroom, who looked the part
of the expendable nephew in movies like *Miami Syndicate.* "I gotta
get the kids," the bride whimpered. "I gotta pick up the sitter, I
gotta get to the midnight show." "What you gotta get," the bridegroom said, opening the door of a Cadillac Coupe de Ville and
watching her crumple on the seat, "is sober.") But Las Vegas
seems to offer something other than "convenience"; it is merchan-
dising "niceness," the facsimile of proper ritual, to children who
do not know how else to find it, how to make the arrangements,
how to do it "right." All day and evening long on the Strip, one
sees actual wedding parties, waiting under the harsh lights at a

crosswalk, standing uneasily in the parking lot of the Frontier while the photographer hired by The Little Church of the West ("Wedding Place of the Stars") certifies the occasion, takes the picture: the bride in a veil and white satin pumps, the bridegroom usually in a white dinner jacket, and even an attendant or two, a sister or a best friend in hot-pink *peau de soie*, a flirtation veil, a carnation nosegay. "When I Fall in Love It Will Be Forever," the organist plays, and then a few bars of Lohengrin. The mother cries; the stepfather, awkward in his role, invites the chapel hostess to join them for a drink at the Sands. The hostess declines with a professional smile; she has already transferred her interest to the group waiting outside. One bride out, another in, and again the sign goes up on the chapel door: "One moment please—Wedding."

5   I sat next to one such wedding party in a Strip restaurant the last time I was in Las Vegas. The marriage had just taken place; the bride still wore her dress, the mother her corsage. A bored waiter poured out a few swallows of pink champagne ("on the house") for everyone but the bride, who was too young to be served. "You'll need something with more kick than that," the bride's father said with heavy jocularity to his new son-in-law; the ritual jokes about the wedding night had a certain Panglossian character, since the bride was clearly several months pregnant. Another round of pink champagne, this time not on the house, and the bride began to cry. "It was just as nice," she sobbed, "as I hoped and dreamed it would be."

QUESTIONS

Ideas

1. Didion jumps into this essay without the usual introductory announcement of the theme. Does she, in fact, give us one later on? What is it, in your own words?

2. What contrast does Didion hope the reader will see between the "candlelight satin . . . wedding dress" and the Las Vegas chapels? Just what does Las Vegas have to offer these young people? Is it false or real? Does that matter to them? To Didion? To you? You need to consider the implications of the title, of course.

3. What is Didion's purpose in the essay? To entertain? To persuade? To ridicule? What is she suggesting about Las Vegas marriages and

about the cast of characters involved in them? On a more general level, what does the contrast between the traditional "Norman Rockwell" wedding and the chapels in Las Vegas suggest about America? Is this the same theme Didion develops in "On Going Home"?

4.   Are we meant to laugh at the scene in the last paragraph?

5.   On a more abstract level, what is the function of ritual in our lives? Can we do without it? Should we?

Organization

6.   Didion organized this piece as a blend of description, narration, and exposition. She provides the essay with a narrative frame: we begin with Mr. Brennan, then move on to the show girl section, and then to the restaurant scene. How effective is this structure? Could Didion have organized the essay differently? How?

7.   Notice the connecting devices between each of the paragraphs. What is the connection between the first and last sentences of paragraph 2? Between the first sentence of paragraph 2 and the last sentence of paragraph 1?

8.   Paragraph 2 has a different function than paragraphs 1 and 3. And it contains a different kind of information. How does that information help us to understand the details of the first and third paragraphs?

Sentences

9.   Didion makes extensive use of direct quotation in this essay. Three paragraphs, in fact, end with a direct statement (1, 4, and 5). What is the effect of these quotations?

10.   Do the sentences in the second paragraph seem more complicated than those in either the first or last? What might be the reason for this?

Words

11.   When Didion uses a simile in comparing marriage in Las Vegas to playing craps (paragraph 3), what does the use of that device suggest about her attitude toward the Strip chapels? What other comparisons does she use, and what is she implying by the comparisons?

12.   Is the title effective? Can you think of an alternate title? How about "Marriage in Las Vegas"? Is Didion's title better? Why or why not?

13.   Irony is often conveyed by writing one thing but meaning another. We are not, it seems, meant to be impressed by Mr. Brennan's con-

cern for the individual just because he doesn't marry people en masse. Didion uses irony throughout her essay for a variety of purposes. What are some other examples of Didion's use of irony? Look especially at the last paragraph. What effect is she trying to achieve? Does she assume you will agree with her view of the people in Las Vegas? Do you? Would the bride of the last paragraph agree with the thesis of this essay? Why does she cry? Does the last sentence surprise you?

Suggestions for Writing

A. Try rewriting one or two quotations (from paragraphs 1, 4, or 5), converting the direct speech into an indirectly reported statement without quotation marks. Which do you prefer? What is different about them?

B. Write an essay combining narration and description about a place you have a strong feeling about. Try to let the details indicate what your attitude is, i.e., avoid stating an explicit theme while still communicating a central impression.

C. Write an essay about something you are critical of—violent sports, TV game shows, political conventions, shopping centers, fast-food eateries, commercials, whatever. Try to describe your subject without explicitly stating your viewpoint and attitude. Carefully select specific details to convey your point by implication. When you read your essay to a friend, ask him or her to state your attitude. See how close it comes to your intentions. Perhaps you will want to select new details or add to those you have after receiving this feedback.

The White Album

1.

1   WE TELL OURSELVES STORIES in order to live. The princess is caged in the consulate. The man with the candy will lead the children into the sea. The naked woman on the ledge outside the window on the sixteenth floor is a victim of accidie, or the naked woman is an exhibitionist, and it would be "interesting" to know which. We tell ourselves that it makes some difference whether the naked woman is about to commit a mortal sin or is about to register a political protest or is about to be, the

Aristophanic view, snatched back to the human condition by the fireman in priest's clothing just visible in the window behind her, the one smiling at the telephoto lens. We look for the sermon in the suicide, for the social or moral lesson in the murder of five. We interpret what we see, select the most workable of the multiple choices. We live entirely, especially if we are writers, by the imposition of a narrative line upon disparate images, by the "ideas" with which we have learned to freeze the shifting phantasmagoria which is our actual experience.

3.

2   IT WAS SIX, seven o'clock of an early spring evening in 1968 and I was sitting on the cold vinyl floor of a sound studio on Sunset Boulevard, watching a band called The Doors record a rhythm track. On the whole my attention was only minimally engaged by the preoccupations of rock-and-roll bands (I had already heard about acid as a transitional stage and also about the Maharishi and even about Universal Love, and after a while it all sounded like marmalade skies to me), but The Doors were different, The Doors interested me. The Doors seemed unconvinced that love was brotherhood and the Kama Sutra. The Doors' music insisted that love was sex and sex was death and therein lay salvation. The Doors were the Norman Mailers of the Top Forty, missionaries of apocalyptic sex. *Break on through*, their lyrics urged, and *Light my fire*, and:

> Come on baby, gonna take a little ride
> Goin' down by the ocean side
> Gonna get real close
> Get real tight
> Baby gonna drown tonight—
> Goin' down, down, down.

3   On this evening in 1968 they were gathered together in uneasy symbiosis to make their third album, and the studio was too cold and the lights were too bright and there were masses of wires and banks of the ominous blinking electronic circuitry with which musicians live so easily. There were three of the four Doors.

There was a bass player borrowed from a band called Clear Light. There were the producer and the engineer and the road manager and a couple of girls and a Siberian husky named Nikki with one gray eye and one gold. There were paper bags half filled with hard-boiled eggs and chicken livers and cheeseburgers and empty bottles of apple juice and California rosé. There was everything and everybody The Doors needed to cut the rest of this third album except one thing, the fourth Door, the lead singer, Jim Morrison, a 24-year-old graduate of U.C.L.A. who wore black vinyl pants and no underwear and tended to suggest some range of the possible just beyond a suicide pact. It was Morrison who had described The Doors as "erotic politicians." It was Morrison who had defined the group's interests as "anything about revolt, disorder, chaos, about activity that appears to have no meaning." It was Morrison who got arrested in Miami in December of 1967 for giving an "indecent" performance. It was Morrison who wrote most of The Doors' lyrics, the peculiar character of which was to reflect either an ambiguous paranoia or a quite unambiguous insistence upon the love-death as the ultimate high. And it was Morrison who was missing. It was Ray Manzarek and Robby Krieger and John Densmore who made The Doors sound the way they sounded, and maybe it was Manzarek and Krieger and Densmore who made seventeen out of twenty interviewees on *American Bandstand* prefer The Doors over all other bands, but it was Morrison who got up there in his black vinyl pants with no underwear and projected the idea, and it was Morrison they were waiting for now.

4   "Hey listen," the engineer said. "I was listening to an FM station on the way over here, they played three Doors songs, first they played 'Back Door Man' and then 'Love Me Two Times' and 'Light My Fire.'"

5   "I heard it," Densmore muttered. "I heard it."

6   "So what's wrong with somebody playing three of your songs?"

7   "This cat dedicates it to his family."

8   "Yeah? To his family?"

9   "To his family. Really crass."

10   Ray Manzarek was hunched over a Gibson keyboard. "You think *Morrison*'s going to come back?" he asked to no one in particular.

11   No one answered.

12   "So we can do some *vocals?*" Manzarek said.

13   The producer was working with the tape of the rhythm track they had just recorded. "I hope so," he said without looking up.

14   "Yeah," Manzarek said. "So do I."

15   My leg had gone to sleep, but I did not stand up; unspecific tensions seemed to be rendering everyone in the room catatonic. The producer played back the rhythm track. The engineer said that he wanted to do his deep-breathing exercises. Manzarek ate a hard-boiled egg. "Tennyson made a mantra out of his own name," he said to the engineer. "I don't know if he said 'Tennyson Tennyson Tennyson' or 'Alfred Alfred Alfred' or 'Alfred Lord Tennyson,' but anyway, he did it. Maybe he just said 'Lord Lord Lord.'"

16   "Groovy," the Clear Light bass player said. He was an amiable enthusiast, not at all a Door in spirit.

17   "I wonder what Blake said," Manzarek mused. "Too bad *Morrison*'s not here. *Morrison* would know."

18   It was a long while later. Morrison arrived. He had on his black vinyl pants and he sat down on a leather couch in front of the four big blank speakers and he closed his eyes. The curious aspect of Morrison's arrival was this: no one acknowledged it. Robby Krieger continued working out a guitar passage. John Densmore tuned his drums. Manzarek sat at the control console and twirled a corkscrew and let a girl rub his shoulders. The girl did not look at Morrison, although he was in her direct line of sight. An hour or so passed, and still no one had spoken to Morrison. Then Morrison spoke to Manzarek. He spoke almost in a whisper, as if he were wresting the words from behind some disabling aphasia.

19   "It's an hour to West Covina," he said. "I was thinking maybe we should spend the night out there after we play."

20   Manzarek put down the corkscrew. "Why?" he said.

21   "Instead of coming back."

22   Manzarek shrugged. "We were planning to come back."

23   "Well, I was thinking, we could rehearse out there."

24   Manzarek said nothing.

25   "We could get in a rehearsal, there's a Holiday Inn next door."

26   "We could do that," Manzarek said. "Or we could rehearse Sunday, in town."

27   "I guess so." Morrison paused. "Will the place be ready to rehearse Sunday?"

28   Manzarek looked at him for a while. "No," he said then.

29   I counted the control knobs on the electronic console. There were seventy-six. I was unsure in whose favor the dialogue had been resolved, or if it had been resolved at all. Robby Krieger picked at his guitar, and said that he needed a fuzz box. The producer suggested that he borrow one from the Buffalo Springfield, who were recording in the next studio. Krieger shrugged. Morrison sat down again on the leather couch and leaned back. He lit a match. He studied the flame awhile and then very slowly, very deliberately, lowered it to the fly of his black vinyl pants. Manzarek watched him. The girl who was rubbing Manzarek's shoulders did not look at anyone. There was a sense that no one was going to leave the room, ever. It would be some weeks before The Doors finished recording this album. I did not see it through.

QUESTIONS

Ideas

1. What stories does our country tell itself "in order to live"? What about your family, your university, yourself?

2. When Didion refers to our "actual experience," is she suggesting that any "narrative line" is fictive? What does she mean when she says "we interpret what we see"? Is everything we see filtered through our own personal psychological and social lens?

3. When Didion says, "it all sounded like marmalade skies to me," is she being ironic, sarcastic, contemptuous, affectionate, or something else?

4. Why doesn't Didion see The Doors' session through? Is it because she can't figure out a "narrative line"? What might a plausible one be?

Organization

5. In the essay "The White Album," Didion uses "flash cuts," a device from film, to organize over a dozen little anecdotes or narratives. Although part of her point is that in the sixties there were few normal stories, she does seem to use a conventional structure within these "flash cuts." How would you describe the structure here? Is there a beginning, middle, and end, for example?

Sentences

6. Look at the length of Didion's sentences in the opening paragraph. Is there a strategy here?
7. Didion's sentences tend to the subject, verb, object pattern. Point to some variations.

Words

8. Didion uses several unusual words: accidie, phantasmagoria, Aristophanic, symbiosis, aphasia. What do they mean? Are these words part of your reading, writing, or speaking vocabulary?
9. Didion seems to use "catatonic" as a statement of fact. Why might she use this word?

Writing Suggestions

A. Write a paraphrase (a summary in your own words) of the first paragraph. Be as clear, as straightforward, as you can.
B. Write a narrative of an event that you had trouble understanding, one that you could not figure out, one whose neat "narrative line" escaped you.
C. Write an essay in which you give examples of different kinds of "stories" we tell ourselves as individuals, as a school, a region, or a country.

Miami

---

1   On my first visits to Miami I was always being told that there were places I should not go. There were things I should and should not do. I should not walk the block and a half from the Omni to the *Herald* alone after dark. I should lock my car doors when I drove at night. If I hit a red light as I was about to enter I-95 I should not stop but look both ways, and accelerate. I should not drive through Liberty City, or walk around Overtown. If I had occasion to drive through what was called "the black Grove," those several dozen blocks of project housing which separated the expensive greenery of Coral Gables from the expensive greenery of Coconut Grove, I should rethink my route, avoid at all costs the territory of the disentitled, which in fact was hard to do, since Miami was a city, like so many to the south of it, in which it was

possible to pass from walled enclaves to utter desolation while changing stations on the car radio.

2   In the end I went without incident to all of the places I had been told not to go, and did not or did do most of the things I had been told to do or not to do, but the subtext of what I had been told, that this was a city in which black people and white people viewed each other with some discontent, stayed with me, if only because the most dramatic recent season of that discontent, the spring of 1980, the season when certain disruptive events in Havana happened to coincide with a drama then being played out in a Florida courtroom, still figured so large in the local memory. Many people in Miami mentioned the spring of 1980 to me, speaking always of its "mood," which appeared to have been one of collective fever. In the spring of 1980 everyone had been, it was said, "nervous," or "tense." This tension had built, it was said, "to a point of just no return," or "to the breaking point." "It could drive you mad, just waiting for something to happen," one woman said. "The Cuban kids were all out leaning on their horns and the blacks were all out sitting on their porches," someone else said. "You knew it was going to happen but you didn't know when. And anyway it was going to happen. There was no doubt about that. It was like, well, a bad dream. When you try to wake up and you can't."

3   The Miami part of what happened that spring, the part people in Miami refer to as "McDuffie," had its proximate beginning early on the morning of December 17, 1979, when a thirty-three-year-old black insurance agent named Arthur McDuffie was said by police to have made a rolling stop at a red light, to have executed the maneuver called "popping a wheelie" on his borrowed Kawasaki motorcycle, and to have given the finger to a Dade County Public Safety Department officer parked nearby. The officer gave chase. By the time Arthur McDuffie was apprehended, eight minutes later, more than a dozen Dade County and city of Miami police units had converged on the scene.

4   Accounts of the next several minutes conflict. What is known is that at some point a rescue unit was called, for the victim of an "accident," and that four days later Arthur McDuffie died, without regaining consciousness, in Jackson Memorial Hospital. On March 31, 1980, four Dade County Public Safety Department officers, all four of them white, each charged with having played some role in the beating of Arthur McDuffie or in the subsequent attempt to make his injuries seem the result of a motorcycle accident, went on trial before an all-white jury in Tampa, where the

case had been moved after a Miami judge granted a change of venue with these words: "This case is a time bomb. I don't want to see it go off in my courtroom or in this community."

2

5   The Havana part of what happened in the spring of 1980 was also a time bomb. There had been all that spring a dispute between Fidel Castro and the government of Peru over the disposition of a handful of disaffected Cubans who had claimed asylum at the Peruvian embassy in Havana. Castro wanted the Cubans turned out. Peru insisted that they be brought to Lima. It was April 4, four days after jury selection began in the McDuffie case in Tampa, when the Cuban government, as an apparently quixotic move in this dispute, bulldozed down the gates at the Peruvian embassy in Havana and set into motion, whether deliberately or inadvertently, that chain of events referred to as "Mariel," by which people in Miami mean not just the place and not just the boatlift and not just what many see as the "trick," the way in which Fidel Castro managed to take his own problem and make it Miami's, but the entire range of dislocations attendant upon the unloading of 125,000 refugees, 26,000 of them with prison records, onto an already volatile community.

6   The first Mariel refugees arrived in South Florida on April 21, 1980. By May 17, the day the McDuffie case went to the jury in Tampa, there were already some 57,000 Mariels camped under the bleachers at the Orange Bowl and in makeshift tent cities in the Orange Bowl parking area and on the public land under I-95, downtown, in the most visible and frequently traveled part of the city, in case it had escaped anybody's notice that the needs of the black community might not in the immediate future have Miami's full attention. May 17 was a Saturday. The temperature was in the mid-seventies. There was, in Miami, no rain in view.

3

4   There appears to have been an astonishing innocence about what happened that day. In another part of the country the judge in a trial as sensitive as the McDuffie trial might not have allowed the case to go to the jury on a clear Saturday morning,

but the judge in Tampa did. In another part of the country the jury in such a case might not have brought in its verdicts, complete acquittal for all four defendants, in just two hours and forty-five minutes, which came down to something less than forty-two minutes per defendant, but the jury in Tampa did, in many ways predictably, for among the citizens of South Florida the urge to conciliate one another remained remarkably undeveloped. The president of the Orange Bowl Committee, which pretty much represents the established order in Miami, thought as recently as 1985, and said so, for attribution, that it was "not offensive" for the committee to entertain the participating college teams at the Indian Creek Country Club, which admitted no blacks or Jews as members but did allow them to visit the club as guests at private parties. "At the hospital where I work, the black doctors are intellectually fine and wonderful people, but they aren't able to handle the cosmopolitan aspects of circulating in society," a Miami surgeon said a few weeks later, also for attribution, to the *Herald* reporter who had asked him about restrictive policies at another local institution, the Bath Club, on Collins Avenue in Miami Beach.

8   Symbolic moves seemed to be missing here. A University of Miami study released the month of the 1968 Miami Riot had found it necessary to suggest that local black males resented being addressed by police as "boy," or "nigger." When a delegation of black citizens had asked the same year that a certain police officer be transferred, after conduct which had troubled the community, off his Liberty City beat, they were advised by the Miami chief of police that their complaint was "silly." Several weeks later it was reported that the officer in question and his partner had picked up a black seventeen-year-old, charged him with carrying a concealed knife, forced him to strip naked, and dangled him by his heels a hundred feet over the Miami River, from an unfinished span of the Dolphin Expressway.

9   During the twelve years between the 1968 Miami Riot and the Saturday in 1980 when the McDuffie case went to the jury, there had been, in Dade County, thirteen occasions on which the rage of some part of the black community went, for periods of time ranging from a few hours to a few days, out of control. This regular evidence of discontent notwithstanding, those gestures with which other troubled cities gradually learn to accommodate their citizens seemed not, in South Florida, to take hold. Blacks continued to be excluded for cause from juries in trials involving police officers accused of killing blacks. The juries in such cases

continued to stay out two hours, and to bring in acquittals, on clear days, in the summer.

4

10   The McDuffie acquittals were on the Associated Press wire, that clear Saturday in 1980, by 2:42 P.M. The first police call reporting rioting in Liberty City came in at 6:02 P.M., from Miami Police Department Unit 621. By 9:44 P.M., when a call was placed to Tallahassee asking that the National Guard be sent in, there was rioting not only in Liberty City but in Overtown and in the black Grove and around the entire Metro Justice complex, where doctors and nurses answering emergency calls to Jackson Memorial Hospital were being stoned and beaten and the Metro Justice building itself was being torched. Four days later, when the 1980 Liberty City Riot, called that because Liberty City was where it had begun, had run its course, there were eighteen dead or fatally injured, eight of them whites who had driven down the wrong streets and been stoned or doused with gasoline and set afire or, in the case of one, a twenty-two-year-old Burdines warehouse loader on his way home from a day at the beach with his girlfriend and younger brother, dragged from the car to be beaten, kicked, struck not only with bottles and bricks and a twenty-three-pound chunk of concrete but also with a *Miami Herald* street dispenser, shot, stabbed with a screwdriver, run over by a green Cadillac and left, one ear cut off and lying on his chest and his tongue cut out, with a red rose in his mouth.

11   An instinct for self-preservation would have seemed at this point to encourage negotiations, or at least the appearance of negotiations, but few lessons get learned in tropical cities under attack from their own citizens. Lines only harden. Positions become more fixed, and privileges more fiercely defended. In December of 1982 another police killing of another black man occasioned another riot, the 1982 Overtown Riot, on the second night of which there happened to be held, in the ballroom of the Surf Club on Collins Avenue, which numbered among its 680 members no blacks and no Jews, one of the most expensive parties given that year in Miami, a debutante party at which actors performed the story of Little Red Riding Hood under two hundred freshly cut fir trees arranged to represent the Black

Forest of Bavaria. In this case too the police officer in question, a Cuban, was eventually tried before an all-white jury,
which again stayed out two hours and again brought in an acquittal. This verdict came in early one Thursday evening in March of
1984, and order was restored in Miami just after midnight on
Saturday morning, which was applauded locally as progress, not
even a riot.

5

12   There are between the street and the lobby levels of
the Omni International Hotel on Biscayne Boulevard, one block
east of the hundred-block area sealed off by police during the
1982 Overtown Riot, two levels of shops and movie theaters and
carnival attractions: a mall, so designed that the teenagers, most
of them black and most of them male, who hang out around the
carousel in the evenings, waiting for a movie to break or for a turn
at the Space Walk or at the Sea of Balls or just for something to
happen, can look up to the Omni ballroom and lobby levels, but
only with some ingenuity reach them, since a steel grille blocks
the floating stairway after dark and armed security men patrol the
elevator areas. The visible presence of this more or less forbidden
upstairs lends the mall in the evening an unspecific atmosphere
of incipient trouble, an uneasiness which has its equivalent in the
hotel itself, where the insistent and rather sinister music from the
carousel downstairs comes to suggest, particularly on those weekend nights when the mall is at its loosest and the hotel often given
over to one or another of the lavish *quinces* or charity galas which
fill the local Cuban calendar, a violent night world just underfoot,
and perhaps not underfoot for long.

13   Not often does a social dynamic seem to present itself in a
single tableau, but at the Omni in Miami one did, and during the
time I spent there I came to see the hotel and its mall as the most
theatrical possible illustration of how a native proletariat can be
left behind in a city open to the convulsions of the Third World,
something which had happened in the United States first and
most dramatically in Miami but had been happening since in
other parts of the country. Black Miami had of course been particularly unprepared to have the world move in. Its common experience was of the cracker South. Black assertiveness had been virtu-

ally nonexistent, black political organization absent. Into the 1960s, according to *The Miami Riot of 1980*, a study of the Liberty City Riot by Bruce Porter of Brooklyn College and Marvin Dunn of Florida International University, the latter a black candidate for mayor of Miami who lost in 1985 to a Cuban, Xavier Suarez, Miami blacks did not swim at Dade County beaches. When Miami blacks paid taxes at the Dade County Courthouse they did so at a separate window, and when Miami blacks shopped at Burdines, where they were allowed to buy although not to try on clothes, they did so without using the elevators.

14   This had been a familiar enough pattern throughout the South, but something else had happened here. Desegregation had not just come hard and late to South Florida but it had also coincided, as it had not in other parts of the South, with another disruption of the local status quo, the major Cuban influx, which meant that jobs and services which might have helped awaken an inchoate black community went instead to Cubans, who tended to be overtrained but willing. Havana bankers took jobs as inventory clerks at forty-five dollars a week. Havana newspaper publishers drove taxis. That these were the men in black tie who now danced with the women in the Chanel and Valentino evening dresses on the ballroom level of the Omni was an irony lost in its precise detail, although not in its broad outline, on the sons of the men who did not get jobs as inventory clerks or taxi drivers, the children downstairs, in the high-topped sneakers, fanning in packs through the dim avenues of the locked-up mall.

QUESTIONS

Ideas

1. What specific lines can you point to that suggest that Didion is blaming the white power structure for the racial troubles in Miami?

2. In the second paragraph of the last section, Didion writes that "not often does a social dynamic seem to present itself in a single tableau." Describe what you think the important notions of that dynamic are?

3. In the second paragraph of the fourth section, Didion says, "Lines only harden." Did you take this as fatalism, a belief that the problems are too complicated to solve? Does she suggest a solution? Is there a solution?

Organization

4. Some rhetoric textbooks suggest that writers use specific organizational patterns. Professional writers, however, often create plans for their writing based specifically on the piece they are working on. Didion uses five sections here. What do they have to do with each other? Is there a central thread running through each? Give titles to each section.

Sentences

5. Look at the last sentence of each paragraph and the first sentence of the next in sections 1 and 2. Comment on how she uses these as transitions.

6. Didion's sentences are sometimes meant ironically. Choose a couple and explain why you think she is not quite serious about the literal meaning.

Words

7. Choose specific words or phrases from the first section that you think suggest the mood of the ghettos.

8. Didion has a reputation for carefully selecting appropriate details. Point to places in the text that you think are effectively specific.

Suggestions for Writing

A. Write an essay in which you imitate Didion's strategy of placing events or places or ideas one after the other for contrast. Although photographs often do this most effectively, try to create in words the difference between the two events (or places or ideas) while specifically coming to a conclusion.

B. Write a letter to "the president of the Orange Bowl Committee," mentioned in section 3, agreeing or disagreeing with his views.

Salvador

1   During the week before I flew down to El Salvador a Salvadoran woman who works for my husband and me in Los Angeles gave me repeated instructions about what we must and

must not do. We must not go out at night. We must stay off the
street whenever possible. We must never ride in buses or taxis,
never leave the capital, never imagine that our passports would
protect us. We must not even consider the hotel a safe place: people were killed in hotels. She spoke with considerable vehemence,
because two of her brothers had been killed in Salvador in August
of 1981, in their beds. The throats of both brothers had been
slashed. Her father had been cut but stayed alive. Her mother had
been beaten. Twelve of her other relatives, aunts and uncles and
cousins, had been taken from their houses one night the same
August, and their bodies had been found some time later, in a
ditch. I assured her that we would remember, we would be careful, we would in fact be so careful that we would probably (trying
for a light touch) spend all our time in church.

2   She became still more agitated, and I realized that I had spoken as a *norteamericana:* churches had not been to this woman the
neutral ground they had been to me. I must remember:
Archbishop Romero killed saying mass in the chapel of the Divine
Providence Hospital in San Salvador. I must remember: more
than thirty people killed at Archbishop Romero's funeral in the
Metropolitan Cathedral in San Salvador. I must remember: more
than twenty people killed before that on the steps of the
Metropolitan Cathedral. CBS had filmed it. It had been on television, the bodies jerking, those still alive crawling over the dead as
they tried to get out of range. I must understand: the Church was
dangerous.

3   I told her that I understood, that I knew all that, and I did,
abstractly, but the specific meaning of the Church she knew elud-
ed me until I was actually there, at the Metropolitan Cathedral in
San Salvador, one afternoon when rain sluiced down its corrugat-
ed plastic windows and puddled around the supports of the Sony
and Phillips billboards near the steps. The effect of the
Metropolitan Cathedral is immediate, and entirely literary. This is
the cathedral that the late Archbishop Oscar Arnulfo Romero
refused to finish, on the premise that the work of the Church
took precedence over its display, and the high walls of raw concrete bristle with structural rods, rusting now, staining the concrete, sticking out at wrenched and violent angles. The wiring is
exposed. Fluorescent tubes hang askew. The great high altar is
backed by warped plyboard. The cross on the altar is of bare
incandescent bulbs, but the bulbs, that afternoon, were unlit:

there was in fact no light at all on the main altar, no light on the cross, no light on the globe of the world that showed the northern American continent in gray and the southern in white; no light on the dove above the globe, *Salvador del Mundo*. In this vast brutalist space that was the cathedral, the unlit altar seemed to offer a single ineluctable message: at this time and in this place the light of the world could be construed as out, off, extinguished.

4   In many ways the Metropolitan Cathedral is an authentic piece of political art, a statement for El Salvador as *Guernica* was for Spain. It is quite devoid of sentimental relief. There are no decorative or architectural references to familiar parables, in fact no stories at all, not even the Stations of the Cross. On the afternoon I was there the flowers laid on the altar were dead. There were no traces of normal parish activity. The doors were open to the barricaded main steps, and down the steps there was a spill of red paint, lest anyone forget the blood shed there. Here and there on the cheap linoleum inside the cathedral there was what seemed to be actual blood, dried in spots, the kind of spots dropped by a slow hemorrhage, or by a woman who does not know or does not care that she is menstruating.

5   There were several women in the cathedral during the hour or so I spent there, a young woman with a baby, an older woman in house slippers, a few others, all in black. One of the women walked the aisles as if by compulsion, up and down, across and back, crooning loudly as she walked. Another knelt without moving at the tomb of Archbishop Romero in the right transept. "LOOK A MONSENOR ROMERO," the crude needlepoint tapestry by the tomb read, "Praise to Monsignor Romero from the Mothers of the Imprisoned, the Disappeared, and the Murdered," the *Comité de Madres y Familiares de Presos, Desaparecidos, y Asesinados Politicos de El Salvador.*

6   The tomb itself was covered with offerings and petitions, notes decorated with motifs cut from greeting cards and cartoons. I recall one with figures cut from a Bugs Bunny strip, and another with a pencil drawing of a baby in a crib. The baby in this drawing seemed to be receiving medication or fluid or blood intravenously, through the IV line shown on its wrist. I studied the notes for a while and then went back and looked again at the unlit altar, and at the red paint on the main steps, from which it was possible to see the guardsmen on the balcony of the National Palace hunching back to avoid the rain. Many Salvadorans are offended by the

Metropolitan Cathedral, which is as it should be, because the place remains perhaps the only unambiguous political statement in El Salvador, a metaphorical bomb in the ultimate power station. . . .

7   ". . . I had nothing more to do in San Salvador. I had given a lecture on the topic that had occurred to me on the train to Tapachula: Little-known Books by Famous American Authors—*Pudd'nhead Wilson, The Devil's Dictionary, The Wild Palms.* I had looked at the university; and no one could explain why there was a mural of Marx, Engels, and Lenin in the university of this rightwing dictatorship."

                              —PAUL THEROUX, *The Old Patagonian Express.*

8   The university Paul Theroux visited in San Salvador was the National University of El Salvador. This visit (and, given the context, this extraordinary lecture) took place in the late seventies, a period when the National University was actually open. In 1972 the Molina government had closed it, forcibly, with tanks and artillery and planes, and had kept it closed until 1974. In 1980 the Duarte government again moved troops onto the campus, which then had an enrollment of about 30,000, leaving fifty dead and offices and laboratories systematically smashed. By the time I visited El Salvador a few classes were being held in storefronts around San Salvador, but no one other than an occasional reporter had been allowed to enter the campus since the day the troops came in. Those reporters allowed to look had described walls still splashed with the spray-painted slogans left by the students, floors littered with tangled computer tape and with copies of what the National Guardsmen in charge characterized as *subversivo* pamphlets, for example a reprint of an article on inherited enzyme deficiency from *The New England Journal of Medicine.*

9   In some ways the closing of the National University seemed another of those Salvadoran situations in which no one came out well, and everyone was made to bleed a little, not excluding the National Guardsmen left behind to have their ignorance exposed by *gringo* reporters. The Jesuit university, UCA, or La Universidad Centroamericana José Simeón Cañas, had emerged as the most important intellectual force in the country, but the Jesuits had been so widely identified with the left that some local scholars would not attend lectures or seminars held on the UCA campus. (Those Jesuits still in El Salvador had in fact been under a cate-

gorical threat of death from the White Warriors Union since 1977. The Carter administration forced President Romero to protect the Jesuits, and on the day the killing was to have begun, July 22, 1977, the National Police are said to have sat outside the Jesuit residence in San Salvador on their motorcycles, with UZIs.) In any case UCA could manage an enrollment of only about 5,000. The scientific disciplines, which never had a particularly tenacious hold locally, had largely vanished from local life.

10   Meanwhile many people spoke of the National University in the present tense, as if it still existed, or as if its closing were a routine event on some long-term academic calendar. I recall talking one day to a former member of the faculty at the National University, a woman who had not seen her office since the morning she noticed the troops massing outside and left it. She lost her books and her research and the uncompleted manuscript of the book she was then writing, but she described this serenely, and seemed to find no immediate contradiction in losing her work to the Ministry of Defense and the work she did later with the Ministry of Education. The campus of the National University is said to be growing over, which is one way contradictions get erased in the tropics.

11   I was invited one morning to a gathering of Salvadoran writers, a kind of informal coffee hour arranged by the American embassy. For some days there had been a question about where to hold this *café literario,* since there seemed to be no single location that was not considered off-limits by at least one of the guests, and at one point the ambassador's residence was put forth as the most neutral setting. On the day before the event it was finally decided that UCA was the more appropriate place ("and just never mind," as one of the embassy people put it, that some people would not go to UCA), and at ten the next morning we gathered there in a large conference room and drank coffee and talked, at first in platitudes, and then more urgently.

12   These are some of the sentences spoken to me that morning: *It's not possible to speak of intellectual life in El Salvador. Every day we lose more. We are regressing constantly. Intellectual life is drying up. You are looking at the intellectual life of El Salvador. Here. In this room. We are the only survivors. Some of the others are out of the country, others are not writing because they are engaged in political activity. Some have been disappeared, many of the teachers have been disappeared. Teaching is very dangerous, if a student misinterprets what a teacher says, then the*

teacher may be arrested. Some are in exile, the rest are dead. Los muertos, you know? We are the only ones left. There is no one after us, no young ones. It is all over, you know? At noon there was an exchange of books and *curricula vitae.* The cultural attaché from the embassy said that she, for one, would like to see this *café literario* close on a hopeful note, and someone provided one: it was a hopeful note that *norteamericanos* and *centroamericanos* could have such a meeting. This is what passed for a hopeful note in San Salvador in the summer of 1982.

QUESTIONS

Ideas

1. If someone told you about the events described in the first two paragraphs, would you still travel there as a journalist? Why or why not?

2. Although Didion describes the cathedral's actual appearance, much of what she says about it is interpretation. What, for example, are possible reasons for Salvadorans being offended by Metropolitan Cathedral? What reason does Didion offer? How does this support the first sentence of paragraph 4?

3. In the last two or three sentences of paragraph 3 Didion seems to be "reading" the cathedral as a critic would read a poem, finding meaning in little details. What does she "find"? Is this fair to do?

4. Didion often makes her point indirectly, by selecting particular details for certain effects. What response is she after with the journal example in the last sentence of paragraph 8?

5. What tone do you detect in the last sentence? What is the effect of the phrase "what passed for"?

6. Based on these observations from Didion, what is your impression of life in El Salvador? Do you think our State Department is influenced by writers like Didion?

Organization

7. In the first sentence of paragraphs 2–6 and 8–12, underline the words or phrase that serves as a link to the previous paragraph. Comment on these transitions. Are they forced? Do they work? Are there different types?

8. How do the opening paragraphs of Didion's portrait of the Salvadorean church and university (or the spirit and the mind) set the mood for her concluding thoughts in each section?

Sentences

9. In the first two paragraphs Didion repeats two sentence patterns for rhetorical effect. Which series of sentences do you find more effective? Why?

10. Didion uses the colon a good deal in this essay. Examine half a dozen examples. Describe her method. If you were writing a rule for its use based on this essay, what would it be? Give an original example.

Words

11. What is the effect of using the three words at the end of paragraph 3?

12. Make a list of words or phrases that you think Didion means to be taken ironically? Compare your list with those of your classmates. Is this a matter of interpretation? Is irony in the mind of the reader?

Suggestions for Writing

A. Find an interesting place that you can describe in some detail, perhaps a church, a section of a mall, a deserted house, or a wooded area. Write about it, noting its specific details and, most importantly, interpreting its meaning.

B. Find a reproduction of *Guernica* (paragraph 4) in an art history text. What do you think Didion meant by her comparison between that painting and the Metropolitan Cathedral?

Why I Write

---

1   Of course I stole the title for this talk, from George Orwell. One reason I stole it was that I like the sound of the words: *Why I Write.* There you have three short unambiguous words that share a sound, and the sound they share is this:

I
I
I

2   In many ways writing is the act of saying *I*, of imposing oneself upon other people, of saying *listen to me, see it my way, change your mind.* It's an aggressive, even a hostile act. You can disguise its

aggressiveness all you want with veils of subordinate clauses and
qualifiers and tentative subjunctives, with ellipses and evasions—
with the whole manner of intimating rather than claiming, of
alluding rather than stating—but there's no getting around the
fact that setting words on paper is the tactic of a secret bully, an
invasion, an imposition of the writer's sensibility on the reader's
most private space.

3   I stole the title not only because the words sounded right
but because they seemed to sum up, in a no-nonsense way, all I
have to tell you. Like many writers I have only this one "subject,"
this one "area": the act of writing. I can bring you no reports from
any other front. I may have other interests: I am "interested," for
example, in marine biology, but I don't flatter myself that you
would come out to hear me talk about it. I am not a scholar. I am
not in the least an intellectual, which is not to say that when I
hear the word "intellectual" I reach for my gun, but only to say
that I do not think in abstracts. During the years when I was an
undergraduate at Berkeley I tried, with a kind of hopeless late-
adolescent energy, to buy some temporary visa into the world of
ideas, to forge for myself a mind that could deal with the abstract.

4   In short I tried to think. I failed. My attention veered inex-
orably back to the specific, to the tangible, to what was generally
considered, by everyone I knew then and for that matter have
known since, the peripheral. I would try to contemplate the
Hegelian dialectic and would find myself concentrating instead
on a flowering pear tree outside my window and the particular
way the petals fell on my floor. I would try to read linguistic theory and would find myself wondering instead if the lights were on
in the bevatron up the hill. When I say that I was wondering if the
lights were on in the bevatron you might immediately suspect, if
you deal in ideas at all, that I was registering the bevatron as a
political symbol, thinking in shorthand about the military-indus-
trial complex and its role in the university community, but you
would be wrong. I was only wondering if the lights were on in the
bevatron, and how they looked. A physical fact.

5   I had trouble graduating from Berkeley, not because of this
inability to deal with ideas—I was majoring in English, and I could
locate the house-and-garden imagery in "The Portrait of a Lady"
as well as the next person, "imagery" being by definition the kind
of specific that got my attention—but simply because I had
neglected to take a course in Milton. For reasons which now

sound baroque I needed a degree by the end of that summer, and the English department finally agreed, if I would come down from Sacramento every Friday and talk about the cosmology of "Paradise Lost," to certify me proficient in Milton. I did this. Some Fridays I took the Greyhound bus, other Fridays I caught the Southern Pacific's City of San Francisco on the last leg of its transcontinental trip. I can no longer tell you whether Milton put the sun or the earth at the center of his universe in "Paradise Lost," the central question of at least one century and a topic about which I wrote 10,000 words that summer, but I can still recall the exact rancidity of the butter in the City of San Francisco's dining car, and the way the tinted windows on the Greyhound bus cast the oil refineries around Carquinez Straits into a grayed and obscurely sinister light. In short my attention was always on the periphery, on what I could see and taste and touch, on the butter, and the Greyhound bus. During those years I was traveling on what I knew to be a very shaky passport, forged papers: I knew that I was no legitimate resident in any world of ideas. I knew I couldn't think. All I knew then was what I couldn't do. All I knew then was what I wasn't, and it took me some years to discover what I was

6   Which was a writer.

7   By which I mean not a "good" writer or a "bad" writer but simply a writer, a person whose most absorbed and passionate hours are spent arranging words on pieces of paper. Had my credentials been in order I would never have become a writer. Had I been blessed with even limited access to my own mind there would have been no reason to write. I write entirely to find out what I'm thinking, what I'm looking at, what I see and what it means. What I want and what I fear. Why did the oil refineries around Carquinez Straits seem sinister to me in the summer of 1956? Why have the night lights in the bevatron burned in my mind for twenty years? *What is going on in these pictures in my mind?*

8   When I talk about pictures in my mind I am talking, quite specifically, about images that shimmer around the edges. There used to be an illustration in every elementary psychology book showing a cat drawn by a patient in varying stages of schizophrenia. This cat had a shimmer around it. You could see the molecular structure breaking down at the very edges of the cat: the cat became the background and the background the cat, everything interacting, exchanging ions. People on hallucinogens describe

the same perception of objects. I'm not a schizophrenic, nor do I
take hallucinogens, but certain images do shimmer for me. Look
hard enough, and you can't miss the shimmer. It's there. You
can't think too much about these pictures that shimmer. You just
lie low and let them develop. You stay quiet. You don't talk to
many people and you keep your nervous system from shorting out
and you try to locate the cat in the shimmer, the grammar in the
picture.

9   Just as I meant "shimmer" literally I mean "grammar" literally. Grammar is a piano I play by ear, since I seem to have been out
of school the year the rules were mentioned. All I know about
grammar is its infinite power. To shift the structure of a sentence
alters the meaning of that sentence, as definitely and inflexibly as
the position of a camera alters the meaning of the object photographed. Many people know about camera angles now, but not
so many know about sentences. The arrangement of the words
matters, and the arrangement you want can be found in the picture in your mind. The picture dictates the arrangement. The picture dictates whether this will be a sentence with or without clauses, a sentence that ends hard or a dying-fall sentence, long or
short, active or passive. The picture tells you how to arrange the
words and the arrangement of the words tells you, or tells me,
what's going on in the picture. *Nota bene:*

10   It tells you.

11   You don't tell it.

12   Let me show you what I mean by pictures in the mind. I
began "Play It As It Lays" just as I have begun each of my novels,
with no notion of "character" or "plot" or even "incident." I had
only two pictures in my mind, more about which later, and a technical intention, which was to write a novel so elliptical and fast
that it would be over before you noticed it, a novel so fast that it
would scarcely exist on the page at all. About the pictures: the first
was of white space. Empty space. This was clearly the picture that
dictated the narrative intention of the book—a book in which
anything that happened would happen off the page, a "white"
book to which the reader would have to bring his or her own bad
dreams—and yet this picture told me no "story," suggested no situation. The second picture did. This second picture was of something actually witnessed. A young woman with long hair and a
short white halter dress walks through the casino at the Riviera in
Las Vegas at one in the morning. She crosses the casino alone and

picks up a house telephone. I watch her because I have heard her paged, and recognize her name: she is a minor actress I see around Los Angeles from time to time, in places like Jax and once in a gynecologist's office in the Beverly Hills Clinic, but have never met. I know nothing about her. Who is paging her? Why is she here to be paged? How exactly did she come to this? It was precisely this moment in Las Vegas that made "Play It As It Lays" begin to tell itself to me, but the moment appears in the novel only obliquely, in a chapter which begins:

13   "Maria made a list of things she would never do. She would never: walk through the Sands or Caesar's alone after midnight. She would never: ball at a party, do S-M unless she wanted to, borrow furs from Abe Lipsey, deal. She would never: carry a Yorkshire in Beverly Hills."

14   That is the beginning of the chapter and that is also the end of the chapter, which may suggest what I meant by "white space."

15   I recall having a number of pictures in my mind when I began the novel I just finished, "A Book of Common Prayer." As a matter of fact one of these pictures was of that bevatron I mentioned, although I would be hard put to tell you a story in which nuclear energy figured. Another was a newspaper photograph of a hijacked 707 burning on the desert in the Middle East. Another was the night view from a room in which I once spent a week with paratyphoid, a hotel room on the Colombian coast. My husband and I seemed to be on the Colombian coast representing the United States of America at a film festival (I recall invoking the name "Jack Valenti" a lot, as if its reiteration could make me well), and it was a bad place to have fever, not only because my indisposition offended our hosts but because every night in this hotel the generator failed. The lights went out. The elevator stopped. My husband would go to the event of the evening and make excuses for me and I would stay alone in this hotel room, in the dark. I remember standing at the window trying to call Bogotá (the telephone seemed to work on the same principle as the generator) and watching the night wind come up and wondering what I was doing eleven degrees off the equator with a fever of 103. The view from that window definitely figures in "A Book of Common Prayer," as does the burning 707, and yet none of these pictures told me the story I needed.

16   The picture that did, the picture that shimmered and made these other images coalesce, was the Panama airport at 6 A.M. I

was in this airport only once, on a plane to Bogotá that stopped for an hour to refuel, but the way it looked that morning remained superimposed on everything I saw until the day I finished "A Book of Common Prayer." I lived in that airport for several years. I can still feel the hot air when I step off the plane, can see the heat already rising off the tarmac at 6 A.M. I can feel my skirt damp and wrinkled on my legs. I can feel the asphalt stick to my sandals. I remember the big tail of a Pan American plane floating motionless down at the end of the tarmac. I remember the sound of a slot machine in the waiting room. I could tell you that I remember a particular woman in the airport, an American woman, a *norteamericana,* a thin *norteamericana* about 40 who wore a big square emerald in lieu of a wedding ring, but there was no such woman there.

17   I put this woman in the airport later. I made this woman up, just as I later made up a country to put the airport in, and a family to run the country. This woman in the airport is neither catching a plane nor meeting one. She is ordering tea in the airport coffee shop. In fact she is not simply "ordering" tea but insisting that the water be boiled, in front of her, for twenty minutes. Why is this woman in this airport? Why is she going nowhere, where has she been? Where did she get that big emerald? What derangement, or disassociation, makes her believe that her will to see the water boiled can possibly prevail?

18   "She had been going to one airport or another for four months, one could see it, looking at the visas on her passport. All those airports where Charlotte Douglas's passport had been stamped would have looked alike. Sometimes the sign on the tower would say 'Bienvenidos' and sometimes the sign on the tower would say 'Bienvenue,' some places were wet and hot and others dry and hot, but at each of these airports the pastel concrete walls would rust and stain and the swamp off the runway would be littered with the fuselages of cannibalized Fairchild F-227's and the water would need boiling.

19   "I knew why Charlotte went to the airport even if Victor did not."

20   "I knew about airports."

21   These lines appear about halfway through "A Book of Common Prayer," but I wrote them during the second week I worked on the book, long before I had any idea where Charlotte Douglas had been or why she went to airports. Until I wrote these

lines I had no character called "Victor" in mind: the necessity for mentioning a name, and the name "Victor," occurred to me as I wrote the sentence. *I knew why Charlotte went to the airport* sounded incomplete. *I knew why Charlotte went to the airport even if Victor did not* carried a little more narrative drive. Most important of all, until I wrote these lines I did not know who "I" was, who was telling the story. I had intended until that moment that the "I" be no more than the voice of the author, a 19th-century omniscient narrator. But there it was:

22   "I knew why Charlotte went to the airport even if Victor did not."

23   "I knew about airports."

24   This "I" was the voice of no author in my house. This "I" was someone who not only knew why Charlotte went to the airport but also knew someone called "Victor." Who was Victor? Who was this narrator? Why was this narrator telling me this story? Let me tell you one thing about why writers write: had I known the answer to any of these questions I would never have needed to write a novel.

QUESTIONS

1. Why does Didion write? Do her reasons make sense to you? What reason for writing is suggested in the last paragraph? How does that reason tie in with the ones given in paragraph 7?

2. How does Didion begin the process of writing? What does she start with and from? What do you think of her method? Of her compulsion? Are there any advantages to starting this way? Any disadvantages?

3. Didion says she stole her title from George Orwell. Is her theft legitimate? Can one writer steal from another? How far can any writer, including you, legitimately go in this kind of stealing?

4. Didion likes her title because she says it's no-nonsense. What does she mean? Are her first three paragraphs also no-nonsense paragraphs?

5. In the second paragraph Didion says writers are bullies, and in the first paragraph she suggests that they are egocentric. Is she convincing here? Do you feel this way? Compare this with what E. B. White says about writers in "The Essayist."

6. In paragraphs 4 and 5 Didion makes a lot of her alleged inability to think abstractly and generally. Reread these paragraphs carefully

and make a list of the general ideas she includes and of the specific details she sets up as counters to them and illustrations of them.

7. What does Didion mean when she says: "To shift the structure of a sentence alters the meaning of that sentence." Can you provide an example either by altering the structure of one of Didion's sentences or by altering one of your own? How does the analogy that follows this statement help to clarify her meaning: "as the position of a camera alters the meaning of the object photographed"?

Suggestions for Writing

A. Explain, in an essay, why you write. Has writing helped you to see or to think in ways you wouldn't without writing? Has it hindered or hurt you in any way? You might describe your own composing process—that is, exactly what you do from the time you first sit down to write until you turn your essay in. Or you might write an essay about why you don't write, and how and why you avoid it.

B. In another essay, "On Keeping a Notebook," Didion writes: "The point of my keeping a notebook has never been, nor is it now, to have an accurate factual record of what I have been doing or thinking." Her instinct, as she explains it, is neither for reality nor for history. It is rather, she insists, a personal impulse—a desire to remember who she was at different points in her life, an urge to recall how things felt, what they seemed like then. "It is a good idea, then," she continues, "to keep in touch, and I suppose that keeping in touch is what notebooks are all about." Try for a week, a month, or longer if you like, to keep some kind of notebook or journal of responses to things you do, see, hear, encounter. Avoid making it either a diary so private you'd want no one to read it, or simply a record of trivial and uninteresting actions ("I got up, ate, and went to work"). Instead, make it a re-acting notebook, literally a book of notes on your thoughts and feelings, your ideas and attitudes about any and every thing.

On Keeping a Notebook

1   " 'THAT WOMAN ESTELLE,' " the note reads, " 'is partly the reason why George Sharp and I are separated today.' *Dirty crepe-de-Chine wrapper, hotel bar, Wilmington RR, 9:45 a.m. August Monday morning.*"

2   Since the note is in my notebook, it presumably has some meaning to me. I study it for a long while. At first I have only the most general notion of what I was doing on an August Monday morning in the bar of the hotel across from the Pennsylvania Railroad station in Wilmington, Delaware (waiting for a train? missing one? 1960? 1961? why Wilmington?), but I do remember being there. The woman in the dirty crepe-de-Chine wrapper had come down from her room for a beer, and the bartender had heard before the reason why George Sharp and she were separated today. "Sure," he said, and went on mopping the floor. "You told me." At the other end of the bar is a girl. She is talking, pointedly, not to the man beside her but to a cat lying in the triangle of sunlight cast through the open door. She is wearing a plaid silk dress from Peck & Peck, and the hem is coming down.

3   Here is what it is: the girl has been on the Eastern Shore, and now she is going back to the city, leaving the man beside her, and all she can see ahead are the viscous summer sidewalks and the 3 a.m. long-distance calls that will make her lie awake and then sleep drugged through all the steaming mornings left in August (1960? 1961?). Because she must go directly from the train to lunch in New York, she wishes that she had a safety pin for the hem of the plaid silk dress, and she also wishes that she could forget about the hem and the lunch and stay in the cool bar that smells of disinfectant and malt and make friends with the woman in the crepe-de-Chine wrapper. She is afflicted by a little self-pity, and she wants to compare Estelles. That is what that was all about.

4   Why did I write it down? In order to remember, of course, but exactly what was it I wanted to remember? How much of it actually happened? Did any of it? Why do I keep a notebook at all? It is easy to deceive oneself on all those scores. The impulse to write things down is a peculiarly compulsive one, inexplicable to those who do not share it, useful only accidentally, only secondarily, in the way that any compulsion tries to justify itself. I suppose that it begins or does not begin in the cradle. Although I have felt compelled to write things down since I was five years old, I doubt that my daughter ever will, for she is a singularly blessed and accepting child, delighted with life exactly as life presents itself to her, unafraid to go to sleep and unafraid to wake up. Keepers of private notebooks are a different breed altogether, lonely and resistant rearrangers of things, anxious malcontents, children afflicted apparently at birth with some presentiment of loss.

5   My first notebook was a Big Five tablet, given to me by my
mother with the sensible suggestion that I stop whining and learn
to amuse myself by writing down my thoughts. She returned the
tablet to me a few years ago; the first entry is an account of a
woman who believed herself to be freezing to death in the Arctic
night, only to find, when day broke, that she had stumbled onto
the Sahara Desert, where she would die of the heat before lunch.
I have no idea what turn of a five-year-old's mind could have
prompted so insistently "ironic" and exotic a story, but it does
reveal a certain predilection for the extreme which has dogged
me into adult life; perhaps if I were analytically inclined I would
find it a truer story than any I might have told about Donald
Johnson's birthday party or the day my cousin Brenda put Kitty
Litter in the aquarium.

6   So the point of my keeping a notebook has never been, nor
is it now, to have an accurate factual record of what I have been
doing or thinking. That would be a different impulse entirely, an
instinct for reality which I sometimes envy but do not possess. At
no point have I ever been able successfully to keep a diary; my
approach to daily life ranges from the grossly negligent to the
merely absent, and on those few occasions when I have tried dutifully to record a day's events, boredom has so overcome me that
the results are mysterious at best. What is this business about
"shopping, typing piece, dinner with E, depressed"? Shopping for
what? Typing what piece? Who is E? Was this "E" depressed, or
was I depressed? Who cares?

7   In fact I have abandoned altogether that kind of pointless
entry; instead I tell what some would call lies. "That's simply not
true," the members of my family frequently tell me when they
come up against my memory of a shared event. "The party was *not*
for you, the spider was *not* a black widow, *it wasn't that way at all.*"
Very likely they are right, for not only have I always had trouble
distinguishing between what happened and what merely might
have happened, but I remain unconvinced that the distinction,
for my purposes, matters. The cracked crab that I recall having
for lunch the day my father came home from Detroit in 1945
must certainly be embroidery, worked into the day's pattern to
lend verisimilitude; I was ten years old and would not now remember the cracked crab. The day's events did not turn on cracked
crab. And yet it is precisely that fictitious crab that makes me see

the afternoon all over again, a home movie run all too often, the father bearing gifts, the child weeping, an exercise in family love and guilt. Or that is what it was to me. Similarly, perhaps it never did snow that August in Vermont; perhaps there never were flurries in the night wind, and maybe no one else felt the ground hardening and summer already dead even as we pretended to bask in it, but that was how it felt to me, and it might as well have snowed, could have snowed, did snow.

8   *How it felt to me:* that is getting closer to the truth about a notebook. I sometimes delude myself about why I keep a notebook, imagine that some thrifty virtue derives from preserving everything observed. See enough and write it down, I tell myself, and then some morning when the world seems drained of wonder, some day when I am only going through the motions of doing what I am supposed to do, which is write—on that bankrupt morning I will simply open my notebook and there it will all be, a forgotten account with accumulated interest, paid passage back to the world out there: dialogue overheard in hotels and elevators and at the hat-check counter in Pavillon (one middle-aged man shows his hat check to another and says, "That's my old football number"); impressions of Bettina Aptheker and Benjamin Sonnenberg and Teddy ("Mr. Acapulco") Stauffer; careful *aperçus* about tennis bums and failed fashion models and Greek shipping heiresses, one of whom taught me a significant lesson (a lesson I could have learned from F. Scott Fitzgerald, but perhaps we all must meet the very rich for ourselves) by asking, when I arrived to interview her in her orchid-filled sitting room on the second day of a paralyzing New York blizzard, whether it was snowing outside.

9   I imagine, in other words, that the notebook is about other people. But of course it is not. I have no real business with what one stranger said to another at the hat-check counter in Pavillon; in fact I suspect that the line "That's my old football number" touched not my own imagination at all, but merely some memory of something once read, probably "The Eighty-Yard Run." Nor is my concern with a woman in a dirty crepe-de-Chine wrapper in a Wilmington bar. My stake is always, of course, in the unmentioned girl in the plaid silk dress. *Remember what it was to be me:* that is always the point.

10   It is a difficult point to admit. We are brought up in the ethic that others, any others, all others, are by definition more

interesting than ourselves; taught to be diffident, just this side of self-effacing. ("You're the least important person in the room and don't forget it," Jessica Mitford's governess would hiss in her ear on the advent of any social occasion; I copied that into my notebook because it is only recently that I have been able to enter a room without hearing some such phrase in my inner ear.) Only the very young and the very old may recount their dreams at breakfast, dwell upon self, interrupt with memories of beach picnics and favorite Liberty lawn dresses and the rainbow trout in a creek near Colorado Springs. The rest of us are expected, rightly, to affect absorption in other people's favorite dresses, other people's trout.

11 And so we do. But our notebooks give us away, for however dutifully we record what we see around us, the common denominator of all we see is always, transparently, shamelessly, the implacable "I." We are not talking here about the kind of notebook that is patently for public consumption, a structural conceit for binding together a series of graceful *pensées;* we are talking about something private, about bits of the mind's string too short to use, an indiscriminate and erratic assemblage with meaning only for its maker.

12 And sometimes even the maker has difficulty with the meaning. There does not seem to be, for example, any point in my knowing for the rest of my life that, during 1964, 720 tons of soot fell on every square mile of New York City, yet there it is in my notebook, labeled "FACT." Nor do I really need to remember that Ambrose Bierce liked to spell Leland Stanford's name "£eland $tanford" or that "smart women almost always wear black in Cuba," a fashion hint without much potential for practical application. And does not the relevance of these notes seem marginal at best?:

> In the basement museum of the Inyo County Courthouse in Independence, California, sign pinned to a mandarin coat: "This MANDARIN COAT was often worn by Mrs. Minnie S. Brooks when giving lectures on her TEAPOT COLLECTION."

> Redhead getting out of car in front of Beverly Wilshire Hotel, chinchilla stole, Vuitton bags with tags reading:
> MRS LOU FOX
> HOTEL SAHARA
> VEGAS

13   Well, perhaps not entirely marginal. As a matter of fact, Mrs. Minnie S. Brooks and her MANDARIN COAT pull me back into my own childhood, for although I never knew Mrs. Brooks and did not visit Inyo County until I was thirty, I grew up in just such a world, in houses cluttered with Indian relics and bits of gold ore and ambergris and the souvenirs my Aunt Mercy Farnsworth brought back from the Orient. It is a long way from that world to Mrs. Lou Fox's world, where we all live now, and is it not just as well to remember that? Might not Mrs. Minnie S. Brooks help me to remember what I am? Might not Mrs. Lou Fox help me to remember what I am not?

14   But somtimes the point is harder to discern. What exactly did I have in mind when I noted down that it cost the father of someone I know $650 a month to light the place on the Hudson in which he lived before the Crash? What use was I planning to make of this line by Jimmy Hoffa: "I may have my faults, but being wrong ain't one of them"? And although I think it interesting to know where the girls who travel with the Syndicate have their hair done when they find themselves on the West Coast, will I ever make suitable use of it? Might I not be better off just passing it on to John O'Hara? What is a recipe for sauerkraut doing in my notebook? What kind of magpie keeps this notebook? *"He was born the night the Titanic went down."* That seems a nice enough line, and I even recall who said it, but is it not really a better line in life than it could ever be in fiction?

15   But of course that is exactly it: not that I should ever use the line, but that I should remember the woman who said it and the afternoon I heard it. We were on her terrace by the sea, and we were finishing the wine left from lunch, trying to get what sun there was, a California winter sun. The woman whose husband was born the night the *Titanic* went down wanted to rent her house, wanted to go back to her children in Paris. I remember wishing that I could afford the house, which cost $1,000 a month. "Someday you will," she said lazily. "Someday it all comes." There in the sun on her terrace it seemed easy to believe in someday, but later I had a low-grade afternoon hangover and ran over a black snake on the way to the supermarket and was flooded with inexplicable fear when I heard the checkout clerk explaining to the man ahead of me why she was finally divorcing her husband. "He left me no choice," she said over and over as she punched the

register. "He has a little seven-month-old baby by her, he left me
no choice." I would like to believe that my dread then was for the
human condition, but of course it was for me, because I wanted a
baby and did not then have one and because I wanted to own the
house that cost $1,000 a month to rent and because I had a hang-
over.

16   It all comes back. Perhaps it is difficult to see the value in
having one's self back in that kind of mood, but I do see it; I think
we are well advised to keep on nodding terms with the people we
used to be, whether we find them attractive company or not.
Otherwise they turn up unannounced and surprise us, come hammering on the mind's door at 4 a.m. of a bad night and demand
to know who deserted them, who betrayed them, who is going to
make amends. We forget all too soon the things we thought we
could never forget. We forget the loves and the betrayals alike,
forget what we whispered and what we screamed, forget who we
were. I have already lost touch with a couple of people I used to
be; one of them, a seventeen-year-old, presents little threat,
although it would be of some interest to me to know again what it
feels like to sit on a river levee drinking vodka-and-orange-juice
and listening to Les Paul and Mary Ford and their echoes sing
"How High the Moon" on the car radio. (You see I still have the
scenes, but I no longer perceive myself among those present, no
longer could even improvise the dialogue.) The other one, a
twenty-three-year-old, bothers me more. She was always a good
deal of trouble, and I suspect she will reappear when I least want
to see her, skirts too long, shy to the point of aggravation, always
the injured party, full of recriminations and little hurts and stories
I do not want to hear again, at once saddening me and angering
me with her vulnerability and ignorance, an apparition all the
more insistent for being so long banished.

17   It is a good idea, then, to keep in touch, and I suppose that
keeping in touch is what notebooks are all about. And we are all
on our own when it comes to keeping those lines open to ourselves: your notebook will never help me, nor mine you. *So what's
new in the whiskey business?* What could that possibly mean to you?
To me it means a blonde in a Pucci bathing suit sitting with a couple of fat men by the pool at the Beverly Hills Hotel. Another man
approaches, and they all regard one another in silence for a
while. "So what's new in the whiskey business?" one of the fat men
finally says by way of welcome, and the blonde stands up, arches

one foot and dips it in the pool, looking all the while at the cabaña where Baby Pignatari is talking on the telephone. That is all there is to that, except that several years later I saw the blonde coming out of Saks Fifth Avenue in New York with her California complexion and a voluminous mink coat. In the harsh wind that day she looked old and irrevocably tired to me, and even the skins in the mink coat were not worked the way they were doing them that year, not the way she would have wanted them done, and there is the point of the story. For a while after that I did not like to look in the mirror, and my eyes would skim the newspapers and pick out only the deaths, the cancer victims, the premature coronaries, the suicides, and I stopped riding the Lexington Avenue IRT because I noticed for the first time that all the strangers I had seen for years—the man with the seeing-eye dog, the spinster who read the classified pages every day, the fat girl who always got off with me at Grand Central—looked older than they once had.

18   It all comes back. Even that recipe for sauerkraut: even that brings it back. I was on Fire Island when I first made that sauerkraut, and it was raining, and we drank a lot of bourbon and ate the sauerkraut and went to bed at ten, and I listened to the rain and the Atlantic and felt safe. I made the sauerkraut again last night and it did not make me feel any safer, but that is, as they say, another story.

QUESTIONS

Ideas

1. Didion seems to be working toward an understanding of her own motives in this piece, admitting that she sometimes deludes herself about why she keeps a notebook. What, finally, do you think her purpose is in keeping a notebook?

2. Do you agree with Didion's opening statement in paragraph 17 that it is a good idea to keep in touch with former selves? Why?

3. What do you think Didion means in the first sentence of paragraph 7 when she claims that she tells what "some would call lies"?

4. As a college student, what advantages do you see in keeping a notebook? What do you make of Didion's rather negative interpretation of notebook-keepers in the last sentence of paragraph 4?

Organization

5. List several stages in Didion's thinking, beginning with "it presumably has some meaning to me" in paragraph 2.

6. Look at the opening sentences in paragraphs 10 through 15. Describe the techniques Didion uses to link one group of thoughts to another.

7. There are four major sections here, indicated by a space after paragraphs 5, 9, and 13. What would be an appropriate title for each?

Sentences

8. Revise Didion's long third sentence in paragraph 8. First try for several shorter sentences, then try to change the sequence. What happens?

9. Where does Didion's conclusion begin? Describe what she does in her conclusion.

Words

10. What do the following words mean? "viscous" (paragraph 3); "*aperçus*" (paragraph 8); "presentiment" (paragraph 4); "predilection" (paragraph 5); "*pensées*" (paragraph 11); "apparition" (paragraph 16). Can you suggest more appropriate synonyms?

Suggestions for Writing

A. Using one of the following statements from Didion's essay as your focus, write a personal essay:

> We forget all too soon the things we thought we could never forget. (paragraph 16)

> The rest of us are expected, rightly, to affect absorption in other people's favorite dresses, other people's trout. (paragraph 10)

B. In paragraph 16 Didion says it would be of some interest to her to know again what it feels like to sit on a river levee drinking vodka-and-orange-juice. Try to remember some comparable situation from your past and write a paragraph about how it felt.

FOUR

Annie Dillard

(1945–   )

Annie Dillard's writing is rooted in an impassioned awe of the natural world. In prose by turns taut and expansive she reveals both the delights of this world and its terrors. Something of a visionary with a mystical strain, Dillard writes prose that often reads more like poetry or fiction than like nonfiction prose. The range of her published writing testifies to her imaginative sensibility as her books include a collection of poems, *Tickets for a Prayer Wheel* (1974); works of philosophical speculation, *Holy the Firm* (1977), and literary theory, *Living by Fiction* (1979); and a collection of essays, *Teaching a Stone to Talk* (1982).

In *An American Childhood* (1987), she has written about her early life in Pittsburgh, where she went to private girls' schools. She remembers most her fierce commitment to reading, a passion that deeply shaped her consciousness. In the excerpt given here, "Skating," Dillard discovers intolerance in others and superstition in herself. The selection from *The Writing Life* (1989) explores the pain, pleasure, and lonely habits of the professional writer.

Her first book, *Pilgrim at Tinker Creek* (1974), was a best seller, and won a Pulitzer Prize. In this work Dillard describes what she saw while patiently observing nature at Tinker Creek in the Roanoke Valley in Virginia. Throughout the book, Dillard moves from a careful exploration of the natural world to the largest of philosophical and theological questions, questions about the design and purpose of the universe and of our place in it;

questions about pain, cruelty, suffering, and death—
unanswerable yet inescapable questions all.

Meaning and design are central not only as subjects
of Dillard's writing, but also as dimensions of its substance and form. Her essays, that is, are attempts to
explore and explain the meanings hidden in nature; however, Dillard's essays also raise questions about the meaning of life and the purpose of nature. Moreover, just as
Dillard seeks to discover patterns of form and structure in
nature, in her chance encounters with mystery, so too do
her essays both reveal and conceal intricacies of structure and form. (Perhaps we ought to read Dillard
with the same attention and deliberation she lavishes
on nature.)

What is apparent from even a casual reading of her
work is its intensity, its seriousness. There's nothing chatty about her tone, nothing superficial about her subjects
or her ideas. In "Jest and Earnest," an excerpt from the
first chapter of *Pilgrim at Tinker Creek,* Dillard describes a
shocking event: a frog being drained of its internal
organs, reduced to juice by a powerful enzyme of the
giant water bug. This event stirs Dillard, provoking her to
ask a series of questions about God, nature, beauty, and
terror. The writing, highly charged with feeling, relies
heavily on an accumulation of verbs in the descriptive section and on a pile-up of questions in the speculative part.
This is typical of the way Dillard arranges her essays. She
often starts with a close description of something she has
seen or heard about—a frog, a bird, a fire, a dream, an
airplane accident. From description she moves out
through a series of questions and provisional answers into
speculation and argument.

Her concern throughout *Pilgrim* is with seeing. Her
interest, however, is less in what we see than in how we
see; less in what we know than in how we come to know.
Chapter Two, entitled "Seeing," is an investigation of
what it means to really see something; it is an exploration
of the different ways of seeing, knowing, and understanding available to us. In another book, *Holy the Firm* (1977),
Dillard raises other questions, exploring the meaning of
suffering, particularly the seemingly senseless suffering of
children. The essay is casual in structure, angry in tone,
and passionate in its agonized quest for meaning in a
chance tragic event.

One of the things Dillard seeks to understand is nature, especially the relationship between human and animal life. She explores this subject in "Living Like Weasels," in which she describes her own stunning encounter with a weasel, and in which she explores the questions the encounter gave rise to. In "Transfiguration" she describes the death of a moth by incineration, seeing in its burning brightness an image of the writer. Dillard has described herself as "an explorer" and "a stalker"— both of the natural world and of the meanings locked within it. Both naturalist and symbolist, Dillard searches in and through nature for transcendent truths. Her intense scrutiny of nature is fueled by a passionate search for meaning. And the risks she takes in describing the marvelous steep her writing in wonder and make it a continual vehicle of insight.

Jest and Earnest

1   A couple of summers ago I was walking along the edge of the island to see what I could see in the water, and mainly to scare frogs. Frogs have an inelegant way of taking off from invisible positions on the bank just ahead of your feet, in dire panic, emitting a froggy "Yike!" and splashing into the water. Incredibly, this amused me, and, incredibly, it amuses me still. As I walked along the grassy edge of the island, I got better and better at seeing frogs both in and out of the water. I learned to recognize, slowing down, the difference in texture of the light reflected from mudbank, water, grass, or frog. Frogs were flying all around me. At the end of the island I noticed a small green frog. He was exactly half in and half out of the water, looking like a schematic diagram of an amphibian, and he didn't jump.

2   He didn't jump; I crept closer. At last I knelt on the island's winterkilled grass, lost, dumbstruck, staring at the frog in the creek just four feet away. He was a very small frog with wide, dull eyes. And just as I looked at him, he slowly crumpled and began to sag. The spirit vanished from his eyes as if snuffed. His skin emptied and drooped; his very skull seemed to collapse and settle

like a kicked tent. He was shrinking before my eyes like a deflating football. I watched the taut, glistening skin on his shoulders ruck, and rumple, and fall. Soon, part of his skin, formless as a pricked balloon, lay in floating folds like bright scum on top of the water: it was a monstrous and terrifying thing. I gaped bewildered, appalled. An oval shadow hung in the water behind the drained frog; then the shadow glided away. The frog skin bag started to sink.

3   I had read about the giant water bug, but never seen one. "Giant water bug" is really the name of the creature, which is an enormous, heavy-bodied brown beetle. It eats insects, tadpoles, fish, and frogs. Its grasping forelegs are mighty and hooked inward. It seizes a victim with these legs, hugs it tight, and paralyzes it with enzymes injected during a vicious bite. That one bite is the only bite it ever takes. Through the puncture shoot the poisons that dissolve the victim's muscles and bones and organs—all but the skin—and through it the giant water bug sucks out the victim's body, reduced to a juice. This event is quite common in warm fresh water. The frog I saw was being sucked by a giant water bug. I had been kneeling on the island grass; when the unrecognizable flap of frog skin settled on the creek bottom, swaying, I stood up and brushed the knees of my pants. I couldn't catch my breath.

4   Of course, many carnivorous animals devour their prey alive. The usual method seems to be to subdue the victim by downing or grasping it so it can't flee, then eating it whole or in a series of bloody bites. Frogs eat everything whole, stuffing prey into their mouths with their thumbs. People have seen frogs with their wide jaws so full of live dragonflies they couldn't close them. Ants don't even have to catch their prey: in the spring they swarm over newly hatched, featherless birds in the nest and eat them tiny bite by bite.

5   That it's rough out there and chancy is no surprise. Every live thing is a survivor on a kind of extended emergency bivouac. But at the same time we are also created. In the Koran, Allah asks, "The heaven and the earth and all in between, thinkest thou I made them *in jest?*" It's a good question. What do we think of the created universe, spanning an unthinkable void with an unthinkable profusion of forms? Or what do we think of nothingness, those sickening reaches of time in either direction? If the giant water bug was not made in jest, was it then made in earnest?

Pascal uses a nice term to describe the notion of the creator's, once having called forth the universe, turning his back to it: *Deus Absconditus*. Is this what we think happened? Was the sense of it there, and God absconded with it, ate it, like a wolf who disappears round the edge of the house with the Thanksgiving turkey? "God is subtle," Einstein said, "but not malicious." Again, Einstein said that "nature conceals her mystery by means of her essential grandeur, not by her cunning." It could be that God has not absconded but spread, as our vision and understanding of the universe have spread, to a fabric of spirit and sense so grand and subtle, so powerful in a new way, that we can only feel blindly of its hem. In making the thick darkness a swaddling band for the sea, God "set bars and doors" and said, "Hitherto shalt thou come, but no further." But have we come even that far? Have we rowed out to the thick darkness, or are we all playing pinochle in the bottom of the boat?

6   Cruelty is a mystery, and the waste of pain. But if we describe a world to compass these things, a world that is a long, brute game, then we bump against another mystery: the inrush of power and light, the canary that sings on the skull. Unless all ages and races of men have been deluded by the same mass hypnotist (who?), there seems to be such a thing as beauty, a grace wholly gratuitous. About five years ago I saw a mockingbird make a straight vertical descent from the roof gutter of a four-story building. It was an act as careless and spontaneous as the curl of a stem or the kindling of a star.

7   The mockingbird took a single step into the air and dropped. His wings were still folded against his sides as though he were singing from a limb and not falling, accelerating thirty-two feet per second per second, through empty air. Just a breath before he would have been dashed to the ground, he unfurled his wings with exact, deliberate care, revealing the broad bars of white, spread his elegant, white-banded tail, and so floated onto the grass. I had just rounded a corner when his insouciant step caught my eye; there was no one else in sight. The fact of his free fall was like the old philosophical conundrum about the tree that falls in the forest. The answer must be, I think, that beauty and grace are performed whether or not we will or sense them. The least we can do is try to be there.

8   Another time I saw another wonder: sharks off the Atlantic coast of Florida. There is a way a wave rises about the ocean hori-

zon, a triangular wedge against the sky. If you stand where the ocean breaks on a shallow beach, you see the raised water in a wave is translucent, shot with lights. One late afternoon at low tide a hundred big sharks passed the beach near the mouth of a tidal river in a feeding frenzy. As each green wave rose from the churning water, it illuminated within itself the six- or eight-foot-long bodies of twisting sharks. The sharks disappeared as each wave rolled toward me; then a new wave would swell above the horizon, containing in it, like scorpions in amber, sharks that roiled and heaved. The sight held awesome wonders: power and beauty, grace tangled in a rapture with violence.

9   We don't know what's going on here. If these tremendous events are random combinations of matter run amok, the yield of millions of monkeys at millions of typewriters, then what is it in us, hammered out of those same typewriters, that they ignite? We don't know. Our life is a faint tracing on the surface of mystery, like the idle, curved tunnels of leaf miners on the face of a leaf. We must somehow take a wider view, look at the whole landscape, really see it, and describe what's going on here. Then we can at least wail the right question into the swaddling band of darkness, or, if it comes to that, choir the proper praise.

10   At the time of Lewis and Clark, setting the prairies on fire was a well-known signal that meant, "Come down to the water." It was an extravagant gesture, but we can't do less. If the landscape reveals one certainty, it is that the extravagant gesture is the very stuff of creation. After the one extravagant gesture of creation in the first place, the universe has continued to deal exclusively in extravagances, flinging intricacies and colossi down aeons of emptiness, heaping profusions on profligacies with ever-fresh vigor. The whole show has been on fire from the word go. I come down to the water to cool my eyes. But everywhere I look I see fire; that which isn't flint is tinder, and the whole world sparks and flames.

QUESTIONS

Ideas

1.   Good writing often begins with seeing, with close observation. What does Dillard look at closely and then describe for us to see?

2. Dillard's seeing does not end with literal observation. It extends outward into thought. What ideas does Dillard develop out of her seeing?

3. The first two paragraphs present a description—a shocking one. Following this comes a pair of informative paragraphs and a paragraph that offers speculation about the information and description presented up to that point. Label paragraphs 6–10 as primarily descriptive, informative, or speculative.

4. What is the connection between paragraphs 5 and 6? Look especially at the first two sentences of paragraph 6, where a link is made. If the first sentence of paragraph 6 sums up what Dillard has been saying in the preceding paragraph, what does the second sentence do? And how do the sentences following that develop the point of paragraph 6?

5. Why does Dillard separate paragraph 7 from the one before it? Why does she bother including this paragraph at all? Does she need this mockingbird section? How does it fit in with what Dillard has shown up to that point?

6. The essay can be thought of or approached in terms of the three creatures described: frog, mockingbird, shark. Why is each included, and how are the three related in the context of Dillard's idea?

7. Is the final paragraph of the essay necessary? What does it contribute to the idea of the piece? To the effect?

Sentences

8. Most of the essay consists of declarative sentences, of statements. In paragraphs 5 and 6, however, Dillard uses many questions. What is the effect of these questions and what is the tone of the paragraphs?

9. Dillard uses participles to extend sentences in paragraphs 2 and 7. Here is one example: "At last I knelt on the island's winterkilled grass, lost, dumbstruck, staring at the frog in the creek just four feet away." If you ended the sentence after "dumbstruck," beginning a new sentence after it, you might get this: At last I knelt on the island's winterkilled grass, lost, dumbstruck. I stared at the frog in the creek just four feet away. What advantage—in this instance—does the participial sentence have over the two shorter sentences?

10. In paragraph 3 Dillard writes an inverted sentence: "Through the puncture shoot the poisons that dissolve the victim's bones and muscles and organs. . . ." Here is an alternate version: The poisons that dissolve the victim's bones and muscles and organs shoot through the puncture. Which version do you prefer and why?

11. Return once more to the frog description, this time for a look at Dillard's punctuation. After examining the sentences with semi-colons, try to formulate a general rule for their use. What is the relationship, in each sentence, of the part before the semicolon to the part after it? Here are the important sentences: "He didn't jump; I crept closer." "His skin emptied and drooped; his very skull seemed to collapse and settle like a kicked tent." "An oval shadow hung in the water behind the drained frog; then the shadow glided away."

12. Dillard uses the colon in paragraphs 4, 6, and 8. For all three sentences, decide whether a period or comma could replace the colon. For each sentence, explain the relationship between the two parts—the part to the left of the colon and the part to the right.

Words

13. Examine the verbs in the first three sentences of paragraph 7. Compare the number and kind of verbs with the number and type of verbs in paragraph 2. What do you notice?

14. In the frog description Dillard uses a number of comparisons. What do they have in common? What is their purpose and what is their cumulative effect?

15. Imagery of light and darkness appears throughout the essay. Explain how the fire of paragraph 10 is related to the darkness of paragraphs 5, 6, and 9. What does Dillard mean when she writes: "But everywhere I look I see fire, that which isn't flint is tinder, and the whole world sparks and flames"?

16. In paragraph 5 Dillard alludes to and quotes from Einstein, Pascal, and the Koran. What is the purpose of each of these quotations and allusions? Could Dillard have made her point as well without quotation and allusion?

Suggestions for Writing

A. Write imitations of the sentences discussed in questions 9–12.

B. Write variations of some of the sentences discussed in questions 9–12. For example, you might change the punctuation or the word order of the sentences.

C. Look closely at something. Be attentive to details of shape, color, form, texture, background, line. If you like, observe a place with a considerable amount of action such as a restaurant, supermarket, or intersection. List the things you see. From your list select three or four items that stand out. Write freely, jotting down thoughts as they occur about each of the items on your list.

D. For each of the following poems explain what the speaker is looking at. Notice that in both poems a passage of explanation, generalization, or speculation accompanies the passage of description. What point does each poem make? How necessary is the descriptive, "seeing" part of each to its idea? In each poem, how is what is seen related to or connected with what is thought?

DESIGN

I found a dimpled spider, fat and white,
On a white heal-all, holding up a moth
Like a white piece of rigid satin cloth—
Assorted characters of death and blight
Mixed ready to begin the morning right,
Like the ingredients of a witches' broth—
A snow-drop spider, a flower like a froth,
And dead wings carried like a paper kite.

What had that flower to do with being white,
The wayside blue and innocent heal-all?
What brought the kindred spider to that height,
Then steered the white moth thither in the night?
What but design of darkness to appall?—
If design govern in a thing so small.

ROBERT FROST

MUSÉE DES BEAUX ARTS

About suffering they were never wrong,
The Old Masters: how well they understood
Its human position; how it takes place
While someone else is eating or opening a window or just walking
    dully along;
How, when the aged are reverently, passionately waiting
For the miraculous birth, there always must be
Children who did not specially want it to happen, skating
On a pond at the edge of the wood:
They never forgot
That even the dreadful martyrdom must run its course
Anyhow in a corner, some untidy spot
Where the dogs go on with their doggy life and the torturer's horse
Scratches its innocent behind on a tree.

In Brueghel's *Icarus*, for instance: how everything turns away
Quite leisurely from the disaster; the ploughman may
Have heard the splash, the forsaken cry,
But for him it was not an important failure; the sun shone
As it had to on the white legs disappearing into the green
Water: and the expensive delicate ship that must have seen
Something amazing, a boy falling out of the sky,
Had somewhere to get to and sailed calmly on.

W. H. AUDEN

Living Like Weasels

I

1   A weasel is wild. Who knows what he thinks? He sleeps in his underground den, his tail draped over his nose. Sometimes he lives in his den for two days without leaving. Outside, he stalks rabbits, mice, muskrats, and birds, killing more bodies than he can eat warm, and often dragging the carcasses home. Obedient to instinct, he bites his prey at the neck, either splitting the jugular vein at the throat or crunching the brain at the base of the skull, and he does not let go. One naturalist refused to kill a weasel who was socketed into his hand deeply as a rattlesnake. The man could in no way pry the tiny weasel off, and he had to walk half a mile to water, the weasel dangling from his palm, and soak him off like a stubborn label.

2   And once, says Ernest Thompson Seton—once, a man shot an eagle out of the sky. He examined the eagle and found the dry skull of a weasel fixed by the jaws to his throat. The supposition is that the eagle had pounced on the weasel and the weasel swiveled and bit as instinct taught him, tooth to neck, and nearly won. I would like to have seen that eagle from the air a few weeks or months before he was shot: was the whole weasel still attached to his feathered throat, a fur pendant? Or did the eagle eat what he could reach, gutting the living weasel with his talons before his breast, bending his beak, cleaning the beautiful airborne bones?

II

3   I have been reading about weasels because I saw one last week. I startled a weasel who startled me, and we exchanged a long glance.

4   Twenty minutes from my house, through the woods by the quarry and across the highway, is Hollins Pond, a remarkable piece of shallowness, where I like to go at sunset and sit on a tree trunk. Hollins Pond is also called Murray's Pond; it covers two acres of bottomland near Tinker Creek with six inches of water and six thousand lily pads. In winter, brown-and-

white steers stand in the middle of it, merely dampening their hooves; from the distant shore they look like miracle itself, complete with miracle's nonchalance. Now, in summer, the steers are gone. The water lilies have blossomed and spread to a green horizontal plane that is terra firma to plodding blackbirds, and tremulous ceiling to black leeches, crayfish, and carp.

5   This is, mind you, suburbia. It is a five-minute walk in three directions to rows of houses, though none is visible here. There's a 55 mph highway at one end of the pond, and a nesting pair of wood ducks at the other. Under every bush is a muskrat hole or a beer can. The far end is an alternating series of fields and woods, fields and woods, threaded everywhere with motorcycle tracks—in whose bare clay wild turtles lay eggs.

6   So. I had crossed the highway, stepped over two low barbed-wire fences, and traced the motorcycle path in all gratitude through the wild rose and poison ivy of the pond's shoreline up into high grassy fields. Then I cut down through the woods to the mossy fallen tree where I sit. This tree is excellent. It makes a dry, upholstered bench at the upper, marshy end of the pond, a plush jetty raised from the thorny shore between a shallow blue body of water and a deep blue body of sky.

7   The sun had just set. I was relaxed on the tree trunk, ensconced in the lap of lichen, watching the lily pads at my feet tremble and part dreamily over the thrusting path of a carp. A yellow bird appeared to my right and flew behind me. It caught my eye; I swiveled around—and the next instant, inexplicably, I was looking down at a weasel, who was looking up at me.

III

8   Weasel! I'd never seen one wild before. He was ten inches long, thin as a curve, a muscled ribbon, brown as fruitwood, soft-furred, alert. His face was fierce, small and pointed as a lizard's; he would have made a good arrowhead. There was just a dot of chin, maybe two brown hairs' worth, and then the pure white fur began that spread down his underside. He had two black eyes I didn't see, any more than you see a window.

9   The weasel was stunned into stillness as he was emerging from beneath an enormous shaggy wild rose bush four feet away. I

was stunned into stillness twisted backward on the tree trunk. Our
eyes locked, and someone threw away the key.

10   Our look was as if two lovers, or deadly enemies, met unexpectedly on an overgrown path when each had been thinking of
something else: a clearing blow to the gut. It was also a bright
blow to the brain, or a sudden beating of brains, with all the
charge and intimate grate of rubbed balloons. It emptied our
lungs. It felled the forest, moved the fields, and drained the
pond; the world dismantled and tumbled into that black hole
of eyes. If you and I looked at each other that way, our skulls
would split and drop to our shoulders. But we don't. We keep our
skulls. So.

11   He disappeared. This was only last week, and already I don't
remember what shattered the enchantment. I think I blinked, I
think I retrieved my brain from the weasel's brain, and tried to
memorize what I was seeing, and the weasel felt the yank of separation, the careening splashdown into real life and the urgent current of instinct. He vanished under the wild rose. I waited motionless, my mind suddenly full of data and my spirit with pleadings,
but he didn't return.

12   Please do not tell me about "approach-avoidance conflicts."
I tell you I've been in that weasel's brain for sixty seconds, and he
was in mine. Brains are private places, muttering through unique
and secret tapes—but the weasel and I both plugged into another
tape simultaneously, for a sweet and shocking time. Can I help it
if it was a blank?

13   What goes on in his brain the rest of the time? What does a
weasel think about? He won't say. His journal is tracks in clay, a
spray of feathers, mouse blood and bone: uncollected, unconnected, loose-leaf, and blown.

                        IV

14   I would like to learn, or remember, how to live. I come
to Hollins Pond not so much to learn how to live as, frankly, to
forget about it. That is, I don't think I can learn from a wild animal how to live in particular—shall I suck warm blood, hold my
tail high, walk with my footprints precisely over the prints of my
hands?—but I might learn something of mindlessness, something
of the purity of living in the physical senses and the dignity
of living without bias or motive. The weasel lives in necessity and

we live in choice, hating necessity and dying at the last ignobly in its talons. I would like to live as I should, as the weasel lives as he should. And I suspect that for me the way is like the weasel's: open to time and death painlessly, noticing everything, remembering nothing, choosing the given with a fierce and point- ed will.

V

15   I missed my chance. I should have gone for the throat. I should have lunged for that streak of white under the weasel's chin and held on, held on through mud and into the wild rose, held on for a dearer life. We could live under the wild rose wild as weasels, mute and uncomprehending. I could very calmly go wild. I could live two days in the den, curled, leaning on mouse fur, sniffing bird bones, blinking, licking, breathing musk, my hair tangled in the roots of grasses. Down is a good place to go, where the mind is single. Down is out, out of your ever-loving mind and back to your careless senses. I remem ber muteness as a prolonged and giddy fast, where every momriit is a feast of utterance received. Time and events are merely poured, unremarked, and ingested directly, like blood pulsed into my gut through a jugular vein. Could two live that way? Could two live under the wild rose, and explore by the pond, so that the smooth mind of each is as everywhere present to the other, and as received and as unchallenged, as falling snow?

16   We could, you know. We can live any way we want. People take vows of poverty, chastity, and obedience—even of silence— by choice. The thing is to stalk your calling in a certain skilled and supple way, to locate the most tender and live spot and plug into that pulse. This is yielding, not fighting. A weasel doesn't "attack" anything; a weasel lives as he's meant to, yield- ing at every moment to the perfect freedom of single neces- sity.

VI

17   I think it would be well, and proper, and obedient, and pure, to grasp your one necessity and not let it go, to dangle from

it limp wherever it takes you. Then even death, where you're going no matter how you live, cannot you part. Seize it and let it seize you up aloft even, till your eyes burn out and drop; let your musky flesh fall off in shreds, and let your very bones unhinge and scatter, loosened over fields, over fields and woods, lightly, thoughtless, from any height at all, from as high as eagles.

QUESTIONS

Ideas

1. What does Dillard mean by suggesting we can live like the weasel? What does the weasel come to represent?
2. What is Dillard's primary purpose in this essay? To provide us with facts about weasels? To entertain us with surprising anecdotes? To convince us of something?
3. What does Dillard suggest about how humans can relate to animals? How far can their communication go? Why?

Organization

4. One way of considering the structure of this essay is to divide it into four segments: paragraphs 1–2; 3–7; 8–13; and 14–17. What are the focus and concern of each section, and how are the sections related? Why do you think the author arranged the essay in six sections?
5. Consider alternative introductions—paragraphs 3–7 or paragraphs 8–13. If the essay were to begin with either of these sections, what other changes in organization would be necessitated?

Sentences

6. Many of Dillard's sentences are short, particularly those at the beginning of paragraphs. What effects do her short sentences have?
7. Dillard employs frequent questions. Why? What is her purpose in interrogating us?

Words

8. List the words in the essay that suggest violence. How many of these are verbs? What is their cumulative effect?
9. Identify and comment on the purpose and effectiveness of the comparisons Dillard employs in paragraphs 1, 8, 10, 12, and 15.

Suggestions for Writing

A. Write an essay analyzing "Living Like Weasels." Discuss the ideas and the style of the essay.

B. Discuss an experience involving nature that led you to reflect on your relationship to the natural world.

C. Write imitations of any two sentences you think especially attractive.

Transfiguration

---

1   I live on northern Puget Sound, in Washington State, alone. I have a gold cat, who sleeps on my legs, named Small. In the morning I joke to her blank face, Do you remember last night? Do you remember? I throw her out before breakfast, so I can eat.

2   There is a spider, too, in the bathroom, with whom I keep a sort of company. Her little outfit always reminds me of a certain moth I helped to kill. The spider herself is of uncertain lineage, bulbous at the abdomen and drab. Her six-inch mess of a web works, works somehow, works miraculously, to keep her alive and me amazed. The web itself is in a corner behind the toilet, connecting tile wall to tile wall and floor, in a place where there is, I would have thought, scant traffic. Yet under the web are sixteen or so corpses she has tossed to the floor.

3   The corpses appear to be mostly sow bugs, those little armadillo creatures who live to travel flat out in houses, and die round. There is also a new shred of earwig, three old spider skins crinkled and clenched, and two moth bodies, wingless and huge and empty, moth bodies I drop to my knees to see.

4   Today the earwig shines darkly and gleams, what there is of him: a dorsal curve of thorax and abdomen, and a smooth pair of cerci by which I knew his name. Next week, if the other bodies are any indication, he will be shrunken and gray, webbed to the floor with dust. The sow bugs beside him are hollow and empty of color, fragile, a breath away from brittle fluff. The spider skins lie on their sides, translucent and ragged, their legs drying in knots. And the moths, the empty moths, stagger against each other,

headless, in a confusion of arching strips of chitin like peeling var-
nish, like a jumble of buttresses for cathedral domes, like nothing
resembling moths, so that I should hesitate to call them moths,
except that I have had some experience with the figure Moth
reduced to a nub.

5   Two summers ago I was camping alone in the Blue Ridge
Mountains in Virginia. I had hauled myself and gear up there to
read, among other things, James Ramsey Ullman's *The Day on Fire*,
a novel about Rimbaud that had made me want to be a writer
when I was sixteen; I was hoping it would do it again. So I read,
lost, every day sitting under a tree by my tent, while warblers
swung in the leaves overhead and bristle worms trailed their inches over the twiggy dirt at my feet; and I read every night by candlelight, while barred owls called in the forest and pale moths
massed round my head in the clearing, where my light made a
ring.
6   Moths kept flying into the candle. They would hiss and
recoil, lost upside down in the shadows among my cooking pans.
Or they would singe their wings and fall, and their hot wings, as if
melted, would stick to the first thing they touched—a pan, a lid, a
spoon—so that the snagged moths could flutter only in tiny arcs,
unable to struggle free. These I could release by a quick flip with
a stick; in the morning I would find my cooking stuff gilded with
torn flecks of moth wings, triangles of shiny dust here and there
on the aluminum. So I read, and boiled water, and replenished
candles, and read on.
7   One night a moth flew into the candle, was caught, burnt
dry, and held. I must have been staring at the candle, or maybe I
looked up when a shadow crossed my page; at any rate, I saw it all.
A golden female moth, a biggish one with a two-inch wing-span,
flapped into the fire, dropped her abdomen into the wet wax,
stuck, flamed, frazzled and fried in a second. Her moving wings
ignited like tissue paper, enlarging the circle of light in the clearing and creating out of the darkness the sudden blue sleeves of
my sweater, the green leaves of jewelweed by my side, the ragged
red trunk of a pine. At once the light contracted again and the
moth's wings vanished in a fine, foul smoke. At the same time her
six legs clawed, curled, blackened, and ceased, disappearing utterly. And her head jerked in spasms, making a spattering noise; her
antennae crisped and burned away and her heaving mouth parts

crackled like pistol fire. When it was all over, her head was, so far as I could determine, gone, gone the long way of her wings and legs. Had she been new, or old? Had she mated and laid her eggs, had she done her work? All that was left was the glowing horn shell of her abdomen and thorax—a fraying, partially collapsed gold tube jammed upright in the candle's round pool.

8   And then this moth-essence, this spectacular skeleton, began to act as a wick. She kept burning. The wax rose in the moth's body from her soaking abdomen to her thorax to the jagged hole where her head should be, and widened into flame, a saffron-yellow flame that robed her to the ground like any immolating monk. That candle had two wicks, two flames of identical height, side by side. The moth's head was fire. She burned for two hours, until I blew her out.

9   She burned for two hours without changing, without bending or leaning—only glowing within, like a building fire glimpsed through silhouetted walls, like a hollow saint, like a flame-faced virgin gone to God, while I read by her light, kindled, while Rimbaud in Paris burnt out his brains in a thousand poems, while night pooled wetly at my feet.

10   And that is why I believe those hollow crisps on the bathroom floor are moths. I think I know moths, and fragments of moths, and chips and tatters of utterly empty moths, in any state. How many of you, I asked the people in my class, which of you want to give your lives and be writers? I was trembling from coffee, or cigarettes, or the closeness of faces all around me. (Is this what we live for? I thought; is this the only final beauty: the color of any skin in any light, and living, human eyes?) All hands rose to the question. (You, Nick? Will you? Margaret? Randy? Why do I want them to mean it?) And then I tried to tell them what the choice must mean: you can't be anything else. You must go at your life with a broadax. . . . They had no idea what I was saying. (I have two hands, don't I? And all this energy, for as long as I can remember. I'll do it in the evenings, after skiing, or on the way home from the bank, or after the children are asleep. . . .) They thought I was raving again. It's just as well.

11   I have three candles here on the table which I disentangle from the plants and light when visitors come. Small usually avoids them, although once she came too close and her tail caught fire; I rubbed it out before she noticed. The flames move light over

everyone's skin, draw light to the surface of the faces of my friends. When the people leave I never blow the candles out, and after I'm asleep they flame and burn.

QUESTIONS

Ideas

1. What is the main point of this essay, and where is it made most directly? Is Dillard saying something about moths? About monks? About writers? About something else? Explain.

2. Explain the central analogy that governs the essay. What connection does Dillard establish between a writer and her moth? And how is Rimbaud's life related to what she says?

Organization

3. How do paragraphs 1–4 serve to introduce the essay? What would be gained or lost if Dillard had omitted them and begun the essay with paragraph 5?

4. Dillard's essay appears above in three sections: paragraphs 1–4; 5–7; 8–11. Explain the logic of this division. Then propose another and compare its merits with the division as it now exists.

5. Consider the way Dillard organizes time in this essay. Where does she describe past and where present events?

Sentences

6. Consider the way Dillard stacks and balances details in the following sentence. It has been arranged on the page to highlight its parallelism.

> Her moving wings ignited like tissue paper,
> enlarging the circle of light in the clearing
> and creating out of the darkness
> the sudden blue sleeves of my sweater,
> the green leaves of jewelweed by my side,
> the ragged red trunk of a pine.

7. Notice the way Dillard varies the length and type of her sentences throughout the essay. Analyze a couple of paragraphs from this standpoint, considering the effects of rhythm and sound with the varied forms and lengths of sentences.

Words

8. Consider the profusion of verbs in the third and sixth sentences of paragraph 7: *flapped, dropped, stuck, flamed, frazzled,* and *fried; clawed, curled, blackened,* and *ceased.* Which contain the most vivid pictures? Which, if any, are unfamiliar?

9. Discuss the way Dillard employs images of light and fire. Comment, especially, on the point and effect of the light image in the last sentence.

10. In paragraph 7, Dillard describes the death of the moth. What makes her description engaging and effective?

11. Identify and comment on the comparisons in paragraphs 8 and 9.

12. Look up the meanings of the following words: *transfiguration, gilded* (6), *replenished* (6), *essence* (8), *immolating* (8).

Suggestions for Writing

A. Write imitations of the sentences in questions 6 and 7. Write an imitation of paragraph 7 or 8—or both.

B. Compare and contrast Dillard's essay with White's "Death of a Pig." Consider each writer's purpose, point, tone, and style.

Skating

1 There was a big snow that same year, 1950. Traffic vanished; in the first week, nothing could move. The mailman couldn't get to us; the milkman couldn't come. Our long-legged father walked four miles with my sled to the dairy across Fifth Avenue and carried back milk.

2 We had a puppy, who was shorter than the big snow. Our parents tossed it for fun in the yard and it disappeared, only to pop up somewhere else at random like a loon in a lake. After a few days of this game, the happy puppy went crazy and died. It had distemper. While it was crazy it ran around the house crying, upstairs and down.

3 One night during the second week of the big snow I saw Jo Ann Sheehy skating on the street. I remembered this sight for its beauty and strangeness.

4   I was aware of the Sheehy family; they were Irish Catholics from a steep part of the neighborhood. One summer when I was walking around the block, I had to walk past skinny Tommy Sheehy and his fat father, who were hunched on their porch doing nothing. Tommy's eleven-year-old sister, Jo Ann, brought them iced tea.

5   "Go tell your maid she's a nigger," Tommy Sheehy said to me.

6   What?

7   He repeated it, and I did it, later, when I got home. That night, Mother came into our room after Amy was asleep. She explained, and made sure I understood. She was steely. Where had my regular mother gone? Did she hate me? She told me a passel of other words that some people use for other people. I was never to use such words, and never to associate with people who did so long as I lived; I was to apologize to Margaret Butler first thing in the morning; and I was to have no further dealings with the Sheehys.

8   The night Jo Ann Sheehy skated on the street, it was dark inside our house. We were having dinner in the dining room—my mother, my father, my sister Amy, who was two, and I. There were lighted ivory candles on the table. The only other light inside was the blue fluorescent lamp over the fish tank, on a sideboard. Inside the tank, neon tetras, black mollies, and angelfish circled, illuminated, through the light-shot water. When I turned the fluorescent lamp off, I had learned, the fish still circled their tank in the dark. The still water in the tank's center barely stirred.

9   Now we sat in the dark dining room, hushed. The big snow outside, the big snow on the roof, silenced our words and the scrape of our forks and our chairs. The dog was gone, the world outside was dangerously cold, and the big snow held the houses down and the people in.

10   Behind me, tall chilled windows gave out onto the narrow front yard and the street. A motion must have caught my mother's eye; she rose and moved to the windows, and Father and I followed. There we saw the young girl, the transfigured Jo Ann Sheehy, skating alone under the streetlight.

11   She was turning on ice skates inside the streetlight's yellow cone of light—illuminated and silent. She tilted and spun. She wore a short skirt, as if Edgerton Avenue's asphalt had been the ice of an Olympic arena. She wore mittens and a red knitted cap below

which her black hair lifted when she turned. Under her skates the street's packed snow shone; it illumined her from below, the cold light striking her under her chin.

12   I stood at the tall window, barely reaching the sill; the glass fogged before my face, so I had to keep moving or hold my breath. What was she doing out there? Was everything beautiful so bold? I expected a car to run over her at any moment: the open street was a fatal place, where I was forbidden to set foot.

13   Once, the skater left the light. She winged into the blackness beyond the streetlight and sped down the street; only her white skates showed, and the white snow. She emerged again under another streetlight, in the continuing silence, just at our corner stop sign where the trucks' brakes hissed. Inside that second cone of light she circled backward and leaning. Then she reversed herself in an abrupt half-turn—as if she had skated backward into herself, absorbed her own motion's impetus, and rebounded from it; she shot forward into the dark street and appeared again becalmed in the first streetlight's cone. I exhaled; I looked up. Distant over the street, the night sky was moonless and foreign, a frail, bottomless black, and the cold stars speckled it without moving.

14   This was for many years the center of the maze, this still, frozen evening inside, the family's watching through glass the Irish girl skate outside on the street. Here were beauty and mystery outside the house, and peace and safety within. I watched passive and uncomprehending, as in summer I watched Lombardy poplar leaves turn their green sides out, and then their silver sides out—watched as if the world were a screen on which played interesting scenes for my pleasure. But there was danger in this radiant sight, in the long glimpse of the lone girl skating, for it was night, and killingly cold. The open street was fatal and forbidden. And the apparently invulnerable girl was Jo Ann Sheehy, Tommy Sheehy's sister, part of the Sheehy family, whose dark ways were a danger and a crime.

15   "Tell your maid she's a nigger," he had said, and when I said to Margaret, "You're a nigger," I had put myself in danger—I felt at the time, for Mother was so enraged—of being put out, tossed out in the cold, where I would go crazy and die like the dog.

16   That night Jo Ann alone outside in the cold had performed recklessly. My parents did not disapprove; they loved the beauty of

it, and the queerness of skating on a street. The next morning I saw from the dining-room windows the street shrunken again and ordinary, tracked by tires, and the streetlights inconspicuous, and Jo Ann Sheehy walking to school in a blue plaid skirt.

17   Jo Ann Sheehy and the Catholic schoolchildren carried brown-and-tan workbooks, which they filled, I knew, with gibberish they not only had to memorize, they had to believe.

18   Every morning they filed into the subterranean maw of St. Bede's, the low stone school attached to the high stone church just a block up Edgerton Avenue. From other Protestant children, I gathered St. Bede's was a cave where Catholic children had to go to fill their brown-and-tan workbooks in the dark, possibly kneeling; they wrote down whatever the Pope said. (Whatever the Pope said, I thought, it was no prize; it didn't work; our Protestant lives were much sunnier, without our half trying.) Every afternoon, authorities "let out" the surviving children to return to their lightless steep houses, where they knelt before writhing crucifixes, bandied racial epithets about, and ate stewed fish.

19   One afternoon the following spring, I was sitting stilled on the side-yard swing; I was watching transparent circles swim in the sky. When I focused on them, the circles parted, as fish flew from a finger poked in their tank. Apparently it was my eyes, and not the sky, that produced the transparent circles, each with a dimple or nucleus, but I always failed to find any in my eyes in a mirror; I had tried the night before.

20   Now St. Bede's was, as the expression had it, letting out; Jo Ann Sheehy would walk by again, and all the other Catholic children, and perhaps the nuns. I kept an eye out for the nuns.

21   From my swing seat I saw the girls appear in bunches. There came Jo Ann Sheehy up the dry sidewalk with two other girls; her black hair fell over her blue blazer's back. Behind them, running back and forth across the street, little boys were throwing gravel bits. The boys held their workbooks tightly. Probably, if they lost them, they would be put to death.

22   In the leafy distance up Edgerton I could see a black phalanx. It blocked the sidewalk; it rolled footlessly forward like a tank. The nuns were coming. They had no bodies, and imitation faces. I quitted the swing and banged through the back door and ran in to Mother in the kitchen.

23   I didn't know the nuns taught the children; the Catholic children certainly avoided them on the streets, almost as much as I did. The nuns seemed to be kept in St. Bede's as in a prison, where their faces had rotted away—or they lived cycless in the dark by choice, like bats. Parts of them were manufactured. Other parts were made of mushrooms.

24   In the kitchen, Mother said it was time I got over this. She took me by the hand and hauled me back outside; we crossed the street and caught up with the nuns. "Excuse me," Mother said to the black phalanx. It wheeled around. "Would you just please say hello to my daughter here? If you could just let her see your faces."

25   I saw the white, conical billboards they had as mock-up heads; I couldn't avoid seeing them, those white boards like pillories with circles cut out and some bunched human flesh pressed like raw pie crust into the holes. Like mushrooms and engines, they didn't have hands. There was only that disconnected saucerful of whitened human flesh at their tops. The rest, concealed by a chassis of soft cloth over hard cloth, was cylinders, drive shafts, clean wiring, and wheels.

26   "Why, hello," some of the top parts said distinctly. They teetered toward me. I was delivered to my enemies, and had no place to hide; I could only wail for my young life so unpityingly snuffed.

QUESTIONS

Ideas

1. Dillard wonders, as she watches Jo Ann Sheehy skate, whether everything beautiful is so bold. What do you think she means by this?

2. Can you remember an incident from your childhood in which you were brought face to face with the reality of racial or ethnic difference?

3. Dillard describes herself as "passive and uncomprehending" as she watches the skater. She says she "watched as if the world were a screen on which played interesting scenes for my pleasure." She seems to imply that there are alternatives to this sort of passivity. What might they be?

Organization

4. Dillard begins with two anecdotes—one about a puppy, the other about Tommy Sheehy. At the end of the essay, she returns to these anecdotes briefly. How does each serve as a frame for the essay?

5. Why does Dillard include a description of the fish tank in paragraph 8?

Sentences

6. Dillard is fond of the semicolon. Pick two sentences in which she uses this form of punctuation and comment on how the semicolon is effective.

7. Why does the last sentence of the chapter seem to be a satisfying conclusion to the episode?

Words

8. Notice the words in paragraph 13 that are used to describe the actions of the skater. Pick out three verbs that you find particularly effective. Why do they work so well?

9. Dillard's diction in this piece seems much simpler than that in many of her other writings. Why might this be the case?

Suggestions for Writing

A. Write a brief essay describing the first time you encountered the reality of racial prejudice.

B. Describe an incident in which you watched someone you knew perform—in sports, music, or the arts—in a way that surprised you.

The Writing Life

1

1   When you write, you lay out a line of words. The line of words is a miner's pick, a woodcarver's gouge, a surgeon's probe. You wield it, and it digs a path you follow. Soon you find yourself deep in new territory. Is it a dead end, or have you located the real subject? You will know tomorrow, or this time next year.

2   You make the path boldly and follow it fearfully. You go where the path leads. At the end of the path, you find a box canyon. You hammer out reports, dispatch bulletins.

3   The writing has changed, in your hands, and in a twinkling, from an expression of your notions to an epistemological tool. The new place interests you because it is not clear. You attend. In your humility, you lay down the words carefully, watching all the angles. Now the earlier writing looks soft and careless. Process is nothing; erase your tracks. The path is not the work. I hope your tracks have grown over; I hope birds ate the crumbs; I hope you will toss it all and not look back.

4   The line of words is a hammer. You hammer against the walls of your house. You tap the walls, lightly, everywhere. After giving many years' attention to these things, you know what to listen for. Some of the walls are bearing walls; they have to stay, or everything will fall down. Other walls can go with impunity; you can hear the difference. Unfortunately, it is often a bearing wall that has to go. It cannot be helped. There is only one solution, which appalls you, but there it is. Knock it out. Duck.

5   Courage utterly opposes the bold hope that this is such fine stuff the work needs it, or the world. Courage, exhausted, stands on bare reality: this writing weakens the work. You must demolish the work and start over. You can save some of the sentences, like bricks. It will be a miracle if you can save some of the paragraphs, no matter how excellent in themselves or hard-won. You can waste a year worrying about it, or you can get it over with now. (Are you a woman, or a mouse?)

6   The part you must jettison is not only the best-written part; it is also, oddly, that part which was to have been the very point. It is the original key passage, the passage on which the rest was to hang, and from which you yourself drew the courage to begin. Henry James knew it well, and said it best. In his preface to *The Spoils of Poynton*, he pities the writer, in a comical pair of sentences that rises to a howl: "Which is the work in which he hasn't surrendered, under dire difficulty, the best thing he meant to have kept? In which indeed, before the dreadful *done*, doesn't he ask himself what has become of the thing all for the sweet sake of which it was to proceed to that extremity?"

7   So it is that a writer writes many books. In each book, he intended several urgent and vivid points, many of which he sacrificed as the book's form hardened. "The youth gets together

his materials to build a bridge to the moon," Thoreau noted mournfully, "or perchance a palace or temple on the earth, and at length the middle-aged man concludes to build a wood-shed with them." The writer returns to these materials, these passionate subjects, as to unfinished business, for they are his life's work.

2

8   It is the beginning of a work that the writer throws away.

9   A painting covers its tracks. Painters work from the ground up. The latest version of a painting overlays earlier versions, and obliterates them. Writers, on the other hand, work from left to right. The discardable chapters are on the left. The latest version of a literary work begins somewhere in the work's middle, and hardens toward the end. The earlier version remains lumpishly on the left; the work's beginning greets the reader with the wrong hand. In those early pages and chapters anyone may find bold leaps to nowhere, read the brave beginnings of dropped themes, hear a tone since abandoned, discover blind alleys, track red herrings, and laboriously learn a setting now false.

10   Several delusions weaken the writer's resolve to throw away work. If he has read his pages too often, those pages will have a necessary quality, the ring of the inevitable, like poetry known by heart; they will perfectly answer their own familiar rhythms. He will retain them. He may retain those pages if they possess some virtues, such as power in themselves, though they lack the cardinal virtue, which is pertinence to, and unity with, the book's thrust. Sometimes the writer leaves his early chapters in place from gratitude; he cannot contemplate them or read them without feeling again the blessed relief that exalted him when the words first appeared—relief that he was writing anything at all. That beginning served to get him where he was going, after all; surely the reader needs it, too, as groundwork. But no.

11   Every year the aspiring photographer brought a stack of his best prints to an old, honored photographer, seeking his judgment. Every year the old man studied the prints and painstakingly ordered them into two piles, bad and good. Every year the old man moved a certain landscape print into the bad stack. At length

he turned to the young man: "You submit this same landscape every year, and every year I put it on the bad stack. Why do you like it so much?" The young photographer said, "Because I had to climb a mountain to get it."

12   A cabdriver sang his songs to me, in New York. Some we sang together. He had turned the meter off; he drove around midtown, singing. One long song he sang twice; it was the only dull one. I said, You already sang that one; let's sing something else. And he said, "You don't know how long it took me to get that one together."

13   How many books do we read from which the writer lacked courage to tie off the umbilical cord? How many gifts do we open from which the writer neglected to remove the price tag? Is it pertinent, is it courteous, for us to learn what it cost the writer personally?

3

14   The written word is weak. Many people prefer life to it. Life gets your blood going, and it smells good. Writing is mere writing, literature is mere. It appeals only to the subtlest senses— the imagination's vision, and the imagination's hearing—and the moral sense, and the intellect. This writing that you do, that so thrills you, that so rocks and exhilarates you, as if you were dancing next to the band, is barely audible to anyone else. The reader's ear must adjust down from loud life to the subtle, imaginary sounds of the written word. An ordinary reader picking up a book can't yet hear a thing; it will take half an hour to pick up the writing's modulations, its ups and downs and louds and softs.

15   An intriguing entomological experiment shows that a male butterfly will ignore a living female butterfly of his own species in favor of a painted cardboard one, if the cardboard one is big. If the cardboard one is bigger than he is, bigger than any female butterfly ever could be. He jumps the piece of cardboard. Over and over again, he jumps the piece of cardboard. Nearby, the real, living female butterfly opens and closes her wings in vain.

16   Films and television stimulate the body's senses too, in big ways. A nine-foot handsome face, and its three-foot-wide smile, are irresistible. Look at the long legs on that man, as high as a wall,

and coming straight toward you. The music builds. The moving,
lighted screen fills your brain. You do not like filmed car chases?
See if you can turn away. Try not to watch. Even knowing you are
manipulated, you are still as helpless as the male butterfly drawn
to painted cardboard.

17   That is the movies. That is their ground. The printed word
cannot compete with the movies on their ground, and should not.
You can describe beautiful faces, car chases, or valleys full of
Indians on horseback until you run out of words, and you will not
approach the movies' spectacle. Novels written with film contracts
in mind have a faint but unmistakable, and ruinous, odor. I cannot name what, in the text, alerts the reader to suspect the writer
of mixed motives; I cannot specify which sentences, in several
books, have caused me to read on with increasing dismay, and
finally close the books because I smelled a rat. Such books seem
uneasy being books; they seem eager to fling off their disguises
and jump onto screens.

18   Why would anyone read a book instead of watching big people move on a screen? Because a book can be literature. It is a
subtle thing—a poor thing, but our own. In my view, the more literary the book—the more purely verbal, crafted sentence by sentence, the more imaginative, reasoned, and deep—the more likely people are to read it. The people who read are the people who
like literature, after all, whatever that might be. They like, or
require, what books alone have. If they want to see films that
evening, they will find films. If they do not like to read, they will
not. People who read are not too lazy to flip on the television;
they prefer books. I cannot imagine a sorrier pursuit than struggling for years to write a book that attempts to appeal to people
who do not read in the first place.

4

19   On the Fourth of July, my husband and our friends
drove into the city, Roanoke, to see the fireworks. I begged off; I
wanted to keep working. I was working hard, although of course it
did not seem hard enough at the time—a finished chapter every
few weeks. I castigated myself daily for writing too slowly. Even
when passages seemed to come easily, as though I were copying
from a folio held open by smiling angels, the manuscript revealed

the usual signs of struggle—bloodstains, teethmarks, gashes, and burns.

20　　This night, as on most nights, I entered the library at dusk. The building was locked and dark. I had a key. Every night I let myself in, climbed the stairs, found my way between the tall stacks in the dark, located and unlocked my study's door, and turned on the light. I remembered how many stacks I had to hit with my hand in the dark before I turned down the row to my study. Even if I left only to get a drink of water, I felt and counted the stacks with my hand again to find my room. Once, in daylight, I glanced at a book on a stack's corner, a book I presumably touched every night with my hand. The book was *The World I Live In*, by Helen Keller. I read it at once: it surprised me by its strong and original prose.

21　　When I flicked on my carrel light, there it all was: the bare room with yellow cinder-block walls; the big, flattened venetian blind and my drawing taped to it; two or three quotations taped up on index cards; and on a far table some ever-changing books, the fielder's mitt, and a yellow bag of chocolate-covered peanuts. There was the long, blond desk and its chair, and on the desk a dozen different-colored pens, some big index cards in careful, splayed piles, and my messy yellow legal pads. As soon as I saw that desktop, I remembered the task: the chapter, its problems, its phrases, its points.

22　　This night I was concentrating on the chapter. The horizon of my consciousness was the contracted circle of yellow light inside my study—the lone lamp in the enormous, dark library. I leaned over the desk. I worked by hand. I doodled deliriously in the legal-pad margins. I fiddled with the index cards. I reread a sentence maybe a hundred times, and if I kept it I changed it seven or eight times, often substantially.

23　　Now a June bug was knocking at my window. I was wrestling inside a sentence. I must have heard it a dozen times before it registered—before I noticed that I had been hearing a bug knock for half an hour. It made a hollow, bonking sound. Some people call the same fumbling, heavy insects "May beetles." It must have been attracted to my light—what little came between the slats of the blind. I dislike June bugs. Back to work. Knock again, knock again, and finally, to learn what monster of a fat, brown June bug could fly up to a second story and thump so insistently at my window as though it wanted admittance—at last, unthinkingly, I parted the venetian blind slats with my fingers, to look out.

24   And there were the fireworks, far away. It was the Fourth of July. I had forgotten. They were red and yellow, blue and green and white; they blossomed high in the black sky many miles away. The fireworks seemed as distant as the stars, but I could hear the late banging their bursting made. The sound, those bangs so muffled and out of sync, accompanied at random the silent, far sprays of color widening and raining down. It was the Fourth of July, and I had forgotten all of wide space and all of historical time. I opened the blinds a crack like eyelids, and it all came exploding in on me at once—oh yes, the world.

5

25   Here is a fairly sober version of what happens in the small room between the writer and the work itself. It is similar to what happens between a painter and the canvas.

26   First you shape the vision of what the projected work of art will be. The vision, I stress, is no marvelous thing: it is the work's intellectual structure and aesthetic surface. It is a chip of mind, a pleasing intellectual object. It is a vision of the work, not of the world. It is a glowing thing, a blurred thing of beauty. Its structure is at once luminous and translucent; you can see the world through it. After you receive the initial charge of this imaginary object, you add to it at once several aspects, and incubate it most gingerly as it grows into itself.

27   Many aspects of the work are still uncertain, of course; you know that. You know that if you proceed you will change things and learn things, that the form will grow under your hands and develop new and richer lights. But that change will not alter the vision or its deep structures; it will only enrich it. You know that, and you are right.

28   But you are wrong if you think that in the actual writing, or in the actual painting, you are filling in the vision. You cannot fill in the vision. You cannot even bring the vision to light. You are wrong if you think that you can in any way take the vision and tame it to the page. The page is jealous and tyrannical; the page is made of time and matter; the page always wins. The vision is not

so much destroyed, exactly, as it is, by the time you have finished, forgotten. It has been replaced by this changeling, this bastard, this opaque lightless chunky ruinous work.

29   Here is how it happens. The vision is, *sub specie aeternitatis*, a set of mental relationships, a coherent series of formal possibilities. In the actual rooms of time, however, it is a page or two of legal paper filled with words and questions; it is a terrible diagram, a few books' names in a margin, an ambiguous doodle, a corner folded down in a library book. These are memos from the thinking brain to witless hope.

30   Nevertheless, ignoring the provisional and pathetic nature of these scraps, and bearing the vision itself in mind—having it before your sights like the very Grail—you begin to scratch out the first faint marks on the canvas, on the page. You begin the work proper. Now you have gone and done it. Now the thing is no longer a vision: it is paper.

31   Words lead to other words and down the garden path. You adjust the paints' values and hues not to the world, not to the vision, but to the rest of the paint. The materials are stubborn and rigid; push is always coming to shove. You can fly—you can fly higher than you thought possible—but you can never get off the page. After every passage another passage follows, more sentences, more everything on drearily down. Time and materials hound the work; the vision recedes ever farther into the dim realms.

32   And so you continue the work, and finish it. Probably by now you have been forced to toss the most essential part of the vision. But this is a concern for mere nostalgia now: for before your eyes, and stealing your heart, is this fighting and frail finished product, entirely opaque. You can see nothing through it. It is only itself, a series of well-known passages, some colored paint. Its relationship to the vision that impelled it is the relationship between any energy and any work, anything unchanging to anything temporal.

33   The work is not the vision itself, certainly. It is not the vision filled in, as if it had been a coloring book. It is not the vision reproduced in time; that were impossible. It is rather a simulacrum and a replacement. It is a golem. You try—you try every time—to reproduce the vision, to let your light so shine before men. But you can only come along with your bushel and hide it.

6

34   Who will teach me to write? a reader wanted to know.

35   The page, the page, that eternal blankness, the blankness of
eternity which you cover slowly, affirming time's scrawl as a right
and your daring as necessity; the page, which you cover woodenly,
ruining it, but asserting your freedom and power to act, acknowledging that you ruin everything you touch but touching it nevertheless, because acting is better than being here in mere opacity;
the page, which you cover slowly with the crabbed thread of your
gut; the page in the purity of its possibilities; the page of your
death, against which you pit such flawed excellences as you can
muster with all your life's strength: that page will teach you to
write.

36   There is another way of saying this. Aim for the chopping
block. If you aim for the wood, you will have nothing. Aim past
the wood, aim through the wood; aim for the chopping block.

QUESTIONS

1. What does Dillard mean when she describes a "line of words" as a
    tool? Discuss the appropriateness of the various metaphors she uses.

2. Discuss the meaning of the anecdote about the young photogra-
    pher. How is it related to the anecdote about the cabdriver? How
    are they both related to writing?

3. What is Dillard getting at when she says, "Aim for the chopping
    block" at the end of the selection?

4. What are some of the differences between the written word and the
    movies? According to Dillard, why do people read books? Does this
    fit with your own experience?

5. Suggest some concrete definitions of the "vision" she discusses.

6. Why does Dillard quote Henry James and Thoreau? Does this
    strengthen her essay? Why or why not?

7. Notice the space breaks and lines with which Dillard separates dif-
    ferent sections of her essay. What does this indicate to the reader
    about how the piece is to be read?

8. In the fourth paragraph of section 4, Dillard describes herself at
    work. What do you notice about these sentences? How do they con-
    vey her deep concentration?

9. Why does Dillard use so many adjectives in describing her "opaque
    lightless chunky ruinous work"?

10. To what does Dillard allude when she speaks of "let your light so shine before men" and "hide it under a bushel"? What is a bushel? What does this phrase mean?

11. What do the following words mean: "epistemological," "jettison," "red herrings," "castigated"? Look each word up and then use each in a sentence of your own.

Suggestions for Writing

A. Describe in a couple of paragraphs a situation in which you have been able to achieve intense concentration. Did you have to work carefully to control your environment, as Dillard seems to have done? Do you ever concentrate so hard that you forget the world around you?

B. Describe the comparisons Dillard makes between painting and writing. Are there other activities to which writing might profitably be compared? Think of one and write about the comparison.

C. Are you a writer in the sense that Dillard sees herself as one? Can you relate to these descriptions of writing? Describe in a brief essay your own experiences of writing.

FIVE

Loren Eiseley

(1907–1977)

Many critics bemoan the increasingly narrow focus of both scientists and humanists. Unfortunately, the age of specialization asks us to probe deep but not wide. Loren Eiseley is different. He is the rare individual who can range far, wide, and deep in both cultures. He is a renowned anthropologist and archaeologist, a naturalist and a philosopher, an essayist and poet. Eiseley bridges the gulf between science and the humanities by returning to nature the wonder and mystery that reason often takes away. Although gifted with a mature and acute perception of nature's secrets, he is able in his nonfiction to maintain the child's capacity for wonder and surprise. He feels that the man of science needs balance, needs both analysis and intuition. At the end of his scientific career as a museum curator and university professor, he wrote: "When the human mind exists in the light of reason and no more than reason, we may say with absolute certainty that man and all that made him will be in that instant gone."

Eiseley did not even realize that he wanted to be a scientist until graduate school. Until then he felt he was rootless: spending his childhood on the plains of western Nebraska, attending college, riding the freight trains during the Depression, recuperating from an illness in a cabin in Colorado. For much of this time he was unhappy and lonely. In his autobiography, *All the Strange Hours* (1975), he recounts the frustration and pain of growing up in poverty in a tumultuous, neurotic family. Specifically, in "The Running Man" he tries to understand how several encounters from his childhood shaped the man he has become. He is especially obsessed with his mother and his awkward, scarring relationship with her. His description of one dramatic and public episode forms the center of this essay. It is painful and honest, haunting and lyrical.

Even though Eiseley's reputation as a scientist was firmly established through his articles in scholarly journals, it was not until his collection of popular essays, *The Immense Journey* (1957), was published that he became known to the general public.

This book marked the beginning of a new career for Eiseley as a writer of the "concealed essay," a form in which personal observations lead to thoughts of a more general, objective nature. Eiseley, like Annie Dillard, is willing to read cosmic significance into small incidents— in the flight of birds, the web of a spider, in a run-in with a neighborhood bully, and in a chance encounter with a young fox. In these essays Eiseley, as narrator, is a knowing and helpful presence, but he is also there with the reader as an observer, questioning and puzzling over the inexplicable. In "The Judgment of the Birds," for example, he comes across an improbable and transitory web, built by a spider who refuses to succumb to the weather. He observes the spider carefully, then speculates: "Maybe man himself will fight like this in the end." The everyday event reverberates in the scientist's mind until it awakens the artist. This is characteristic of Eiseley's vision: the mundane is "refracted, transmuted and clarified through the prism of his poetic imagination." In this way, the scientist looks beyond logic to beauty and mystery that defy explanation. And so wonder is returned to nature.

One of Eiseley's most persistent themes is the mystery and complexity of time—an appropriate topic for an archaeologist. Eiseley treats it with the intellectual rigor and curiosity of a scientist, without neglecting eloquence and sensitivity. His style and tone are filled with poetic sensibility and an amateur's sense of wonder and reverence. Somehow he can simultaneously observe, speculate, and dream. In "The Time of Man," an early essay on evolution (1962), the following passages are characteristic of Eiseley's incantatory, lyrical prose:

A strange animal, indeed: so very quiet when one turns over the mineral-hardened skull in a gravel bed, or peers into that little dark space which has housed so much cruelty and delight. One feels that something should be there still, some indefinable essence, some jinni to be evoked out of this little space which may contain at the same time the words of Jesus and the blasphemous megatons of modern physics. They are all in there together, inextricably intermixed. . . .

Those ancient bestial stirrings which still claw at sanity are part, also, of that dark continent we long chose to forget. But we do not forget, because man in contemplation reveals something that is characteristic of no other form of life known to us: he suffers because of what he is, and wishes to become something else. The moment we cease to hunger to be otherwise, our soul is dead. Long ago we began that hunger: long ago we painted on the walls of caverns and buried the revered dead. More and more, because our brain lays hold upon and seeks to shape the future, we are conscious of what we are, and what we might be. "No man," wrote John Donne, "doth exalt Nature to the height it would beare." He saw the great discrepancy between the dream and the reality.

Loren Eiseley learned not just to study nature but to participate in it. His essays are written in the same spirit: the reader is urged to be an active voyager. Eiseley once wrote that animals understand their roles, but that man, "bereft of instinct, must search continually for meanings." These essays are a rich source for such a journey.

The Long Loneliness

1   There is nothing more alone in the universe than man. He is alone because he has the intellectual capacity to know that he is separated by a vast gulf of social memory and experiment from the lives of his animal associates. He has entered into the strange world of history, of social and intellectual change, while his brothers of the field and forest remain subject to the invisible laws of biological evolution. Animals are molded by natural forces they do not comprehend. To their minds there is no past and no future. There is only the everlasting present of a single generation—its trails in the forest, its hidden pathways of the air and in the sea.

2   Man, by contrast, is alone with the knowledge of his history
until the day of his death. When we were children we wanted to
talk to animals and struggled to understand why this was impossible. Slowly we gave up the attempt as we grew into the solitary
world of human adulthood; the rabbit was left on the lawn, the
dog was relegated to his kennel. Only in acts of inarticulate compassion, in rare and hidden moments of communion with nature,
does man briefly escape his solitary destiny. Frequently in science
fiction he dreams of worlds with creatures whose communicative
power is the equivalent of his own.

3   It is with a feeling of startlement, therefore, and eager interest touching the lost child in every one of us, that the public has
received the recent accounts of naval research upon the intelligence of one of our brother mammals—the sea-dwelling bottle-
nosed porpoise or dolphin.

4   These small whales who left the land millions of years ago to
return to the great mother element of life, the sea, are now being
regarded by researchers as perhaps the most intelligent form of
life on our planet next to man. Dr. John Lilly of the Com-
munications Research Institute in the Virgin Islands reports that
the brain of the porpoise is 40 per cent larger than man's and is
just as complex in its functional units. Amazed by the rapidity with
which captive porpoises solved problems that even monkeys
found difficult, Dr. Lilly is quoted as expressing the view that
"man's position at the top of the hierarchy [of intelligence]
begins to be questioned."

5   Dr. Lilly found that his captives communicated in a series of
underwater whistles and that, in addition, they showed an amazing "verbalizing" ability in copying certain sounds heard in the
laboratory. The experimental animal obviously hoped to elicit by
this means a reproduction of the pleasurable sensations he had
been made to experience under laboratory conditions. It is
reported that in spite of living in a medium different from the
one that man inhabits, and therefore having quite a different
throat structure, one of the porpoises even uttered in a Donald-
Duckish voice a short number series it had heard spoken by one
of the laboratory investigators.

6   The import of these discoveries is tremendous and may not
be adequately known for a long time. An animal from a little-
explored medium, which places great barriers in the way of the
psychologist, has been found to have not only a strong social orga-

nization but to show a degree of initiative in experimental communicative activity unmatched by man's closest relatives, the great apes. The porpoises reveal, moreover, a touching altruism and friendliness in their attempts to aid injured companions. Can it be, one inevitably wonders, that man is so locked in his own type of intelligence—an intelligence that is linked to a prehensile, grasping hand giving him power over his environment—that he is unable to comprehend the intellectual life of a highly endowed creature from another domain such as the sea?

7   Perhaps the water barrier has shut us away from a potentially communicative and jolly companion. Perhaps we have some things still to learn from the natural world around us before we turn to the far shores of space and whatever creatures may await us there. After all, the porpoise is a mammal. He shares with us an ancient way of birth and affectionate motherhood. His blood is warm, he breathes air as we do. We both bear in our bodies the remnants of a common skeleton torn asunder for divergent purposes far back in the dim dawn of mammalian life. The porpoise has been superficially streamlined like a fish.

8   His are not, however, the cold-blooded ways of the true fishes. Far higher on the tree of life than fishes, the dolphin's paddles are made-over paws, rather than fins. He is an ever-constant reminder of the versatility of life and its willingness to pass through strange dimensions of experience. There are environmental worlds on earth every bit as weird as what we may imagine to revolve by far-off suns. It is our superficial familiarity with this planet that inhibits our appreciation of the unknown until a porpoise, rearing from a tank to say Three-Two-Three, re-creates for us the utter wonder of childhood.

9   Unless we are specialists in the study of communication and its relation to intelligence, however, we are apt to oversimplify or define poorly what intelligence is, what communication and language are, and thus confuse and mystify both ourselves and others. The mysteries surrounding the behavior of the bottle-nosed porpoise, and even of man himself, are not things to be probed simply by the dissector's scalpel. They lie deeper. They involve the whole nature of the mind and its role in the universe.

10   We are forced to ask ourselves whether native intelligence in another form than man's might be as high as or even higher than his own, yet be marked by no such material monuments as man has placed upon the earth. At first glance we are alien to this idea,

because man is particularly a creature who has turned the tables
on his environment so that he is now engrossed in shaping it,
rather than being shaped by it. Man expresses himself upon his
environment through the use of tools. We therefore tend to
equate the use of tools in a one-to-one relationship with intelligence.

11   The question we must now ask ourselves, however, is
whether this involves an unconsciously man-centered way of looking at intelligence. Let us try for a moment to enter the dolphin's
kingdom and the dolphin's body, retaining, at the same time, our
human intelligence. In this imaginative act, it may be possible to
divest ourselves of certain human preconceptions about our kind
of intelligence and at the same time to see more clearly why mind,
even advanced mind, may have manifestations other than the
tools and railroad tracks and laboratories that we regard as evidence of intellect. If we are particularly adept in escaping from
our own bodies, we may even learn to discount a little the kind of
world of rockets and death that our type of busy human curiosity,
linked to a hand noted for its ability to open assorted Pandora's
boxes, has succeeded in foisting upon the world as a symbol of
universal intelligence.

12   We have now sacrificed, in our imagination, our hands for
flippers and our familiar land environment for the ocean. We will
go down into the deep waters as naked of possessions as when we
entered life itself. We will take with us one thing alone that exists
among porpoises as among men: an ingrained biological gregari-
ousness—a sociality that in our new world will permit us to run in
schools, just as early man ran in the packs that were his ancient
anthropoid heritage. We will assume in the light of Dr. Lilly's
researches that our native intelligence, as distinguished from our
culturally transmitted habits, is very high. The waters have closed
finally over us, our paws have been sacrificed for the necessary
flippers with which to navigate.

13   The result is immediately evident and quite clear: No matter
how well we communicate with our fellows through the water
medium we will never build drowned empires in the coral; we will
never inscribe on palace walls the victorious boasts of porpoise
kings. We will know only water and the wastes of water beyond the
power of man to describe. We will be secret visitors in hidden
canyons beneath the mouths of torrential rivers. We will survey in
innocent astonishment the flotsam that pours from the veins of

continents—dead men, great serpents, giant trees—or perhaps
the little toy boat of a child loosed far upstream will come floating
past. Bottles with winking green lights will plunge by us into the
all-embracing ooze. Meaningless appearances and disappearances
will comprise our philosophies. We will hear the earth's heart ticking in its thin granitic shell. Volcanic fires will growl ominously in
steam-filled crevices. Vapor, bird cries, and sea wrack will com-
pose our memories. We will see death in many forms and, on
occasion, the slow majestic fall of battleships through the green
light that comes from beyond our domain.

14   Over all that region of wondrous beauty we will exercise no
more control than the simplest mollusk. Even the octopus with
flexible arms will build little shelters that we cannot imitate.
Without hands we will have only the freedom to follow the
untrammeled sea winds across the planet.

15   Perhaps if those whistling sounds that porpoises make are
truly symbolic and capable of manipulation in our brains, we will
wonder about the world in which we find ourselves—but it will be
a world not susceptible to experiment. At best we may nuzzle in
curiosity a passing shipbottom and be harpooned for our pains.
Our thoughts, in other words, will be as limited as those of the
first men who roved in little bands in the times before fire and the
writing that was to open to man the great doorway of his past.

16   Man without writing cannot long retain his history in his
head. His intelligence permits him to grasp some kind of succession of generations; but without writing, the tale of the past rapidly degenerates into fumbling myth and fable. Man's greatest epic,
his four long battles with the advancing ice of the great continental glaciers, has vanished from human memory without a trace.
Our illiterate fathers disappeared and with them, in a few scant
generations, died one of the great stories of all time. This episode
has nothing to do with the biological quality of a brain as between
then and now. It has to do instead with a device, an invention
made possible by the hand. That invention came too late in time
to record eyewitness accounts of the years of the Giant Frost.

17   Primitives of our own species, even today, are historically
shallow in their knowledge of the past. Only the poet who writes
speaks his message across the millennia to other hearts. Only in
writing can the cry from the great cross on Golgotha still be heard
in the minds of men. The thinker of perceptive insight, even if we
allow him for the moment to be a porpoise rather than a man,

has only his individual glimpse of the universe until such time as he can impose that insight upon unnumbered generations. In centuries of pondering, man has come upon but one answer to this problem: speech translated into writing that passes beyond human mortality.

18   Writing, and later printing, is the product of our adaptable many-purposed hands. It is thus, through writing, with no increase in genetic, inborn capacity since the last ice advance, that modern man carries in his mind the intellectual triumphs of all his predecessors who were able to inscribe their thoughts for posterity.

19   All animals which man has reason to believe are more than usually intelligent—our relatives the great apes, the elephant, the raccoon, the wolverine, among others—are problem solvers, and in at least a small way manipulators of their environment. Save for the instinctive calls of their species, however, they cannot communicate except by direct imitation. They cannot invent words for new situations nor get their fellows to use such words. No matter how high the individual intelligence, its private world remains a private possession locked forever within a single, perishable brain. It is this fact that finally balks our hunger to communicate even with the sensitive dog who shares our fireside.

20   Dr. Lilly insists, however, that the porpoises communicate in high-pitched, underwater whistles that seem to transmit their wishes and problems. The question then becomes one of ascertaining whether these sounds represent true language—in the sense of symbolic meanings, additive, learned elements—or whether they are simply the instinctive signals of a pack animal. To this there is as yet no clear answer, but the eagerness with which laboratory sounds and voices were copied by captive porpoises suggests a vocalizing ability extending perhaps to or beyond the threshold of speech.

21   Most of the intelligent land animals have prehensile, grasping organs for exploring their environment—hands in man and his anthropoid relatives, the sensitive inquiring trunk in the elephant. One of the surprising things about the porpoise is that his superior brain is unaccompanied by any type of manipulative organ. He has, however, a remarkable range-finding ability involving some sort of echo-sounding. Perhaps this acute sense—far more accurate than any man has been able to devise artificially—brings him greater knowledge of his watery surroundings than

might at first seem possible. Human beings think of intelligence as geared to things. The hand and the tool are to us the unconscious symbols of our intellectual achievement. It is difficult for us to visualize another kind of lonely, almost disembodied intelligence floating in the wavering green fairyland of the sea—an intelligence possibly near or comparable to our own but without hands to build, to transmit knowledge by writing, or to alter by one hairsbreadth the planet's surface. Yet at the same time there are indications that this is a warm, friendly and eager intelligence quite capable of coming to the assistance of injured companions and striving to rescue them from drowning. Porpoises left the land when mammalian brains were still small and primitive. Without the stimulus provided by agile exploring fingers, these great sea mammals have yet taken a divergent road toward intelligence of a high order. Hidden in their sleek bodies is an impressively elaborated instrument, the reason for whose appearance is a complete enigma. It is as though both man and porpoise were each part of some great eye which yearned to look both outward on eternity and inward to the sea's heart—that fertile entity so like the mind in its swarming and grotesque life.

92   Perhaps man has something to learn after all from fellow creatures without the ability to drive harpoons through living flesh, or poison with strontium the planetary winds. One is reminded of those watery blue vaults in which, as in some idyllic eternity, Herman Melville once saw the sperm whales nurse their young. And as Melville wrote of the sperm whale, so we might now paraphrase his words in speaking of the porpoise. "Genius in the porpoise? Has the porpoise ever written a book, spoken a speech? No, his great genius is declared in his doing nothing particular to prove it. It is declared in his pyramidical silence." If man had sacrificed his hands for flukes, the moral might run, he would still be a philosopher, but there would have been taken from him the devastating power to wreak his thought upon the body of the world. Instead he would have lived and wandered, like the porpoise, homeless across currents and winds and oceans, intelligent, but forever the lonely and curious observer of unknown wreckage falling through the blue light of eternity. This role would now be a deserved penitence for man. Perhaps such a transformation would bring him once more into that mood of childhood innocence in which he talked successfully to all things living but had no power and no urge to harm. It is worth at least a wistful

thought that someday the porpoise may talk to us and we to him. It would break, perhaps, the long loneliness that has made man a frequent terror and abomination even to himself.

QUESTIONS

Ideas

1. Do you believe that certain animals have an intelligence that we cannot fathom? Did you ever "communicate" with an animal?
2. If we were to de-evolve, losing our hands, speculate on how our culture would change.
3. Eiseley puts great emphasis on writing. Explain its significance in making our culture different from that of dolphins.
4. Do you think cultures that do not write are necessarily shallow? Does Eiseley suggest that we might be stuck in our own definition of intelligence?
5. Why does Eiseley fantasize that it would be a good penance for humans to roam the oceans "forever the lonely and curious observer?"?

Organization

6. Eiseley uses the third paragraph to explain the occasion of this essay. Write a brief sentence outline of his thinking starting with "Man is alone because he is separated from animals by history and intellectual change."
7. Explain how Eiseley does or doesn't bring things together in the last paragraph.

Sentences

8. Eiseley uses dashes in a number of sentences. Explain how he uses them and comment on their effectiveness.
9. Eiseley varies his sentence structure from the usual subject, verb, object of the first sentence. Give several examples of variations you think are effective.

Words

10. What do you think Eiseley means by "pyramidical silence" in the concluding paragraph?

11. Unpack what you think is the meaning of the following words in the last sentence: "loneliness," "man," "terror," and "abomination."

Suggestions for Writing

A. If porpoises could communicate directly with us and us with them, what would we tell each other? Create an imaginary dialogue.

B. Write a brief essay in which you discuss the difficulty of defining intelligence.

C. Do some research on some specific aspect of animal communication. Write a brief report.

The Judgment of the Birds

1 It is a commonplace of all religious thought, even the most primitive, that the man seeking visions and insight must go apart from his fellows and live for a time in the wilderness. If he is of the proper sort, he will return with a message. It may not be a message from the god he set out to seek, but even if he has failed in that particular, he will have had a vision or seen a marvel, and these are always worth listening to and thinking about.

2 The world, I have come to believe, is a very queer place, but we have been part of this queerness for so long that we tend to take it for granted. We rush to and fro like Mad Hatters upon our peculiar errands, all the time imagining our surroundings to be dull and ourselves quite ordinary creatures. Actually, there is nothing in the world to encourage this idea, but such is the mind of man, and this is why he finds it necessary from time to time to send emissaries into the wilderness in the hope of learning of great events, or plans in store for him, that will resuscitate his waning taste for life. His great news services, his worldwide radio network, he knows with a last remnant of healthy distrust will be of no use to him in this matter. No miracle can withstand a radio broadcast, and it is certain that it would be no miracle if it could. One must seek, then, what only the solitary approach can give—a natural revelation.

3 Let it be understood that I am not the sort of man to whom is entrusted direct knowledge of great events or prophecies. A nat-

uralist, however, spends much of his life alone, and my life is no exception. Even in New York City there are patches of wilderness, and a man by himself is bound to undergo certain experiences falling into the class of which I speak. I set mine down, therefore: a matter of pigeons, a flight of chemicals, and a judgment of birds, in the hope that they will come to the eye of those who have retained a true taste for the marvelous, and who are capable of discerning in the flow of ordinary events the point at which the mundane world gives way to quite another dimension.

4   New York is not, on the whole, the best place to enjoy the downright miraculous nature of the planet. There are, I do not doubt, many remarkable stories to be heard there and many strange sights to be seen, but to grasp a marvel fully it must be savored from all aspects. This cannot be done while one is being jostled and hustled along a crowded street. Nevertheless, in any city there are true wildernesses where a man can be alone. It can happen in a hotel room, or on the high roofs at dawn.

5   One night on the twentieth floor of a midtown hotel I awoke in the dark and grew restless. On an impulse I climbed upon the broad old-fashioned window sill, opened the curtains, and peered out. It was the hour just before dawn, the hour when men sigh in their sleep or, if awake, strive to focus their wavering eyesight upon a world emerging from the shadows. I leaned out sleepily through the open window. I had expected depths, but not the sight I saw.

6   I found I was looking down from that great height into a series of curious cupolas or lofts that I could just barely make out in the darkness. As I looked, the outlines of these lofts became more distinct because the light was being reflected from the wings of pigeons who, in utter silence, were beginning to float outward upon the city. In and out through the open slits in the cupolas passed the white-winged birds on their mysterious errands. At this hour the city was theirs, and quietly, without the brush of a single wing tip against stone in that high, eerie place, they were taking over the spires of Manhattan. They were pouring upward in a light that was not yet perceptible to human eyes, while far down in the black darkness of the alleys it was still midnight.

7   As I crouched half-asleep across the sill, I had a moment's illusion that the world had changed in the night, as in some immense snowfall, and that, if I were to leave, it would have to be as these other inhabitants were doing, by the window. I should

have to launch out into that great bottomless void with the simple confidence of young birds reared high up there among the familiar chimney pots and interposed horrors of the abyss.

8   I leaned farther out. To and fro went the white wings, to and fro. There were no sounds from any of them. They knew man was asleep and this light for a little while was theirs. Or perhaps I had only dreamed about man in this city of wings—which he could surely never have built. Perhaps I, myself, was one of these birds dreaming unpleasantly a moment of old dangers far below as I teetered on a window ledge.

9   Around and around went the wings. It needed only a little courage, only a little shove from the window ledge, to enter that city of light. The muscles of my hands were already making little premonitory lunges. I wanted to enter that city and go away over the roofs in the first dawn. I wanted to enter it so badly that I drew back carefully into the room and opened the hall door. I found my coat on the chair, and it slowly became clear to me that there was a way down through the floors, that I was, after all, only a man.

10   I dressed then and went back to my own kind, and I have been rather more than usually careful ever since not to look into the city of light. I had seen, just once, man's greatest creation from a strange inverted angle, and it was not really his at all. I will never forget how those wings went round and round, and how, by the merest pressure of the fingers and a feeling for air, one might go away over the roofs. It is a knowledge, however, that is better kept to oneself. I think of it sometimes in such a way that the wings, beginning far down in the black depths of the mind, begin to rise and whirl till all the mind is lit by their spinning, and there is a sense of things passing away, but lightly, as a wing might veer over an obstacle.

11   To see from an inverted angle, however, is not a gift allotted merely to the human imagination. I have come to suspect that within their degree it is sensed by animals, though perhaps as rarely as among men. The time has to be right; one has to be, by chance or intention, upon the border of two worlds. And sometimes these two borders may shift or interpenetrate and one sees the miraculous.

12   I once saw this happen to a crow.

13   This crow lives near my house, and though I have never injured him, he takes good care to stay up in the very highest

trees and, in general, to avoid humanity. His world begins at about the limit of my eyesight.

14   On the particular morning when this episode occurred, the whole countryside was buried in one of the thickest fogs in years. The ceiling was absolutely zero. All planes were grounded, and even a pedestrian could hardly see his outstretched hand before him.

15   I was groping across a field in the general direction of the railroad station, following a dimly outlined path. Suddenly out of the fog, at about the level of my eyes, and so closely that I flinched, there flashed a pair of immense black wings and a huge beak. The whole bird rushed over my head with a frantic cawing outcry of such hideous terror as I have never heard in a crow's voice before and never expect to hear again.

16   He was lost and startled, I thought, as I recovered my poise. He ought not to have flown out in this fog. He'd knock his silly brains out.

17   All afternoon that great awkward cry rang in my head. Merely being lost in a fog seemed scarcely to account for it—especially in a tough, intelligent old bandit such as I knew that particular crow to be. I even looked once in the mirror to see what it might be about me that had so revolted him that he had cried out in protest to the very stones.

18   Finally, as I worked my way homeward along the path, the solution came to me. It should have been clear before. The borders of our worlds had shifted. It was the fog that had done it. That crow, and I knew him well, never under normal circumstances flew low near men. He had been lost all right, but it was more than that. He had thought he was high up, and when he encountered me looming gigantically through the fog, he had perceived a ghastly and, to the crow mind, unnatural sight. He had seen a man walking on air, desecrating the very heart of the crow kingdom, a harbinger of the most profound evil a crow mind could conceive of—air-walking men. The encounter, he must have thought, had taken place a hundred feet over the roofs.

19   He caws now when he sees me leaving for the station in the morning, and I fancy that in that note I catch the uncertainty of a mind that has come to know things are not always what they seem. He has seen a marvel in his heights of air and is no longer as other crows. He has experienced the human world from an

unlikely perspective. He and I share a viewpoint in common: our worlds have interpenetrated, and we both have faith in the miraculous.

20   It is a faith that in my own case has been augmented by two remarkable sights. I once saw some very odd chemicals fly across a waste so dead it might have been upon the moon, and once, by an even more fantastic piece of luck, I was present when a group of birds passed a judgment upon life.

21   On the maps of the old voyageurs it is called *Mauvaises Terres*, the evil lands, and, slurred a little with the passage through many minds, it has come down to us anglicized as the badlands. The soft shuffle of moccasins has passed through its canyons on the grim business of war and flight, but the last of those slight disturbances of immemorial silences died out almost a century ago. The land, if one can call it a land, is a waste as lifeless as that valley in which lie the kings of Egypt. Like the Valley of the Kings, it is a mausoleum, a place of dry bones in what once was a place of life. Now it has silences as deep as those in the moon's airless chasms.

22   Nothing grows among its pinnacles; there is no shade except under great toadstools of sandstone whose bases have been eaten to the shape of wine glasses by the wind. Everything is flaking, cracking, disintegrating, wearing away in the long, imperceptible weather of time. The ash of ancient volcanic outbursts still sterilizes its soil, and its colors in that waste are the colors that flame in the lonely sunsets on dead planets. Men come there but rarely, and for one purpose only, the collection of bones.

23   It was a late hour on a cold, wind-bitten autumn day when I climbed a great hill spined like a dinosaur's back and tried to take my bearings. The tumbled waste fell away in waves in all directions. Blue air was darkening into purple along the bases of the hills. I shifted my knapsack, heavy with the petrified bones of long-vanished creatures, and studied my compass. I wanted to be out of there by nightfall, and already the sun was going sullenly down in the west.

24   It was then that I saw the flight coming on. It was moving like a little close-knit body of black specks that danced and darted and closed again. It was pouring from the north and heading toward me with the undeviating relentlessness of a compass needle. It streamed through the shadows rising out of monstrous gorges. It rushed over towering pinnacles in the red light of the sun or momentarily sank from sight within their shade. Across

that desert of eroding clay and wind-worn stone they came with a faint wild twittering that filled all the air about me as those tiny living bullets hurtled past into the night.

25   It may not strike you as a marvel. It would not, perhaps, unless you stood in the middle of a dead world at sunset, but that was where I stood. Fifty million years lay under my feet, fifty million years of bellowing monsters moving in a green world now gone so utterly that its very light was traveling on the farther edge of space. The chemicals of all that vanished age lay about me in the ground. Around me still lay the shearing molars of dead titanotheres, the delicate sabers of soft-stepping cats, the hollow sockets that had held the eyes of many a strange, outmoded beast. Those eyes had looked out upon a world as real as ours; dark, savage brains had roamed and roared their challenges into the steaming night.

26   Now they were still here, or, put it as you will, the chemicals that made them were here about me in the ground. The carbon that had driven them ran blackly in the eroding stone. The stain of iron was in the clays. The iron did not remember the blood it had once moved within, the phosphorus had forgot the savage brain. The little individual moment had ebbed from all those strange combinations of chemicals as it would ebb from our living bodies into the sinks and runnels of oncoming time.

27   I had lifted up a fistful of that ground. I held it while that wild flight of south-bound warblers hurtled over me into the oncoming dark. There went phosphorus, there went iron, there went carbon, there beat the calcium in those hurrying wings. Alone on a dead planet I watched that incredible miracle speeding past. It ran by some true compass over field and waste land. It cried its individual ecstasies into the air until the gullies rang. It swerved like a single body, it knew itself, and, lonely, it bunched close in the racing darkness, its individual entities feeling about them the rising night. And so, crying to each other their identity, they passed away out of my view.

28   I dropped my fistful of earth. I heard it roll inanimate back into the gully at the base of the hill: iron, carbon, the chemicals of life. Like men from those wild tribes who had haunted these hills before me seeking visions, I made my sign to the great darkness. It was not a mocking sign, and I was not mocked. As I walked into my camp late that night, one man, rousing from his blankets beside the fire, asked sleepily, "What did you see?"

₉₀ "I think, a miracle," I said softly, but I said it to myself. Behind me that vast waste began to glow under the rising moon.

₉₀ I have said that I saw a judgment upon life, and that it was not passed by men. Those who stare at birds in cages or who test minds by their closeness to our own may not care for it. It comes from far away out of my past, in a place of pouring waters and green leaves. I shall never see an episode like it again if I live to be a hundred, nor do I think that one man in a million has ever seen it, because man is an intruder into such silences. The light must be right, and the observer must remain unseen. No man sets up such an experiment. What he sees, he sees by chance.

31 You may put it that I had come over a mountain, that I had slogged through fern and pine needles for half a long day, and that on the edge of a little glade with one long, crooked branch extending across it, I had sat down to rest with my back against a stump. Through accident I was concealed from the glade, although I could see into it perfectly.

32 The sun was warm there, and the murmurs of forest life blurred softly away into my sleep. When I awoke, dimly aware of some commotion and outcry in the clearing, the light was slanting down through the pines in such a way that the glade was lit like some vast cathedral. I could see the dust motes of wood pollen in the long shaft of light, and there on the extended branch sat an enormous raven with a red and squirming nestling in his beak.

33 The sound that awoke me was the outraged cries of the nestling's parents, who flew helplessly in circles about the clearing. The sleek black monster was indifferent to them. He gulped, whetted his beak on the dead branch a moment, and sat still. Up to that point the little tragedy had followed the usual pattern. But suddenly, out of all that area of woodland, a soft sound of complaint began to rise. Into the glade fluttered small birds of half a dozen varieties drawn by the anguished outcries of the tiny parents.

34 No one dared to attack the raven. But they cried there in some instinctive common misery, the bereaved and the unbereaved. The glade filled with their soft rustling and their cries. They fluttered as though to point their wings at the murderer. There was a dim intangible ethic he had violated, that they knew. He was a bird of death.

35   And he, the murderer, the black bird at the heart of life, sat
on there, glistening in the common light, formidable, unmoving,
unperturbed, untouchable.

36   The sighing died. It was then I saw the judgment. It was the
judgment of life against death. I will never see it again so forcefully presented. I will never hear it again in notes so tragically prolonged. For in the midst of protest, they forgot the violence.
There, in that clearing, the crystal note of a song sparrow lifted
hesitantly in the hush. And finally, after painful fluttering, another took the song, and then another, the song passing from one
bird to another, doubtfully at first, as though some evil thing were
being slowly forgotten. Till suddenly they took heart and sang
from many throats joyously together as birds are known to sing.
They sang because life is sweet and sunlight beautiful. They sang
under the brooding shadow of the raven. In simple truth they had
forgotten the raven, for they were the singers of life, and not of
death.

37   I was not of that airy company. My limbs were the heavy
limbs of an earthbound creature who could climb mountains,
even the mountains of the mind, only by a great effort of will. I
knew I had seen a marvel and observed a judgment, but the mind
which was my human endowment was sure to question it and to
be at me day by day with its heresies until I grew to doubt the
meaning of what I had seen. Eventually darkness and subtleties
would ring me round once more.

38   And so it proved until, on the top of a stepladder, I made
one more observation upon life. It was cold that autumn evening,
and, standing under a suburban street light in a spate of leaves
and beginning snow, I was suddenly conscious of some huge and
hairy shadows dancing over the pavement. They seemed attached
to an odd, globular shape that was magnified above me. There
was no mistaking it. I was standing under the shadow of an orb-
weaving spider. Gigantically projected against the street, she was
about her spinning when everything was going underground.
Even her cables were magnified upon the sidewalk and already I
was half-entangled in their shadows.

39   "Good Lord," I thought, "she has found herself a kind of
minor sun and is going to upset the course of nature."

40   I procured a ladder from my yard and climbed up to inspect
the situation. There she was, the universe running down around

her, warmly arranged among her guy ropes attached to the lamp supports—a great black and yellow embodiment of the life force, not giving up to either frost or stepladders. She ignored me and went on tightening and improving her web.

41   I stood over her on the ladder, a faint snow touching my cheeks, and surveyed her universe. There were a couple of iridescent green beetle cases turning slowly on a loose strand of web, a fragment of luminescent eye from a moth's wing and a large indeterminable object, perhaps a cicada, that had struggled and been wrapped in silk. There were also little bits and slivers, little red and blue flashes from the scales of anonymous wings that had crashed there.

42   Some days, I thought, they will be dull and gray and the shine will be out of them; then the dew will polish them again and drops hang on the silk until everything is gleaming and turning in the light. It is like a mind, really, where everything changes but remains, and in the end you have these eaten-out bits of experience like beetle wings.

43   I stood over her a moment longer, comprehending somewhat reluctantly that her adventure against the great blind forces of winter, her seizure of this warming globe of light, would come to nothing and was hopeless. Nevertheless it brought the birds back into my mind, and that faraway song which had traveled with growing strength around a forest clearing years ago—a kind of heroism, a world where even a spider refuses to lie down and die if a rope can still be spun on to a star. Maybe man himself will fight like this in the end, I thought, slowly realizing that the web and its threatening yellow occupant had been added to some luminous store of experience, shining for a moment in the fogbound reaches of my brain.

44   The mind, it came to me as I slowly descended the ladder, is a very remarkable thing; it has gotten itself a kind of courage by looking at a spider in a street lamp. Here was something that ought to be passed on to those who will fight our final freezing battle with the void. I thought of setting it down carefully as a message to the future: *In the days of the frost seek a minor sun.*

45   But as I hesitated, it became plain that something was wrong. The marvel was escaping—a sense of bigness beyond man's power to grasp, the essence of life in its great dealings with the universe. It was better, I decided, for the emissaries returning from the wilderness, even if they were merely descending from a

stepladder, to record their marvel, not to define its meaning. In that way it would go echoing on through the minds of men, each grasping at that beyond out of which the miracles emerge, and which, once defined, ceases to satisfy the human need for symbols.

46   In the end I merely made a mental note: One specimen of Epeira observed building a web in a street light. Late autumn and cold for spiders. Cold for men, too. I shivered and left the lamp glowing there in my mind. The last I saw of Epeira she was hauling steadily on a cable. I stepped carefully over her shadow as I walked away.

QUESTIONS

Ideas

1. Near the end of this essay, Eiseley talks about recording events without trying to define their meaning. Does he—or can you—define the meaning of the events recorded in this essay?

2. How does the following excerpt from another Eiseley essay bear on "The Judgment of the Birds"?

    It is a funny thing what the brain will do with memories and how it will treasure them and finally bring them into odd juxtapositions with other things, as though it wanted to make a design, or get some meaning out of them, whether you want it or not, or even see it.

3. In paragraph 2 Eiseley uses the term "a natural revelation." What does he mean? (Consider the meaning of the word "reveal.")

4. In this essay and in the other Eiseley essays included in this book, Eiseley calls himself a "naturalist." What is his sense of the word?

5. In paragraphs 9 and 19, Eiseley describes a peculiar feeling that he had. What is this feeling and why is it important? (Can it be compared with his impulse to dance with the frogs? Why or why not?)

6. What does Eiseley mean by "In the days of the frost seek a minor sun"? Why does he step carefully over the spider's shadow?

Organization

7. How is the essay organized? How many parts does it have and how are they related? How does Eiseley move from one section to another? How does he link them?

8. Where does the introduction end? Where does the conclusion begin? Could paragraphs 19–28 be omitted? Why or why not?

Sentences

9. Paragraph 35 is a single sentence, as is paragraph 12. Why?
10. How does the style of Eiseley's mental note in the last paragraph differ from the syntax of the previous one?
11. In paragraphs 3 and 18 Eiseley uses the colon. What is the relationship of the right-hand part of each statement to the left-hand part? Rewrite the sentences without the colon. How are the sentences different—in tone, in rhythm, in effect?
12. Notice how dashes are used in the sentences of paragraphs 2 and 17. Rewrite the sentences without the dashes. What is different about them? Compare the sentences using dashes with those using the colon. How do they differ? Can you suggest any guidelines for using the colon or the dash?

Words

13. What words and phrases indicating attentiveness appear in the first five paragraphs? What is the effect of the language of the final sentence of paragraph 5: "I had expected depths, but not the sight I saw"?
14. Near the end of the essay (paragraph 41), Eiseley describes a spider's web, comparing the human mind to the web. How is the mind like a spider's web? What does the spider represent?

Suggestions for Writing

A. Rewrite the following sentence in normal word order: "To and fro went the white wings, to and fro." What is the difference? Do the same with this sentence: "Around and around went the wings."
B. Rewrite the following sentence: "And he, the murderer, the black bird at the heart of life, sat there, glistening in the common light, formidable, unmoving, unperturbed, untouchable."
C. Write an essay in which you examine Eiseley's ideas about nature. Consider his view of himself as a naturalist. Use at least two of his essays.
D. Compare the following passages about webs with Eiseley's comparison of the mind to a spider's web. Write an essay exploring the idea implied by one or more of the web passages—including Eiseley's.

> Experience is never limited, and it is never complete; it is an immense sensibility, a kind of huge spiderweb of the finest silken

threads suspended in the chamber of consciousness, and catching
every airborne particle in its tissue.

—Henry James, from *"The Art of Fiction"*

The world is like an enormous spider web and if you touch it, however lightly, at any point, the vibration ripples to the remotest
perimeter and the drowsy spider feels the tingle and is drowsy no
more but springs out to fling the gossamer coils about you who
have touched the web and then inject the black, numbing poison
under your hide. It does not matter whether or not you meant to
brush the web of things.

—Robert Penn Warren, from *All the King's Men*

The Dance of the Frogs

I

1   He was a member of the Explorers Club, and he had
never been outside the state of Pennsylvania. Some of us who
were world travelers used to smile a little about that, even though
we knew his scientific reputation had been, at one time, great. It is
always the way of youth to smile. I used to think of myself as something of an adventurer, but the time came when I realized that
old Albert Dreyer, huddling with his drink in the shadows close to
the fire, had journeyed farther into the Country of Terror than
any of us would ever go, God willing, and emerge alive.

2   He was a morose and aging man, without family and without
intimates. His membership in the club dated back into the
decades when he was a zoologist famous for his remarkable experiments upon amphibians—he had recovered and actually produced the adult stage of the Mexican axolotl, as well as achieving
remarkable tissue transplants in salamanders. The club had been
flattered to have him then, travel or no travel, but the end was not
fortunate. The brilliant scientist had become the misanthrope;
the achievement lay all in the past, and Albert Dreyer kept to his solitary room, his solitary drink, and his accustomed spot by the fire.

3   The reason I came to hear his story was an odd one. I had
been north that year, and the club had asked me to give a little
talk on the religious beliefs of the Indians of the northern forest,

the Naskapi of Labrador I had long been a student of the strange mélange of superstition and woodland wisdom that makes up the religious life of the nature peoples. Moreover, I had come to know something of the strange similarities of the "shaking tent rite" to the phenomena of the modern medium's cabinet.

4   "The special tent with its entranced occupant is no different from the cabinet," I contended. "The only difference is the type of voices that emerge. Many of the physical phenomena are identical—the movement of powerful forces shaking the conical hut, objects thrown, all this is familiar to Western physical science. What is different are the voices projected. Here they are the cries of animals, the voices from the swamp and the mountain—the solitary elementals before whom the primitive man stands in awe, and from whom he begs sustenance. Here the game lords reign supreme; man himself is voiceless."

5   A low, halting query reached me from the back of the room. I was startled, even in the midst of my discussion, to note that it was Dreyer.

6   "And the game lords, what are they?"

7   "Each species of animal is supposed to have gigantic leaders of more than normal size," I explained. "These beings are the immaterial controllers of that particular type of animal. Legend about them is confused. Sometimes they partake of human qualities, will and intelligence, but they are of animal shape. They control the movements of game, and thus their favor may mean life or death to man."

8   "Are they visible?" Again Dreyer's low, troubled voice came from the back of the room.

9   "Native belief has it that they can be seen on rare occasions," I answered. "In a sense they remind one of the concept of the archetypes, the originals behind the petty show of our small, transitory existence. They are the immortal renewers of substance—the force behind and above animate nature."

10   "Do they dance?" persisted Dreyer.

11   At this I grew nettled. Old Dreyer in a heckling mood was something new. "I cannot answer that question," I said acidly. "My informants failed to elaborate upon it. But they believe implicitly in these monstrous beings, talk to and propitiate them. It is their voices that emerge from the shaking tent."

12   "The Indians believe it," pursued old Dreyer relentlessly, "but do *you* believe it?"

13   "My dear fellow"—I shrugged and glanced at the smiling audience—"I have seen many strange things, many puzzling things, but I am a scientist." Dreyer made a contemptuous sound in his throat and went back to the shadow out of which he had crept in his interest. The talk was over. I headed for the bar.

II

14   The evening passed. Men drifted homeward or went to their rooms. I had been a year in the woods and hungered for voices and companionship. Finally, however, I sat alone with my glass, a little mellow, perhaps, enjoying the warmth of the fire and remembering the blue snowfields of the North as they should be remembered—in the comfort of warm rooms.

15   I think an hour must have passed. The club was silent except for the ticking of an antiquated clock on the mantel and small night noises from the street. I must have drowsed. At all events it was some time before I grew aware that a chair had been drawn up opposite me. I started.

16   "A damp night," I said.

17   "Foggy," said the man in the shadow musingly. "But not too foggy. They like it that way."

18   "Eh?" I said. I knew immediately it was Dreyer speaking. Maybe I had missed something; on second thought, maybe not.

19   "And spring," he said. "Spring. That's part of it. God knows why, of course, but we feel it, why shouldn't they? And more intensely."

20   "Look—" I said. "I guess—" The old man was more human than I thought. He reached out and touched my knee with the hand that he always kept a glove over—burn, we used to speculate—and smiled softly.

21   "You don't know what I'm talking about," he finished for me. "And, besides, I ruffled your feelings earlier in the evening. You must forgive me. You touched on an interest of mine, and I was perhaps overeager. I did not intend to give the appearance of heckling. It was only that . . ."

22   "Of course," I said. "Of course." Such a confession from Dreyer was astounding. The man might be ill. I rang for a drink and decided to shift the conversation to a safer topic, more appropriate to a scholar.

23   "Frogs," I said desperately, like any young ass in a china shop. "Always admired your experiments. Frogs. Yes."

24   I give the old man credit. He took the drink and held it up and looked at me across the rim. There was a faint stir of sardonic humor in his eyes.

25   "Frogs, no," he said, "or maybe yes. I've never been quite sure. Maybe yes. But there was no time to decide properly." The humor faded out of his eyes. "Maybe I should have let go," he said. "It was what they wanted. There's no doubting that at all, but it came too quick for me. What would you have done?"

26   "I don't know," I said honestly enough and pinched myself.

27   "You had better know," said Albert Dreyer severely, "if you're planning to become an investigator of primitive religions. Or even not. I wasn't, you know, and the things came to me just when I least suspected—But I forget, you don't believe in them."

28   He shrugged and half rose, and for the first time, really, I saw the black-gloved hand and the haunted face of Albert Dreyer and knew in my heart the things he had stood for in science. I got up then, as a young man in the presence of his betters should get up, and I said, and I meant it, every word: "Please, Dr. Dreyer, sit down and tell me. I'm too young to be saying what I believe or don't believe in at all. I'd be obliged if you'd tell me."

29   Just at that moment a strange, wonderful dignity shone out of the countenance of Albert Dreyer, and I knew the man he was. He bowed and sat down, and there were no longer the barriers of age and youthful ego between us. There were just two men under a lamp, and around them a great waiting silence. Out to the ends of the universe, I thought fleetingly, that's the way with man and his lamps. One has to huddle in, there's so little light and so much space. One—

III

30   "It could happen to anyone," said Albert Dreyer. "And especially in the spring. Remember that. And all I did was to skip. Just a few feet, mark you, but I skipped. Remember that, too.

31   "You wouldn't remember the place at all. At least not as it was then." He paused and shook the ice in his glass and spoke more easily.

32   "It was a road that came out finally in a marsh along
the Schuylkill River. Probably all industrial now. But I had a little house out there with a laboratory thrown in. It was convenient to the marsh, and that helped me with my studies of
amphibia. Moreover, it was a wild, lonely road, and I wanted
solitude. It is always the demand of the naturalist. You understand that?"

33   "Of course," I said. I knew he had gone there, after the
death of his young wife, in grief and loneliness and despair. He
was not a man to mention such things. "It is best for the naturalist," I agreed.

34   "Exactly. My best work was done there." He held up his
black-gloved hand and glanced at it meditatively. "The work on
the axolotl, newt neoteny. I worked hard. I had—" he hesitated—
"things to forget. There were times when I worked all night. Or
diverted myself, while waiting the result of an experiment, by midnight walks. It was a strange road. Wild all right, but paved and
close enough to the city that there were occasional street lamps.
All uphill and downhill, with bits of forest leaning in over it, till
you walked in a tunnel of trees. Then suddenly you were in the
marsh, and the road ended at an old, unused wharf."

35   "A place to be alone. A place to walk and think. A place for
shadows to stretch ahead of you from one dim lamp to another
and spring back as you reached the next. I have seen them get
tall, tall, but never like that night. It was like a road into space."

36   "Cold?" I asked.

37   "No. I shouldn't have said 'space.' It gives the wrong effect.
Not cold. Spring. Frog time. The first warmth, and the leaves coming. A little fog in the hollows. The way they like it then in the wet
leaves and bogs. No moon, though; secretive and dark, with just
those street lamps wandered out from the town. I often wondered
what graft had brought them there. They shone on nothing—
except my walks at midnight and the journeys of toads, but
still . . ."

38   "Yes?" I prompted, as he paused.

39   "I was just thinking. The web of things. A politician in town
gets a rake-off for selling useless lights on a useless road. If it
hadn't been for that, I might not have seen them. I might not
even have skipped. Or, if I had, the effect—How can you tell
about such things afterwards? Was the effect heightened? Did it
magnify their power? Who is to say?"

40 "The skip?" I said, trying to keep things casual. "I don't understand. You mean, just skipping? Jumping?"

41 Something like a twinkle came into his eyes for a moment. "Just that," he said. "No more. You are a young man. Impulsive? You should understand."

42 "I'm afraid—" I began to counter.

43 "But of course," he cried pleasantly. "I forget. You were not there. So how could I expect you to feel or know about this skipping. Look, look at me now. A sober man, eh?"

44 I nodded. "Dignified," I said cautiously.

45 "Very well. But, young man, there is a time to skip. On country roads in the spring. It is not necessary that there be girls. You will skip without them. You will skip because something within you knows the time—frog time. Then you will skip."

46 "Then I will skip," I repeated, hypnotized. Mad or not, there was a force in Albert Dreyer. Even there under the club lights, the night damp of an unused road began to gather.

IV

47 "It was a late spring," he said. "Fog and mist in those hollows in a way I had never seen before. And frogs, of course. Thousands of them, and twenty species, trilling, gurgling, and grunting in as many keys. The beautiful keen silver piping of spring peepers arousing as the last ice leaves the ponds—if you have heard that after a long winter alone, you will never forget it." He paused and leaned forward, listening with such an intent inner ear that one could almost hear that far-off silver piping from the wet meadows of the man's forgotten years.

48 I rattled my glass uneasily, and his eyes came back to me.

49 "They come out then," he said more calmly. "All amphibia have to return to the water for mating and egg laying. Even toads will hop miles across country to streams and waterways. You don't see them unless you go out at night in the right places as I did, but that night—

50 "Well, it was unusual, put it that way, as an understatement. It was late, and the creatures seemed to know it. You could feel the forces of mighty and archaic life welling up from the very ground. The water was pulling them—not water as we know it, but the mother, the ancient life force, the thing that made us in the

days of creation, and that lurks around us still, unnoticed in our sterile cities.

51 "I was no different from any other young fool coming home on a spring night, except that as a student of life, and of amphibia in particular, I was, shall we say, more aware of the creatures. I had performed experiments"—the black glove gestured before my eyes. "I was, as it proved, susceptible.

52 "It began on that lost stretch of roadway leading to the river, and it began simply enough. All around, under the street lamps, I saw little frogs and big frogs hopping steadily toward the river. They were going in my direction.

53 "At that time I had my whimsies, and I was spry enough to feel the tug of that great movement. I joined them. There was no mystery about it. I simply began to skip, to skip gaily, and enjoy the great bobbing shadow I created as I passed onward with that leaping host all headed for the river.

54 "Now skipping along a wet pavement in spring is infectious, particularly going downhill, as we were. The impulse to take mightier leaps, to soar farther, increases progressively. The madness worked into me. I bounded till my lungs labored, and my shadow, at first my own shadow, bounded and labored with me.

55 "It was only midway in my flight that I began to grow conscious that I was not alone. The feeling was not strong at first. Normally a sober pedestrian, I was ecstatically preoccupied with the discovery of latent stores of energy and agility which I had not suspected in my subdued existence.

56 "It was only as we passed under a street lamp that I noticed, beside my own bobbing shadow, another great, leaping grotesquerie that had an uncanny suggestion of the frog world about it. The shocking aspect of the thing lay in its size, and the fact that, judging from the shadow, it was soaring higher and more gaily than myself.

57 "'Very well,' you will say"—and here Dreyer paused and looked at me tolerantly—"'Why didn't you turn around? That would be the scientific thing to do.'

58 "It would be the scientific thing to do, young man, but let me tell you it is not done—not on an empty road at midnight— not when the shadow is already beside your shadow and is joined by another, and then another.

59   "No, you do not pause. You look neither to left nor right, for fear of what you might see there. Instead, you dance on madly, hopelessly. Plunging higher, higher, in the hope the shadows will be left behind, or prove to be only leaves dancing, when you reach the next street light. Or that whatever had joined you in this midnight bacchanal will take some other pathway and depart.

60   "You do not look—you cannot look—because to do so is to destroy the universe in which we move and exist and have our transient being. You dare not look, because, beside the shadows, there now comes to your ears the loose-limbed slap of giant batrachian feet, not loud, not loud at all, but there, definitely there, behind you at your shoulder, plunging with the utter madness of spring, their rhythm entering your bones until you too are hurtling upward in some gigantic ecstasy that it is not given to mere flesh and blood to long endure.

61   "I was part of it, part of some mad dance of the elementals behind the show of things. Perhaps in that night of archaic and elemental passion, that festival of the wetlands, my careless hopping passage under the street lights had called them, attracted their attention, brought them leaping down some fourth-dimensional roadway into the world of time.

62   "Do not suppose for a single moment I thought so coherently then. My lungs were bursting, my physical self exhausted, but I sprang, I hurtled, I flung myself onward in a company I could not see, that never outpaced me, but that swept me with the mighty ecstasies of a thousand springs, and that bore me onward exultantly past my own doorstep, toward the river, toward some pathway long forgotten, toward some unforgettable destination in the wetlands and the spring.

63   "Even as I leaped, I was changing. It was this, I think, that stirred the last remnants of human fear and human caution that I still possessed. My will was in abeyance; I could not stop. Furthermore, certain sensations, hypnotic or otherwise, suggested to me that my own physical shape was modifying, or about to change. I was leaping with a growing ease. I was—

64   "It was just then that the wharf lights began to show. We were approaching the end of the road, and the road, as I have said, ended in the river. It was this, I suppose, that startled me back into some semblance of human terror. Man is a land animal.

He does not willingly plunge off wharfs at midnight in the monstrous company of amphibious shadows.

65   "Nevertheless their power held me. We pounded madly toward the wharf, and under the light that hung above it, and the beam that made a cross. Part of me struggled to stop, and part of me hurtled on. But in that final frenzy of terror before the water below engulfed me I shrieked, *'Help! In the name of God, help me! In the name of Jesus, stop!'*"

66   Dreyer paused and drew in his chair a little closer under the light. Then he went on steadily.

67   "I was not, I suppose, a particularly religious man, and the cries merely revealed the extremity of my terror. Nevertheless this is a strange thing, and whether it involves the crossed beam, or the appeal to a Christian deity, I will not attempt to answer.

68   "In one electric instant, however, I was free. It was like the release from demoniac possession. One moment I was leaping in an inhuman company of elder things, and the next moment I was a badly shaken human being on a wharf. Strangest of all, perhaps, was the sudden silence of that midnight hour. I looked down in the circle of the arc light, and there by my feet hopped feebly some tiny froglets of the great migration. There was nothing impressive about them, but you will understand that I drew back in revulsion. I have never been able to handle them for research since. My work is in the past."

69   He paused and drank, and then, seeing perhaps some lingering doubt and confusion in my eyes, held up his black-gloved hand and deliberately pinched off the glove.

70   A man should not do that to another man without warning, but I suppose he felt I demanded some proof. I turned my eyes away. One does not like a webbed batrachian hand on a human being.

71   As I rose embarrassedly, his voice came up to me from the depths of the chair.

72   "It is not the hand," Dreyer said. "It is the question of choice. Perhaps I was a coward, and ill prepared. Perhaps"—his voice searched uneasily among his memories—"perhaps I should have taken them and that springtime without question. Perhaps I should have trusted them and hopped onward. Who knows? They were gay enough, at least."

73   He sighed and set down his glass and stared so intently into empty space that, seeing I was forgotten, I tiptoed quietly away.

QUESTIONS

Ideas

1. Does Eiseley mean us to take this essay as fact or fiction? What might be the point of such a story?

2. Regardless of your belief, what are some possible explanations for what happens in this essay? Try to construct reasons along a continuum from fact to fantasy.

3. How would you describe the narrator's personality? How does his attitude toward Dreyer change?

4. What is the significance of the following line from part II: "Maybe I should have let go . . . it was what they wanted, there's no doubting that at all, but it came too quick for me"?

Organization

5. How are the two stories here, Eiseley's and Dreyer's, related?

6. What is the purpose of part I? Look especially at the exchange between Dreyer and Eiseley. What conflict of perspective, of viewpoint, is being shown here?

7. Part IV is the longest and most detailed. Why? What is its point?

8. What is the overall structure of the four parts? What is the purpose of each?

Sentences

9. Most of this essay is told in dialogue. Compare the narrator's voice in part I with Dreyer's in the last dozen paragraphs of part IV. What differences do you find in tone, diction, and sentence structure?

Words

10. In part I, the narrator refers to Dreyer as a "misanthrope." Do you think this is accurate?

11. What does "mélange" mean? How about "propitiate," "implicitly," "nettled," "whimsies," "infectious," "uncanny"?

Suggestions for Writing

A. Write down your thoughts about each of the following questions. Write quickly on each one for about five minutes:

1. What are the advantages and disadvantages of believing in events such as these?

2.   What are some of the things you accept on faith?

3.   Is there absolute Truth within the scientific community?

Based on your responses, write an essay that explores the idea of belief in the supernatural.

B.   Compare the theme of the following poem by Eiseley to "The Dance of the Frogs."

NOCTURNE IN SILVER

Here where the barbed wire straggles in the marsh
And alkali crusts all the weeds like frost,
I have come home, I have come home to hear
The new young frogs that cry along the lost

Wild ditches where at midnight only cows
And fools with eery marsh fire in their brains
Blunder toward midnight. Silvery and clear
Cry the new frogs; the blood runs in my veins

Coldly and clearly. I am mottled, too,
And feel a silver bubble in my throat.
Lock doors, turn keys, or follow in your fear.
My eyes are green, and warily afloat

In the June darkness. I am done with fire.
Water quicksilver-like that slips through stone
Has quenched my madness—if you find me here
My lineage squat and warty will be known.

The Running Man

1   While I endured the months in the Colorado cabin, my mother, who had been offered a safe refuge in the home of her sister, quarreled and fought with everyone. Finally, in her own inelegant way of putting things, she had "skipped town" to work as a seamstress, domestic, or housekeeper upon farms. She was stone deaf. I admired her courage, but I also knew by then that she was paranoid, neurotic and unstable. What ensued on these various short-lived adventures I neither know to this day, nor wish to know.

2   It comes to me now in retrospect that I never saw my mother weep; it was her gift to make others suffer instead. She was an untutored, talented artist and she left me, if anything, a capacity

for tremendous visual impressions just as my father, a one-time itinerant actor, had in that silenced household of the stone age—a house of gestures, of daylong facial contortion—produced for me the miracle of words when he came home. My mother had once been very beautiful. It is only thus that I can explain the fatal attraction that produced me. I have never known how my parents chanced to meet.

3   There will be those to say, in this mother-worshipping culture, that I am harsh, embittered. They will be quite wrong. Why should I be embittered? It is far too late. A month ago, after a passage of many years, I stood above her grave in a place called Wyuka. We, she and I, were close to being one now, lying like the skeletons of last year's leaves in a fence corner. And it was all nothing. Nothing, do you understand? All the pain, all the anguish. Nothing. We were, both of us, merely the debris life always leaves in its passing, like the maimed, discarded chicks in the hatchery trays—no more than that. For a little longer I would see and hear, but it was nothing, and to the world it would mean nothing.

4   I murmured to myself and tried to tell her this belatedly: Nothing, mama, nothing. Rest. You could never rest. That was your burden. But now, sleep. Soon I will join you, although, forgive me, not here. Neither of us then would rest. I will go far to lie down; the time draws on; it is unlikely that I will return. Now you will understand, I said, touching the October warmth of the gravestone. It was for nothing. It has taken me all my life to grasp this one fact.

5   I am, it is true, wandering out of time and place. This narrative is faltering. To tell the story of a life one is bound to linger above gravestones where memory blurs and doors can be pushed ajar, but never opened. Listen, or do not listen, it is all the same.

6   I am every man and no man, and will be so to the end. This is why I must tell the story as I may. Not for the nameless name upon the page, not for the trails behind me that faded or led nowhere, not for the rooms at nightfall where I slept from exhaustion or did not sleep at all, not for the confusion of where I was to go, or if I had a destiny recognizable by any star. No, in retrospect it was the loneliness of not knowing, not knowing at all.

7   I was a child of the early century, American man, if the term may still be tolerated. A creature molded of plains' dust and the seed of those who came west with the wagons. The names Corey,

Hollister, Appleton, McKee lie strewn in graveyards from New England to the broken sticks that rotted quickly on the Oregon trail. That ancient contingent, with a lost memory and a gene or two from the Indian, is underscored by the final German of my own name.

8   How, among all these wanderers, should I have absorbed a code by which to live? How should I have answered in turn to the restrained Puritan, and the long hatred of the beaten hunters? How should I have curbed the flaring rages of my maternal grandfather? How should—

9   But this I remember out of deepest childhood—I remember the mad Shepards as I heard the name whispered among my mother's people. I remember the pacing, the endless pacing of my parents after midnight, while I lay shivering in the cold bed and tried to understand the words that passed between my mother and my father.

10   Once, a small toddler, I climbed from bed and seized their hands, pleading wordlessly for sleep, for peace, peace. And surprisingly they relented, even my unfortunate mother. Terror, anxiety, ostracism, shame; I did not understand the words. I learned only the feelings they represent. I repeat, I am an American whose profession, even his life, is no more than a gambler's throw by the firelight of a western wagon.

11   What have I to do with the city in which I live? Why, far to the west, does my mind still leap to great windswept vistas of grass or the eternal snows of the Cascades? Why does the sight of wolves in cages cause me to avert my eyes?

12   I will tell you only because something like this was at war in the heart of every American at the final closing of the westward trails. One of the most vivid memories I retain from my young manhood is of the wagon ruts of the Oregon trail still visible on the unplowed short-grass prairie. They stretched half a mile in width and that was only yesterday. In his young years, my own father had carried a gun and remembered the gamblers at the green tables in the cow towns. I dream inexplicably at times of a gathering of wagons, of women in sunbonnets and black-garbed, bewhiskered men. Then I wake and the scene dissolves.

13   I have strayed from the Shepards. It was a name to fear but this I did not learn for a long time. I thought they were the people pictured in the family Bible, men with white beards and long crooks with which they guided sheep.

14   In that house, when my father was away and my mother's people came to visit, the Shepards were spoken of in whispers. They were the mad Shepards, I slowly gathered, and they lay somewhere in my line of descent. When I was recalcitrant the Shepards were spoken of and linked with my name.

15   In that house there was no peace, yet we loved each other fiercely. Perhaps the adults were so far on into the midcountry that mistakes were never rectifiable, flight disreputable. We were Americans of the middle border where the East was forgotten and the one great western road no longer crawled with wagons.

16   A silence had fallen. I was one of those born into that silence. The bison had perished; the Sioux no longer rode. Only the yellow dust of the cyclonic twisters still marched across the landscape. I knew the taste of that dust in my youth. I knew it in the days of the dust bowl. No matter how far I travel it will be a fading memory upon my tongue in the hour of my death. It is the taste of one dust only, the dust of a receding ice age.

17   So much for my mother, the mad Shepards, and the land, but this is not all, certainly not. Some say a child's basic character is formed by the time he is five. I can believe it, I who begged for peace at four and was never blessed for long by its presence.

18   The late W. H. Auden once said to me over a lonely little dinner in New York before he left America, "What public event do you remember first from childhood?" I suppose the massive old lion was in his way encouraging a shy man to speak. Being of the same age we concentrated heavily upon the subject.

19   "I think for me, the Titanic disaster," he ventured thoughtfully.

20   "Of course," I said. "That would be 1912. She was a British ship and you British have always been a sea people."

21   "And you?" he questioned, holding me with his seamed features that always gave him the aspect of a seer.

22   I dropped my gaze. Was it 1914? Was it Pancho Villa's raid into New Mexico in 1916? All westerners remembered that. We wandered momentarily among dead men and long-vanished events. Auden waited patiently.

23   "Well," I ventured, for it was a long-held personal secret, "It was an escape, just an escape from prison."

24   "Your own?" Auden asked with a trace of humor.

25   "No," I began, "it was the same year as the Titanic sinking. He blew the gates with nitroglycerin. I was five years old, like you."

Then I paused, considering the time. "You are right," I admitted hesitantly. "I was already old enough to know one should flee from the universe but I did not know where to run." I identified with the man as I always had across the years. "We never made it," I added glumly, and shrugged. "You see, there was a warden, a prison, and a blizzard. Also there was an armed posse and a death." I could feel the same snow driving beside the window in New York. "We never made it," I repeated unconsciously.

26   Auden sighed and looked curiously at me. I knew he was examining the pronoun. "There are other things that constitute a child," I added hastily. "Sandpiles, for example. There was a lot of building being done then on our street. I used to spend hours turning over the gravel. Why, I wouldn't know. Finally I had a box of pretty stones and some fossils. I prospected for hours alone. It was like today in book stores, old book stores," I protested defensively.

27   Auden nodded in sympathy.

28   "I still can't tell what started it," I went on. "I was groping, I think, childishly into time, into the universe. It was to be my profession but I never understood in the least, not till much later. No other child on the block wasted his time like that. I have never understood my precise motivation, never. For actually I was retarded in the reading of clock time. Was it because, in the things found in the sand, I was already lost and wandering instinctively—amidst the debris of vanished eras?"

29   "Ah," Auden said kindly, "who knows these things?"

30   "Then there was the period of the gold crosses," I added. "Later, in another house, I had found a little bottle of liquid gilt my mother used on picture frames. I made some crosses, carefully whittled out of wood, and gilded them till they were gold. Then I placed them over an occasional dead bird I buried. Or, if I read of a tragic, heroic death like those of the war aces, I would put the clipping—I could read by then—into a little box and bury it with a gold cross to mark the spot. One day a mower in the empty lot beyond our backyard found the little cemetery and carried away all of my carefully carved crosses. I cried but I never told anyone. How could I? I had sought in my own small way to preserve the memory of what always in the end perishes: life and great deeds. I wonder what the man with the scythe did with my crosses. I wonder if they still exist."

31   "Yes, it was a child's effort against time," commented Auden. "And perhaps the archaeologist is just that child grown up."

32   It was time for Auden to go. We stood and exchanged polite amenities while he breathed in that heavy, sad way he had. "Write me at Oxford," he had said at the door. But then there was Austria and soon he was gone. Besides one does not annoy the great. Their burdens are too heavy. They listen kindly with their eyes far away.

33   After that dinner I was glumly despondent for days. Finally a rage possessed me, started unwittingly by that gentle, gifted man who was to die happily after a recitation of his magnificent verse. For nights I lay sleepless in a New York hotel room and all my memories in one gigantic catharsis were bad, spewed out of hell's mouth, invoked by that one dinner, that one question, *what do you remember first?* My God, they were all firsts. My brain was so scarred it was a miracle it had survived in any fashion.

34   For example, I remembered for the first time a ruined farmhouse that I had stumbled upon in my solitary ramblings after school. The road was one I had never taken before. Rain was falling. Leaves lay thick on the abandoned road. Hesitantly I approached and stood in the doorway. Plaster had collapsed from the ceiling; wind mourned through the empty windows. I crunched tentatively over shattered glass upon the floor. Papers lay scattered about in wild disorder. Some looked like school examination papers. I picked one up in curiosity, but this, my own mature judgment tells me, no one will believe. The name Eiseley was scrawled across the cover. I was too shocked even to read the paper. No such family had ever been mentioned by my parents. We had come from elsewhere. But here, in poverty like our own, at the edge of town, had subsisted in this ruined house a boy with my own name. Gingerly I picked up another paper. There was the scrawled name again, not too unlike my own rough signature. The date was what might have been expected in that tottering clapboard house. It read from the last decade of the century before. They were gone, whoever they were, and another Eiseley was tiptoeing through the ruined house.

35   All that remained in a room that might in those days have been called the parlor were two dice lying forlornly amidst the plaster, forgotten at the owners' last exit. I picked up the pretty cubes uncertainly in the growing sunset through the window, and on impulse cast them. I did not know how adults played, I merely cast and cast again, making up my own game as I played. Sometimes I thought I won and murmured to myself as children

will. Sometimes I thought I lost, but I liked the clicking sound before I rolled the dice. For what stakes did I play, with my childish mind gravely considering? I think I was too naive for such wishes as money and fortune. I played, and here memory almost fails me. I think I played against the universe as the universe was represented by the wind, stirring papers on the plaster-strewn floor. I played against time, remembering my stolen crosses, I played for adventure and escape. Then, clutching the dice, but not the paper with my name, I fled frantically down the leaf-sodden unused road, never to return. One of the dice survives still in my desk drawer. The time is sixty years away.

36   I have said that, though almost ostracized, we loved each other fiercely there in the silent midcountry because there was nothing else to love, but was it true? Was the hour of departure nearing? My mother lavished affection upon me in her tigerish silent way, giving me cakes when I should have had bread, attempting protection when I was already learning without brothers the grimness and realities of the street.

37   There had been the time I had just encountered the neighborhood bully. His father's shoulder had been long distorted and rheumatic from the carrying of ice, and the elder son had just encountered the law and gone to prison. My antagonist had inherited his brother's status in the black Irish gang that I had heretofore succeeded in avoiding by journeying homeward from school through alleys and occasional thickets best known to me. But now brother replaced brother. We confronted each other on someone's lawn.

38   "Get down on your knees," he said contemptuously, knowing very well what was coming. He had left me no way out. At that moment I hit him most inexpertly in the face, whereupon he began very scientifically, as things go in childish circles, to cut me to ribbons. My nose went first.

39   But then came the rage, the utter fury, summoned up from a thousand home repressions, adrenalin pumped into me from my Viking grandfather, the throwback from the long ships, the berserk men who cared nothing for living when the mood came on them and they stormed the English towns. It comes to me now that the Irishman must have seen it in my eyes. By nature I was a quiet reclusive boy, but then I went utterly mad.

40   The smashed nose meant nothing, the scientific lefts and rights slicing up my features meant nothing. I went through them

with body punches and my eyes. When I halted we were clear across the street and the boy was gone, running for home. Typically I, too, turned homeward but not for succor. All I wanted was access to the outside watertap to wash off the blood cascading down my face. This I proceeded to do with the stoical indifference of one who expected no help.

41   As I went about finishing my task, my mother, peering through the curtains, saw my face and promptly had hysterics. I turned away then. I always turned away. In the end, not too far distant, there would be an unbridgeable silence between us. Slowly I was leaving the world she knew and desperation marked her face.

42   I was old enough that I obeyed my father's injunction, reluctantly given out of his own pain. "Your mother is not responsible, son. Do not cross her. Do you understand?" He held me with his eyes, a man I loved, who could have taken the poor man's divorce, desertion, at any moment. The easy way out. He stayed for me. That was the simple reason. He stayed when his own closest relatives urged him to depart.

43   I cast down my eyes. "Yes, father," I promised, but I could not say for always. I think he knew it, but work and growing age were crushing him. We looked at each other in a blind despair.

44   I was like a rag doll upon whose frame skins were tightening in a distorted crippling sequence; the toddler begging for peace between his parents at midnight; the lad suppressing fury till he shook with it; the solitary with his books; the projected fugitive running desperately through the snows of 1912; the dice player in the ruined house of his own name. Who was he, really? The man, so the psychologists would say, who had to be shaped or found in five years' time. I was inarticulate but somewhere, far forward, I would meet the running man; the peace I begged for between my parents would, too often, leave me sleepless. There was another thing I could not name to Auden. The fact that I remember it at all reveals the beginning of adulthood and a sense of sin beyond my years.

45   To grow is a gain, an enlargement of life; is not this what they tell us? Yet it is also a departure. There is something lost that will not return. We moved one fall to Aurora, Nebraska, a sleepy country town near the Platte. A few boys gathered to watch the van unload. "Want to play?" ventured one. "Sure," I said. I followed them off over a rise to a creek bed. "We're making a cave in

the bank," they explained. It was a great raw gaping hole obviously worked on by more than one generation of troglodytes. They giggled. "But first you've got to swear awful words. We'll all swear."

46   I was a silent boy, who went by reading. My father did not use these words. I was, in retrospect, a very funny little boy. I was so alone I did not know how to swear, but clamoring they taught me. I wanted to belong, to enter the troglodytes' existence. I shouted and mouthed the uncouth, unfamiliar words with the rest.

47   Mother was restless in the new environment, though again my father had wisely chosen a house at the edge of town. The population was primarily Scandinavian. She exercised arbitrary judgment. She drove good-natured, friendly boys away if they seemed big, and on the other hand encouraged slighter youngsters whom I had every reason to despise.

48   Finally, because it was farmland over which children roamed at will, mother's ability to keep track of my wide-ranging absences faltered. On one memorable occasion her driving, possessive restlessness passed out of bounds. She pursued us to a nearby pasture and in the rasping voice of deafness ordered me home.

49   My comrades of the fields stood watching. I was ten years old by then. I sensed my status in this gang was at stake. I refused to come. I had refused a parental order that was arbitrary and uncalled for and, in addition, I was humiliated. My mother was behaving in the manner of a witch. She could not hear, she was violently gesticulating without dignity, and her dress was somehow appropriate to the occasion.

50   Slowly I turned and looked at my companions. Their faces could not be read. They simply waited, doubtless waited for me to break the apron strings that rested lightly and tolerably upon themselves. And so in the end I broke my father's injunction; I ran, and with me ran my childish companions, over fences, tumbling down haystacks, chuckling, with the witch, her hair flying, her clothing disarrayed, stumbling after. Escape, escape, the first stirrings of the running man. Miles of escape.

51   Of course she gave up. Of course she never caught us. Walking home alone in the twilight I was bitterly ashamed. Ashamed for the violation of my promise to my father. Ashamed at what I had done to my savage and stone-deaf mother who could not grasp the fact that I had to make my way in a world

unknown to her. Ashamed for the story that would penetrate the neighborhood. Ashamed for my own weakness. Ashamed, ashamed.

52   I do not remember a single teacher from that school, a single thing I learned there. Men were then drilling in a lot close to our house. I watched them every day. Finally they marched off. It was 1917. I was ten years old. I wanted to go. Either that or back to sleeping the troglodyte existence we had created in the cave bank. But never home, not ever. Even today, as though in a far-off crystal, I can see my running, gesticulating mother and her distorted features cursing us. And they laughed, you see, my companions. Perhaps I, in anxiety to belong, did also. That is what I could not tell Auden. Only an unutterable savagery, my savagery at myself, scrawls it once and once only on this page.

QUESTIONS

Ideas

1   Eiseley's images seem especially vivid in this remembrance. What one comes immediately to your mind? Eiseley uses narrative, anecdotes, and significant moments from his experiences, but what do these pictures convey to you? Who is this essay about? Is it about Eiseley as a child or as an adult? Or is it about his mother?

2.   What is Eiseley's purpose in writing this essay? Does he hope to do something for himself? Is he trying to learn something, discover something? Consider especially paragraphs 5 and 6.

3.   Does Eiseley himself realize that he is not "sticking to the topic" as the essay opens, that he seems to be wandering? But does he? Read the first and the last four paragraphs again. Do you see connections to the rest of the piece?

4.   What is all this business about being an "American man"? Is Eiseley trying to connect his life to yours in some way? Do you accept the notion that one life can represent the experiences of all Americans?

5.   Eiseley denies that he is "harsh, embittered" about his relationship with his mother. What do you think? In this sense, what do you make of the last paragraph? How about the first sentence of paragraph 2?

6.   What exactly do you think Eiseley means by "It was for nothing"?

7.   What do you make of Eiseley's comment on the writing of autobiography: "To tell the story of a life one is bound to linger about grave-

stones where memory blurs and doors can be pushed ajar, but never opened"? What does Eiseley seem to be implying in this paragraph about the difference between writing about one's life and living it? Look especially at the last sentence.

8. Based on paragraphs 11 and 12, what do you make of Eiseley's wagon dream?

9. Before Eiseley begins his anecdote about Auden (paragraph 18) he writes a short "introductory" paragraph about inner peace. Why does he do this, and what expectations does this raise about the subsequent narrative?

10. In the tale Eiseley tells Auden, what do you think he means by "I was already old enough to know one should flee from the universe but I did not know where to run"?

11. Why did a rage possess Eiseley after his dinner with Auden? In his attempts to remember, Eiseley narrates a series of anecdotes: about his finding dice in a ruined farmhouse, his encounter with the neighborhood bully, and, finally, his running from his "violently gesticulating" mother. What is the point of these stories? Do they make concrete and specific a generalization? Look especially at the concluding paragraph to his bully story ("As I went about . . .") and the elaborate build-up to the running-away scene (the four paragraphs preceding "Finally, because it was farm land . . .). Do you see common threads among these tales? Are they in sequence, leading somewhere?

12. Why could he not tell Auden this last episode, yet could "scrawl it once and once only on this page"?

13. What is meant by "The Running Man"? Try to suggest several different possibilities.

Organization

14. Eiseley begins and ends this essay with thoughts of his mother. Where does the introduction end? The conclusion begin?

15. List in order all the incidents in this piece. What holds them all together?

Sentences

16. Eiseley has a reputation for lyrical, evocative prose. Cite some examples. What makes them poetic?

17. Read the last three paragraphs out loud. What do you notice about Eiseley's style? How does he use repetition? Modifiers? Sentence fragments? Parallelism? Sentence length?

Words

18.   Make a list of all the words Eiseley uses to describe himself. What impressions do they add up to? Do the same for words describing his mother.

Suggestions for Writing

From vividly drawn episodes in his life, Eiseley tries to assemble recurring patterns to define himself, to create an image of who he is. Try to remember two or three incidents from your childhood. Just free-write for fifteen minutes on each one, until some narrative line begins to emerge.

Read over your writing, looking for possible consistent themes, key terms, gestures, beginnings, and endings. That is, can you, like Eiseley, see in that distant self beginnings of your adult self; can you see hopes, fears, likes, curiosities, needs, predictable reactions, in these brief jottings of yours? Be aware that defining yourself in a narrative is often as much a process of interpretation as of discovery.

Now try to arrange your writing in a simple pattern. Begin with a generalization, a broad theme (see Eiseley's paragraph "To grow is a gain . . .") and then get more specific about yourself. Then support that assertion with one or two brief anecdotes. Conclude with a present view of that incident (see especially Eiseley's penultimate paragraph, "Of course she gave up . . .").

SIX

Ellen Goodman

(1941–)

Ellen Goodman, a columnist for *The Boston Globe,* has described her job as "telling people what I think." This she has been doing for many years with honesty, intelligence, and verve. Collected in three books—*Close to Home, At Large,* and *Making Sense*—Goodman's essays range over many subjects, both public and private: family life, television, friendship, the relations between men and women (and between adults and children), anxiety, violence, the role of women, and trends, fads, and established traditions.

Her writing about these and other issues is clear, direct, and personal. Because her essays are confined to a 750-word column, she writes to the point. Because she addresses a general audience—her work is nationally syndicated—she writes clearly and simply, without pomposity or ostentation. Prizing the personal, the concrete, and the familiar, Goodman fills her essays with anecdotes, vignettes, and characters; she tells stories with real people in them. This is her way of bringing important public issues down to earth or, as she puts it, "close to home."

In "The Company Man" Goodman describes Phil, a man who "worked himself to death" at fifty-one. In a few quick strokes she sketches Phil: a man who worked six days a week, had no interests beyond his job, and "ate egg salad sandwiches at his desk." Throughout "The Company Man" Goodman works by implication rather than outright statement. She presents facts about Phil's life and work along with comments from the wife and children he rarely saw and hardly knew. She allows her readers to draw their own conclusions, with the result that her argument, inviting the reader's participation, is the more powerfully advanced by remaining implicit.

Her views in another essay are more explicitly aired. In "It's Failure, Not Success" Goodman argues against the ideas in Michael Korda's book *Success!* Countering Korda's advice to look out for Number One, to be greedy and selfish, she asserts that "it's not OK to be greedy, Machiavellian, dishonest. It's not always OK to be rich." Questioning the assumptions on which *Success!* rests, Goodman gets to the heart of the issue—an ethical one— and from her counterperspective claims that Korda's book is less about success than about failure.

Besides possessing a talent for description and a flair for argument and debate, Goodman is a shrewd and sensitive social analyst. In "The Tapestry of Friendships" she sharply contrasts the bonding styles of men and women, setting her ideas in the context of how friends are portrayed in a few recent films. Although the tone of the piece is authoritative, even judgmental, the thought is more speculative than polemical. The confident yet reasonable tone of this and many of her essays enhances their persuasiveness.

But whatever her subject and however pointedly expressed her views, Goodman is consistently witty, intelligent, and provocative. She entertains as she enlightens. Perhaps best of all, her essays reveal her as she wants to be revealed: as "a person, not a pontificator," as a writer who enjoys her work, one who communicates with intelligence and civility.

On Being a Journalist

1   When my daughter Katie was seven years old, I overheard her telling a friend, "My mommy is a columnist." "What's that?" asked the other little girl, reasonably enough. Katie thought about it awhile and finally said, "Well, my mother gets paid for telling people what she thinks."

2   All in all, that's not such a bad job description. The pieces collected in this book represent several years of "telling people what I think." They also represent two of the main qualifications for this business: nerve and endurance.

3   To write a column you need the egocentric confidence that your view of the world is important enough to be read. Then you need the pacing of a long-distance runner to write day after day, week after week, year after year. One journalist who dropped out of this endurance contest with a sigh of relief said that writing a column was like being married to a nymphomaniac: every time you think you're through, you have to start all over again. This was an unenlightened, but fairly accurate, analogy.

4   To meet my "quota," I need two opinions a week, although I assure you that some weeks I overflow with ideas, percolate opinions, while other weeks I can't decide what I think about the weather. Moreover, I have to fit these thoughts into a carefully reserved piece of newspaper property. I am allotted approximately the same number of words whether I am writing about life, love or the world-shattering problem of a zucchini that is sterile.

5   Despite these constraints, I tend to go through life like a vacuum cleaner, inhaling all the interesting tidbits in my path, using almost everything I observe, read or report. For me at least, this makes life more interesting and more integrated. I don't "go" to work or "return" to home life. The lines between the personal and professional sides of my life are far less rigidly drawn in this job than in virtually any other.

6   I suppose that is because I do write close to home.

7   I never wanted to be a package tour sort of columnist who covered thirteen countries in twenty-seven days. Nor do I want to write at arm's length about the Major Issues of Our Times. I think it's more important for all of us to be able to make links between our personal lives and public issues.

8   The most vital concerns can't be divided into internal and external affairs. What is more private a concern than the public policy decisions made about the family? What is more public a concern than the impact of divorce, or the new isolation, or the two-worker family? The ups and downs of presidential polls are no more crucial to our society than the way we raise our children.

9   As a writer, I've wanted to be seen as a person, not a pontificator. Why should people believe what I have to say if they know nothing about me? I don't want to present myself as a dis-

embodied voice of authority but as a thirty-eight-year-old woman, mother, vegetable gardener, failed jogger and expert on only one subject: the ambivalence of life.

10   I see myself in these pieces, and in fact, as a fellow struggler. In that sense too I write close to home.

11   What else can I say about the collection? The pieces show that I am more comfortable observing—people, change, events— than judging. I am more concerned with the struggles between conflicting values than the struggles between conflicting political parties. I don't think there is anything undignified about being silly when all about me are grave.

12   And maybe these columns also show how much I like my work.

QUESTIONS

1. How does Goodman define herself? Does she give you a good idea of what she does and why she does it?

2. What personal characteristics and attributes does a columnist need to do the job well? Does Goodman seem to possess these?

3. What does Goodman see as proper subjects for a columnist? What does she mean by saying she writes "close to home"?

4. Throughout this essay Goodman establishes a sense of her priorities by setting up a series of contrasts. Single out one or two of these and explain what point she makes in presenting the contrast. (See especially paragraphs 5–11.)

5. Goodman frequently uses comparisons to clarify her ideas. Explain the idea behind each of the following comparisons:

    Writing a column is like being married to a nymphomaniac: every time you think you're through, you have to start all over again.

    I tend to go through life like a vacuum cleaner, inhaling all the interesting tidbits in my path. . . .

6. One of the notable features of Goodman's style—in this piece as well as in her others—is a high degree of concreteness, of specificity. She talks about *things,* things you can get your hands on, things from everyday life. Make a list of all the specific things, the details that Goodman includes in this essay.

7. In paragraph 4 Goodman mentions one of the constraints of writing a column: limitations of space. How well does she succeed in saying what she has to, in making her point? What kind of audience is she writing for?

Suggestions for Writing

A. Write an essay in which you identify or define yourself. Try to imitate Goodman's down-to-earth tone and concreteness, even to the point of using comparisons from everyday life.

B. After you read what E. B. White or Edward Hoagland suggests about writing essays, assess Goodman's writing according to their standards and goals.

The Company Man

---

1   He worked himself to death, finally and precisely, at 3:00 A.M. Sunday morning.

2   The obituary didn't say that, of course. It said that he died of a coronary thrombosis—I think that was it—but everyone among his friends and acquaintances knew it instantly. He was a perfect Type A, a workaholic, a classic, they said to each other and shook their heads—and thought for five or ten minutes about the way they lived.

3   This man who worked himself to death finally and precisely at 3:00 A.M. Sunday morning—on his day off—was fifty-one years old and a vice-president. He was, however, one of six vice-presidents, and one of three who might conceivably—if the president died or retired soon enough—have moved to the top spot. Phil knew that.

4   He worked six days a week, five of them until eight or nine at night, during a time when his own company had begun the four-day week for everyone but the executives. He worked like the Important People. He had no outside "extracurricular interests," unless, of course, you think about a monthly golf game that way. To Phil, it was work. He always ate egg salad sandwiches at his desk. He was, of course, overweight, by 20 or 25 pounds. He thought it was okay, though, because he didn't smoke.

5   On Saturdays, Phil wore a sports jacket to the office instead of a suit, because it was the weekend.

6   He had a lot of people working for him, maybe sixty, and most of them liked him most of the time. Three of them will be seriously considered for his job. The obituary didn't mention that.

7   But it did list his "survivors" quite accurately. He is survived by his wife, Helen, forty-eight years old, a good woman of no particular marketable skills, who worked in an office before marrying and mothering. She had, according to her daughter, given up trying to compete with his work years ago, when the children were small. A company friend said, "I know how much you will miss him." And she answered, "I already have."

8   "Missing him all these years," she must have given up part of herself which had cared too much for the man. She would be "well taken care of."

9   His "dearly beloved" eldest of the "dearly beloved" children is a hard-working executive in a manufacturing firm down South. In the day and a half before the funeral, he went around the neighborhood researching his father, asking the neighbors what he was like. They were embarrassed.

10   His second child is a girl, who is twenty-four and newly married. She lives near her mother and they are close, but whenever she was alone with her father, in a car driving somewhere, they had nothing to say to each other.

11   The youngest is twenty, a boy, a high-school graduate who has spent the last couple of years, like a lot of his friends, doing enough odd jobs to stay in grass and food. He was the one who tried to grab at his father, and tried to mean enough to him to keep the man at home. He was his father's favorite. Over the last two years, Phil stayed up nights worrying about the boy.

12   The boy once said, "My father and I only board here."

13   At the funeral, the sixty-year-old company president told the forty-eight-year-old widow that the fifty-one-year-old deceased had meant much to the company and would be missed and would be hard to replace. The widow didn't look him in the eye. She was afraid he would read her bitterness and, after all, she would need him to straighten out the finances—the stock options and all that.

14   Phil was overweight and nervous and worked too hard. If he wasn't at the office, he was worried about it. Phil was a Type A, a heart-attack natural. You could have picked him out in a minute from a lineup.

15   So when he finally worked himself to death, at precisely 3:00 A.M. Sunday morning, no one was really surprised.

16   By 5:00 P.M. the afternoon of the funeral, the company president had begun, discreetly of course, with care and taste, to make

inquiries about his replacement. One of three men. He asked around: "Who's been working the hardest?"

QUESTIONS

Ideas

1. Goodman uses Phil as an example, a type of something. Of what is he a representative, and what is her attitude toward him and toward what he represents? What point does she make about the more general situation of which he is only a part?

2. What is implied by the boss's question at the end of the essay? Would this point have been more effective if made explicitly rather than by implication?

3. Why, in an essay about a company man, does Goodman include discussion of his family? What does this discussion contribute to her point?

Organization

4. Consider the structure of this essay. How could it be diagrammed? What figure could represent its structure—circle, square, triangle? Look at paragraph 1 in relation to paragraph 15, and at paragraphs 2 and 3 in relation to paragraph 16.

5. Paragraphs 1, 3, and 15 repeat a particular point—the time of Phil's death. Does Goodman employ other forms of repetition? For what purpose?

Sentences

6. In paragraphs 2 and 3 Goodman includes sentences that make use of the double dash. Explain the function and tone of the information included between the dashes in each sentence. Could the "sandwiched-in" information be left out of any of these sentences? Why or why not?

7. Goodman ends a number of her paragraphs with short, emphatic sentences—paragraphs 3, 4, 6, 7, 8, 9, 14, and 15. In fact, one paragraph—14—consists of four consecutive short sentences. What tone is established with these short, almost staccato sentences?

8. Another thing to notice about Goodman's sentences in this essay is their uniformity of pattern, in this case, subject-verb-object. Almost all begin with a noun or pronoun; many begin with "Phil," "He," or

"His." Is this uniformity of structure monotonous? What is the effect of such heavy use of repeated sentence forms?

Words

9. Why does Goodman repeatedly use generic terms like "the widow," "the company man," "the company president"? What is the tone of these?

10. Why are so many words and phrases in quotation marks? What tone is established through their use?

Suggestions for Writing

A. Write an essay explaining what it means to be a company man or a company woman. You might want to consider the pleasures and pressures, the liabilities and assets, the opportunities and obligations such a position accords.

B. Write an essay in which you use something that happened as an occasion to explore an idea that the event illustrates. You might consider treating the description of what happened ironically, as Goodman does in "The Company Man."

C. Imagine that you are the president of the company for which Phil worked. Write a letter to Phil's wife. Decide what you want the purpose and tone of the letter to be.

D. Imagine that you are Phil's wife. Write a letter to the company president. You might want to write the letter before Phil dies. Or you could do it after. In either case, decide what the purpose and tone of your letter should be.

It's Failure, Not Success

---

1   I knew a man who went into therapy about three years ago because, as he put it, he couldn't live with himself any longer. I didn't blame him. The guy was a bigot, a tyrant and a creep.

2   In any case, I ran into him again after he'd finished therapy. He was still a bigot, a tyrant and a creep, *but* . . . he had learned to live with himself.

3   Now, I suppose this was an accomplishment of sorts. I mean, nobody else could live with him. But it seems to me that there are an awful lot of people running around and writing around these

days encouraging us to feel good about what we should feel terrible about, and to accept in ourselves what we should change.

4   The only thing they seem to disapprove of is disapproval. The only judgment they make is against being judgmental, and they assure us that we have nothing to feel guilty about except guilt itself. It seems to me that they are all intent on proving that I'm OK and You're OK, when in fact, I may be perfectly dreadful and you may be unforgivably dreary, and it may be—gasp!— *wrong.*

5   What brings on my sudden attack of judgmentitis is success, or rather, *Success!*—the latest in a series of exclamation-point books all concerned with How to Make It.

6   In this one, Michael Korda is writing a recipe book for success. Like the other authors, he leapfrogs right over the "Shoulds" and into the "Hows." He eliminates value judgments and edits out moral questions as if he were Fanny Farmer and the subject was the making of a blueberry pie.

7   It's not that I have any reason to doubt Mr. Korda's advice on the way to achieve success. It may very well be that successful men wear handkerchiefs stuffed neatly in their breast pockets, and that successful single women should carry suitcases to the office on Fridays whether or not they are going away for the weekend.

8   He may be realistic when he says that "successful people generally have very low expectations of others." And he may be only slightly cynical when he writes: "One of the best ways to ensure success is to develop expensive tastes or marry someone who has them."

9   And he may be helpful with his handy hints on how to sit next to someone you are about to overpower.

10   But he simply finesses the issues of right and wrong—silly words, embarrassing words that have been excised like warts from the shiny surface of the new how-to books. To Korda, guilt is not a prod, but an enemy that he slays on page four. Right off the bat, he tells the would-be successful reader that:

- It's OK to be greedy.
- It's OK to look out for Number One.
- It's OK to be Machiavellian (if you can get away with it).
- It's OK to recognize that honesty is not always the best policy (provided you don't go around saying so).
- And it's always OK to be rich.

11   Well, in fact, it's not OK. It's not OK to be greedy, Machiavellian, dishonest. It's not always OK to be rich. There is a qualitative difference between succeeding by making napalm or by making penicillin. There is a difference between climbing the ladder of success, and macheteing a path to the top.

12   Only someone with the moral perspective of a mushroom could assure us that this was all OK. It seems to me that most Americans harbor ambivalence toward success, not for neurotic reasons, but out of a realistic perception of what it demands.

13   Success is expensive in terms of time and energy and altered behavior—the sort of behavior he describes in the grossest of terms: "If you can undermine your boss and replace him, fine, do so, but never express anything but respect and loyalty for him while you're doing it."

14   This author—whose *Power!* topped the best-seller list last year—is intent on helping rid us of that ambivalence which is a signal from our conscience. He is like the other "Win!" "Me First!" writers, who try to make us comfortable when we should be uncomfortable.

15   They are all Doctor Feelgoods, offering us placebo prescriptions instead of strong medicine. They give us a way to live with ourselves, perhaps, but not a way to live with each other. They teach us a whole lot more about "Failure!" than about success.

QUESTIONS

Ideas

1. How well does the title fit the essay? Where does Goodman echo the title and with what point?

2. Both near the beginning of the essay (paragraph 5) and at the end (paragraphs 14 and 15), Goodman goes beyond discussion of Korda's *Success!* Why does she do this, and what does she say about other books of this type? What is her main objection to Korda's book in particular?

Organization

3. Divide the essay into two major parts. Provide a subtitle for each and explain how they are related. Then divide the essay into three or four parts, and again provide subtitles and show how the parts are related.

4. One thing that quickly strikes the reader of this essay is the short-
ness of its paragraphs. Reorganize and rearrange the paragraphs,
combining as many as you think can be logically connected. What
differences do you detect between this new version and Goodman's
present arrangement? Which do you prefer and why?

Sentences

5. Throughout the essay Goodman uses parallel sentences. She does
this most noticeably in paragraphs 10, 11, and 15. Explain what is
gained by use of the parallel structure.

> There is a qualitative difference between succeeding
> by making napalm
> or by making penicillin.

> There is a   difference between
> climbing the ladder of success
> or machete-ing a path to the top.

6. Examine the first four paragraphs, noting especially how Goodman
varies the length of her sentences. Consider where and how she uses
short sentences.

Words

7. What words and phrases are responsible for the personal, even
familiar tone of the essay?

8. What point does Goodman make by comparing Korda with Fanny
Farmer? How does the comparison convey her attitude toward
Korda and his book?

9. Explain the function and effect of the comparisons used in paragraph 10:

> But he simply finesses the issues of right and wrong—silly words,
> embarrassing words that have been excised like warts from the
> shiny surface of the new how-to books.

> To Korda, guilt is not a prod, but an enemy that he slays on page
> four. . . .

Suggestions for Writing

A. Write an essay about a book you've read—perhaps a practical, how-to
book or a self-help book such as Korda's. In your essay, summarize
the author's views, then explain why you agree or disagree with
them.

B. Write a how-to essay. Assume the role of a confident and comfortable and experienced person who knows and believes in the advice being given. If you like, you can write a humorous essay rather than a "straight" or serious one. Possible titles: "How to Annoy Your Friends"; "How to Con Your Teachers"; "How to Feel Good (or Bad) about Yourself." Try to make the essay an offering of general advice about the subject rather than a set of directions.

C. Write an essay defining and illustrating what you mean by Failure— or Success, and defending or refuting Goodman's claims.

The Tapestry of Friendships

---

1   It was, in many ways, a slight movie. Nothing actually happened. There was no big-budget chase scene, no bloody shoot-out. The story ended without any cosmic conclusions.

2   Yet she found Claudia Weill's film *Girlfriends* gentle and affecting. Slowly, it panned across the tapestry of friendship— showing its fragility, its resiliency, its role as the connecting tissue between the lives of two young women.

3   When it was over, she thought about the movies she'd seen this year—*Julia, The Turning Point* and now *Girlfriends*. It seemed that the peculiar eye, the social lens of the cinema, had drastically shifted its focus. Suddenly the Male Buddy movies had been replaced by the Female Friendship flicks.

4   This wasn't just another binge of trendiness, but a kind of *cinéma vérité*. For once the movies were reflecting a shift, not just from men to women but from one definition of friendship to another.

5   Across millions of miles of celluloid, the ideal of friendship had always been male—a world of sidekicks and "pardners," of Butch Cassidys and Sundance Kids. There had been something almost atavistic about these visions of attachments—as if producers culled their plots from some pop anthropology book on male bonding. Movies portrayed the idea that only men, those direct descendants of hunters and Hemingways, inherited a primal capacity for friendship. In contrast, they portrayed women picking on each other, the way they once picked berries.

6　　Well, that duality must have been mortally wounded in some shootout at the You're OK, I'm OK Corral. Now, on the screen, they were at least aware of the subtle distinction between men and women as buddies and friends.

7　　About 150 years ago, Coleridge had written, "A woman's friendship borders more closely on love than man's. Men affect each other in the reflection of noble or friendly acts, whilst women ask fewer proofs and more signs and expressions of attachment."

8　　Well, she thought, on the whole, men had buddies, while women had friends. Buddies bonded, but friends loved. Buddies faced adversity together, but friends faced each other. There was something palpably different in the way they spent their time. Buddies seemed to "do" things together; friends simply "were" together.

9　　Buddies came linked, like accessories, to one activity or another. People have golf buddies and business buddies, college buddies and club buddies. Men often keep their buddies in these categories, while women keep a special category for friends.

10　　A man once told her that men weren't real buddies until they'd been "through the wars" together—corporate or athletic or military. They had to soldier together, he said. Women, on the other hand, didn't count themselves as friends until they'd shared three loathsome confidences.

11　　Buddies hang tough together; friends hang onto each other.

12　　It probably had something to do with pride. You don't show off to a friend; you show need. Buddies try to keep the worst from each other; friends confess it.

13　　A friend of hers once telephoned her lover, just to find out if he were home. She hung up without a hello when he picked up the phone. Later, wretched with embarrassment, the friend moaned, "Can you believe me? A thirty-five-year-old lawyer, making a chicken call?" Together they laughed and made it better.

14　　Buddies seek approval. But friends seek acceptance.

15　　She knew so many men who had been trained in restraint, afraid of each other's judgment or awkward with each other's affection. She wasn't sure which. Like buddies in the movies, they would die for each other, but never hug each other.

16　　She'd reread *Babbitt* recently, that extraordinary catalogue of male grievances. The only relationship that gave meaning to the claustrophobic life of George Babbitt had been with Paul

Riesling. But not once in the tragedy of their lives had one been able to say to the other: You make a difference.

17   Even now men shocked her at times with their description of friendship. Does this one have a best friend? "Why, of course, we see each other every February." Does that one call his most intimate pal long distance? "Why, certainly, whenever there's a real reason." Do those two old chums ever have dinner together? "You mean alone? Without our wives?"

18   Yet, things were changing. The ideal of intimacy wasn't this parallel playmate, this teammate, this trenchmate. Not even in Hollywood. In the double standard of friendship, for once the female version was becoming accepted as the general ideal.

19   After all, a buddy is a fine life-companion. But one's friends, as Santayana once wrote, "are that part of the race with which one can be human."

QUESTIONS

Ideas

1. What does Goodman see as the main difference between male and female friendships? Do you agree that men "bond" and "buddy" whereas women "love" and "befriend" one another? Why or why not?

2. How do the movies that Goodman mentions tie in with her main point? Are these movie references necessary?

Organization

3. The essay falls roughly into three parts: paragraphs 1–6; paragraphs 7–17; paragraphs 18–19. What would have been gained and lost if Goodman had omitted paragraphs 1–6?

4. Two paragraphs (11 and 14) are very short, even for journalism. Should these short paragraphs have been attached to the paragraphs before or after them? Why or why not? Could they be omitted?

Sentences

5. A notable feature of Goodman's style in this essay is her use of antithetical sentences such as the following:

Buddies bonded, but friends loved. (8)

Buddies try to keep the worst from each other; friends confess it. (12)

Buddies seek approval. But friends seek acceptance. (14)

The basic thrust and the general idea of the three sentences are the same; the sentence structure is slightly different in the three instances. Find other sentences that make contrastive, antithetical points about buddies and friends—in still other, slightly different ways.

6. In the sentences that follow, Goodman uses the dash to set off part of her idea. For each, explain how the sentence would be different if a comma replaced the dash. And explain also whether the sentence could (or should) end where the dash occurs. (That is, imagine a period where the dash is with the words after the period omitted.)

    Slowly, it panned across the tapestry of friendship—showing its fragility, its resiliency, its role as the connecting tissue between the lives of two young women. (2)

    When it was over, she thought about the movies she'd seen this year—*Julia, The Turning Point* and now *Girlfriends*. (3)

    Across millions of miles of celluloid, the ideal of friendship had always been male—a world of sidekicks and "pardners," of Butch Cassidys and Sundance Kids. (5)

    A man once told her that men weren't real buddies until they'd been "through the wars" together—corporate or athletic or military. (10)

7. In paragraph 17 Goodman asks a series of questions and then provides answers in quotation marks. What are the tone and the point of these questions (and of this paragraph)?

8. Goodman twice introduces quotations into the essay—Coleridge in paragraph 7 and Santayana at the end. What is the point of each quotation, and how well does each tie in with Goodman's main idea?

Words

9. In writing of herself in this essay, Goodman uses the third person: she refers to herself as "she," rather than as the more conventional and expected "I." What is the effect of this third-person self-reference? Try reading two or three paragraphs, mentally changing the "she" to "I." How does the tone change?

10. In the first five paragraphs Goodman uses the language of film, perhaps more so than she actually needs to. What is her purpose in using film language?

11. Explain the tone and word play of each of the following sentences:

   Buddies faced adversity together, but friends faced each other. (8)

   Buddies hang tough together; friends hang onto each other. (11)

   You don't show off to a friend; you show need. (12)

Suggestions for Writing

A. Write imitations of the sentences discussed in questions 5, 6, and 7.

B. Write your own essay on the meaning and value of friendship.

C. Attend a film—or several films—and write an essay examining the kinds of friendships portrayed.

D. Argue for or against Goodman's ideas about friendship in an essay of your own.

In the Male Direction

---

1 Boston—There was a time in my life, I confess, when I thought that the only inherent differences between men and women were the obvious ones.

2 In my callous youth, I scoffed at the mental gymnastics of sociobiologists who leaped to conclusions about men and women from long years spent studying bugs. I suspected the motives of brain researchers who split the world of the sexes into left and right hemispheres.

3 But now, in my midlife, I can no longer deny the evidence of my senses or experiences.

4 Like virtually every woman in America who has spent time beside a man behind a wheel, like every woman in America who has ever been a lost passenger outward bound with a male driver, I know that there is one way in which the male sex is innately different from the female: Men are by their very nature congenitally unable to ask directions.

5 The historical record of their unwillingness was always clear. Consider, for example, the valiant 600 cavalrymen who plunged

into the Valley of Death . . . because they refused to ask if there wasn't some other way around the cannons.

6   Consider the entire wagon train that drove into the Donner Pass . . . because the wagon master wouldn't stop at the station marked Last Gas before the Disaster.

7   Consider even my own childhood. My father—a man with a great sense of humor and no sense of direction—constantly led us on what he referred to as "scenic routes."

8   But for centuries we assumed that this refusal was a weird idiosyncrasy. We never dreamed that it came with the testosterone.

9   In recent years, I have from time to time found myself sitting beside men who would not admit they were lost until I lit matches under their fingertips in an attempt to read maps in a box canyon.

10   One particular soul would consult an astronomical chart for his whereabouts before he would consult a police officer. Another would use a divining rod or a compass before he would use a gas station attendant.

11   In the 1970s, people believed in roles instead of genes, and I assumed that this behavior came from growing up male in America. I figured that males were taught that being lost was a challenge and seeking help was a cop-out. I assumed that the lost highwayman thought of himself as the Daniel Boone of Route 66.

12   Finally, however, the new breed of scientists are offering us new insights, not into upbringing but into biology and brains.

13   The male brain, according to researchers, is organized differently than the female. Men have better spatial abilities; women have better verbal abilities. Thus, we see the problem: Men read maps and women read people. The average man uses instruments. The average woman uses the voice.

14   Due to this fact, the husband who is able to adequately drive into a toll booth and roll down the car window is handicapped with the inability to then ask the question: "Where is Route Twenty?" A man who can stick-shift and double-clutch, using his right hemisphere, is handicapped by his left hemisphere when it comes to asking, "Do we take a right here?"

15   It isn't his fault, you understand. It has to do with our Darwinian roots (what doesn't these days?). The primeval hunter couldn't ask a highway patrolman which way the antelopes were running. He had to shut up and follow the tracks. A good berry picker, on the other hand, could follow advice.

16   These primitive differences have all the value of the
appendix. They are likely to rupture in modern life. In my own
life, the differences between the sexes have led to all sorts of misunderstandings and midnight hysterics. In other cases, they have
led to deserted roadways, and divorce instead of doorsteps.

17   It is time for the female who finds herself in the passenger
seat on a scenic tour to take the wheel or to be more understanding. After all, anatomy may not be destiny—but it has a lot to do
with destination.

QUESTIONS

Ideas

1.   What is Goodman's point in this essay? That men are "congenitally
      unable to ask directions"? That differences between men and
      women encompass the emotional and psychological realms as well
      as the physical? Something else?

2.   Goodman alludes to the nature vs. nurture explanation of male
      behavior when she says that she "believed in roles instead of genes."
      Which does she now see as more influential in determining why
      men act in the ways they do?

Organization

3.   How is Goodman's essay organized? Identify its introduction, body,
      and conclusion.

4.   What evidence does Goodman advance in the course of developing
      her argument? Where is this evidence most heavily concentrated?
      How is it arranged?

Sentences

5.   Goodman's sentences, like her paragraphs, are mostly short. Why
      might she have chosen this option? What is the effect of using so
      many short sentences (and paragraphs)?

6.   Goodman uses balanced sentences in paragraph 13. She sets up
      neat pairs of contrasting details. Has she made use of such explicit
      syntactic contrastive patterns elsewhere in the essay?

Words

7.   Goodman's diction in the essay ranges from the formal and techni-
      cal (testosterone, sociobiologists) to the casually informal (copout,

stick-shift). Find examples of each level of diction, and comment on the effect of their coexistence.

8. Goodman's point may be serious, but her tone is humorous. Find examples of words and phrases that seem amusing or funny.

Suggestions for Writing

A. Write imitations of the balanced sentences in paragraph 13.

B. Write a short essay in which you use a common, everyday experience to illustrate a significant difference between men and women.

SEVEN

Stephen Jay Gould

(1941–   )

Most people dare not doubt the findings of modern science, thinking it an objective, dispassionate march toward truth. They assume that scientists carefully gather and analyze a multitude of facts and then come to logical conclusions. Geology and evolutionary biology, for example, are thought to be neutral inquiries, free from the social and political prejudices that distort most of our other intellectual pursuits. But not according to Stephen Jay Gould. For him, science is a creative activity, its findings deeply intertwined with the personal opinions and biases of fallible and impressionable investigators. It is this kind of iconoclastic position that lends excitement and power to Gould's science writing.

In "This View of Life," a monthly column in *Natural History,* Gould helps us understand the impact of social and political pressures on a range of supposedly objective disciplines, from paleontology and geology to zoology and evolutionary biology. Since Gould is not writing for specialists here, he switches from the technical language common in academic circles to a style that both entertains and teaches. Most first-rate scientists find this quite difficult. Only a handful have been able to popularize their specialties without also trivializing them. Along with Lewis Thomas and Loren Eiseley, Gould is able to write clearly about complicated ideas in a strong, elegant style. But even more than the intellectual content and graceful prose, the reader senses Gould's enthusiasm, his passion for ideas and rigorous thinking.

This fiery commitment began early. As a young boy in New York, Stephen's father took him to the Museum of Natural History where, like most children, his imagination and sense of wonder were electrified by the great dinosaurs. He even dedicated his first popular success, an anthology of essays, *Ever Since Darwin—Reflections in Natural History* (1977), to his father, "who took me to see the Tyrannosaurus when I was five." Now, as a professor of geology, biology, and the history of science at Harvard, and as the winner of several prestigious book awards, Gould does a good deal more than put bones together. Besides his many professional responsibilities, his major task today is to develop and expand our understanding of how life evolves. Although his topics seem diverse, in one way or another, all his popular essays deal with Darwinian evolutionary theory: "I am a tradesman, not a polymath; what I know of planets and politics lies at their intersection with biological evolution."

In describing his own writing, Gould is equally straightforward, claiming he uses "Darwin's evolutionary perspective as an antidote to our cosmic arrogance." In other words, Gould wants us to understand that humanity is not necessarily the ultimate goal of evolution. In fact, our presence and current domination of earth is more chance than purpose, more luck than destiny. The revolutionary ideas of Copernicus and Freud served comparable decentering and humbling functions, demonstrating that we are neither the center of the universe nor complete masters of our own actions.

Gould is a devoted scientist who reveals the power and the limitations of his profession; an insider who cares about the scientific ideas of those of us on the outside. His column demystifies science which he holds is neither magic nor religion. It is a human activity, accessible to all educated people, its findings subject to the same cultural pressures as literature and philosophy. There should really be nothing surprising about this, but science has operated in a privileged sphere for so long we easily forget that scientists can be as disturbed or myopic as anyone else. Gould's essays show us that very little that we do is free from the subjectivity of emotion and opinion. All of us reflect the values of our time, the limitations of our place. The myth of objectivity is, then, one of Gould's favorite targets, as are biological theories past and present that exploit science to justify the social superiority of one group over another.

In the prologue to his anthology *Bully for Brontosaurus* (1991), excerpted here, Gould defends science writing for the nonprofessional reader, and acknowledges an evolution in his own writing as he explores the improbable "lateral connections" between science and the world of political and social issues. Although he has moved toward a more discursive style, he remains a master of argumentation. A study of his shrewd and vigorous method will indicate that Gould has carefully arranged his evidence while also paying attention to the psychology involved in trying to be persuasive to alert readers. In "Flaws in a Victorian Veil" from *The Panda's Thumb*, Gould questions the assumption that ideas can be "objective" or politically neutral by presenting a telling example.

In the anthologies *Hen's Teeth and Horse's Toes* (1983) and *The Panda's Thumb* (1982), Gould is clearly angered and saddened both by the sexism of early experiments that demonstrated the innate superiority of white, middle-class males, and the distortions of "scientific creationism." In "Women's Brains," Gould does some historical research to unravel the theory and practice of the now discredited science of craniometry, an inquiry which measured intelligence by the size of the skull and the weight of the brain. It is shocking for some readers to see how an apparently meticulous science, one that seemed "particularly invulnerable to refutation," could, in fact, be heavily influenced by prevailing cultural assumptions; in this case, the common notion in the last century that women were intellectually inferior to men. Gould's talents as a writer are clear as he moves from explaining Broca's theories, to making contemporary connections, to making a plea to avoid biological labeling of disadvantaged groups.

As a writer and thinker, Gould is at his controversial best in "Evolution as Fact and Theory," a vigorous and learned rebuttal of certain religious fundamentalists, especially those on the evangelical right who challenge the theory of evolution. This is Gould's best-known piece. It appeared in *Discovery*, a magazine with a wider and more general audience than *Natural History*. Gould is not polite in his attack. He thinks the attempt to introduce "scientific creationism" into classrooms on an equal footing with modern biology is an issue of politics and power, not religion. He claims that dogmatism and distortion are more relevant motivators than religious feeling and that this issue is an ongoing replay of the Scopes trial of half a century ago. Because of his strong denunciation of the creationists and their methods, Gould has become one of the fundamentalists' major targets. Gould seems to enjoy this controversy, believing that the issues are important enough to step outside the ivory tower and fight for what he values. His strong social conscience makes him think he owes it to the integrity of science and the continuation of the separation of church and state.

There is no denying that Gould makes his readers think. He is always calling into question ideas we take for granted, ideas that form the backbone of Western thought. For example, there is a popular version of evolution that holds that we are invariably evolving into ever higher beings, that we are evolving for positive reasons, toward harmony and order, that progress is inevitable. It is hard not to believe in this optimistic account. But Gould boldly asserts that evolution has no purpose or direction or meaning. He teaches us that science provides facts, but we interpret, and that purpose and meaning are, therefore, in the eye of the beholder.

Since truth in this view is a social construct, Gould gives us not only a crucial insight, he gives us authority and responsibility. For finally that's what these essays are all about: the need for educated people to be involved, to understand that science is fallible, to be active inquiring citizens, and not to abdicate our opinions to those who claim that objectivity and truth are theirs alone.

Prologue

---

1   In France, they call this genre *vulgarisation*—but the implications are entirely positive. In America, we call it "popular (or pop) writing" and its practitioners are dubbed "science writers" even if, like me, they are working scientists who love to share the power and beauty of their field with people in other professions.

2   In France (and throughout Europe), *vulgarisation* ranks within the highest traditions of humanism, and also enjoys an ancient pedigree—from St. Francis communing with animals to Galileo choosing to write his two great works in Italian, as dia-

logues between professor and students, and not in the formal
Latin of churches and universities. In America, for reasons that I
do not understand (and that are truly perverse), such writing for
nonscientists lies immured in deprecations "adulteration," "sim-
plification," "distortion for effect," "grandstanding," "whizbang." I
do not deny that many American works deserve these designations—but poor and self-serving items, even in vast majority, do
not invalidate a genre. "Romance" fiction has not banished love as
a subject for great novelists.

3   I deeply deplore the equation of popular writing with pap
and distortion for two main reasons. First, such a designation
imposes a crushing professional burden on scientists (particularly
young scientists without tenure) who might like to try their hand
at this expansive style. Second, it denigrates the intelligence of
millions of Americans eager for intellectual stimulation without
patronization. If we writers assume a crushing mean of mediocrity
and incomprehension, then not only do we have contempt for
our neighbors, but we also extinguish the light of excellence. The
"perceptive and intelligent" layperson is no myth. They exist in
millions—a low percentage of Americans perhaps, but a high
absolute number with influence beyond their proportion in the
population. I know this in the most direct possible way—by thousands of letters received from nonprofessionals during my twenty
years of writing these essays, and particularly from the large number written by people in their eighties and nineties, and still striving, as intensely as ever, to grasp nature's richness and add to a
lifetime of understanding.

4   We must all pledge ourselves to recovering accessible science as an honorable intellectual tradition. The rules are simple:
no compromises with conceptual richness; no bypassing of ambiguity or ignorance; removal of jargon, of course, but no dumbing
down of ideas (any conceptual complexity can be conveyed in
ordinary English). Several of us are pursuing this style of writing
in America today. And we enjoy success if we do it well. Thus, our
primary task lies in public relations: We must be vigorous in identifying what we are and are not, uncompromising in our claims to
the humanistic lineages of St. Francis and Galileo, not to the
sound bites and photo ops in current ideologies of persuasion—
the ultimate in another grand old American tradition (the dark
side of anti-intellectualism, and not without a whiff of appeal to
the unthinking emotionalism that can be a harbinger of fascism).

5   Humanistic natural history comes in two basic lineages. I call
them Franciscan and Galilean in the light of my earlier discussion. Franciscan writing is nature poetry—an exaltation of organic
beauty by corresponding choice of words and phrase. Its lineage
runs from St. Francis to Thoreau on Walden Pond, W. H. Hudson
on the English downs, to Loren Eiseley in our generation.
Galilean composition delights in nature's intellectual puzzles and
our quest for explanation and understanding. Galileans do not
deny the visceral beauty, but take greater delight in the joy of
causal comprehension and its powerful theme of unification. The
Galilean (or rationalist) lineage has roots more ancient than its
eponym—from Aristotle dissecting squid to Galileo reversing the
heavens, to T. H. Huxley inverting our natural place, to P. B.
Medawar dissecting the follies of our generation.

6   I love good Franciscan writing but regard myself as a fervent,
unrepentant, pure Galilean—and for two major reasons. First, I
would be an embarrassing flop in the Franciscan trade. Poetic
writing is the most dangerous of all genres because failures are so
conspicuous, usually as the most ludicrous form of purple prose.
Cobblers should stick to their lasts and rationalists to their measured style. Second, Wordsworth was right. The child is father to
the man. My youthful "splendor in the grass" was the bustle and
buildings of New York. My adult joys have been walks in cities,
amidst stunning human diversity of behavior and architecture—
from the Quirinal to the Piazza Navona at dusk, from the
Georgian New Town to the medieval Old Town of Edinburgh at
dawn—more than excursions in the woods. I am not insensible to
natural beauty, but my emotional joys center on the improbable
yet sometimes wondrous works of that tiny and accidental evolutionary twig called *Homo sapiens*. And I find, among these works,
nothing more noble than the history of our struggle to understand nature—a majestic entity of such vast spatial and temporal
scope that she cannot care much for a little mammalian
afterthought with a curious evolutionary invention, even if that
invention has, for the first time in some four billion years of life
on earth, produced recursion as a creature reflects back upon its
own production and evolution. Thus, I love nature primarily for
the puzzles and intellectual delights that she offers to the first
organ capable of such curious contemplation.

7   Franciscans may seek a poetic oneness with nature, but we
Galilean rationalists have a program of unification as well—nature

made mind and mind now returns the favor by trying to comprehend the source of production.

8   A final thought on Franciscans and Galileans in the light of our environmental concerns as a tattered planet approaches the millennium (by human reckoning—as nature, dealing in billions, can only chuckle). Franciscans engage the glory of nature by direct communion. Yet nature is so massively indifferent to us and our suffering. Perhaps this indifference, this majesty of years in uncaring billions (before we made a belated appearance), marks her true glory. Omar Khayyám's old quatrain grasped this fundamental truth (though he should have described his Eastern hotel, his metaphor for the earth, as grand rather than battered):

> Think, in this battered caravanserai
> Whose portals are alternate night and day,
> How sultan after sultan with his pomp
> Abode his destined hour, and went his way.

9   The true beauty of nature is her amplitude; she exists neither for nor because of us, and possesses a staying power that all our nuclear arsenals cannot threaten (much as we can easily destroy our puny selves).

10   The hubris that got us into trouble in the first place, and that environmentalists seek to avoid as the very definition of their (I should say our) movement, often creeps back in an unsuspected (and therefore potentially dangerous) form in two tenets frequently advanced by "green" movements: (1) that we live on a fragile planet subject to permanent ruin by human malfeasance; (2) that humans must act as stewards of this fragility in order to save our planet.

11   We should be so powerful! (Read this sentence with my New York accent as a derisive statement about our false sense of might, not as a literal statement of desire.) For all our mental and technological wizardry, I doubt that we can do much to derail the earth's history in any permanent sense by the proper planetary time scale of millions of years. Nothing within our power can come close to conditions and catastrophes that the earth has often passed through and beyond. The worst scenario of global warming under greenhouse models yields an earth substantially cooler than many happy and prosperous times of a prehuman

past. The megatonnage of the extraterrestrial impact that probably triggered the late Cretaceous mass extinction has been estimated at 10,000 times greater than all the nuclear bombs now
stockpiled on earth. And this extinction, wiping out some 50 percent of marine species, was paltry compared to the granddaddy of
all—the Permian event some 225 million years ago that might
have dispatched up to 95 percent of species. Yet the earth recovered from these superhuman shocks, and produced some interesting evolutionary novelties as a result (consider the potential for
mammalian domination, including human emergence, following
the removal of dinosaurs).

12   But recovery and restabilization occur at planetary, not
human, time scales—that is, millions of years after the disturbing
event. At this scale, we are powerless to harm; the planet will take
care of itself, our puny foolishnesses notwithstanding. But this
time scale, though natural for planetary history, is not appropriate
in our legitimately parochial concern for our own species, and the
current planetary configurations that now support us. For these
planetary instants—our millennia—we do hold power to impose
immense suffering (I suspect that the Permian catastrophe was
decidedly unpleasant for the nineteen of twenty species that
didn't survive).

13   We certainly cannot wipe out bacteria (they have been the
modal organisms on earth right from the start, and probably shall
be until the sun explodes); I doubt that we can wreak much permanent havoc upon insects as a whole (whatever our power to
destroy local populations and species). But we can surely eliminate our fragile selves—and our well-buffered earth might then
breathe a metaphorical sigh of relief at the ultimate failure of an
interesting but dangerous experiment in consciousness. Global
warming is worrisome because it will flood our cities (built so
often at sea level as ports and harbors), and alter our agricultural
patterns to the severe detriment of millions. Nuclear war is an ultimate calamity for the pain and death of billions, and the genetic
maiming of millions in future generations.

14   Our planet is not fragile at its own time scale, and we, pitiful
latecomers in the last microsecond of our planetary year, are stewards of nothing in the long run. Yet no political movement is
more vital and timely than modern environmentalism—because
we must save ourselves (and our neighbor species) from our own
immediate folly. We hear so much talk about an environmental

ethic. Many proposals embody the abstract majesty of a Kantian categorical imperative. Yet I think that we need something far more grubby and practical. We need a version of the most useful and ancient moral principle of all—the precept developed in one form or another by nearly every culture because it acts, in its legitimate appeal to self-interest, as a doctrine of stability based upon mutual respect. No one has ever improved upon the golden rule. If we execute such a compact with our planet, pledging to cherish the earth as we would wish to be treated ourselves, she may relent and allow us to muddle through. Such a limited goal may strike some readers as cynical or blinkered. But remember that, to an evolutionary biologist, persistence is the ultimate reward. And human brainpower, for reasons quite unrelated to its evolutionary origin, has the damnedest capacity to discover the most fascinating things, and think the most peculiar thoughts. So why not keep this interesting experiment around, at least for another planetary second or two?

QUESTIONS

Ideas

1. What contrast does Stephen Jay Gould make between European and American attitudes toward writing for the general reader? What reasons does Gould give for his own position on the question? Do you agree with his statement in paragraph 4 that "any conceptual complexity can be conveyed in ordinary English"? What is the difference between the "dumbing down of ideas" and a simplicity of language? Why is material written for experts in a field usually difficult for nonprofessionals to read? Taking paragraph 14 as an example, explain why you think that Gould does or doesn't practice what he preaches.

2. What does Gould mean in paragraph 4 by "sound bites and photo ops in current ideologies of persuasion"? When he speaks of an American tradition of anti-intellectualism that appeals primarily to emotion, can you think of examples of this sort of persuasion?

3. Gould separates writers of "humanistic natural history" into two types: Franciscans and Galileans. What attitudes toward nature and corresponding use of language are characterized by each type? Do you agree with Gould that these points of view are mutually exclusive, or could they be mixed or alternated by the same writer? How

does Gould relate this dichotomy to environmental movements? How would you group other nature writers that you have read?

Organization

4. How does Gould, in his second paragraph, foreshadow his later use of St. Francis and Galileo as contrasting thinkers? Does he give any indication of their importance to the essay's structure at this point? What effect does Gould's juxtaposition of animals and academics have on you as a reader?

5. Beginning with paragraph 3, Gould structures four paragraphs in essentially the same way. What is this structure? Is it effective? Why might this type of structure be useful to writers in scientific fields?

Sentences

6. Count the number of times that Gould uses parenthetical asides in this piece, including both parentheses and dashes. What sort of information does he include in this way? What effect does this have on sentences and on the formality of the writing? Do you think that he would use this device as often if he were writing for a scholarly journal?

7. Analyze the sentences in paragraph 4 according to their length and complexity. Note the use of colons, semicolons, dashes, and parentheses. How are sentences placed in the paragraph relative to their length and complexity? Does he use the same sort of variation in other paragraphs? How do you respond as a reader to the pacing and rhythm of Gould's writing?

Words

8. In paragraphs 1 and 2, Gould discusses the positive and (mostly) negative implications of terms often used to designate science writing directed toward nonscientists. Discuss specific implications of the words Gould lists here and of *vulgarization* as English speakers might use it, listing synonyms, definitions, and your own connotations for each word. What do the words on Gould's list say about attitudes toward the American public and people who write for this audience?

9. Introducing Galileo and St. Francis, Gould uses the words "communing" and "dialogues." Look up the dictionary definitions of "communion" and "dialogue." What qualitative difference is implied simply from this choice of words? Do you see this as a legitimate dichotomy?

Suggestions for Writing

A. Both St. Francis of Assisi and Galileo shook the thinking of the established church. Given Gould's position in evolution/creation controversies, challenged or misquoted by biblical literalists and by some traditional evolutionists, his choice to contrast the thinking of these particular historical figures reflects his own embattled position as a science writer. Research one of the controversies that Gould, Galileo, or St. Francis has been involved in and write a report that outlines both sides of the controversy and the intellectual and social ramifications of each side. You needn't be "objective."

B. Choose a subject in the natural world with which you are familiar. Try writing about it as a Franciscan thinker might, then as a Galilean. Also write about your writing process in each case. Which did you find easier? In what specific ways was the writing different?

Flaws in a Victorian Veil

1   The Victorians left some magnificent, if lengthy, novels. But they also foisted upon an apparently willing world a literary genre probably unmatched for tedium and inaccurate portrayal: the multivolumed "life and letters" of eminent men. These extended encomiums, usually written by grieving widows or dutiful sons and daughters, masqueraded as humbly objective accounts, simple documentation of words and activities. If we accepted these works at face value, we would have to believe that eminent Victorians actually lived by the ethical values they espoused—a fanciful proposition that Lytton Strachey's *Eminent Victorians* put to rest more than fifty years ago.

2   Elizabeth Cary Agassiz—eminent Bostonian, founder and first president of Radcliffe College, and devoted wife of America's premier naturalist—had all the right credentials for authorship (including a departed and lamented husband). Her *Life and Correspondence of Louis Agassiz* turned a fascinating, cantankerous, and not overly faithful man into a paragon of restraint, statesmanship, wisdom, and rectitude.

3   I write this essay in the structure that Louis Agassiz built in 1859—the original wing of Harvard's Museum of Comparative Zoology. Agassiz, the world's leading student of fossil fishes, pro-

tégé of the great Cuvier left his native Switzerland for an American career in the late 1840s. As a celebrated European and a charming man, Agassiz was lionized in social and intellectual circles from Boston to Charleston. He led the study of natural history in America until his death in 1873.

4   Louis's public utterances were always models of propriety, but I expected that his private letters would match his ebullient personality. Yet Elizabeth's book, ostensibly a verbatim report of Louis's letters, manages to turn this focus of controversy and source of restless energy into a measured and dignified gentleman.

5   Recently, in studying Louis Agassiz's views on race and prompted by some hints in E. Lurie's biography *(Louis Agassiz: a life in science)*, I encountered some interesting discrepancies between Elizabeth's version and Louis's original letters. I then discovered that Elizabeth simply expurgated the text and didn't even insert ellipses (those annoying three dots) to indicate her deletions. Harvard has the original letters, and a bit of sleuthing on my part turned up some spicy material.

6   During the decade before the Civil War, Agassiz expressed strong opinions on the status of blacks and Indians. As an adopted son of the north, he rejected slavery, but as an upper crust Caucasian, he certainly didn't link this rejection to any notion of racial equality.

7   Agassiz presented his racial attitudes as sober and ineluctable deductions from first principles. He maintained that species are static, created entities (at his death in 1873, Agassiz stood virtually alone among biologists as a holdout against the Darwinian tide). They are not placed upon the earth in a single spot, but created simultaneously over their entire range. Related species are often created in separate geographic regions, each adapted to prevailing environments of its own area. Since human races met these criteria before commerce and migration mixed us up, each race is a separate biological species.

8   Thus, America's leading biologist came down firmly on the wrong side of a debate that had been raging in America for a decade before he arrived: Was Adam the progenitor of all people or only of white people? Are blacks and Indians our brothers or merely our look-alikes? The *polygenists,* Agassiz among them, held that each major race had been created as a truly separate species;

the *monogenists* advocated a single origin and ranked races by their unequal degeneration from the primeval perfection of Eden—the debate included no egalitarians. In logic, separate needn't mean unequal, as the victors in Plessy vs. Ferguson argued in 1896. But, as the winners in Brown vs. the Topeka Board of Education maintained in 1954, a group in power always conflates separation with superiority. I know of no American polygenist who did not assume that whites were separate *and* superior.

9   Agassiz insisted that his defense of polygeny had nothing to do with political advocacy or social prejudice. He was, he argued, merely a humble and disinterested scholar, trying to establish an intriguing fact of natural history.

> It has been charged upon the views here advanced that they tend to the support of slavery. . . . Is that a fair objection to a philosophical investigation? Here we have to do only with the question of the origin of men; let the politicians, let those who feel themselves called upon to regulate human society, see what they can do with the results. . . . We disclaim all connection with any question involving political matters. . . . Naturalists have a right to consider the questions growing out of men's physical relations as merely scientific questions, and to investigate them without reference to either politics or religion.

10   Despite these brave words, Agassiz ends this major statement on race (published in the *Christian Examiner*, 1850) with some definite social recommendations. He begins by affirming the doctrine of separate and unequal: "There are upon earth different races of men, inhabiting different parts of its surface . . . and this fact presses upon us the obligation to settle the relative rank among these races." The resulting hierarchy is self-evident: "The indomitable, courageous, proud Indian—in how different a light he stands by the side of the submissive, obsequious, imitative negro, or by the side of the tricky, cunning, and cowardly Mongolian! Are not these facts indications that the different races do not rank upon one level in nature." Finally, if he hadn't made his political message clear by generalization, Agassiz ends by advocating specific social policy—thus contravening his original pledge to abjure politics for the pure life of the mind. Education, he argues, must be tailored to innate ability; train blacks in hand work, whites in mind work.

> What would be the best education to be imparted to the different
> races in consequence of their primitive difference. . . . We enter-
> tain not the slightest doubt that human affairs with reference to
> the colored races would be far more judiciously conducted if, in
> our intercourse with them, we were guided by a full consciousness
> of the real differences existing between us and them, and a desire
> to foster those dispositions that are eminently marked in them,
> rather than by treating them on terms of equality.

11   Since these "eminently marked" dispositions are submissiveness, obsequiousness, and imitation, we can well imagine what
Agassiz had in mind.

12   Agassiz had political clout, largely because he spoke as a scientist, supposedly motivated only by the facts of his case and the
abstract theory they embodied. In this context, the actual source
of Agassiz's ideas on race becomes a matter of some importance.
Did he really have no ax to grind, no predisposition, no impetus
beyond his love for natural history? The passages expurgated
from *Life and Correspondence* shed considerable light. They show a
man with strong prejudices based primarily on immediate visceral
reactions and deep sexual fears.

13   The first passage, almost shocking in its force, even 130
years later, recounts Agassiz's first experience with black people
(he had never encountered blacks in Europe). He first visited
America in 1846 and sent his mother a long letter detailing
his experiences. In the section about Philadelphia, Elizabeth
Agassiz records only his visits to museums and the private
homes of scientists. She expunges, without ellipses, his first
impression of blacks—a visceral reaction to waiters in a hotel
restaurant. In 1846 Agassiz still believed in human unity, but this
passage exposes an explicit, stunningly nonscientific basis for
his conversion to polygeny. For the first time, then, without
omissions:

> It was in Philadelphia that I first found myself in prolonged contact
> with negroes; all the domestics in my hotel were men of color. I
> can scarcely express to you the painful impression that I received,
> especially since the sentiment that they inspired in me is contrary
> to all our ideas about the confraternity of the human type and the
> unique origin of our species. But truth before all. Nevertheless, I
> experienced pity at the sight of this degraded and degenerate race,
> and their lot inspired compassion in me in thinking that they are

really men. Nonetheless, it is impossible for me to repress the feeling that they are not of the same blood as us. In seeing their black faces with their thick lips and grimacing teeth, the wool on their head, their bent knees, their elongated hands, their large curved nails, and especially the livid color of the palms of their hands, I could not take my eyes off their faces in order to tell them to stay far away. And when they advanced that hideous hand towards my plate in order to serve me, I wished I were able to depart in order to eat a piece of bread elsewhere, rather than to dine with such service. What unhappiness for the white race—to have tied their existence so closely with that of negroes in certain countries! God preserve us from such a contact!

14   The second set of documents comes from the midst of the Civil War. Samuel Howe, husband of Julia Ward Howe (author of *The Battle Hymn of the Republic*) and a member of President Lincoln's Inquiry Commission, wrote to ask Agassiz his opinion about the role of blacks in a reunited nation. During August 1863, Agassiz responded in four long and impassioned letters. Elizabeth Agassiz bowdlerized them to render Louis's case as a soberly stated opinion (despite its peculiar content), derived from first principles and motivated only by a love of truth.

15   Louis argued, in short, that races should be kept separate lest white superiority be diluted. This separation should occur naturally since mulattoes, as a weak strain, will eventually die out. Blacks will leave the northern climates so unsuited to them (since they were created as a separate species for Africa); they will move south in droves and will eventually prevail in a few lowland states, although whites will maintain dominion over the seashore and elevated ground. We will have to recognize these states, even admit them to the Union, as the best solution to a bad situation; after all, we do recognize "Haity and Liberia."

16   Elizabeth's substantial deletions display Louis's motivation in a very different light. They radiate raw fear and blind prejudice. She systematically eliminates three kinds of statements. First, she omits the most denigrating references to blacks: "In everything unlike other races," Louis writes, "they may but be compared to children, grown in the stature of adults, while retaining a childlike mind." Second, she removes all elitist claims about the correlation of wisdom, wealth, and social position within races. In these passages, we begin to sense Louis's real fears about miscegenation.

I shudder from the consequences. We have already to struggle, in our progress, against the influence of universal equality, in consequence of the difficulty of preserving the acquisitions of individual eminence, the wealth of refinement and culture growing out of select associations. What would be our condition if to these difficulties were added the far more tenacious influences of physical disability. Improvements in our system of education . . . may sooner or later counterbalance the effects of the apathy of the uncultivated and of the rudeness of the lower classes and raise them to a higher standard. But how shall we eradicate the stigma of a lower race when its blood has once been allowed to flow freely into that of our children.

17   Third, and of greatest significance, she expunges several long passages on interbreeding that place the entire correspondence in a different setting from the one she fashioned. In them, we grasp Louis's intense, visceral revulsion toward the idea of sexual contact between races. This deep and irrational fear was as strong a driving force within him as any abstract notion about separate creation: "The production of half-breeds," he writes, "is as much a sin against nature, as incest in a civilized community is a sin against purity of character. . . . I hold it to be a perversion of every natural sentiment."

18   This natural aversion is so strong that abolitionist sentiment cannot reflect any innate sympathy for blacks but must arise because many "blacks" have substantial amounts of white blood and whites instinctively sense this part of themselves: "I have no doubt in my mind that the sense of abhorrence against slavery, which has led to the agitation now culminating in our civil war, has been chiefly if unconsciously fostered by the recognition of our own type in the offspring of southern gentlemen, moving among us as negros *[sic]* , which they are not."

19   But if races naturally repel each other, how then do "southern gentlemen" take such willing advantage of their bonded women? Agassiz blames the mulatto house slaves. Their whiteness renders them attractive; their blackness, lascivious. The poor, innocent young men are enticed and entrapped.

As soon as the sexual desires are awakening in the young men of the South, they find it easy to gratify themselves by the readiness with which they are met by colored [mulatto] house servants. [This contact] blunts his better instincts in that direction and leads him gradually to seek more spicy partners, as I have heard the full blacks called by fast young men. One thing is certain, that there is no elevating element whatever conceivable in the connection of individuals of different races; there is neither love, nor desire for improvement of any kind. It is altogether a physical connection.

How a previous generation of gentlemen overcame their aversion to produce the first mulattoes, we are not told.

20   We cannot know in detail why Elizabeth chose her deletions. I doubt that a conscious desire to convert Louis's motives from prejudice to logical implication prompted all her actions. Simple Victorian prudery probably led her to reject a public airing of any statement about sex. In any case, her deletions did distort Louis Agassiz's thought and did render his intentions according to the fallacious and self-serving model favored by scientists—that opinions arise from dispassionate surveys of raw information.

21   These restorations show that Louis Agassiz was jolted to consider the polygenist theory of races as separate species by his initial, visceral reaction to contact with blacks. They also demonstrate that his extreme views on racial mixing were powered more by intense sexual revulsion than by any abstract theory of hybridity.

22   Racism has often been buttressed by scientists who present a public façade of objectivity to mask their guiding prejudices. Agassiz's case may be distant, but its message rings through our century as well.

QUESTIONS

Ideas

1.   Stephen Jay Gould says that Victorian biographies often "masqueraded as humbly objective accounts" (paragraph 1) and that scientists have and may continue to "present a public façade of objectivity to mask their guiding prejudices" (paragraph 23). Is it possible for a writer to be unbiased and free of political ideology, to be "a humble and disinterested scholar," as Agassiz claimed to be? Or is "objectivity" always a cover for hidden or unexamined ideas? How would you define "objective" writing? How does Gould's writing fit into this definition?

2.   In paragraph 8, Gould says: "In logic, separate needn't mean unequal. . . . But . . . a group in power always conflates separation

with superiority." Discuss this idea in terms of groups who choose separatism to maintain group identity, even though they are not the group in power. Should differences be ignored, aiming for a "melting pot" ideal? Is it possible for a person to be "racist" (or "sexist") if he or she is not a member of the dominant group? How might the situation Gould describes be changed so that marginalized groups could keep valued differences, yet have an equal voice politically and socially?

3. Do you think that the educational policies suggested by Agassiz (paragraph 10) have been eliminated from schools? How might "tracking" or "ability grouping" and culturally biased testing continue to separate students according to race, even when official policies deny such separation occurs? Can you think of examples of Agassiz's logic that you have heard in recent years?

Organization

4. Gould has stated that his favorite method of writing is "beginning with something small and curious and then working outward and onward by a network of lateral connections." What "small and curious" discrepancies led Gould to write this essay? How does he use the repetition of words and ideas to achieve cohesiveness among seemingly unrelated bits of information? How do the concluding paragraphs work to tie the essay together? Does the essay have a thesis statement, i.e., one sentence that summarizes one main idea? What would you say is the main idea of this essay?

5. In his characterization of Agassiz in paragraph 2, Gould includes the phrase "not overly faithful." What reasons could Gould have for including this comment? Does it relate to later content about sexuality? Is it irrelevant? What is its effect at this point in the essay?

Sentences

6. Paragraph 20 begins with a question. What effect does this usage have on your reading of Agassiz's opinions which directly follow? What function does the final sentence of the paragraph seem to play? Find other instances of Gould's use of questions or implied questions. What is their rhetorical effect?

7. Gould's essay contains a great many quotations and paraphrases of Louis Agassiz's ideas. Note several ways in which Gould structures sentences which contain or introduce quotations and/or paraphrases. Can you pinpoint any factors that may come into play when Gould chooses how to cite Agassiz's opinions?

Words

8. The title of this essay, "Flaws in a Victorian Veil," uses words with connotations beyond their dictionary definitions for most readers. List a few of the connotations the words "Victorian" or "veil" have for you. Throughout his essay, Gould uses words that refer to things being covered up, hidden, or taken out of view. See how many examples you can find of these words. What is the etymology of the word "bowdlerized"?

9. Gould often uses the word "visceral" in his writing, as in paragraph 18 of this essay. What does this word mean? Do you think it is effective in this context?

10. In paragraph 19, what does the term *sic* mean? Why is it used here? Why is it in brackets? According to Gould in paragraph 5, what are ellipses? Can you expand his definition?

Suggestions for Writing

A. Imagine that someone has written a letter to the editor, using one of the quotations from the "noted scientist Louis Agassiz" that we have read here. (You choose the quotation.) Write a letter to the editor that refutes Agassiz's statement by pointing out the flaws in his logic and in his interpretations of the behavior and physical characteristics of African-Americans of his day.

B. Write an encomium to someone you know well and admire. Read it. Then write an analysis of your tribute, describing your writing process. What sorts of things did you decide to omit? What factors influenced your decisions? Did audience play a part? Were you being "objective"?

Women's Brains

1   In the prelude to *Middlemarch*, George Eliot lamented the unfulfilled lives of talented women:

> Some have felt that these blundering lives are due to the inconvenient indefiniteness with which the Supreme Power has fashioned the natures of women: if there were one level of feminine incompe-

tence as strict as the ability to count three and no more, the social
lot of women might be treated with scientific certitude.

2   Eliot goes on to discount the idea of innate limitation, but
while she wrote in 1872, the leaders of European anthropometry
were trying to measure "with scientific certitude" the inferiority of
women. Anthropometry, or measurement of the human body, is
not so fashionable a field these days, but it dominated the human
sciences for much of the nineteenth century and remained popular until intelligence testing replaced skull measurement as a
favored device for making invidious comparisons among races,
classes, and sexes. Craniometry, or measurement of the skull,
commanded the most attention and respect. Its unquestioned
leader, Paul Broca (1824–80), professor of clinical surgery at the
Faculty of Medicine in Paris, gathered a school of disciples and
imitators around himself. Their work, so meticulous and apparently irrefutable, exerted great influence and won high esteem as
a jewel of nineteenth-century science.

3   Broca's work seemed particularly invulnerable to refutation.
Had he not measured with the most scrupulous care and accuracy? (Indeed, he had. I have the greatest respect for Broca's meticulous procedure. His numbers are sound. But science is an inferential exercise, not a catalog of facts. Numbers, by themselves,
specify nothing. All depends upon what you do with them.) Broca
depicted himself as an apostle of objectivity, a man who bowed
before facts and cast aside superstition and sentimentality. He
declared that "there is no faith, however respectable, no interest,
however legitimate, which must not accommodate itself to the
progress of human knowledge and bend before truth." Women,
like it or not, had smaller brains than men and, therefore, could
not equal them in intelligence. This fact, Broca argued, may reinforce a common prejudice in male society, but it is also a scientific
truth. L. Manouvrier, a black sheep in Broca's fold, rejected the
inferiority of women and wrote with feeling about the burden
imposed upon them by Broca's numbers:

> Women displayed their talents and their diplomas. They also
> invoked philosophical authorities. But they were opposed by *num-*
> *bers* unknown to Condorcet or to John Stuart Mill. These numbers
> fell upon poor women like a sledge hammer, and they were accom-
> panied by commentaries and sarcasms more ferocious than the

most misogynist imprecations of certain church fathers. The theologians had asked if women had a soul. Several centuries later, some scientists were ready to refuse them a human intelligence.

4   Broca's argument rested upon two sets of data: the larger brains of men in modern societies, and a supposed increase in male superiority through time. His most extensive data came from autopsies performed personally in four Parisian hospitals. For 292 male brains, he calculated an average weight of 1,325 grams; 140 female brains averaged 1,144 grams for a difference of 181 grams, or 14 percent of the male weight. Broca understood, of course, that part of this difference could be attributed to the greater height of males. Yet he made no attempt to measure the effect of size alone and actually stated that it cannot account for the entire difference because we know, a priori, that women are not as intelligent as men (a premise that the data were supposed to test, not rest upon):

> We might ask if the small size of the female brain depends exclusively upon the small size of her body. Tiedemann has proposed this explanation. But we must not forget that women are, on the average, a little less intelligent than men, a difference which we should not exaggerate but which is, nonetheless, real. We are therefore permitted to suppose that the relatively small size of the female brain depends in part upon her physical inferiority and in part upon her intellectual inferiority.

5   In 1873, the year after Eliot published *Middlemarch*, Broca measured the cranial capacities of prehistoric skulls from L'Homme Mort cave. Here he found a difference of only 99.5 cubic centimeters between males and females, while modern populations range from 129.5 to 220.7. Topinard, Broca's chief disciple, explained the increasing discrepancy through time as a result of differing evolutionary pressures upon dominant men and passive women:

> The man who fights for two or more in the struggle for existence, who has all the responsibility and the cares of tomorrow, who is constantly active in combating the environment and human rivals, needs more brain than the woman whom he must protect and nourish, the sedentary woman, lacking any interior occupations, whose role is to raise children, love, and be passive.

6   In 1879, Gustave Le Bon, chief misogynist of Broca's school, used these data to publish what must be the most vicious attack upon women in modern scientific literature (no one can top Aristotle). I do not claim his views were representative of Broca's school, but they were published in France's most respected anthropological journal. Le Bon concluded:

> In the most intelligent races, as among the Parisians, there are a large number of women whose brains are closer in size to those of gorillas than to the most developed male brains. This inferiority is so obvious that no one can contest it for a moment; only its degree is worth discussion. All psychologists who have studied the intelligence of women, as well as poets and novelists, recognize today that they represent the most inferior forms of human evolution and that they are closer to children and savages than to an adult, civilized man. They excel in fickleness, inconstancy, absence of thought and logic, and incapacity to reason. Without doubt there exist some distinguished women, very superior to the average man, but they are as exceptional as the birth of any monstrosity, as, for example, of a gorilla with two heads; consequently, we may neglect them entirely.

7   Nor did Le Bon shrink from the social implications of his views. He was horrified by the proposal of some American reformers to grant women higher education on the same basis as men:

> A desire to give them the same education, and, as a consequence, to propose the same goals for them, is a dangerous chimera. . . . The day when, misunderstanding the inferior occupations which nature has given her, women leave the home and take part in our battles; on this day a social revolution will begin, and everything that maintains the sacred ties of the family will disappear.

Sound familiar?

8   I have reexamined Broca's data, the basis for all this derivative pronouncement, and I find his numbers sound but his interpretation ill-founded, to say the least. The data supporting his claim for increased difference through time can be easily dismissed. Broca based his contention on the samples from L'Homme Mort alone—only seven male and six female skulls in all. Never have so little data yielded such far ranging conclusions.

9   In 1888, Topinard published Broca's more extensive data on the Parisian hospitals. Since Broca recorded height and age as

well as brain size, we may use modern statistics to remove their effect. Brain weight decreases with age, and Broca's women were, on average, considerably older than his men. Brain weight increases with height, and his average man was almost half a foot taller than his average woman. I used multiple regression, a technique that allowed me to assess simultaneously the influence of height and age upon brain size. In an analysis of the data for women, I found that, at average male height and age, a woman's brain would weigh 1,212 grams. Correction for height and age reduces Broca's measured difference of 181 grams by more than a third, to 113 grams.

10   I don't know what to make of this remaining difference because I cannot assess other factors known to influence brain size in a major way. Cause of death has an important effect: degenerative disease often entails a substantial diminution of brain size. (This effect is separate from the decrease attributed to age alone.) Eugene Schreider, also working with Broca's data, found that men killed in accidents had brains weighing, on average, 60 grams more than men dying of infectious diseases. The best modern data I can find (from American hospitals) records a full 100-gram difference between death by degenerative arteriosclerosis and by violence or accident. Since so many of Broca's subjects were very elderly women, we may assume that lengthy degenerative disease was more common among them than among the men.

11   More importantly, modern students of brain size still have not agreed on a proper measure for eliminating the powerful effect of body size. Height is partly adequate, but men and women of the same height do not share the same body build. Weight is even worse than height, because most of its variation reflects nutrition rather than intrinsic size—fat versus skinny exerts little influence upon the brain. Manouvrier took up this subject in the 1880s and argued that muscular mass and force should be used. He tried to measure this elusive property in various ways and found a marked difference in favor of men, even in men and women of the same height. When he corrected for what he called "sexual mass," women actually came out slightly ahead in brain size.

12   Thus, the corrected 113-gram difference is surely too large; the true figure is probably close to zero and may as well favor women as men. And 113 grams, by the way, is exactly the average

difference between a 5 foot 4 inch and a 6 foot 4 inch male in Broca's data. We would not (especially us short folks) want to ascribe greater intelligence to tall men. In short, who knows what to do with Broca's data? They certainly don't permit any confident claim that men have bigger brains than women.

13   To appreciate the social role of Broca and his school, we must recognize that his statements about the brains of women do not reflect an isolated prejudice toward a single disadvantaged group. They must be weighed in the context of a general theory that supported contemporary social distinctions as biologically ordained. Women, blacks, and poor people suffered the same disparagement, but women bore the brunt of Broca's argument because he had easier access to data on women's brains. Women were singularly denigrated but they also stood as surrogates for other disenfranchised groups. As one of Broca's disciples wrote in 1881: "Men of the black races have a brain scarcely heavier than that of white women." This juxtaposition extended into many other realms of anthropological argument, particularly to claims that, anatomically and emotionally, both women and blacks were like white children—and that white children, by the theory of recapitulation, represented an ancestral (primitive) adult stage of human evolution. I do not regard as empty rhetoric the claim that women's battles are for all of us.

14   Maria Montessori did not confine her activities to educational reform for young children. She lectured on anthropology for several years at the University of Rome, and wrote an influential book entitled *Pedagogical Anthropology* (English edition, 1913). Montessori was no egalitarian. She supported most of Broca's work and the theory of innate criminality proposed by her compatriot Cesare Lombroso. She measured the circumference of children's heads in her schools and inferred that the best prospects had bigger brains. But she had no use for Broca's conclusions about women. She discussed Manouvrier's work at length and made much of his tentative claim that women, after proper correction of the data, had slightly larger brains than men. Women, she concluded, were intellectually superior, but men had prevailed heretofore by dint of physical force. Since technology has abolished force as an instrument of power, the era of women may soon be upon us: "In such an epoch there will really be superior human beings, there will really be men strong in morality and in sentiment. Perhaps in this way the reign of women is approach-

ing, when the enigma of her anthropological superiority will be deciphered. Woman was always the custodian of human sentiment, morality and honor."

15   This represents one possible antidote to "scientific" claims for the constitutional inferiority of certain groups. One may affirm the validity of biological distinctions but argue that the data have been misinterpreted by prejudiced men with a stake in the outcome, and that disadvantaged groups are truly superior. In recent years, Elaine Morgan has followed this strategy in her *Descent of Woman,* a speculative reconstruction of human prehistory from the woman's point of view—and as farcical as more famous tall tales by and for men.

16   I prefer another strategy. Montessori and Morgan followed Broca's philosophy to reach a more congenial conclusion. I would rather label the whole enterprise of setting a biological value upon groups for what it is: irrelevant and highly injurious. George Eliot well appreciated the special tragedy that biological labeling imposed upon members of disadvantaged groups. She expressed it for people like herself—women of extraordinary talent. I would apply it more widely—not only to those whose dreams are flouted but also to those who never realize that they may dream—but I cannot match her prose. In conclusion, then, the rest of Eliot's prelude to *Middlemarch:*

> The limits of variation are really much wider than anyone would imagine from the sameness of women's coiffure and the favorite love stories in prose and verse. Here and there a cygnet is reared uneasily among the ducklings in the brown pond, and never finds the living stream in fellowship with its own oary-footed kind. Here and there is born a Saint Theresa, foundress of nothing, whose loving heartbeats and sobs after an unattained goodness tremble off and are dispersed among hindrances instead of centering in some long-recognizable deed.

QUESTIONS

Ideas

1. In the parenthetical sentences in paragraph 3, Gould claims that science "is an inferential exercise, not a catalog of facts." Is this what you have been taught in your science class?

2. At the end of paragraph 4, Gould places another important observation in parentheses. What do you understand by this comment about basing conclusions on *a priori* (before examination) assumptions? Do you think this happens in science today?

3. When Gould writes "Sound familiar?" at the end of paragraph 7, what do you think he has in mind?

4. How do you interpret Gould's statement in the last sentence of paragraph 13?

5. What conclusion about women's brains does Gould finally arrive at?

6. Gould assumes he is writing for an audience that shares his values. Look, for example, at the second sentence in paragraph 2. Do you think intelligence testing is a way of making harmful comparisons among races? Find other comments like this that indicate Gould's strong opinions.

Organization

7. Gould begins and ends this essay with quotes from *Middlemarch*. What point is made in each quote?

8. In arranging his argument, Gould first describes Broca's work on skull measurement. In paragraph 8 Gould begins a new phase of his attack on craniometry. Describe what he attempts to do in this paragraph and where his argument then goes.

9. What role does Montessori play in the structure of Gould's argument?

Sentences

10. Read the two passages from George Eliot out loud. Do they sound different than the sentences of Gould in, say, paragraph 14? Try to describe why.

11. Gould uses parentheses and dashes throughout this piece. Locate examples of each. What purpose do they serve? Are there effective alternatives?

Words

12. What do the following words mean in their contexts: "invidious" (paragraph 2); "disparagement" (paragraph 13); "surrogates" (paragraph 13); "juxtaposition" (paragraph 13); "rhetoric" (paragraph 13); "scientific" (paragraph 15); "farcical" (paragraph 15).

13. Paraphrase Eliot's opening quote (paragraph 1), using words a sixth-grader would easily understand.

Suggestions for Writing

A. From your own contemporary perspective, write a letter in response to the Gustave Le Bon excerpt in paragraph 6.

B. From your own experiences, opinions, and feelings write a position paper for or against the Le Bon quote in paragraph 7.

Evolution as Fact and Theory

---

1   Kirtley Mather, who died last year at age ninety, was a pillar of both science and Christian religion in America and one of my dearest friends. The difference of a half-century in our ages evaporated before our common interests. The most curious thing we shared was a battle we each fought at the same age. For Kirtley had gone to Tennessee with Clarence Darrow to testify for evolution at the Scopes trial of 1925. When I think that we are enmeshed again in the same struggle for one of the best documented, most compelling and exciting concepts in all of science, I don't know whether to laugh or cry.

2   According to idealized principles of scientific discourse, the arousal of dormant issues should reflect fresh data that give renewed life to abandoned notions. Those outside the current debate may therefore be excused for suspecting that creationists have come up with something new, or that evolutionists have generated some serious internal trouble. But nothing has changed; the creationists have presented not a single new fact or argument. Darrow and Bryan were at least more entertaining than we lesser antagonists today. The rise of creationism is politics, pure and simple; it represents one issue (and by no means the major concern) of the resurgent evangelical right. Arguments that seemed kooky just a decade ago have reentered the mainstream.

3   The basic attack of modern creationists falls apart on two general counts before we even reach the supposed factual details of their assault against evolution. First, they play upon a vernacular misunderstanding of the word "theory" to convey the false impression that we evolutionists are covering up the rotten core of our edifice. Second, they misuse a popular philosophy of science to argue that they are behaving scientifically in attacking

evolution. Yet the same philosophy demonstrates that their own belief is not science, and that "scientific creationism" is a meaningless and self-contradictory phrase, an example of what Orwell called "newspeak."

4   In the American vernacular, "theory" often means "imperfect fact"—part of a hierarchy of confidence running downhill from fact to theory to hypothesis to guess. Thus, creationists can (and do) argue: evolution is "only" a theory, and intense debate now rages about many aspects of the theory. If evolution is less than a fact, and scientists can't even make up their minds about the theory, then what confidence can we have in it? Indeed, President Reagan echoed this argument before an evangelical group in Dallas when he said (in what I devoutly hope was campaign rhetoric): "Well, it is a theory. It is a scientific theory only, and it has in recent years been challenged in the world of science—that is, not believed in the scientific community to be as infallible as it once was."

5   Well, evolution *is* a theory. It is also a fact. And facts and theories are different things, not rungs in a hierarchy of increasing certainty. Facts are the world's data. Theories are structures of ideas that explain and interpret facts. Facts do not go away while scientists debate rival theories for explaining them. Einstein's theory of gravitation replaced Newton's, but apples did not suspend themselves in mid-air pending the outcome. And human beings evolved from apelike ancestors whether they did so by Darwin's proposed mechanism or by some other, yet to be discovered.

6   Moreover, "fact" does not mean "absolute certainty." The final proofs of logic and mathematics flow deductively from stated premises and achieve certainty only because they are *not* about the empirical world. Evolutionists make no claim for perpetual truth, though creationists often do (and then attack us for a style of argument that they themselves favor). In science, "fact" can only mean "confirmed to such a degree that it would be perverse to withhold provisional assent." I suppose that apples might start to rise tomorrow, but the possibility does not merit equal time in physics classrooms.

7   Evolutionists have been clear about this distinction between fact and theory from the very beginning, if only because we have always acknowledged how far we are from completely understanding the mechanisms (theory) by which evolution (fact) occurred. Darwin continually emphasized the difference between his two

great and separate accomplishments: establishing the fact of evolution, and proposing a theory—natural selection—to explain the
mechanism of evolution. He wrote in *The Descent of Man:* "I had
two distinct objects in view; firstly, to show that species had not
been separately created, and secondly, that natural selection had
been the chief agent of change . . . Hence if I have erred in . . .
having exaggerated its [natural selection's] power . . . I have at
least, as I hope, done good service in aiding to overthrow the
dogma of separate creations."

8   Thus Darwin acknowledged the provisional nature of natural selection while affirming the fact of evolution. The fruitful the-
oretical debate that Darwin initiated has never ceased. From the
1940s through the 1960s, Darwin's own theory of natural selection
did achieve a temporary hegemony that it never enjoyed in his
lifetime. But renewed debate characterizes our decade, and, while
no biologist questions the importance of natural selection, many
now doubt its ubiquity. In particular, many evolutionists argue
that substantial amounts of genetic change may not be subject to
natural selection and may spread through populations at random.
Others are challenging Darwin's linking of natural selection with
gradual, imperceptible change through all intermediary degrees;
they are arguing that most evolutionary events may occur far
more rapidly than Darwin envisioned.

9   Scientists regard debates on fundamental issues of theory as
a sign of intellectual health and a source of excitement. Science
is—and how else can I say it?—most fun when it plays with interesting ideas, examines their implications, and recognizes that old
information may be explained in surprisingly new ways.
Evolutionary theory is now enjoying this uncommon vigor. Yet
amidst all this turmoil no biologist has been led to doubt the fact
that evolution occurred; we are debating *how* it happened. We are
all trying to explain the same thing: the tree of evolutionary
descent linking all organisms by ties of genealogy. Creationists
pervert and caricature this debate by conveniently neglecting the
common conviction that underlies it, and by falsely suggesting
that we now doubt the very phenomenon we are struggling to
understand.

10   Secondly, creationists claim that "the dogma of separate creations," as Darwin characterized it a century ago, is a scientific theory meriting equal time with evolution in high school biology curricula. But a popular viewpoint among philosophers of science

belies this creationist argument. Philosopher Karl Popper has argued for decades that the primary criterion of science is the falsifiability of its theories. We can never prove absolutely, but we can falsify. A set of ideas that cannot, in principle, be falsified is not science.

11   The entire creationist program includes little more than a rhetorical attempt to falsify evolution by presenting supposed contradictions among its supporters. Their brand of creationism, they claim, is "scientific" because it follows the Popperian model in trying to demolish evolution. Yet Popper's argument must apply in both directions. One does not become a scientist by the simple act of trying to falsify a rival and truly scientific system; one has to present an alternative system that also meets Popper's criterion—it too must be falsifiable in principle.

12   "Scientific creationism" is a self-contradictory, nonsense phrase precisely because it cannot be falsified. I can envision observations and experiments that would disprove any evolutionary theory I know, but I cannot imagine what potential data could lead creationists to abandon their beliefs. Unbeatable systems are dogma, not science. Lest I seem harsh or rhetorical, I quote creationism's leading intellectual, Duane Gish, Ph.D., from his recent (1978) book, *Evolution? The Fossils Say No!* "By creation we mean the bringing into being by a supernatural Creator of the basic kinds of plants and animals by the process of sudden, or fiat, creation. We do not know how the Creator created, what processes He used, *for He used processes which are not now operating anywhere in the natural universe* [Gish's italics]. This is why we refer to creation as special creation. We cannot discover by scientific investigations anything about the creative processes used by the Creator." Pray tell, Dr. Gish, in the light of your last sentence, what then is "scientific" creationism?

13   Our confidence that evolution occurred centers upon three general arguments. First, we have abundant, direct, observational evidence of evolution in action, from both field and laboratory. This evidence ranges from countless experiments on change in nearly everything about fruit flies subjected to artificial selection in the laboratory to the famous populations of British moths that became black when industrial soot darkened the trees upon which the moths rest. (Moths gain protection from sharp-sighted bird predators by blending into the background.) Creationists do not deny these observations; how could they? Creationists have

tightened their act. They now argue that God only created "basic kinds," and allowed for limited evolutionary meandering within them. Thus toy poodles and Great Danes come from the dog kind and moths can change color, but nature cannot convert a dog to a cat or a monkey to a man.

14   The second and third arguments for evolution—the case for major changes—do not involve direct observation of evolution in action. They rest upon inference, but are no less secure for that reason. Major evolutionary change requires too much time for direct observation on the scale of recorded human history. All historical sciences rest upon inference, and evolution is no different from geology, cosmology, or human history in this respect. In principle, we cannot observe processes that operated in the past. We must infer them from results that still surround us: living and fossil organisms for evolution, documents and artifacts for human history, strata and topography for geology.

15   The second argument—that the imperfection of nature reveals evolution—strikes many people as ironic, for they feel that evolution should be most elegantly displayed in the nearly perfect adaptation expressed by some organisms—the camber of a gull's wing, or butterflies that cannot be seen in ground litter because they mimic leaves so precisely. But perfection could be imposed by a wise creator or evolved by natural selection. Perfection covers the tracks of past history. And past history—the evidence of descent—is the mark of evolution.

16   Evolution lies exposed in the *imperfections* that record a history of descent. Why should a rat run, a bat fly, a porpoise swim, and I type this essay with structures built of the same bones unless we all inherited them from a common ancestor? An engineer, starting from scratch, could design better limbs in each case. Why should all the large native mammals of Australia be marsupials, unless they descended from a common ancestor isolated on this island continent? Marsupials are not "better," or ideally suited for Australia; many have been wiped out by placental mammals imported by man from other continents. This principle of imperfection extends to all historical sciences. When we recognize the etymology of September, October, November, and December (seventh, eighth, ninth, and tenth), we know that the year once started in March, or that two additional months must have been added to an original calendar of ten months.

17   The third argument is more direct: transitions are often found in the fossil record. Preserved transitions are not common—and should not be, according to our understanding of evolution . . .—but they are not entirely wanting, as creationists often claim. The lower jaw of reptiles contains several bones, that of mammals only one. The non-mammalian jawbones are reduced, step by step, in mammalian ancestors until they become tiny nubbins located at the back of the jaw. The "hammer" and "anvil" bones of the mammalian ear are descendants of these nubbins. How could such a transition be accomplished? the creationists ask. Surely a bone is either entirely in the jaw or in the ear. Yet paleontologists have discovered two transitional lineages of therapsids (the so-called mammal-like reptiles) with a double jaw joint—one composed of the old quadrate and articular bones (soon to become the hammer and anvil), the other of the squamosal and dentary bones (as in modern mammals). For that matter, what better transitional form could we expect to find than the oldest human, *Australopithecus afarensis,* with its apelike palate, its human upright stance, and a cranial capacity larger than any ape's of the same body size but a full 1,000 cubic centimeters below ours? If God made each of the half-dozen human species discovered in ancient rocks, why did he create in an unbroken temporal sequence of progressively more modern features— increasing cranial capacity, reduced face and teeth, larger body size? Did he create to mimic evolution and test our faith thereby?

18   Faced with these facts of evolution and the philosophical bankruptcy of their own position, creationists rely upon distortion and innuendo to buttress their rhetorical claim. If I sound sharp or bitter, indeed I am—for I have become a major target of these practices.

19   I count myself among the evolutionists who argue for a jerky, or episodic, rather than a smoothly gradual, pace of change. In 1972 my colleague Niles Eldredge and I developed the theory of punctuated equilibrium. We argued that two outstanding facts of the fossil record—geologically "sudden" origin of new species and failure to change thereafter (stasis)—reflect the predictions of evolutionary theory, not the imperfections of the fossil record. In most theories, small isolated populations are the source of new species, and the process of speciation takes thousands or tens of thousands of years. This amount of time, so long when measured against our lives, is a geological microsecond. It represents much less than 1 per cent of the average life-span for a fossil

invertebrate species—more than ten million years. Large, widespread, and well established species, on the other hand, are not expected to change very much. We believe that the inertia of large populations explains the stasis of most fossil species over millions of years.

20   We proposed the theory of punctuated equilibrium largely to provide a different explanation for pervasive trends in the fossil record. Trends, we argued, cannot be attributed to gradual transformation within lineages, but must arise from the differential success of certain kinds of species. A trend, we argued, is more like climbing a flight of stairs (punctuations and stasis) than rolling up an inclined plane.

21   Since we proposed punctuated equilibria to explain trends, it is infuriating to be quoted again and again by creationists— whether through design or stupidity, I do not know—as admitting that the fossil record includes no transitional forms. Transitional forms are generally lacking at the species level, but they are abundant between larger groups. Yet a pamphlet entitled "Harvard Scientists Agree Evolution Is a Hoax" states: "The facts of punctuated equilibrium which Gould and Eldredge . . . are forcing Darwinists to swallow fit the picture that Bryan insisted on, and which God has revealed to us in the Bible."

22   Continuing the distortion, several creationists have equated the theory of punctuated equilibrium with a caricature of the beliefs of Richard Goldschmidt, a great early geneticist. Goldschmidt argued, in a famous book published in 1940, that new groups can arise all at once through major mutations. He referred to these suddenly transformed creatures as "hopeful monsters." (I am attracted to some aspects of the non-caricatured version, but Goldschmidt's theory still has nothing to do with punctuated equilibrium.) Creationist Luther Sunderland talks of the "punctuated equilibrium hopeful monster theory" and tells his hopeful readers that "it amounts to tacit admission that anti-evolutionists are correct in asserting there is no fossil evidence supporting the theory that all life is connected to a common ancestor." Duane Gish writes, "According to Goldschmidt, and now apparently according to Gould, a reptile laid an egg from which the first bird, feathers and all, was produced." Any evolutionist who believed such nonsense would rightly be laughed off the intellectual stage; yet the only theory that could ever envision such a scenario for the origin of birds is creationism—with God acting in the egg.

23   I am both angry at and amused by the creationists; but mostly I am deeply sad. Sad for many reasons. Sad because so many people who respond to creationist appeals are troubled for the right reason, but venting their anger at the wrong target. It is true that scientists have often been dogmatic and elitist. It is true that we have often allowed the white-coated, advertising image to represent us—"Scientists say that Brand X cures bunions ten times faster than . . ." We have not fought it adequately because we derive benefits from appearing as a new priesthood. It is also true that faceless and bureaucratic state power intrudes more and more into our lives and removes choices that should belong to individuals and communities. I can understand that school curricula, imposed from above and without local input, might be seen as one more insult on all these grounds. But the culprit is not, and cannot be, evolution or any other fact of the natural world. Identify and fight your legitimate enemies by all means, but we are not among them.

24   I am sad because the practical result of this brouhaha will not be expanded coverage to include creationism (that would also make me sad), but the reduction or excision of evolution from high school curricula. Evolution is one of the half dozen "great ideas" developed by science. It speaks to the profound issues of genealogy that fascinate all of us—the "roots" phenomenon writ large. Where did we come from? Where did life arise? How did it develop? How are organisms related? It forces us to think, ponder, and wonder. Shall we deprive millions of this knowledge and once again teach biology as a set of dull and unconnected facts, without the thread that weaves diverse material into a supple unity?

25   But most of all I am saddened by a trend I am just beginning to discern among my colleagues. I sense that some now wish to mute the healthy debate about theory that has brought new life to evolutionary biology. It provides grist for creationist mills, they say, even if only by distortion. Perhaps we should lie low and rally around the flag of strict Darwinism, at least for the moment—a kind of old-time religion on our part.

26   But we should borrow another metaphor and recognize that we too have to tread a straight and narrow path, surrounded by roads to perdition. For if we ever begin to suppress our search to understand nature, to quench our own intellectual excitement in a misguided effort to present a united front where it does not and should not exist, then we are truly lost.

QUESTIONS

Ideas

1 How can evolution be both a theory and a fact? What do these terms mean? What is the problem in defining them? What objection does Gould raise to President Reagan's statement, "It is a scientific theory only"?

2. How does Gould's assertion, "Unbeatable systems are dogma, not science," relate to creationism's leading theorist in paragraph 12?

3. What are the three major arguments that evolution is based on? According to Gould, what tactics do creationists rely on in the face of these arguments? How does he support his accusations?

4. In writing an argument, support for one's own ideas is important, as is the careful refutation of the opposition. But equally important is the writer's persona, or voice—how the writer sounds to you. Do you trust Gould's persona here? Does he sound credible? Is he too harsh on the opposition? If you were his editor, would you advise him to change his tone in any way? Why or why not?

5. Do you find Gould's personal response in the last three paragraphs effective? Were you impressed by his aggressive stance in the last paragraph? Do you think presenting a "united front" more important than an individual's search for understanding?

Organization

6. Most theories of argument suggest that the writer first spend some time refuting the opposition's position before presenting evidence. How does Gould pay attention to this?

7. If you were to divide this essay into sections, how would you describe the purpose of each? Write a brief sentence outline of the major divisions.

8. Look at how Gould organizes paragraphs 23, 24, and 25. He begins with a focus ("but mostly I am deeply sad"). Describe how he develops this idea in the next three paragraphs.

Sentences

9. Compare the sentence patterns in paragraphs 3 and 23. Do they seem different, similar? What is Gould's purpose in each paragraph?

10. Note how Gould's sentence length varies; see for example, paragraphs 5, 6, and 7. Does he vary them enough? Is there a purpose in writing long sentences or short sentences?

Words

11. Go through this essay as if you were editing it for a junior high school class. Choose a dozen words you think you would have to explain in a glossary, then write brief definitions.

12. In the last sentence of paragraph 18, Gould admits he is sharp and bitter. Underline words or phrases that could be used to support this.

Suggestions for Writing

A. In paragraph 24 Gould says evolution is one of six "great ideas." Write an essay in which you explain, in layman's terms, other great ideas that might be included.

B. Write a 150-word summary of this essay by first going through the piece underlining key sentences. Then focus on just those sentences, changing them into your own words. Revise and edit this draft, paying attention to economy and transition between sentences.

EIGHT

Maxine Hong Kingston
(1940–   )

Although she had a novel published in 1989
(Tripmaster Monkey: His Fake Book), Maxine Hong Kingston
is best known for her earlier mixed-genre works, *The
Woman Warrior* (1976) and *China Men* (1980), winner of
the American Book Award. Kingston has described the
earlier work as the book of her mother since it is filled
with stories her mother told her, stories about Chinese
women, her Asian ancestors whom Kingston describes as
the ghosts of her girlhood. *China Men,* by contrast, is her
father's book since it tells the stories of her male ancestors, including her father and grandfathers—though she
learned these male stories too from women, especially
from her mother. Both books are filled with stories. Both
mix fact and fiction, autobiography and legend, combining in imaginative ways family history with fictional invention.

Kingston's books are, thus, difficult to classify. They
refuse to sit still and accept the tidy categories we devise
for prose narrative. The selections excerpted here from
these two family chronicles reflect the curious and striking effects Kingston achieves throughout them with her
blending of myth and legend with autobiography and
family history. Moreover, in addition to their provocative
combinations of fact and fiction, the two books possess
another striking quality: their compelling voices.
Kingston's narratives retell heard stories, stories told by
her and stories told to her. Her stories derive from an
oral tradition—the "talk story"—sustained largely by
Chinese women. Kingston thus simultaneously inherits

this oral narrative tradition and participates in it. Perhaps even more importantly, however, by inscribing her mother's stories and imagining her own variants of them, Kingston marks that tradition with her own distinctive imaginative imprint. In doing so, she demonstrates the power of these stories to enthrall readers outside the Chinese cultural tradition.

Maxine Hong Kingston was born and raised in Stockton, California, where her immigrant parents operated a laundry. She graduated from the University of California at Berkeley in 1962, and she has taught high school and college English, primarily in Hawaii, where she lived for seventeen years before moving to Oakland, California.

Kingston's autobiographical impulse appears strongly in "Silence," an excerpt from *The Woman Warrior*. In "Silence" we see Kingston begin to negotiate the struggle between the Chinese culture she inherited and the American culture she was born into. Her silence powerfully illustrates her uncertainty about how to invoke one cultural perspective without revoking or violating the other. A similar conflict of cultures emerges in "The Wild Man from the Green Swamp," an excerpt from *China Men*. Although not primarily a story about herself, this story also touches her experience, as is evident from the autobiographical conclusion to what begins as a report of a newspaper story. The significantly different voices in these pieces reveal Kingston's versatility in letting the voices of others speak through her.

This ventriloquil ability, however, is even more powerfully manifested in "No Name Woman," the opening section of *The Woman Warrior*. As Esther Schor has pointed out in *Women's Voices,* the first voice we hear in "No Name Woman" is the voice of her mother, who "ironically . . . admonishes the daughter to silence even as she nourishes her with stories." Kingston's instincts as a writer are revealed not only in the stories she chooses to tell, but in the voices she creates to tell them. This is as true for the multiple voices we hear in "No Name Woman" as for the singularly different voices that sound in the other tales Kingston narrates in both books, including the brief parable, "On Discovery," which turns gender role and power inside out.

To some extent Kingston is a woman's writer precisely because she gives public voice to what women had spoken only in private or what they had to keep silent. To some extent also she is an ethnic writer, one who transmits stories of her Cantonese heritage. Her artistry and imaginative sympathy, however, transcend the limits of both gender and culture, as Kingston invents a world and constructs a self that appear both strange and familiar, at once "other" and recognizably our own.

No Name Woman

1   "You must not tell anyone," my mother said, "what I am about to tell you. In China your father had a sister who killed herself. She jumped into the family well. We say that your father has all brothers because it is as if she had never been born.

2   "In 1924 just a few days after our village celebrated seventeen hurry-up weddings— to make sure that every young man who went 'out on the road' would responsibly come home—your father and his brothers and your grandfather and his brothers and your aunt's new husband sailed for America, the Gold Mountain. It was your grandfather's last trip. Those lucky enough to get contracts waved good-bye from the decks. They fed and guarded the stowaways and helped them off in Cuba, New York, Bali, Hawaii, 'We'll meet in California next year,' they said. All of them sent money home.

3   "I remember looking at your aunt one day when she and I were dressing; I had not noticed before that she had such a protruding melon of a stomach. But I did not think, 'She's pregnant,' until she began to look like other pregnant women, her shirt pulling and the white tops of her black pants showing. She could not have been pregnant, you see, because her husband had been gone for years. No one said anything. We did not discuss it. In early summer she was ready to have the child, long after the time when it could have been possible.

4   "The village had also been counting. On the night the baby was to be born the villagers raided our house. Some were crying. Like a great saw, teeth strung with lights, files of people walked

zigzag across our land, tearing the rice. Their lanterns doubled in the disturbed black water, which drained away through the broken bunds. As the villagers closed in, we could see that some of them, probably men and women we knew well, wore white masks. The people with long hair hung it over their faces. Women with short hair made it stand up on end. Some had tied white bands around their foreheads, arms, and legs.

5   "At first they threw mud and rocks at the house. Then they threw eggs and began slaughtering our stock. We could hear the animals scream their deaths—the roosters, the pigs, a last great roar from the ox. Familiar wild heads flared in our night windows; the villagers encircled us. Some of the faces stopped to peer at us, their eyes rushing like searchlights. The hands flattened against the panes, framed heads, and left red prints.

6   "The villagers broke in the front and the back doors at the same time, even though we had not locked the doors against them. Their knives dripped with the blood of our animals. They smeared blood on the doors and walls. One woman swung a chicken, whose throat she had slit, splattering blood in red arcs about her. We stood together in the middle of our house, in the family hall with the pictures and tables of the ancestors around us, and looked straight ahead.

7   "At that time the house had only two wings. When the men came back, we would build two more to enclose our courtyard and a third one to begin a second courtyard. The villagers pushed through both wings, even your grandparents' rooms, to find your aunt's, which was also mine until the men returned. From this room a new wing for one of the younger families would grow. They ripped up her clothes and shoes and broke her combs, grinding them underfoot. They tore her work from the loom. They scattered the cooking fire and rolled the new weaving in it. We could hear them in the kitchen breaking our bowls and banging the pots. They overturned the great waist-high earthenware jugs; duck eggs, pickled fruits, vegetables burst out and mixed in acrid torrents. The old woman from the next field swept a broom through the air and loosed the spirits-of-the-broom over our heads. 'Pig.' 'Ghost.' 'Pig,' they sobbed and scolded while they ruined our house.

8   "When they left, they took sugar and oranges to bless themselves. They cut pieces from the dead animals. Some of them took bowls that were not broken and clothes that were not torn. Afterward we swept up the rice and sewed it back up into sacks.

But the smells from the spilled preserves lasted. Your aunt gave birth in the pigsty that night. The next morning when I went for the water, I found her and the baby plugging up the family well.

9   "Don't let your father know that I told you. He denies her. Now that you have started to menstruate, what happened to her could happen to you. Don't humiliate us. You wouldn't like to be forgotten as if you had never been born. The villagers are watchful."

10   Whenever she had to warn us about life, my mother told stories that ran like this one, a story to grow up on. She tested our strength to establish realities. Those in the emigrant generations who could not reassert brute survival died young and far from home. Those of us in the first American generations have had to figure out how the invisible world the emigrants built around our childhoods fits in solid America.

11   The emigrants confused the gods by diverting their curses, misleading them with crooked streets and false names. They must try to confuse their offspring as well, who, I suppose, threaten them in similar ways—always trying to get things straight, always trying to name the unspeakable. The Chinese I know hide their names; sojourners take new names when their lives change and guard their real names with silence.

12   Chinese-Americans, when you try to understand what things in you are Chinese, how do you separate what is peculiar to childhood, to poverty, insanities, one family, your mother who marked your growing with stories, from what is Chinese? What is Chinese tradition and what is the movies?

13   If I want to learn what clothes my aunt wore, whether flashy or ordinary, I would have to begin, "Remember Father's drowned-in-the-well sister?" I cannot ask that. My mother has told me once and for all the useful parts. She will add nothing unless powered by Necessity, a riverbank that guides her life. She plants vegetable gardens rather than lawns; she carries the odd-shaped tomatoes home from the fields and eats food left for the gods.

14   Whenever we did frivolous things, we used up energy; we flew high kites. We children came up off the ground over the melting cones our parents brought home from work and the American movie on New Year's Day—*Oh, You Beautiful Doll* with Betty Grable one year, and *She Wore a Yellow Ribbon* with John Wayne another year. After the one carnival ride each, we paid in guilt; our tired father counted his change on the dark walk home.

15   Adultery is extravagance. Could people who hatch their own chicks and eat the embryos and the heads for delicacies and boil the feet in vinegar for party food, leaving only the gravel, eating even the gizzard lining—could such people engender a prodigal aunt? To be a woman, to have a daughter in starvation time was a waste enough. My aunt could not have been the lone romantic who gave up everything for sex. Women in the old China did not choose. Some man had commanded her to lie with him and be his secret evil. I wonder whether he masked himself when he joined the raid on her family.

16   Perhaps she had encountered him in the fields or on the mountain where the daughters-in-law collected fuel. Or perhaps he first noticed her in the marketplace. He was not a stranger because the village housed no strangers. She had to have dealings with him other than sex. Perhaps he worked an adjoining field, or he sold her the cloth for the dress she sewed and wore. His demand must have surprised, then terrified her. She obeyed him; she always did as she was told.

17   When the family found a young man in the next village to be her husband, she had stood tractably beside the best rooster, his proxy, and promised before they met that she would be his forever. She was lucky that he was her age and she would be the first wife, an advantage secure now. The night she first saw him, he had sex with her. Then he left for America. She had almost forgotten what he looked like. When she tried to envision him, she only saw the black and white face in the group photograph the men had had taken before leaving.

18   The other man was not, after all, much different from her husband. They both gave orders: she followed. "If you tell your family, I'll beat you. I'll kill you. Be here again next week." No one talked sex, ever. And she might have separated the rapes from the rest of living if only she did not have to buy her oil from him or gather wood in the same forest. I want her fear to have lasted just as long as rape lasted so that the fear could have been contained. No drawn-out fear. But women at sex hazarded birth and hence lifetimes. The fear did not stop but permeated everywhere. She told the man, "I think I'm pregnant." He organized the raid against her.

19   On nights when my mother and father talked about their life back home, sometimes they mentioned an "outcast table" whose business they still seemed to be settling, their voices tight.

In a commensal tradition, where food is precious, the powerful older people made wrongdoers eat alone. Instead of letting them start separate new lives like the Japanese, who could become samurais and geishas, the Chinese family, faces averted but eyes glowering sideways, hung on to the offenders and fed them leftovers. My aunt must have lived in the same house as my parents and eaten at an outcast table. My mother spoke about the raid as if she had seen it, when she and my aunt, a daughter-in-law to a different household, should not have been living together at all. Daughters-in-law lived with their husbands' parents, not their own; a synonym for marriage in Chinese is "taking a daughter-in-law." Her husband's parents could have sold her, mortgaged her, stoned her. But they had sent her back to her own mother and father, a mysterious act hinting at disgraces not told me. Perhaps they had thrown her out to deflect the avengers.

20   She was the only daughter; her four brothers went with her father, husband, and uncles "out on the road" and for some years became western men. When the goods were divided among the family, three of the brothers took land, and the youngest, my father, chose an education. After my grandparents gave their daughter away to her husband's family, they had dispensed all the adventure and all the property. They expected her alone to keep the traditional ways, which her brothers, now among the barbarians, could fumble without detection. The heavy, deep-rooted women were to maintain the past against the flood, safe for returning. But the rare urge west had fixed upon our family, and so my aunt crossed boundaries not delineated in space.

21   The work of preservation demands that the feelings playing about in one's guts not be turned into action. Just watch their passing like cherry blossoms. But perhaps my aunt, my forerunner, caught in a slow life, let dreams grow and fade and after some months or years went toward what persisted. Fear at the enormities of the forbidden kept her desires delicate, wire and bone. She looked at a man because she liked the way the hair was tucked behind his ears, or she liked the question-mark line of a long torso curving at the shoulder and straight at the hip. For warm eyes or a soft voice or a slow walk—that's all—a few hairs, a line, a brightness, a sound, a pace, she gave up family. She offered us up for a charm that vanished with tiredness, a pigtail that didn't toss when the wind died. Why, the wrong lighting could erase the dearest thing about him.

22   It could very well have been, however, that my aunt did not take subtle enjoyment of her friend, but, a wild woman, kept rollicking company. Imagining her free with sex doesn't fit, though. I don't know any women like that, or men either. Unless I see her life branching into mine, she gives me no ancestral help.

23   To sustain her being in love, she often worked at herself in the mirror, guessing at the colors and shapes that would interest him, changing them frequently in order to hit on the right combination. She wanted him to look back.

24   On a farm near the sea, a woman who tended her appearance reaped a reputation for eccentricity. All the married women blunt-cut their hair in flaps about their ears or pulled it back in tight buns. No nonsense. Neither style blew easily into heart-catching tangles. And at their weddings they displayed themselves in their long hair for the last time. "It brushed the backs of my knees," my mother tells me. "It was braided, and even so, it brushed the backs of my knees."

25   At the mirror my aunt combined individuality into her bob. A bun could have been contrived to escape into black streamers blowing in the wind or in quiet wisps about her face, but only the older women in our picture album wear buns. She brushed her hair back from her forehead, tucking the flaps behind her ears. She looped a piece of thread, knotted into a circle between her index fingers and thumbs, and ran the double strand across her forehead. When she closed her fingers as if she were making a pair of shadow geese bite, the string twisted together catching the little hairs. Then she pulled the thread away from her skin, ripping the hairs out neatly, her eyes watering from the needles of pain. Opening her fingers, she cleaned the thread, then rolled it along her hairline and the tops of her eyebrows. My mother did the same to me and my sisters and herself. I used to believe that the expression "caught by the short hairs" meant a captive held with a depilatory string. It especially hurt at the temples, but my mother said we were lucky we didn't have to have our feet bound when we were seven. Sisters used to sit on their beds and cry together, she said, as their mothers or their slave removed the bandages for a few minutes each night and let the blood gush back into their veins. I hope that the man my aunt loved appreciated a smooth brow, that he wasn't just a tits-and-ass man.

26   Once my aunt found a freckle on her chin, at a spot that the almanac said predestined her for unhappiness. She dug it out with a hot needle and washed the wound with peroxide.

27   More attention to her looks than these pullings of hairs and pickings at spots would have caused gossip among the villagers. They owned work clothes and good clothes, and they wore good clothes for feasting the new seasons. But since a woman combing her hair hexes beginnings, my aunt rarely found an occasion to look her best. Women looked like great sea snails—the corded wood, babies, and laundry they carried were the whorls on their backs. The Chinese did not admire a bent back; goddesses and warriors stood straight. Still there must have been a marvelous freeing of beauty when a worker laid down her burden and stretched and arched.

28   Such commonplace loveliness, however, was not enough for my aunt. She dreamed of a lover for the fifteen days of New Year's, the time for families to exchange visits, money, and food. She plied her secret comb. And sure enough she cursed the year, the family, the village, and herself.

29   Even as her hair lured her imminent lover, many other men looked at her. Uncles, cousins, nephews, brothers would have looked, too, had they been home between journeys. Perhaps they had already been restraining their curiosity, and they left, fearful that their glances, like a field of nesting birds, might be startled and caught. Poverty hurt, and that was their first reason for leaving. But another, final reason for leaving the crowded house was the never-said.

30   She may have been unusually beloved, the precious only daughter, spoiled and mirror gazing because of the affection the family lavished on her. When her husband left, they welcomed the chance to take her back from the in-laws; she could live like the little daughter for just a while longer. There are stories that my grandfather was different from other people, "crazy ever since the little Jap bayoneted him in the head." He used to put his naked penis on the dinner table, laughing. And one day he brought home a baby girl, wrapped up inside his brown western-style greatcoat. He had traded one of his sons, probably my father, the youngest, for her. My grandmother made him trade back. When he finally got a daughter of his own, he doted on her. They must have all loved her, except perhaps my father, the only brother who never went back to China, having once been traded for a girl.

31   Brothers and sisters, newly men and women, had to efface their sexual color and present plain miens. Disturbing hair and eyes, a smile like no other, threatened the ideal of five genera-

tions living under one roof. To focus blurs, people shouted face to face and yelled from room to room. The immigrants I know have loud voices, unmodulated to American tones even after years away from the village where they called their friendships out across the fields. I have not been able to stop my mother's screams in public libraries or over telephones. Walking erect (knees straight, toes pointed forward, not pigeon-toed, which is Chinese-feminine) and speaking in an inaudible voice, I have tried to turn myself American-feminine. Chinese communication was loud, public. Only sick people had to whisper. But at the dinner table, where the family members came nearest one another, no one could talk, not the outcasts nor any eaters. Every word that falls from the mouth is a coin lost. Silently they gave and accepted food with both hands. A preoccupied child who took his bowl with one hand got a sideways glare. A complete moment of total attention is due everyone alike. Children and lovers have no singularity here, but my aunt used a secret voice, a separate attentiveness.

32   She kept the man's name to herself throughout her labor and dying; she did not accuse him that he be punished with her. To save her inseminator's name she gave silent birth.

33   He may have been somebody in her own household, but intercourse with a man outside the family would have been no less abhorrent. All the village were kinsmen, and the titles shouted in loud country voices never let kinship be forgotten. Any man within visiting distance would have been neutralized as a lover— "brother," "younger brother," "older brother"—one hundred and fifteen relationship titles. Parents researched birth charts probably not so much to assure good fortune as to circumvent incest in a population that has but one hundred surnames. Everybody has eight million relatives. How useless then sexual mannerisms, how dangerous.

34   As if it came from an atavism deeper than fear, I used to add "brother" silently to boys' names. It hexed the boys, who would or would not ask me to dance, and made them less scary and as familiar and deserving of benevolence as girls.

35   But, of course, I hexed myself also—no dates. I should have stood up, both arms waving, and shouted out across libraries, "Hey, you! Love me back." I had no idea, though, how to make attraction selective, how to control its direction and magnitude. If I made myself American-pretty so that the five or six Chinese boys in the class fell in love with me, everyone else—the Caucasian,

Negro, and Japanese boys—would too. Sisterliness, dignified and honorable, made much more sense.

36 Attraction eludes control so stubbornly that whole societies designed to organize relationships among people cannot keep order, not even when they bind people to one another from childhood and raise them together. Among the very poor and the wealthy, brothers married their adopted sisters, like doves. Our family allowed some romance, paying adult brides' prices and providing dowries so that their sons and daughters could marry strangers. Marriage promises to turn strangers into friendly relatives—a nation of siblings.

37 In the village structure, spirits shimmered among the live creatures, balanced and held in equilibrium by time and land. But one human being flaring up into violence could open up a black hole, a maelstrom that pulled in the sky. The frightened villagers, who depended on one another to maintain the real, went to my aunt to show her a personal, physical representation of the break she had made in the "roundness." Misallying couples snapped off the future, which was to be embodied in true offspring. The villagers punished her for acting as if she could have a private life, secret and apart from them.

38 If my aunt had betrayed the family at a time of large grain yields and peace, when many boys were born, and wings were being built on many houses, perhaps she might have escaped such severe punishment. But the men—hungry, greedy, tired of planting in dry soil—and had been forced to leave the village in order to send food-money home. There were ghost plagues, bandit plagues, wars with the Japanese, floods. My Chinese brother and sister had died of an unknown sickness. Adultery, perhaps only a mistake during good times, became a crime when the village needed food.

39 The round moon cakes and round doorways, the round tables of graduated size that fit one roundness inside another, round windows and rice bowls—these talismans had lost their power to warn this family of the law: a family must be whole, faithfully keeping the descent line by having sons to feed the old and the dead, who in turn look after the family. The villagers came to show my aunt and her lover-in-hiding a broken house. The villagers were speeding up the circling of events because she was too shortsighted to see that her infidelity had already harmed the village, that waves of consequences would return unpredictably, sometimes in disguise, as now, to hurt her. This roundness had to

be made coin-sized so that she would see its circumference: punish her at the birth of her baby. Awaken her to the inexorable. People who refused fatalism because they could invent small resources insisted on culpability. Deny accidents and wrest fault from the stars.

40   After the villagers left, their lanterns now scattering in various directions toward home, the family broke their silence and cursed her. "Aiaa, we're going to die. Death is coming. Death is coming. Look what you've done. You've killed us. Ghost! Dead ghost! Ghost! You've never been born." She ran out into the fields, far enough from the house so that she could no longer hear their voices, and pressed herself against the earth, her own land no more. When she felt the birth coming, she thought that she had been hurt. Her body seized together. "They've hurt me too much," she thought. "This is gall, and it will kill me." With forehead and knees against the earth, her body convulsed and then relaxed. She turned on her back, lay on the ground. The black well of sky and stars went out and out and out forever; her body and her complexity seemed to disappear. She was one of the stars, a bright dot in blackness, without home, without a companion, in eternal cold and silence. An agoraphobia rose in her, speeding higher and higher, bigger and bigger; she would not be able to contain it; there would be no end to fear.

41   Flayed, unprotected against space, she felt pain return, focusing her body. This pain chilled her—a cold, steady kind of surface pain. Inside, spasmodically, the other pain, the pain of the child, heated her. For hours she lay on the ground, alternately body and space. Sometimes a vision of normal comfort obliterated reality: she saw the family in the evening gambling at the dinner table, the young people massaging their elders' backs. She saw them congratulating one another, high joy on the mornings the rice shoots came up. When these pictures burst, the stars drew yet further apart. Black space opened.

42   She got to her feet to fight better and remembered that old-fashioned women gave birth in their pigsties to fool the jealous, pain-dealing gods, who do not snatch piglets. Before the next spasms could stop her, she ran to the pigsty, each step a rushing out into emptiness. She climbed over the fence and knelt in the dirt. It was good to have a fence enclosing her, a tribal person alone.

43   Laboring, this woman who had carried her child as a foreign

growth that sickened her every day, expelled it at last. She reached down to touch the hot, wet, moving mass, surely smaller than anything human, and could feel that it was human after all— fingers, toes, nails, nose. She pulled it up on to her belly, and it lay curled there, butt in the air, feet precisely tucked one under the other. She opened her loose shirt and buttoned the child inside. After resting, it squirmed and thrashed and she pushed it up to her breast. It turned its head this way and that until it found her nipple. There, it made little snuffling noises. She clenched her teeth at its preciousness, lovely as a young calf, a piglet, a little dog.

44   She may have gone to the pigsty as a last act of responsibility: she would protect this child as she had protected its father. It would look after her soul, leaving supplies on her grave. But how would this tiny child without family find her grave when there would be no marker for her anywhere, neither in the earth nor the family hall? No one would give her a family hall name. She had taken the child with her into the wastes. At its birth the two of them had felt the same raw pain of separation, a wound that only the family pressing tight could close. A child with no descent line would not soften her life but only trail after her, ghostlike, begging her to give it purpose. At dawn the villagers on their way to the fields would stand around the fence and look.

45   Full of milk, the little ghost slept. When it awoke, she hardened her breasts against the milk that crying loosens. Toward morning she picked up the baby and walked to the well.

46   Carrying the baby to the well shows loving. Otherwise abandon it. Turn its face into the mud. Mothers who love their children take them along. It was probably a girl; there is some hope of forgiveness for boys.

47   "Don't tell anyone you had an aunt. Your father does not want to hear her name. She has never been born." I have believed that sex was unspeakable and words so strong and fathers so frail that "aunt" would do my father mysterious harm. I have thought that my family, having settled among immigrants who had also been their neighbors in the ancestral land, needed to clean their name, and a wrong word would incite the kinspeople even here. But there is more to this silence: they want me to participate in her punishment. And I have.

48   In the twenty years since I heard this story I have not asked

for details nor said my aunt's name; I do not know it. People who can comfort the dead can also chase after them to hurt them further—a reverse ancestor worship. The real punishment was not the raid swiftly inflicted by the villagers, but the family's deliberately forgetting her. Her betrayal so maddened them, they saw to it that she would suffer forever, even after death. Always hungry, always needing, she would have to beg food from other ghosts, snatch and steal it from those whose living descendants give them gifts. She would have to fight the ghosts massed at crossroads for the buns a few thoughtful citizens leave to decoy her away from village and home so that the ancestral spirits could feast unharassed. At peace, they could act like gods, not ghosts, their descent lines providing them with paper suits and dresses, spirit money, paper houses, paper automobiles, chicken, meat, and rice into eternity—essences delivered up in smoke and flames, steam and incense rising from each rice bowl. In an attempt to make the Chinese care for people outside the family, Chairman Mao encourages us now to give our paper replicas to the spirits of outstanding soldiers and workers, no matter whose ancestors they may be. My aunt remains forever hungry. Goods are not distributed evenly among the dead.

49   My aunt haunts me—her ghost drawn to me because now, after fifty years of neglect, I alone devote pages of paper to her, though not origamied into houses and clothes. I do not think she always means me well. I am telling on her, and she was a spite suicide, drowning herself in the drinking water. The Chinese are always very frightened of the drowned one, whose weeping ghost, wet hair hanging and skin bloated, waits silently by the water to pull down a substitute.

QUESTIONS

Ideas

1. What is the point of the story about the writer's aunt, the "no name woman"? How does Kingston reveal its significance?

2. What ideas about cultural origins emerge from this selection? How important are the cultural origins that Kingston describes? Which does she feature most prominently? Why?

3. How are women portrayed? What details does Kingston select to represent relations between men and woman?

Organization

4. Kingston begins this piece with a shocking family story. What is the effect of opening with this story rather than working it in later?
5. Kingston, in part, fictionalizes her aunt's story, imagining her possible motives and feelings. How does the writer shape, organize, and dramatize these details?

Sentences

6. Choose two sentences that you find particularly effective. Explain the source of their power and your pleasure.

Words

7. Kingston describes the Chinese family "circle" and what she calls the "roundness" of family life. Explain the significance of these words and comment on their aptness.
8. Another set of words haunting this essay concerns secrecy and silence. Find examples of such words and explain their significance.

Suggestions for Writing

A. Tell a family story that has been part of your family lore. It may be serious or humorous, one well known in your family or one that has been kept secret.
B. Compare the way Kingston blends fact and fiction in this piece with the way Richard Selzer combines fact and fiction in "Imelda."

On Discovery

---

1   Once upon a time, a man, named Tang Ao, looking for the Gold Mountain, crossed an ocean, and came upon the Land of Women. The women immediately captured him, not on guard against ladies. When they asked Tang Ao to come along, he followed; if he had had male companions, he would've winked over his shoulder.

2   "We have to prepare you to meet the queen," the women said. They locked him in a canopied apartment equipped with pots of makeup, mirrors, and a woman's clothes. "Let us help you

off with your armor and boots," said the women. They slipped his coat off his shoulders, pulled it down his arms, and shackled his wrists behind him. The women who kneeled to take off his shoes chained his ankles together.

3   A door opened, and he expected to meet his match, but it was only two old women with sewing boxes in their hands. "The less you struggle, the less it'll hurt," one said, squinting a bright eye as she threaded her needle. Two captors sat on him while another held his head. He felt an old woman's dry fingers trace his ear; the long nail on her little finger scraped his neck. "What are you doing?" he asked. "Sewing your lips together," she joked, blackening needles in a candle flame. The ones who sat on him bounced with laughter. But the old woman did not sew his lips together. They pulled his earlobes taut and jabbed a needle through each of them. They had to poke and probe before puncturing the layers of skin correctly, the hole in the front of the lobe in line with the one in back, the layers of skin sliding about so. They worked the needle through—a last jerk for the needle's wide eye ("needle's nose" in Chinese). They strung his raw flesh with silk threads; he could feel the fibers.

4   The women who sat on him turned to direct their attention to his feet. They bent his toes so far backward that his arched foot cracked. The old ladies squeezed each foot and broke many tiny bones along the sides. They gathered his toes, toes over and under one another like a knot of ginger root. Tang Ao wept with pain. As they wound the bandages tight and tighter around his feet, the women sang footbinding songs to distract him: "Use aloe for binding feet and not for scholars."

5   During the months of a season, they fed him on women's food: the tea was thick with white chrysanthemums and stirred the cool female winds inside his body; chicken wings made his hair shine; vinegar soup improved his womb. They drew the loops of thread through the scabs that grew daily over the holes in his earlobes. One day they inserted gold hoops. Every night they unbound his feet, but his veins had shrunk, and the blood pumping through them hurt so much, he begged to have his feet rewrapped tight. They forced him to wash his used bandages, which were embroidered with flowers and smelled of rot and cheese. He hung the bandages up to dry, streamers that drooped and draped wall to wall. He felt embarrassed; the wrappings were like underwear, and they were his.

6   One day his attendants changed his gold hoops to jade studs and strapped his feet to shoes that curved like bridges. They plucked out each hair on his face, powdered him white, painted his eyebrows like a moth's wings, painted his cheeks and lips red. He served a meal at the queen's court. His hips swayed and his shoulders swiveled because of his shaped feet. "She's pretty, don't you agree?" the diners said, smacking their lips at his dainty feet as he bent to put dishes before them.

7   In the Women's Land there are no taxes and no wars. Some scholars say that that country was discovered during the reign of Empress Wu (A.D. 694–705), and some say earlier than that, A.D. 441, and it was in North America.

QUESTIONS

Ideas

1. What is Kingston's point here? To what extent is her piece about gender? About roles? About power?
2. How important is it that Kingston describes a *man* becoming a woman? To what extent does the effect, power, and point of this selection hinge upon and depend upon a man's suffering the fate of a woman?

Organization

3. How has Kingston arranged this story to foreground its ironies? What are those ironies?
4. What is the purpose of the final sentence? Why is it separated from the story proper, and what is its relation to the story?

Sentences

5. How does Kingston achieve a simplicity and directness of style suitable to a parable like this? Identify three sentences that illustrate such stylistic directness and simplicity.
6. How would you describe the tone of the piece? What do the half dozen uses of dialogue contribute to this tone?

Words

7. Identify all the words Kingston uses to indicate physical action. What is their cumulative effect? (Pay particular attention to verbs.)

8. Select two uses of comparison, explain their significance, and comment on their effectiveness.

Suggestions for Writing

A. Discuss the following comment by Simone de Beauvoir in relation to "On Discovery": "One Is Not Born a Woman; One Becomes a Woman."

B. In the spirit of Kingston's parable, write your own story describing a reversal of gender roles.

C. Compare Kingston's depiction of gender roles and their reversal here with Gretel Ehrlich's discussion of gender attitudes in "About Men."

The Wild Man of the Green Swamp

---

1   For eight months in 1975, residents on the edge of Green Swamp, Florida, had been reporting to the police that they had seen a Wild Man. When they stepped toward him, he made strange noises as in a foreign language and ran back into the saw grass. At first, authorities said the Wild Man was a mass hallucination. Man-eating animals lived in the swamp, and a human being could hardly find a place to rest without sinking. Perhaps it was some kind of a bear the children had seen.

2   In October, a game officer saw a man crouched over a small fire, but as he approached, the figure ran away. It couldn't have been a bear because the Wild Man dragged a burlap bag after him. Also, the fire was obviously man-made.

3   The fish-and-game wardens and the sheriff's deputies entered the swamp with dogs but did not search for long; no one could live in the swamp. The mosquitoes alone would drive him out.

4   The Wild Man made forays out of the swamp. Farmers encountered him taking fruit and corn from the turkeys. He broke into a house trailer, but the occupant came back, and the Wild Man escaped out a window. The occupant said that a bad

smell came off the Wild Man. Usually, the only evidence of him were his abandoned campsites. At one he left the remains of a four-foot-long alligator, of which he had eaten the feet and tail.

5   In May a posse made an air and land search; the plane signaled down to the hunters on the ground, who circled the Wild Man. A fish-and-game warden "brought him down with a tackle," according to the news. The Wild Man fought, but they took him to jail. He looked Chinese, so they found a Chinese in town to come translate.

6   The Wild Man talked a lot to the translator. He told him his name. He said he was thirty-nine years old, the father of seven children, who were in Taiwan. To support them, he had shipped out on a Liberian freighter. He had gotten very homesick and asked everyone if he could leave the ship and go home. But the officers would not let him off. They sent messages to China to find out about him. When the ship landed, they took him to the airport and tried to put him on an airplane to some foreign place. Then, he said, the white demons took him to Tampa Hospital, which is for insane people, but he escaped, just walked out and went into the swamp.

7   The interpreter asked how he lived in the swamp. He said he ate snakes, turtles, armadillos, and alligators. The captors could tell how he lived when they opened up his bag, which was not burlap but a pair of pants with the legs knotted. Inside, he had carried a pot, a piece of sharpened tin, and a small club, which he had made by sticking a railroad spike into a section of aluminum tubing.

8   The sheriff found the Liberian freighter that the Wild Man had been on. The ship's officers said that they had not tried to stop him from going home. His shipmates had decided that there was something wrong with his mind. They had bought him a plane ticket and arranged his passport to send him back to China. They had driven him to the airport, but there he began screaming and weeping and would not get on the plane. So they had found him a doctor, who sent him to Tampa Hospital.

9   Now the doctors at the jail gave him medicine for the mosquito bites, which covered his entire body, and medicine for his stomachache. He was getting better, but after he'd been in jail for three days, the U.S. Border Patrol told him they were sending him back. He became hysterical. That night, he fastened his belt to the bars, wrapped it around his neck, and hung himself.

10   In the newspaper picture he did not look very wild, being led by the posse out of the swamp. He did not look dirty, either. He wore a checkered shirt unbuttoned at the neck, where his white undershirt showed; his shirt was tucked into his pants; his hair was short. He was surrounded by men in cowboy hats. His fingers stretching open, his wrists pulling apart to the extent of the handcuffs, he lifted his head, his eyes screwed shut, and cried out.

11   There was a Wild Man in our slough too, only he was a black man. He wore a shirt and no pants, and some mornings when we walked to school, we saw him asleep under the bridge. The police came and took him away. The newspaper said he was crazy; it said the police had been on the lookout for him for a long time, but we had seen him every day.

QUESTIONS

Ideas

1. What is the central concern of this piece? Madness? Survival? Cultural difference? Something else?
2. Why does the Wild Man not want to return to Taiwan? Why does he live as he does? Why does he hang himself?

Organization

3. Kingston includes two different time frames in this piece: the past, in which she describes a memory from her youth; the present, in which she tells the story of the Wild Man. What connection exists between these two stories?
4. What is the advantage of beginning with the later story—that of the Wild Man—rather than with her childhood memory?

Sentences

5. Kingston keeps her sentences and paragraphs short. Why? With what effect?
6. Notice how many of Kingston's sentences follow the subject-verb-object pattern. Notice too how often her sentences begin with nouns and pronouns: "he," "they," "the Wild Man," "the inter-

prefer," "the deputy," "the sheriff," "the occupant," etc. What is the effect of this feature of sentence style in this piece?

Words

7. Why does Kingston continue to describe the Chinese man as the "Wild Man" even when his name becomes known? Why does she capitalize the term?
8. Look back at the selection of details in paragraph 10. Account for the references to "posse" and "cowboy hats" and comment on the effect of the description of the Wild Man.

Suggestions for Writing

A. Consider a time when something you read or saw in the news triggered a childhood memory. Describe the news account and reconstruct the memory. Then explain their connection.
B. Discuss what this selection implies about language and culture, especially about linguistic and cultural differences. You might like to compare the depiction of the Wild Man as an "other" with Kingston's portrayal of "otherness" in "No Name Woman."

Silence

---

1   When I went to kindergarten and had to speak English for the first time, I became silent. A dumbness—a shame—still cracks my voice in two, even when I want to say "hello" casually, or ask an easy question in front of the check-out counter, or ask directions of a bus driver. I stand frozen, or I hold up the line with the complete, grammatical sentence that comes squeaking out at impossible length. "What did you say?" says the cab driver, or "Speak up," so I have to perform again, only weaker the second time. A telephone call makes my throat bleed and takes up that day's courage. It spoils my day with self-disgust when I hear my broken voice come skittering out into the open. It makes people wince to hear it. I'm getting better, though. Recently I asked the postman for special-issue stamps; I've waited since childhood for postmen to give me some of their own accord. I am making progress, a little every day.

2   My silence was thickest—total—during the three years that I
covered my school paintings with black paint. I painted layers of
black over houses and flowers and suns, and when I drew on the
blackboard, I put a layer of chalk on top. I was making a stage curtain, and it was the moment before the curtain parted or rose.
The teachers called my parents to school, and I saw they had been
saving my pictures, curling and cracking, all alike and black. The
teachers pointed to the pictures and looked serious, talked seriously too, but my parents did not understand English. ("The parents and teachers of criminals were executed," said my father.) My
parents took the pictures home. I spread them out (so black and
full of possibilities) and pretended the curtains were swinging
open, flying up, one after another, sunlight underneath, mighty
operas.

3   During the first silent year I spoke to no one at school, did
not ask before going to the lavatory, and flunked kindergarten.
My sister also said nothing for three years, silent in the playground and silent at lunch. There were other quiet Chinese girls
not of our family, but most of them got over it sooner than we
did. I enjoyed the silence. At first it did not occur to me I was supposed to talk or to pass kindergarten. I talked at home and to one
or two of the Chinese kids in class. I made motions and even
made some jokes. I drank out of a toy saucer when the water
spilled out of the cup, and everybody laughed, pointing at me, so
I did it some more. I didn't know that Americans don't drink out
of saucers.

4   I liked the Negro students (Black Ghosts) best because they
laughed the loudest and talked to me as if I were a daring talker
too. One of the Negro girls had her mother coil braids over her
ears Shanghai-style like mine; we were Shanghai twins except that
she was covered with black like my paintings. Two Negro kids
enrolled in Chinese school, and the teachers gave them Chinese
names. Some Negro kids walked me to school and home, protecting me from the Japanese kids, who hit me and chased me and
stuck gum in my ears. The Japanese kids were noisy and tough.
They appeared one day in kindergarten, released from concentration camp, which was a tic-tac-toe mark, like barbed wire, on the
map.

5   It was when I found out I had to talk that school become a
misery, that the silence became a misery. I did not speak and felt
bad each time that I did not speak. I read aloud in first grade,

though, and heard the barest whisper with little squeaks come out of my throat. "Louder," said the teacher, who scared the voice away again. The other Chinese girls did not talk either, so I knew the silence had to do with being a Chinese girl.

6   Reading out loud was easier than speaking because we did not have to make up what to say, but I stopped often, and the teacher would think I'd gone quiet again. I could not understand "I." The Chinese "I" has seven strokes, intricacies. How could the American "I," assuredly wearing a hat like the Chinese, have only three strokes, the middle so straight? Was it out of politeness that this writer left off the strokes the way a Chinese has to write her own name small and crooked? No, it was not politeness; "I" is a capital and "you" is lower-case. I stared at that middle line and waited so long for its black center to resolve into tight strokes and dots that I forgot to pronounce it. The other troublesome word was "here," no strong consonant to hang on to, and so flat, when "here" is two mountainous ideographs. The teacher, who had already told me every day how to read "I" and "here," put me in the low corner under the stairs again, where the noisy boys usually sat.

7   When my second grade class did a play, the whole class went to the auditorium except the Chinese girls. The teacher, lovely and Hawaiian, should have understood about us, but instead left us behind in the classroom. Our voices were too soft or nonexistent, and our parents never signed the permission slips anyway. They never signed anything unnecessary. We opened the door a crack and peeked out, but closed it again quickly. One of us (not me) won every spelling bee, though.

8   I remember telling the Hawaiian teacher, "We Chinese can't sing 'land where our fathers died.'" She argued with me about politics, while I meant because of curses. But how can I have that memory when I couldn't talk? My mother says that we, like the ghosts, have no memories.

9   After American school, we picked up our cigar boxes, in which we had arranged books, brushes, and an inkbox neatly, and went to Chinese school, from 5:00 to 7:30 P.M. There we chanted together, voices rising and falling, loud and soft, some boys shouting, everybody reading together, reciting together and not alone with one voice. When we had a memorization test, the teacher let each of us come to his desk and say the lesson to him privately, while the rest of the class practiced copying or tracing. Most of

the teachers were men. The boys who were so well behaved in the American school played tricks on them and talked back to them. The girls were not mute. They screamed and yelled during recess, when there were no rules; they had fistfights. Nobody was afraid of children hurting themselves or of children hurting school property. The glass doors to the red and green balconies with the gold joy symbols were left wide open so that we could run out and climb the fire escapes. We played capture-the-flag in the auditorium, where Sun Yat-sen and Chiang Kai-shek's pictures hung at the back of the stage, the Chinese flag on their left and the American flag on their right. We climbed the teak ceremonial chairs and made flying leaps off the stage. One flag headquarters was behind the glass door and the other on stage right. Our feet drummed on the hollow stage. During recess the teachers locked themselves up in their office with the shelves of books, copybooks, inks from China. They drank tea and warmed their hands at a stove. There was no play supervision. At recess we had the school to ourselves, and also we could roam as far as we could go—downtown, Chinatown stores, home—as long as we returned before the bell rang.

10   At exactly 7:30 the teacher again picked up the brass bell that sat on his desk and swung it over our heads, while we charged down the stairs, our cheering magnified in the stairwell. Nobody had to line up.

11   Not all of the children who were silent at American school found voice at Chinese school. One new teacher said each of us had to get up and recite in front of the class, who was to listen. My sister and I had memorized the lesson perfectly. We said it to each other at home, one chanting, one listening. The teacher called on my sister to recite first. It was the first time a teacher had called on the second-born to go first. My sister was scared. She glanced at me and looked away; I looked down at my desk. I hoped that she could do it because if she could, then I would have to. She opened her mouth and a voice came out that wasn't a whisper, but it wasn't a proper voice either. I hoped that she would not cry, fear breaking up her voice like twigs underfoot. She sounded as if she were trying to sing through weeping and strangling. She did not pause or stop to end the embarrassment. She kept going until she said the last word, and then she sat down. When it was my turn, the same voice came out, a crippled animal running on broken legs. You could hear splinters in my voice, bones rubbing

jagged against one another. I was loud, though. I was glad I didn't whisper.

12   How strange that the emigrant villagers are shouters, hollering face to face. My father asks, "Why is it I can hear Chinese from blocks away? Is it that I understand the language? Or is it they talk loud?" They turn the radio up full blast to hear the operas, which do not seem to hurt their ears. And they yell over the singers that wail over the drums, everybody talking at once, big arm gestures, spit flying. You can see the disgust on American faces looking at women like that. It isn't just the loudness. It is the way Chinese sounds, ching-chong ugly, to American ears, not beautiful like Japanese sayonara words with the consonants and vowels as regular as Italian. We make guttural peasant noise and have Ton Duc Thang names you can't remember. And the Chinese can't hear Americans at all; the language is too soft and western music unhearable. I've watched a Chinese audience laugh, visit, talk-story, and holler during a piano recital, as if the musician could not hear them. A Chinese-American, somebody's son, was playing Chopin, which has no punctuation, no cymbals, no gongs. Chinese piano music is five black keys. Normal Chinese women's voices are strong and bossy. We American-Chinese girls had to whisper to make ourselves American-feminine. Apparently we whispered even more softly than the Americans. Once a year the teachers referred my sister and me to speech therapy, but our voices would straighten out, unpredictably normal, for the therapists. Some of us gave up, shook our heads, and said nothing, not one word. Some of us could not even shake our heads. At times shaking my head no is more self-assertion than I can manage. Most of us eventually found some voice, however faltering. We invented an American-feminine speaking personality.

QUESTIONS

Ideas

1. Why was Kingston silent in school for so long? Explain the extent to which her silence was culturally conditioned.

2. Consider Kingston's comments about the pronoun "I." What troubles her about it? Why does it pose a problem not only for her but for other Chinese immigrant girls as well?

3. Explain what you think Kingston means when she says that she and
    her friend "eventually found some voice" and that they "invented an
    American-feminine speaking personality."

Organization

4. Kingston arranges her piece partly by contrasting silence with noise.
    Identify and explain the significant features of this noise-silence
    contrast.
5. Explain the logic of development in this selection. Comment on the
    writer's developing thought as she advances from one paragraph to
    the next. Explain how the various facets of her thought emerge.

Sentences

6. Examine the questions Kingston raises in paragraphs 6 and 11.
    What is the effect of including questions in these paragraphs?
    Would they have been better as statements? Why or why not?
7. In paragraphs 1, 2, and 9 Kingston interrupts the flow of her sen-
    tences with double-dash interpolations. Comment on the point and
    purpose of each use of the double dash.

Words

8. Identify the words Kingston uses to refer to speech and silence.
    Explain their significance.
9. Consider the comparisons Kingston employs in paragraph 11.
    Comment on their point, purpose, and effect.

Suggestions for Writing

A. Discuss a time when you were more comfortable with silence than
    with speech. Identify the circumstances, describe your feelings, and
    explain how you moved from silence to speech—or how you did not.
B. Compare Kingston's discussion of culturally induced silence with
    that of Richard Rodriquez.

NINE

Barry Lopez
(1945–   )

In our newspapers and magazines we read about
and are impressed by the need for ecological responsibility. And so we recycle what we can; we conserve energy; we
are concerned about our water, our air; we bemoan the
damage done to our surroundings by oil spills, toxic
dumpsites, and industrial and auto pollution. Although
growing numbers of concerned citizens are trying to
understand how we could have been so oblivious to the
declining condition of the natural world, a large part of
our culture still seems unaffected by the crisis in our environment. Perhaps this is so because many Americans live
in cities where our actual contact with nature is so limited
and so distorted by steel and concrete that we no longer
have a feel for what the natural world might be. Perhaps
we suffer from a massive, culturally self-induced, disorien-
tation; perhaps we can no longer see ourselves blending
into the natural world. With our ancient memories
repressed, we see the natural world as merely a vacation
possibility, as entertainment and spectacle; we see other
forms of life who live there as alien things, removed from
our concern. We are skeptical that nature or animals can
teach us how to live in corporate America.

Such a situation cries out for a special voice, one
that can remind us of the interconnectedness of humans
and the natural world. For the past fifteen years or so
Barry Lopez has been a lyrical, informed, and passionate
advocate for a renewed connection between our cultural
and individual imaginations and wild places, for a re-
enchantment with natural landscapes that can teach us

who we are, where we came from, and where we might
tragically go if we do not find again our place in nature.

Barry Lopez, who lives on the McKenzie River in the
Oregon woods with his wife, was born just outside New
York City, but spent his childhood in Southern California,
an emotionally imprinting experience that greatly
influenced his attachment to the West. He returned to
Manhattan to go to high school and then went to the
University of Notre Dame where he received his B.A. in
1966 and a master's in teaching two years later. Although
he has been a distinguished visiting writer at the
University of Iowa and a distinguished visiting naturalist
at Carlton College, as well as an editor at *Harper's* and the
North American Review, he makes his living writing about
the wilderness.

Growing out of his graduate work in folklore,
Lopez's first book, *Giving Birth to Thunder, Sleeping With
His Daughter,* was a retelling of Native American tales
about the coyote as a trickster figure. In 1978 he published *Of Wolves and Men,* a book that began as an assignment for the magazine *Smithsonian,* and turned into one
of the most highly praised nature books of the decade.
Although Lopez did prodigious research, focusing on the
ancient history of wolves, how they have been portrayed
in books and myth in various cultures, what Eskimos knew
of them as well as what responsible scientific studies
revealed about their behavior, Lopez still maintains that
he wants his readers to see the wolf as a symbol of our
uninformed treatment of all animals. Lopez tries to
understand those who abused the wolf, especially the
hunters, ranchers, and biased scientists who were social-
ized in a different cultural framework when the wolf was
considered evil. As a writer he doesn't assign blame;
instead, he gives his readers new sources of knowledge
about wolves. He hopes our culture might arrive at a
more rational and compassionate view of the rightful
place of animals in nature.

*Arctic Dream: Imagination and Desire in a Northern
Landscape* (1986) won for Lopez the National Book Award
for nonfiction. Reviews described it as "a splendid book,
passionate and compassionate, by a man who is both a
first-rate writer and an uncompromising defender of the
wild country and its native inhabitants." Edward Hoagland, writing in the *New York Times Book Review,* says that

Lopez is "a master nature writer" who has "brought his
talent for close observation, empathy, freshness and wonder to a major effort north of the treeline . . . the gift of
sight (and second sight) focused here upon the ocean,
ice, skyscapes, landscapes, and wildlife is extraordinary."
Here are a few short but typical passages from *Arctic
Dreams:*

> I looked up at the icebergs. They so embodied the land.
> Austere. Implacable. Harsh but not antagonistic. Creatures of
> pale light. Once, a friend had said, gazing off across a broad
> glacial valley of soft greens and straw browns, that it was so beau-
> tiful it made you cry. . . . I looked out at the icebergs. They
> were so beautiful they also made you afraid.

> To the explorer, the land becomes large, alive like an ani-
> mal; it humbles him in a way he cannot pronounce. It is not that
> the land is simply beautiful but that it is powerful. Its power
> derives from the tension between its obvious beauty and its
> capacity to take life. Its power flows into the mind from a real-
> ization of how darkness and light are bound together within it,
> and the feeling that this is the floor of creation.

As in *Of Wolves and Men,* this expansive book is filled
with a wealth of factual information. His definition of
landscape is so inclusive, involving animals, trees, vegetation, temperature, sounds, even drainage, that his perspective and range are truly interdisciplinary. Lopez also
demonstrates his ability as a vigorous, lyrical prose stylist
that one reviewer called "deft and vivid." Another writes
that he "infuses each sentence with grace." Yet he always
uses his evocative prose for a purpose: he wants us to
question our place in the universe, to wonder if we can
find a way to adapt to the natural world before we destroy
it. He also hopes we can lose our desire to think of our
planet as so much clay we can mold to our desires, our
whims. He uses his knowledge and skill to persuade us.
His travels in the Arctic have a deep purpose. His odyssey
across the dazzling Arctic landscape is "a symphony of
movement—massive migrations, swirling storms, graceful
floes . . . solar and lunar rings, haloes, coronas, mountainous mirages, and the awesome aurora borealis."
Lopez wants to draw us into this place so that it may grip
our hearts and our imaginations and so that finally, long
after we've finished reading the book, we will be left with

a renewed respect for the necessity to understand our interrelationship with the planet.

Crossing Open Ground (1989) brings together over a dozen of Lopez's published essays from such magazines as *Harper's* and *Antaeus* on a range of topics from bull riders, seals, and whales to narrative theory and Cortes. One reviewer writes that "Barry Lopez is the best nature writer of our decade, repeatedly reminding us of the age-old ties between the wild places and humanity." Another claims that he makes readers feel at home with themselves and the world: "Anyone who has ever felt lost should read this book." With these essays, Lopez establishes himself as a nature writer in the same class as Annie Dillard, Loren Eiseley, and Edward Hoagland. Like these writers, Lopez combines his intricate knowledge of nature and his sensitivity to its elusive nuances with a commitment to say something significant about the human condition. Even his novels, *Winter Count* and *River Notes* (1979), focus on the wilderness as an illuminating place where wonder and imagination can be a respite from television, political chicanery, and crass materialism. There is, he notes, a "clarity in stillness."

In our first selection, "The Stone Horse," Lopez crosses genres, blends cultural history, personal experience, description, and speculation. Like essayists from Montaigne to E. B. White, Lopez uses personal experience as an occasion for an intriguing mental journey through history to make a philosophical observation about the values of the past. In "The Clamor of Justification," Lopez tries to understand how the wolf could have become such an object of hatred and fear. Like a critic reading a poem, Lopez interprets both the stone horse and the wolf in the light of his own cultural values. Although Lopez doesn't have any children, "Children in the Woods" takes as its focus the responsibility of adults to help children understand the ethics of ecology. In "Perspective" Lopez speculates on a long-standing conundrum among philosophers: "Do we shape language or does it shape us?" In this selection from *Arctic Dreams,* Lopez uses examples from the Hopi and Eskimo languages to make his point.

For all his impressive ability as a writer, Lopez is not concerned that he be thought of as a great artist. In an interview, he maintains that he is more interested in having the reader feel the wisdom, power, and life-blood of a wild scene. The writer, he feels, is a conduit for the reader to eventual insight and understanding. Like the storyteller in aboriginal cultures, Lopez uses his narrative and descriptive skills to shape his experiences and knowledge in such a way that readers are encouraged to think about their own ideas, not the writer's. Even though Lopez wants his readers to sense the ethical and moral dimensions so prominent in his work, especially his emphasis on tolerance and dignity, he also hopes that the ego of the writer can creatively disappear. Although Lopez believes writing is an "extraordinary act of self-assertion," his purpose is finally communal, to elevate and heal, to illuminate and inspire, to give greater dimension to our lives, to transform our wounded planet.

The Stone Horse

---

1   The deserts of southern California, the high, relatively cooler and wetter Mojave and the hotter, dryer Sonoran to the south of it, carry the signatures of many cultures. Prehistoric rock drawings in the Mojave's Coso Range, probably the greatest concentration of petroglyphs in North America, are at least three thousand years old. Big game hunting cultures that flourished six or seven thousand years before that are known from broken spear tips, choppers, and burins left scattered along the shores of great Pleistocene lakes, long since evaporated. Weapons and tools discovered at China Lake may be thirty thousand years old; and worked stone from a quarry in the Calico Mountains is, some argue, evidence that human beings were here more than two hundred thousand years ago.

2   Because of the long-term stability of such arid environments, much of this prehistoric stone evidence still lies exposed on the ground, accessible to anyone who passes by—the studious, the acquisitive, the indifferent, the merely curious. Archaeologists do not agree on the sequence of cultural history beyond about twelve thousand years ago, but it is clear that these broken bits of chalcedony, chert, and obsidian, like the animal drawings and geometric designs etched on walls of basalt throughout the desert,

anchor the earliest threads of human history, the first record of human endeavor here.

3   Western man did not enter the California desert until the end of the eighteenth century, 250 years after Coronado brought his soldiers into the Zuni pueblos in a bewildered search for the cities of Cibola. The earliest appraisals of the land were cursory, hurried. People traveled *through* it, en route to Santa Fe or the California coastal settlements. Only miners tarried. In 1823 what had been Spain's became Mexico's and in 1848 what had been Mexico's became America's; but the bare, jagged mountains and dry lake beds, the vast and uniform plains of creosote bush and yucca plants, remained as obscure as the northern Sudan until the end of the nineteenth century.

4   Before 1940 the tangible evidence of twentieth-century man's passage here consisted of very little—the hard tracery of travel corridors; the widely scattered, relatively insignificant evidence of mining operations; and the fair expanse of irrigated fields at the desert's periphery. In the space of a hundred years or so the wagon roads were paved, railroads were laid down, and canals and high-tension lines were built to bring water and electricity across the desert to Los Angeles from the Colorado River. The dark mouths of gold, talc, and tin mines yawned from the bony flanks of desert ranges. Dust-encrusted chemical plants stood at work on the lonely edges of dry lake beds. And crops of grapes, lettuce, dates, alfalfa, and cotton covered the Coachella and Imperial valleys, north and south of the Salton Sea, and the Palo Verde Valley along the Colorado.

5   These developments proceeded with little or no awareness of earlier human occupations by cultures that preceded those of the historic Indians—the Mohave, the Chemehuevi, the Quechan. (Extensive irrigation began to actually change the climate of the Sonoran Desert, and human settlements, the railroads, and farming introduced many new, successful plants and animals into the region.)

6   During World War II, the American military moved into the desert in great force, to train troops and to test equipment. They found the clear weather conducive to year-round flying, the dry air, and isolation very attractive. After the war, a complex of training grounds, storage facilities, and gunnery and test ranges was permanently settled on more than three million

acres of military reservations. Few perceived the extent or significance of the destruction of aboriginal sites that took place during tank maneuvers and bombing runs or in the laying out of highways, railroads, mining districts, and irrigated fields. The few who intuited that something like an American Dordogne Valley lay exposed here were (only) amateur archaeologists; even they reasoned that the desert was too vast for any of this to matter.

7   After World War II, people began moving out of the crowded Los Angeles basin into homes in Lucerne, Apple, and Antelope valleys in the western Mojave. They emigrated as well to a stretch of resort land at the foot of the San Jacinto Mountains that included Palm Springs, and farther out to old railroad and military towns like Twentynine Palms and Barstow. People also began exploring the desert, at first in military-surplus jeeps and then with a variety of all-terrain and off-road vehicles that became available in the 1960s. By the mid-1970s, the number of people using such vehicles for desert recreation had increased exponentially. Most came and went in innocent curiosity; the few who didn't wreaked a havoc all out of proportion to their numbers. The disturbance of previously isolated archaeological sites increased by an order of magnitude. Many sites were vandalized before archaeologists, themselves late to the desert, had any firm grasp of the bounds of human history in the desert. It was as though in the same moment an Aztec library had been discovered intact various lacunae had begun to appear.

8   The vandalism was of three sorts: the general disturbance usually caused by souvenir hunters and by the curious and the oblivious; the wholesale stripping of a place by professional thieves for black-market sale and trade; and outright destruction, in which vehicles were actually used to ram and trench an area. By 1980, the Bureau of Land Management estimated that probably thirty-five percent of the archaeological sites in the desert had been vandalized. The destruction at some places by rifles and shotguns, or by power winches mounted on vehicles, was, if one cared for history, demoralizing to behold.

9   In spite of public education, land closures, and stricter law enforcement in recent years, the BLM estimates that, annually, about one percent of the archaeological record in the desert continues to be destroyed or stolen.

2

10   A BLM archaeologist told me, with understandable reluctance, where to find the intaglio. I spread my Automobile Club of Southern California map of Imperial County out on his desk, and he traced the route with a pink felt-tip pen. The line crossed Interstate 8 and then turned west along the Mexican border.

11   "You can't drive any farther than about here," he said, marking a small *x*. "There's boulders in the wash. You walk up past them."

12   On a separate piece of paper he drew a route in a smaller scale that would take me up the arroyo to a certain point where I was to cross back east, to another arroyo. At its head, on higher ground just to the north, I would find the horse.

13   "It's tough to spot unless you know it's there. Once you pick it up . . ." He shook his head slowly, in a gesture of wonder at its existence.

14   I waited until I held his eye. I assured him I would not tell anyone else how to get there. He looked at me with stoical despair, like a man who had been robbed twice, whose belief in human beings was offered without conviction.

15   I did not go until the following day because I wanted to see it at dawn. I ate breakfast at 4 A.M. in El Centro and then drove south. The route was easy to follow, though the last section of road proved difficult, broken and drifted over with sand in some spots. I came to the barricade of boulders and parked. It was light enough by then to find my way over the ground with little trouble. The contours of the landscape were stark, without any masking vegetation. I worried only about rattlesnakes.

16   I traversed the stone plain as directed, but, in spite of the frankness of the land, I came on the horse unawares. In the first moment of recognition I was without feeling. I recalled later being startled, and that I held my breath. It was laid out on the ground with its head to the east, three times life size. As I took in its outline I felt a growing concentration of all my senses, as though my attentiveness to the pale rose color of the morning sky and other peripheral images had now ceased to be important. I was aware that I was straining for sound in the windless air and I felt the uneven pressure of the earth hard against my feet. The horse, outlined in a standing profile on the dark ground, was as vivid before me as a bed of tulips.

17   I've come upon animals suddenly before, and felt a similar tension, a precipitate heightening of the senses. And I have felt the inexplicable but sharply boosted intensity of a wild moment in the bush, where it is not until some minutes later that you discover the source of electricity—the warm remains of a grizzly bear kill, or the still moist tracks of a wolverine.

18   But this was slightly different. I felt I had stepped into an unoccupied corridor. I had no familiar sense of history, the temporal structure in which to think: This horse was made by Quechan people three hundred years ago. I felt instead a headlong rush of images: people hunting wild horses with spears on the Pleistocene veld of southern California; Cortés riding across the causeway into Montezuma's Tenochtitlán; a short-legged Comanche, astride his horse like some sort of ferret, slashing through cavalry lines of young men who rode like farmers. A hoof exploding past my face one morning in a corral in Wyoming. These images had the weight and silence of stone.

19   When I released my breath, the images softened. My initial feeling, of facing a wild animal in a remote region, was replaced with a calm sense of antiquity. It was then that I became conscious, like an ordinary tourist, of what was before me, and thought: This horse was probably laid out by Quechan people. But when, I wondered? The first horses they saw, I knew, might have been those that came north from Mexico in 1692 with Father Eusebio Kino. But Cocopa people, I recalled, also came this far north on occasion, to fight with their neighbors, the Quechan. And *they* could have seen horses with Melchior Díaz, at the mouth of the Colorado River in the fall of 1540. So, it could be four hundred years old. (No one in fact knows.)

20   I still had not moved. I took my eyes off the horse for a moment to look south over the desert plain into Mexico, to look east past its head at the brightening sunrise, to situate myself. Then, finally, I brought my trailing foot slowly forward and stood erect. Sunlight was running like a thin sheet of water over the stony ground and it threw the horse into relief. It looked as though no hand had ever disturbed the stones that gave it its form.

21   The horse had been brought to life on ground called desert pavement, a tight, flat matrix of small cobbles blasted smooth by sand-laden winds. The uniform, monochromatic blackness of the stones, a patina of iron and magnesium oxides called desert var-

nish, is caused by long-term exposure to the sun. To make this type of low-relief ground glyph, or intaglio, the artist either selectively turns individual stones over to their lighter side or removes areas of stone to expose the lighter soil underneath, creating a negative image. This horse, about eighteen feet from brow to rump and eight feet from withers to hoof, had been made in the latter way, and its outline was bermed at certain points with low ridges of stone a few inches high to enhance its three-dimensional qualities. (The left side of the horse was in full profile; each leg was extended at 90 degrees to the body and fully visible, as though seen in three-quarter profile.)

22   I was not eager to move. The moment I did I would be back in the flow of time, the horse no longer quivering in the same way before me. I did not want to feel again the sequence of quotidian events—to be drawn off into deliberation and analysis. A human being, a four-footed animal, the open land. That was all that was present—and a "thoughtless" understanding of the very old desires bearing on this particular animal: to hunt it, to render it, to fathom it, to subjugate it, to honor it, to take it as a companion.

23   What finally made me move was the light. The sun now filled the shallow basin of the horse's body. The weighted line of the stone berm created the illusion of a mane and the distinctive roundness of an equine belly. The change in definition impelled me. I moved to the left, circling past its rump, to see how the light might flesh the horse out from various points of view. I circled it completely before squatting on my haunches. Ten or fifteen minutes later I chose another view. The third time I moved, to a point near the rear hooves, I spotted a stone tool at my feet. I stared at it a long while, more in awe than disbelief, before reaching out to pick it up. I turned it over in my left palm and took it between my fingers to feel its cutting edge. It is always difficult, especially with something so portable, to rechannel the desire to steal.

24   I spent several hours with the horse. As I changed positions and as the angle of the light continued to change I noticed a number of things. The angle at which the pastern carried the hoof away from the ankle was perfect. Also, stones had been placed within the image to suggest, at precisely the right spot, the left shoulder above the foreleg. The line that joined thigh and hock was similarly accurate. The muzzle alone seemed distorted— but perhaps these stones had been moved by a later hand. It was an admirably accurate representation, but not what a breeder

would call perfect conformation. There was the suggestion of a bowed neck and an undershot jaw, and the tail, as full as a winter coyote's, did not appear to be precisely to scale.

25   The more I thought about it, the more I felt I was looking at an individual horse, a unique combination of generic and specific detail. It was easy to imagine one of Kino's horses as a model, or a horse that ran off from one of Coronado's columns. What kind of horses would these have been, I wondered? In the sixteenth century the most sought-after horses in Europe were Spanish, the offspring of Arabian stock and Barbary horses that the Moors brought to Iberia and bred to the older, eastern European strains brought in by the Romans. The model for this horse, I speculated, could easily have been a palomino, or a descendant of horses trained for lion-hunting in North Africa.

26   A few generations ago, cowboys, cavalry quartermasters, and draymen would have taken this horse before me under consideration and not let up their scrutiny until they had its heritage fixed to their satisfaction. Today, the distinction between draft and harness horses is arcane knowledge, and no image may come to mind for a blue roan or a claybank horse. The loss of such refinement in everyday conversation leaves me unsettled. People praise the Eskimo's ability to distinguish among forty types of snow but forget the skill of others who routinely differentiate between overo and tobiano pintos. Such distinctions are made for the same reason. You have to do it to be able to talk clearly about the world.

27   For parts of two years I worked as a horse wrangler and packer in Wyoming. It is dim knowledge now; I would have to think to remember if a buckskin was a kind of dun horse. And I couldn't throw a double-diamond hitch over a set of panniers—the packer's basic tie-down—without guidance. As I squatted there in the desert, however, these more personal memories seemed tenuous in comparison with the sweep of this animal in human time. My memories had no depth. I thought of the Hittite cavalry riding against the Syrians 3500 years ago. And the first of the Chinese emperors, Ch'in Shih Huang, buried in Shensi Province in 210 B.C. with thousands of life-size horses and soldiers, a terra-cotta guardian army. What could I know of what was in the mind of whoever made this horse? Was there some racial memory of it as an animal that had once fed the artist's ancestors and then disappeared from North America? And then returned in this strange alliance with another race of men?

28   Certainly, whoever it was, the artist had observed the animal very closely. Certainly the animal's speed had impressed him. Among the first things the Quechan would have learned from an encounter with Kino's horses was that their own long-distance runners—men who could run down mule deer—were no match for this animal.

29   From where I squatted I could look far out over the Mexican plain. Juan Bautista de Anza passed this way in 1774, extending El Camino Real into Alta California from Sinaloa. He was followed by others, all of them astride the magical horse; *gente de razón,* the people of reason, coming into the country of *los primitivos.* The horse, like the stone animals of Egypt, urged these memories upon me. And as I drew them up from some forgotten corner of my mind—huge horses carved in the white chalk downs of southern England by an Iron Age people; Spanish horses rearing and wheeling in fear before alligators in Florida—the images seemed tethered before me. With this sense of proportion, a memory of my own—the morning I almost lost my face to a horse's hoof— now had somewhere to fit.

30   I rose up and began to walk slowly around the horse again. I had taken the first long measure of it and was looking now for a way to depart, a new angle of light, a fading of the image itself before the rising sun, that would break its hold on me. As I circled, feeling both heady and serene at the encounter, I realized again how strangely vivid it was. It had been created on a barren bajada between two arroyos, as nondescript a place as one could imagine. The only plant life here was a few wands of ocotillo cactus. The ground beneath my shoes was so hard it wouldn't take the print of a heavy animal even after a rain. The only sounds I had heard here were the voices of quail.

31   The archaeologist had been correct. For all its forcefulness, the horse is inconspicuous. If you don't care to see it you can walk right past it. That pleases him, I think. Unmarked on this bleak shoulder of the plain, the site signals to no one; so he wants no protective fences here, no informative plaque, to act as beacons. He would rather take a chance that no motorcyclist, no aimless wanderer with a flair for violence and a depth of ignorance, will ever find his way here.

32   The archaeologist had given me something before I left his office that now seemed peculiar—an aerial photograph of the horse. It is widely believed that an aerial view of an intaglio pro-

vides a fair and accurate description. It does not. In the photograph the horse looks somewhat crudely constructed; from the ground it appears far more deftly rendered. The photograph is of a single moment, and in that split second the horse seems vaguely impotent. I watched light pool in the intaglio at dawn; I imagine you could watch it withdraw at dusk and sense the same animation I did. In those prolonged moments its shape and so, too, its general character changed—noticeably. The living quality of the image, its immediacy to the eye, was brought out by the light-in-time, not, at least here, in the camera's frozen instant.

33   Intaglios, I thought, were never meant to be seen by gods in the sky above. They were meant to be seen by people on the ground, over a long period of shifting light. This could even be true of the huge figures on the Plain of Nazca in Peru, where people could walk for the length of a day beside them. It is our own impatience that leads us to think otherwise.

34   This process of abstraction, almost unintentional, drew me gradually away from the horse. I came to a position of attention at the edge of the sphere of its influence. With a slight bow I paid my respects to the horse, its maker, and the history of us all, and departed.

3

35   A short distance away I stopped the car in the middle of the road to make a few notes. I had not been able to write down what I was thinking when I was with the horse. It would have seemed disrespectful, and it would have required another kind of attention. So now I patiently drained my memory of the details it had fastened itself upon. The road I'd stopped on was adjacent to the All American Canal, the major source of water for the Imperial and Coachella valleys. The water flowed west placidly. A disjointed flock of coots, small, dark birds with white bills, was paddling against the current, foraging in the rushes.

36   I was peripherally aware of the birds as I wrote, the only movement in the desert; and of a series of sounds from a village a half-mile away. The first sounds from this collection of ramshackle houses in a grove of cottonwoods were the distracted dawn voices of dogs. I heard them intermingled with the cries of a rooster. Later, the high-pitched voices of children calling out to each

other came disembodied through the dry desert air. Now, a little after seven, I could hear someone practicing on the trumpet, the same rough phrases played over and over. I suddenly remembered how as children we had tried to get the rhythm of a galloping horse with hands against our thighs, or by fluttering our tongues against the roofs of our mouths.

37   After the trumpet, the impatient calls of adults, summoning children. Sunday morning. Wood smoke hung like a lens in the trees. The first car starts—a cold, eight-cylinder engine, of Chrysler extraction perhaps, goosed to life, then throttled back to murmur through dual mufflers, the obbligato music of a shade-tree mechanic. The rote bark of mongrel dogs at dawn, the jagged outcries of men and women, an engine coming to life. Like a thousand villages from West Virginia to Guadalajara.

38   I finished my notes—where was I going to find a description of the horses that came north with the conquistadors? Did their manes come forward prominently over the brow, like this one's, like the forelocks of Blackfeet and Assiniboine men in nineteenth-century paintings? I set the notes on the seat beside me.

39   The road followed the canal for a while and then arced north, toward Interstate 8. It was slow driving and I fell to thinking how the desert had changed since Anza had come through. New plants and animals—the MacDougall cottonwood, the English house sparrow, the chukar from India—have about them now the air of the native-born. Of the native species, some—no one knows how many—are extinct. The populations of many others, especially the animals, have been sharply reduced. The idea of a desert impoverished by agricultural poisons and varmint hunters, by off-road vehicles and military operations, did not seem as disturbing to me, however, as this other horror, now that I had been those hours with the horse. The vandals, the few who crowbar rock art off the desert's walls, who dig up graves, who punish the ground that holds intaglios, are people who devour history. Their self-centered scorn, their disrespect for ideas and images beyond their ken, create the awful atmosphere of loose ends in which totalitarianism thrives, in which the past is merely curious or wrong.

40   I thought about the horse sitting out there on the unprotected plain. I enumerated its qualities in my mind until a sense of its vulnerability receded and it became an anchor for something else. I remembered that history, a history like this one, which ran

deeper than Mexico, deeper than the Spanish, was a kind of medicine. It permitted the great breadth of human expression to reverberate, and it did not urge you to locate its apotheosis in the present.

41   Each of us, individuals and civilizations, has been held upside down like Achilles in the River Styx. The artist mixing his colors in the dim light of Altamira; an Egyptian ruler lying still now, wrapped in his byssus, stored against time in a pyramid; the faded Dorset culture of the Arctic; the Hmong and Samburu and Walbiri of historic time; the modern nations. This great, imperfect stretch of human expression is the clarification and encouragement, the urging and the reminder, we call history. And it is inscribed everywhere in the face of the land, from the mountain passes of the Himalayas to a nameless bajada in the California desert.

42   Small birds rose up in the road ahead, startled, and flew off. I prayed no infidel would ever find that horse.

QUESTIONS

Ideas

1. The central incident—the discovery of the stone horse—becomes for Lopez cause for an extended meditation on history, horses, and his own experiences. What "reading" of the glyph seems most interesting to you? Which of his observations on the horse seems most unusual?

2. Speculate about what the original intention of the artist who created the horse might have been. Since we can almost certainly never recover the original purpose of the stone glyph, are we free to interpret it as we may? Is it possible to ever fully understand the art of the past?

3. How does Lopez's thinking change after he says his farewell to the horse?

4. What do you make of his idea that the horse is a "kind of medicine"?

5. Why does he use the word "infidel" in the last sentence instead of, say, vandal or thief?

Organization

6. Give a title to each of the three sections. Describe briefly the purpose of each. Is there an overall purpose?

7. Lopez deftly blends narrative, description, exposition, and meditation. Try to describe his train of thought when he comes upon the
horse. Is there a "logic" to his ruminations?

Sentences

8. In the middle of the second section, read the paragraph that begins, "I was not eager to move." Is there a sentence fragment here?
Why? Explain the structure of the last sentence.

9. Lopez uses a wide array of sentence types, beginnings, and lengths.
Give examples of this flexibility.

Words

10. Is it clear from the context what a petroglyph is? Can you "guess" at
other words before you look them up? How about "chalcedony,"
"creosote," "winches," "arroyo," "ken"?

Suggestions for Writing

A. Write a summary of this essay, trying to keep Lopez's tone and attitudes intact.

B. Using the last three paragraphs in section three as a focus, write an
essay about something in our own culture that future civilizations
might come upon with wonder.

C. Agree or disagree in a brief essay with the following idea: We can
never understand anything but our own moment in time.

The Clamor of Justification

---

1   In the course of writing [*Of Wolves and Men*] I had a
chance to talk with many people, and to come into contact with
several different points of view about wolves. I enjoyed being in
the field with biologists. I enjoyed the range and subtlety of
Indian and Eskimo ideas. My only discomfort came when I talked
with men who saw nothing wrong with killing wolves, who felt it
was basically a good thing to be doing. For the most part, they
were men who had matured in a different time and under different circumstances than I. We didn't share the same feelings

toward animals, but I could understand their positions. Some were professional trappers. Others had lost stock to wolves. There was a larger context.

2   There were a few I spoke with, however, who were quite different. It was as though these men had broken down at some point in their lives and begun to fill with bile, and that bile had become an unreasoned hatred of many things. Of laws. Of governments. Of wolves. They hated wolves because—they would struggle to put it into words—because wolves seemed better off than they were. And that seemed perverse. They killed wolves habitually, with a trace of vengeance, with as little regret as a boy shooting rats at a dump.

3   They were few in number but their voices, screaming for the wolf's head, were often the loudest, the ones that set the tone at a grange meeting and precipitated the wolf's extirpation in the lower forty-eight states.

4   These men, and others, killed no one will ever know how many thousands of wolves in America, mostly to control predation against livestock. At the time, toward the close of the nineteenth century, it was a legitimate undertaking. Wolves, deprived of buffalo and other wild game, had turned to cattle and sheep; if you wanted to raise stock in America you had little choice but to kill wolves. But the killing was a complicated business, it was never as clearly reasoned as that. On the spur of the moment men offered ridiculous reasons—because the wolves loafed and didn't have to work for their food, they would say.

5   It is easy to condemn these men now, to look at what they did—destroy a national wildlife heritage—and feel a sense of loss. But they are, perhaps, too easily blamed. We forget how little, really, separates us from the times and circumstances in which we, too, would have killed wolves. Besides, blaming them for the loss is too simplistic. We are forced to a larger question: when a man cocked a rifle and aimed at a wolf's head, what was he trying to kill? And other questions. Why didn't we quit, why did we go on killing long after the need was gone? And when the craven and deranged tortured wolves, why did so many of us look the other way?

6   In an historical sense, we are all to blame for the loss of wolves. In the nineteenth century when the Indians on the plains were telling us that the wolf was a brother, we were preaching another gospel. Manifest Destiny. What rankles us now, I think, is

that an alternative gospel still remains largely unarticulated. You want to say there never should have been a killing, but you don't know what to put in its place.

• • •

7   Ever since man first began to wonder about wolves—to make dogs of their descendants, to admire them as hunters—he has made a regular business of killing them. At first glance the reasons are simple enough, and justifiable. Wolves are predators. When men come into a land to "tame" it, they replace wild game with domestic animals. The wolves prey on these creatures, the men kill them in turn, and reduce the wolf population generally, as a preventive measure to secure their economic investment. The two just can't live side by side. A step removed from this, perhaps, in terms of its justification, is the action of Fish and Game departments that kill wolves to sustain or increase the yield of big game animals so human hunters can kill them. This kind of "predator control" has historically accommodated economic and political interests ahead of ecological interests. And it has acted occasionally from a basis of bar stool and barbershop biology, not wildlife science.

8   Wolf killing goes much beyond predator control, of course. Bounty hunters kill wolves for money; trappers kill them for pelts; scientists kill them for data; big game hunters kill them for trophies. The arguments for killing here are harder to sustain, yet many people see nothing at all wrong with these activities. Indeed, this is the way we commonly treat all predators—bobcats, bears, and mountain lions included. But the wolf is fundamentally different because the history of killing wolves shows far less restraint and far more perversity. A lot of people didn't just kill wolves; they tortured them. They set wolves on fire and tore their jaws out and cut their Achilles tendons and turned dogs loose on them. They poisoned them with strychnine, arsenic, and cyanide, on such a scale that *millions* of other animals—raccoons, black-footed ferrets, red foxes, ravens, red-tailed hawks, eagles, ground squirrels, wolverines—were killed incidentally in the process. In the thick of the wolf fever they even poisoned themselves, and burned down their own property torching the woods to get rid of wolf havens. In the United States in the period between 1865 and 1885 cattlemen killed wolves with almost pathological dedication.

In the twentieth century people pulled up alongside wolves in air-planes and snowmobiles and blew them apart with shotguns for sport. In Minnesota in the 1970s people choked Eastern timber wolves to death in snares to show their contempt for the animal's designation as an endangered species.

9   This is not predator control, and it goes beyond the casual cruelty sociologists say manifests itself among people under stress, or where there is no perception of responsibility. It is the violent expression of a terrible assumption: that men have the right to kill other creatures not for what they do but for what we fear they may do. I almost wrote "or for no reason," but there are always reasons. Killing wolves has to do with fear based on superstitions. It has to do with "duty." It has to do with proving manhood (abstractly, perhaps, this is nothing more than wanting either to possess or to destroy the animal's soul). And sometimes, I think, because the killing is so righteously pursued and yet so entirely without conscience, killing wolves has to do with murder.

10   Historically, the most visible motive, and the one that best explains the excess of killing, is a type of fear: theriophobia. Fear of the beast. Fear of the beast as an irrational, violent, insatiable creature. Fear of the projected beast in oneself. The fear is composed of two parts: self-hatred; and anxiety over the human loss of inhibitions that are common to other animals who do not rape, murder, and pillage. At the heart of theriophobia is the fear of one's own nature. In its headiest manifestations theriophobia is projected onto a single animal, the animal becomes a scapegoat, and it is annihilated. That is what happened to the wolf in America. The routes that led there, however, were complex.

11   Those days are past. There is little to be gained now by condemning the aerial "sport" hunting of wolves (the activity is banned in the United States by federal law), or by railing against the cattle industry for the excesses of its founders. But there is something to be gained from learning where the fear and hatred originated, and where the one thing besides cruelty to the animal that sets wolf hunting apart from other kinds of hunting—the "righteousness" of it—comes from.

12   The hatred has religious roots: the wolf was the Devil in disguise. And it has secular roots: wolves killed stock and made men poor. At a more general level it had to do, historically, with feelings about wilderness. What men said about the one, they general-

ly meant about the other. To celebrate wilderness was to celebrate
the wolf; to want an end to wilderness and all it stood for was to
want the wolf's head.

13   In setting down a base for our antipathy toward wilderness,
the historian Roderick Nash has singled out religious and secular
antecedents. In *Beowulf,* for example, there is an expression of the
secular (i.e., nonreligious) wilderness that is constituted of unin-
habited forest—a region whose dank, cold depths, with its miasmic swamps and windswept crags, harbor foul creatures that prey
on men. In the Bible, wilderness is defined as the place without
God—a sere and barren desert. This twined sense of wilderness as
a place innately dangerous and godless was something that
attached itself, inevitably, to the wolf—the most feared denizen of
gloomy wilderness. As civilized man matured and came to measure his own progress by his subjugation of the wilderness—both
clearing trees for farms and clearing pagan minds for Christian
ideas—the act of killing wolves became a symbolic act, a way to
lash out at that enormous, inchoate obstacle: wilderness. Man
demonstrated his own prodigious strength as well as his allegiance
to God by killing wolves. I greatly oversimplify, but there is not
much distinction in motive between the Christian missionaries
who set fire to England's woods to deprive Druids of a place to
worship and the residents of Arkansas who set fire to thousands of
acres of the Ouachita National Forest in 1928 to deprive wolves of
hiding places.

14   In America in the eighteenth century Cotton Mather and
other Puritan ministers preached against wilderness as an insult to
the Lord, as a challenge to man to show the proof of his religious
conviction by destroying it. Mather, and others, urged the
colonists to make of the "howling wilderness" a "fruitful field." In
1756 John Adams wrote that when the colonists arrived in
America, "the whole continent was one continued dismal wilderness, the haunt of wolves and bears and more savage men. Now
the forests are removed, the land covered with fields of corn,
orchards bending with fruit and the magnificent habitations of
rational and civilized people." In Europe at the same time the
subjugation and ordering of shabby wilderness had reached its
exaggerated apotheosis in the excessive neatness of the Versailles
gardens.

15   The drive to tame wilderness in America never let up. The
wagonmaster of the 1840s "opened the road west"; he was fol-

lowed by the farmer, who cleared the fields, and the logger, who "let daylight into the swamp." One hundred years after Adams wrote of dismal wilderness, the railroad barons and cattle barons were speaking of Manifest Destiny and man's right and obligation as God's steward to "make something of the land." And where they made it into towns, fields, and pastures, there was no place for the wolf. The wolf became the symbol of what you wanted to kill—memories of man's primitive origins in the wilderness, the remnant of his bestial nature which was all that held him back in America from building the greatest empire on the face of the earth. The wolf represented "a fierce, bloodsucking persecutor" (as Roger Williams called him) of everything that was high-born in man. Theodore Roosevelt, his hand on the Bible, his eye riveting the attention of men of commerce, spoke gravely of wolf predation on his ranch in North Dakota, of the threat to progress represented by the wolf. He called him "the beast of waste and desolation."

QUESTIONS

Ideas

1. Lopez suggests that in another time we too would scream for "the wolf's head." Do you think that's true? What does this imply about the values we currently hold?

2. Can you remember stories or movies or TV programs from your childhood about wolves? Were they made to be sinister or terrible? What was or is your view of them and where did those ideas come from?

3. Lopez says killing wolves was a symbolic act. Do you think the modern hunter is acting in comparable ways?

4. Are we still trying to conquer the wilderness, hoping to control nature? Give examples.

Organization

5. Examine the structure of paragraphs 7 and 8. Describe in your own words the relationship between a sentence and the one that follows it.

6. Choose two paragraphs with clear topic sentences that are developed with examples.

Sentences

7. In paragraph 8, notice the second sentence. Can you suggest alter-
    native ways of writing it? Choose another sentence in paragraph 8
    and rearrange its structure. Comment on the differences.
8. Explain the use of the colon in the first two sentences of paragraph 12.

Words

9. Why does Lopez put the words sport, duty, and righteousness in
    quotes?
10. What does "apotheosis" mean? "miasmic"? "pathological"?

Suggestions for Writing

A. Write an essay in which you argue that the hunting of wild animals
    should be abolished or allowed.
B. Can you think of other animals that have also received "bad press" in
    our culture. Write an essay that tries to explain why.

Children in the Woods

1   When I was a child growing up in the San Fernando
Valley in California, a trip into Los Angeles was special. The sensation of movement from a rural area into an urban one was sharp.
On one of these charged occasions, walking down a sidewalk with
my mother, I stopped suddenly, caught by a pattern of sunlight
trapped in a spiraling imperfection in a windowpane. A stranger,
an elderly woman in a cloth coat and a dark hat, spoke out spontaneously, saying how remarkable it is that children notice these
things.
2   I have never forgotten the texture of this incident. Whenever I recall it I am moved not so much by any sense of my young
self but by a sense of responsibility toward children, knowing how
acutely I was affected in that moment by that woman's words. The
effect, for all I know, has lasted a lifetime.
3   Now, years later, I live in a rain forest in western Oregon, on
the banks of a mountain river in relatively undisturbed country,
surrounded by 150-foot-tall Douglas firs, delicate deer-head
orchids, and clearings where wild berries grow. White-footed mice

and mule deer, mink and coyote move through here. My wife and I do not have children, but children we know, or children whose parents we are close to, are often here. They always want to go into the woods. And I wonder what to tell them.

4   In the beginning, years ago, I think I said too much. I spoke with an encyclopedic knowledge of the names of plants or the names of birds passing through in season. Gradually I came to say less. After a while the only words I spoke, beyond answering a question or calling attention quickly to the slight difference between a sprig of red cedar and a sprig of incense cedar, were to elucidate single objects.

5   I remember once finding a fragment of a raccoon's jaw in an alder thicket. I sat down alongside the two children with me and encouraged them to find out who this was—with only the three teeth still intact in a piece of the animal's maxilla to guide them. The teeth told by their shape and placement what this animal ate. By a kind of visual extrapolation its size became clear. There were other clues, immediately present, which told, with what I could add of climate and terrain, how this animal lived, how its broken jaw came to be lying here. Raccoon, they surmised. And tiny tooth marks along the bone's broken edge told of a mouse's hunger for calcium.

6   We set the jaw back and went on.

7   If I had known more about raccoons, finer points of osteology, we might have guessed more: say, whether it was male or female. But what we deduced was all we needed. Hours later, the maxilla, lost behind us in the detritus of the forest floor, continued to effervesce. It was tied faintly to all else we spoke of that afternoon.

8   In speaking with children who might one day take a permanent interest in natural history—as writers, as scientists, as filmmakers, as anthropologists—I have sensed that an extrapolation from a single fragment of the whole is the most invigorating experience I can share with them. I think children know that nearly anyone can learn the names of things; the impression made on them at this level is fleeting. What takes a lifetime to learn, they comprehend, is the existence and substance of myriad relationships: it is these relationships, not the things themselves, that ultimately hold the human imagination.

9   The brightest children, it has often struck me, are fascinated by metaphor—with what is shown in the set of relationships bearing on the raccoon, for example, to lie quite beyond the raccoon.

In the end, you are trying to make clear to them that everything found at the edge of one's senses—the high note of the winter wren, the thick perfume of propolis that drifts downwind from spring willows, the brightness of wood chips scattered by beaver—that all this fits together. The indestructibility of these associations conveys a sense of permanence that nurtures the heart, that cripples one of the most insidious of human anxieties, the one that says, you do not belong here, you are unnecessary.

10   Whenever I walk with a child, I think how much I have seen disappear in my own life. What will there be for this person when he is my age? If he senses something ineffable in the landscape, will I know enough to encourage it?—to somehow show him that, yes, when people talk about violent death, spiritual exhilaration, compassion, futility, final causes, they are drawing on forty thousand years of human meditation on *this*—as we embrace Douglas firs, or stand by a river across whose undulating back we skip stones, or dig out a camas bulb, biting down into a taste so much wilder than last night's potatoes.

11   The most moving look I ever saw from a child in the woods was on a mud bar by the footprints of a heron. We were on our knees, making handprints beside the footprints. You could feel the creek vibrating in the silt and sand. The sun beat down heavily on our hair. Our shoes were soaking wet. The look said: I did not know until now that I needed someone much older to confirm this, the feeling I have of life here. I can now grow older, knowing it need never be lost.

12   The quickest door to open in the woods for a child is the one that leads to the smallest room, by knowing the name each thing is called. The door that leads to the cathedral is marked by a hesitancy to speak at all, rather to encourage by example a sharpness of the senses. If one speaks it should only be to say, as well as one can, how wonderfully all this fits together, to indicate what a long, fierce peace can derive from this knowledge.

QUESTIONS

Ideas

1. What is it the child in the penultimate paragraph is saying with a look?

2. What is it Lopez most wants to share with children? How can adults do this? Was this ever done to you?

Organization

3. Like many essayists, Lopez begins with a specific anecdote from his own experience and uses that to make broader generalizations. He combines this within a then/now framework. Comment on the time frame of each paragraph.

4. Rather than beginning with a thesis, Lopez seems to end with one. Comment on the usefulness of each approach.

Sentences

5. Lopez often uses the standard pattern: subject, verb, object. But he varies this frequently. Give examples of different patterns.

6. Notice sentences that begin with the conjunctions "and" and "but." Why does he use them? Were you allowed to use them in high school?

Words

7. What do you think Lopez means by "cathedral" in the last paragraph?

8. What do "detritus" and "effervesce" mean? Are these effective words?

Suggestions for Writing

A. Can you remember an incident involving something an adult said to you as a child which, like Lopez, you never forgot? Narrate the event and speculate about why it has lasted.

B. Write a brief essay focusing on nature in which you recall events that demonstrated either "a sense of permanence that nurtures the heart" or one that suggested that "you do not belong here, you are unnecessary."

Perspective

---

1   In the 1930s a man named Benjamin Lee Whorf began to clarify an insight he had had into the structure of the Hopi language. Hopi has only limited tenses, noted Whorf, makes

no reference to time as an entity distinct from space, and, though relatively poor in nouns, is rich in verbs. It is a language that projects a world of movement and changing relationships, a continuous "fabric" of time and space. It is better suited than the English language to describing quantum mechanics. English divides time into linear segments by making use of many tenses. It is a noun-rich, verb-poor tongue that contrasts fixed space with a flow of time. It is a language of static space, more suited, say, to architectural description. All else being equal, a Hopi child would have little difficulty comprehending the theory of relativity in his own language, while an American child could more easily master history. A Hopi would be confounded by the idea that time flowed from the past into the present.

2   In 1936 Whorf wrote that many aboriginal languages "abound in finely wrought, beautifully logical discriminations about causation, action, result, dynamic and energetic quality, directness of experience, etc. . . ." He made people see that there were no primitive languages; and that there was no pool of thought from which all cultures drew their metaphysics. "All observers," he cautioned, "are not led by the same physical evidence to the same picture of the universe."

3   These ideas were anticipated to some extent by the anthropologist Franz Boas, who emphasized the individual integrity of different aboriginal cultures. His was a reaction against the predominant Victorian view that considered all cultures reducible to a set of "true" observations about the world. (Boas's "functionalist" approach has since been replaced by a "structuralist" view, which knowingly imposes abstract and subjective patterns on a culture.)

4   Whorf, Boas, and others in this tradition urged people after the turn of the century to see human culture as a mechanism for ordering reality. These realities were separate, though they might be simultaneously projected onto the same landscape. And there was no ultimate reality—any culture that would judge the perceptions of another, particularly one outside its own traditions, should proceed cautiously.

5   In recent years the writing of people like Joseph Campbell and Claude Lévi-Strauss has illuminated the great panorama of human perceptual experience, pointing up not only the different approaches we take to the background that contains us (the landscape) but the similarities we seem to share. For hunting peoples,

for example, says Lévi-Strauss, an animal is held in high totemic regard not merely because it is food and therefore good to eat but because it is "good to think." The animal is "good to imagine."

6 In the Arctic, researchers such as Richard Nelson, Edmund Carpenter, and Hugh Brody, each addressing a different aspect of Eskimo existence, have reiterated these themes in studying the land. Their work has made clear the integrity and coherence of a different vision of the Arctic; misunderstandings that arise when a view of reality similar to our own is assumed to exist; and the ways in which the Eskimo's view of the land presents us with growing ethical, political, and economic problems, because we would prefer that ours was the mind of record in that landscape.

7 I have already referred to Nelson's work on natural history and hunting. Brody has been influential in the development of land-use-and-occupancy studies. Carpenter has written cogently on Eskimo art and Eskimo perceptions of space. Not surprisingly, each has emphasized that a knowledge of the language, the pertinent regional dialect, is critical to an understanding of what Eskimos are talking about when they talk about the land. Says Nelson, an understanding of the behavior of sea ice off the coast at Wainwright, where the ice is very active, is "difficult to acquire, especially without a full understanding" of Eskimo terminology. Brody, discussing Eskimo concepts of intimacy with the land, says, flatly, "The key terms are not translatable."

8 Carpenter discerns a correspondence between the Inuktitut language and Eskimo carving: the emphasis in both is on what is dynamic, and on observations made from a variety of viewpoints. In our language, says Carpenter, we lavish attention on concepts of time; Eskimos give their attention to varieties of space. We assume all human beings are oriented similarly in space and therefore regard objects from the same point of view—the top is the top, the bottom the bottom; that direction is north and this south. In describing a distant place, however, says Carpenter, an Eskimo will often make no reference to the mass of the land in between (which would impress us, and which we would describe in terms of distance), but only to geographical points, and not necessarily as seen from the point of one's approach. Thus, to a non-Eskimo observer, the Eskimo might seem to have "no sense of direction." And because he travels somewhat like the arctic fox—turning aside to investigate something unusual, or moving

ahead in a series of steps punctuated by short stops for tea,
instead of in a straight, relentless dash for a "goal"—the Eskimo
might be thought poorly self-disciplined or improvident. But it
would only have to do with how the Eskimo saw himself in the fabric of space and time, how he conceived of "proceeding" through
the world, where he placed lines or points in the stream of dura-
tion.

9   The Eskimo's different but still sophisticated mind is largely
inaccessible without recourse to his language. And, of course, it
works the other way around. Each for the other is a kind of primitive.

10   The Eskimo language reaches its apogee in describing the
land and man's activity in it. Young people in modern Eskimo villages, especially in the eastern Arctic, say that when they are out
on the land with their parents, they find it much more difficult to
speak Inuktitut, though they speak it at home all the time. It is
not so much a lack of vocabulary as a difficulty with constructions,
with idioms, a lost fluency that confuses them. It is out on the
land, in the hunting camps and traveling over the ice, that the
language comes alive. The Eskimo language is seasonal—terms
for the many varieties of snow emerge in winter, while those for
whaling come into use in the spring. Whole areas of the language
are starting to disappear because they refer to activities no longer
much practiced, like traveling with dogs; or to the many different
parts of an animal like the walrus that are no longer either eaten
or used; or to activities that are discouraged, such as the intercession of shamans.

11   For Whorf, language was something man created in his
mind and projected onto reality, something he imposed on the
landscape, as though the land were a receptacle for his imagination. I think there are possibly two things wrong with this thought.
First, the landscape is not inert; and it is precisely because it is
alive that it eventually contradicts the imposition of a reality that
does not derive from it. Second, language is not something man
imposes on the land. It evolves in his conversation with the land—
in testing the sea ice with the toe of a *kamik,* in the eating of a wild
berry, in repairing a sled by the light of a seal-oil lamp. A long-
lived inquiry produces a discriminating language. The very order
of the language, the ecology of its sounds and thoughts, derives
from the mind's intercourse with the landscape. To learn the
indigenous language, then, is to know what the speakers of the
language have made of the land.

QUESTIONS

Ideas

1. Instead of the nouns "tree" or "man," the Hopi use the verbs "tree-ing" and "manning." How might this affect their notion of reality? Might they, for example, see people as less static and fixed than we do?

2. When Lopez says "each for the other is a kind of primitive," might that also apply to other cultural interactions, for example, between the British and Indians, the Puritans and the Indians, the French and the African? What are the implications here for understanding the Other?

Organization

3. Lopez, like many writers, tries to move between the concrete and the abstract, the specific and the general. Give examples.

Sentences

4. Can you point to sentences that might be examples of imposing language on reality? What, for example, is the force of "is" in "the animal is 'good to imagine'"? Do all uses of "to be" distort the world? Is a person good or bad, or is it just our perspective that makes it seem so?

Words

5. What kinds of words do we have for roads? for machines? for sports? for entertainment? What would someone from, say, the Eskimo culture make of these terms?

Suggestions for Writing

A. Agree or disagree with the Whorfian idea that language shapes our perceptions of reality, that it is not only the vehicle of our thought but the driver as well. Try to give concrete examples.

B. Does the Whorfian idea hold for subcultures within our society as well? That is, can we understand surfers or heavy metal rockers or Christians or farmers without knowing their lingo? Discuss in a brief essay.

TEN

John
McPhee

(1931–   )

John McPhee is a master of detail, a poet of information, an artist of the factual. His passion for getting it
right is almost obsessive. If he were a painter, he would
probably be a photo-realist; if a filmmaker, he would
broaden the artistic possibilities of the documentary. In
fact, according to one critic, he has already "stretched the
artistic dimensions of reportage." His book *Oranges*
(1967) is typical of his literary nonfiction. Although we
learn an enormous amount about citrus botany and history, about international customs and economic realities,
we are also aesthetically entertained by the craft and photographic precision of his prose—by the clarity of his
accurate and authentic details.

Unlike Tom Wolfe and Joan Didion, John McPhee
is not a New Journalist: his presence is barely noticeable
in the events he is describing, and he almost never tells
the reader what he is thinking. He is self-effacing. The
persona he adopts as a narrator reveals little; instead he
usually lets his carefully arranged details convey his feelings. In a traditional sense, he tries for objectivity.
However, because writing is a process of selecting, rejecting, and arranging information, a writer cannot possibly
be completely objective. McPhee has to leave some material out; he has to put other material in. All writers have
to choose. In McPhee's case it is easy enough to infer his
attitude. He leaves many traces.

McPhee is interested in the values that people live
by, and he usually writes about people he likes. They can
be basketball players, scientists, headmasters, or canoe

makers. He clearly admires the finesse and dedication of the former basketball player Bill Bradley and likes the independence and pluck of Fred Brown, a piney backwoodsman. Very often his heroes possess competence, self-assurance, modesty, and self-discipline. Many critics attribute these same qualities to McPhee.

But he is more interested in giving the reader a precisely rendered account of the people he writes about than in extolling them. When we encounter the people of the Pine Barrens, we find out about their lives and the codes they live by through details that have been meticulously researched and verified. McPhee gains authority through fact and layers of details. We trust his persona because he has mastered his material. He has done his homework. His scholarly attention to creating a particular atmosphere makes his nonfiction as complex as a novel. His refined, economically controlled portraits make his characters breathe. McPhee once said that "factual characters can live as much on the page as any fictional character . . . writing is more than just the delivery of information *per se.*"

None of this comes easy, of course. In fact, McPhee says that writing "gets harder and harder the older you get. Not easier." He claims that as a young writer he "would thread my bathrobe sash through the spokes of the chair and tie myself in." Even today McPhee finds the life of a writer difficult. Although he is a staff writer for *The New Yorker* and has an office there, he does all his writing in a study on Main Street in Princeton, New Jersey. He arrives at 8:30 in the morning and doesn't leave until 8:30 at night. He maintains, however, that he gets only two or three hours of good writing done. "The rest of the time I wander around in here going nuts—trying to bring it all into focus."

To make the process of composing easier, McPhee tries to follow a pattern that he feels comfortable with, one that fits his personality. He does not use a tape recorder, preferring instead to fill up notebooks in longhand with the results of interviews, observations, and library research. After reading and rereading these notes, he looks for gaps that will need future research. Then he jots down possible structures, later trying possible opening paragraphs. He then arranges his notes according to a tentative structure.

Unlike many writers, McPhee does most of his planning in his head instead of on paper. He decides whether to use a prearranged pattern or to let the material suggest an organic pattern. Generally he prefers a logical, simple form. Then he writes his first draft. A critic described his composing processes: "Some authors overwrite and later boil down; he culls before ever typing a phrase."

McPhee's first draft is for him the most difficult. After that he edits, pruning and polishing his sentences. Because of the "laborious planning and composing" that McPhee goes through in the early stages of his writing, he can concentrate on style in the closing stages.

Although he doesn't begin to write until the end of his planning stage, his overall composing sequence is comparable to that of many other experienced writers who spend up to 80 percent of their composing effort in preparation for the first good draft. For most writers, revising that draft involves a good deal of rearranging, refocusing, and reseeing. However, McPhee feels he has already laid a solid foundation and so makes few changes in the original structure. His purpose in choosing an organization is to create an unobtrusive design, one so logical and simple that the reader's attention will be drawn only to meaning, to content; not to the window, but to the scene beyond.

His style is as unaffected as his organization. His prose is strong, direct, and economical. His most characteristic sentence pattern is the straightforward assertion: "Bradley is not an innovator" or "Bradley's graceful hook shot is a masterpiece of eclecticism." These sentences are often placed first in a paragraph so that he can follow them with supporting details. And these specifics are concrete and knowledgeable. He achieves some of his authority by absorbing the vocabulary, the "sound" of whatever he is writing about. If it is pinballs, he will use the right jargon: "Ballys" and "Gottliebs," "reinforcing" and "death channels." If it is oranges, we will hear about "Maltese Ovals" and "Luc Gim Gongs," "zygotic seedlings" and "pomologists." His use of the concrete suggests a writer deeply involved in his subject, a person totally in touch with his surroundings. Readers trust a writer who sounds as if he knows what he is talking about.

John McPhee uses disciplined hard work to let readers see, to make us understand. With *The Pine Barrens*

(1968), *Coming Into the Country* (1979), and *Basin and Range* (1981), he earned a reputation as one of the most versatile and literate journalists in America, a reporter who creates living art out of inert information. Through a patient and textured prose filled with carefully selected details, he shows us how it was to be there. By standing back and letting his sentences evoke special people and special places, McPhee invites the reader to activate his prose. In his *La Place de la Concorde Suisse* (1985), he has perfected his persona as the "invisible interlocutor," in prose so clean and controlled it almost seems too effortless, too simple. But that is just the illusion a skilled artisan like McPhee wants to achieve. Lucid prose does not come easily. McPhee works all day, every day on his writing, constantly revising. It is this dedication to the writing process that makes McPhee's prose so readable.

In *The Control of Nature* (1989), McPhee turns his attention to the strategies and tactics people have tried to use to control rivers and mountains, lava and debris flows. In the selection given here, the almost tragic narrative of a family's confrontation with the San Gabriel Mountains contains a message about our ingenuity and foolishness. The excerpt from *Looking For a Ship* (1990) is a surprising narrative about contemporary pirates that McPhee actually encountered when he decided to live aboard a merchant marine ship for several months as it traveled to South America.

Los Angeles against the Mountains

---

1   In Los Angeles versus the San Gabriel Mountains, it is not always clear which side is losing. For example, the Genofiles, Bob and Jackie, can claim to have lost and won. They live on an acre of ground so high that they look across their pool and past the trunks of big pines at an aerial view over Glendale and across Los Angeles to the Pacific bays. The setting, in cool dry air, is serene and Mediterranean. It has not been everlastingly serene.

2   On a February night some years ago, the Genofiles were awakened by a crash of thunder—lightning striking the mountain

front. Ordinarily, in their quiet neighborhood, only the creek beside them was likely to make much sound, dropping steeply out of Shields Canyon on its way to the Los Angeles River. The creek, like every component of all the river systems across the city from mountains to ocean, had not been left to nature. Its banks were concrete. Its bed was concrete. When boulders were running there, they sounded like a rolling freight. On a night like this, the boulders should have been running. The creek should have been a torrent. Its unnatural sound was unnaturally absent. There was, and had been, a lot of rain.

3   The Genofiles had two teen-age children, whose rooms were on the uphill side of the one-story house. The window in Scott's room looked straight up Pine Cone Road, a cul-de-sac, which, with hundreds like it, defined the northern limit of the city, the confrontation of the urban and the wild. Los Angeles is over-matched on one side by the Pacific Ocean and on the other by very high mountains. With respect to these principal boundaries, Los Angeles is done sprawling. The San Gabriels, in their state of tectonic youth, are rising as rapidly as any range on earth. Their loose inimical slopes flout the tolerance of the angle of repose. Rising straight up out of the megalopolis, they stand ten thousand feet above the nearby sea, and they are not kidding with this city. Shedding, spalling, self-destructing, they are disintegrating at a rate that is also among the fastest in the world. The phalanxed communities of Los Angeles have pushed themselves hard against these mountains, an aggression that requires a deep defense bud-get to contend with the results. Kimberlee Genofile called to her mother, who joined her in Scott's room as they looked up the street. From its high turnaround, Pine Cone Road plunges down-hill like a ski run, bending left and then right and then left and then right in steep christiania turns for half a mile above a three-hundred-foot straightaway that aims directly at the Genofiles' house. Not far below the turnaround, Shields Creek passes under the street, and there a kink in its concrete profile had been plugged by a six-foot boulder. Hence the silence of the creek. The water was now spreading over the street. It descended in heavy sheets. As the young Genofiles and their mother glimpsed it in the all but total darkness, the scene was suddenly illuminated by a blue electrical flash. In the blue light they saw a massive blackness, moving. It was not a landslide, not a mudslide, not a rock avalanche; nor by any means was it the front of a conventional

flood. In Jackie's words, "It was just one big black thing coming at us, rolling, rolling with a lot of water in front of it, pushing the water, this big black thing. It was just one big black hill coming toward us."

4   In geology, it would be known as a debris flow. Debris flows amass in stream valleys and more or less resemble fresh concrete. They consist of water mixed with a good deal of solid material, most of which is above sand size. Some of it is Chevrolet size. Boulders bigger than cars ride long distances in debris flows. Boulders grouped like fish eggs pour downhill in debris flows. The dark material coming toward the Genofiles was not only full of boulders; it was so full of automobiles it was like bread dough mixed with raisins. On its way down Pine Cone Road, it plucked up cars from driveways and the street. When it crashed into the Genofiles' house, the shattering of safety glass made terrific explosive sounds. A door burst open. Mud and boulders poured into the hall. We're going to go, Jackie thought. Oh, my God, what a hell of a way for the four of us to die together.

5   The parents' bedroom was on the far side of the house. Bob Genofile was in there kicking through white satin draperies at the panelled glass, smashing it to provide an outlet for water, when the three others ran in to join him. The walls of the house neither moved nor shook. As a general contractor, Bob had built dams, department stores, hospitals, six schools, seven churches, and this house. It was made of concrete block with steel reinforcement, sixteen inches on center. His wife had said it was stronger than any dam in California. His crew had called it "the fort." In those days, twenty years before, the Genofiles' acre was close by the edge of the mountain brush, but a developer had come along since then and knocked down thousands of trees and put Pine Cone Road up the slope. Now Bob Genofile was thinking, I hope the roof holds. I hope the roof is strong enough to hold. Debris was flowing over it. He told Scott to shut the bedroom door. No sooner was the door closed than it was battered down and fell into the room. Mud, rock, water poured in. It pushed everybody against the far wall. "Jump on the bed," Bob said. The bed began to rise. Kneeling on it—on a gold velvet spread—they could soon press their palms against the ceiling. The bed also moved toward the glass wall. The two teen-agers got off, to try to control the motion, and were pinned between the bed's brass railing and the wall. Boulders went up against the railing, pressed it into their

legs, and held them fast. Bob dived into the muck to try to move the boulders, but he failed. The debris flow, entering through windows as well as doors, continued to rise. Escape was still possible for the parents but not for the children. The parents looked at each other and did not stir. Each reached for and held one of the children. Their mother felt suddenly resigned, sure that her son and daughter would die and she and her husband would quickly follow. The house became buried to the eaves. Boulders sat on the roof. Thirteen automobiles were packed around the building, including five in the pool. A din of rocks kept banging against them. The stuck horn of a buried car was blaring. The family in the darkness in their fixed tableau watched one another by the light of a directional signal, endlessly blinking. The house had filled up in six minutes, and the mud stopped rising near the children's chins.

6   It was assumed that the Genofiles were dead. Firemen and paramedics who came into the neighborhood took one glance at the engulfed house and went elsewhere in search of people needing help. As the family remained trapped, perhaps an hour went by. They have no idea.

7   "We didn't know why it had come or how long it was going to last."

8   They lost all sense of time. The stuck horn went on blaring, the directional signal eerily blinking. They imagined that more debris was on the way.

9   "We didn't know if the whole mountain was coming down."

10   As they waited in the all but total darkness, Jackie thought of neighbors' children. "I thought, Oh, my gosh, all those little kids are dead. Actually, they were O.K. And the neighbors thought for sure we were all gone. All our neighbors thought we were gone."

11   At length, a neighbor approached their house and called out, "Are you alive?"

12   "Yes. But we need help."

13   As the debris flow hit the Genofiles' house, it also hit a six-ton truck from the L.A.C.F.C.D., the vigilant bureau called Flood. Vigilance was about all that the L.A.C.F.C.D. had been able to offer. The patrolling vehicle and its crew of two were as helpless as everyone else. Each of the crewmen had lived twenty-six years, and each came close to ending it there. Minutes before the flow arrived, the truck labored up Pine Cone Road—a forty-one-per-

cent grade, steep enough to stiff a Maserati. The two men meant
to check on a debris basin at the top. Known as Upper Shields, it
was less than two years old, and had been built in anticipation of
the event that was about to occur. Oddly enough, the Genofiles
and their neighbors were bracketed with debris basins—Upper
Shields above them, Shields itself below them, six times as large.
Shields Debris Basin, with its arterial concrete feeder channels,
was prepared to catch fifty thousand tons. The Genofiles' house
looked out over Shields as if it were an empty lake, its shores
hedged about with oleander. When the developer extended Pine
Cone Road up into the brush, the need for Upper Shields was
apparent. The new basin came in the nick of time but—with a
capacity under six thousand cubic yards—not in the nick of space.
Just below it was a chain-link gate. As the six-ton truck approached
the gate, mud was oozing through. The basin above had filled in
minutes, and now, suddenly, boulders shot like cannonballs over
the crest of the dam, with mud, cobbles, water, and trees. Chris
Terracciano, the driver, radioed to headquarters, "It's coming
over." Then he whipped the truck around and fled. The debris
flow came through the chain-link barrier as if the links were made
of paper. Steel posts broke off. As the truck accelerated down the
steep hill, the debris flow chased and caught it. Boulders bounced
against it. It was hit by empty automobiles spinning and revolving
in the muck. The whole descending complex gathered force with
distance. Terracciano later said, "I thought I was dead the whole
way." The truck finally stopped when it bashed against a tree and
a cement-block wall. The rear window shattered. Terracciano's
partner suffered a broken leg. The two men crawled out through
the window and escaped over the wall.

14   Within a few miles, other trapped patrols were calling in to
say, "It's coming over." Zachau went over—into Sunland. Haines
went over—into Tujunga. Dunsmuir went over—into Highway
Highlands. As bulldozers plow out the streets after events like
these, the neighborhoods of northern Los Angeles assume a
macabre resemblance to New England villages under deep snow:
the cleared paths, the vehicular rights-of-way, the parking meters
buried within the high banks, the half-covered drift-girt homes. A
street that is lined with palms will have debris berms ten feet up
the palms. In the Genofiles' front yard, the drift was twelve feet
deep. A person, without climbing, could walk onto the roof.
Scott's bedroom had a few inches of space left at the top.

Kimberlee's had mud on the ceiling. On the terrace, the crushed
vehicles, the detached erratic wheels suggested bomb damage,
artillery hits, the track of the Fifth Army. The place looked like a
destroyed pillbox. No wonder people assumed that no one had
survived inside

15   There was a white sedan under the house eaves crushed to
half its height, with two large boulders resting on top of it. Near
the pool, a Volkswagen bug lay squashed. Another car was literally
wrapped around a tree, like a C-clamp, its front and rear bumpers
pointing in the same direction. A crushed pickup had boulders all
over it, each a good deal heavier than anything a pickup could
carry. One of the cars in the swimming pool was upside down, its
tires in the air. A Volkswagen was on top of it. Bob Genofile—
owner, contractor, victim—walked around in rubber boots, a
visored construction cap, a foul-weather jacket, studying the damage, mostly guessing at what he couldn't see. A big, strongly built,
leonine man with prematurely white hair, he looked like a middle
linebacker near the end of a heavy day. He wondered if the house
was still on its foundation, but there was no telling in this profound chaos, now hardening and cracking like bad concrete. In
time, as his house was excavated from the inside, he would find
that it had not budged. Not one wall had so much as cracked. He
was uninsured, but down in the rubble was a compensation of
greater value than insurance. Forever, he could say, as he quietly
does when he tells the story, "I built it, man."

16   Kimberlee's birthday came two days after the debris. She was
a college student, turning nineteen, and her father had had a gift
for her that he was keeping in his wallet. "I had nineteen fifty-dol-
lar bills to give her for her birthday, but my pants and everything
was gone."

17   Young Scott, walking around in the wreckage, saw a belt
sticking out of the muck like a night crawler after rain. He pulled
at it, and the buried pants came with it. The wallet was still in the
pants. The wallet still contained what every daughter wants for her
birthday: an album of portraits of U.S. Grant, no matter if Ulysses
is wet or dry.

18   The living room had just been decorated, and in six minutes
the job had been destroyed—"the pale tangerines and greens,
Italian-style furniture with marble, and all that." Jackie Genofile
continues the story: "We had been out that night, and, you know,
you wear your better jewelry. I came home like an idiot and put

mine on the dresser. Bob put his on the dresser. Three weeks later, when some workers were cleaning debris out of the bedroom, they found his rings on the floor. They did not find mine. But—can you believe it?—a year and a half later Scott was down in the debris basin with one of his friends, and the Flood Control had these trucks there cleaning it out, and Scott saw this shiny thing, and he picked it up, and it was my ring that Bob had given me just before the storm."

19   Before the storm, they had not in any way felt threatened. Like their neighbors, they were confident of the debris basins, of the concrete liners of the nearby stream. After the storm, neighbors moved away. Where Pine Cone Road swung left or right, the debris had made centrifugal leaps, breaking into houses. A hydrant snapped off, and arcing water shot through an upstairs window. A child nearly drowned inside his own house. The family moved. "Another family that moved owned one of the cars that ended up in our pool," Jackie told me. "The husband said he'd never want to live here again, you know. And she was in real estate."

20   After the storm, the Genofiles tended to wake in the night, startled and anxious. They still do. "I wake up once in a while really uptight," Bob said. "I can just feel it—go through the whole thing, you know."

21   Jackie said that when rain pounds on a roof, anywhere she happens to be, she will become tense. Once, she took her dog and her pillow and went to sleep in Bob's office—which was then in Montrose, down beyond Foothill Boulevard.

22   Soon after the storm, she said, "Scotty woke up one night, and he had a real high temperature. You see, he was sixteen, and he kept hearing the mud and rock hitting the window. He kept thinking it was going to come again. Kim used to go four-wheeling, and cross streams, and she had to get out once, because they got stuck, and when she felt the flow of water and sand on her legs, she said, she could have panicked."

23   Soon after the storm, the family gathered to make a decision. Were they going to move or were they going to dig out their house and rebuild it? Each of them knew what might have happened. Bob said, "If it had been a frame house, we would be dead down in the basin below."

24   But it was not a frame house. It was the fort. "The kids said rebuild. So we rebuilt."

25　　As he sat in his new living room telling the story, Bob was dressed in a Pierre Cardin jumper and pants, and Jackie was beside him in a pale-pink jumpsuit by Saint Germain. The house had a designer look as well, with its railings and balconies and Italianate marbles under the tall dry trees. It appeared to be worth a good deal more than the half-million dollars Bob said it might bring. He had added a second story and put all bedrooms there. The original roof spread around them like a flaring skirt. He changed a floor-length window in the front hall, filling the lower half of it with cement block.

26　　I asked what other structural changes he had made.

27　　He said, "None."

28　　The Genofiles sued Los Angeles County. They claimed that Upper Shields Debris Basin had not been cleaned out and that the channel below was improperly designed. Los Angeles settled for three hundred and thirty-seven thousand five hundred dollars.

29　　From the local chamber of commerce the family later received the Beautification Award for Best Home. Two of the criteria by which houses are selected for this honor are "good maintenance" and "a sense of drama."

QUESTIONS

Ideas

1. McPhee is interested in strong narratives and concrete detail, not in strong conclusions. He assumes, of course, that active readers will find significance in this narrative of catastrophe. Read over the last five or six paragraphs and write your own explicit, one-sentence conclusion.

2. Is there some ambiguity in both the title of this essay as well as in the last phrase? Explain.

3. Is it irrational for people to want to live in dangerous locales? Do you get a sense that McPhee thinks the catastrophe could have been avoided?

Organization

4. Actually, these are two separate narratives. We have deleted a long related piece for more coherence. Comment on McPhee's narrative sequence? Is it simply, this happens and then this? Is McPhee actual-

ly present at the scene as the events are happening? Are there observations that suggests he is?

5. There are only five paragraphs in the first section, two of which
   seem quite long. Can you justify McPhee's organizational decision
   here?

Sentences

6. Notice the sentences in the long third and fifth paragraphs.
   Describe some of the different ways he begins sentences. Count the
   number of words in each sentence. Is there a rhythm to those various lengths?

7. McPhee will occasionally use short sentences of three to five words.
   Find some of these and comment on their purpose. Does he save
   them for some special effect?

Words

8. Pick out the similes and metaphors in these two passages. Are there
   similarities? To what end?

9. Where does "phalanxed" come from? How about "christiana turns"?
   What does "spalling" mean?

Suggestions for Writing

A. Write a narrative about a time when you were in some danger or
   difficulty because of nature, for example, some encounter with
   extreme cold or heat, a storm, rain, snow, an earthquake, hurricane,
   or tornado.

B. Explain why you would stay in a place you loved even if it were dangerous. Explain why you might leave.

Pirates, Stowaways, Drugs

1   And now it is 5:49 A.M., August 18th, and Vernon
McLaughlin turns the helm over to Calvin King, saying, "Zero-
three-nine. Automatic. All is well, and the pirates are waiting for
us." Three degrees south of the equator, we are crossing the Gulf
of Guayaquil. For the second time, we approach the Guayas. The

sea is flat. The temperature is cool (in the sixties). In the weeks since we were here before, the pirate talk has never really stopped, but now, as we prepare once more to go upstream, the talk intensifies. "This place is becoming a God-damned war zone," Mac says. "When you board a ship that is docking, how much more brazen can you get? That is real defiance."

2   "We didn't sign anything saying that we would defend this ship with our lives," Andy remarks.

3   In the past couple of months in Guayaquil, pirates have attacked the Allison Lykes once, the Mallory Lykes once, and the Stella Lykes three times. Late one evening, some of Stella's crew saw pirates boarding a vessel berthed a cable length away. The port authorities were notified. Meanwhile, the spectators watched goods from containers being lowered into small boats from the stern of the other ship. They witnessed the arrival of police, who had a look around and left. The pirates resumed work. Thirteen boatloads went to the mangrove swamps.

4   One attack occurred at noon. Obviously, the pirates have no fear of confrontation. "They know our routines," the captain remarks. "They know if we're eating supper. They know if we're heaving up the anchor. They know where every man on the ship is. They have free run of the harbor. They've come aboard with manifests. They go around looking for the containers with the TVs, the containers with the computers. Piracy is a way of life here. It has been for four hundred years. We've had 'em steal the flag halyards, the mooring lines. Any kind of metal. The sounding caps out of the deck. The deck telephones. Mooring lines are chained down and locked. They can cut those chains like they're paper. What can we do? We'll have roving patrols, crew members on the stern with walkie-talkies, searchlights."

5   J. Peter Fritz, the chief mate, says, "They carry firearms. They have bolt cutters. They know their way around the ship in darkness. They know our lashing gear. They know our docking procedures. They must have walkie-talkies. They must have people with spyglasses."

6   A couple of trips ago, in Guayaquil, an A.B. named Bill Haisten went aft at dawn to run up the flag and cut some lights. When he didn't return, Luke Midgett sent Calvin and Peewee to investigate. They found Haisten tied to a king post. Seven pirates had come over the stern and surprised him. In their needle boat, they had come up the river under the stern of the ship before the

day's first light. They were armed mainly with knives. One of them held a hacksaw blade at Haisten's throat while others tied him up. A sailor named Ron Just, who was taking "a morning stroll," happened to pick the wrong moment to stroll across the stern. They tied him to the lashing rods of a container. A pirate pointed at the men's watches and said, "Give me." When Just showed signs of not cooperating, the pirate threatened to cut off Just's arm with a hacksaw. Haisten and Just surrendered the watches. The pirate looked at Haisten's watch and gave it back.

7   Breaking into four containers, the pirates stole a load of yard goods. Then they went over the side and away in their boat. "But, hey," the captain says. "Hey! They take whole containers in New York, in Boston. They don't board from private boats. You're safe until the longshoremen and the labor gangs come aboard. They think it's part of their pay. No one outsteals the Boston longshoremen. They wouldn't *have* that. Ever since man put two logs together and made a raft, people stole from it. During the war, when I was an able seaman somewhere in North Africa I watched two Arabs work two hours to take a mattress through a porthole. They got a corner of it up there—they twisted and pulled and they twisted and pulled, and they finally got that whole mattress through the porthole. Then the chief mate took it away from them. But, hey! Piracy is a different ballgame. Sooner or later, they start killing people."

8   Off Singapore, when merchant ships make the slow tight move between Raffles Lighthouse and Buffalo Rock they might as well be passing through a pirate tollhouse. It is most especially that part of the Strait of Malacca which is in a category with the approaches to Lagos, with various ports in the Bight of Benin, with Guayaquil. After pirate attacks in the Malacca Strait, it has been reported that the pirates were wearing uniforms. They use gunboats. They have sprayed merchant ships with automatic weapons.

9   To throw a grappling hook over a stern rail and climb a line to board a ship requires conditioned strength. The pirates have that kind of strength. Our quinquagenarian and sexagenarian crewmen—so many of whom appear to be in their third trimester—are no match for such invaders. The day may come when merchant ships are beribboned with concertina wire, railed with chain-link fencing.

10   In Charleston, Captain Ron Crook told me that he had once

lain at anchor off the delta of the Ganges for two weeks as he waited to transfer cargo to a German ship. Every night, in heavy rain, pirates came down the river in black mahogany boats. These were oar-powered boats, each holding ten or fifteen pirates. Crook blew his whistle and shouted commands—including "Repel boarders!"—while the crew shot water into the boats from high-pressure hoses. The pirates had bamboo poles with hooks on the end. They climbed them to the deck. The crew fought the boarders with axe handles, broom handles, and three-cell flashlights. At last, the Germans arrived. They brought two hundred Indians of both sexes and all ages to unload the ship by hand, to lighten it enough to go up the shallow Ganges to Calcutta. The Indians camped on Crook's deck, where they built fires and made curries. Crook is a great-great-great-nephew of Brigadier General George Crook, commander of the Department of the Platte, who was one of the most celebrated soldiers of the Old West, and who stood out in his time for the integrity with which he dealt with Indians.

11 In 1974, when Ron Crook was third mate on the Mormacscan, armed pirates boarded her in Brazilian waters, went directly to a container said to contain two hundred thousand dollars' worth of Kodak film, offloaded all the film, and sped away in a small, fast boat.

12 Captain Washburn says, "Hey, Cartagena it happens. Buenaventura. In Buenaventura, a while back, they boarded ships while they were under way. It took the United Nations to stop it. In Buenaventura, while the Mason Lykes was steaming around the sea buoy—waiting for daylight *because* of piracy—a pirate grappled the rail, came aboard with a gun, held up the third mate, took his wallet and watch, and disappeared. But, hey, a couple of guys disguised as longshoremen went on a Waterman ship in Barbour's Cut, Houston, Texas, and walked right into the captain's office, made him open the safe, took the money, and shot him dead. Pretty soon—down here on the west coast of South America—it's going to get violent. Right now you'll see armed guards. That's fairly new. Pretty soon these pirates will start shooting back if they get shot at."

13 In Callao, after a new pilot ladder worth five thousand dollars went over the side and into a waiting boat, Louis Smothers said, "What goes around comes back." In case anyone misunderstood him, he explained that we, as a nation, "stole people's lands and destroyed their minds," and are now getting what we deserve.

Smothers, an A.B. on the twelve-to-four, was the assistant pastor of
a church in York, Pennsylvania, before he moved to Jacksonville.
There he has become an intraurban itinerant preacher, preaching every Sunday in a different church when he is home from the
sea. He has been shipping out with the Merchant Marine for
twenty-seven years. Before that, he was in theological seminary,
and before that he spent many years in the army. He once owned
what he describes as "the largest black detective agency in the
state of Maryland." He often wears shorts. They reveal the legs of
a football player. On his dark-blue baseball cap are the words
"QUEEN MARY," across the brow in gold. "The Peruvians steal a line
or a ladder or something from a container," he went on. "In New
York, they steal your Mercedes and put it *in* a container, and six
days later it's in Panama."

14   On every deck of the Stella Lykes, signs are hung on the
doors that connect the interior of the house to the open outside
spaces:

> THIS DOOR TO BE KEPT CLOSED AND
> DOGGED IN ALL FOREIGN PORTS

The doors are dogged to keep out more than pirates. Captain
Washburn, who happens to be in his quarters now, lathering up
for his morning shave and listening to his tape of "Heartaches,"
says, "This coast is not only the drug-producing capital of the
world; it is also the stowaway-producing capital of the world. Why
the ships here don't have more of each is a mystery. We fight it
and fight it and fight it. We try our best to hold it to a minimum."
Some years ago, the word "contraband" referred, generally, to
souvenirs illegally transported by crewmen, he went on. "When
you are talking about contraband now, you are talking about nar-
cotics—hashish, marijuana, cocaine, heroin. That stuff is doubly
hard to find. Usually it's in very small packages. They can hide it
in a light fixture or a shoe."

15   As for stowaways, Washburn has found very few of them on
ships of which he has been master—and that is most fortunate, he
adds, because stowaways are a major nuisance. If they turn up on
your ship, you pay a fine. You do a great deal of paperwork. You
post a sizable bond. You don't get it back if they escape. When
they go off the ship, you have to hire guards to guard them. You
have to see that they are put on the right plane. "If you bring in

twenty stowaways, you're looking at a couple of hundred thousand dollars. You're looking at big bucks."

16   Once does not have to be a former hobo to understand that the seriousness of the stowaway problem is not in a category with the drug traffic. I cannot help wondering, though, what this son of the side-door sleeping cars, this former rider of the rails, would do with stowaways if he found them on his ship.

17   I ask him, and he says, "I'd take the handcuffs and the leg irons and lock them up."

18   On a dock in Colombia during the previous voyage, Ron Peterson, the third mate, was about to inspect a container when a Colombian longshoreman rushed up and put a Lykes Brothers seal on it. This was to be the last container loaded on the ship, and Peterson knew that it was said to contain nothing and therefore did not require a seal. He described the scene to the chief mate, who came down the gangway, broke the seal, and looked in. Nine faces looked out.

19   Ecuadorian and Colombian longshoremen loading American ships used to build huts deep in the holds and bury stowaways in mountains of coffee. Some ships have diverted steam lines into cargo compartments and used a steam smothering system to flush out possible stowaways. Some have used whistles at deafening frequencies. After Delta Lines did that, Colombia complained to the United Nations. Not long ago, the Sheldon Lykes arrived in Mobile, Alabama, with twenty-one Colombian stowaways aboard. A West German ship turned up in Jacksonville with four Ethiopians. The youngest was twelve, the oldest fifteen. Heading south, the crew of the Allison Lykes found a stowaway who had got on in New York.

20   At the end of another recent voyage, the Allison arrived in Port Newark carrying a container said to contain chocolate and addressed to a warehouse in Long Island. The United States Customs Service drilled into the chocolate and found a filling of cocaine. They resealed the container. It was offloaded, set on a tractor trailer, and driven away. Customs agents followed. At the Long Island warehouse, they arrested the recipients of the chocolate, who were members of the Medellín Cartel. Inside the chocolate was four hundred and eighty million dollars' worth of cocaine—the largest single shipment of cocaine ever seized in a United States port north of Florida.

21   "They just try to catch what they can," Washburn comments.

"They figure they stop less than ten per cent of it." When the
Customs people appeared in Newark with fifteen dogs and
unloaded seventy of Stella's containers right there on the dock,
they found nothing. Nevertheless, they charged the people to
whom the containers were addressed seventy-five dollars per container. When they do discover drugs, they not only will fine the
shipping company but will confiscate whole ships. They fined
Evergreen, of the Taiwan flag, fifty-nine and a half million dollars
after eleven thousand pounds of marijuana turned up in New
Orleans.

22   "It's our problem, but there's nothing we can do about it,"
Washburn continues. "The letter of the law is that a ship is
responsible for everything it brings in. But we're not there when
the containers are packed. When they deliver a container down
here, you certainly don't make them take the cargo out of it.
They've now got containers that are built to smuggle. They've got
a double wall. You couldn't detect it if you were in there. We pick
up containers and we load them, and there's absolutely no way we
can check the contents. We've got a piece of paper that says
what's in there. 'Said to contain'—that's all we've got. Half of
these drugs are smuggled in in household articles—like they've
got refrigerators and dryers just full of them, and overstuffed furniture. But the real kingpins are much more sophisticated than
that. It's a computerized business today. It's not piecemeal or haphazard. Where they've got three or four hundred million dollars'
worth coming in, the cartel may have spent two years setting that
one delivery up. They even start when they're refining it. They
say, 'O.K., we're refining this amount. It's eventually going to go
to New York in *this* type of container.' They'll even *build* a container for that special shipment. These clever Colombians—they trap
wild dogs and keep them penned up. They use the urine of the
wild dogs to smear on the packages of cocaine that they're sending in to the United States. These domestic dogs that we're using
smell that wild-dog urine and they're afraid, and they don't go
near that stuff. There'll be a day that these dogs will be useless to
us and we'll be using pigs. They find something. We combat it.
They find something else. The drug lords threaten everyone. Oh,
they're tough. They've caught American drug enforcers, and
they've killed more than one, and they didn't kill 'em quick,
either. It took some of them two or three days to die. Just like the
old days, you know—two or three days and just begging for death.

These Colombians don't just kill a person. They'll kill a guy's mother and father, his wife, his children. They kill the whole family. There's a viciousness about these present drug dealers that the old Mafia—the old underworld—never had. The old underworld treated each other bad enough, but they weren't vicious to the general populace, ever. It was bad for business. They thought nothing of shooting or blowing up their adversary, but they never thought about hitting a guy's women and children. It wasn't their nature. But, man, these drug lords—they'll terrorize a whole community to have their way. They had one prosecutor in Colombia that the drug lords told him they were going to kill him and they told him there was nowhere he could hide. They told him, 'Between the North Pole and the South Pole there is nowhere you can go that we won't find you. There's no such place.' I think it was Sofia, Bulgaria, they caught up with him and killed him. That's what an honest official is up against. In Ecuador, my gosh, they're killing a prosecutor or a judge every day in the week."

23   On one of Stella's voyages, under another captain, a Colombian brought to the ship a twenty-kilogram carton labeled as coffee. He said it was for the bosun, and he departed. Crew members routinely buy Colombian coffee, but not the brand mentioned on the carton. The bosun said he had purchased none. Lock it up, said the captain. After the ship sailed, he ordered an inspection. According to Peewee, who was working that voyage, the box contained well over a million dollars' worth of uncut crack—twelve tightly wrapped packets of white powder, at any rate, each weighing more than three and a half pounds. The captain told the mate to break open the packets and pour the contents into the ocean. "That saved a lot of paperwork," Peewee said as he finished telling the story. "A lot of paperwork and a lot of jive." The deliveryman had evidently erred. Not long before he reached the dock, another ship had sailed for the United States.

24   Some years ago, after a sailor just off the Joseph Lykes was found with two million dollars' worth of cocaine, Lykes Brothers was fined two hundred thousand dollars. Washburn believes that American sailors do very little smuggling anymore. Among other things, they have come to know that people who sell drugs to Americans are likely to go straight to the American Embassy and report the transaction in order to claim a finder's fee. The United States pays finder's fees of up to fifty thousand dollars.

25   Washburn likes to tell a story about an old Lykes Brothers
stick ship that "brought a couple and their camper-type van from
the Gulf down to either Colombia or Ecuador on this run, and
put them off." He continues, "What these people were going to
do was tour South America, and then they were going to come
back on this same ship to the United States. They left the ship in
either Guayaquil or Buenaventura—I forget which. Weeks later,
the couple came aboard, with their ticket and everything, and the
ship was loading their camper. The chief mate happened to
notice that the ship's cargo gear—those single-stick booms—
could hardly pick that camper up. They got it aboard, but just
barely. And he became suspicious, and they searched that
camper, and there was three tons of cocaine in a special-built
floor in the bottom of the camper. It was not in there haphazard.
It was almost like that camper had been rebuilt. Three tons of
cocaine is worth about a hundred and eighty million dollars."

26   Washburn stares for a while into the passing mangroves, the
ragged edge of the olive river. Then he says, "The basis of the
problem is the American appetite for this stuff. I can put everybody else down, but *we're the customers*. I'm sittin' here puttin'
Colombia, Bolivia, and Ecuador down, and *we're* the customers.
It's *our* ferocious appetite. It's an illness. And if anybody has it we
all have it. Hey, if I caught my son with that stuff I would bag him
quicker than I would anyone else. I'd bag him first. If I knew it
was in my house, I wouldn't send for the city police, I'd send for
the narcs, and they could have him. He'd be gone—gee oh enn
ee. It's sick, disgusting, debasing, dehumanizing."

QUESTIONS

Ideas

1.   Do you think the captain is trying to understand why the pirates
     steal—or is he trying to rationalize or excuse it?

2.   Captain Washburn claims that the pirates will shoot back "if they get
     shot at." Does this suggest that armed police are partly responsible
     for the violence of criminals?

3.   In describing some of the problems of today's merchant marine,
     McPhee describes pirates, stowaways, and drugs. Although McPhee
     tries to efface himself and his values, are all three problems treated
     the same? Can you sense McPhee's opinions?

4. Do you agree with Washburn's accusation in the last paragraph?

Organization

5. Describe how McPhee manages his transitions from pirates to stowaways to drugs.
6. McPhee blends narrative with dialogue throughout his writing, but sometimes he will have whole paragraphs of narration and then large sections of quoted material. Find examples and comment on the effectiveness of each technique.

Sentences

7. McPhee has a reputation for writing clear, precise sentences. Some readers might even consider them flat. Choose several examples of sentences that could be considered either exact or colorless.
8. Choose a long paragraph and comment on McPhee's variations in sentence length and openings.

Words

9. In describing the crew, McPhee calls them quinqungenarian and sexagenarian. What do these terms mean? Should McPhee have used simpler language? Did you notice any technical nautical terms? Can you figure out plausible definitions from the context?

Suggestions for Writing

A. Write a response to Captain Washburn's closing statement, especially his comment about his son.
B. Lurking in the background of this piece might be the suggestion that human nature is corrupt. Do you agree or are pirates, drugs, and stowaways merely social problems? Write an essay in which you explore both possibilities.

The Pineys

---

1   While isolation in the woods was bringing out self-reliance, it was also contributing to other developments that eventually attracted more attention. After the pine towns lost touch, to

a large extent, with the outside world, some of the people slid into illiteracy, and a number slid further than that. Marriages were pretty casual in the pines late in the nineteenth century and early in the twentieth. For lawful weddings, people had to travel beyond the woods, to a place like Mt. Holly. Many went to native "squires," who performed weddings for a fee of one dollar. No questions were asked, even if the squires recognized the brides and the grooms as people they had married to other people a week or a month before. Given the small population of the pines, the extreme rarity of new people coming in, and the long span of time that most families had been there, some relationships were extraordinarily complicated and a few were simply incestuous. To varying degrees, there was a relatively high incidence in the pines of what in the terms of the era was called degeneracy, feeblemindedness, or mental deficiency.

2   In 1913, startling publicity was given to the most unfortunate stratum of the pine society, and the effects have not yet faded. In that year, Elizabeth Kite, a psychological researcher, published a report called "The Pineys," which had resulted from two years of visits to cabins in the pines. Miss Kite worked for the Vineland Training School, on the southern edge of the Pine Barrens, where important early work was being done with people of subnormal intelligence, and she was a fearless young woman who wore spotless white dresses as she rode in a horse-drawn wagon through the woods. Her concern for the people there became obvious to the people themselves, who grew fond of her, and even dependent upon her, and a colony for the care of the "feebleminded" was founded in the northern part of the Pine Barrens as a result of her work. Her report told of children who shared their bedrooms with pigs, of men who could not count beyond three, of a mother who walked nine miles with her children almost every day to get whiskey, of a couple who took a wheelbarrow with them when they went out drinking, so that one could wheel the other home. "In the heart of the region, scattered in widely separated huts over miles of territory, exists today a group of human beings as distinct in morals and manners as to excite curiosity and wonder in the mind of any outsider brought into contact with them," Miss Kite wrote. "They are recognized as a distinct people by the normal communities living on the borders of their forests." The report included some extremely gnarled family trees, such as one headed by Sam Bender, who

conceived a child with his daughter, Mollie Bender Brooks, whose husband, Billie Brooks, sometimes said the child had been fathered by his wife's brother rather than her father, both possibilities being strong ones. When a district nurse was sent around to help clean up Mollie's house, chickens and a pig were found in the kitchen, and the first implement used in cleaning the house was a hoe. Mollie, according to Miss Kite, was "good-looking and sprightly, which fact, coupled with an utter lack of sense of decency, made her attractive even to men of otherwise normal intelligence." When Billie and all of their children were killed in a fire, Mollie said cheerfully, "Well, they was all insured. I'm still young and can easy start another family." Miss Kite reported some relationships that are almost impossible to follow. Of the occupants of another cabin, she wrote, "That May should call John 'Uncle' could be accounted for on the basis of a childish acceptance of 'no-matter-what' conditions, for the connection was that her mother was married to the brother of John's other woman's second man, and her mother's sister had had children by John. This bond of kinship did not, however, keep the families long together." Miss Kite also told of a woman who came to ask for food at a state almshouse on a bitter winter day. The people at the almshouse gave her a large burlap sack containing a basket of potatoes, a basket of turnips, three cabbages, four pounds of pork, five pounds of rye flour, two pounds of sugar, and some tea. The woman shouldered the sack and walked home cross-country through snow. Thirty minutes after she reached her home, she had a baby. No one helped her deliver it, nor had anyone helped her with the delivery of her nine other children.

3   Miss Kite's report was made public. Newspapers printed excerpts from it. All over the state, people became alarmed about conditions in the Pine Barrens—a region most of them had never heard of. James T. Fielder, the governor of New Jersey, travelled to the pines, returned to Trenton, and sought to increase his political momentum by recommending to the legislature that the Pine Barrens be somehow segregated from the rest of New Jersey in the interest of the health and safety of the people of the state at large. "I have been shocked at the conditions I have found," he said. "Evidently these people are a serious menace to the State of New Jersey because they produce so many persons that inevitably become public charges. They have inbred, and led lawless and scandalous lives, till they have become a race of imbeciles, crimi-

nals, and defectives." Meanwhile, H. H. Goddard, director of the research laboratory at the Vineland Training School and Miss Kite's immediate superior, had taken the genealogical charts that Miss Kite had painstakingly assembled, pondered them, extrapolated a bit, and published what became a celebrated treatise on a family called Kallikak—a name that Goddard said he had invented to avoid doing harm to real people. According to the theory set forth in the treatise, nearly all pineys were descended from one man. This man, Martin Kallikak, conceived an illegitimate son with an imbecile barmaid. Martin's bastard was said to be the forebear of generations of imbeciles, prostitutes, epileptics, and drunks. Martin himself, however, married a normal girl, and among their progeny were generations of normal and intelligent people, including doctors, lawyers, politicians, and a president of Princeton University. Goddard coined the name Kallikak from the Greek *kalós* and *kakós*—"good" and "bad." Goddard's work has been discredited, but its impact, like that of Governor Fielder's proposal to segregate the Pine Barrens, was powerful in its time. Even Miss Kite seemed to believe that there was some common flaw in the blood of all the people of the pines. Of one pinelands woman, Miss Kite wrote, "Strangely enough, this woman belonged originally to good stock. No piney blood flowed in her veins."

4   The result of all this was a stigma that has never worn off. A surprising number of people in New Jersey today seem to think that the Pine Barrens are dark backlands inhabited by hostile and semiliterate people who would as soon shoot an outsider as look at him. A policeman in Trenton who had never been to the pines—"only driven through on the way downa shore," as people usually say—once told me, in an anxious tone, that if I intended to spend a lot of time in the Pine Barrens I was asking for trouble. Some of the gentlest of people—botanists, canoemen, campers— spent a great deal of time in the pines, but their influence has not been sufficient to correct an impression, vivid in some parts of the state for fifty years, that the pineys are weird and sometimes dangerous barefoot people who live in caves, marry their sisters, and eat snakes. Pineys are, for the most part, mild and shy, but their resentment is deep, and they will readily and forcefully express it. The unfortunate people that Miss Kite described in her report were a minor fraction of the total population of the Pine Barrens, and the larger number suffered from it, and are still suffering

from it. This appalled Elizabeth Kite, who said to an interviewer in 1940, some years before her death, "Nothing would give me greater pleasure than to correct the idea that has unfortunately been given by the newspapers regarding the pines. Anybody who lived in the pines was a piney. I think it a most terrible calamity that the newspapers publicly took the term and gave it the degenerate sting. Those families who were not potential state cases did not interest me as far as my study was concerned. I have no language in which I can express my admiration for the pines and the people who live there."

5   The people of the Pine Barrens turn cold when they hear the word "piney" spoken by anyone who is not a native. Over the years since 1913, in many places outside the pines, the stigma of degeneracy has been concentrated in that word. A part of what hurts them is that they themselves are fond of the word. They refer to one another freely, and frequently, as pineys. They have a strong regional pride, and, in a way that is not at all unflattering to them, they *are* different from the run of the people of the state. A visitor who stays awhile in the Pine Barrens soon feels that he is in another country, where attitudes and ambitions are at variance with the American norm. People who drive around in the pines and see houses like Fred Brown's, with tarpaper peeling from the walls, and automobiles overturned in the front yard, often decide, as they drive on, that they have just looked destitution in the face. I wouldn't call it that. I have yet to meet anyone living in the Pine Barrens who has in any way indicated envy of people who live elsewhere. One reason there are so many unpainted houses in the Pine Barrens is that the pineys believe, correctly, that their real-estate assessments would be higher if their houses were painted. Some pineys who make good money in blueberries or cranberries or in jobs on the outside would never think of painting their houses. People from other parts of New Jersey will say of Pine Barrens people, "They don't like to work. They can't seem to hold jobs." This, too, is a judgment based on outside values. What the piney usually says is "I hate to be tied down long to any one job." That remark is made so often in the pines that it is almost a local slogan. It expresses an attitude born of the old pines cycle—sphagnum in the spring, berries in the summer, coaling when the weather is cold. With the plenitude of the woodland around them—and, historically, behind them—pineys are bored with the

idea of doing the same thing all year long, in every weather. Many of them have to, of course. Many work at regular jobs outside the woods. But many try that and give it up, preferring part-time labor—always at rest in the knowledge that no one who knows the woods and is willing to do a little work on his own is ever going to go hungry. The people have no difficulty articulating what it is that gives them a special feeling about the landscape they live in; they know that their environment is unusual and they know why they value it. Some, of course, put it with more finesse than others do. "I'm just a woods boy," a fellow named Jim Leek said to me one day. "There ain't nobody bothers you here. You can be alone. I'm just a woods boy. I wouldn't want to live in a town." When he said "town," he meant one of the small communities in the pines; he preferred living in the woods to living in a Pine Barrens town. When pineys talk about going to "the city," they usually mean Mt. Holly or the Moorestown Mall or the Two Guys from Harrison store on Route 206. When Jim Leek said "nobody bothers you" and "you can be alone," he was sounding two primary themes of the pines. Bill Wasovwich said one day, "The woods just look nice and it's more quieter. It's quiet anywhere in the pines. That's why I like it here." Another man, Scorchy Jones, who works for the state Fish and Game Division, said this to an interviewer from a small New Jersey radio station: "A sense of security is high among us. We were from pioneers. We know how to survive in the woods. Here in these woods areas, you have a reputation. A dishonest person can't survive in the community. You have to maintain your reputation, or you would have to jump from place to place. A man lives by his reputation and by his honesty and by his ambition to work. If he doesn't have it, he would be an outcast. These people have the reputations of their parents and grandparents ahead of them—and they are proud of them, and they want to maintain that same standard. They don't worship gold. All they want is necessities. They would rather live than make a lot of money. They live by this code. They're the best citizens in this country." Later in the interview, Jones said, "Unless these wild areas are preserved, we're going to get to the point where dense population is going to work on the nervous systems of the people, and the more that takes place, the poorer neighbors they become. Eventually, like birds or animals confined to too small an area, they will fight among themselves. Man is an animal as well." People known in the pines as "the old-time pineys"—those who lived wholly by the cycle, and seldom, if ever, saw an outsider—are gone now. When the United States Army built Camp Dix on the northwestern edge of the Pine Barrens during the First World War, civilian jobs were created, and many people of the pines first got to know what money was and how to use it. Paved roads first crossed the pines in the nineteen-twenties. Electrical lines, the Second World War, and television successively brought an end to the utter isolation of the pineys. But so far all this has not materially changed their attitudes. They are apparently a tolerant people, with an attractive spirit of live and let live. They seem to like hard work, if not steady work, and they like to brag about working hard. When they say they will do something, they do it. They seem shy, like the people who went before them, but when they get to know an outsider they are not shy and will generously share their tables, which often include new-potato stews and cranberry potpies. I have met Pine Barrens people who have, at one time or another, moved to other parts of the country. Most of them tried other lives for a while, only to return unreluctantly to the pines. One of them explained to me, "It's a privilege to live in these woods."

QUESTIONS

Ideas

1. How do you explain the behavior of the pineys?
2. What function does Miss Kite serve in this piece?
3. Do you think Mollie is amoral? What principles do the pineys operate on? Do they have a morality or a code that they follow?
4. Do you think it was unusual for the newspapers to have given the pineys such negative publicity?
5. What do you think McPhee thinks about the pineys? How can you tell? Look especially at the extended quotes he uses.
6. If you regarded this piece as a research essay (which, of course, it is), you might find it profitable to examine McPhee's way of integrating facts, details, quotes, dialogue, narration, and commentary into a seamless whole. At the end of this piece the reader knows a good deal. Jot down in phrases what you remember from a first reading, then go back and read the piece again, noting the amount of information McPhee is able to blend almost unnoticed into his account.

Organization

7. As Aristotle perceptively noted, effective pieces of writing tend to have a beginning, a middle, and an end. Composition textbooks often say an introduction, a body, and a conclusion. What kind of pattern is being used here?

8. Can you point to a thematic sentence that suggests the focus of this piece?

9. Look at the first sentence in each paragraph. What function does it serve?

Sentences

10. Is the first sentence in each paragraph shorter than the others, on the average? What might be a reason for this?

11. Notice how McPhee weaves quotes into his sentences to give them authority and force. Based on the second paragraph, write some general rules for using quotes. Include the use of commas, capital letters, and quote marks, and note especially McPhee's technique of using a quote as part of his sentence.

Words

12. What emotional association do you have to these words: "feeble-mindedness," "mental deficiency," "imbeciles," and "degenerate." Can such connotations be changed?

Suggestions for Writing

A. Interview someone in class on a specific topic (favorite guitar player, sports hero, whatever). Copy down exact quotes and indirect quotes (exact meaning but not the specific words used). Now write up the interview using the quotes. Blend as many of the quotes as you can into your own sentences.

B. Do some focused research on a group that typically gets bad publicity. In writing your brief research essay arrange your facts and quotes so as to convey your attitude toward the group. (It can, of course, be positive or negative.)

The Swiss at War

---

1   It seems likely that the two most widely circulated remarks ever made about Switzerland's military prowess were made by Napoleon Bonaparte and Orson Welles.

2   Welles said, "In Italy for thirty years under the Borgias, they had warfare, terror, murder, bloodshed—but they produced Michelangelo, Leonardo da Vinci, and the Renaissance. In Switzerland, they have brotherly love, five hundred years of democracy and peace, and what did that produce? The cuckoo clock."

3   Napoleon said, "The best troops—those in whom you can have the most confidence—are the Swiss."

4   Welles spoke his lines in "The Third Man," a motion picture that deservedly attracted an extensive worldwide audience. The screenplay was written by Graham Greene, who later published the preliminary treatment in book form, but Greene was not the author of the lines about the Borgias and Switzerland. They were interpolated by the ingenious Welles, who may have chosen to suppress in his memory the fact that when Italy was enjoying the Borgias, Switzerland was enjoying a reputation as—to quote Douglas Miller's "The Swiss at War"—"the most powerful and feared military force in Europe." Switzerland was about as neutral in those days as had been Mongolia under Genghis Khan. Not only were the Swiss ready to fight. They fought. They had a militia system that could mobilize fifty-four thousand soldiers. They knew enough warfare and bloodshed to sicken a Borgia. They were so chillingly belligerent that even if they were destroyed in battle they had been known in the same moment to win a war. One afternoon in mid-Renaissance, a few hundred Swiss who were outnumbered fifteen to one elected not to run away but to wade across a river and break into the center of the opposition, where all of them died, but not before they had slaughtered three thousand of their French enemies. The French Army was so unnerved that it struck its tents and fled.

5   It was the Swiss who unhorsed the mounted knight, and in a sense their confederation—their Everlasting League—was formed with that in mind. The peasants of the forest cantons made their pact of mutual defense because they wished not to be the vassals of alien equestrian lords. They waited twenty-four years for the first big test of their ability to resist—ample time to be prepared, to rehearse what they would do. Then, in 1315, two thousand Austrian knights appeared, leading a considerable army, and fatally attempted to make use of Morgarten pass. The knights were aristocrats, accustomed to tournament warfare and not to peasants attacking them from higher ground. The peasants came down on them with tree trunks, halberds, axes, and plummeting

rock. The pass was blocked. The horses and riders became compressed and hopelessly jammed. The peasants rushed among them and hacked them down. Few knights survived. ("In the mountains, mechanization doesn't help you any. You are almost lost with armored cars.")

6   Also in the Renaissance, Swiss soldiers began sewing white crosses on their doublets, so they would recognize one another in the confusion of infantry battle. When mounted knights attacked them in open country, the Swiss formed squares—ten thousand soldiers in a square, bristling with twenty-one-foot pikes: the Porcupine Principle. In the course of time, they developed some interesting equipment. They developed the Lucerne hammer, fundamentally a poleaxe with a brass fist on its head and spikes protruding between the fingers. They developed the Morgenstern, an eight-foot cudgel with a sixteen-spike pineapple head. And they developed the Swiss Army knife.

7   Its precursor was a simple fifteenth-century dagger that every warrior carried. Over a hundred years, it acquired so many additions and complications that only officers and rich citizens could afford it, and it fell into disuse. It was an infantry weapon, but in its advanced stages it acquired built-in forks and other utensils. Competition waxed in the decorating of sheaths with scroll ornaments in gold and silver, and expensive foreign artists—such as the Hans Holbeins—were employed to do the work. The knife every soldier is issued today is jacketed with quilted gray aluminum, has one blade, a can opener, a bottle opener, a hole punch, two screwdrivers, and no corkscrew. On one side is a small red shield bearing the white cross. The knife is made identically by two companies—Victorinox and Wenger—that also make the red knives that in commercial display cases are all stuck apart like swastikas and include fish disgorgers, ski-wax scrapers, international wrenches, magnifying glasses, tweezers, toothpicks, scissors, and saws. The gray army knife resembles the simpler of the commercial offerings, minus the red plastic. Officers included, everyone in the Swiss Army carries a Swiss Army knife. Once, at the end of a long session in driving snow with machine guns firing and grenades exploding—up on the high ground where such practice can be conducted with live ammunition—I walked down with the Fifth Regiment's Colonel Marc-Henri Chaudet, and when he reached the roadhead he discovered that his automobile would not start. It was a gray Mercedes-Benz, and—with its

hood up—its engine looked even grayer, there in the wind and stinging snow, many miles from the nearest garage and almost as many from the nearest warm room. After six hours of storm weather and steep inclines, the Colonel might have been forgiven if he had displayed exasperation. This, after all, was Switzerland, where everything works; Switzerland, where trains run like clocks, and clocks run like watches, and watches are synchronous with the pulse of the universe; Switzerland, where electric eyes watch underground parking spaces and turn on green lights when they are free; Switzerland, where electric eyes watch urinals and flush not only the one under address but the one next to it as well; Switzerland, where switches in mattresses cause rooms to go dark as people get into bed; and now, in Switzerland, the Colonel was inconvenienced by this weather-whipped, tuned-down, one-jewel German car, which wheezed but would not cough. Colonel Chaudet—a Vevey lawyer—gave it a cool glance, sighting along his nose. Tall, slim, handsome—his trousers taut and neatly creased and disappearing inside his boots like a downhill skier's— the Colonel had a certain downplay in the corners of his mouth, suggesting, among other things, detached amusement. Besides, he had complete confidence in his soldiers and their equipment. Observing the difficulty, a corporal stepped forward, removed from a pocket his Swiss Army knife, used a fingernail to expose the can opener, and leaned into the Mercedes. Within ten minutes, the engine was running.

8   The Swiss infantry, six hundred years ago, knew not only how to form a square but also how to break through almost anything. At Sempach—a name of resonance in Switzerland—a soldier named Arnold Winkelried gathered to his body the pike points of many foemen, thus opening on either side of him holes in the Austrian line, through which the Swiss backfield poured, swinging six-foot halberds, while Winkelried died. For each Swiss who died at Sempach, nine Austrians died as well, many of them dismounted knights. Machiavelli called the Swiss "the new Romans." In the Quattrocento, exactly three hundred years before the United States declared its independence, the Swiss won a great victory at a small town called Morat, defeating Burgundian invaders who were threatening the city of Fribourg. Among the Swiss ordnance were mortars that shot chunks of limestone and granite. Four hundred and ten Swiss died at Morat— and twelve thousand Burgundians. A durable legend sprang from

this battle. To wit: a Swiss courier-soldier, carrying a linden branch, ran with the glorious news to Fribourg; all but breathless, he at last approached the ramparts and the towers of the town, and passed through the main gate and into the central square, where anxious Fribourgeois had formed a human circle—magistrates, priests, women on their knees—in the center of which the courier gathered his last three breaths, shouted "Victoire! Victoire! Victoire!" and fell dead, as later recorded, "la face contre terre." It has been suggested that this story is not without companionship in a genre! However that may be, there is an old sick linden in Fribourg that is thought to have grown from the branch the runner carried. Each year, in October, a footrace is run from Morat to Fribourg, and it now attracts about a hundred thousand spectators and eleven thousand runners. The race has been held for fifty years, with runners sometimes preparing for the ordeal by stretching their minds as well as their muscles—chanting in the streets, "Morat! Morat! Morat!" It doesn't matter that the distance is four-tenths of a marathon.

9   Swiss neutrality began in 1515, when the Swiss were thoroughly beaten by a French Army under François I at Marignano, in what is now Italy. "I have conquered those whom only Caesar managed to conquer before me," said the French king, and his words were struck in coin. The confederated cantons, by then thirteen, decided to fight thereafter only as mercenaries in other people's wars. They were a small nation, rustic, poor—nothing at all like the service-industry and manufacturing society we know today—and to embellish their economy they leased their incomparable soldiers. The cantons have always been importantly autonomous, and never more so than in the sixteenth century, when the political bond between Catholics and Protestants was under so much strain. It is unlikely that during the heaviest reverberations of the Reformation a cooperating army could have been assembled from the Protestant and Catholic cantons, and so, regardless of Marignano, neutrality was now less a matter of policy than a de-facto condition of Swiss life. The militia was then, as it has generally remained, cantonal in character. The cantons did the selling of soldiers. The French bought heavily for three hundred years—now twelve thousand Swiss, now seventy thousand Swiss, now a hundred and sixty-three thousand Swiss, depending on the intensity of the problems of France. For all that time, the Compagnie des Cent-Suisses were the personal bodyguards of the

French kings. Scarcely had the Swiss soldiers appeared in the French court when the Pope decided that he wanted some, too; and the Pope, of course, still has them, ninety in all—the only vestige of the Swiss mercenaries.

10   Switzerland is so conscious—not to say proud—of the service of its mercenaries in foreign armies that a château outside Geneva has been refurbished as a Musée des Suisses à l'Étranger. The most eminent mercenary of all was Colonel Louis Pfyffer, Roi des Suisses, who became a Swiss hero by serving four French kings. Jérôme d'Erlach, of Bern, became a Swiss hero as an Austrian field marshal. François Lefort, of Geneva, became a Swiss hero as a Russian general under Peter the Great, as Viceroy of the Grand Duchy of Novgorod, as President of all the Councils of Russia, and as the creator and Grand Admiral of the Russian Navy. Swiss mercenaries fought for the Scandinavian kingdoms, the Holy Roman Empire, the Netherlands, Prussia, Poland, Lorraine, Saxony, Savoy, Spain. In various battles, they fought on both sides. They served the Doge of Genoa, the King of Naples, the Elector of Brandenburg. For a large unnegotiable discount, they served Napoleon. Later, they became one of the perennially toughest components of the French Foreign Legion. In the Château de Penthes—the Musée des Suisses à l'Étranger—hangs a British Union Jack with a prominently inset Swiss white cross.

11   Contracts always specified that if Switzerland was attacked the soldiers would go back to Switzerland. All such contracts have been illegal for something over a hundred years. Meanwhile, by 1830 or so, in places like Bière, the militias of the various cantons were getting together to march, to exercise, to perform military legerdemain before people with parasols and uncorked wine, men in top hats chatting with soldiers in uniform attending the beginning of the federal army. Upward of a hundred thousand people will turn out today to watch the army parade and perform. A retired soldier will visit his unit's refresher course like an old college football player returning to watch a practice. Quite voluntarily, several thousand civilian soldiers annually collect for a thirty-kilometer footrace in which they carry packs and rifles. Beneath the long neutrality, there lies what the Swiss describe as "an aptitude for war." It appears to be an appetite as well—sublimited and under close control. The Landesmuseum in Zurich is the Louvre of the toy soldier. In glass cases there, toy soldiers by the ten thou

sand engage in replica battles. There are eight military museums
in La Suisse Romande alone. In Morges, there are displays not
only of Swiss military exploits but also of Aztec sacrifices, the Siege
of Alesia (52 B.C.), and the Battle of Zama, with elephants. In the
rooms the women come and go talking of Saint-Lô.

QUESTIONS

Ideas

1. Even though it is McPhee's style to efface himself, letting his facts
   do the work, can you still sense his attitude toward the Swiss military
   exploits? Point to specifics that suggest his opinions.
2. What seem to you to be the best examples of the Swiss "aptitude for
   war"?
3. What was your response to the incident at the end of paragraph 4?
4. What impression of modern Switzerland is created? Do you think it
   is accurate?
5. McPhee often tries to make a point by stacking detail upon detail,
   gaining momentum through specifics. What, then, seems to be the
   purpose of paragraph 7?

Organization

6. If you were to use conventional structural designations such as
   beginning, middle, and end—or introduction, body, and conclusion—how would this piece be divided?
7. To some readers McPhee's paragraphs seem too long and dense.
   Might you break up paragraph 7 or does it hold together? How
   about paragraph 8?

Sentences

8. Look carefully at the sentence in paragraph 7 that begins, "This,
   after all, was Switzerland. . . ." Imitate this pattern by writing one of
   your own, substituting "the United States" for the repeated
   "Switzerland."
9. Find other ways McPhee uses repetition in either his sentence
   beginnings or in their structure. Do you find it an effective technique?

Words

10. Look up the weapons McPhee mentions in a dictionary until you locate definitions for all of them. Explain the etymology of one. You might try the *Oxford English Dictionary*.

Suggestions for Writing

A. Write an essay in which you try to describe the American attitude toward war. You should try to take a broad historical perspective.

B. Is the American appetite for war "sublimated and under close control"? Write an essay using this question as a focus.

ELEVEN

Richard Selzer

(1928–   )

Richard Selzer for many years was both a doctor and a writer. Like the American poet and pediatrician, William Carlos Williams, Selzer combined practicing medicine with writing about it. His books include two collections of stories, *Rituals of Surgery* (1974) and *Imagine a Woman* (1991), and four collections of essays—*Mortal Lessons* (1977), *Confessions of a Knife* (1979), *Letters to a Young Doctor* (1982), and *Taking the World in for Repairs* (1986). Throughout his work, Selzer explores the role and image of the physician, the relations between doctor and patient, and the workings of the diseased and healthy body in all its splendor.

Born in Troy, New York, in 1928, Selzer was educated at Union College, Albany Medical College, and Yale University. Since 1960 he has lived in New Haven, where, until his retirement, he taught at the Yale Medical School and conducted a private practice in surgery, his father's medical specialty.

Selzer did not begin his writing career until he was nearly forty, when he experienced a restless urgency to do something besides practice medicine. When he realized that he possessed the talent and the desire to be a writer, Selzer dedicated himself to learning the craft of writing as he had earlier devoted himself to the art of surgery. He began, as he put it, "suturing words together," a suturing he had to teach himself. His major preparation for this writerly work was reading. Among the writers Selzer cites as formative influences were the English essayists, particularly Chesterton, Lamb, and Hazlitt.

Important also were the fiction writers, Poe and Patrick
White, and the Catholic mystics, especially Saint Cath-
erine of Siena and Saint John of the Cross. To these
Selzer adds the French symbolist poets, Rimbaud,
Verlaine, Baudelaire, and Mallarmé. From these writers
Selzer derived a sense of linguistic precision and artistic
passion. His own writing combines these elements in
striking ways.

Selzer has spoken in an interview with Charles
Shuster about the process of writing, which for him is a
solitary one. He writes in longhand, which he says possesses "a special kind of magic" in which "the manual work of
fashioning the words . . . flows out of your hand as
though it were a secretion from your own body." The
energy of writing carries Selzer along as he goes on line
by line "to get it down as the burst comes." Following this
"initial fever" of writing comes what Selzer describes as
the work of the "sly fox" who calculates and manipulates
the draft, tinkering with it, reconstructing and polishing
it. And Selzer enjoys both these stages—the impetuous
commitment to paper of words recording thoughts and
feelings and the disciplined reining in of revision and
editing.

Selzer has calculated that he writes sixty to seventy
polished, publishable pages a year—and hundreds more
from which he distills those. In his published prose he
aims to accomplish a number of things: to evoke experience, to amuse, to inform. Amid his lyric outpourings of
language, his sometimes sensational subjects and details,
Selzer aims to establish, as he points out, "a kinship with
the reader," as if to say, "we're both in this together."
(And by "this" Selzer means both this life about which the
writing centers and also the writing itself.)

Beneath these purposes lie two others: to come to
terms with his vocation and identity as doctor and writer;
to make out of his experiences works of literary art. Selzer
himself put it clearly and forcefully: "I am writing," he
says, "to make art. That's the whole thing. To write the
best I can." And when he is writing to this high standard,
Selzer's words perform a double function: they teach and
they heal. They heal the writer, who makes himself whole
in finding language to express his sense of self and the
world; and they heal the reader, who experiences the
power and pleasure of art. In the act of writing, Selzer the
surgeon of the body becomes a doctor of the soul.

The Pen and the Scalpel

1   I had been a general surgeon for 15 years when, at the age of 40, the psychic energy for writing inexplicably appeared. It was an appearance that was to knock over my life. For 15 years I had studied, practiced and taught surgery at the Yale School of Medicine, all the while enjoying the usefulness and the *handsomeness* of the craft. For the next 16 years, until my recent retirement, I would practice both surgery and writing. But where to fit in the writing when all of my days and half of my nights were fully engaged? Certainly not evenings. In the evening, one visits with one's next-of-kin; in the evening one helps with homework; in the evening, if one is so inclined, one has a martini. Instead, I became the first adult in the state of Connecticut to go to bed in the evening. Having slept from 8:30 P.M. to 1 in the morning, I rose, went down to the kitchen, put on a pot of tea and wrote in long-hand (a typewriter would disturb the household) until 3 o'clock. Then it was back upstairs and to sleep until 6 in the morning, when I began the day's doctoring. Plenty of sleep, only divided by two hours, when I was alone with my pen, and all the light in the world gathered upon a sheet of paper. In this way, I wrote three collections of stories, essays and memoirs.

2   Time was when in the professions—medicine and law—to patronize the arts was respectable; to practice them was not. For a surgeon it was even more questionable. Who wants to know, after all, what a surgeon does in his spare time? When it became known how I was spending my wild nights, my colleagues at the hospital were distressed. "Come, come" they coaxed in (more or less) the words of the poet Richard Wilbur, "Forsake those roses of the mind, and tend the true, the moral flower." But because the subject of my writings was my work as a doctor, the two seemed insep-arable. The one fertilized the other. Why, I wondered, doesn't every surgeon write? A doctor walks in and out of a dozen short stories a day. It is irresistible to write them down. When, at last, the time came to make a choice between my two passions, it had already been made for me. Listen:

3   In the operating room, the patient must be anesthetized in order that he feel no pain. The surgeon too must be "anes-thetized" in order to remain at some distance from the event:

when he cuts the patient, his own flesh must not bleed. It is this seeming lack of feeling that gives the surgeon the image of someone who is out of touch with his humanity, a person wanting only to cut, to perform. I assure you that it is the image only. A measure of insulation against the laying open of the bodies of his fellow human beings is necessary for the well-being of both patient and doctor. In surgery, if nowhere else, dispassion is an attribute. But the surgeon-writer is not anesthetized. He remains awake; sees everything; censors nothing. It is his dual role to open and repair the body of his patient and to report back to the waiting world in the keenest language he can find. By becoming a writer, I had stripped off the protective carapace. It was time to go. A surgeon can unmake himself; a writer cannot.

4   A Faustian bargain, you say? Perhaps, but, truth to tell, New Haven had begun to seem rather like the Beast With a Thousand Gallbladders. And where is it graven in stone that, once having been ordained, a surgeon must remain at the operating table until the scalpel slips from his lifeless fingers? Nor had I any wish to become like the old lion whose claws are long since blunt but not the desire to use them. Still, one does not walk away from the workbench of one's life with a cheery wave of the hand. In the beginning, I felt a strange sense of dislocation. As though I were standing near a river whose banks were flowing while the stream itself stood still. Only now, after two years, have I ceased to have attacks of longing for the labor that so satisfied and uplifted my spirit. Then, too, there was the risk that by withdrawing from the hospital, with its rich cargo of patients and those who tend them, I would be punished as a writer, suffer from impotence of the pen. A writer turns his back upon his native land at his own peril. Besides, to begin the life of a writer at the age of 56 is to toil under the very dart of death. As did another doctor-writer, John Keats, I too "have fears that I may cease to be before my pen has gleaned my teeming brain."

5   In medicine, there is a procedure called transillumination. If, in a darkened room, a doctor holds a bright light against a hollow part of the body, he will see through the outer tissues to the structures within that cavity—arteries, veins, projecting shelves of bone. In such a ruby gloom he can distinguish among a hernia, a hydrocele of the scrotum and a tumor of the testicle. Or he can light up a sinus behind the brow. Unlike surgery, which opens the body to direct examination, transillumination gives an indirect

vision, calling into play the simplest perceptions of the doctor. To write about a patient is like transillumination. You hold the lamp of language against his body and gaze through the covering layers at the truths within.

6   At first glance, it would appear that surgery and writing have little in common, but I think that is not so. For one thing, they are both sub-celestial arts; as far as I know, the angels disdain to perform either one. In each of them you hold a slender instrument that leaves a trail wherever it is applied. In one, there is the shedding of blood; in the other it is ink that is spilled upon a page. In one, the scalpel is restrained; in the other, the pen is given rein. The surgeon sutures together the tissues of the body to make whole what is sick or injured; the writer sews words into sentences to fashion a new version of human experience. A surgical operation is rather like a short story. You make the incision, rummage around inside for a bit, then stitch up. It has a beginning, a middle and an end. If I were to choose a medical specialist to write a novel, it would be a psychiatrist. They tend to go on and on. And on.

7   Despite that I did not begin to write until the middle of my life, I think I must always have been a writer. Like my father who was a general practitioner during the Depression in Troy, N.Y., and who wrote a novel. It was all about a prostitute with a heart of gold (her name was Goldie!) and the doctor who first saves her life, then falls in love with her. Mother read it and told him: "Keep it away from the children."

8   Father's office was on the ground floor of an old brownstone, and we lived upstairs. At night, after office hours, my brother Billy and I (we were 10 and 9 years old) would sneak downstairs to Father's darkened consultation room and there, shamefaced, by the light of a candle stub, we would take down from the shelves his medical textbooks. Our favorite was "The Textbook of Obstetrics and Gynecology."

9   It was there that I first became aware of the rich language of medicine. Some of the best words began with the letter C. *Carcinoma*, I read, and thought it was that aria from "Rigoletto" that mother used to sing while she washed and dried the dishes. *Cerebellum.* I said the word aloud, letting it drip off the end of my tongue like melted chocolate. And I read *choledochojejunostomy*, which later I was to learn as the name of an operation. All those syllables marching off in my mind to that terminal *y!* If that was

the way surgeons talked, I thought, I would be one of them, and
live forever in a state of mellifluous rapture. I do not use these
words in my writing, but I do try to use language that evokes the
sounds of the body—the *lub-dup, lub-dup* of the garrulous heart,
the gasp and wheeze of hard breathing, all the murmur and
splash of anatomy and physiology. And I have tried to make use of
the poetic potential in scientific language. Here, from my diary,
this specimen:

10   How gentle the countryside near Troy, with much farming
everywhere. Farming gives a sense of health to the land. It is
replenishing to watch at dusk as the herd of cattle flows like a
giant amoeba toward the barn. First one cow advances. She pauses. Another pseudopodium is thrust ahead, pulling the others
behind it until all of the cytoplasm, trailing milk, is inside the
barn. All along the banks of the Hudson River, oak, elm and
locust trees have grown very tall. The bark of the locust is thrown
into deep folds coated with lichen and moss. So old are these
trees that, without the least wind, one will drop off a quite large
branch as if to shed a part of its burden. This letting-fall doesn't
seem to do the tree any harm. It is more an anatomical relinquish-
ment of a part so that the whole might remain healthy. Much as a
diabetic will accept amputation of a gangrenous toe in order that
he might once again walk on his foot. How clever of these locust
trees to require no surgeon for their trimmage, only their own
corporeal wisdom.

QUESTIONS

1. Selzer wonders, at one point, why more doctors don't write. Why
    does he write, and why does he think more doctors also ought to
    write?

2. How does Selzer's solution to finding a time to write strike you? Can
    you imagine yourself getting up in the middle of the night to write?
    What might the advantages of such a routine be?

3. What are Selzer's fears about giving up the scalpel for the pen? Why
    does he bring the poet John Keats into his discussion at that point?

4. In paragraph 5 Selzer defines transillumination. Explain how he
    uses this practice of transillumination as a metaphor for writing.

5. Do you find Selzer's comparisons between surgery and writing per-
    suasive? Illuminating? Why or why not?

6. Toward the end of his essay Selzer mentions his love of language,

especially the sounds of words. Find examples elsewhere in this piece of Selzer's pleasure in the play of sound in language.

Suggestions for Writing

A. Write a letter to Richard Selzer responding to his discussion in this piece. Ask him a couple of questions.

B. Develop a paragraph or essay around an extended comparison or analogy—as Selzer does here.

The Knife

---

1   One holds the knife as one holds the bow of a cello or a tulip—by the stem. Not palmed nor gripped nor grasped, but lightly, with the tips of the fingers. The knife is not for pressing. It is for drawing across the field of skin. Like a slender fish, it waits, at the ready, then, go! It darts, followed by a fine wake of red. The flesh parts, falling away to yellow globules of fat. Even now, after so many times, I still marvel at its power—cold, gleaming, silent. More, I am still struck with a kind of dread that it is I in whose hand the blade travels, that my hand is its vehicle, that yet again this terrible steel-bellied thing and I have conspired for a most unnatural purpose, the laying open of the body of a human being.

2   A stillness settles in my heart and is carried to my hand. It is the quietude of resolve layered over fear. And it is this resolve that lowers us, my knife and me, deeper and deeper into the person beneath. It is an entry into the body that is nothing like a caress; still, it is among the gentlest of acts. Then stroke and stroke again, and we are joined by other instruments, hemostats and forceps, until the wound blooms with strange flowers whose looped handles fall to the sides in steely array.

3   There is sound, the tight click of clamps fixing teeth into severed blood vessels, the snuffle and gargle of the suction machine clearing the field of blood for the next stroke, the litany of monosyllables with which one prays his way down and in: *clamp, sponge, suture, tie, cut*. And there is color. The green of the cloth,

the white of the sponges, the red and yellow of the body. Beneath the fat lies the fascia, the tough fibrous sheet encasing the muscles. It must be sliced and the red beef of the muscles separated. Now there are retractors to hold apart the wound. Hands move together, part, weave. We are fully engaged, like children absorbed in a game or the craftsmen of some place like Damascus.

4   Deeper still. The peritoneum, pink and gleaming and membranous, bulges into the wound. It is grasped with forceps, and opened. For the first time we can see into the cavity of the abdomen. Such a primitive place. One expects to find drawings of buffalo on the walls. The sense of trespassing is keener now, heightened by the world's light illuminating the organs, their secret colors revealed—maroon and salmon and yellow. The vista is sweetly vulnerable at this moment, a kind of welcoming. An arc of the liver shines high and on the right, like a dark sun. It laps over the pink sweep of the stomach, from whose lower border the gauzy omentum is draped, and through which veil one sees, sinuous, slow as just-fed snakes, the indolent coils of the intestine.

5   You turn aside to wash your gloves. It is a ritual cleansing. One enters this temple doubly washed. Here is man as microcosm, representing in all his parts the earth, perhaps the universe.

6   I must confess that the priestliness of my profession has ever been impressed on me. In the beginning there are vows, taken with all solemnity. Then there is the endless harsh novitiate of training, much fatigue, much sacrifice. At last one emerges as celebrant, standing close to the truth lying curtained in the Ark of the body. Not surplice and cassock but mask and gown are your regalia. You hold no chalice, but a knife. There is no wine, no wafer. There are only the facts of blood and flesh.

7   In the room the instruments lie on trays and tables. They are arranged precisely by the scrub nurse, in an order that never changes, so that you can reach blindly for a forceps or hemostat without looking away from the operating field. The instruments lie *thus!* Even at the beginning, when all is clean and tidy and no blood has been spilled, it is the scalpel that dominates. It has a figure the others do not have, the retractors and the scissors. The scalpel is all grace and line, a fierceness. It grins. It is like a cat— to be respected, deferred to, but which returns no amiability. To hold it above a belly is to know the knife's force—as though were you to give it slightest rein, it would pursue an intent of its own, driving into the flesh, a wild energy.

8   In a story by Borges, a deadly knife fight between two rivals is depicted. It is not, however, the men who are fighting. It is the knives themselves that are settling their own old score. The men who hold the knives are mere adjuncts to the weapons. The unguarded knife is like the unbridled war-horse that not only carries its helpless rider to his death, but tramples all beneath its hooves. The hand of the surgeon must tame this savage thing. He is a rider reining to capture a pace.

9   So close is the joining of knife and surgeon that they are like the Centaur—the knife, below, all equine energy, the surgeon, above, with his delicate art. One holds the knife back as much as advances it to purpose. One is master of the scissors. One is partner, sometimes rival, to the knife. In a moment it is like the long red fingernail of the Dragon Lady. Thus does the surgeon curb in order to create, restraining the scalpel, governing it shrewdly, setting the action of the operation into a pattern, giving it form and purpose.

10   It is the nature of creatures to live within a tight cuirass that is both their constriction and their protection. The carapace of the turtle is his fortress and retreat, yet keeps him writhing on his back in the sand. So is the surgeon rendered impotent by his own empathy and compassion. The surgeon cannot weep. When he cuts the flesh, his own must not bleed. Here it is all work. Like an asthmatic hungering for air, longing to take just one deep breath, the surgeon struggles not to feel. It is suffocating to press the feeling out. It would be easier to weep or mourn—for you know that the lovely precise world of proportion contains, just beneath, *there*, all disaster, all disorder. In a surgical operation, a risk may flash into reality: the patient dies . . . of *complication*. The patient knows this too, in a more direct and personal way, and he is afraid.

11   And what of that *other*, the patient, you, who are brought to the operating room on a stretcher, having been washed and purged and dressed in a white gown? Fluid drips from a bottle into your arm, diluting you, leaching your body of its personal brine. As you wait in the corridor, you hear from behind the closed door the angry clang of steel upon steel, as though a battle were being waged. There is the odor of antiseptic and ether, and masked women hurry up and down the halls, in and out of rooms. There is the watery sound of strange machinery, the tinny beep

ing that is the transmitted heartbeat of yet another *human being*.
And all the while the dreadful knowledge that soon you will be
taken, laid beneath great lamps that will reveal the secret linings
of your body. In the very act of lying down, you have made a declaration of surrender. One lies down gladly for sleep or for love.
But to give over one's body and will for surgery, to *lie down* for it,
is a yielding of more than we can bear.

12   Soon a man will stand over you, gowned and hooded. In
time the man will take up a knife and crack open your flesh like a
ripe melon. Fingers will rummage among your viscera. Parts of
you will be cut out. Blood will run free. Your blood. All the night
before you have turned with the presentiment of death upon you.
You have attended your funeral, wept with your mourners. You
think, "I should never have had surgery in the springtime." It is
too cruel. Or on a Thursday. It is an unlucky day.

13   Now it is time. You are wheeled in and moved to the table.
An injection is given. "Let yourself go," I say. "It's a pleasant sensation," I say. "Give in," I say.

14   Let go? Give in? When you know that you are being tricked
into the hereafter, that you will end when consciousness ends? As
the monstrous silence of anesthesia falls discourteously across
your brain, you watch your soul drift off.

15   Later, in the recovery room, you awaken and gaze through
the thickness of drugs at the world returning, and you guess, at
first dimly, then surely, that you have not died. In pain and nausea you will know the exultation of death averted, of life restored.

16   What is it, then, this thing, the knife, whose shape is virtually
the same as it was three thousand years ago, but now with its head
grown detachable? Before steel, it was bronze. Before bronze,
stone—then back into unremembered time. Did man invent it or
did the knife precede him here, hidden under ages of vegetation and hoofprints, lying in wait to be discovered, picked up,
used?

17   The scalpel is in two parts, the handle and the blade. Joined,
it is six inches from tip to tip. At one end of the handle is a narrow notched prong upon which the blade is slid, then snapped
into place. Without the blade, the handle has a blind, decapitated
look. It is helpless as a trussed maniac. But slide on the blade,
click it home, and the knife springs instantly to life. It is headed
now, edgy, leaping to mount the fingers for the gallop to its feast.

18   Now is the moment from which you have turned aside, from which you have averted your gaze, yet toward which you have been hastened. Now the scalpel sings along the flesh again, its brute run unimpeded by germs or other frictions. It is a slick slide home, a barracuda spurt, a rip of embedded talon. One listens, and almost hears the whine—nasal, high, delivered through that gleaming metallic snout. The flesh splits with its own kind of moan. It is like the penetration of rape.

19   The breasts of women are cut off, arms and legs sliced to the bone to make ready for the saw, eyes freed from sockets, intestines lopped. The hand of the surgeon rebels. Tension boils through his pores, like sweat. The flesh of the patient retaliates with hemorrhage, and the blood chases the knife wherever it is withdrawn.

20   Within the belly a tumor squats, toadish, fungoid. A gray mother and her brood. The only thing it does not do is croak. It too is hacked from its bed as the carnivore knife lips the blood, turning in it in a kind of ecstasy of plenty, a gluttony after the long fast. It is just for this that the knife was created, tempered, heated, its violence beaten into paper-thin force.

21   At last a little thread is passed into the wound and tied. The monstrous booming fury is stilled by a tiny thread. The tempest is silenced. The operation is over. On the table, the knife lies spent, on its side, the bloody meal smear-dried upon its flanks. The knife rests.

22   And waits.

QUESTIONS

Ideas

1. What does Selzer suggest about the surgeon's knife, the scalpel? What images of the instrument does he present?

2. What impression of the surgeon emerges in this essay? What attitude toward the body does the writer take?

Organization

3. Map out the structure of the essay. What are its major divisions? Provide titles for the sections you identify.

4. In paragraph 8 Selzer alludes to a story by the Argentinian writer
    Jorge Luis Borges. How is this allusion relevant to Selzer's discus-
    sion? What would be gained or lost if this paragraph were omitted?
    Why?

Sentences

5. Notice the balanced phrasing of the following sentence, and com-
    ment on the effect of its repetitions.

> More, I am still struck with a kind of dread
> that it is I in whose hand the blade travels,
> that my hand is its vehicle,
> that yet again I have conspired for a most unnatural purpose,
>   the laying open of the body of a human being.

6. Consider the effect of the following sentences, all of which include
    dashes. Substitute commas for the dashes and comment on the dif-
    ferences in tone you detect.

> One holds the knife as one holds the bow of a cello or a
> tulip—by the stem.

> Even now, after so many times, I still marvel at its power—
> cold, gleaming, silent.

7. Throughout the essay Selzer switches from the informal pronoun,
    "I," to the formal "one," with an occasional use of the second-person
    pronoun, "you." Look, for example, at paragraphs 1, 5, and 6. Try
    making all the pronouns the same. What happens? What are the
    advantages or disadvantages of mixing pronouns as Selzer does
    here?

8. What effects does Selzer achieve with his use of questions in para-
    graphs 11, 12, and 16?

9. Identify and comment on the effectiveness of the sentence frag-
    ments in paragraphs 1, 3, 4, 12, 20, and 22.

Words

10. Identify and comment on the effectiveness of the comparisons in
    the first two paragraphs.

11. Consider the use of onomatopoeia—the use of words to imitate the
    sounds they describe—in paragraph 3: "click," "snuffle," "gargle."

12. Identify the medical terms Selzer employs. Substitute a less techni-
    cal word for each and explain what is gained or lost with the alter-
    ations.

Suggestions for Writing

A. Describe an object that is important in your work or play: a musical instrument, a tool, a vehicle, a piece of equipment—some item you are thoroughly familiar with. Try to see it as possessing a life and set of intentions. Try to see it in different ways. In the process, explain what it does and why it's important.

B. If you've undergone surgery, write an essay describing your perception of the event. Try to remember what the experience was like for you so you can recreate it for your readers.

The Masked Marvel's Last Toehold

MORNING ROUNDS.

1   On the fifth floor of the hospital, in the west wing, I know that a man is sitting up in his bed, waiting for me. Elihu Koontz is seventy-five, and he is diabetic. It is two weeks since I amputated his left leg just below the knee. I walk down the corridor, but I do not go straight into his room. Instead, I pause in the doorway. He is not yet aware of my presence, but gazes down at the place in the bed where his leg used to be, and where now there is the collapsed leg of his pajamas. He is totally absorbed, like an athlete appraising the details of his body. What is he thinking, I wonder. Is he dreaming the outline of his toes? Does he see there his foot's incandescent ghost? Could he be angry? Feel that I have taken from him something for which he yearns now with all his heart? Has he forgotten so soon the pain? It was a pain so great as to set him apart from all other men, in a red-hot place where he had no kith or kin. What of those black gorilla toes and the soupy mess that was his heel? I watch him from the doorway. It is a kind of spying, I know.

2   Save for a white fringe open at the front, Elihu Koontz is bald. The hair has grown too long and is wilted. He wears it as one would wear a day-old laurel wreath. He is naked to the waist, so that I can see his breasts. They are the breasts of Buddha, inverted triangles from which the nipples swing, dark as garnets.

3   I have seen enough. I step into the room, and he sees that I am there.

4   "How did the night go, Elihu?"

5   He looks at me for a long moment. "Shut the door," he says.

6   I do, and move to the side of the bed. He takes my left hand in both of his, gazes at it, turns it over, then back, fondling, at last holding it up to his cheek. I do not withdraw from this loving. After a while he relinquishes my hand, and looks up at me.

7   "How is the pain?" I ask.

8   He does not answer, but continues to look at me in silence. I know at once that he has made a decision.

9   "Ever hear of The Masked Marvel?" He says this in a low voice, almost a whisper.

10   "What?"

11   "The Masked Marvel," he says. "You never heard of him?"

12   "No."

13   He clucks his tongue. He is exasperated.

14   All at once there is a recollection. It is dim, distant, but coming near.

15   "Do you mean the wrestler?"

16   Eagerly, he nods, and the breasts bob. How gnomish he looks, oval as the huge helpless egg of some outlandish lizard. He has very long arms, which, now and then, he unfurls to reach for things—a carafe of water, a get-well card. He gazes up at me, urging. He *wants* me to remember.

17   "Well . . . yes," I say. I am straining backward in time. "I saw him wrestle in Toronto long ago."

18   "Ha!" He smiles. "You saw *me.*" And his index finger, held rigid and upright, bounces in the air.

19   The man has said something shocking, unacceptable. It must be challenged.

20   "You?" I am trying to smile.

21   Again that jab of the finger. "You saw *me.*"

22   "No," I say. But even then, something about Elihu Koontz, those prolonged arms, the shape of his head, the sudden agility with which he leans from his bed to get a large brown envelope from his nightstand, something is forcing me toward a memory. He rummages through his papers, old newspaper clippings, photographs, and I remember . . .

23   It is almost forty years ago. I am ten years old. I have been sent to Toronto to spend the summer with relatives. Uncle Max has bought two tickets to the wrestling match. He is taking me that night.

24   "He isn't allowed," says Aunt Sarah to me. Uncle Max has angina.

25   "He gets too excited," she says.

26   "I wish you wouldn't go, Max," she says.

27   "You mind your own business," he says.

28   And we go. Out into the warm Canadian evening. I am not only abroad, I am abroad in the *evening!* I have never been taken out in the evening. I am terribly excited. The trolleys, the lights, the horns. It is a bazaar. At the Maple Leaf Gardens, we sit high and near the center. The vast arena is dark except for the brilliance of the ring at the bottom.

29   It begins.

30   The wrestlers circle. They grapple. They are all haunch and paunch. I am shocked by their ugliness, but I do not show it. Uncle Max is exhilarated. He leans forward, his eyes unblinking, on his face a look of enormous happiness. One after the other, a pair of wrestlers enter the ring. The two men join, twist, jerk, tug, bend, yank, and throw. Then they leave and are replaced by another pair. At last it is the main event. "The Angel vs. The Masked Marvel."

31   On the cover of the program notes, there is a picture of The Angel hanging from the limb of a tree, a noose of thick rope around his neck. The Angel hangs just so for an hour every day, it is explained, to strengthen his neck. The Masked Marvel's trademark is a black stocking cap with holes for the eyes and mouth. He is never seen without it, states the program. No one knows who The Masked Marvel really is!

32   "Good," says Uncle Max. "Now you'll see something." He is fidgeting, waiting for them to appear. They come down separate aisles, climb into the ring from opposite sides. I have never seen anything like them. It is The Angel's neck that first captures the eye. The shaved nape rises in twin columns to puff into the white hood of a sloped and bosselated skull that is too small. As though, strangled by the sinews of that neck, the skull had long since withered and shrunk. The thing about The Angel is the absence of any mystery in his body. It is simply *there.* A monosyllabic

announcement. A grunt. One looks and knows everything at once, the fat thighs, the gigantic buttocks, the great spine from which hang knotted ropes and pale aprons of beef. And that prehistoric head. He is all of a single hideous piece, The Angel is. No detachables.

33   The Masked Marvel seems dwarfish. His fingers dangle kneeward. His short legs are slightly bowed as if under the weight of the cask they are forced to heft about. He has breasts that swing when he moves! I have never seen such breasts on a man before.

34   There is a sudden ungraceful movement, and they close upon one another. The Angel stoops and hugs The Marvel about the waist, locking his hands behind The Marvel's back. Now he straightens and lifts The Marvel as though he were uprooting a tree. Thus he holds him, then stoops again, thrusts one hand through The Marvel's crotch, and with the other grabs him by the neck. He rears and . . . The Marvel is aloft! For a long moment, The Angel stands as though deciding where to make the toss. Then throws. Was that board or bone that splintered there? Again and again, The Angel hurls himself upon the body of The Masked Marvel.

35   Now The Angel rises over the fallen Marvel, picks up one foot in both of his hands, and twists the toes downward. It is far beyond the tensile strength of mere ligament, mere cartilage. The Masked Marvel does not hide his agony, but pounds and slaps the floor with his hand, now and then reaching up toward The Angel in an attitude of supplication. I have never seen such suffering. And all the while his black mask rolls from side to side, the mouth pulled to a tight slit through which issues an endless hiss that I can hear from where I sit. All at once, I hear a shouting close by.

36   "Break it off! Tear off a leg and throw it up here!"

37   It is Uncle Max. Even in the darkness I can see that he is gray. A band of sweat stands upon his upper lip. He is on his feet now, panting, one fist pressed at his chest, the other raised warlike toward the ring. For the first time I begin to think that something terrible might happen here. Aunt Sarah was right.

38   "Sit down, Uncle Max," I say. "Take a pill, please."

39   He reaches for the pillbox, gropes, and swallows without taking his gaze from the wrestlers. I wait for him to sit down.

40   "That's not fair," I say, "twisting his toes like that."

41   "It's the toehold," he explains.

42 "But it's not *fair*," I say again. The whole of the evil is laid open for me to perceive. I am trembling.

43 And now The Angel does something unspeakable. Holding the foot of The Marvel at full twist with one hand, he bends and grasps the mask where it clings to the back of The Marvel's head. And he pulls. He is going to strip it off! Lay bare an ultimate carnal mystery! Suddenly it is beyond mere physical violence. Now I am on my feet, shouting into the Maple Leaf Gardens.

44 "Watch out," I scream. "Stop him. Please, somebody, stop him."

45 Next to me, Uncle Max is chuckling.

46 Yet The Masked Marvel hears me, I know it. And rallies from his bed of pain. Thrusting with his free heel, he strikes The Angel at the back of the knee. The Angel falls. The Masked Marvel is on top of him, pinning his shoulders to the mat. One! Two! Three! And it is over. Uncle Max is strangely still. I am gasping for breath. All this I remember as I stand at the bedside of Elihu Koontz.

47 Once again, I am in the operating room. It is two years since I amputated the left leg of Elihu Koontz. Now it is his right leg which is gangrenous. I have already scrubbed. I stand to one side wearing my gown and gloves. And . . . *I am masked.* Upon the table lies Elihu Koontz, pinned in a fierce white light. Spinal anesthesia has been administered. One of his arms is taped to a board placed at a right angle to his body. Into this arm, a needle has been placed. Fluid drips here from a bottle overhead. With his other hand, Elihu Koontz beats feebly at the side of the operating table. His head rolls from side to side. His mouth is pulled into weeping. It seems to me that I have never seen such misery.

48 An orderly stands at the foot of the table, holding Elihu Koontz's leg aloft by the toes so that the intern can scrub the limb with antiseptic solutions. The intern paints the foot, ankle, leg, and thigh, both front and back, three times. From a corner of the room where I wait, I look down as from an amphitheater. Then I think of Uncle Max yelling, "Tear off a leg. Throw it up here." And I think that forty years later I am making the catch.

49 "It's not fair," I say aloud. But no one hears me. I step forward to break The Masked Marvel's last toehold.

QUESTIONS

Ideas

1. What are the point and purpose of this essay? What do you think Selzer tries to accomplish here? Does the essay have a single main point or thesis? If so, what do you think it is?
2. In what way(s) does the surgeon break The Masked Marvel's toehold? Consider the various meanings of "break."
3. Compare the reactions of the boy and his uncle as they watch the wrestling match. How do you respond and evaluate the reactions of each? Why?

Organization

4. Selzer arranges his essay in three parts. Explain the relationship among the three sections. Consider how time is shaped—how chronology is broken—and with what effects.
5. What details from the second section parallel those of the first? What parallels exist between parts II and III? (Consider especially the opening paragraph of part III.)

Sentences

6. What are the purpose and effect of the interrogative sentences in the opening paragraph? How would the tone of the paragraph change if these questions were converted to declarative sentences?
7. On occasion Selzer employs sentence fragments, especially in paragraphs 21, 32, and 46. Identify the fragments and consider whether they would be more or less effective if revised into complete sentences.

Words

8. Identify and consider the effectiveness of the similes and metaphors in paragraphs 1 and 32. Explain the purposes and bases of each of the comparisons.
9. Note the profusion and precision of verbs at specific points in the essay—in paragraphs 30 and 34, for example. Account for the accuracy of each verb in these paragraphs. Substitute a few alternative verbs and consider their effectiveness.

Suggestions for Writing

A. Using the questions above, write an essay analyzing "The Masked Marvel's Last Tochold." Interpret the essay, considering not only what Selzer says, but how he says it as well.

B. Describe a climatic moment of an athletic event—or of any kind of performance or contest. Try to recapture your experience of the event and provide the reader with a sense of being there.

C. Write an essay comparing or classifying different kinds of sports fans. You might compare two kinds of wrestling or baseball fans. Or you might identify characteristics that distinguish baseball fans from football fans. As another possibility, consider defining the word *fan* in an essay that highlights and explains the qualities that make a fan what he or she is.

Imelda

I

1   I heard the other day that Hugh Franciscus had died. I knew him once. He was the Chief of Plastic Surgery when I was a medical student at Albany Medical College. Dr. Franciscus was the archetype of the professor of surgery—tall, vigorous, muscular, as precise in his technique as he was impeccable in his dress. Each day a clean lab coat monkishly starched, that sort of thing. I doubt that he ever read books. One book only, that of the human body, took the place of all others. He never raised his eyes from it. He read it like a printed page as though he knew that in the calligraphy there just beneath the skin were all the secrets of the world. Long before it became visible to anyone else, he could detect the first sign of granulation at the base of a wound, the first blue line of new epithelium at the periphery that would tell him that a wound would heal, or the barest hint of necrosis that presaged failure. This gave him the appearance of a prophet. "This skin graft will take," he would say, and you must believe beyond all cyanosis, exudation and inflammation that it would.

2   He had enemies, of course, who said he was arrogant, that he exalted activity for its own sake. Perhaps. But perhaps it was no

more than the honesty of one who knows his own worth. Just look
at a scalpel, after all. What a feeling of sovereignty, megalomania
even, when you know that it is you and you alone who will make
certain use of it. It was said, too, that he was a ladies' man. I don't
know about that. It was all rumor. Besides, I think he had other
things in mind than mere living. Hugh Franciscus was a zealous
hunter. Every fall during the season he drove upstate to hunt
deer. There was a glass-front case in his office where he showed
his guns. How could he shoot a deer? we asked. But he knew better. To us medical students he was someone heroic, someone
made up of several gods, beheld at a distance, and always from a
lesser height. If he had grown accustomed to his miracles, we had
not. He had no close friends on the staff. There was something a
little sad in that. As though once long ago he had been flayed by
friendship and now the slightest breeze would hurt. Confidences
resulted in dishonor. Perhaps the person in whom one confided
would scorn him, betray. Even though he spent his days among
those less fortunate, weaker than he—the sick, after all—
Franciscus seemed aware of an air of personal harshness in his
environment to which he reacted by keeping his own counsel, by
a certain remoteness. It was what gave him the appearance of
being haughty. With the patients he was forthright. All the facts
laid out, every question anticipated and answered with specific
information. He delivered good news and bad with the same dispassion.

3   I was a third-year student, just turned onto the wards for the
first time, and clerking on Surgery. Everything—the operating
room, the morgue, the emergency room, the patients, professors,
even the nurses—was terrifying. One picked one's way among the
mines and booby traps of the hospital, hoping only to avoid the
hemorrhage and perforation of disgrace. The opportunity for
humiliation was everywhere.

4   It all began on Ward Rounds. Dr. Franciscus was demonstrating a cross-leg flap graft he had constructed to cover a large
fleshy defect in the leg of a merchant seaman who had injured
himself in a fall. The man was from Spain and spoke no English.
There had been a comminuted fracture of the femur, much soft
tissue damage, necrosis. After weeks of débridement and dress-
ings, the wound had been made ready for grafting. Now the
patient was in his fifth postoperative day. What we saw was a thick
web of pale blue flesh arising from the man's left thigh, and

which had been sutured to the open wound on the right thigh.
When the surgeon pressed the pedicle with his finger, it
blanched; when he let up, there was a slow return of the viola-
ceous color.

5　　"The circulation is good," Franciscus announced. "It will get
better." In several weeks, we were told, he would divide the tube
of flesh at its site of origin, and tailor it to fit the defect to which,
by then, it would have grown more solidly. All at once, the
webbed man in the bed reached out, and gripping Franciscus by
the arm, began to speak rapidly, pointing to his groin and hip.
Franciscus stepped back at once to disengage his arm from the
patient's grasp.

6　　"Anyone here know Spanish? I didn't get a word of that."

7　　"The cast is digging into him up above," I said. "The edges
of the plaster are rough. When he moves, they hurt."

8　　Without acknowledging my assistance, Dr. Franciscus took a
plaster shears from the dressing cart and with several large snips
cut away the rough edges of the cast.

9　　"*Gracias, gracias.*" The man in the bed smiled. But Franciscus
had already moved on to the next bed. He seemed to me a man
of immense strength and ability, yet without affection for the
patients. He did not want to be touched by them. It was less kind-
ness that he showed them than a reassurance that he would never
give up, that he would bend every effort. If anyone could, he
would solve the problems of their flesh.

10　　Ward Rounds had disbanded and I was halfway down the
corridor when I heard Dr. Franciscus' voice behind me.

11　　"You speak Spanish." It seemed a command.

12　　"I lived in Spain for two years," I told him.

13　　"I'm taking a surgical team to Honduras next week to operate on the natives down there. I do it every year for three weeks,
somewhere. This year, Honduras. I can arrange the time away
from your duties here if you'd like to come along. You will act as
interpreter. I'll show you how to use the clinical camera. What
you'd see would make it worthwhile."

14　　So it was that, a week later, the envy of my classmates, I
joined the mobile surgical unit—surgeons, anesthetists, nurses
and equipment—aboard a Military Air Transport plane to spend
three weeks performing plastic surgery on people who had been
previously selected by an advance team. Honduras. I don't suppose I shall ever see it again. Nor do I especially want to. From the

plane it seemed a country made of clay—burnt umber, raw
sienna, dry. It had a deadweight quality, as though the ground
had no buoyancy, no air sacs through which a breeze might
wander. Our destination was Comayagua, a town in the Central
Highlands. The town itself was situated on the edge of one of the
flatlands that were linked in a network between the granite mountains. Above, all was brown, with only an occasional Spanish cedar
tree; below, patches of luxuriant tropical growth. It was a day's
bus ride from the airport. For hours, the town kept appearing and
disappearing with the convolutions of the road. At last, there it
lay before us, panting and exhausted at the bottom of the
mountain.

15   That was all I was to see of the countryside. From then on,
there was only the derelict hospital of Comayagua, with the smell
of spoiling bananas and the accumulated odors of everyone who
had been sick there for the last hundred years. Of the two, I much
preferred the frank smell of the sick. The heat of the place was
incendiary. So hot that, as we stepped from the bus, our own
words did not carry through the air, but hung limply at our lips
and chins. Just in front of the hospital was a thirsty courtyard
where mobs of waiting people squatted or lay in the meager
shade, and where, on dry days, a fine dust rose through which
untethered goats shouldered. Against the walls of this courtyard,
gaunt, dejected men stood, their faces, like their country, preter-
naturally solemn, leaden. Here no one looked up at the sky. Every
head was bent beneath a wide-brimmed straw hat. In the days that
followed, from the doorway of the dispensary, I would watch the
brown mountains sliding about, drinking the hospital into their
shadow as the afternoon grew later and later, flattening us by
their very altitude.

16   The people were mestizos, of mixed Spanish and Indian
blood. They had flat, broad, dumb museum feet. At first they
seemed to me indistinguishable the one from the other, without
animation. All the vitality, the hidden sexuality, was in their black
hair. Soon I was to know them by the fissures with which each face
was graven. But, even so, compared to us, they were masked, shut
away. My job was to follow Dr. Franciscus around, photograph the
patients before and after surgery, interpret and generally act as
aide-de-camp. It was exhilarating. Within days I had decided that I
was not just useful, but essential. Despite that we spent all day in
each other's company, there were no overtures of friendship from

Dr. Franciscus. He knew my place, and I knew it, too. In the afternoon he examined the patients scheduled for the next day's surgery. I would call out a name from the doorway to the examining room. In the courtyard someone would rise. I would usher the patient in, and nudge him to the examining table where Franciscus stood, always, I thought, on the verge of irritability. I would read aloud the case history, then wait while he carried out his examination. While I took the "before" photographs, Dr. Franciscus would dictate into a tape recorder:

17   "Ulcerating basal cell carcinoma of the right orbit—six by eight centimeters—involving the right eye and extending into the floor of the orbit. Operative plan: wide excision with enucleation of the eye. Later, bone and skin grafting." The next morning we would be in the operating room where the procedure would be carried out.

18   We were more than two weeks into our tour of duty—a few days to go—when it happened. Earlier in the day I had caught sight of her through the window of the dispensary. A thin, dark Indian girl about fourteen years old. A figurine, orange-brown, terra-cotta, and still attached to the unshaped clay from which she had been carved. An older, sun-weathered woman stood behind and somewhat to the left of the girl. The mother was short and dumpy. She wore a broad-brimmed hat with a high crown, and a shapeless dress like a cassock. The girl had long, loose black hair. There were tiny gold hoops in her ears. The dress she wore could have been her mother's. Far too big, it hung from her thin shoulders at some risk of slipping down her arms. Even with her in it, the dress was empty, something hanging on the back of a door. Her breasts made only the smallest imprint in the cloth, her hips none at all. All the while, she pressed to her mouth a filthy, pink, balled-up rag as though to stanch a flow or buttress against pain. I knew that what she had come to show us, what we were there to see, was hidden beneath that pink cloth. As I watched, the woman handed down to her a gourd from which the girl drank, lapping like a dog. She was the last patient of the day. They had been waiting in the courtyard for hours.

19   "Imelda Valdez," I called out. Slowly she rose to her feet, the cloth never leaving her mouth, and followed her mother to the examining-room door. I shooed them in.

20   "You sit up there on the table," I told her. "Mother, you stand over there, please." I read from the chart:

21   "This is a fourteen-year-old girl with a complete, unilateral, left-sided cleft lip and cleft palate. No other diseases or congenital defects. Laboratory tests, chest X ray—negative."

22   "Tell her to take the rag away," said Dr. Franciscus. I did, and the girl shrank back, pressing the cloth all the more firmly.

23   "Listen, this is silly," said Franciscus. "Tell her I've got to see it. Either she behaves, or send her away."

24   "Please give me the cloth," I said to the girl as gently as possible. She did not. She could not. Just then, Franciscus reached up and, taking the hand that held the rag, pulled it away with a hard jerk. For an instant the girl's head followed the cloth as it left her face, one arm still upflung against showing. Against all hope, she would hide herself. A moment later, she relaxed and sat still. She seemed to me then like an animal that looks outward at the infinite, at death, without fear, with recognition only.

25   Set as it was in the center of the girl's face, the defect was utterly hideous—a nude rubbery insect that had fastened there. The upper lip was widely split all the way to the nose. One white tooth perched upon the protruding upper jaw projected through the hole. Some of the bone seemed to have been gnawed away as well. Above the thing, clear almond eyes and long black hair reflected the light. Below, a slender neck where the pulse trilled visibly. Under our gaze the girl's eyes fell to her lap where her hands lay palms upward, half open. She was a beautiful bird with a crushed beak. And tense with the expectation of more shame.

26   "Open your mouth," said the surgeon. I translated. She did so, and the surgeon tipped back her head to see inside.

27   "The palate, too. Complete," he said. There was a long silence. At last he spoke.

28   "What is your name?" The margins of the wound melted until she herself was being sucked into it.

29   "Imelda." The syllables leaked through the hole with a slosh and a whistle.

30   "Tomorrow," said the surgeon, "I will fix your lip. *Mañana.*"

31   It seemed to me that Hugh Franciscus, in spite of his years of experience, in spite of all the dreadful things he had seen, must have been awed by the sight of this girl. I could see it flit across his face for an instant. Perhaps it was her small act of concealment, that he had had to demand that she show him the lip, that he had had to force her to show it to him. Perhaps it was her

resistance that intensified the disfigurement. Had she brought her mouth to him willingly, without shame, she would have been for him neither more nor less than any other patient.

32   He measured the defect with calipers, studied it from different angles, turning her head with a finger at her chin.

33   "How can it ever be put back together?" I asked.

34   "Take her picture," he said. And to her, "Look straight ahead." Through the eye of the camera she seemed more pitiful than ever, her humiliation more complete.

35   "Wait!" The surgeon stopped me. I lowered the camera. A strand of her hair had fallen across her face and found its way to her mouth, becoming stuck there by saliva. He removed the hair and secured it behind her ear.

36   "Go ahead," he ordered. There was the click of the camera. The girl winced.

37   "Take three more, just in case."

38   When the girl and her mother had left, he took paper and pen and with a few lines drew a remarkable likeness of the girl's face.

39   "Look," he said. "If this dot is A, and this one B, this, C and this, D, the incisions are made A to B, then C to D. CD must equal AB. It is all equilateral triangles." All well and good, but then came X and Y and rotation flaps and the rest.

40   "Do you see?" he asked.

41   "It is confusing," I told him.

42   "It is simply a matter of dropping the upper lip into a normal position, then crossing the gap with two triangular flaps. It is geometry," he said.

43   "Yes," I said. "Geometry." And relinquished all hope of becoming a plastic surgeon.

II

44   In the operating room the next morning the anesthesia had already been administered when we arrived from Ward Rounds. The tube emerging from the girl's mouth was pressed against her lower lip to be kept out of the field of surgery. Already, a nurse was scrubbing the face which swam in a reddish-brown lather. The tiny gold earrings were included in the scrub. Now and then, one of them gave a brave flash. The face was washed for the last time, and dried. Green towels were placed

over the face to hide everything but the mouth and nose. The drapes were applied.

45   "Calipers!" The surgeon measured, locating the peak of the distorted Cupid's bow.

46   "Marking pen!" He placed the first blue dot at the apex of the bow. The nasal sills were dotted; next, the inferior philtral dimple, the vermilion line. The A flap and the B flap were out-lined. On he worked, peppering the lip and nose, making sense out of chaos, realizing the lip that lay waiting in that deep essen-tial pink, that only he could see. The last dot and line were placed. He was ready.

47   "Scalpel!" He held the knife above the girl's mouth.

48   "O.K. to go ahead?" he asked the anesthetist.

49   "Yes."

50   He lowered the knife.

51   "No! Wait!" The anesthetist's voice was tense, staccato. "Hold it!"

52   The surgeon's hand was motionless.

53   "What's the matter?"

54   "Something's wrong. I'm not sure. God, she's hot as a pistol. Blood pressure is way up. Pulse one eighty. Get a rectal tempera-ture." A nurse fumbled beneath the drapes. We waited. The nurse retrieved the thermometer.

55   "One hundred seven . . . no . . . eight." There was disbelief in her voice.

56   "Malignant hyperthermia," said the anesthetist. "Ice! Ice! Get lots of ice!" I raced out the door, accosted the first nurse I saw.

57   "Ice!" I shouted. *"Hielo!* Quickly! *Hielo!"* The woman's expression was blank. I ran to another. *"Hielo! Hielo!* For the love of God, ice."

58   *"Hielo?"* She shrugged. *"Nada."* I ran back to the operating room.

59   "There isn't any ice," I reported. Dr. Franciscus had ripped off his rubber gloves and was feeling the skin of the girl's abdomen. Above the mask his eyes were the eyes of a horse in battle.

60   "The EKG is wild . . ."

61   "I can't get a pulse . . ."

62   "What the hell . . ."

63   The surgeon reached for the girl's groin. No femoral pulse.

64   "EKG flat. My God! She's dead!"

65 "She can't be."

66 "She is."

67 The surgeon's fingers pressed the groin where there was no pulse to be felt, only his own pulse hammering at the girl's flesh to be let in.

III

68   It was noon, four hours later, when we left the operating room. It was a day so hot and humid I felt steamed open like an envelope. The woman was sitting on a bench in the courtyard in her dress like a cassock. In one hand she held the piece of cloth the girl had used to conceal her mouth. As we watched, she folded it once neatly, and then again, smoothing it, cleaning the cloth which might have been the head of the girl in her lap that she stroked and consoled.

69   "I'll do the talking here," he said. He would tell her himself, in whatever Spanish he could find. Only if she did not understand was I to speak for him. I watched him brace himself, set his shoulders. How could he tell her? I wondered. What? But I knew he would tell her everything, exactly as it had happened. As much for himself as for her, he needed to explain. But suppose she screamed, fell to the ground, attacked him, even? All that hope of love . . . gone. Even in his discomfort I knew that he was teaching me. The way to do it was professionally. Now he was standing above her. When the woman saw that he did not speak, she lifted her eyes and saw what he held crammed in his mouth to tell her. She knew, and rose to her feet.

70   "*Señora,*" he began, "I am sorry." All at once he seemed to me shorter than he was, scarcely taller than she. There was a place at the crown of his head where the hair had grown thin. His lips were stones. He could hardly move them. The voice dry, dusty.

71   "No one could have known. Some bad reaction to the medicine for sleeping. It poisoned her. High fever. She did not wake up." The last, a whisper. The woman studied his lips as though she were deaf. He tried, but could not control a twitching at the corner of his mouth. He raised a thumb and forefinger to press something back into his eyes.

72   "*Muerte,*" the woman announced to herself. Her eyes were human, deadly.

73   *"Si, muerte."* At that moment he was like someone cast, still
alive, as an effigy for his own tomb. He closed his eyes. Nor did he
open them until he felt the touch of the woman's hand on his
arm, a touch from which he did not withdraw. Then he looked
and saw the grief corroding her face, breaking it down, melting
the features so that eyes, nose, mouth ran together in a distortion,
like the girl's. For a long time they stood in silence. It seemed to
me that minutes passed. At last her face cleared, the features rear-
ranged themselves. She spoke, the words coming slowly to make
certain that he understood her. She would go home now. The
next day her sons would come for the girl, to take her home for
burial. The doctor must not be sad. God has decided. And she was
happy now that the harelip had been fixed so that her daughter
might go to Heaven without it. Her bare feet retreating were the
felted pads of a great bereft animal.

IV

74   The next morning I did not go to the wards, but stood
at the gate leading from the courtyard to the road outside. Two
young men in striped ponchos lifted the girl's body wrapped in a
straw mat onto the back of a wooden cart. A donkey waited. I had
been drawn to this place as one is drawn, inexplicably, to certain
scenes of desolation—executions, battlefields. All at once, the
woman looked up and saw me. She had taken off her hat. The
heavy-hanging coil of her hair made her head seem larger, darker, noble. I pressed some money into her hand.

75   "For flowers," I said. "A priest." Her cheeks shook as though
minutes ago a stone had been dropped into her naval and the ripples were just now reaching her head. I regretted having come to
that place.

76   *"Si, si,"* the woman said. Her own face was stitched with flies.
"The doctor is one of the angels. He has finished the work of
God. My daughter is beautiful."

77   What could she mean! The lip had not been fixed. The girl
had died before he would have done it.

78   "Only a fine line that God will erase in time," she said.

79   I reached into the cart and lifted a corner of the mat in
which the girl had been rolled. Where the cleft had been there

was now a fresh line of tiny sutures. The Cupid's bow was delicate-
ly shaped, the vermilion border aligned. The flattened nostril had
now the same rounded shape as the other one. I let the mat fall
over the face of the dead girl, but not before I had seen the
touching place where the finest black hairs sprang from the temple.

80   *"Adiós, adiós . . ."* And the cart creaked away to the sound
of hooves, a tinkling bell.

V

81   There are events in a doctor's life that seem to mark
the boundary between youth and age, seeing and perceiving. Like
certain dreams, they illuminate a whole lifetime of past behavior.
After such an event, a doctor is not the same as he was before. It
had seemed to me then to have been the act of someone dement
ed, or at least insanely arrogant. An attempt to reorder events.
Her death had come to him out of order. It should have come
after the lip had been repaired, not before. He could have told
the mother that, no, the lip had not been fixed. But he did not.
He said nothing. It had been an act of omission, one of those
strange lapses to which all of us are subject and which we live to
regret. It must have been then, at that moment, that the knowledge of what he would do appeared to him. The words of the
mother had not consoled him; they had hunted him down. He
had not done it for her. The dire necessity was his. He would not
accept that Imelda had died before he could repair her lip.
People who do such things break free from society. They follow
their own lonely path. They have a secret which they can never
reveal. I must never let on that I knew.

VI

82   How often I have imagined it. Ten o'clock at night.
The hospital of Comayagua is all but dark. Here and there
lanterns tilt and skitter up and down the corridors. One of these
lamps breaks free from the others and descends the stone steps to
the underground room that is the morgue of the hospital. This

room wears the expression as if it had waited all night for someone to come. No silence so deep as this place with its cargo of
newly dead. Only the slow drip of water over stone. The door closes gassily and clicks shut. The lock is turned. There are four
tables, each with a body encased in a paper shroud. There is no
mistaking her. She is the smallest. The surgeon takes a knife from
his pocket and slits open the paper shroud, that part in which the
girl's head is enclosed. The wound seems to be living on long
after she has died. Waves of heat emanate from it, blurring his
vision. All at once, he turns to peer over his shoulder. He sees
nothing, only a wooden crucifix on the wall.

83   He removes a package of instruments from a satchel and
arranges them on a tray. Scalpel, scissors, forceps, needle holder.
Sutures and gauze sponges are produced. Stealthy, hunched,
engaged, he begins. The dots of blue dye are still there upon her
mouth. He raises the scalpel, pauses. A second glance into the
darkness. From the wall a small lizard watches and accepts. The
first cut is made. A sluggish flow of dark blood appears. He wipes
it away with a sponge. No new blood comes to take its place. Again
and again he cuts, connecting each of the blue dots until the
whole of the zigzag slice is made, first on one side of the cleft,
then on the other. Now the edges of the cleft are lined with fresh
tissue. He sets down the scalpel and takes up scissors and forceps,
undermining the little flaps until each triangle is attached only at
one side. He rotates each flap into its new position. He must be
certain that they can be swung without tension. They can. He is
ready to suture. He fits the tiny curved needle into the jaws of the
needle holder. Each suture is placed precisely the same number
of millimeters from the cut edge, and the same distance apart. He
ties each knot down until the edges are apposed. Not too tightly.
These are the most meticulous sutures of his life. He cuts each
thread close to the knot. It goes well. The vermilion border with
its white skin roll is exactly aligned. One more stitch and the
Cupid's bow appears as if by magic. The man's face shines with
moisture. Now the nostril is incised around the margin, released,
and sutured into a round shape to match its mate. He wipes the
blood from the face of the girl with gauze that he has dipped in
water. Crumbs of light are scattered on the girl's face. The shroud
is folded once more about her. The instruments are handed into
the satchel. In a moment the morgue is dark and a lone lantern
ascends the stairs and is extinguished.

VII

84   Six weeks later I was in the darkened amphitheater of the Medical School. Tiers of seats rose in a semicircle above the small stage where Hugh Franciscus stood presenting the case material he had encountered in Honduras. It was the highlight of the year. The hall was filled. The night before he had arranged the slides in the order in which they were to be shown. I was at the controls of the slide projector.

85   "Next slide!" he would order from time to time in that military voice which had called forth blind obedience from generations of medical students, interns, residents and patients.

86   "This is a fifty-seven-year-old man with a severe burn contracture of the neck. You will notice the rigid webbing that has fused the chin to the presternal tissues. No motion of the head on the torso is possible. . . . Next slide!"

87   "Click," went the projector.

88   "Here he is after the excision of the scar tissue and with the head in full extension for the first time. The defect was then covered. . . . Next slide!"

89   "Click."

90   ". . . with full-thickness drums of skin taken from the abdomen with the Padgett dermatome. Next slide!"

91   "Click."

92   And suddenly there she was, extracted from the shadows, suspended above and beyond all of us like a resurrection. There was the oval face, the long black hair unbraided, the tiny gold hoops in her ears. And that luminous gnawed mouth. The whole of her life seemed to have been summed up in this photograph. A long silence followed that was the surgeon's alone to break. Almost at once, like the anesthetist in the operating room in Comayagua, I knew that something was wrong. It was not that the man would not speak as that he could not. The audience of doctors, nurses and students seemed to have been infected by the black, limitless silence. My own pulse doubled. It was hard to breathe. Why did he not call out for the next slide? Why did he not save himself? Why had he not removed this slide from the ones to be shown? All at once I knew that he had used his camera on her again. I could see the long black shadows of her hair flowing into the darker shadows of the morgue. The sudden blinding flash . . . The next slide

would be the one taken in the morgue. He would be exposed.

93   In the dim light reflected from the slide, I saw him gazing up at her, seeing not the colored photograph, I thought, but the negative of it where the ghost of the girl was. For me, the amphitheater had become Honduras. I saw again that courtyard littered with patients. I could see the dust in the beam of light from the projector. It was then that I knew that she was his measure of perfection and pain—the one lost, the other gained. He, too, had heard the click of the camera, had seen her wince and felt his mercy enlarge. At last he spoke.

94   "Imelda." It was the one word he had heard her say. At the sound of his voice I removed the next slide from the projector. "Click" . . . and she was gone. "Click" again, and in her place the man with the orbital cancer. For a long moment Franciscus looked up in my direction, on his face an expression that I have given up trying to interpret. Gratitude? Sorrow? It made me think of the gaze of the girl when at last she understood that she must hand over to him the evidence of her body.

95   "This is a sixty-two-year-old man with a basal cell carcinoma of the temple eroding into the bony orbit . . ." he began as though nothing had happened.

96   At the end of the hour, even before the lights went on, there was loud applause. I hurried to find him among the departing crowd. I could not. Some weeks went by before I caught sight of him. He seemed vaguely convalescent, as though a fever had taken its toll before burning out.

97   Hugh Franciscus continued to teach for fifteen years, although he operated a good deal less, then gave it up entirely. It was as though he had grown tired of blood, of always having to be involved with blood, of having to draw it, spill it, wipe it away, stanch it. He was a quieter, softer man, I heard, the ferocity diminished. There were no more expeditions to Honduras or anywhere else.

98   I, too, have not been entirely free of her. Now and then, in the years that have passed, I see that donkey-cart cortège, or his face bent over hers in the morgue. I would like to have told him what I now know, that his unrealistic act was one of goodness, one of those small, persevering acts done, perhaps, to ward off madness. Like lighting a lamp, boiling water for tea, washing a shirt. But, of course, it's too late now.

QUESTIONS

Ideas

1. Identify three ideas that emerge in the essay. Comment briefly on each.

2. Explain the purpose of the essay. How do you think Selzer wants us to respond to Imelda, to Dr. Franciscus, and to himself as a medical student?

Organization

3. "Imelda" is arranged in seven sections. Provide a title and explain the purpose of each.

4. Provide another way of thinking about the organization of the essay, one that comprises fewer than the seven sections Selzer has established. Can any of the short sections be grouped? On what basis?

Sentences

5. Notice the way each of the following sentences employs units of three:

> There was the oval face, the long black hair unbraided, the tiny gold hoops in her ears. (92)
> Like lighting a lamp, boiling water for tea, washing a shirt. (98)
> It was as though he had grown tired of blood, of always having to be involved with blood, of having to draw it, spill it, wipe it away, stanch it. (97)
> The heavy coil of her hair made her head seem larger, darker, noble. (74)
> Then he looked and saw the grief corroding her face, breaking it down, melting the features so that eyes, nose, mouth ran together in a distortion, like the girl's. (73)
> Stealthy, hunched, engaged, he begins. (83)

6. Notice how in the following sentences Selzer preserves a balance of word against word, phrase against phrase, clause against clause.

> There are events in a doctor's life that seem to mark the boundary between youth and age, seeing and perceiving. (81)
> It seemed to me then to have been the act of someone demented, or at least insanely arrogant. (81)
> The words of the mother had not consoled him; they had hunted him down. (81)
> The door closes gassily and clicks shut. (82)
> It was then that I knew that she was his measure of perfection and pain, the one lost, the other gained. (93)

Words

7. Consider carefully the diction (word choices) and images of comparison in section III. Comment on their tone, their effect, their descriptive power, their precision, and their emotional weight.

8. What is the effect of using Spanish words throughout the essay rather than English equivalents? Substitute English for the Spanish and consider the differences.

Suggestions for Writing

A. Write an essay in which you describe your feelings as you were reading "Imelda." Try to account for your state of mind and feeling as you read. Include also your response upon finishing it and after having had some time to think about it.

B. Discuss what you take to be an important idea that emerges in the essay: perhaps something Selzer states in one of the more reflective moments in the piece; perhaps something you discover in its dialogue or action.

C. Write imitations of the sentences referred to in questions 5 and 6.

TWELVE

Lewis Thomas

(1913–   )

Lewis Thomas uses science to tell us something important about the human predicament. But unlike many similar commentators, he does not tell a pessimistic tale. The cosmic melancholy of Loren Eiseley, another acclaimed science writer, is perhaps more typical of the modern outlook. Thomas, instead, celebrates life, seeing "possibilities where others see only doom." Recently, however, even Thomas's optimism has been diminished by thoughts of nuclear war. In "Night Thoughts," he is so upset by the grotesque calm of a defense analyst that he permits his readers to see a rare event: Lewis Thomas in a dark frame of mind.

In "To Err Is Human," he turns our typically negative reaction to error completely around, finding in mistakes progress and growth. He sees hope everywhere. For example, in an essay not included in this collection, "On Natural Death," instead of wincing at the spectacle of a dying field mouse in "the jaws of an amiable household cat," he uses the incident to speculate that, instead of being an abomination, nature is wise and kind. Since there are scientific reasons for thinking that fear releases peptide hormones that have the "pharmacologic properties of opium," it is plausible to think that the mouse does not feel pain. He goes on to cite a passage from Montaigne that suggests that nature will teach us all how to die, "take you no care for it."

This is typical Lewis Thomas: after something in nature is encountered, he lets it reverberate in his mind until he comes to a tentative hypothesis. He then tests it

and invariably arrives at an encouraging vision of both
man and nature. It is a traditional and logical thought
process and one that is made more plausible because of
its simplicity.

Although he doesn't share Eiseley's mood, Thomas
has a similar purpose in writing about scientific matters:
"to communicate truths too mysterious for old-fashioned
common sense." Ironically, even though Eiseley and
Thomas have both contributed significantly to scientific
understanding, they both stress how much we *don't* know
about the workings of nature.

This is not to say that there is not a great deal of scientific information in Thomas's essays. His three collections of essays, *The Lives of a Cell: Notes of a Biology Watcher*
(1974), *The Medusa and the Snail: More Notes of a Biology
Watcher* (1979), *Late Night Thoughts on Listening to Mahler's
Ninth Symphony* (1983), and his memoir *The Youngest
Science: Notes of a Medicine Watcher* (1983), explore a wide
range of complex scientific topics, from pheromones and
embryology to cloning and germs. He is also not afraid to
deal with such diverse subjects as linguistics, music, computers, and literature. In exploring these complex issues,
he is never dogmatic, even when he is clearly the expert.
He always invites the reader to join in, to share with him
the joy of "being dumbfounded."

Indeed, it is refreshing to be told we are better than
we think. In "The Iks," for example, he strongly disagrees
with a famous anthropologist's depressing idea that a
repellent mountain tribe from Uganda is an appropriate
symbol for mankind. Thomas argues that it is society that
corrupts man, not the opposite. At heart, he believes, we
are all good. In his characteristically plain and exact style,
Thomas rejects the view that man is inherently evil with
"He's all right."

In "The Lives of a Cell," he develops another of his
central concerns—our connection to nature. Symbiosis,
in fact, is one of his favorite notions. He seems quite
upset by our nineteenth-century view that man is superior
to and independent from nature. In his graceful, gently
persuasive prose, he argues instead that "man is embedded in nature." We can, he believes, no longer see ourselves as separate and detached entities. In fact, it is an
illusion to see ourselves as autonomous. In this regard he
echoes Annie Dillard's almost mystic urge toward the
total unity of all life.

Even though Chekhov, William Carlos Williams, and other creative writers have been medical doctors, it still seems unusual for a famous pathologist to write about scientific matters with such grace, clarity, and eloquence. For the president of a world-famous cancer center to have the reputation of being one of America's best essayists is a tribute to Thomas's diversity as a scientist and humanist.

The Iks

1   The small tribe of Iks, formerly nomadic hunters and gatherers in the mountain valleys of northern Uganda, have become celebrities, literary symbols for the ultimate fate of disheartened, heartless mankind at large. Two disastrously conclusive things happened to them: the government decided to have a national park, so they were compelled by law to give up hunting in the valleys and become farmers on poor hillside soil, and then they were visited for two years by an anthropologist who detested them and wrote a book about them.

2   The message of the book is that the Iks have transformed themselves into an irreversibly disagreeable collection of unattached, brutish creatures, totally selfish and loveless, in response to the dismantling of their traditional culture. Moreover, this is what the rest of us are like in our inner selves, and we will all turn into Iks when the structure of our society comes all unhinged.

3   The argument rests, of course, on certain assumptions about the core of human beings, and is necessarily speculative. You have to agree in advance that man is fundamentally a bad lot, out for himself alone, displaying such graces as affection and compassion only as learned habits. If you take this view, the story of the Iks can be used to confirm it. These people seem to be living together, clustered in small, dense villages, but they are really solitary, unrelated individuals with no evident use for each other. They talk, but only to make ill-tempered demands and cold refusals. They share nothing. They never sing. They turn the children out to forage as soon as they can walk, and desert the elders to starve whenever they can, and the foraging children snatch food from the mouths of the helpless elders. It is a mean society.

4   They breed without love or even casual regard. They defecate on each other's doorsteps. They watch their neighbors for
signs of misfortune, and only then do they laugh. In the book
they do a lot of laughing, having so much bad luck. Several times
they even laughed at the anthropologist, who found this especially
repellent (one senses, between the lines, that the scholar is not
himself the world's luckiest man). Worse, they took him into the
family, snatched his food, defecated on his doorstep, and hooted
dislike at him. They gave him two bad years.

5   It is a depressing book. If, as he suggests, there is only Ikness
at the center of each of us, our sole hope for hanging on to the
name of humanity will be in endlessly mending the structure of
our society, and it is changing so quickly and completely that we
may never find the threads in time. Meanwhile, left to ourselves
alone, solitary, we will become the same joyless, zestless, untouch-
ing lone animals.

6   But this may be too narrow a view. For one thing, the Iks are
extraordinary. They are absolutely astonishing, in fact. The anthropologist has never seen people like them anywhere, nor have
I. You'd think, if they were simply examples of the common essence of mankind, they'd seem more recognizable. Instead, they
are bizarre, anomalous. I have known my share of peculiar, difficult, nervous, grabby people, but I've never encountered any genuinely, consistently detestable human beings in all my life. The Iks
sound more like abnormalities, maladies.

7   I cannot accept it. I do not believe that the Iks are representative of isolated, revealed man, unobscured by social habits. I
believe their behavior is something extra, something laid on. This
unremitting, compulsive repellence is a kind of complicated ritual. They must have learned to act this way; they copied it, somehow.

8   I have a theory, then. The Iks have gone crazy.

9   The solitary Ik, isolated in the ruins of an exploded culture,
has built a new defense for himself. If you live in an unworkable
society you can make up one of your own, and this is what the Iks
have done. Each Ik has become a group, a one-man tribe on its
own, a constituency.

10   Now everything falls into place. This is why they do seem,
after all, vaguely familiar to all of us. We've seen them before.
This is precisely the way groups of one size or another, ranging
from committees to nations, behave. It is, of course, this aspect of

humanity that has lagged behind the rest of evolution, and this is why the Ik seems so primitive. In his absolute selfishness, his incapacity to give anything away, no matter what, he is a successful committee. When he stands at the door of his hut, shouting insults at his neighbors in a loud harangue, he is city addressing another city.

11   Cities have all the Ik characteristics. They defecate on doorsteps, in rivers and lakes, their own or anyone else's. They leave rubbish. They detest all neighboring cities, give nothing away. They even build institutions for deserting elders out of sight.

12   Nations are the most Iklike of all. No wonder the Iks seem familiar. For total greed, rapacity, heartlessness, and irresponsibility there is nothing to match a nation. Nations, by law, are solitary, self-centered, withdrawn into themselves. There is no such thing as affection between nations, and certainly no nation ever loved another. They bawl insults from their doorsteps, defecate into whole oceans, snatch all the food, survive by detestation, take joy in the bad luck of others, celebrate the death of others, live for the death of others.

13   That's it, and I shall stop worrying about the book. It does not signify that man is a sparse, inhuman thing at his center. He's all right. It only says what we've always known and never had enough time to worry about, that we haven't yet learned how to stay human when assembled in masses. The Ik, in his despair, is acting out this failure, and perhaps we should pay closer attention. Nations have themselves become too frightening to think about, but we might learn some things by watching these people.

QUESTIONS

Ideas

1.   How does Thomas react to the Iks? To the book about them? The anthropologist, in his book, does indeed suggest "that man is a sparse, inhuman thing at his center?" Does Thomas think so? Do you think so? What is Thomas's position in paragraph 3? Does he think man is basically good at heart? Does his view seem reasonable? Fair? Flexible? Why or why not?

2.   Thomas lets us follow his train of thought as he comes to terms with the nature of the Iks and finally with the nature of man. After he

sketches the necessary background, he asserts, in paragraph 5, that this "is a depressing book." Try to outline, in brief sentences, his reasoning from this point on. How does he counter the anthropologist's thesis?

3. What is the effect of "That's it," in the last paragraph? Has he convinced you that "he's all right"? Who is this "he"?

Organization

4. Go back through this essay, reading only the first and last sentences in each paragraph. What does this tell you about Thomas's view of the paragraph's opening sentence? Notice paragraphs 11 and 12. After the opening sentence, what do the rest of the sentences try to do?

5. What do you make of the one-sentence paragraph 8? Is this effective?

6. How is the last sentence of paragraph 3 related to and connected with the five sentences before it?

7. Where does the essay seem to change direction? To shift in ideas?

8. Do you think the organization represents Thomas's actual thinking process? Would the essay have been more effective if he had begun with a thesis and then set out to defend it? What organization would you have chosen?

9. As part of his organization and thematic plan Thomas compares the Iks first to cities, then to nations. How does he do this? What aspects of each does he compare?

Sentences

10. Is the repetition of "they" effective in paragraph 4?

11. When Thomas wants to be emphatic he usually writes short, assertive sentences. Can you point to some that seem especially effective? (Read paragraphs 3 and 4 aloud.)

12. There don't seem to be many compound sentences here. There's one in paragraph 10; can you find others? What is the effect of making sentences simple?

13. Take a close look at Thomas's use of commas in the first sentence. Why does he use the first two? Could he have used a colon instead of the third comma? Can you explain the function of these commas?

Words

14. What words and specific details does Thomas repeat in the essay? To what effect?

15. What words, in paragraphs 5 and 6, carry negative connotations? Which describe or define "Ikness"?

Suggestion for Writing

Write an essay that supports either the anthropologist's or Thomas's position on the Iks. Try to use personal experience to support your stand.

The Lives of a Cell

---

1   We are told that the trouble with Modern Man is that he has been trying to detach himself from nature. He sits in the topmost tiers of polymer, glass, and steel, dangling his pulsing legs, surveying at a distance the writhing life of the planet. In this scenario, Man comes on as a stupendous lethal force, and the earth is pictured as something delicate, like rising bubbles at the surface of a country pond, or flights of fragile birds.

2   But it is illusion to think that there is anything fragile about the life of the earth; surely this is the toughest membrane imaginable in the universe, opaque to probability, impermeable to death. We are the delicate part, transient and vulnerable as cilia. Nor is it a new thing for man to invent an existence that he imagines to be above the rest of life; this has been his most consistent intellectual exertion down the millennia. As illusion, it has never worked out to his satisfaction in the past, any more than it does today. Man is embedded in nature.

3   The biologic science of recent years has been making this a more urgent fact of life. The new, hard problem will be to cope with the dawning, intensifying realization of just how interlocked we are. The old, clung-to notions most of us have held about our special lordship are being deeply undermined.

4   *Item.* A good case can be made for our nonexistence as entities. We are not made up, as we had always supposed, of successively enriched packets of our own parts. We are shared, rented, occupied. At the interior of our cells, driving them, providing the oxidative energy that sends us out for the improvement of each shining day, are the mitochondria, and in a strict sense they are not ours. They turn out to be little separate creatures, the colonial

posterity of migrant prokaryocytes, probably primitive bacteria that swam into ancestral precursors of our eukaryotic cells and stayed here. Ever since, they have maintained themselves and their ways, replicating in their own fashion, privately, with their own DNA and RNA quite different from ours. They are as much symbionts as the rhizobial bacteria in the roots of beans. Without them, we would not move a muscle, drum a finger, think a thought.

5   Mitochondria are stable and responsible lodgers, and I choose to trust them. But what of the other little animals, similarly established in my cells, sorting and balancing me, clustering me together? My centrioles, basal bodies, and probably a good many other more obscure tiny beings at work inside my cells, each with its own special genome, are as foreign, and as essential, as aphids in anthills. My cells are no longer the pure line entities I was raised with; they are ecosystems more complex than Jamaica Bay.

6   I like to think that they work in my interest, that each breath they draw for me, but perhaps it is they who walk through the local park in the early morning, sensing my senses, listening to my music, thinking my thoughts.

7   I am consoled, somewhat, by the thought that the green plants are in the same fix. They could not be plants, or green, without their chloroplasts, which run the photosynthetic enterprise and generate oxygen for the rest of us. As it turns out, chloroplasts are also separate creatures with their own genomes, speaking their own language.

8   We carry stores of DNA in our nuclei that may have come in, at one time or another, from the fusion of ancestral cells and the linking of ancestral organisms in symbiosis. Our genomes are catalogues of instructions from all kinds of sources in nature, filed for all kinds of contingencies. As for me, I am grateful for differentiation and speciation, but I cannot feel as separate an entity as I did a few years ago, before I was told these things, nor, I should think, can anyone else.

9   *Item.* The uniformity of the earth's life, more astonishing than its diversity, is accountable by the high probability that we derived, originally, from some single cell, fertilized in a bolt of lightning as the earth cooled. It is from the progeny of this parent cell that we take our looks; we still share genes around, and the resemblance of the enzymes of grasses to those of whales is a family resemblance.

10   The viruses, instead of being single-minded agents of disease
and death, now begin to look more like mobile genes. Evolution
is still an infinitely long and tedious biologic game, with only the
winners staying at the table, but the rules are beginning to look
more flexible. We live in a dancing matrix of viruses; they dart,
rather like bees, from organism to organism, from plant to insect
to mammal to me and back again, and into the sea, tugging along
pieces of this genome, strings of genes from that, transplanting
grafts of DNA, passing around heredity as though at a great party.
They may be a mechanism for keeping new, mutant kinds of DNA
in the widest circulation among us. If this is true, the odd virus
disease, on which we must focus so much of our attention in
medicine, may be looked on as an accident, something dropped.

11   *Item.* I have been trying to think of the earth as a kind of
organism, but it is no go. I cannot think of it this way. It is too big,
too complex, with too many working parts lacking visible connections. The other night, driving through a hilly, wooded part of
southern New England, I wondered about this. If not like an
organism, what is it like, what is it *most* like? Then, satisfactorily for
that moment, it came to me: it is *most* like a single cell.

QUESTIONS

Ideas

1. From your experience, do you think Thomas's image in the first
    paragraph is correct? Have we been trying to detach ourselves from
    nature?

2. Does his "correction" of this scenario seem more or less optimistic?
    Does it worry you that he claims "we are the delicate part"?

3. In the last paragraph, what difference does it make whether we
    accept Thomas's analogy that the earth is an organism or a single
    cell?

Organization

4. Thomas chooses to put a traditional topic sentence (the assertion of
    an opinion) at the end of the second paragraph. What does he try
    to do in the succeeding paragraphs? Is this exposition (explana-
    tion), or is he trying to persuade you of something? Look especially
    at the last sentence in paragraph 8.

5. Thomas appears to be trying to alter our misconceptions about our "special lordship." In this regard, do you think he arranges his essay effectively?

6. Where does his introduction end? Where does his conclusion begin?

7. How does Thomas support his opening sentence in paragraph 4?

8. How does Thomas get us from paragraph 1 to 2 and on to 3? Underline all the connections; include the syntactic and semantic ways the paragraphs are linked.

9. Look at the ways Thomas begins his sentences in the first two paragraphs. How many follow the normal subject, verb, object (S-V-O) pattern?

10. Look at the first sentence of the second paragraph. The two three-word phrases at the end are free modifiers, meaning they can be moved to other positions in the sentence. Where else might they go?

11. Count the words in each sentence in the second paragraph. Is there a reason for this pattern?

12. In paragraph 9, why did Thomas decide to use a semicolon in the last sentence? Are there other options?

Words

13. Unlike much of "scientific writing," Thomas opens this piece on a technical subject with an attention-getting image. Does this "popular technique" make his argument seem less serious?

14. Do you find Thomas mixing levels of diction, for example, using scientific jargon and informational speech? Where does he do it and for what effect? Does it work?

15. What kind of voice (or persona) do you hear in this essay? Try reading the last two paragraphs out loud. Is this a voice of authority? Is he trying to be down to earth? What voice might you take in handling this subject? Does it depend on your purpose? What do you think Thomas's purpose is?

Suggestions for Writing

A. Throughout the essay, Thomas frequently uses triplets—three words in parallel form, three phrases in parallel structure, three sentences in parallel motion. Paragraph 3 contains two examples, paragraph 5, one. Rewrite these sentences, destroying the parallelism or adding connecting words (like "and") to join the three elements. What is lost in these revisions?

B. Even more frequently than triplets, Thomas uses doublets of words and phrases, of sentences and paragraphs. What kinds of "pairs" can you find in the essay? How effective are they? Consider especially the balances and parallels of paragraphs 6, 7, and 11. Write a short paragraph describing a familiar scene using doublets.

C. Think of a scientific or technical subject that concerns you, say, pollution and protecting (or not protecting) the environment, or cloning, or chemical additives in our food. Try to write about it using the Thomas structure of beginning with a misconception our society shares and then demonstrating why the illusion is false. In writing your piece keep in mind how Thomas combines anecdote, comparison and contrast, exposition, persuasion, and description.

The Tucson Zoo

1   Science gets most of its information by the process of reductionism, exploring the details, then the details of the details, until all the smallest bits of the structure, or the smallest parts of the mechanism, are laid out for counting and scrutiny. Only when this is done can the investigation be extended to encompass the whole organism or the entire system. So we say.

2   Sometimes it seems that we take a loss, working this way. Much of today's public anxiety about science is the apprehension that we may forever be overlooking the whole by an endless, obsessive preoccupation with the parts. I had a brief, personal experience of this misgiving one afternoon in Tucson, where I had time on my hands and visited the zoo, just outside the city. The designers there have cut a deep pathway between two small artificial ponds, walled by clear glass, so when you stand in the center of the path you can look into the depths of each pool, and at the same time you can regard the surface. In one pool, on the right side of the path, is a family of otters; on the other side, a family of beavers. Within just a few feet from your face, on either side, beavers and otters are at play, underwater and on the surface, swimming toward your face and then away, more filled with life than any creatures I have ever seen before, in all my days. Except for the glass, you could reach across and touch them.

3   I was transfixed. As I now recall it, there was only one sensation in my head: pure elation mixed with amazement at such perfection. Swept off my feet, I floated from one side to the other,

swiveling my brain, staring astounded at the beavers, then at the otters. I could hear shouts across my corpus callosum, from one hemisphere to the other. I remember thinking, with what was left in charge of my consciousness, that I wanted no part of the science of beavers and otters; I wanted never to know how they performed their marvels; I wished for no news about the physiology of their breathing, the coordination of their muscles, their vision, their endocrine systems, their digestive tracts. I hoped never to have to think of them as collections of cells. All I asked for was the full hairy complexity, then in front of my eyes, of whole, intact beavers and otters in motion.

4   It lasted, I regret to say, for only a few minutes, and then I was back in the late twentieth century, reductionist as ever, wondering about the details by force of habit, but not, this time, the details of otters and beavers. Instead, me. Something worth remembering had happened in my mind, I was certain of that; I would have put it somewhere in the brain stem; maybe this was my limbic system at work. I became a behavioral scientist, an experimental psychologist, an ethologist, and in the instant I lost all the wonder and the sense of being overwhelmed. I was flattened.

5   But I came away from the zoo with something, a piece of news about myself: I am coded, somehow, for otters and beavers. I exhibit instinctive behavior in their presence, when they are displayed close at hand behind glass, simultaneously below water and at the surface. I have receptors for this display. Beavers and otters possess a "releaser" for me, in the terminology of ethology, and the releasing was my experience. What was released? Behavior. What behavior? Standing, swiveling flabbergasted, feeling exultation and a rush of friendship. I could not, as the result of the transaction, tell you anything more about beavers and otters than you already know. I learned nothing new about them. Only about me, and I suspect also about you, maybe about human beings at large: we are endowed with genes which code out our reaction to beavers and otters, maybe our reaction to each other as well. We are stamped with stereotyped, unalterable patterns of response, ready to be released. And the behavior released in us, by such confrontations, is, essentially, a surprised affection. It is compulsory behavior and we can avoid it only by straining with the full power of our conscious minds, making up conscious excuses all the way. Left to ourselves, mechanistic and autonomic, we hanker for friends.

6   Everyone says, stay away from ants. They have no lessons for us; they are crazy little instruments, inhuman, incapable of con-

trolling themselves, lacking manners, lacking souls. When they are massed together, all touching, exchanging bits of information held in their jaws like memoranda, they become a single animal. Look out for that. It is a debasement, a loss of individuality, a violation of human nature, an unnatural act.

7   Sometimes people argue this point of view seriously and with deep thought. Be individuals, solitary and selfish, is the message. Altruism, a jargon word for what used to be called love, is worse than weakness, it is sin, a violation of nature. Be separate. Do not be a social animal. But this is a hard argument to make convincingly when you have to depend on language to make it. You have to print up leaflets or publish books and get them bought and sent around, you have to turn up on television and catch the attention of millions of other human beings all at once, and then you have to say to all of them, all at once, all collected and paying attention: be solitary; do not depend on each other. You can't do this and keep a straight face.

8   Maybe altruism is our most primitive attribute, out of reach, beyond our control. Or perhaps it is immediately at hand, waiting to be released, disguised now, in our kind of civilization, as affection or friendship or attachment. I don't see why it should be unreasonable for all human beings to have strands of DNA coiled up in chromosomes, coding out instincts for usefulness and helpfulness. Usefulness may turn out to be the hardest test of fitness for survival, more important than aggression, more effective, in the long run, than grabbiness. If this is the sort of information biological science holds for the future, applying to us as well as to ants, then I am all for science.

9   One thing I'd like to know most of all: when those ants have made the Hill, and are all there, touching and exchanging, and the whole mass begins to behave like a single huge creature, and *thinks*, what on earth is that thought? And while you're at it, I'd like to know a second thing: when it happens, does any single ant know about it? Does his hair stand on end?

QUESTIONS

Ideas

1. Think of this essay as a counterpart to "The Iks." Do they have a common theme? What does Thomas hope is bound up in our DNA?

What does this have to do with the Iks' problem? Look especially at the first two sentences in paragraph 8.

2. Like many writers, including Eiseley and Dillard, Thomas uses his response to an experience as a jumping-off place to further thinking. Try to outline the chain of reasoning that the beavers and otters of the Tucson Zoo set off in Thomas's mind.

3. What do you think Thomas means by "full hairy complexity" in paragraph 3? Why does he "want no part of the science of beavers and otters"?

4. What did Thomas learn about himself from his zoo experience? What does he mean by saying he is "coded for beavers"? (Consider paragraph 5 carefully.)

5. Do you agree that our conscious minds fight against the loss of individuality? What is Thomas's rejoinder to those who urge us "not to be a social animal"?

6. Even though Thomas is using the questions in the last paragraph for effect, how might you answer them?

Organization

7. What is the function of the first paragraph? What do you think Thomas intended in the last sentence by, "So we say"?

8. Does Thomas come back to that opening paragraph to summarize or strengthen? Does he do so explicitly, implicitly, or not at all?

9. Why does Thomas begin paragraph 5 with "But"? Is this an effective device?

10. Read the first sentence of paragraphs 2 and 7. How does Thomas connect them to the previous paragraphs?

11. In paragraph 6, what is the relation between the first and the remaining sentences? How are the sentences in this paragraph connected to each other?

12. If you split the essay into two parts, where would you break it and why?

Sentences

13. Thomas is trying to make his prose seem effortless, but we know that prose that is easy to read is hard to write. Thomas's prose did not spontaneously flow from his typewriter. He worked at it, long and hard. All writers do. For example, read paragraph 3 out loud several times. Can you describe some of the techniques Thomas uses here to achieve fluency? Some hints: Do all the sentences begin the same way? How does he vary the S-V-O pattern? How many words are in each sentence?

14. How is the fifth sentence constructed? Why the specific detail (endocrine systems, etc.) and the repetition? Does this paragraph have a beginning, a middle, and an end? How would you partition it?

15. Thomas occasionally uses short sentences, sometimes only two or three words long. Look through paragraphs 1-4, noting those. What is the effect of each?

Words

16. Thomas uses some scientific words in this essay. Do they confuse you? Did you get lost while reading them?

17. Why does Thomas use personal pronouns? See paragraphs 2 (you), 3 and 4 (I), and 5 (we).

Suggestion for Writing

Write a letter to Lewis Thomas agreeing or disagreeing with paragraphs 6, 7, or 8—or with the whole essay.

To Err Is Human

1   Everyone must have had at least one personal experience with a computer error by this time. Bank balances are suddenly reported to have jumped from $379 into the millions, appeals for charitable contributions are mailed over and over to people with crazy-sounding names at your address, department stores send the wrong bills, utility companies write that they're turning everything off, that sort of thing. If you manage to get in touch with someone and complain, you then get instantaneously typed, guilty letters from the same computer, saying, "Our computer was in error, and an adjustment is being made in your account."

2   These are supposed to be the sheerest, blindest accidents. Mistakes are not believed to be part of the normal behavior of a good machine. If things go wrong, it must be a personal, human error, the result of fingering, tampering, a button getting stuck, someone hitting the wrong key. The computer, at its normal best, is infallible.

3   I wonder whether this can be true. After all, the whole point of computers is that they represent an extension of the human brain, vastly improved upon but nonetheless human, superhuman maybe. A good computer can think clearly and quickly enough to beat you at chess, and some of them have even been programmed to write obscure verse. They can do anything we can do, and more besides.

4   It is not yet known whether a computer has its own consciousness, and it would be hard to find out about this. When you walk into one of those great halls now built for the huge machines, and stand listening, it is easy to imagine that the faint, distant noises are the sound of thinking, and the turning of the spools gives them the look of wild creatures rolling their eyes in the effort to concentrate, choking with information. But real thinking, and dreaming, are other matters.

5   On the other hand, the evidences of something like an *unconscious,* equivalent to ours, are all around, in every mail. As extensions of the human brain, they have been constructed with the same property of error, spontaneous, uncontrolled, and rich in possibilities.

6   Mistakes are at the very base of human thought, embedded there, feeding the structure like root nodules. If we were not provided with the knack of being wrong, we could never get anything useful done. We think our way along by choosing between right and wrong alternatives, and the wrong choices have to be made as frequently as the right ones. We get along in life this way. We are built to make mistakes, coded for error.

7   We learn, as we say, by "trial and error." Why do we always say that? Why not "trial and rightness" or "trial and triumph"? The old phrase puts it that way because that is, in real life, the way it is done.

8   A good laboratory, like a good bank or a corporation or government, has to run like a computer. Almost everything is done flawlessly, by the book, and all the numbers add up to the predicted sums. The days go by. And then, if it is a lucky day, and a lucky laboratory, somebody makes a mistake: the wrong buffer, something in one of the blanks, a decimal misplaced in reading counts, the warm room off by a degree and a half, a mouse out of his box, or just a misreading of the day's protocol. Whatever, when the results come in, something is obviously screwed up, and then the action can begin.

9   The misreading is not the important error; it opens the way. The next step is the crucial one. If the investigator can bring himself to say, "But even so, look at that!" then the new finding, whatever it is, is ready for snatching. What is needed, for progress to be made, is the move based on the error.

10   Whenever new kinds of thinking are about to be accomplished, or new varieties of music, there has to be an argument beforehand. With two sides debating in the same mind, haranguing, there is an amiable understanding that one is right and the other wrong. Sooner or later the thing is settled, but there can be no action at all if there are not the two sides, and the argument. The hope is in the faculty of wrongness, the tendency toward error. The capacity to leap across mountains of information to land lightly on the wrong side represents the highest of human endowments.

11   It may be that this is a uniquely human gift, perhaps even stipulated in our genetic instructions. Other creatures do not seem to have DNA sequences for making mistakes as a routine part of daily living, certainly not for programmed error as a guide for action.

12   We are at our human finest, dancing with our minds, when there are more choices than two. Sometimes there are ten, even twenty different ways to go, all but one bound to be wrong, and the richness of selection in such situations can lift us onto totally new ground. This process is called exploration and is based on human fallibility. If we had only a single center in our brains, capable of responding only when a correct decision was to be made, instead of the jumble of different, credulous, easily conned clusters of neurones that provide for being flung off into blind alleys, up trees, down dead ends, out into blue sky, along wrong turnings, around bends, we could only stay the way we are today, stuck fast.

13   The lower animals do not have this splendid freedom. They are limited, most of them, to absolute infallibility. Cats, for all their good side, never make mistakes. I have never seen a maladroit, clumsy, or blundering cat. Dogs are sometimes fallible, occasionally able to make charming minor mistakes, but they get this way by trying to mimic their masters. Fish are flawless in everything they do. Individual cells in a tissue are mindless machines, perfect in their performance, as absolutely inhuman as bees.

14   We should have this in mind as we become dependent on more complex computers for the arrangement of our affairs. Give the computers their heads, I say; let them go their way. If we can learn to do this, turning our heads to one side and wincing while the work proceeds, the possibilities for the future of mankind, and computerkind, are limitless. Your average good computer can make calculations in an instant which would take a lifetime of slide rules for any of us. Think of what we could gain from the near infinity of precise, machine-made miscomputation which is now so easily within our grasp. We could begin the solving of some of our hardest problems. How, for instance, should we go about organizing ourselves for social living on a planetary scale, now that we have become, as a plain fact of life, a single community? We can assume, as a working hypothesis, that all the right ways of doing this are unworkable. What we need, then, for moving ahead, is a set of wrong alternatives much longer and more interesting than the short list of mistaken courses that any of us can think up right now. We need, in fact, an infinite list, and when it is printed out we need the computer to turn on itself and select, at random, the next way to go. If it is a big enough mistake, we could find ourselves on a new level, stunned, out in the clear, ready to move again.

QUESTIONS

Ideas

1. How is the title of this piece relevant? What does it have to do with Thomas's theme? Where is that theme expressed? Underline at least three sentences you think are related to this theme.

2. Do you agree that our ability to make mistakes is a "splendid freedom"? Does our society agree? Does your university, your instructor?

3. Again, Thomas takes an apparently negative topic and makes it seem optimistic. Do you see hope in our "faculty of wrongness, the tendency toward error"?

4. In paragraph 8 Thomas discusses "error." And he makes what at first might seem the rather strange remark ". . . if it is a lucky day, and a lucky laboratory, somebody makes a mistake: . . . when the results come in, something is obviously screwed up, and then the action can begin." Can you explain this paradoxical idea? (Look ahead to paragraph 9 for help.)

5. Why does Thomas celebrate choice and alternative, especially multiple alternatives most of which will be "wrong"? Explain his idea that exploration is based on human fallibility (paragraph 12).

6. Suppose Thomas is "wrong" about what he says in this essay. Does that invalidate his view entirely? Does it make what he says here useless? Why or why not?

7. To err means, of course, to be mistaken. But the original meaning of the word carries the idea of wandering (L. *errare*, to wander). How do Thomas's ideas about error reflect this aspect of the word's meaning?

8. Does what Thomas says about error have any bearing on learning? On writing?

Organization

9. What is the purpose of Thomas's opening two paragraphs? How do they compare to the introductions in "The Iks" and "The Lives of a Cell"?

10. In the overall scheme of these fourteen paragraphs, what is the function of paragraph 6?

11. Where does Thomas support his notion that we are "coded for error"?

12. The last paragraph is rather long for Thomas. What holds it together? Is there an implicit or explicit topic sentence?

13. How many paragraphs have a "this" in the first sentence? Why do you think he does this?

14. Experienced writers try to move between the abstract and the concrete, often supporting general statements with specific details. How does Thomas do this in paragraphs 8, 12, and 13?

Sentences

15. Thomas sometimes adds words, phrases, and clauses to sentences, clarifying an idea, making a general point more specific. See the last sentence, for example. Locate several similar examples.

Words

16. How would you distinguish among "error," "mistake," and "accident"?

17. What does "maladroit" mean? "Haranguing"? "Protocol"?

Suggestion for Writing

Now that Thomas has alerted the reader to the paradox of error, can you see mistakes you made in the past or are continuing to make as enabling you to be "in the clear, ready to move again"? Write an essay involving personal experience to support this optimistic view of error.

Late Night Thoughts on Listening to Mahler's Ninth Symphony

---

1   I cannot listen to Mahler's Ninth Symphony with anything like the old melancholy mixed with the high pleasure I used to take from this music. There was a time, not long ago, when what I heard, especially in the final movement, was an open acknowledgment of death and at the same time a quiet celebration of the tranquillity connected to the process. I took this music as a metaphor for reassurance, confirming my own strong hunch that the dying of every living creature, the most natural of all experiences, has to be a peaceful experience. I rely on nature. The long passages on all the strings at the end, as close as music can come to expressing silence itself, I used to hear as Mahler's idea of leave-taking at its best. But always, I have heard this music as a solitary, private listener, thinking about death.

2   Now I hear it differently. I cannot listen to the last movement of the Mahler Ninth without the door-smashing intrusion of a huge new thought: death everywhere, the dying of everything, the end of humanity. The easy sadness expressed with such gentleness and delicacy by that repeated phrase on faded strings, over and over again, no longer comes to me as old, familiar news of the cycle of living and dying. All through the last notes my mind swarms with images of a world in which the thermonuclear bombs have begun to explode, in New York and San Francisco, in Moscow and Leningrad, in Paris, in Paris, in Paris. In Oxford and Cambridge, in Edinburgh. I cannot push away the thought of a cloud of radioactivity drifting along the Engadin, from the Moloja Pass to Ftan, killing off the part of the earth I love more than any other part.

3   I am old enough by this time to be used to the notion of dying, saddened by the glimpse when it has occurred but only

transiently knocked down, able to regain my feet quickly at the thought of continuity, any day. I have acquired and held in affection until very recently another sideline of an idea which serves me well at dark times: the life of the earth is the same as the life of an organism: the great round being possesses a mind: the mind contains an infinite number of thoughts and memories: when I reach my time I may find myself still hanging around in some sort of midair, one of those small thoughts, drawn back into the memory of the earth: in that peculiar sense I will be alive.

4   Now all that has changed. I cannot think that way anymore. Not while those things are still in place, aimed everywhere, ready for launching.

5   This is a bad enough thing for the people in my generation. We can put up with it, I suppose, since we must. We are moving along anyway, like it or not. I can even set aside my private fancy about hanging around, in midair.

6   What I cannot imagine, what I cannot put up with, the thought that keeps grinding its way into my mind, making the Mahler into a hideous noise close to killing me, is what it would be like to be young. How do the young stand it? How can they keep their sanity? If I were very young, sixteen or seventeen years old, I think I would begin, perhaps very slowly and imperceptibly, to go crazy.

7   There is a short passage near the very end of the Mahler in which the almost vanishing violins, all engaged in a sustained backward glance, are edged aside for a few bars by the cellos. Those lower notes pick up fragments from the first movement, as though prepared to begin everything all over again, and then the cellos subside and disappear, like an exhalation. I used to hear this as a wonderful few seconds of encouragement: we'll be back, we're still here, keep going, keep going.

8   Now, with a pamphlet in front of me on a corner of my desk, published by the Congressional Office of Technology Assessment, entitled *MX Basing,* an analysis of all the alternative strategies for placement and protection of hundreds of these missiles, each capable of creating artificial suns to vaporize a hundred Hiroshimas, collectively capable of destroying the life of any continent, I cannot hear the same Mahler. Now, those cellos sound in my mind like the opening of all the hatches and the instant before ignition.

9   If I were sixteen or seventeen years old, I would not feel the cracking of my own brain, but I would know for sure that the

whole world was coming unhinged. I can remember with some clarity what it was like to be sixteen. I had discovered the Brahms symphonies. I knew that there was something going on in the late Beethoven quartets that I would have to figure out, and I knew that there was plenty of time ahead for all the figuring I would ever have to do. I had never heard of Mahler. I was in no hurry. I was a college sophomore and had decided that Wallace Stevens and I possessed a comprehensive understanding of everything needed for a life. The years stretched away forever ahead, forever. My great-great grandfather had come from Wales, leaving his signature in the family Bible on the same page that carried, a century later, my father's signature. It never crossed my mind to wonder about the twenty-first century; it was just there, given, somewhere in the sure distance.

10   The man on television, Sunday midday, middle-aged and solid, nice-looking chap, all the facts at his fingertips, more dependable looking than most high-school principals, is talking about civilian defense, his responsibility in Washington. It can make an enormous difference, he is saying. Instead of the outright death of eighty million American citizens in twenty minutes, he says, we can, by careful planning and practice, get that number down to only forty million, maybe even twenty. The thing to do, he says, is to evacuate the cities quickly and have everyone get under shelter in the countryside. That way we can recover, and meanwhile we will have retaliated, incinerating all of Soviet society, he says. What about radioactive fallout? he is asked. Well, he says. Anyway, he says, if the Russians know they can only destroy forty million of us instead of eighty million, this will deter them. Of course, he adds, they have the capacity to kill all two hundred and twenty million of us if they were to try real hard, but they know we can do the same to them. If the figure is only forty million this will deter them, not worth the trouble, not worth the risk. Eighty million would be another matter, we should guard ourselves against losing that many all at once, he says.

11   If I were sixteen or seventeen years old and had to listen to that, or read things like that, I would want to give up listening and reading. I would begin thinking up new kinds of sounds, different from any music heard before, and I would be twisting and turning to rid myself of human language.

QUESTIONS

Ideas

1. Thomas's notions of death have obviously been upset. What were they? Specifically, what are the ways Thomas used to deal with death?
2. What does Thomas now hear when he listens to Mahler's Ninth Symphony?
3. What about the man on television who angers Thomas? Does he anger you? How do you keep your sanity in the face of nuclear war? Do you have a defense?
4. What does Thomas mean to suggest about his present pessimism with the phrase "there was plenty of time ahead" in paragraph 9?
5. Do you think it is unusual for something like the MX missile to color someone's perception about music?

Organization

6. Much of this essay is structured on a then-and-now pattern. Point out how Thomas integrates these shifts between the past and the present.
7. In paragraph 6, Thomas makes his point about the difficulty of being young in the last sentence. How does that thought control the remaining five paragraphs?

Sentences

8. Read carefully the second sentence in paragraph 3. Explain how Thomas uses this rarely seen colon sequence. Is it effective? What are some alternatives?
9. Look at the many "if" clauses and sentences in this essay. Are there special rules for them; for example, are the verb tenses different than in normal declarative sentences?

Words

10. Why does Thomas repeat "in Paris" in paragraph 2?
11. What is the effect of calling missiles "those things" in paragraph 4?

Suggestions for Writing

A. Write a paragraph in response to Thomas's last paragraph. Do you agree with him? Is he exaggerating?
B. Write a brief paper using "denial of death" as your initial focus.

THIRTEEN

Barbara Tuchman

(1912–1989)

Barbara Tuchman was not a typical academic historian: she had no graduate degrees, did not teach in a university, and was more interested in telling a story readers
feel compelled to follow than in historical objectivity. She
was, in other words, a popular historian, and after winning two Pulitzer Prizes and numerous honorary degrees,
probably the most eminent in America.

She wrote to inform and enthrall an audience of
average readers, not to impress history professors.
Because she knew her chosen audience would not automatically be interested in her subject, she adopted a lively, colorful style that would keep the reader turning
pages. She tried to win the reader over by ordering her
writing as if she were writing fiction. She built suspense by
selecting and arranging dramatic details from her copi-
ous research notes, discarding the irrelevant, and maintaining a strong story line. The following passage from
The Proud Tower is typical of her approach. She was writing about the reaction to the assassination of Jaurès, a
popular French socialist before World War I.

The news licked through Paris like a flame. Crowds gathered so quickly in the street outside the restaurant that it took
the police fifteen minutes to open a passage for the ambulance.
When the body was carried out a great silence fell. As the ambulance clanged away, escorted by policemen on bicycles, a sudden clamor arose, as if to deny the fact of death, "Jaurès! Jaurès!
Vive Jaurès!" Elsewhere people were stupefied, numb with sorrow. Many wept in the streets. "My heart is breaking," said

Anatole France when he heard. Informed at its night session by
a white-faced aide, the Cabinet was stunned and fearful. Visions
rose of working-class riots and civil strife on the eve of war. The
Premier issued a public appeal for unity and calm. Troops were
alerted but next morning, in the national peril, there was only
deep grief and deep quiet. At Carmaux the miners stopped
work. "They have cut down a mighty oak," said one. In Leipzig a
Spanish Socialist student at the University wandered blindly
through the streets for hours; "everything took on the color of
blood."

These techniques have sometimes drawn criticism
from more traditional historians who say that she
sacrifices depth and intellectual content for the immediacy and literary flavor of dramatic narrative. Barbara
Tuchman insists, however, that although her subject matter is historical, she is a writer first, and her loyalty is primarily to her craft, to the drama, coherence, and color of
good writing. She does not, however, avoid ideas. But
even here she goes her own way, sometimes preferring
bold opinion to scholarly detachment. The "Afterword"
to her book on Europe before World War I, *The Proud
Tower*, provides a good example of her engaging mix of
stylistic flair and intelligent insight:

The four years that followed were, as Graham Wallas
wrote, "four years of the most intense and heroic effort the
human race has ever made." When the effort was over, illusions
and enthusiasms possible up to 1914 slowly sank beneath a sea
of massive disillusionment. For the price it had paid, humanity's
major gain was a painful view of its own limitations.
The proud tower built up through the great age of
European civilization was an edifice of grandeur and passion, of
riches and beauty and dark cellars. Its inhabitants lived, as compared to a later time, with more self-reliance, more confidence,
more hope, greater magnificence, extravagance and elegance;
more careless ease, more gaiety, more pleasure in each other's
company and conversation, more injustice and hypocrisy, more
misery and want, more sentiment including false sentiment, less
sufferance of mediocrity, more dignity in work, more delight in
nature, more zest. The Old World had much that has since
been lost, whatever may have been gained. Looking back on it
from 1915, Emile Verhaeren, the Belgian Socialist poet, dedicated his pages, "With emotion, to the man I used to be."

Since Tuchman is not limited by the usual narrow specializations, her topics spring from her present interests. Her subjects have been diverse. Her first success, *The Guns of August* (1962), dealt with the failures of the early military strategy of World War I. She followed that in 1966 with *The Proud Tower: A Portrait of the World before the War—1890–1914,* filled with thickly described, selective narratives of socialists, patricians, anarchists, and statesmen. Five years later she turned her attention to relations between China and America in *Stilwell and the American Experience in China, 1911–1945,* winning praise from specialists for not sacrificing complexity and for "an admirably structured work that is excellent as narrative and fascinating as history." Her most popular book, the best-selling *A Distant Mirror: The Calamitous Fourteenth Century* (1978), was seen by many critics as Tuchman's greatest achievement. In it she weaves a gripping drama of social, political, and historical events around themes that recur in her work: the complexity of life, the hopes and upheavals of people and nations, and the persistent folly of governments. This last concern dominates her most recent book, *The March of Folly: From Troy to Vietnam* (1984), an indictment of governments that consistently make unwise decisions. In a related essay on political wooden-headedness, Tuchman blames the poor performance of leaders on the passions and the emotions: "greed, fear, facesaving, the instinct to dominate, the needs of the ego, the whole bundle of personal vanities and anxieties."

Herein lies the motivating impulse and moral power of Tuchman's career as a writer. She has a message, a warning that she hopes her readers will assimilate from her work. She believes that the modern world can no longer afford to repeat the mistakes of the past: "Today there are no more cushions." She hopes for reason, for intellect, and is outraged when powerful men seem to follow their baser instincts. She is unsparing, for example, with President Johnson, who seemed to her to have a shaky self-image. "Johnson's showed in his deliberate coarseness and compulsion to humiliate others in crude physical ways. No self-confident man would have needed to do that." Idealistically she hopes instead for the "truest wisdom" of magnanimity, rationality, and fitness of character. She writes history in the hope that an informed electorate might choose leaders with these virtues.

In Search of History

1   One learns to write, I have since discovered, in the
practice thereof. After seven years' apprenticeship in journalism I
discovered that an essential element for good writing is a good
ear. One must *listen* to the sound of one's own prose. This, I
think, is one of the failings of much American writing. Too many
writers do not listen to the sound of their own words. For example, listen to this sentence from the organ of my own discipline,
the *American Historical Review:* "His presentation is not vitiated historically by efforts at expository simplicity." In one short sentence
five long Latin words of four or five syllables each. One has to
read it three times over and take time out to think, before one
can even make out what it means.

2   In my opinion, short words are always preferable to long
ones; the fewer syllables the better, and monosyllables, beautiful
and pure like "bread" and "sun" and "grass," are the best of all.
Emerson, using almost entirely one-syllable words, wrote what I
believe are among the finest lines in English:

> By the rude bridge that arched the flood,
> Their flag to April's breeze unfurled,
>   Here once the embattled farmers stood
> And fired the shot heard round the world.

Out of twenty-eight words, twenty-four are monosyllables. It is
English at its purest, though hardly characteristic of its author.

3   Or take this:

> On desperate seas long wont to roam,
>   Thy hyacinth hair, thy classic face,
> Thy Naiad airs have brought me home
>   To the glory that was Greece
>   And the grandeur that was Rome.

Imagine how it must feel to have composed those lines! Though
coming from a writer satisfied with the easy rhythms of "The
Raven" and "Annabel Lee," they represent, I fear, a fluke. To

quote poetry, you will say, is not a fair comparison. True, but what a lesson those stanzas are in the sound of words! What superb use of that magnificent instrument that lies at the command of all of us—the English language. Quite by chance both practitioners in these samples happen to be Americans, and both, curiously enough, writing about history.

4   To write history so as to enthrall the reader and make the subject as captivating and exciting to him as it is to me has been my goal since that initial failure with my thesis. A prerequisite, as I have said, is to be enthralled one's self and to feel a compulsion to communicate the magic. Communicate to whom? We arrive now at the reader, a person whom I keep constantly in mind. Catherine Drinker Bowen has said that she writes her books with a sign pinned up over her desk asking, "Will the reader turn the page?"

5   The writer of history, I believe, has a number of duties *vis-à-vis* the reader, if he wants to keep him reading. The first is to distill. He must do the preliminary work for the reader, assemble the information, make sense of it, select the essential, discard the irrelevant—above all, discard the irrelevant—and put the rest together so that it forms a developing dramatic narrative. Narrative, it has been said, is the lifeblood of history. To offer a mass of undigested facts, of names not identified and places not located, is of no use to the reader and is simple laziness on the part of the author, or pedantry to show how much he has read. To discard the unnecessary requires courage and also extra work, as exemplified by Pascal's effort to explain an idea to a friend in a letter which rambled on for pages and ended, "I am sorry to have wearied you with so long a letter but I did not have time to write you a short one." The historian is continually being beguiled down fascinating byways and sidetracks. But the art of writing—the test of the artist—is to resist the beguilement and cleave to the subject.

6   Should the historian be an artist? Certainly a conscious art should be part of his equipment. Macaulay describes him as half poet, half philosopher. I do not aspire to either of these heights. I think of myself as a storyteller, a narrator, who deals in true stories, not fiction. The distinction is not one of relative values; it is simply that history interests me more than fiction. I agree with Leopold von Ranke, the great nineteenth-century German historian, who said that when he compared the portrait of Louis XI in Scott's *Quentin Durward* with the portrait of the same king in the

memoirs of Philippe de Comines, Louis' minister, he found "the truth more interesting and beautiful than the romance."

7 It was Ranke, too, who set the historian's task: to find out *wie es eigentlich gewesen ist,* what really happened, or, literally, how it really was. His goal is one that will remain forever just beyond our grasp for reasons I explained in a "Note on Sources" in *The Guns of August* (a paragraph that no one ever reads but *I* think is the best thing in the book). Summarized, the reasons are that we who write about the past were not there. We can never be certain that we have recaptured it as it really was. But the least we can do is to stay within the evidence.

8 I do not invent anything, even the weather. One of my readers told me he particularly liked a passage in *The Guns* which tells how the British Army landed in France and how on that afternoon there was a sound of summer thunder in the air and the sun went down in a blood-red glow. He thought it an artistic touch of doom, but the fact is it was true. I found it in the memoirs of a British officer who landed on that day and heard the thunder and saw the blood-red sunset. The art, if any, consisted only in selecting it and ultimately using it in the right place.

9 Selection is what determines the ultimate product, and that is why I use material from primary sources only. My feeling about secondary sources is that they are helpful but pernicious. I use them as guides at the start of a project to find out the general scheme of what happened, but I do not take notes from them because I do not want to end up simply rewriting someone else's book. Furthermore, the facts in a secondary source have already been pre-selected, so that in using them one misses the opportunity of selecting one's own.

10 I plunge as soon as I can into the primary sources: the memoirs and the letters, the generals' own accounts of their campaigns, however tendentious, not to say mendacious, they may be. Even an untrustworthy source is valuable for what it reveals about the personality of the author, especially if he is an actor in the events, as in the case of Sir John French, for example. Bias in a primary source is to be expected. One allows for it and corrects it by reading another version. I try always to read two or more for every episode. Even if an event is not controversial, it will have been seen and remembered from different angles of view by different observers. If the event *is* in dispute, one has extra obligation to examine both sides. As the lion in Aesop said to the Man,

"There are many statues of men slaying lions, but if only the lions were sculptors there might be quite a different set of statues."

11   The most primary source of all is unpublished material: private letters and diaries or the reports, orders, and messages in government archives. There is an immediacy and intimacy about them that reveals character and makes circumstances come alive. I remember Secretary of State Robert Lansing's desk diary, which I used when I was working on *The Zimmermann Telegram*. The man himself seemed to step right out from his tiny neat handwriting and his precise notations of every visitor and each subject discussed. Each day's record opened and closed with the Secretary's time of arrival and departure from the office. He even entered the time of his lunch hour, which invariably lasted sixty minutes: "Left at 1:10; returned at 2:10." Once, when he was forced to record his morning arrival at 10:15, he added, with a worried eye on posterity, "Car broke down."

12   Inside the National Archives even the memory of Widener paled. Nothing can compare with the fascination of examining material in the very paper and ink of its original issue. A report from a field agent with marginal comments by the Secretary of War, his routing directions to State and Commerce, and the scribbled initials of subsequent readers can be a little history in itself. In the Archives I found the original decode of the Zimmermann Telegram, which I was able to have declassified and photostated for the cover of my book.

13   Even more immediate is research on the spot. Before writing *The Guns* I rented a little Renault and in another August drove over the battle areas of August 1914, following the track of the German invasion through Luxembourg, Belgium, and northern France. Besides obtaining a feeling of the geography, distances, and terrain involved in military movements, I saw the fields ripe with grain which the cavalry would have trampled, measured the grain which the cavalry would have trampled, measured the great width of the Meuse at Liège, and saw how the lost territory of Alsace looked to the French soldiers who gazed down upon it from the heights of the Vosges. I learned the discomfort of the Belgian *pavé* and discovered, in the course of losing my way almost permanently in a tangle of country roads in a hunt for the house that had been British Headquarters, why a British motorcycle dispatch rider in 1914 had taken three hours to cover twenty-five miles. Clearly, owing to the British officers' preference for

country houses, he had not been able to find Headquarters either. French army commanders, I noticed, located themselves in *towns,* with railroad stations and telegraph offices.

14   As to the mechanics of research, I take notes on four-by-six index cards, reminding myself about once an hour of a rule I read long ago in a research manual, "Never write on the back of anything." Since copying is a chore and a bore, use of the cards, the smaller the better, forces one to extract the strictly relevant, to distill from the very beginning, to pass the material through the grinder of one's own mind, so to speak. Eventually, as the cards fall into groups according to subject or person or chronological sequence, the pattern of my story will emerge. Besides, they are convenient, as they can be filed in a shoebox and carried around in a pocketbook. When ready to write I need only take along a packet of them, representing a chapter, and I am equipped to work anywhere; whereas if one writes surrounded by a pile of books, one is tied to a single place, and furthermore likely to be too much influenced by other authors.

15   The most important thing about research is to know when to stop. How does one recognize the moment? When I was eighteen or thereabouts, my mother told me that when out with a young man I should always leave a half-hour before I wanted to. Although I was not sure how this might be accomplished, I recognized the advice as sound, and exactly the same rule applies to research. One must stop *before* one has finished; otherwise, one will never stop and never finish. I had an object lesson in this once in Washington at the Archives. I was looking for documents in the case of Perdicaris, an American—or supposed American— who was captured by Moroccan brigands in 1904. The Archives people introduced me to a lady professor who had been doing research in United States relations with Morocco all her life. She had written her Ph.D. thesis on the subject back in, I think, 1936, and was still coming for six months each year to work in the Archives. She was in her seventies and, they told me, had recently suffered a heart attack. When I asked her what year was her cutoff point, she looked at me in surprise and said she kept a file of newspaper clippings right up to the moment. I am sure she knew more about United States–Moroccan relations than anyone alive, but would she ever leave off her research in time to write that definitive history and tell the world what she knew? I feared the answer. Yet I know how she felt. I too feel compelled to follow

every lead and learn everything about a subject, but fortunately I have an even more overwhelming compulsion to see my work in print. That is the only thing that saves me.

16   Research is endlessly seductive; writing is hard work. One has to sit down on that chair and think and transform thought into readable, conservative, interesting sentences that both make sense and make the reader turn the page. It is laborious, slow, often painful, sometimes agony. It means rearrangement, revision, adding, cutting, rewriting. But it brings a sense of excitement, almost of rapture; a moment on Olympus. In short, it is an act of creation.

QUESTIONS

Ideas

1.   What does Tuchman mean by her opening question in paragraph 6? How does she answer her own question? How would you?

2.   Tuchman's goal is to find out "how it really was." To do that she tries to stay "within the evidence." What is evidence, how do you think a historian finds it, judges it, and decides what to use? How do the historian's own values and experiences influence choices?

3.   In reference to paragraph 15, how do you know "when to stop" researching or writing? How does Tuchman describe her composing process in writing history? What seems most important to her? What does it mean to enthrall the reader?

4.   What writing techniques that Tuchman describes might be most useful to your own writing?

5.   Below is the selection from *The Guns of August* that Tuchman mentions in paragraph 7. Do you agree with her definition of "truth"? Are there absolute facts we could all agree on?

    SOURCES

        A full bibliography of the subject would fill a book. No other episode in history has been more fully documented by its participants. They seem to have known, while they lived it, that like the French Revolution, the First World War was one of the great convulsions of history, and each felt the hand of history heavily on his own shoulder. When it was over, despite courage, skill, and sacrifice, the war they had fought proved to have been, on the whole, a monument of failure, tragedy, and disillusion. It had not led to a better world. Men who had taken part at the command level, political and military, felt driven to explain their decisions and actions. Men who had fallen from high command, whether for cause or as scapegoats—and these included most of the commanders of August—wrote their private justifications. As each account appeared, inevitably shifting responsibility or blame to someone else, another was provoked. Private feuds became public; public controversies expanded. Men who would otherwise have remained mute were stung to publish, as Sir Horace Smith-Dorrien by Sir John French. Books proliferated. Whole schools of partisans, like those of Gallieni and Joffre, produced libraries of controversy.

Through this forest of special pleading the historian gropes his way, trying to recapture the truth of past events and find out "what really happened." He discovers that truth is subjective and separate, made up of little bits seen, experienced, and recorded by different people. It is like a design seen through a kaleidoscope; when the cylinder is shaken the countless colored fragments form a new picture. Yet they are the same fragments that made a different picture a moment earlier. This is the problem inherent in the records left by actors in past events. That famous goal, *"wie es wirklich war,"* is never wholly within our grasp.

Organization

6. In describing her writing philosophy Tuchman arranges her ideas in a particular way. Why does she choose this sequence, does she put the most important ideas first or last? Try to find an explanation, a pattern.

7. Look at the organization of paragraph 5: describe the relationship between her sentences. Is there one umbrella sentence under which the others might fit?

Sentences

8. Take a look at the last sentence in each paragraph and then the first sentences in the following paragraph. Are they connected?

9. Does Tuchman try to vary her sentence length? Count the number of words in each sentence in paragraphs 4 and 16, for example.

Words

10. Does Tuchman follow the advice she gives in paragraph 2?

11. Throughout this and other essays Tuchman consistently uses "he" or "him" even when she is talking about herself (e.g., in paragraph 5). Do you think she should have used "her" or some other alternative?

Suggestions for Writing

A. Look again at the second paragraph in "Sources." Based on this notion of truth, how might a historian tell what really happened in your life; in the semester you are in; in the specific class you are sitting in?

B. Think of some famous historical event and write about it from a perspective that would surprise or shock us and alter our usual expectations.

The Idea and the Deed

1   So enchanting was the vision of a stateless society, without government, without law, without ownership of property, in which, corrupt institutions having been swept away, man would be free to be good as God intended him, that six heads of state were assassinated for its sake in the twenty years before 1914. They were President Carnot of France in 1894, Premier Canovas of Spain in 1897, Empress Elizabeth of Austria in 1898, King Humbert of Italy in 1900, President McKinley of the United States in 1901, and another Premier of Spain, Canalejas, in 1912. Not one could qualify as a tyrant. Their deaths were the gestures of desperate or deluded men to call attention to the Anarchist idea.

2   No single individual was the hero of the movement that swallowed up these lives. The Idea was its hero. It was, as a historian of revolt has called it, "a daydream of desperate romantics." It had its theorists and thinkers, men of intellect, sincere and earnest, who loved humanity. It also had its tools, the little men whom misfortune or despair or the anger, degradation and hopelessness of poverty made susceptible to the Idea until they became possessed by it and were driven to act. These became the assassins. Between the two groups there was no contact. The thinkers in press and pamphlet constructed marvelous paper models of the Anarchist millennium; poured out tirades of hate and invective upon the ruling class and its despised ally, the bourgeoisie; issued trumpet calls for action, for a "propaganda of the deed" to accomplish the enemy's overthrow. Whom were they calling? What deed were they asking for? They did not say precisely. Unknown to

them, down in the lower depths of society lonely men were listening. They heard echoes of the tirades and the trumpets and
caught a glimpse of the shining millennium that promised a life
without hunger and without a boss. Suddenly one of them, with a
sense of injury or a sense of mission, would rise up, go out and
kill—and sacrifice his own life on the altar of the Idea.

3   They came from the warrens of the poor, where hunger and
dirt were king, where consumptives coughed and the air was thick
with the smell of latrines, boiling cabbage and stale beer, where
babies wailed and couples screamed in sudden quarrels, where
roofs leaked and unmended windows let in the cold blasts of winter, where privacy was unimaginable, where men, women, grandparents and children lived together, eating, sleeping, fornicating,
defecating, sickening and dying in one room, where a teakettle
served as a wash boiler between meals, old boxes served as chairs,
heaps of foul straw as beds, and boards propped across two crates
as tables, where sometimes not all the children in a family could
go out at one time because there were not enough clothes to go
round, where decent families lived among drunkards, wife-beat-
ers, thieves and prostitutes, where life was a seesaw of unemploy-
ment and endless toil, where a cigar-maker and his wife earning
13 cents an hour worked seventeen hours a day seven days a week
to support themselves and three children, where death was the
only exit and the only extravagance and the scraped savings of a
lifetime would be squandered on a funeral coach with flowers and
a parade of mourners to ensure against the anonymity and last
ignominy of Potter's Field.

4   The Anarchists believed that with Property, the monarch of
all evil, eliminated, no man could again live off the labour of
another and human nature would be released to seek its natural
level of justice among men. The role of State would be replaced
by voluntary cooperation among individuals and the role of the
law by the supreme law of the general welfare. To this end no
reform of existing social evils through vote or persuasion was of
any use, for the ruling class would never give up its property or
the powers and laws which protected ownership of property.
Therefore, the necessity of violence. Only revolutionary overturn
of the entire malignant existing system would accomplish the
desired result. Once the old structure was in rubble, a new social
order of utter equality and no authority, with enough of everything for everybody, would settle smilingly upon the earth. So rea-

sonable seemed the proposition that once apprised of it the oppressed classes could not fail to respond. The Anarchist task was to awaken them to the Idea by propaganda of the word and of the Deed, and one day, one such deed would flash the signal for revolt.

5   During the first and formulative period of Anarchism, beginning around the time of the revolutionary year 1848, its two major prophets were Pierre Proudhon of France and his disciple, Michael Bakunin, a Russian exile who became the active leader of the movement.

6   "Whoever lays his hand on me to govern me," Proudhon proclaimed, "is a usurper and a tyrant; I declare him to be my enemy. . . . Government of man by man is slavery" and its laws are "cobwebs for the rich and chains of steel for the poor." The "highest perfection" for free society is no government, to which Proudhon was the first to give the name "An-archy." He excoriated government in a passion of contempt. "To be governed is to be watched, inspected, spied on, regulated, indoctrinated, preached at, controlled, ruled, censored, by persons who have neither wisdom nor virtue. It is every action and transaction to be registered, stamped, taxed, patented, licensed, assessed, measured, reprimanded, corrected, frustrated. Under pretext of the public good it is to be exploited, monopolized, embezzled, robbed and then, at the least protest or word of complaint, to be fined, harassed, vilified, beaten up, bludgeoned, disarmed, judged, condemned, imprisoned, shot, garroted, deported, sold, betrayed, swindled, deceived, outraged, dishonored. That's government, that's its justice, that's its morality! And imagine that among us there are democrats who believe government to be good, socialists who in the name of liberty, equality and fraternity support this ignominy, proletarians who offer themselves candidates for President of the Republic! What hypocrisy!"

7   Proudhon believed that the "abstract idea of right" would obviate the need of revolution and man would be persuaded to adopt the stateless society through reason. What Bakunin added, learning from Russia under Nicholas I, was the necessity of violent revolution. As opposed to his rival, Karl Marx, who maintained that revolution would come only from an industrial proletariat, organized and trained for the task, Bakunin believed that immediate revolution could explode in one of the more economically backward countries—Italy, Spain or Russia—where the workers,

though untrained, unorganized and illiterate, with no understanding of their own wants, would be ready to rise because they
had nothing to lose. The task of the conscientious revolutionist
was to popularize the Idea among the masses, hitherto bound in
ignorance and prejudice by the ruling class. It was necessary to
make them conscious of their own wants and "evoke" from them
thoughts to match their impulses, thoughts of revolt. When this
happened the workers would know their own will and then "their
power will be irresistible." Bakunin, however, lost control of the
First International to Marx, who believed in organization.

8   There was an inherent paradox within the body of Anarchism that frustrated progress. Anarchism rejected the political
party, which Proudhon had called a mere "variety of absolutism";
yet to bring about a revolution it was necessary to submit to
authority, organization and discipline. Whenever Anarchists met
to prepare a program, this terrible necessity rose up to face them.
Loyal to their Idea, they rejected it. Revolution would burst from
the masses spontaneously. All that was needed was the Idea—and
a spark.

9   Each strike or bread riot or local uprising the Anarchist
hoped—and the capitalist feared—might be the spark. Mme
Hennebau, the manager's wife in Zola's *Germinal,* watching the
march of the striking miners under the bloody gleam of the setting sun, saw "the red vision of revolution that on some sombre
evening at the end of the century would carry everything away.
Yes, on that evening people, unbridled at last, would make the
blood of the middle class flow, . . . in a thunder of boots the
same terrible troop, with their dirty skins and tainted breath,
would sweep away the old world. . . . Fires would flame, there
would be nothing left, not a *sou* of the great fortunes, not a title
deed of acquired properties."

10   Yet each time, as when Zola's miners faced the guns of the
gendarmerie, the spark was stamped out. The magic moment
when the masses would awaken to their wants and their power did
not come. The Paris Commune flared and died in 1871 and failed
to signal a general insurrection. "We reckoned without the masses
who did not want to be roused to passion for their own freedom,"
wrote Bakunin, disillusioned, to his wife. "The passion being
absent what good did it do us to have been right theoretically? We
were powerless." He despaired of saving the world and died, disillusioned, in 1876, a Columbus, as Alexander Herzen said, without
America.

11   Meanwhile, in his native land his ideas took root in the Narodniki, or Populists, otherwise the Party of the People's Will, founded in 1879. Because of communal use of land peculiar to the Russian peasant, reformers worshipped the peasant as a natural Socialist who needed only the appearance of a Messiah to be awakened from his lethargy and impelled upon the march to revolution. The bomb was to be the Messiah. "Terrorist activity," stated the Narodniki program, "consisting in destroying the most harmful person in government, aims to undermine the prestige of the government and arouse in this manner the revolutionary spirit of the people and their confidence in the success of the cause."

12   In 1881 the Narodniki struck a blow that startled the world: they assassinated the Czar, Alexander II. It was a triumphant coup, equal, they imagined, to the battering down of the Bastille. It would shout aloud their protest, summon the oppressed and terrorize the oppressors. Instead it ushered in reaction. The dead Czar, whose crown may have been the symbol of autocracy but who in person was the "Liberator" of the serfs, was mourned by the peasants, who believed "the gentry had murdered the Czar to get back the land." His ministers opened a campaign of savage repression, the public, abandoning all thoughts of reform, acquiesced, and the revolutionary movement, "broken and demoralized, withdrew into the conspirators' cellar." There Anarchism's first period came to an end.

13   Before the movement burst into renewed bloom in the nineties, a single terrible event which enlarged the stature of Anarchism took place, not in Europe, but in America, in the city of Chicago. There in August, 1886, eight Anarchists were sentenced by Judge Joseph Gary to be hanged for the murder of seven police killed on the previous May 4 by a bomb hurled into the midst of an armed police force who were about to break up a strikers' meeting in Haymarket Square.

14   The occasion was the climax of a campaign for the eight-hour day, which in itself was the climax of a decade of industrial war centering on Chicago. In every clash the employers fought with the forces of law—police, militia and courts—as their allies. The workers' demands were met with live ammunition and lockouts and with strikebreakers protected by Pinkertons who were armed and sworn in as deputy sheriffs. In the war between the classes, the State was not neutral. Driven by misery and injustice, the workers' anger grew and with it the employers' fear, their

sense of a rising menace and their determination to stamp it out. Even a man as remote as Henry James sensed a "sinister anarchic underworld heaving in its pain, its power and its hate."

15   Anarchism was not a labour movement and was no more than one element in the general upheaval of the lower class. But Anarchists saw in the struggles of labour the hot coals of revolution and hoped to blow them into flame. "A pound of dynamite is worth a bushel of bullets," cried August Spies, editor of Chicago's German-language Anarchist daily, *Die Arbeiter-Zeitung.* "Police and militia, the bloodhounds of capitalism, are ready to murder!" In this he was right, for in the course of a clash between workers and strikebreakers, the police fired, killing two. "Revenge! Revenge! Workingmen to arms!" shrieked handbills printed and distributed by Spies that night. He called for a protest meeting the next day. It took place in Haymarket Square, the police marched to break it up, the bomb was thrown. Who threw it has never been discovered.

18   The defendants' speeches to the court after sentence, firm in Anarchist principle and throbbing with consciousness of martyrdom, resounded throughout Europe and America and provided the best propaganda Anarchism ever had. In the absence of direct evidence establishing their guilt, they knew and loudly stated that they were being tried and sentenced for the crime, not of murder, but of Anarchism. "Let the world know," cried August Spies, "that in 1886 in the state of Illinois eight men were sentenced to death because they believed in a better future!" Their belief had included the use of dynamite, and society's revenge matched its fright. In the end the sentences of three of the condemned were commuted to prison terms. One, Louis Lingg, the youngest, handsomest and most fervent, who was shown by evidence at the trial to have made bombs, blew himself up with a capsule of fulminate of mercury on the night before the execution and wrote in his blood before he died, "Long live anarchy!" His suicide was regarded by many as a confession of guilt. The remaining four, including Spies, were hanged on November 11, 1887.

17   For years afterward the silhouette of the gallows and its four hanging bodies decorated Anarchist literature, and the anniversary of November 11 was celebrated by Anarchists in Europe and America as a revolutionary memorial. The public conscience, too, was made aware by the gallows' fruit of the misery, protest and upheaval in the working class.

18   Men who were Anarchists without knowing it stood on every street corner. Jacob Riis, the New York police reporter who described in 1890 *How the Other Half Lives*, saw one on the corner of Fifth Avenue and Fourteenth Street. The man suddenly leaped at a carriage carrying two fashionable ladies on an afternoon's shopping and slashed at the sleek and shining horses with a knife. When arrested and locked up, he said, "They don't have to think of tomorrow. They spend in an hour what would keep me and my little ones for a year." He was the kind from which Anarchists of the Deed were made.

19   Most of them were voiceless or could speak their protest only in the wail of a dispossessed Irish peasant spading his field for the last time, who was asked by a visitor what he wanted. "What is it I am wantin'?" cried the old man, shaking his fist at the sky. "I want the Day av Judgment!"

20   The poor lived in a society in which power, wealth and magnificent spending were never more opulent, in which the rich dined on fish, fowl and red meat at one meal, lived in houses of marble floors and damask walls and of thirty or forty or fifty rooms, wrapped themselves in furs in winter and were cared for by a retinue of servants who blacked their boots, arranged their hair, drew their baths and lit their fires. In this world, at a luncheon for Mme Nellie Melba at the Savoy, when perfect peaches, a delicacy of the season, were served up "fragrant and delicious in their cotton wool," the surfeited guests made a game of throwing them at passers-by beneath the windows.

21   These were the rulers and men of property whose immense possessions could, it seemed, only be explained as having been accumulated out of the pockets of the exploited masses. "What is Property?" asked Proudhon in a famous question and answered, "Property is theft." "Do you not know," cried Enrico Malatesta in his *Talk Between Two Workers,* an Anarchist classic of the nineties, "that every bit of bread they eat is taken from your children, every fine present they give to their wives means the poverty, hunger, cold, even perhaps prostitution of yours?"

22   If in their economics the Anarchists were hazy, their hatred of the ruling class was strong and vibrant. They hated "all mankind's tormentors," as Bakunin called them, "priests, monarchs, statesmen, soldiers, officials, financiers, capitalists, moneylenders, lawyers." To the workers themselves it was not the faraway rich but their visible representatives, the landlord, the factory owner, the boss, the policeman, who were the Enemy.

23   They could hate but only a few were rebels. Most existed in apathy, stupefied by poverty. Some gave up. A woman with four children who made match boxes at 4½ cents a gross, and by working fourteen hours could make seven gross a day for a total of 31½ cents, threw herself out of the window one day and was carried from the street dead. She was "discouraged," a neighbor said. A young man who had a sick mother and had lost his job was charged in magistrate's court with attempted suicide. The lockkeeper's wife who pulled him out of the river testified how "as fast as I pulled to get him out, he crawled back" until some workmen came to assist her. When the magistrate congratulated the woman on her muscular powers, the courtroom laughed, but an observer named Jack London wrote, "All I could see was a boy on the threshold of life passionately crawling to a muddy death."

24   The failure of practical attempts at Anarchism in Bakunin's period caused Anarchist theory and practice to veer off in a direction not toward the earth but toward the clouds. In the new period beginning in the nineties, its aims, always idyllic, became even more utopian and its deeds less than ever connected with reality. It became impatient. It despised the puny efforts of Socialists and trade unionists to achieve the eight-hour day. "Eight hours of work for the boss is eight hours too much," proclaimed the Anarchist paper, *La Révolte*. "We know that what is wrong with our society is not that the worker works ten, twelve or fourteen hours, but that the boss exists."

QUESTIONS

Ideas

1.   How would you define the Anarchist Idea? Do you think it has value as a political theory? Could you imagine a situation in which you could become an Anarchist?

2.   At times Tuchman seems sympathetic to the Anarchists, at other times, critical. Where do these feelings seem most obvious?

3.   Some political thinkers say that human nature is basically corrupt and needs strong controls if we are to have an orderly society. Others say we are basically good; it is our institutions that are flawed. Which position do the Anarchists favor? Which do you?

4. Where does Tuchman believe the Anarchists went wrong? Was it a tactical or a conceptual error? In retrospect, could they have succeeded? How?

5. Based on the evidence Tuchman gives in paragraphs 13–16, do you think Spies should have been hanged?

6. How do you respond to paragraphs 20–23? What might be the solution to the condition described?

Organization

7. History is a story. How that narrative is arranged by the historian is crucial to the reader's understanding. Tuchman, for example, could have given us heart-rending sketches of the families of the policemen who were blown up. She didn't. Does that suggest she is unsympathetic? Is her organizational scheme fair-minded?

8. This essay might be seen as an attempt at cause and effect. How does Tuchman set this up? Where does she narrate the causes of anarchism, where the effects?

9. Paragraph 13 begins the second part of this essay. How does Tuchman arrange this section? Write a brief one-sentence description of all twelve paragraphs. How would you describe the movement of her thinking here?

Sentences

10. The third paragraph is one long cumulative sentence. The first eight words form the base clause. Tuchman just adds adverbial clauses on to that foundation. Why do you think she decided to use such a dramatic sentence? Read it out loud. What effect does it have on you?

11. Now read paragraph 23. Tuchman's purpose here might be the same as in paragraph 3, but her sentence strategy is different. What kinds of sentences does she use here? Try to change these sentences into the pattern she used in the third paragraph: base clause plus additions (such as phrases or clauses).

Words

12. Describe the words used by Proudhon in the sixth paragraph. Do they differ from Tuchman's?

13. Make a list of the words (nouns, adjectives, adverbs) Tuchman uses to describe the Anarchists. Make another list for the rich and the establishment. Is she balanced, fair?

Suggestions for Writing

A. The anecdotes in paragraphs 20 and 23 seem effective. Try to reverse
    the effect Tuchman is after by substituting positive incidents for the
    rich and negative ones for the poor.
B. Write an extended definition of "the Anarchist Idea" that Bakunin
    would agree is fair and accurate.
C. Imagine that you are either the lawyer prosecuting or defending the
    Haymarket Square Anarchists. Write a summation speech to the jury
    trying to get the Anarchists freed or hanged.

The Black Death

---

1   In October 1347, two months after the fall of Calais,
Genoese trading ships put into the harbor of Messina in Sicily
with dead and dying men at the oars. The ships had come from
the Black Sea port of Caffa (now Feodosiya) in the Crimea, where
the Genoese maintained a trading post. The diseased sailors
showed strange black swellings about the size of an egg or an
apple in the armpits and groin. The swellings oozed blood and
pus and were followed by spreading boils and black blotches on
the skin from internal bleeding. The sick suffered severe pain and
died quickly within five days of the first symptoms. As the disease
spread, other symptoms of continuous fever and spitting of blood
appeared instead of the swellings or buboes. These victims
coughed and sweated heavily and died even more quickly, within
three days or less, sometimes in 24 hours. In both types everything
that issued from the body—breath, sweat, blood from the buboes
and lungs, bloody urine, and blood-blackened excrement—
smelled foul. Depression and despair accompanied the physical
symptoms, and before the end "death is seen seated on the face."
2   The disease was bubonic plague, present in two forms: one
that infected the bloodstream, causing the buboes and internal
bleeding, and was spread by contact; and a second, more virulent
pneumonic type that infected the lungs and was spread by respiratory infection. The presence of both at once caused the high mortality and speed of contagion. So lethal was the disease that cases
were known of persons going to bed well and dying before they

woke, of doctors catching the illness at a bedside and dying before the patient. So rapidly did it spread from one to another that to a French physician, Simon de Covino, it seemed as if one sick person "could infect the whole world." The malignity of the pestilence appeared more terrible because its victims knew no prevention and no remedy.

3   The physical suffering of the disease and its aspect of evil mystery were expressed in a strange Welsh lament which saw "death coming into our midst like black smoke, a plague which cuts off the young, a rootless phantom which has no mercy for fair countenance. Woe is me of the shilling in the armpit! It is seething, terrible . . . a head that gives pain and causes a loud cry . . . a painful angry knob . . . Great is its seething like a burning cinder . . . a grievous thing of ashy color." Its eruption is ugly like the "seeds of black peas, broken fragments of brittle sea-coal . . . the early ornaments of black death, cinders of the peelings of the cockle weed, a mixed multitude, a black plague like halfpence, like berries. . . ."

4   Rumors of a terrible plague supposedly arising in China and spreading through Tartary (Central Asia) to India and Persia, Mesopotamia, Syria, Egypt, and all of Asia Minor had reached Europe in 1346. They told of a death toll so devastating that all of India was said to be depopulated, whole territories covered by dead bodies, other areas with no one left alive. As added up by Pope Clement VI at Avignon, the total of reported dead reached 23,840,000. In the absence of a concept of contagion, no serious alarm was felt in Europe until the trading ships brought their black burden of pestilence into Messina while other infected ships from the Levant carried it to Genoa and Venice.

5   By January 1348 it penetrated France via Marseille and North Africa via Tunis. Shipborne along coasts and navigable rivers, it spread westward from Marseille through the ports of Languedoc to Spain and northward up the Rhône to Avignon, where it arrived in March. It reached Narbonne, Montpellier, Carcassonne, and Toulouse between February and May, and at the same time in Italy spread to Rome and Florence by their hinterlands. Between June and August it reached Bordeaux, Lyon, and Paris, spread to Burgundy and Normandy, and crossed the Channel from Normandy into southern England. From Italy during the same summer it crossed the Alps into Switzerland and reached eastward to Hungary.

6   In a given area the plague accomplished its kill within four to six months and then faded, except in the larger cities, where, rooting into the close-quartered population, it abated during the winter, only to reappear in spring and rage for another six months.

7   In 1349 it resumed in Paris, spread to Picardy, Flanders, and the Low Countries, and from England to Scotland and Ireland as well as to Norway, where a ghost ship with a cargo of wool and a dead crew drifted offshore until it ran aground near Bergen. From there the plague passed into Sweden, Denmark, Prussia, Iceland, and as far as Greenland. Leaving a strange pocket of immunity in Bohemia, and Russia unattacked until 1351, it had passed from most of Europe by mid-1350. Although the mortality rate was erratic, ranging from one fifth in some places to nine tenths or almost total elimination in others, the overall estimate of modern demographers has settled—for the area extending from India to Iceland—around the same figure expressed in Froissart's casual words: "a third of the world died." His estimate, the common one at the time, was not an inspired guess but a borrowing of St. John's figure for mortality from plague in Revelation, the favorite guide to human affairs of the Middle Ages.

8   A third of Europe would have meant about 20 million deaths. No one knows in truth how many died. Contemporary reports were an awed impression, not an accurate count. In crowded Avignon, it was said, 400 died daily; 7,000 houses emptied by death were shut up; a single graveyard received 11,000 corpses in six weeks; half the city's inhabitants reportedly died, including 9 cardinals or one third of the total, and 70 lesser prelates. Watching the endlessly passing death carts, chroniclers let normal exaggeration take wings and put the Avignon death toll at 62,000 and even at 120,000, although the city's total population was probably less than 50,000.

9   When graveyards filled up, bodies at Avignon were thrown into the Rhône until mass burial pits were dug for dumping the corpses. In London in such pits corpses piled up in layers until they overflowed. Everywhere reports speak of the sick dying too fast for the living to bury. Corpses were dragged out of homes and left in front of doorways. Morning light revealed new piles of bodies. In Florence the dead were gathered up by the Compagnia della Misericordia—founded in 1244 to care for the sick—whose members wore red robes and hoods masking the face except for

the eyes. When their efforts failed, the dead lay putrid in the streets for days at a time. When no coffins were to be had, the bodies were laid on boards, two or three at once, to be carried to graveyards or common pits. Families dumped their own relatives into the pits, or buried them so hastily and thinly "that dogs dragged them forth and devoured their bodies."

10   Amid accumulating death and fear of contagion, people died without last rites and were buried without prayers, a prospect that terrified the last hours of the stricken. A bishop in England gave permission to laymen to make confession to each other as was done by the Apostles, "or if no man is present then even to a woman," and if no priest could be found to administer extreme unction, "then faith must suffice." Clement VI found it necessary to grant remissions of sin to all who died of the plague because so many were unattended by priests. "And no bells tolled," wrote a chronicler of Siena, "and nobody wept no matter what his loss because almost everyone expected death. . . . And people said and believed, 'This is the end of the world.' "

11   In Paris, where the plague lasted through 1349, the reported death rate was 800 a day, in Pisa 500, in Vienna 500 to 600. The total dead in Paris numbered 50,000 or half the population. Florence, weakened by the famine of 1347, lost three to four fifths of its citizens, Venice two thirds, Hamburg and Bremen, though smaller in size, about the same proportion. Cities, as centers of transportation, were more likely to be affected than villages, although once a village was infected, its death rate was equally high. At Givry, a prosperous village in Burgundy of 1,200 to 1,500 people, the parish register records 615 deaths in the space of fourteen weeks, compared to an average of thirty deaths a year in the previous decade. In three villages of Cambridgeshire, manorial records show a death rate of 47 percent, 57 percent, and in one case 70 percent. When the last survivors, too few to carry on, moved away, a deserted village sank back into the wilderness and disappeared from the map altogether, leaving only a grass-covered ghostly outline to show where mortals once had lived.

12   In enclosed places such as monasteries and prisons, the infection of one person usually meant that of all, as happened in the Franciscan convents of Carcassonne and Marseille, where every inmate without exception died. Of the 140 Dominicans at Montpellier only seven survived. Petrarch's brother Gherardo, member of a Carthusian monastery, buried the prior and 34 fel-

low monks one by one, sometimes three a day, until he was left
alone with his dog and fled to look for a place that would take
him in. Watching every comrade die, men in such places could
not but wonder whether the strange peril that filled the air had
not been sent to exterminate the human race. In Kilkenny,
Ireland, Brother John Clyn of the Friars Minor, another monk left
alone among dead men, kept a record of what had happened lest
"things which should be remembered perish with time and vanish
from the memory of those who come after us." Sensing "the
whole world, as it were, placed within the grasp of the Evil One,"
and waiting for death to visit him too, he wrote, "I leave parch-
ment to continue this work, if perchance any man survive and any
of the race of Adam escape this pestilence and carry on the work
which I have begun." Brother John, as noted by another hand,
died of the pestilence, but he foiled oblivion.

13   The largest cities of Europe, with populations of about
100,000, were Paris and Florence, Venice and Genoa. At the next
level, with more than 50,000, were Ghent and Bruges in Flanders,
Milan, Bologna, Rome, Naples, and Palermo, and Cologne. London hovered below 50,000, the only city in England except York
with more than 10,000. At the level of 20,000 to 50,000 were
Bordeaux, Toulouse, Montpellier, Marseille, and Lyon in France,
Barcelona, Seville, and Toledo in Spain, Siena, Pisa, and other
secondary cities in Italy, and the Hanseatic trading cities of the
Empire. The plague raged through them all, killing anywhere
from one third to two thirds of their inhabitants. Italy, with a total
population of 10 to 11 million, probably suffered the heaviest toll.
Following the Florentine bankruptcies, the crop failures and
workers' riots of 1346–47, the revolt of Cola di Rienzi that
plunged Rome into anarchy, the plague came as the peak of suc-
cessive calamities. As if the world were indeed in the grasp of the
Evil One, its first appearance on the European mainland in
January 1348 coincided with a fearsome earthquake that carved a
path of wreckage from Naples up to Venice. Houses collapsed,
church towers toppled, villages were crushed, and the destruction
reached as far as Germany and Greece. Emotional response,
dulled by horrors, underwent a kind of atrophy epitomized by the
chronicler who wrote, "And in these days was burying without sor-
rowe and wedding without friendschippe."

14   In Siena, where more than half the inhabitants died of the
plague, work was abandoned on the great cathedral, planned to

be the largest in the world, and never resumed, owing to loss
of workers and master masons and "the melancholy and grief"
of the survivors. The cathedral's truncated transept still stands
in permanent witness to the sweep of death's scythe. Agnolo di
Tura, a chronicler of Siena, recorded the fear of contagion
that froze every other instinct. "Father abandoned child, wife
husband, one brother another," he wrote, "for this plague
seemed to strike through the breath and sight. And so they
died. And no one could be found to bury the dead for money
or friendship. . . . And I, Agnolo di Tura, called the Fat, buried
my five children with my own hands, and so did many others
likewise."

15   There were many to echo his account of inhumanity and few
to balance it, for the plague was not the kind of calamity that
inspired mutual help. Its loathsomeness and deadliness did not
herd people together in mutual distress, but only prompted their
desire to escape each other. "Magistrates and notaries refused to
come and make the wills of the dying," reported a Franciscan friar
of Piazza in Sicily; what was worse, "even the priests did not come
to hear their confessions." A clerk of the Archbishop of
Canterbury reported the same of English priests who "turned
away from the care of their benefices from fear of death." Cases of
parents deserting children and children their parents were reported across Europe from Scotland to Russia. The calamity
chilled the hearts of men, wrote Boccaccio in his famous account
of the plague in Florence that serves as introduction to the
Decameron. "One man shunned another . . . kinsfolk held aloof,
brother was forsaken by brother, oftentimes husband by wife; nay,
what is more, and scarcely to be believed, fathers and mothers
were found to abandon their own children to their fate, untended, unvisited as if they had been strangers." Exaggeration and literary pessimism were common in the 14th century, but the Pope's
physician, Guy de Chauliac, was a sober, careful observer who
reported the same phenomenon: "A father did not visit his son,
nor the son his father. Charity was dead."

16   Yet not entirely. In Paris, according to the chronicler Jean
de Venette, the nuns of the Hôtel Dieu or municipal hospital,
"having no fear of death, tended the sick with all sweetness and
humility." New nuns repeatedly took the places of those who died,
until the majority "many times renewed by death now rest in
peace with Christ as we may piously believe."

17   When the plague entered northern France in July 1348, it settled first in Normandy and, checked by winter, gave Picardy a deceptive interim until the next summer. Either in mourning or warning, black flags were flown from church towers of the worst-stricken villages of Normandy. "And in that time," wrote a monk of the abbey of Fourcarment, "the mortality was so great among the people of Normandy that those of Picardy mocked them." The same unneighborly reaction was reported of the Scots, separated by a winter's immunity from the English. Delighted to hear of the disease that was scourging the "southrons," they gathered forces for an invasion, "laughing at their enemies." Before they could move, the savage mortality fell upon them too, scattering some in death and the rest in panic to spread the infection as they fled.

18   In Picardy in the summer of 1349 the pestilence penetrated the castle of Coucy to kill Enguerrand's mother, Catherine, and her new husband. Whether her nine-year-old son escaped by chance or was perhaps living elsewhere with one of his guardians is unrecorded. In nearby Amiens, tannery workers, responding quickly to losses in the labor force, combined to bargain for higher wages. In another place villagers were seen dancing to drums and trumpets, and on being asked the reason, answered that, seeing their neighbors die day by day while their village remained immune, they believed they could keep the plague from entering "by the jollity that is in us. That is why we dance." Further north in Tournai on the border of Flanders, Gilles li Muisis, Abbot of St. Martin's, kept one of the epidemic's most vivid accounts. The passing bells rang all day and night, he recorded, because sextons were anxious to obtain their fees while they could. Filled with the sound of mourning, the city became oppressed by fear, so that the authorities forbade the tolling of bells and the wearing of black and restricted funeral services to two mourners. The silencing of funeral bells and of criers' announcements of deaths was ordained by most cities. Siena imposed a fine on the wearing of mourning clothes by all except widows.

19   Flight was the chief recourse of those who could afford it or arrange it. The rich fled to their country places like Boccaccio's young patricians of Florence, who settled in a pastoral palace "removed on every side from the roads" with "wells of cool water and vaults of rare wines." The urban poor died in their burrows, "and only the stench of their bodies informed neighbors of their

death." That the poor were more heavily afflicted than the rich was clearly remarked at the time, in the north as in the south. A Scottish chronicler, John of Fordun, stated flatly that pest "attacked especially the meaner sort and common people—seldom the magnates." Simon de Covino of Montpellier made the same observation. He ascribed it to the misery and want and hard lives that made the poor more susceptible, which was half the truth. Close contact and lack of sanitation was the unrecognized other half. It was noticed too that the young died in greater proportion than the old; Simon de Covino compared the disappearance of youth to the withering of flowers in the fields.

20   In the countryside peasants dropped dead on the roads, in the fields, in their houses. Survivors in growing helplessness fell into apathy, leaving ripe wheat uncut and livestock untended. Oxen and asses, sheep and goats, pigs and chickens ran wild and they too, according to local reports, succumbed to the pest. English sheep, bearers of the precious wool, died throughout the country. The chronicler Henry Knighton, canon of Leicester Abbey, reported 5,000 dead in one field alone, "their bodies so corrupted by the plague that neither beast nor bird would touch them," and spreading an appalling stench. In the Austrian Alps wolves came down to prey upon sheep and then, "as if alarmed by some invisible warning, turned and fled back into the wilderness." In remote Dalmatia bolder wolves descended upon a plague-stricken city and attacked human survivors. For want of herdsmen, cattle strayed from place to place and died in hedgerows and ditches. Dogs and cats fell like the rest.

21   The dearth of labor held a fearful prospect because the 14th century lived close to the annual harvest both for food and for next year's seed. "So few servants and laborers were left," wrote Knighton, "that no one knew where to turn for help." The sense of a vanishing future created a kind of dementia of despair. A Bavarian chronicler of Neuberg on the Danube recorded that "Men and woman . . . wandered around as if mad" and let their cattle stray "because no one had any inclination to concern themselves about the future." Fields went uncultivated, spring seed unsown. Second growth with nature's awful energy crept back over cleared land, dikes crumbled, salt water reinvaded and soured the lowlands. With so few hands remaining to restore the work of centuries, people felt, in Walsingham's words, that "the world could never again regain its former prosperity,"

22   Ignorance of the cause augmented the sense of horror. Of the real carriers, rats and fleas, the 14th century had no suspicion, perhaps because they were so familiar. Fleas, though a common household nuisance, are not once mentioned in contemporary plague writings, and rats only incidentally, although folklore commonly associated them with pestilence. The legend of the Pied Piper arose from an outbreak of 1284. The actual plague bacillus, *Pasturella pestis,* remained undiscovered for another 500 years. Living alternately in the stomach of the flea and the bloodstream of the rat who was the flea's host, the bacillus in its bubonic form was transferred to humans and animals by the bite of either rat or flea. It traveled by virtue of *Rattus rattus,* the small medieval black rat that lived on ships, as well as by the heavier brown or sewer rat. What precipitated the turn of the bacillus from innocuous to virulent form is unknown, but the occurrence is now believed to have taken place not in China but somewhere in central Asia and to have spread along the caravan routes. Chinese origin was a mistaken notion of the 14th century based on real but belated reports of huge death tolls in China from drought, famine, and pestilence which have since been traced to the 1330s, too soon to be responsible for the plague that appeared in India in 1346.

23   The phantom enemy had no name. Called the Black Death only in later recurrences, it was known during the first epidemic simply as the Pestilence or Great Mortality. Reports from the East, swollen by fearful imaginings, told of strange tempests and "sheets of fire" mingled with huge hailstones that "slew almost all," or a "vast rain of fire" that burned up men, beasts, stones, trees, villages, and cities. In another version, "foul blasts of wind" from the fires carried the infection to Europe "and now as some suspect it cometh round the seacoast." Accurate observation in this case could not make the mental jump to ships and rats because no idea of animal- or insect-borne contagion existed.

24   The earthquake was blamed for releasing sulfurous and foul fumes from the earth's interior, or as evidence of a titanic struggle of planets and oceans causing waters to rise and vaporize until fish died in masses and corrupted the air. All these explanations had in common a factor of poisoned air, of miasmas and thick, stinking mists traced to every kind of natural or imagined agency from stagnant lakes to malign conjunction of the planets, from the hand of the Evil One to the wrath of God. Medical thinking,

trapped in the theory of astral influences, stressed air as the communicator of disease, ignoring sanitation or visible carriers. The existence of two carriers confused the trail, the more so because the flea could live and travel independently of the rat for as long as a month and, if infected by the particularly virulent septicemic form of the bacillus, could infect humans without reinfecting itself from the rat. The simultaneous presence of the pneumonic form of the disease, which was indeed communicated through the air, blurred the problem further.

25   The mystery of the contagion was "the most terrible of all the terrors," as an anonymous Flemish cleric in Avignon wrote to a correspondent in Bruges. Plagues had been known before, from the plague of Athens (believed to have been typhus) to the prolonged epidemic of the 6th century A.D., to the recurrence of sporadic outbreaks in the 12th and 13th centuries, but they had left no accumulated store of understanding. That the infection came from contact with the sick or with their houses, clothes, or corpses was quickly observed but not comprehended. Gentile da Foligno, renowned physician of Perugia and doctor of medicine at the universities of Bologna and Padua, came close to respiratory infection when he surmised that poisonous material was "communicated by means of air breathed out and in." Having no idea of microscopic carriers, he had to assume that the air was corrupted by planetary influences. Planets, however, could not explain the ongoing contagion. The agonized search for an answer gave rise to such theories as transference by sight. People fell ill, wrote Guy de Chauliac, not only by remaining with the sick but "even by looking at them." Three hundred years later Joshua Barnes, the 17th century biographer of Edward III, could write that the power of infection had entered into beams of light and "darted death from the eyes."

26   Doctors struggling with the evidence could not break away from the terms of astrology, to which they believed all human physiology was subject. Medicine was the one aspect of medieval life, perhaps because of its links with the Arabs, not shaped by Christian doctrine. Clerics detested astrology, but could not dislodge its influence. Guy de Chauliac, physician to three popes in succession, practiced in obedience to the zodiac. While his *Cirurgia* was the major treatise on surgery of its time, while he understood the use of anesthesia made from the juice of opium, mandrake, or hemlock, he nevertheless prescribed bleeding and

purgatives by the planets and divided chronic from acute diseases
on the basis of one being under the rule of the sun and the other
of the moon.

26   In October 1348 Philip VI asked the medical faculty of the
University of Paris for a report on the affliction that seemed to
threaten human survival. With careful thesis, antithesis, and
proofs, the doctors ascribed it to a triple conjunction of Saturn,
Jupiter, and Mars in the 40th degree of Aquarius said to have
occurred on March 20, 1345. They acknowledged, however,
effects "whose cause is hidden from even the most highly trained
intellects." The verdict of the masters of Paris became the official
version. Borrowed, copied by scribes, carried abroad, translated
from Latin into various vernaculars, it was everywhere accepted,
even by the Arab physicians of Cordova and Granada, as the
scientific if not the popular answer. Because of the terrible interest of the subject, the translations of the plague tracts stimulated
use of national languages. In that one respect, life came from
death.

QUESTIONS

Ideas

1.   Are you surprised by the reported decline of social concern during
     the plague? Take, for example, paragraphs 14 and 15.
2.   Do you think events like this are a thing of the past and that compa-
     rable events are not likely to occur again?
3.   List the causes given for the plague. Do any still sound plausible? Is
     it clear that we are better able to cope with the unknown than our
     ancestors?
4.   What do you think your community's reaction would be to such an
     event? What should it be?

Organization

5.   Tuchman often develops paragraphs by combining explicit topic
     sentences—general ideas—with concrete examples and facts.
     Sometimes she puts her general ideas first, sometimes last. Find
     examples of both.
6.   In what order and in what ways does Tuchman answer the journal-
     ist's questions: who, what, when, where, why, and how?

Sentences

7. Throughout this essay Tuchman uses many quotes, for example, paragraphs 10 and 19. Describe the ways she does this. Are they effective?

8. The most common sentence pattern in English is subject, verb, object. Study a paragraph and see how many times and in what ways Tuchman varies this pattern.

Words

9. What is the meaning of the following phrases Tuchman uses or quotes: "virulent pneumonic" (paragraph 2); "fair countenance" (paragraph 3); "foiled oblivion" (paragraph 12); "truncated transept" (paragraph 14); "dementia of despair" (paragraph 21); "thesis, antithesis, and proofs" (paragraph 27).

10. Do you find any contradictions here to Tuchman's position in paragraph 2 or in "In Search of History"?

Suggestions for Writing

A. Write a brief explanation of this disease that you think might convince a fourteenth-century audience.

B. Imagine that you have been transported to 1348, to a house in the middle of London. What would you do, how would you try to survive? Assuming you could communicate with your neighbors, what would you advise them to do, if anything?

C. Are there lessons to be learned from this event? Write a brief response to this question.

Is History a Guide to the Future?

---

1   The commonest question asked of historians by laymen is whether history serves a purpose. Is it useful? Can we learn from the lessons of history?

2   When people want history to be utilitarian and teach us lessons, that means they also want to be sure that it meets scientific standards. This, in my opinion, it cannot do, for reasons which I will come to in a moment. To practice history as a science

is sociology, an altogether different discipline which I personally find antipathetic—although I suppose the sociologists would consider that my deficiency rather than theirs. The sociologists plod along with their noses to the ground assembling masses of statistics in order to arrive at some obvious conclusion which a reasonably perceptive historian, not to mention a large part of the general public, knows anyway, simply from observation—that social mobility is increasing, for instance, or that women have different problems from men. One wishes they would just cut loose someday, lift up their heads, and look at the world around them.

3   If history were a science, we should be able to get a grip on her, learn her ways, establish her patterns, know what will happen tomorrow. Why is it that we cannot? The answer lies in what I call the Unknowable Variable—namely, man. Human beings are always and finally the subject of history. History is the record of human behavior, the most fascinating subject of all, but illogical and so crammed with an unlimited number of variables that it is not susceptible of the scientific method nor of systematizing.

4   I say this bravely, even in the midst of the electronic age when computers are already chewing at the skirts of history in the process called Quantification. Applied to history, quantification, I believe, has its limits. It depends on a method called "data manipulation," which means that the facts, or data, of the historical past—that is, of human behavior—are manipulated into named categories so that they can be programmed into computers. Out comes—hopefully—a pattern. I can only tell you that for history "data manipulation" is a built-in invalidator, because to the degree that you manipulate your data to suit some extraneous requirement, in this case the requirements of the machine, to that degree your results will be suspect—and run the risk of being invalid. Everything depends on the naming of the categories and the assigning of facts to them, and this depends on the quantifier's individual judgment at the very base of the process. The categories are not revealed doctrine nor are the results scientific truth.

5   The hope for quantification, presumably, is that by processing a vast quantity of material far beyond the capacity of the individual to encompass, it can bring to light and establish reliable patterns. That remains to be seen, but I am not optimistic. History has a way of escaping attempts to imprison it in patterns. Moreover, one of its basic data is the human soul. The conventional

historian, at least the one concerned with truth, not propaganda, will try honestly to let his "data" speak for themselves, but data which are shut up in prearranged boxes are helpless. Their nuances have no voice. They must carry one fixed meaning or another and weigh the result accordingly. For instance, in a quantification study of the origins of World War I which I have seen, the operators have divided all the diplomatic documents, messages, and utterances of the July crisis into categories labeled "hostility," "friendship," "frustration," "satisfaction," and so on, with each statement rated for intensity on a scale from one to nine, including fractions. But no pre-established categories could match all the private character traits and public pressures variously operating on the nervous monarchs and ministers who were involved. The massive effort that went into this study brought forth a mouse—the less than startling conclusion that the likelihood of war increased in proportion to the rise in hostility of the messages.

6   Quantification is really only a new approach to the old persistent effort to make history fit a pattern, but *reliable* patterns, or what are otherwise called the lessons of history, remain elusive.

7   For instance, suppose Woodrow Wilson had not been President of the United States in 1914 but instead Theodore Roosevelt, who had been his opponent in the election of 1912. Had that been the case, America might have entered the war much earlier, perhaps at the time of the *Lusitania* in 1915, with possible shortening of the war and incalculable effects on history. Well, it happens that among the Anarchists in my book *The Proud Tower* is an obscure Italian named Miguel Angiolillo, whom nobody remembers but who shot dead Premier Canovas of Spain in 1897. Canovas was a strong man who was just about to succeed in quelling the rebels in Cuba when he was assassinated. Had he lived, there might have been no extended Cuban insurrection for Americans to get excited about, no Spanish-American War, no San Juan Hill, no Rough Riders, no Vice-Presidency for Theodore Roosevelt to enable him to succeed when another accident, another Anarchist, another unpredictable human being, killed McKinley. If Theodore had never been President, there would have been no third party in 1912 to split the Republicans, and Woodrow Wilson would not have been elected. The speculations from that point on are limitless. To me it is comforting rather than otherwise to feel that history is determined by the illogical

human record and not by large immutable scientific laws beyond
our power to deflect.

8   I know very little (a euphemism for "nothing") about laboratory science, but I have the impression that conclusions are supposed to be logical; that is, from a given set of circumstances a
predictable result should follow. The trouble is that in human
behavior and history it is impossible to isolate or repeat a given set
of circumstances. Complex human acts cannot be either reproduced or deliberately initiated—or counted upon like the phenomena of nature. The sun comes up every day. Tides are so obedient to schedule that a timetable for them can be printed like
that for trains, though more reliable. In fact, tides and trains
sharply illustrate my point: One depends on the moon and is certain; the other depends on man and is uncertain.

9   In the absence of dependable recurring circumstance, too
much confidence cannot be placed on the lessons of history.

10   There *are* lessons, of course, and when people speak of
learning from them, they have in mind, I think, two ways of applying past experience: One is to enable us to avoid past mistakes
and to manage better in similar circumstances next time; the
other is to enable us to anticipate a future course of events. (History could tell us something about Vietnam, I think, if we would
only listen.) To manage better next time is within our means; to
anticipate does not seem to be.

11   World War II, for example, with the experience of the previous war as an awful lesson, was certainly conducted, once we got
into it, more intelligently than World War I. Getting into it was
another matter. When it was important to anticipate the course of
events, Americans somehow failed to apply the right lesson. Pearl
Harbor is the classic example of failure to learn from history.
From hindsight we now know that what we should have anticipated was a surprise attack by Japan in the midst of negotiations.
Merely because this was dishonorable, did that make it unthinkable? Hardly. It was exactly the procedure Japan had adopted in
1904 when she opened the Russo-Japanese War by surprise attack
on the Russian fleet at Port Arthur.

12   In addition we had every possible physical indication. We
had broken the Japanese code, we had warnings on radar, we had
a constant flow of accurate intelligence. What failed? Not information but *judgment*. We had all the evidence and refused to interpret it correctly, just as the Germans in 1944 refused to believe

the evidence of a landing in Normandy. Men will not believe what does not fit in with their plans or suit their prearrangements. The flaw in all military intelligence, whether twenty or fifty or one hundred percent accurate, is that it is no better than the judgment of its interpreters, and this judgment is the product of a mass of individual, social, and political biases, prejudgments, and wishful thinkings; in short, it is human and therefore fallible. If man can break the Japanese code and yet not believe what it tells him, how can he be expected to learn from the lessons of history?

13   Would a computer do better? In the case of Pearl Harbor, probably yes. If one could have fed all the pieces of intelligence available in November 1941 into a computer, it could have hardly failed to reply promptly, "Air attack, Hawaii, Philippines" and probably even "December 7." But will this work every time? Can we trust the lessons of history to computers? I think not, because history will fool them. They may make the right deductions and draw the right conclusions, but a twist occurs, someone sneezes, history swerves and takes another path. Had Cleopatra's nose been shorter, said Pascal, the whole aspect of the world would have been changed. Can a computer account for Cleopatra?

14   Once long ago when the eternal verities seemed clear—that is, during the Spanish Civil War—I thought the lessons of history were unmistakable. It appeared obvious beyond dispute that if fascism under Franco won, Spain in the foreshadowed European war would become a base for Hitler and Mussolini, the Mediterranean would become an Italian lake, Britain would lose Gibraltar and be cut off from her empire east of Suez. The peril was plain, the logic of the thing implacable, every sensible person saw it, and I, just out of college, wrote a small book published in England to point it up, all drawn from the analogy of history. The book showed how, throughout the eighteenth and nineteenth centuries, Britain had consistently interposed herself against the gaining of undue influence over Spain by whatever power dominated the continent. The affair of the Spanish marriages, the campaigns of Wellington, the policies of Castlereagh, Canning, and Palmerston all were directed toward the same objective: The strongest continental power must be prevented from controlling Spain. My treatise was, I thought, very artful and very telling. It did not refer to the then current struggle, but let the past speak for itself and make the argument. It was an irrefutable one—until history refuted it. Franco, assisted by Hitler and Mussolini, *did* win, European

war *did* follow, yet unaccountably Spain remained neutral—at least nominally. Gibraltar did not fall, the portals of the Mediterranean did *not* close. I, not to mention all the other "premature" anti-fascists, as we were called, while morally right about the general danger of fascism, had been wrong about a particular outcome. The lessons of history I had so carefully set forth simply did not operate. History misbehaved.

15   Pearl Harbor and Spain demonstrate two things: One, that man fails to profit from the lessons of history because his prejudgments prevent him from drawing the indicated conclusions; and, two, that history will often capriciously take a different direction from that in which her lessons point. Herein lies the flaw in systems of history.

16   When it comes to systems, history played her greatest betrayal on Karl Marx. Never was a prophet so sure of his premises, never were believers so absolutely convinced of a predicted outcome, never was there an interpretation of history that seemed so foolproof. Analyzing the effects of the Industrial Revolution, Marx exposed the terrible riddle of the nineteenth century: that the greater the material progress, the wider and deeper the resulting poverty, a process which could only end, he decided, in the violent collapse of the existing order brought on by revolution. From this he formulated the doctrine of *Verelendung* (progressive impoverishment) and *Zusammenbruch* (collapse) and decreed that since working-class self-consciousness increased in proportion to industrialization, revolution would come first in the most industrialized country.

17   Marx's analysis was so compelling that it seemed impossible history could follow any other course. His postulates were accepted by followers of his own and later generations as if they had been graven on the tablets of Sinai. Marxism as the revealed truth of history was probably the most convincing dogma ever enunciated. Its influence was tremendous, incalculable, continuing. The founder's facts were correct, his thinking logical and profound; he was right in everything but his conclusions. Developing events did not bear him out. The working class grew progressively better, not worse, off. Capitalism did not collapse. Revolution came in the least, not the most, industrialized country. Under collectivism the state did not wither but extended itself in power and function and in its grip on society. History, ignoring Marx, followed her own mysterious logic, and went on her own way.

18   When it developed that Marx was wrong, men in search of determinism rushed off to submit history to a new authority—Freud. His hand is now upon us. The Unconscious is king. At least it was. There are new voices, I believe, claiming that the Unconscious is a fraud—iconoclasm has reached even Freud. Nevertheless, in his effect on the modern outlook, Freud, I believe, unquestionably was the greatest influence for change between the nineteenth and twentieth centuries. It may well be that our time may one day be named for him and the Freudian Era said to have succeeded the Victorian Era. Our understanding of human motivation has taken on a whole new dimension since his ideas took hold. Yet it does not seem to me that unconscious sexual and psychological drives are as relevant in all circumstances as they are said to be by the Freudians, who have become as fixed in their system as were the orthodox Marxists. They can supply historians with insights but not with guidance to the future because man *en masse* cannot be relied upon to behave according to pattern. All salmon swim back to spawn in the headwaters of their birth; that is universal for salmon. But man lives in a more complicated world than a fish. Too many influences are at work on him to make it applicable that every man is driven by an unconscious desire to swim back to the womb.

19   It has always seemed to me unfortunate, for instance, that Freud chose the experiences of two royal families to exemplify his concept of the Oedipus and Elektra complexes. Royalty lives under special circumstances, particularly as regards the issue of power between the sovereign and his heir, which are not valid as universal experience. The legend of Oedipus killing his father may have derived from the observed phenomenon that every royal heir has always hated his father, not because he wants to sleep with his mother but because he wants to ascend the throne. If the parental sovereign happens to be his mother, he hates her just as much. She will dislike him equally from birth because she knows he is destined to take her place, as in the case of Queen Victoria and her eldest son, who became Edward VII. That is not Freudian, it is simply dynastic.

20   As for Elektra, it is hard to know what to make of that tale. The House of Atreus was a very odd family indeed. More was going on there than just Elektra being in love with her father. How about Orestes, who helped her to kill their mother, or killed her himself, according to another version? Was not that the

wrong parent? How come he did not kill his father? How about Iphigenia, the sister, whom Agememnon killed as a sacrifice? What is the Freudian explanation for that? They do not say, which is not being historical. A historian cannot pick and choose his facts; he must deal with all the evidence.

21   Or take Martin Luther. As you know, Professor Erik Erikson of Harvard has discovered that Luther was constipated from childhood and upon this interesting physiological item he has erected a system which explains everything about his man. This is definitely the most camp thing that has happened to history in years. It even made Broadway. Nevertheless I do not think Luther pinned the 95 Theses on the church door at Wittenberg solely or even mainly because of the activity, or inactivity rather, of his anal muscle. His personal motive for protest may have had an anal basis for all I know, but what is important historically is the form the protest took, and this had to do with old and deep social grievances concerned with the worldliness of the church, the sale of indulgences, corruption of the clergy, and so on. If it had not been Luther who protested, it would have been someone else; Protestantism would have come with or without him, and its causes had nothing whatever to do with his private physiological impediment. Professor Erikson, I am sure, was attempting to explain Luther, not Protestantism, but his book has started a fad for psycho-history among those without the adequate knowledge or training to use it.

22   Following Freud there flourished briefly a minor prophet, Oswald Spengler, who proclaimed the Decline of the West, based on an elaborate study of the lessons of history. Off and on since then people have been returning to his theme, especially since World War II and the end of colonialism. The rise of China and the rash of independence movements in Asia and Africa have inspired many nervous second looks at Spengler. Europe is finished, say the knowing ones; the future belongs to the colored races and all that.

23   People have been burying Europe for quite some time. I remember a political thinker for whom I had great respect telling me in the thirties that Europe's reign was over; the future belonged to America, Russia, and China. It was a new and awful thought to me then and I was immensely impressed. As I see it now, his grouping has not been justified. I do not think Russia and America can be disassociated from Europe; rather, we are extensions of Europe. I hesitate to be dogmatic about Russia, but I am

certain about the United States. American culture stems from Europe, our fortunes are linked with hers, in the long run we are aligned. My impression is that Europe, and by extension the white race, is far from finished. Europe's vitality keeps reviving; as a source of ideas she is inexhaustible. Nuclear fission, the most recent, if unwanted, advance, came from the work of a whole series of Europeans: Max Planck, the Curies, Einstein, Rutherford, Fermi, Nils Bohr, Szilard. Previously the three great makers of the modern mind, Darwin, Marx, and Freud, were Europeans. I do not know of an original idea to have importantly affected the *modern* world which has come from Asia or Africa (except perhaps for Gandhi's concept of non-violent resistance or civil disobedience, and, after all, Thoreau had the same idea earlier).

24   It does not seem to me a passing phenomenon or an accident that the West, in ideas and temporal power, has been dominant for so long. Far from falling behind, it seems to be extending its lead, except in the fearful matter of mere numbers and I like to think the inventiveness of the West will somehow eventually cope with that. What is called the emergence of the peoples of Asia and Africa is taking place in Western terms and is measured by the degree to which they take on Western forms, political, industrial, and otherwise. That they are losing their own cultures is sad, I think, but I suppose it cannot be helped. The new realm is space, and that too is being explored by the West. So much for Spengler.

25   Theories of history go in vogues which, as is the nature of vogues, soon fade and give place to new ones. Yet this fails to discourage the systematizers. They believe as firmly in this year's as last year's, for, as Isaiah Berlin says, the "obstinate craving for unity and symmetry at the expense of experience" is always with us. When I grew up, the economic interpretation of history, as formulated with stunning impact by Charles Beard, was the new gospel—as incontrovertible as if it had been revealed to Beard in a burning bush. Even to question that financial interests motivated our Founding Fathers in the separation from Britain, or that equally mercenary considerations decided our entrance into the First World War, was to convict oneself of the utmost naïveté. Yet lately the fashionable—indeed, what appears to be the required—exercise among historians has been jumping on Beard with both feet. He and the considerable body of his followers who added to

his system and built it up into a dogma capable of covering any historical situation have been knocked about, analyzed, dissected, and thoroughly disposed of. Presently the historical establishment has moved on to dispose of Frederick Jackson Turner and his theory of the Frontier. I do not know what the new explanation is, but I am sure there must be some thesis, for, as one academic historian recently ruled, the writing of history requires a "large organizing idea."

26   I visualize the "large organizing idea" as one of those iron chain mats pulled behind by a tractor to smooth over a plowed field. I see the professor climbing up on the tractor seat and away he goes, pulling behind his large organizing idea over the bumps and furrows of history until he has smoothed it out to a nice, neat, organized surface—in other words, into a system.

27   The human being—you, I, or Napoleon—is unreliable as a scientific factor. In combination of personality, circumstance, and historical moment, each man is a package of variables impossible to duplicate. His birth, his parents, his siblings, his food, his home, his school, his economic and social status, his first job, his first girl, and the variables inherent in all of these, make up that mysterious compendium, personality—which then combines with another set of variables: country, climate, time, and historical circumstance. Is it likely, then, that all these elements will meet again in their exact proportions to reproduce a Moses, or Hitler, or De Gaulle, or for that matter Lee Harvey Oswald, the man who killed Kennedy?

28   So long as man remains the Unknowable Variable—and I see no immediate prospect of his ever being pinned down in every facet of his infinite variety—I do not see how his actions can be usefully programmed and quantified. The eager electronic optimists will go on chopping up man's past behavior into the thousands of little definable segments which they call Input, and the machine will whirr and buzz and flash its lights and in no time at all give back Output. But will Output be dependable? I would lay ten to one that history will pay no more attention to Output than it did to Karl Marx. It will still need historians. Electronics will have its uses, but it will not, I am confident, transform historians into button-pushers or history into a system.

QUESTIONS

Ideas

1. Are there historical events in your memory that could illustrate Tuchman's point that "history misbehaves"? For example, can you narrate events that would illustrate the "illogical human record" Tuchman refers to in paragraph 7?

2. In the last paragraph Tuchman says there will always be a need for historians. Why does she feel a need to say this? Is she answering an opposing view?

3. Why do you think Tuchman is opposed to the "large organizing idea" she mentions in the last line of paragraph 25? What are examples of these master theories?

4. Is Tuchman saying that Freud's theories should not be used to interpret the behavior of historical figures? Is she implying that Marx's influence on history was insignificant? How do you think students at the University of Moscow would respond to that question?

5. Do you think Tuchman's discussion of the non-Decline of the West in paragraphs 22 through 24 is fair? Do you think university students in, say, Japan or Kenya would agree with Tuchman's last sentence in paragraph 23?

6. Based on your reading this essay, how do you think Tuchman would describe human nature?

7. In your opinion, what purposes does the study of history serve? Who should write history? Should there be a women's history? Should minorities be encouraged to write a separate history or should they be assimilated into a larger perspective? Are historical events open to interpretation like poems?

Organization

8. What is the function of paragraphs 6, 9, and 15?

9. An essay with 28 paragraphs is usually divided into parts, with maybe four or five paragraphs used to develop an idea in some detail. Find examples of these "discourse blocks" in the last half of the essay.

10. Divide this essay into five parts. What might be an appropriate title for each?

Sentences

11. Paragraph 13 contains a number of questions. In fact, there are a large number of questions throughout. Do you think this is an effec-

tive device? Might the fact that this is a talk have something to do
with her choice?

12. Look again at paragraph 18, reading it out loud. Are the sentences
     varied in type, length, and beginning?

13. Tuchman often uses the colon (e.g., the first sentence in paragraph
     15). Find other examples, then write some of your own sentences in
     imitation of this pattern.

Words

14. Why do you think Tuchman uses German words in paragraph 16?

15. A euphemism is a polite word or phrase used to cover up an
     unpleasant fact (e.g., *departed* for *dead, strategic backward movement* for
     retreat). Can you find some examples in paragraph 21?

Suggestions for Writing

A. Write a brief letter to Barbara Tuchman disagreeing with one of the
    ideas she presents.

B. Try to write a paragraph in Tuchman's style that would fit into this
    essay and go unnoticed by a reader.

C. Write an essay that argues that we can learn from history. Give exam-
    ples.

FOURTEEN

Alice
Walker

(1944–   )

Born in Georgia in 1944, Alice Walker is the youngest of eight children of black sharecroppers. She attended Spelman College and Sarah Lawrence, from which she graduated with a B.A. During her college years she became deeply involved in the civil rights movement and worked for a variety of social programs, including voter registration, welfare rights, and Head Start. She has also taught at a number of colleges including Jackson State, Wellesley, Brandeis, and the University of California at Berkeley.

Alice Walker's prose has been highly acclaimed for its passion, its honesty, and its beauty. Walker is perhaps best known for her fiction, which includes two collections of short stories and four novels, the most popular of which, *The Color Purple,* won both the Pulitzer Prize and the American Book Award. Her essays, from which the selections that follow were taken, are collected in her 1983 volume, *In Search of Our Mothers' Gardens.*

Throughout her nonfictional prose, Walker ranges over subjects such as family relations, race relations, and the relations between the sexes. In "Brothers and Sisters" she explores family relationships, which, in another context, she has described as "sacred." Walker believes that "love, cohesion, and support" are crucial for the survival of the family, especially the black family. In "Choice" she pays tribute to Martin Luther King, Jr., explaining how his courage and devotion to freedom inspired her. In an essay not included in this volume, Walker pays similar tribute to Zora Neale Hurston, a black woman writer

433

whose work and life provided her with a model of independence and integrity. In the title essay of her book, *In
Search of Our Mothers' Gardens,* she raises questions about
artistic creativity, inviting us to consider how, despite prejudice and oppression, poor black women such as
Walker's own mother found outlets for their considerable
artistic talent. And, finally, in "Beauty: When the Other
Dancer Is the Self," Walker writes movingly of how she
came to terms with a physical disfigurement.

Walker's writing is frequently polemical: she has a
position to argue from and a case to advance. Writing as a
black feminist, Walker reveals the tremendous suffering,
frustration, and waste in the lives of the poor black
women she considers to be "among America's greatest
heroes." Yet, while she makes the lives of such women her
most frequent subject, she occasionally transcends this
subject, enlarging it to explore questions about our common humanity. On such occasions the impact of her writing is felt across boundaries of race, sex, and social class,
largely because Walker offers us a vision of survival, suggesting, as one of her reviewers has written, that her work
exemplifies the capacity of human beings "to live in spiritual health and beauty" in such a way that "their inner
selves can blossom."

One additional quality of her character and writing
remains to be noted: her gratitude. Walker gives thanks,
throughout her essays, for her past, for her rich Southern
experience, and especially for her family. She is grateful
for her skill as a writer and for the dedicated support she
has had in the forms of both public grants and of private
encouragement. And she is grateful, finally, for the strong
and inspiring models she so lovingly memorializes.

Brothers and Sisters

1   We lived on a farm in the South in the fifties, and my
brothers, the four of them I knew (the fifth had left home when I
was three years old), were allowed to watch animals being mated.
This was not unusual; nor was it considered unusual that my older

sister and I were frowned upon if we even asked, innocently, what was going on. One of my brothers explained the mating one day, using words my father had given him: "The bull is getting a little something on his stick," he said. And he laughed. "What stick?" I wanted to know. "Where did he get it? How did he pick it up? Where did he put it?" All my brothers laughed.

2   I believe my mother's theory about raising a large family of five boys and three girls was that the father should teach the boys and the mother teach the girls the facts, as one says, of life. So my father went around talking about bulls getting something on their sticks and she went around saying girls did not need to know about such things. They were "womanish" (a very bad way to be in those days) if they asked.

3   The thing was, watching the matings filled my brothers with an aimless sort of lust, as dangerous as it was unintentional. They knew enough to know that cows, months after mating, produced calves, but they were not bright enough to make the same connection between women and their offspring.

4   Sometimes, when I think of my childhood, it seems to me a particularly hard one. But in reality, everything awful that happened to me didn't seem to happen to *me* at all, but to my older sister. Through some incredible power to negate my presence around people I did not like, which produced invisibility (as well as an ability to appear mentally vacant when I was nothing of the kind), I was spared the humiliation she was subjected to, though at the same time, I felt every bit of it. It was as if she suffered for my benefit, and I vowed early in my life that none of the things that made existence so miserable for her would happen to me.

5   The fact that she was not allowed at official matings did not mean she never saw any. While my brothers followed my father to the mating pens on the other side of the road near the barn, she stationed herself near the pigpen, or followed our many dogs until they were in a mating mood, or, failing to witness something there, she watched the chickens. On a farm it is impossible *not* to be conscious of sex, to wonder about it, to dream . . . but to whom was she to speak of her feelings? Not to my father, who thought all young women perverse. Not to my mother, who pretended all her children grew out of stumps she magically found in the forest. Not to me, who never found anything wrong with this lie.

6   When my sister menstruated she wore a thick packet of clean rags between her legs. It stuck out in front like a penis. The boys laughed at her as she served them at the table. Not knowing any better, and because our parents did not dream of actually *discussing* what was going on, she would giggle nervously at herself. I hated her for giggling, and it was at those times I would think of her as dim-witted. She never complained, but she began to have strange fainting fits whenever she had her period. Her head felt as if it were splitting, she said, and everything she ate came up again. And her cramps were so severe she could not stand. She was forced to spend several days of each month in bed.

7   My father expected all of his sons to have sex with women. "Like bulls," he said, "a man *needs* to get a little something on his stick." And so, on Saturday nights, into town they went, chasing the girls. My sister was rarely allowed into town alone, and if the dress she wore fit too snugly at the waist, or if her cleavage dipped too far below her collarbone, she was made to stay home.

8   "But why can't I go too," she would cry, her face screwed up with the effort not to wail.

9   "They're boys, your brothers, *that's* why they can go."

10   Naturally, when she got the chance, she responded eagerly to boys. But when this was discovered she was whipped and locked up in her room.

11   I would go in to visit her.

12   "Straight Pine," she would say, "you don't know what it *feels* like to want to be loved by a man."

13   "And if this is what you get for feeling like it I never will," I said, with—I hoped—the right combination of sympathy and disgust.

14   "Men smell so good," she would whisper ecstatically. "And when they look into your eyes, you just melt."

15   Since they were so hard to catch, naturally she thought almost any of them terrific.

16   "Oh, that Alfred!" she would moon over some mediocre, square-headed boy, "he's so *sweet!*" And she would take his ugly picture out of her bosom and kiss it.

17   My father was always warning her not to come home if she ever found herself pregnant. My mother constantly reminded her that abortion was a sin. Later, although she never became pregnant, her period would not come for months at a time. The painful symptoms, however, never varied or ceased. She fell for

the first man who loved her enough to beat her for looking at someone else, and when I was still in high school, she married him.

18 My fifth brother, the one I never knew, was said to be different from the rest. He had not liked matings. He would not watch them. He thought the cows should be given a choice. My father had disliked him because he was soft. My mother took up for him. "Jason is just tenderhearted," she would say in a way that made me know he was her favorite; "he takes after me." It was true that my mother cried about almost anything.

19 Who was the oldest brother? I wondered.

20 "Well," said my mother, "he was someone who always loved you. Of course he was a great big boy when you were born and out working on his own. He worked on a road gang building roads. Every morning before he left he would come in the room where you were and pick you up and give you the biggest kisses. He used to look at you and just smile. It's a pity you don't remember him."

21 I agreed.

22 At my father's funeral I finally "met" my oldest brother. He is tall and black with thick gray hair above a young-looking face. I watched my sister cry over my father until she blacked out from grief. I saw my brothers sobbing, reminding each other of what a great father he had been. My oldest brother and I did not shed a tear between us. When I left my father's grave he came up and introduced himself, "You don't ever have to walk alone," he said, and put his arms around me.

23 One out of five ain't *too* bad, I thought, snuggling up.

24 But I didn't discover until recently his true uniqueness: He is the only one of my brothers who assumes responsibility for all his children. The other four all fathered children during those Saturday-night chases of twenty years ago. Children—my nieces and nephews whom I will probably never know—they neither acknowledge as their own, provide for, or even see.

25 It was not until I became a student of women's liberation ideology that I could understand and forgive my father. I needed an ideology that would define his behavior in context. The black movement had given me an ideology that helped explain his colorism (he *did* fall in love with my mother partly because she was so light; he never denied it). Feminism helped explain his sexism. I was relieved to know his sexist behavior was not something uniquely his own, but, rather, an imitation of the behavior of the society around us.

26   All partisan movements add to the fullness of our understanding of society as a whole. They never detract; or, in any case,
one must not allow them to do so. Experience adds to experience.
"The more things the better," as O'Connor and Welty both have
said, speaking, one of marriage, the other of Catholicism.

27   I desperately needed my father and brothers to give me
male models I could respect, because white men (for example;
being particularly handy in this sort of comparison)—whether in
films or in person—offered man as dominator, as killer, and
always as hypocrite.

28   My father failed because he copied the hypocrisy. And my
brothers—except for one—never understood they must represent
half the world to me, as I must represent the other half to them.

QUESTIONS

Ideas

1. What ideas about family life emerge in this essay? What sexual
    stereotypes appear?
2. What is Walker's attitude toward her brothers and sister? Where is
    her feeling about them most directly expressed?

Organization

3. Divide the essay into two, three, or four parts. Provide titles for each
    part and explain the relationship of one part to another.
4. Explain how the last paragraphs return the essay to concerns voiced
    earlier. What do these paragraphs add to those concerns?

Sentences

5. Explain the purpose and effect of the parenthetical interpolations
    in sentences from paragraphs 1, 2, 4, 25, and 27.
6. Paragraphs 4 and 5 include a variety of moderately long, well-con-
    trolled sentences. Consider carefully the structure of the last two
    sentences of paragraph 4 and the second sentence of paragraph 5.
    Notice also the parallelism Walker establishes at the end of para-
    graph 5 by repeating with variations the following sentence open-
    ing:

    Not to my father . . . Not to my mother . . . Not to me . . .

Words

7. Characterize and explain the language of the following bits of dialogue:

> The bull is getting a little something on his stick.
> Oh that Alfred, he's so *sweet!*
> You don't ever have to walk alone.

8. What do you think Walker means by the following words: *colorism, feminism, sexism, movement,* and *ideology*—all from paragraph 25.

Suggestions for Writing

A. Agree or disagree with Walker's contention that "all partisan movements add to the fullness of our understanding of our society as a whole." In what sense do you think this statement may be true or not, whether you think of women's liberation or of any other movement or ideology?

B. Write an essay explaining and responding to the idea you think Walker advances in paragraph 27 or 28.

C. Reflect on your own relations with your brothers and sisters. Write an essay exploring some aspect of sibling relationship.

D. Write an imitation of paragraph 4 or 5. Attend particularly to the punctuation, length, and rhythms of Walker's sentences.

Choice: A Tribute to Dr. Martin Luther King, Jr.

---

1 My great-great-great-grandmother walked as a slave from Virginia to Eatonton, Georgia—which passes for the Walker ancestral home—with two babies on her hips. She lived to be a hundred and twenty-five years old and my own father knew her as a boy. (It is in memory of this walk that I choose to keep and to embrace my "maiden" name, Walker.)

2 There is a cemetery near our family church where she is buried; but because her marker was made of wood and rotted years ago, it is impossible to tell exactly where her body lies. In the same cemetery are most of my mother's people, who have lived in

Georgia for so long nobody even remembers when they came. And all of my great-aunts and -uncles are there, and my grandfather and grandmother, and, very recently, my own father.

3   If it is true that land does not belong to anyone until they have buried a body in it, then the land of my birthplace belongs to me, dozens of times over. Yet the history of my family, like that of all black Southerners, is a history of dispossession. We loved the land and worked the land, but we never owned it; and even if we bought land, as my great-grandfather did after the Civil War, it was always in danger of being taken away, as his was, during the period following Reconstruction.

4   My father inherited nothing of material value from his father, and when I came of age in the early sixties I awoke to the bitter knowledge that in order just to continue to love the land of my birth, I was expected to leave it. For black people—including my parents—had learned a long time ago that to stay willingly in a beloved but brutal place is to risk losing the love and being forced to acknowledge only the brutality.

5   It is a part of the black Southern sensibility that we treasure memories; for such a long time, that is all of our homeland those of us who at one time or another were forced away from it have been allowed to have.

6   I watched my brothers, one by one, leave our home and leave the South. I watched my sisters do the same. This was not unusual; abandonment, except for memories, was the common thing, except for those who "could not do any better," or those whose strength or stubbornness was so colossal they took the risk that others could not bear.

7   In 1960, my mother bought a television set, and each day after school I watched Hamilton Holmes and Charlayne Hunter as they struggled to integrate—fair-skinned as they were—the University of Georgia. And then, one day, there appeared the face of Dr. Martin Luther King, Jr. What a funny name, I thought. At the moment I first saw him, he was being handcuffed and shoved into a police truck. He had dared to claim his rights as a native son, and had been arrested. He displayed no fear, but seemed calm and serene, unaware of his own extraordinary courage. His whole body, like his conscience, was at peace.

8   At the moment I saw his resistance I knew I would never be able to live in this country without resisting everything that sought

to disinherit me, and I would never be forced away from the land of my birth without a fight.

9   He was The One, The Hero, The One Fearless Person for whom we had waited. I hadn't even realized before that we *had* been waiting for Martin Luther King, Jr., but we had. And I knew it for sure when my mother added his name to the list of people she prayed for every night.

10   I sometimes think that it was literally the prayers of people like my mother and father, who had bowed down in the struggle for such a long time, that kept Dr. King alive until five years ago. For years we went to bed praying for his life, and awoke with the question "Is the 'Lord' still here?"

11   The public acts of Dr. King you know. They are visible all around you. His voice you would recognize sooner than any other voice you have heard in this century—this in spite of the fact that certain municipal libraries, like the one in downtown Jackson, do not carry recordings of his speeches, and the librarians chuckle cruelly when asked why they do not.

12   You know, if you have read his books, that his is a complex and revolutionary philosophy that few people are capable of understanding fully or have the patience to embody in themselves. Which is our weakness, which is our loss.

13   And if you know anything about good Baptist preaching, you can imagine what you missed if you never had a chance to hear Martin Luther King, Jr., preach at Ebenezer Baptist Church.

14   You know of the prizes and awards that he tended to think very little of. And you know of his concern for the disinherited: the American Indian, the Mexican-American, and the poor American white—for whom he cared much.

15   You know that this very room, in this very restaurant, was closed to people of color not more than five years ago. And that we eat here together tonight largely through his efforts and his blood. We accept the common pleasures of life, assuredly, in his name.

16   But add to all of these things the one thing that seems to me second to none in importance: He gave us back our heritage. He gave us back our homeland; the bones and dust of our ancestors, who may now sleep within our caring *and* our hearing. He gave us the blueness of the Georgia sky in autumn as in summer; the col-

ors of the Southern winter as well as glimpses of the green of vacation-time spring. Those of our relatives we used to invite for a visit we now can ask to stay. . . . He gave us full-time use of our own woods, and restored our memories to those of us who were forced to run away, as realities we might each day enjoy and leave for our children.

17   He gave us continuity of place, without which community is ephemeral. He gave us home.

QUESTIONS

Ideas

1.   There's no question that Walker thinks highly of King. Why does she value him and how does she characterize him?
2.   Before referring specifically to King, Walker talks about the South—her home. What does she say about the South and about her relation to it?

Organization

3.   "Choice" can be divided into two parts: paragraphs 1–7 and paragraphs 8–17. Explain how the two final paragraphs can be related to the concerns of the first seven. Comment on the effectiveness of returning at the end of the essay to its opening.
4.   Consider paragraph 3 or 5 as an alternative introductory paragraph for the essay. Which makes a better lead? How would you reorganize the first seven paragraphs to accommodate either 5 or 3 as a new introduction?

Sentences

5.   How effective is the sentence fragment in paragraph 12?

     Which is our weakness, which is our loss.

     Would it be better in this alternative version?

     This has been both our weakness and our loss.

     How effective is the fragment in paragraph 15?
6.   What is the rhetorical purpose of the colon in the opening sentence of paragraph 16? Explain the relationship of the information on the two sides of the colon.

7. Explain the effect in paragraphs 14–17 of Walker's use of similar patterns of sentence opening.

> You know of . . . And you know of . . . You know that . . . And that . . .
> He gave us back . . . He gave us back . . . He gave us . . . He gave us . . .

Words

8. Notice how Walker repeats key words in paragraph 4: love–beloved–love; knowledge–acknowledge; brutal–brutality. What is the effect of such repetition and variation? Locate and comment on another example from another paragraph.

9. In paragraphs 11–15 Walker addresses her readers directly as "you." What is the effect of this choice of pronoun on the tone of the piece? Why does Walker shift from *you* to *we* in the concluding paragraphs (16–17) and how effective is this shift?

Suggestions for Writing

A. Write an essay or a speech in which you extol the virtues of a public figure you value. Consider imitating Walker's style in the last four paragraphs of "Choice."

B. Write imitations of the dash sentences in paragraphs 1, 4, 7, 11, and 14.

Beauty: When the Other Dancer Is the Self

1   It is a bright summer day in 1947. My father, a fat, funny man with beautiful eyes and a subversive wit, is trying to decide which of his eight children he will take with him to the county fair. My mother, of course, will not go. She is knocked out from getting most of us ready: I hold my neck stiff against the pressure of her knuckles as she hastily completes the braiding and then beribboning of my hair.

2   My father is the driver for the rich old white lady up the road. Her name is Miss Mey. She owns all the land for miles

around, as well as the house in which we live. All I remember about her is that she once offered to pay my mother thirty-five cents for cleaning her house, raking up piles of her magnolia leaves, and washing her family's clothes, and that my mother—she of no money, eight children, and a chronic earache—refused it. But I do not think of this in 1947. I am two and a half years old. I want to go everywhere my daddy goes. I am excited at the prospect of riding in a car. Someone has told me fairs are fun. That there is room in the car for only three of us doesn't faze me at all. Whirling happily in my starchy frock, showing off my biscuit-polished patent-leather shoes and lavender socks, tossing my head in a way that makes my ribbons bounce, I stand, hands on hips, before my father. "Take me, Daddy," I say with assurance; "I'm the prettiest!"

3   Later, it does not surprise me to find myself in Miss Mey's shiny black car, sharing the back seat with the other lucky ones. Does not surprise me that I thoroughly enjoy the fair. At home that night I tell the unlucky ones all I can remember about the merry-go-round, the man who eats live chickens, and the teddy bears, until they say: that's enough, baby Alice. Shut up now, and go to sleep.

4   It is Easter Sunday, 1950. I am dressed in a green, flocked, scalloped-hem dress (handmade by my adoring sister, Ruth) that has its own smooth satin petticoat and tiny hot-pink roses tucked into each scallop. My shoes, new T-strap patent leather, again highly biscuit-polished. I am six years old and have learned one of the longest Easter speeches to be heard that day, totally unlike the speech I said when I was two: "Easter lilies/pure and white/blossom in/the morning light." When I rise to give my speech I do so on a great wave of love and pride and expectation. People in the church stop rustling their new crinolines. They seem to hold their breath. I can tell they admire my dress, but it is my spirit, bordering on sassiness (womanishness), they secretly applaud.

5   "That girl's a little *mess*," they whisper to each other, pleased.

6   Naturally I say my speech without stammer or pause, unlike those who stutter, stammer, or, worst of all, forget. This is before the word "beautiful" exists in people's vocabulary, but "Oh, isn't she the *cutest* thing!" frequently floats my way. "And got so much sense!" they gratefully add . . . for which thoughtful addition I thank them to this day.

7   *It was great fun being cute. But then, one day, it ended.*

8   I am eight years old and a tomboy. I have a cowboy hat, cowboy boots, checkered shirt and pants, all red. My playmates are my brothers, two and four years older than I. Their colors are black and green, the only difference in the way we are dressed. On Saturday nights we all go to the picture show, even my mother; Westerns are her favorite kind of movie. Back home, "on the ranch," we pretend we are Tom Mix, Hopalong Cassidy, Lash LaRue (we've even named one of our dogs Lash LaRue); we chase each other for hours rustling cattle, being outlaws, delivering damsels from distress. Then my parents decide to buy my brothers guns. These are not "real" guns. They shoot "BBs," copper pellets my brothers say will kill birds. Because I am a girl, I do not get a gun. Instantly I am relegated to the position of Indian. Now there appears a great distance between us. They shoot and shoot at everything with their new guns. I try to keep up with my bow and arrows.

9   One day while I am standing on top of our makeshift "garage"—pieces of tin nailed across some poles—holding my bow and arrow and looking out toward the fields, I feel an incredible blow in my right eye. I look down just in time to see my brother lower his gun.

10   Both brothers rush to my side. My eye stings, and I cover it with my hand. "If you tell," they say, "we will get a whipping. You don't want that to happen, do you?" I do not. "Here is a piece of wire," says the older brother, picking it up from the roof; "say you stepped on one end of it and the other flew up and hit you." The pain is beginning to start. "Yes," I say. "Yes, I will say that is what happened." If I do not say this is what happened, I know my brothers will find ways to make me wish I had. But now I will say anything that gets me to my mother.

11   Confronted by our parents we stick to the lie agreed upon. They place me on a bench on the porch and I close my left eye while they examine the right. There is a tree growing from underneath the porch that climbs past the railing to the roof. It is the last thing my right eye sees. I watch as its trunk, its branches, and then its leaves are blotted out by the rising blood.

12   I am in shock. First there is intense fever, which my father tries to break using lily leaves bound around my head. Then there are chills: my mother tries to get me to eat soup. Eventually, I do not know how, my parents learn what has happened. A week after the "accident" they take me to see a doctor. "Why did you wait so

long to come?" he asks, looking into my eye and shaking his head. "Eyes are sympathetic," he says. "If one is blind, the other will likely become blind too."

13   This comment of the doctor's terrifies me. But it is really how I look that bothers me most. Where the BB pellet struck there is a glob of whitish scar tissue, a hideous cataract, on my eye. Now when I stare at people—a favorite pastime, up to now—they will stare back. Not at the "cute" little girl, but at her scar. For six years I do not stare at anyone, because I do not raise my head.

14   Years later, in the throes of a mid-life crisis, I ask my mother and sister whether I changed after the "accident." "No," they say, puzzled. "What do you mean?"

15   *What do I mean?*

16   I am eight, and, for the first time, doing poorly in school, where I have been something of a whiz since I was four. We have just moved to the place where the "accident" occurred. We do not know any of the people around us because this is a different county. The only time I see the friends I knew is when we go back to our old church. The new school is the former state penitentiary. It is a large stone building, cold and drafty, crammed to overflowing with boisterous, ill-disciplined children. On the third floor there is a huge circular imprint of some partition that has been torn out.

17   "What used to be here?" I ask a sullen girl next to me on our way past it to lunch.

18   "The electric chair," says she.

19   At night I have nightmares about the electric chair, and about all the people reputedly "fried" in it. I am afraid of the school, where all the students seem to be budding criminals.

20   "What's the matter with your eye?" they ask, critically.

21   When I don't answer (I cannot decide whether it was an "accident" or not), they shove me, insist on a fight.

22   My brother, the one who created the story about the wire, comes to my rescue. But then brags so much about "protecting" me, I become sick.

23   After months of torture at the school, my parents decide to send me back to our old community, to my old school. I live with my grandparents and the teacher they board. But there is no room for Phoebe, my cat. By the time my grandparents decide there *is* room, and I ask for my cat, she cannot be found. Miss Yarborough, the boarding teacher, takes me under her wing, and begins to teach me to play the piano. But soon she marries an

African—a "prince," she says—and is whisked away to his continent.

24   At my old school there is at least one teacher who loves me. She is the teacher who "knew me before I was born" and bought my first baby clothes. It is she who makes life bearable. It is her presence that finally helps me turn on the one child at the school who continually calls me "one-eyed bitch." One day I simply grab him by his coat and beat him until I am satisfied. It is my teacher who tells me my mother is ill.

25   My mother is lying in bed in the middle of the day, something I have never seen. She is in too much pain to speak. She has an abscess in her ear. I stand looking down on her, knowing that if she dies, I cannot live. She is being treated with warm oils and hot bricks held against her cheek. Finally a doctor comes. But I must go back to my grandparents' house. The weeks pass but I am hardly aware of it. All I know is that my mother might die, my father is not so jolly, my brothers still have their guns, and I am the one sent away from home.

26   "You did not change," they say.

27   *Did I imagine the anguish of never looking up?*

28   I am twelve. When relatives come to visit I hide in my room. My cousin Brenda, just my age, whose father works in the post office and whose mother is a nurse, comes to find me. "Hello," she says. And then she asks, looking at my recent school picture, which I did not want taken, and on which the "glob," as I think of it, is clearly visible, "You still can't see out of that eye?"

29   "No," I say, and flop back on the bed over my book.

30   That night, as I do almost every night, I abuse my eye. I rant and rave at it, in front of the mirror. I plead with it to clear up before morning. I tell it I hate and despise it. I do not pray for sight. I pray for beauty.

31   "You did not change," they say.

32   I am fourteen and baby-sitting for my brother Bill, who lives in Boston. He is my favorite brother and there is a strong bond between us. Understanding my feelings of shame and ugliness he and his wife take me to a local hospital, where the "glob" is removed by a doctor named O. Henry. There is still a small bluish crater where the scar tissue was, but the ugly white stuff is gone. Almost immediately I become a different person from the girl who does not raise her head. Or so I think. Now that I've raised

my head I win the boyfriend of my dreams. Now that I've raised my head I have plenty of friends. Now that I've raised my head classwork comes from my lips as faultlessly as Easter speeches did, and I leave high school as valedictorian, most popular student, and *queen,* hardly believing my luck. Ironically, the girl who was voted most beautiful in our class (and was) was later shot twice through the chest by a male companion, using a "real" gun, while she was pregnant. But that's another story in itself. Or is it?

33   "You did not change," they say.

34   It is now thirty years since the "accident." A beautiful journalist comes to visit and to interview me. She is going to write a cover story for her magazine that focuses on my latest book. "Decide how you want to look on the cover," she says. "Glamorous, or whatever."

35   Never mind "glamorous," it is the "whatever" that I hear. Suddenly all I can think of is whether I will get enough sleep the night before the photography session: if I don't, my eye will be tired and wander, as blind eyes will.

36   At night in bed with my lover I think up reasons why I should not appear on the cover of a magazine. "My meanest critics will say I've sold out," I say. "My family will now realize I write scandalous books."

37   "But what's the real reason you don't want to do this?" he asks.

38   "Because in all probability," I say in a rush, "my eye won't be straight."

39   "It will be straight enough," he says. Then, "Besides, I thought you'd made your peace with that."

40   And I suddenly remember that I have.

41   *I remember:*

42   I am talking to my brother Jimmy, asking if he remembers anything unusual about the day I was shot. He does not know I consider that day the last time my father, with his sweet home remedy of cool lily leaves, chose me, and that I suffered and raged inside because of this. "Well," he says, "all I remember is standing by the side of the highway with Daddy, trying to flag down a car. A white man stopped, but when Daddy said he needed somebody to take his little girl to the doctor, he drove off."

43   *I remember:*

44   I am in the desert for the first time. I fall totally in love with it. I am so overwhelmed by its beauty, I confront for the first time, consciously, the meaning of the doctor's words years ago: "Eyes

are sympathetic. If one is blind, the other will likely become blind too." I realize I have dashed about the world madly, looking at this, looking at that, storing up images against the fading of the light. *But I might have missed seeing the desert!* The shock of that possibility—and gratitude for over twenty-five years of sight—sends me literally to my knees. Poem after poem comes—which is perhaps how poets pray.

ON SIGHT

I am so thankful I have seen
The Desert
And the creatures in the desert
And the desert Itself.

The desert has its own moon
Which I have seen
With my own eye.

There is no flag on it.
Trees of the desert have arms
All of which are always up
That is because the moon is up
The sun is up
Also the sky
The stars
Clouds
None with flags.

If there *were* flags, I doubt
the trees would point.
Would you?

45   *But mostly, I remember this:*

46   I am twenty-seven, and my baby daughter is almost three. Since her birth I have worried about her discovery that her mother's eyes are different from other people's. Will she be embarrassed? I think. What will she say? Every day she watches a television program called "Big Blue Marble." It begins with a picture of the earth as it appears from the moon. It is bluish, a little battered-looking, but full of light, with whitish clouds swirling around it. Every time I see it I weep with love, as if it is a picture of Grandma's house. One day when I am putting Rebecca down for her

nap, she suddenly focuses on my eye. Something inside me cringes, gets ready to try to protect myself. All children are cruel about physical differences, I know from experience, and that they don't always mean to be is another matter. I assume Rebecca will be the same.

47   But no-o-o-o. She studies my face intently as we stand, her inside and me outside her crib. She even holds my face maternally between her dimpled little hands. Then, looking every bit as serious and lawyerlike as her father, she says, as if it may just possibly have slipped my attention: "Mommy, there's a *world* in your eye." (As in, "Don't be alarmed, or do anything crazy.") And then, gently, but with great interest: "Mommy, where did you *get* that world in your eye?"

48   For the most part, the pain left then. (So what, if my brothers grew up to buy even more powerful pellet guns for their sons and to carry real guns themselves. So what, if a young "Morehouse man" once nearly fell off the steps of Trevor Arnett Library because he thought my eyes were blue.) Crying and laughing I ran to the bathroom, while Rebecca mumbled and sang herself off to sleep. Yes indeed, I realized, looking into the mirror. There *was* a world in my eye. And I saw that it was possible to love it: that in fact, for all it had taught me of shame and anger and inner vision, I *did* love it. Even to see it drifting out of orbit in boredom, or rolling up out of fatigue, not to mention floating back at attention in excitement (bearing witness, a friend has called it), deeply suitable to my personality, and even characteristic of me.

49   That night I dream I am dancing to Stevie Wonder's song "Always" (the name of the song is really "As," but I hear it as "Always"). As I dance, whirling and joyous, happier than I've ever been in my life, another bright-faced dancer joins me. We dance and kiss each other and hold each other through the night. The other dancer has obviously come through all right, as I have done. She is beautiful, whole and free. And she is also me.

QUESTIONS

Ideas

1. In what ways does the young Alice Walker change after the injury to her eye? What effect has the injury had on her as an adult?

2. Discuss whether Walker has overreacted to her injury. Consider how an injury can alter our perception of ourselves or our sense of how others perceive and respond to us.

Organization

3. How is the essay organized? How does Walker signal her changes of focus and emphasis? What ties the various sections of the essay together?
4. Cite at least one example of a repeated sentence and comment on Walker's purpose in using it.

Sentences

5. Consider the effect in paragraph 32 of the use of a repeated sentence pattern: "Now that I've . . ." In the same paragraph comment on the effect of these two short sentences: "Or so I think." "Or is it?"
6. Explain the effect of the double dashes in the following sentence:

   But soon she marries an African—a "prince," she says—and is whisked away to his continent. (23)

   The shock of that possibility—and gratitude for over twenty five years of sight—sends me literally to my knees. (44)

Consider the differences in tone that would result if the dashes were replaced either with parentheses or with commas.

Words

7. Cite three uses of dialogue you think effective and explain what makes them so.
8. At the end of the essay Walker invokes the image of a dancer—another dancer who joins her in a dance. She also makes reference to a world in her eye. What do you think is the point and purpose of each of these images?

Suggestions for Writing

A. Describe a time when an accident or other turn of events damaged your self-image, made you feel insecure or unhappy with yourself. Explain how you came to terms with your situation and what the consequences for your later life have been or might be.
B. Compare Walker's discussion of her injury and its effects with Richard Rodriguez's essay "Complexion," or with Nancy Mairs's essay "On Being a Cripple."

In Search of Our Mothers' Gardens

MOTHEROOT

Creation often
needs two hearts
one to root
and one to flower
One to sustain
in time of drouth
and hold fast
against winds of pain
the fragile bloom
that in the glory
of its hour
affirms a heart
unsung, unseen.

—MARILOU AWIAKTA,
ABIDING APPALACHIA

I described her own nature and temperament. Told how they needed a larger life for their expression. . . . I pointed out that in lieu
of proper channels, her emotions had overflowed into paths that
dissipated them. I talked, beautifully I thought, about an art that
would be born, an art that would open the way for women the likes
of her. I asked her to hope, and build up an inner life against the
coming of that day. . . . I sang, with a strange quiver in my voice, a
promise song.

—JEAN TOOMER, "AVEY,"
CANE

1   The poet speaking to a prostitute who falls asleep while he's
talking—

2   When the poet Jean Toomer walked through the South in
the early twenties, he discovered a curious thing: black women
whose spirituality was so intense, so deep, so *unconscious,* that they

were themselves unaware of the richness they held. They stumbled blindly through their lives: creatures so abused and mutilated in body, so dimmed and confused by pain, that they considered themselves unworthy even of hope. In the selfless
abstractions their bodies became to the men who used them, they
became more than "sexual objects," more even than mere
women: they became "Saints." Instead of being perceived as whole
persons, their bodies became shrines: what was thought to be
their minds became temples suitable for worship. These crazy
Saints stared out at the world, wildly, like lunatics—or quietly, like
suicides; and the "God" that was in their gaze was as mute as a
great stone.

3   Who were these Saints? These crazy, loony, pitiful women?

4   Some of them, without a doubt, were our mothers and
grandmothers.

5   In the still heat of the post-Reconstruction South, this is how
they seemed to Jean Toomer: exquisite butterflies trapped in an
evil honey, toiling away their lives in an era, a century, that did
not acknowledge them, except as "the *mule* of the world." They
dreamed dreams that no one knew—not even themselves, in any
coherent fashion—and saw visions no one could understand.
They wandered or sat about the countryside crooning lullabies to
ghosts, and drawing the mother of Christ in charcoal on courthouse walls.

6   They forced their minds to desert their bodies and their
striving spirits sought to rise, like frail whirlwinds from the hard
red clay. And when those frail whirlwinds fell, in scattered parti-
cles, upon the ground, no one mourned. Instead, men lit candles
to celebrate the emptiness that remained, as people do who enter
a beautiful but vacant space to resurrect a God.

7   Our mothers and grandmothers, some of them: moving to
music not yet written. And they waited.

8   They waited for a day when the unknown thing that was in
them would be made known; but guessed, somehow in their darkness, that on the day of their revelation they would be long dead.
Therefore to Toomer they walked, and even ran, in slow motion.
For they were going nowhere immediate, and the future was not
yet within their grasp. And men took our mothers and grandmothers, "but got no pleasure from it." So complex was their passion and their calm.

9   To Toomer, they lay vacant and fallow as autumn fields, with harvest time never in sight: and he saw them enter loveless marriages, without joy; and become prostitutes, without resistance; and become mothers of children, without fulfillment.

10   For these grandmothers and mothers of ours were not Saints, but Artists; driven to a numb and bleeding madness by the springs of creativity in them for which there was no release. They were Creators, who lived lives of spiritual waste, because they were so rich in spirituality—which is the basis of Art—that the strain of enduring their unused and unwanted talent drove them insane. Throwing away this spirituality was their pathetic attempt to lighten the soul to a weight their work-worn, sexually abused bodies could bear.

11   What did it mean for a black woman to be an artist in our grandmothers' time? In our great-grandmothers' day? It is a question with an answer cruel enough to stop the blood.

12   Did you have a genius of a great-great-grandmother who died under some ignorant and depraved white overseer's lash? Or was she required to bake biscuits for a lazy backwater tramp, when she cried out in her soul to paint watercolors of sunsets, or the rain falling on the green and peaceful pasturelands? Or was her body broken and forced to bear children (who were more often than not sold away from her)—eight, ten, fifteen, twenty children—when her one joy was the thought of modeling heroic figures of rebellion, in stone or clay?

13   How was the creativity of the black woman kept alive, year after year and century after century, when for most of the years black people have been in America, it was a punishable crime for a black person to read or write? And the freedom to paint, to sculpt, to expand the mind with action did not exist. Consider, if you can bear to imagine it, what might have been the result if singing, too, had been forbidden by law. Listen to the voices of Bessie Smith, Billie Holiday, Nina Simone, Roberta Flack, and Aretha Franklin, among others, and imagine those voices muzzled for life. Then you may begin to comprehend the lives of our "crazy," "Sainted" mothers and grandmothers. The agony of the lives of women who might have been Poets, Novelists, Essayists, and Short-Story Writers (over a period of centuries), who died with their real gifts stifled within them.

14   And, if this were the end of the story, we would have cause to cry out in my paraphrase of Okot p'Bitek's great poem:

> O, my clanswomen
> Let us all cry together!
> Come,
> Let us mourn the death of our mother,
> The death of a Queen
> The ash that was produced
> By a great fire!
> O, this homestead is utterly dead
> Close the gates
> With *lacari* thorns,
> For our mother
> The creator of the Stool is lost!
> And all the young women
> Have perished in the wilderness!

15   But this is not the end of the story, for all the young women—our mothers and grandmothers, *ourselves*—have not perished in the wilderness. And if we ask ourselves why, and search for and find the answer, we will know beyond all efforts to erase it from our minds, just exactly who, and of what, we black American women are.

16   One example, perhaps the most pathetic, most misunderstood one, can provide a backdrop for our mothers' work: Phillis Wheatley, a slave in the 1700s.

17   Virginia Woolf, in her book *A Room of One's Own*, wrote that in order for a woman to write fiction she must have two things, certainly: a room of her own (with key and lock) and enough money to support herself.

18   What then are we to make of Phillis Wheatley, a slave, who owned not even herself? This sickly, frail black girl who required a servant of her own at times—her health was so precarious—and who, had she been white, would have been easily considered the intellectual superior of all the women and most of the men in the society of her day.

19   Virginia Woolf wrote further, speaking of course not of our Phillis, that "any woman born with a great gift in the sixteenth century [insert "eighteenth century," insert "black woman," insert "born or made a slave"] would certainly have gone crazed, shot herself, or ended her days in some lonely cottage outside the village, half witch, half wizard [insert "Saint"], feared and mocked at. For it needs little skill and psychology to be sure that a highly

gifted girl who had tried to use her gift for poetry would have
been so thwarted and hindered by contrary instincts [add "chains,
guns, the lash, the ownership of one's body by someone else, sub-
mission to an alien religion"], that she must have lost her health
and sanity to a certainty."

20   The key words, as they relate to Phillis, are "contrary
instincts." For when we read the poetry of Phillis Wheatley—as
when we read the novels of Nella Larsen or the oddly false-sound-
ing autobiography of that freest of all black women writers, Zora
Hurston—evidence of "contrary instincts" is everywhere. Her loy-
alties were completely divided, as was, without question, her
mind.

21   But how could this be otherwise? Captured at seven, a slave
of wealthy, doting whites who instilled in her the "savagery" of the
Africa they "rescued" her from . . . one wonders if she was even
able to remember her homeland as she had known it, or as it really was.

22   Yet, because she did try to use her gift for poetry in a world
that made her a slave, she was "so thwarted and hindered by . . .
contrary instincts, that she . . . lost her health. . . ." In the last
years of her brief life, burdened not only with the need to express
her gift but also with a penniless, friendless "freedom" and several
small children for whom she was forced to do strenuous work to
feed, she lost her health, certainly. Suffering from malnutrition
and neglect and who knows what mental agonies, Phillis Wheatley
died.

23   So torn by "contrary instincts" was black, kidnapped,
enslaved Phillis that her description of "the Goddess"—as she
poetically called the Liberty she did not have—is ironically, cruelly humorous. And, in fact, has held Phillis up to ridicule for more
than a century. It is usually read prior to hanging Phillis's memory
as that of a fool. She wrote:

> The Goddess comes, she moves divinely fair,
> Olive and laurel binds her *golden* hair.
> Wherever shines this native of the skies,
> Unnumber'd charms and recent graces rise. [My italics]

24   It is obvious that Phillis, the slave, combed the "Goddess's"
hair every morning; prior, perhaps, to bringing in the milk, or

fixing her mistress's lunch. She took her imagery from the one thing she saw elevated above all others.

25   With the benefit of hindsight we ask, "How could she?"

26   But at last, Phillis, we understand. No more snickering when your stiff, struggling, ambivalent lines are forced on us. We know now that you were not an idiot or a traitor; only a sickly little black girl, snatched from your home and country and made a slave; a woman who still struggled to sing the song that was your gift, although in a land of barbarians who praised you for your bewildered tongue. It is not so much what you sang, as that you kept alive, in so many of our ancestors, *the notion of song.*

27   Black women are called, in the folklore that so aptly identifies one's status in society, "the *mule* of the world," because we have been handed the burdens that everyone else—*everyone* else—refused to carry. We have also been called "Matriarchs," "Superwomen," and "Mean and Evil Bitches." Not to mention "Castraters" and "Sapphire's Mama." When we have pleaded for understanding, our character has been distorted; when we have asked for simple caring, we have been handed empty inspirational appellations, then stuck in the farthest corner. When we have asked for love, we have been given children. In short, even our plainer gifts, our labors of fidelity and love, have been knocked down our throats. To be an artist and a black woman, even today, lowers our status in many respects, rather than raises it: and yet, artists we will be.

28   Therefore we must fearlessly pull out of ourselves and look at and identify with our lives the living creativity some of our great-grandmothers were not allowed to know. I stress *some* of them because it is well known that the majority of our great-grandmothers knew, even without "knowing" it, the reality of their spirituality, even if they didn't recognize it beyond what happened in the singing at church—and they never had any intention of giving it up.

29   How they did it—those millions of black women who were not Phillis Wheatley, or Lucy Terry or Frances Harper or Zora Hurston or Nella Larsen or Bessie Smith; or Elizabeth Catlett, or Katherine Dunham, either—brings me to the title of this essay, "In Search of Our Mothers' Gardens," which is a personal account that is yet shared, in its theme and its meaning, by all of us. I

found, while thinking about the far-reaching world of the creative
black woman, that often the truest answer to a question that really
matters can be found very close.

30   In the late 1920s my mother ran away from home to marry
my father. Marriage, if not running away, was expected of seventeen-year-old girls. By the time she was twenty, she had two children and was pregnant with a third. Five children later, I was
born. And this is how I came to know my mother: she seemed a
large, soft, loving-eyed woman who was rarely impatient in our
home. Her quick, violent temper was on view only a few times a
year, when she battled with the white landlord who had the misfortune to suggest to her that her children did not need to go to
school.

31   She made all the clothes we wore, even my brothers' over-
alls. She made all the towels and sheets we used. She spent the
summers canning vegetables and fruits. She spent the winter
evenings making quilts enough to cover all our beds.

32   During the "working" day, she labored beside—not
behind—my father in the fields. Her day began before sunup,
and did not end until late at night. There was never a moment for
her to sit down, undisturbed, to unravel her own private thoughts;
never a time free from interruption—by work or the noisy
inquiries of her many children. And yet, it is to my mother—and
all our mothers who were not famous—that I went in search of
the secret of what has fed that muzzled and often mutilated, but
vibrant, creative spirit that the black woman has inherited, and
that pops out in wild and unlikely places to this day.

33   But when, you will ask, did my overworked mother have time
to know or care about feeding the creative spirit?

34   The answer is so simple that many of us have spent years discovering it. We have constantly looked high, when we should have
looked high—and low.

35   For example: in the Smithsonian Institution in Washington,
D.C., there hangs a quilt unlike any other in the world. In fanciful, inspired, and yet simple and identifiable figures, it portrays
the story of the Crucifixion. It is considered rare, beyond price.
Though it follows no known pattern of quilt-making, and though
it is made of bits and pieces of worthless rags, it is obviously the
work of a person of powerful imagination and deep spiritual feel-

ing. Below this quilt I saw a note that says it was made by "an anonymous Black woman in Alabama, a hundred years ago."

36 If we could locate this "anonymous" black woman from Alabama, she would turn out to be one of our grandmothers—an artist who left her mark in the only materials she could afford, and in the only medium her position in society allowed her to use.

37 As Virginia Woolf wrote further, in *A Room of One's Own:*

> Yet genius of a sort must have existed among women as it must have existed among the working class. [Change this to "slaves" and "the wives and daughters of sharecroppers."] Now and again an Emily Brontë or a Robert Burns [change this to "a Zora Hurston or a Richard Wright"] blazes out and proves its presence. But certainly it never got itself on to paper. When, however, one reads of a witch being ducked, of a woman possessed by devils [or "Sainthood"], of a wise woman selling herbs [our root workers], or even a very remarkable man who had a mother, then I think we are on the track of a lost novelist, a suppressed poet, of some mute and inglorious Jane Austen. . . . Indeed, I would venture to guess that Anon, who wrote so many poems without signing them, was often a woman. . . .

38 And so our mothers and grandmothers have, more often than not anonymously, handed on the creative spark, the seed of the flower they themselves never hoped to see: or like a sealed letter they could not plainly read.

39 And so it is, certainly, with my own mother. Unlike "Ma" Rainey's songs, which retained their creator's name even while blasting forth from Bessie Smith's mouth, no song or poem will bear my mother's name. Yet so many of the stories that I write, that we all write, are my mother's stories. Only recently did I fully realize this: that through years of listening to my mother's stories of her life, I have absorbed not only the stories themselves, but something of the manner in which she spoke, something of the urgency that involves the knowledge that her stories—like her life —must be recorded. It is probably for this reason that so much of what I have written is about characters whose counterparts in real life are so much older than I am.

40 But the telling of these stories, which came from my mother's lips as naturally as breathing, was not the only way my mother

showed herself as an artist. For stories, too, were subject to being distracted, to dying without conclusion. Dinners must be started, and cotton must be gathered before the big rains. The artist that was and is my mother showed itself to me only after many years. This is what I finally noticed:

41   Like Mem, a character in *The Third Life of Grange Copeland,* my mother adorned with flowers whatever shabby house we were forced to live in. And not just your typical straggly country stand of zinnias, either. She planted ambitious gardens—and still does—with over fifty different varieties of plants that bloom profusely from early March until late November. Before she left home for the fields, she watered her flowers, chopped up the grass, and laid out new beds. When she returned from the fields she might divide clumps of bulbs, dig a cold pit, uproot and replant roses, or prune branches from her taller bushes or trees—until night came and it was too dark to see.

42   Whatever she planted grew as if by magic, and her fame as a grower of flowers spread over three counties. Because of her creativity with her flowers, even my memories of poverty are seen through a screen of blooms—sunflowers, petunias, roses, dahlias, forsythia, spirea, delphiniums, verbena . . . and on and on.

43   And I remember people coming to my mother's yard to be given cuttings from her flowers; I hear again the praise showered on her because whatever rocky soil she landed on, she turned into a garden. A garden so brilliant with colors, so original in its design, so magnificent with life and creativity, that to this day people drive by our house in Georgia—perfect strangers and imperfect strangers—and ask to stand or walk among my mother's art.

44   I notice that it is only when my mother is working in her flowers that she is radiant, almost to the point of being invisible—except as Creator: hand and eye. She is involved in work her soul must have. Ordering the universe in the image of her personal conception of Beauty.

45   Her face, as she prepares the Art that is her gift, is a legacy of respect she leaves to me, for all that illuminates and cherishes life. She has handed down respect for the possibilities—and the will to grasp them.

46   For her, so hindered and intruded upon in so many ways, being an artist has still been a daily part of her life. This ability to hold on, even in very simple ways, is work black women have done for a very long time.

47   This poem is not enough, but it is something, for the woman who literally covered the holes in our walls with sunflowers:

> They were women then
> My mama's generation
> Husky of voice—Stout of
> Step
> With fists as well as
> Hands
> How they battered down
> Doors
> And ironed
> Starched white
> Shirts
> How they led
> Armies
> Headragged Generals
> Across mined
> Fields
> Booby-trapped
> Kitchens
> To discover books
> Desks
> A place for us
> How they knew what we
> *Must* know
> Without knowing a page
> Of it
> Themselves.

48   Guided by my heritage of a love of beauty and a respect for strength—in search of my mother's garden, I found my own.

49   And perhaps in Africa over two hundred years ago, there was just such a mother; perhaps she painted vivid and daring decorations in oranges and yellows and greens on the walls of her hut; perhaps she sang—in a voice like Roberta Flack's—*sweetly* over the compounds of her village; perhaps she wove the most stunning mats or told the most ingenious stories of all the village storytellers. Perhaps she was herself a poet—though only her daughter's name is signed to the poems that we know.

50   Perhaps Phillis Wheatley's mother was also an artist.

51   Perhaps in more than Phillis Wheatley's biological life is her mother's signature made clear.

QUESTIONS

Ideas

1. What does Walker propose as an answer to the question she asks in paragraph 11: "What did it mean for a black woman to be an artist in our grandmothers' time?" How about the question she asks in paragraph 13: "How was the creativity of the black woman kept alive . . . century after century?"

2. Explain the relationships Walker postulates between sainthood, madness, and artistic creation.

3. Define in your own words the main point and purpose of this piece.

Organization

4. If the introductory portion of this essay comprises paragraphs 1–14, what constitutes its body and its conclusion?

5. What function do the paragraphs about Phillis Wheatley serve? What would be lost if they were to be omitted? Would anything be gained?

Sentences

6. Single out for analysis and study two sentences that strike you as arresting or beautiful. Account for their power.

7. What are the function and effect of the interrogative sentences in paragraphs 11, 12, 13, and 18?

Words

8. What is the point of the description in the opening of the essay of southern black women as saints?

9. What are the force and effect of the comparisons Walker alludes to in paragraph 9?

10. Explain the function and effect of the garden and flower images in paragraphs 41–45.

Suggestions for Writing

A. Write an essay recording your debt to someone or something in your past. Explain how the person or event has helped you become who and what you are. If a tribute seems in order, pay tribute—as Walker does.

B. Write an essay analyzing Walker's piece. Consider its main ideas; its structure, purpose, and tone; its language and imagery.

C. Compare this essay with Walker's tribute to Martin Luther King, Jr. in her essay, "Choice."

FIFTEEN

E. B. White

(1899–1985)

E. B. White is generally recognized as one of America's finest writers. Long associated with *The New Yorker,* for which he wrote stories, sketches, essays, and editorials, White has also contributed to another prominent magazine, *Harper's,* writing a monthly column, "One Man's Meat," from 1938 to 1943. These columns were collected and published with a few additional pieces from *The New Yorker* as *One Man's Meat* (1944). This book was followed by two other collections of miscellany, *The Second Tree from the Corner* (1954) and *The Points of My Compass* (1962). Besides these collections, White published, over a slightly longer span of years, three children's books: *Stuart Little* (1945), *Charlotte's Web* (1952), and *The Trumpet of the Swan* (1970). In 1976, White published a selection of his best essays, those, as he says, which had "an odor of durability clinging to them." *The Essays of E. B. White* were followed a year later by a selection of White's letters, entitled simply enough, *Letters of E. B. White. Poems and Sketches of E. B. White* appeared in 1981.

Though not a complete bibliography of White's published work, this list does suggest something of White's range and versatility, as well as something about the way writing has been for him steady work over a long stretch of time. And the steadiest of White's work, in both senses of the word, has been his essays. In fact, it is an essayist that White is best known and most highly acclaimed. And it is as an essayist that he identifies himself, defining an essayist as "a self-liberated man sustained by the childish belief that everything he thinks about, everything that happens to him, is of general interest." And again, as one who is "content with living a free life and enjoying the satisfactions of a somewhat undisciplined existence."

Edward Hoagland has recently noted that White's name has become almost synonymous with "essay." And for good reason, we might add, since it is the form most congenial to his temperament, a form that allows him the latitude he needs to roam freely in thought, a form that he has been able to stamp with his own imprint. This imprint is reflected in the following elements: a scrupulous respect for his readers; an uncanny accuracy in the use of language; and an uncommon delight in common, everyday things. White sees the extraordinary in the ordinary, noticing and valuing what most of us either overlook or take for granted. And from his repeated and respectful acts of attention flow reminiscences, speculations, explorations, and questions about our common humanity, about our relationships with one another, with the past, with the worlds of technology and nature.

White is a writer whose insights derive directly from his literal observations, from what he sees. Thoreau, one of White's favorite writers—and one with whom White has much in common—once remarked that "you can't say more than you can see." White's writing bears this out. The relationship between sight and insight, between observation and speculation, is evident in essays such as "The Ring of Time," which begins with a description of a circus act and ends with speculations about time and change, and "Once More to the Lake," in which White reminisces about his boyhood summer holidays in Maine, both describing the place with startling vividness and offering unsettling speculations about the meaning of his memories. In these and in other essays, White's writing is rooted in the crucial act of vision, a vision which sees into and beyond the surface of his subjects.

White's best writing, however, is more than a record of what he has seen and thought. It is also art, literature. His best work is crafted, shaped, formed with the same attention to details of structure, texture, image, and tone that poets or painters, sculptors or novelists gives their work. In "The Ring of Time" and "Once More to the Lake," matters of fact, details of time, place, and circumstance give way to larger concerns. The circus is more than a circus ring: it becomes an emblem of time and change; the lake is more than a summer vacation place: it becomes an image of serenity and a reminder of time, change, even death. The images of light and water, the symbolism of circus ring and lake, along with a concern for understanding the present in relation to the past and the future—these lift their respective essays beyond the merely personal and reminiscent, beyond the ordinary and the everyday into the extraordinary universality of art.

About writing itself White has said a good deal, and said it well. In the chapter he contributed to the now famous *Elements of Style*, White notes that when we speak of a writer's style we mean "the sound his words make on paper." The voice that we hear is what distinguishes one writer from another; and it is one good reason why, to get a good sense of a writer's style, we should read his work aloud. Beyond this concern for hearing what language can do, White notes that a writer's style "reveals something of his spirit, his habits, his capacities, his bias . . . it is the Self escaping into the open." And, as White suggests, this Self cannot be hidden, for a writer's style "reveals his identity as surely as would his fingerprints."

Recognizing that writing is hard work requiring endurance, thought, and revision ("revising is part of writing"), White advises that the beginning writer let his ear be his guide, that he avoid all tricks and mannerisms, that he see writing as "one way to go about thinking," and, finally, that he achieve style both by affecting none and by believing "in the truth and worth of the scrawl."

Throughout his years as a writer, White has often been asked for advice about writing. To one seeker he wrote: "Remember that writing is translation, and the opus to be translated is yourself." On another occasion he responded to a seventeen-year-old girl this way:

You asked me about writing—how I did it. There is no trick to it. If you like to write and want to write, you write, no matter where you are or what else you are doing or whether anyone pays any heed. . . . If you want to write about feelings, about the end of summer, about growing, write about it. A great deal of writing is not "plotted"—most of my essays have no plot structure, they are a ramble in the woods, or a ramble in the basement of my mind.

There is a naturalness, an ease about White's writing, both in these offhand remarks from his letters and in his more elaborately plotted essays. It is an case that derives in part from a refusal to be either pompous or pedantic; it is an ease that derives also from a consistent attempt to be honest, to achieve the candor he admires in Montaigne; and it is a naturalness that is reflected in his style, a style that mingles the high subject and the low, the big word and the small, without flamboyance or ostentation. White's style, in short, is a badge of his character—intelligent, honest, witty, exact, and fundamentally endearing.

The Essayist

1   The essayist is a self-liberated man, sustained by the childish belief that everything he thinks about, everything that happens to him, is of general interest. He is a fellow who thoroughly enjoys his work, just as people who take bird walks enjoy theirs. Each new excursion of the essayist, each new "attempt," differs from the last and takes him into new country. This delights him. Only a person who is congenitally self-centered has the effrontery and the stamina to write essays.

2   There are as many kinds of essays as there are human attitudes or poses, as many essay flavors as there are Howard Johnson ice creams. The essayist arises in the morning and, if he has work to do, selects his garb from an unusually extensive wardrobe: he can pull on any sort of shirt, be any sort of person, according to his mood or his subject matter—philosopher, scold, jester, raconteur, confidant, pundit, devil's advocate, enthusiast. I like the essay, have always liked it, and even as a child was at work, attempting to inflict my young thoughts and experiences on others by putting them on paper. I early broke into print in the pages of *St. Nicholas.* I tend still to fall back on the essay form (or lack of form) when an idea strikes me, but I am not fooled about the place of the essay in twentieth-century American letters—it stands a short distance down the line. The essayist, unlike the novelist, the poet, and the playwright, must be content in his self-imposed role of second-class citizen. A writer who has his sights trained on the Nobel Prize or other earthly triumphs had best write a novel, a poem, or a play, and leave the essayist to ramble about, content with living a free life and enjoying the satisfactions of a somewhat

undisciplined existence. (Dr. Johnson called the essay "an irregular, undigested piece"; this happy practitioner has no wish to quarrel with the good doctor's characterization.)

3   There is one thing the essayist cannot do, though—he cannot indulge himself in deceit or in concealment, for he will be found out in no time. Desmond MacCarthy, in his introductory remarks to the 1928 E. P. Dutton & Company edition of Montaigne, observes that Montaigne "had the gift of natural candour. . . ." It is the basic ingredient. And even the essayist's escape from discipline is only a partial escape: the essay, although a relaxed form, imposes its own disciplines, raises its own problems, and these disciplines and problems soon become apparent and (we all hope) act as a deterrent to anyone wielding a pen merely because he entertains random thoughts or is in a happy or wandering mood.

4   I think some people find the essay the last resort of the egoist, a much too self-conscious and self-serving form for their taste; they feel that it is presumptuous of a writer to assume that his little excursions or his small observations will interest the reader. There is some justice in their complaint. I have always been aware that I am by nature self-absorbed and egotistical; to write of myself to the extent I have done indicates a too great attention to my own life, not enough to the lives of others. I have worn many shirts, and not all of them have been a good fit. But when I am discouraged or downcast I need only fling open the door of my closet, and there, hidden behind everything else, hangs the mantle of Michel de Montaigne, smelling slightly of camphor.

5   The essays in this collection cover a long expanse of time, a wide variety of subjects. I have chosen the ones that have amused me in the rereading, along with a few that seemed to have the odor of durability clinging to them. Some, like "Here is New York," have been seriously affected by the passage of time and now stand as period pieces. I wrote about New York in the summer of 1948, during a hot spell. The city I described has disappeared, and another city has emerged in its place—one that I'm not familiar with. But I remember the former one, with longing and with love. David McCord, in his book *About Boston* tells of a journalist from abroad visiting this country and seeing New York for the first time. He reported that it was "inspiring but temporary in appearance." I know what he means. The last time I visited New York, it seemed to have suffered a personality change, as though it had a brain tumor as yet undetected.

6   Two of the Florida pieces have likewise experienced a sea change. My remarks about the condition of the black race in the South have happily been nullified, and the pieces are merely prophetic, not definitive.

7   To assemble these essays I have rifled my other books and have added a number of pieces that are appearing for the first time between covers. Except for extracting three chapters, I have let "One Man's Meat" alone, since it is a sustained report of about five years of country living—a report I prefer not to tamper with. The arrangement of the book is by subject matter or by mood or by place, not by chronology. Some of the pieces in the book carry a dateline, some do not. Chronology enters into the scheme, but neither the book nor its sections are perfectly chronological. Sometimes the reader will find me in the city when he thinks I am in the country, and the other way round. This may cause a mild confusion; it is unavoidable and easily explained. I spent a large part of the first half of my life as a city dweller, a large part of the second half as a countryman. In between, there were periods when nobody, including myself, quite knew (or cared) where I was: I thrashed back and forth between Maine and New York for reasons that seemed compelling at the time. Money entered into it, affection for *The New Yorker* magazine entered in. And affection for the city.

8   I have finally come to rest.

QUESTIONS

1. Why does White write? What image of the writer does he present? Why do you write, and more generally, why does anybody write?

2. What does White enjoy about being an essayist? What does he mean when he says that the essayist is "self-liberated"? Liberated from what and for what?

3. White defines an essay as an "attempt" and an "excursion." An attempt at what and an excursion where? And for what purpose?

4. What, according to White, distinguishes the essay from the novel, the story, and the poem? Do you agree with White's (and Dr. Johnson's) characterization of the essay as "an irregular undigested piece"? Why or why not?

5. At more than one point in this essay, White suggests that essayists are egoists. Is White an egocentric writer? Are you? Explain.

6. Explain the point of White's comparisons in paragraph 2, the comparisons between essays and ice cream, and between essays and clothes.

7. "The Essayist" can be divided into two parts: paragraphs 1–4 and paragraphs 5–8. What are the purpose and the point of each part?

Suggestions for Writing

A. White mentions that the essential characteristic of any essayist must be "candor." Discuss why you think this is or is not an essential quality of good writing. Include some discussion of other qualities you think a good essayist ought to possess, and why.

B. Examine the writing of one of the authors in this book for one or more of the following qualities: candor, humor, wit, subtlety, charm, egotism, arrogance, irony, satire, mystery, power.

C. White identifies himself as an essayist, a writer of essays. This is an important aspect of his self-image. Think of some aspect of your identity, or think of something you do that is important to your sense of who and what you are. Write an essay on the meaning and value of this— whatever it is.

The Sea and the Wind
That Blows

---

1 Waking or sleeping, I dream of boats—usually of rather small boats under a slight press of sail. When I think how great a part of my life has been spent dreaming the hours away and how much of this total dream life has concerned small craft, I wonder about the state of my health, for I am told that it is not a good sign to be always voyaging into unreality, driven by imaginary breezes.

2 I have noticed that most men, when they enter a barber shop and must wait their turn, drop into a chair and pick up a magazine. I simply sit down and pick up the thread of my sea wandering, which began more than fifty years ago and is not quite ended. There is hardly a waiting room in the East that has not served as my cockpit, whether I was waiting to board a train or to

see a dentist. And I am usually still trimming sheets when the train starts or the drill begins to whine.

3   If a man must be obsessed by something, I suppose a boat is as good as anything, perhaps a bit better than most. A small sailing craft is not only beautiful, it is seductive and full of strange promise and the hint of trouble. If it happens to be an auxiliary cruising boat, it is without question the most compact and ingenious arrangement for living ever devised by the restless mind of man—a home that is stable without being stationary, shaped less like a box than like a fish or a bird or a girl, and in which the homeowner can remove his daily affairs as far from shore as he has the nerve to take them, close-hauled or running free—parlor, bedroom, and bath, suspended and alive.

4   Men who ache all over for tidiness and compactness in their lives often find relief for their pain in the cabin of a thirty-foot sailboat at anchor in a sheltered cove. Here the sprawling panoply of The Home is compressed in orderly miniature and liquid delirium, suspended between the bottom of the sea and the top of the sky, ready to move on in the morning by the miracle of canvas and the witchcraft of rope. It is small wonder that men hold boats in the secret place of their mind, almost from the cradle to the grave.

5   Along with my dream of boats has gone the ownership of boats, a long succession of them upon the surface of the sea, many of them makeshift and crank. Since childhood I have managed to have some sort of sailing craft and to raise a sail in fear. Now, in my seventies, I still own a boat, still raise my sail in fear in answer to the summons of the unforgiving sea. Why does the sea attract me in the way it does? Whence comes this compulsion to hoist a sail, actually or in dream? My first encounter with the sea was a case of hate at first sight. I was taken, at the age of four, to a bathing beach in New Rochelle. Everything about the experience frightened and repelled me: the taste of salt in my mouth, the foul chill of the wooden bathhouse, the littered sand, the stench of the tide flats. I came away hating and fearing the sea. Later, I found that what I had feared and hated, I now feared and loved.

6   I returned to the sea of necessity, because it would support a boat; and although I knew little of boats, I could not get them out of my thoughts. I became a pelagic boy. The sea became my unspoken challenge: the wind, the tide, the fog, the ledge, the bell,

the gull that cried help, the never-ending threat and bluff of weather. Once having permitted the wind to enter the belly of my sail, I was not able to quit the helm; it was as though I had seized hold of a high-tension wire and could not let go.

7   I liked to sail alone. The sea was the same as a girl to me—I did not want anyone else along. Lacking instruction, I invented ways of getting things done, and usually ended by doing them in a rather queer fashion, and so did not learn to sail properly, and still cannot sail well, although I have been at it all my life. I was twenty before I discovered that charts existed; all my navigating up to that time was done with the wariness and the ignorance of the early explorers. I was thirty before I learned to hang a coiled halyard on its cleat as it should be done. Until then I simply coiled it down on deck and dumped the coil. I was always in trouble and always returned, seeking more trouble. Sailing became a compulsion: there lay the boat, swinging to her mooring, there blew the wind; I had no choice but to go. My earliest boats were so small that when the wind failed, or when I failed, I could switch to manual control—I could paddle or row home. But then I graduated to boats that only the wind was strong enough to move. When I first dropped off my mooring in such a boat, I was an hour getting up the nerve to cast off the pennant. Even now, with a thousand little voyages notched in my belt, I still feel a memorial chill on casting off, as the gulls jeer and the empty mainsail claps.

8   Of late years, I have noticed that my sailing has increasingly become a compulsive activity rather than a simple source of pleasure. There lies the boat, there blows the morning breeze— it is a point of honor, now, to go. I am like an alcoholic who cannot put his bottle out of his life. With me, I cannot not sail. Yet I know well enough that I have lost touch with the wind and, in fact, do not like the wind anymore. It jiggles me up, the wind does, and what I really love are windless days, when all is peace. There is a great question in my mind whether a man who is against wind should longer try to sail a boat. But this is an intellectual response —the old yearning is still in me, belonging to the past, to youth, and so I am torn between past and present, a common disease of later life.

9   When does a man quit the sea? How dizzy, how bumbling must he be? Does he quit while he's ahead, or wait till he makes some major mistake, like falling overboard or being flattened by an accidental jibe? This past winter I spent hours arguing the

question with myself. Finally, deciding that I had come to the end
of the road, I wrote a note to the boatyard, putting my boat up for
sale. I said I was "coming off the water." But as I typed the sentence, I doubted that I meant a word of it.

10   If no buyer turns up, I know what will happen: I will instruct
the yard to put her in again—"just till somebody comes along."
And then there will be the old uneasiness, the old uncertainty, as
the mild southeast breeze ruffles the cove, a gentle, steady, morning breeze, bringing the taint of the distant wet world, the smell
that takes a man back to the very beginning of time, linking him
to all that has gone before. There will lie the sloop, there will blow
the wind, once more I will get under way. And as I reach across to
the red nun off the Torry Islands, dodging the trap buoys and tog-
gles, the shags gathered on the ledge will note my passage. "There
goes the old boy again," they will say. "One more rounding of his
little Horn, one more conquest of his Roaring Forties." And with
the tiller in my hand, I'll feel again the wind imparting life to a
boat, will smell again the old menace, the one that imparts life to
me: the cruel beauty of the salt world, the barnacle's tiny knives,
the sharp spine of the urchin, the stinger of the sun jelly, the claw
of the crab.

QUESTIONS

Ideas

1. How does White suggest the strength of his attraction to sailing?
   What, specifically, attracts him?

2. There is evidence that White is writing of more than his love of sailing. What else is his subject? Where do you find hints of deeper
   meanings?

Organization

3. White begins by writing that he often dreams of sailing. Where does
   he go from there? Chart the course of White's thought by identifying how he gets from one aspect of his subject to another.

4. The essay can be divided into three sections: paragraphs 1–4, 5–7,
   and 8–10. What are the concerns of each section and how are the
   sections related?

Sentences

5. In paragraphs 5 and 6 White stacks details, piling them up behind a
    colon. Examine the following examples:

    (a) Everything about the experience frightened and repelled me:
         the taste of salt in my mouth,
         the foul chill of the wooden bathhouse,
         the littered sand,
         the stench of the tide flats.

    Should White have put the word "and" between the last two details?

    (b) The sea became my unspoken challenge:
                    the wind,
                    the tide,
                    the fog,
                    the ledge,
                    the bell,
                    the gull that cried help,
                    the never-ending threat and bluff of weather.

    Would it make much difference if the details were reordered? Try
    moving the items around. Compare your versions with those of
    other students and with White's original. Which version do you pre-
    fer and why?

    (c) And with the tiller in my hand
                 I'll feel again the wind imparting life to a boat,
                 will smell again the old menace,
                    the one that imparts life to me:
                        the cruel beauty of the salt world,
                        the barnacle's tiny knives,
                        the sharp spine of the urchin,
                        the stinger of the sun jelly,
                        the claw of the crab.

    In this last example you can see the balance of phrasing White
    achieves in the second and third lines and in the third and fourth,
    and of course in the stacked details of lines 5–9.

6. Twice in the essay, in paragraphs 5 and 9, White strings questions
    together. Why? What do these questions accomplish? Would a con-
    version to statements alter the meaning or change the effect of
    either paragraph? Why or why not?

7. As the final sentence of paragraph 4 White wrote:

          It is small wonder that men hold boats in the secret place of
       their mind, almost from the cradle to the grave.

    How do these revisions compare with White's original?

    (a) It is small wonder that boats are so important to men.

(b) It is small wonder that men hold boats in such high regard.

Reread this sentence in context (paragraph 4). What unusual words and phrases provide a contrasting backdrop to its easy familiarity? What other conversational phrases occur in the paragraph?

8. In paragraph 8 White writes a brief striking sentence:

With me, I cannot not sail.

If we eliminate the double negative we get: With me, I can sail. What is the difference?

Words

9. White uses many specific details and much concrete language. Select one passage in which precise, specific language enables you to envision or imagine what White describes.

10. Throughout the essay, White uses comparisons—for different reasons and with different effects. Explain the meaning and the feeling behind each of the following comparisons:

   a) the miracle of canvas and the witchcraft of rope. (4)
   b) I am like an alcoholic who cannot put his bottle out of his life. (8)
   c) it was as though I had seized hold of a high-tension wire and could not let go. (6)

What comparison is developed in paragraph 3? What does it imply about White's attitude toward boats and the sea?

11. In the final paragraph, you will notice quotation marks around some phrases and sentences. Why are they there? Can they be omitted?

Suggestions for Writing

A. In the beginning and at the end of paragraph 5 White repeats words and phrases. Rewrite the paragraph without the repetitions. Compare your version with those of other students and with White's paragraph.

B. Write imitations of the sentences in questions 5, 6, 7, and 8.

C. Write an imitation of either paragraph 5 or paragraph 9.

D. Most of us are strongly attracted to some special activity or hobby. In an essay, discuss one of your favorite activities, explaining what draws you to it. Try to explain why it attracts you as powerfully as it does.

Death of a Pig

Autumn 1947

1   I spent several days and nights in mid-September with an ailing pig and I feel driven to account for this stretch of time, more particularly since the pig died at last, and I lived, and things might easily have gone the other way round and none left to do the accounting. Even now, so close to the event, I cannot recall the hours sharply and am not ready to say whether death came on the third night or the fourth night. This uncertainty afflicts me with a sense of personal deterioration; if I were in decent health I would know how many nights I had sat up with a pig.

2   The scheme of buying a spring pig in blossomtime, feeding it through summer and fall, and butchering it when the solid cold weather arrives, is a familiar scheme to me and follows an antique pattern. It is a tragedy enacted on most farms with perfect fidelity to the original script. The murder, being premeditated, is in the first degree but is quick and skillful, and the smoked bacon and ham provide a ceremonial ending whose fitness is seldom questioned.

3   Once in a while something slips—one of the actors goes up in his lines and the whole performance stumbles and halts. My pig simply failed to show up for a meal. The alarm spread rapidly. The classic outline of the tragedy was lost. I found myself cast suddenly in the role of pig's friend and physician—a farcical character with an enema bag for a prop. I had a presentiment, the very first afternoon, that the play would never regain its balance and that my sympathies were now wholly with the pig. This was slapstick—the sort of dramatic treatment that instantly appealed to my old dachshund, Fred, who joined the vigil, held the bag, and, when all was over, presided at the interment. When we slid the body into the grave, we both were shaken to the core. The loss we felt was not the loss of ham but the loss of pig. He had evidently become precious to me, not that he represented a distant nourishment in a hungry time, but that he had suffered in a suffering world. But I'm running ahead of my story and shall have to go back.

4   My pigpen is at the bottom of an old orchard below the house. The pigs I have raised have lived in a faded building that

once was an ice-house. There is a pleasant yard to move about in, shaded by an apple tree that overhangs the low rail fence. A pig couldn't ask for anything better—or none has, at any rate. The sawdust in the icehouse makes a comfortable bottom in which to root, and a warm bed. This sawdust, however, came under suspicion when the pig took sick. One of my neighbors said he thought the pig would have done better on new ground—the same principle that applies in planting potatoes. He said there might be something unhealthy about that sawdust, that he never thought well of sawdust.

5　　It was about four o'clock in the afternoon when I first noticed that there was something wrong with the pig. He failed to appear at the trough for his supper, and when a pig (or a child) refuses supper a chill wave of fear runs through any household, or ice-household. After examining my pig, who was stretched out in the sawdust inside the building, I went to the phone and cranked it four times. Mr. Dameron answered. "What's good for a sick pig?" I asked. (There is never any identification needed on a country phone; the person on the other end knows who is talking by the sound of the voice and by the character of the question.)

6　　"I don't know, I never had a sick pig," said Mr. Dameron, "but I can find out quick enough. You hang up and I'll call Henry."

7　　Mr. Dameron was back on the line again in five minutes. "Henry says roll him over on his back and give him two ounces of castor oil or sweet oil, and if that doesn't do the trick give him an injection of soapy water. He says he's almost sure the pig's plugged up, and even if he's wrong, it can't do any harm."

8　　I thanked Mr. Dameron. I didn't go right down to the pig, though. I sank into a chair and sat still for a few minutes to think about my troubles, and then I got up and went to the barn, catching up on some odds and ends that needed tending to. Unconsciously I held off, for an hour, the deed by which I would officially recognize the collapse of the performance of raising a pig; I wanted no interruption in the regularity of feeding, the steadiness of growth, the even succession of days. I wanted no interruption, wanted no oil, no deviation. I just wanted to keep on raising a pig, full meal after full meal, spring into summer into fall. I didn't even know whether there were two ounces of castor oil on the place.

9　　Shortly after five o'clock I remembered that we had been

invited out to dinner that night and realized that if I were to dose
a pig there was no time to lose. The dinner date seemed a familiar
conflict: I move in a desultory society and often a week or two will
roll by without my going to anybody's house to dinner or anyone's
coming to mine, but when an occasion does arise, and I am summoned, something usually turns up (an hour or two in advance)
to make all human intercourse seem vastly inappropriate. I have
come to believe that there is in hostesses a special power of divina-
tion, and that they deliberately arrange dinners to coincide with
pig failure or some other sort of failure. At any rate, it was after
five o'clock and I knew I could put off no longer the evil hour.

10   When my son and I arrived at the pigyard, armed with a
small bottle of castor oil and a length of clothesline, the pig had
emerged from his house and was standing in the middle of his
yard, listlessly. He gave us a slim greeting. I could see that he felt
uncomfortable and uncertain. I had brought the clothesline
thinking I'd have to tie him (the pig weighed more than a hundred pounds) but we never used it. My son reached down,
grabbed both front legs, upset him quickly, and when he opened
his mouth to scream I turned the oil into his throat—a pink, cor-
rugated area I had never seen before. I had just time to read the
label while the neck of the bottle was in his mouth. It said
Puretest. The screams, slightly muffled by oil, were pitched in the
hysterically high range of pig-sound, as though torture were being
carried out, but they didn't last long: it was all over rather suddenly, and, his legs released, the pig righted himself.

11   In the upset position the corners of his mouth had been
turned down, giving him a frowning expression. Back on his feet
again, he regained the set smile that a pig wears even in sickness.
He stood his ground, sucking slightly at the residue of oil; a few
drops leaked out of his lips while his wicked eyes, shaded by their
coy little lashes, turned on me in disgust and hatred. I scratched
him gently with oily fingers and he remained quiet, as though trying to recall the satisfaction of being scratched when in health,
and seeming to rehearse in his mind the indignity to which he
had just been subjected. I noticed, as I stood there, four or five
small dark spots on his back near the tail end, reddish brown in
color, each about the size of a housefly. I could not make out
what they were. They did not look troublesome but at the same
time they did not look like mere surface bruises or chafe marks.
Rather they seemed blemishes of internal origin. His stiff white

bristles almost completely hid them and I had to part the bristles with my fingers to get a good look.

12   Several hours later, a few minutes before midnight, having dined well and at someone else's expense, I returned to the pig-house with a flashlight. The patient was asleep. Kneeling, I felt his ears (as you might put your hand on the forehead of a child) and they seemed cool, and then with the light made a careful examination of the yard and the house for sign that the oil had worked. I found none and went to bed.

13   We had been having an unseasonable spell of weather—hot, close days, with the fog shutting in every night, scaling for a few hours in midday, then creeping back again at dark, drifting in first over the trees on the point, then suddenly blowing across the fields, blotting out the world and taking possession of houses, men, and animals. Everyone kept hoping for a break, but the break failed to come. Next day was another hot one. I visited the pig before breakfast and tried to tempt him with a little milk in his trough. He just stared at it, while I made a sucking sound through my teeth to remind him of past pleasures of the feast. With very small, timid pigs, weanlings, this ruse is often quite successful and will encourage them to eat; but with a large, sick pig the ruse is senseless and the sound I made must have made him feel, if anything, more miserable. He not only did not crave food, he felt a positive revulsion to it. I found a place under the apple tree where he had vomited in the night.

14   At this point, although a depression had settled over me, I didn't suppose that I was going to lose my pig. From the lustiness of a healthy pig a man derives a feeling of personal lustiness; the stuff that goes into the trough and is received with such enthusiasm is an earnest of some later feast of his own, and when this suddenly comes to an end and the food lies stale and untouched, souring in the sun, the pig's imbalance becomes the man's, vicariously, and life seems insecure, displaced, transitory.

15   As my own spirits declined, along with the pig's, the spirits of my vile old dachshund rose. The frequency of our trips down the footpath through the orchard to the pigyard delighted him, although he suffers greatly from arthritis, moves with difficulty, and would be bedridden if he could find anyone willing to serve him meals on a tray.

16   He never missed a chance to visit the pig with me, and he

made many professional calls on his own. You could see him down there at all hours, his white face parting the grass along the fence as he wobbled and stumbled about, his stethoscope dangling—a happy quack, writing his villainous prescriptions and grinning his corrosive grin. When the enema bag appeared, and the bucket of warm suds, his happiness was complete, and he managed to squeeze his enormous body between the two lowest rails of the yard and then assumed full charge of the irrigation. Once, when I lowered the bag to check the flow, he reached in and hurriedly drank a few mouthfuls of the suds to test their potency. I have noticed that Fred will feverishly consume any substance that is associated with trouble—the bitter flavor is to his liking. When the bag was above reach, he concentrated on the pig and was everywhere at once, a tower of strength and inconvenience. The pig, curiously enough, stood rather quietly through this colonic carnival, and the enema, though ineffective, was not as difficult as I had anticipated.

17   I discovered, though, that once having given a pig an enema there is no turning back, no chance of resuming one of life's more stereotyped roles. The pig's lot and mine were inextricably bound now, as though the rubber tube were the silver cord. From then until the time of his death I held the pig steadily in the bowl of my mind; the task of trying to deliver him from his misery became a strong obsession. His suffering soon became the embodiment of all earthly wretchedness. Along toward the end of the afternoon, defeated in physicking, I phoned the veterinary twenty miles away and placed the case formally in his hands. He was full of questions, and when I casually mentioned the dark spots on the pig's back, his voice changed its tone.

18   "I don't want to scare you," he said, "but when there are spots, erysipelas has to be considered."

19   Together we considered erysipelas, with frequent interruptions from the telephone operator, who wasn't sure the connection had been established.

20   "If a pig has erysipelas can he give it to a person?" I asked.

21   "Yes, he can," replied the vet.

22   "Have they answered?" asked the operator.

23   "Yes, they have," I said. Then I addressed the vet again. "You better come over here and examine this pig right away."

24   "I can't come myself," said the vet, "but McFarland can come this evening if that's all right. Mac knows more about pigs than I

do anyway. You needn't worry too much about the spots. To indicate erysipelas they would have to be deep hemorrhagic infarcts."

25   "Deep hemorrhagic what?" I asked.

26   "Infarcts," said the vet.

27   "Have they answered?" asked the operator.

28   "Well," I said, "I don't know what you'd call these spots, except they're about the size of a housefly. If the pig has erysipelas I guess I have it, too, by this time, because we've been very close lately."

29   "McFarland will be over," said the vet.

30   I hung up. My throat felt dry and I went to the cupboard and got a bottle of whiskey. Deep hemorrhagic infarcts—the phrase began fastening its hooks in my head. I had assumed that there could be nothing much wrong with a pig during the months it was being groomed for murder; my confidence in the essential health and endurance of pigs had been strong and deep, particularly in the health of pigs that belonged to me and that were part of my proud scheme. The awakening had been violent and I minded it all the more because I knew that what could be true of my pig could be true also of the rest of my tidy world. I tried to put this distasteful idea from me, but it kept recurring. I took a short drink of the whiskey and then, although I wanted to go down to the yard and look for fresh signs, I was scared to. I was certain I had erysipelas.

31   It was long after dark and the supper dishes had been put away when a car drove in and McFarland got out. He had a girl with him. I could just make her out in the darkness—she seemed young and pretty. "This is Miss Owen," he said. "We've been having a picnic supper on the shore, that's why I'm late."

32   McFarland stood in the driveway and stripped off his jacket, then his shirt. His stocky arms and capable hands showed up in my flashlight's gleam as I helped him find his coverall and get zipped up. The rear seat of his car contained an astonishing amount of paraphernalia, which he soon overhauled, selecting a chain, a syringe, a bottle of oil, a rubber tube, and some other things I couldn't identify. Miss Owen said she'd go along with us and see the pig. I led the way down the warm slope of the orchard, my light picking out the path for them, and we all three climbed the fence, entered the pighouse, and squatted by the pig while McFarland took a rectal reading. My flashlight picked up the glitter of an engagement ring on the girl's hand.

33   "No elevation," said McFarland, twisting the thermometer in the light. "You needn't worry about erysipelas." He ran his hand slowly over the pig's stomach and at one point the pig cried out in pain.

34   "Poor piggledy-wiggledy!" said Miss Owen.

35   The treatment I had been giving the pig for two days was then repeated, somewhat more expertly, by the doctor, Miss Owen and I handing him things as he needed them—holding the chain that he had looped around the pig's upper jaw, holding the syringe, holding the bottle stopper, the end of the tube, all of us working in darkness and in comfort, working with the instinctive teamwork induced by emergency conditions, the pig unprotesting, the house shadowy, protecting, intimate. I went to bed tired but with a feeling of relief that I had turned over part of the responsibility of the case to a licensed doctor. I was beginning to think, though, that the pig was not going to live.

36   He died twenty-four hours later, or it might have been forty-eight—there is a blur in time here, and I may have lost or picked up a day in the telling and the pig one in the dying. At intervals during the last day I took cool fresh water down to him and at such times as he found the strength to get to his feet he would stand with head in the pail and snuffle his snout around. He drank a few sips but no more; yet it seemed to comfort him to dip his nose in water and bobble it about, sucking in and blowing out through his teeth. Much of the time, now, he lay indoors half buried in sawdust. Once, near the last, while I was attending him I saw him try to make a bed for himself but he lacked the strength, and when he set his snout into the dust he was unable to plow even the little furrow he needed to lie down in.

37   He came out of the house to die. When I went down, before going to bed, he lay stretched in the yard a few feet from the door. I knelt, saw that he was dead, and left him there; his face had a mild look, expressive neither of deep peace nor of deep suffering, although I think he had suffered a good deal. I went back up to the house and to bed, and cried internally—deep hemorrhagic intears. I didn't wake till nearly eight the next morning, and when I looked out the open window the grave was already being dug, down beyond the dump under a wild apple. I could hear the spade strike against the small rocks that blocked the way. Never send to know for whom the grave is dug, I said to myself,

it's dug for thee. Fred, I well knew, was supervising the work of digging, so I ate breakfast slowly.

38   It was a Saturday morning. The thicket in which I found the gravediggers at work was dark and warm, the sky overcast. Here, among alders and young hackmatacks, at the foot of the apple tree, Lennie had dug a beautiful hole, five feet long, three feet wide, three feet deep. He was standing in it, removing the last spadefuls of earth while Fred patrolled the brink in simple but impressive circles, disturbing the loose earth of the mound so that it trickled back in. There had been no rain in weeks and the soil, even three feet down, was dry and powdery. As I stood and stared, an enormous earthworm which had been partially exposed by the spade at the bottom dug itself deeper and made a slow withdrawal, seeking even remoter moistures at even lonelier depths. And just as Lennie stepped out and rested his spade against the tree and lit a cigarette, a small green apple separated itself from a branch overhead and fell into the hole. Everything about this last scene seemed overwritten—the dismal sky, the shabby woods, the imminence of rain, the worm (legendary bedfellow of the dead), the apple (conventional garnish of a pig).

39   But even so, there was a directness and dispatch about animal burial, I thought, that made it a more decent affair than human burial: there was no stopover in the undertaker's foul parlor, no wreath nor spray; and when we hitched a line to the pig's hind legs and dragged him swiftly from his yard, throwing our weight into the harness and leaving a wake of crushed grass and smoothed rubble over the dump, ours was a businesslike procession, with Fred, the dishonorable pallbearer, staggering along in the rear, his perverse bereavement showing in every seam in his face; and the post-mortem performed handily and swiftly right at the edge of the grave, so that the inwards that had caused the pig's death preceded him into the ground and he lay at last resting squarely on the cause of his own undoing.

40   I threw in the first shovelful, and then we worked rapidly and without talk, until the job was complete. I picked up the rope, made it fast to Fred's collar (he is a notorious ghoul), and we all three filed back up the path to the house, Fred bringing up the rear and holding back every inch of the way, feigning unusual stiffness. I noticed that although he weighed far less than the pig, he was harder to drag, being possessed of the vital spark.

41   The news of the death of my pig traveled fast and far, and I

received many expressions of sympathy from friends and neighbors, for no one took the event lightly and the premature expiration of a pig is, I soon discovered, a departure which the community marks solemnly on its calendar, a sorrow in which it feels fully involved. I have written this account in penitence and in grief, as a man who failed to raise his pig, and to explain my deviation from the classic course of so many raised pigs. The grave in the woods is unmarked, but Fred can direct the mourner to it unerringly and with immense good will, and I know he and I shall often revisit it, singly and together, in seasons of reflection and despair, on flagless memorial days of our own choosing.

QUESTIONS

Ideas

1. What is the tone of the opening paragraph? Of the second paragraph? How far is this tone sustained throughout the essay? In what ways is it modified?

2. What is the main point of White's essay? What is the essayist's purpose?

3. What connections does White make between pigs and men? Why do the pig's illness and death matter to him?

Organization

4. The essay could easily begin with paragraph 2. Why? Could it begin as readily with paragraph 3 or 4? Why or why not?

5. How is the essay organized? How important is chronology to the essay?

Sentences

6. As the final sentence of paragraph 9 White has written:

   > At any rate, it was after five o'clock and I knew I could put off no longer the evil hour.

   Consider this alternative:

   > At any rate it was after five o'clock and I knew I could put off the evil hour no longer.

7. Analyze the following sentence, paying attention particularly to its use of present participles (*ing* verbs):

> We had been having an unseasonable spell of weather—hot,
> close days, with the fog shutting in every night,
> scaling for a few hours in midday,
> then creeping back again at dark,
> drifting in first over the trees on the point,
> then suddenly blowing across the fields,
> blotting out the world
> and taking possession of houses,
> men,
> and animals.

Words

8. What is the effect of White's comparing the pig to a child in paragraphs 5 and 12? What other comparisons with the pig does White make? What is their point and how effective are they?

9. Comment on the underlined words in the following phrases:

> [Fred] was everywhere at once, a tower of strength and inconvenience. (16)
> I held the pig steadily in the bowl of my mind. (17)
> The pig's imbalance becomes the man's, vicariously. (14)
> He would stand with his head in the pail and snuffle his snout around. (36)
> I went back up to the house and cried internally—deep hemorrhagic intears. (37)

Suggestions for Writing

A. Write imitations of any two of White's sentences.

B. Write an essay recounting the death of an animal.

C. Compare White's treatment of the death of a pig with Dillard's of the death of a moth. Consider the writers' purposes, tones, ideas, and styles.

The Ring of Time

Fiddler Bayou, March 22, 1956

1   After the lions had returned to their cages, creeping angrily through the chutes, a little bunch of us drifted away and into an open doorway nearby, where we stood for a while in semi-

darkness, watching a big brown circus horse go harumphing around the practice ring. His trainer was a woman of about forty, and the two of them, horse and woman, seemed caught up in one of those desultory treadmills of afternoon from which there is no apparent escape. The day was hot, and we kibitzers were grateful to be briefly out of the sun's glare. The long rein, or tape, by which the woman guided her charge counterclockwise in his dull career formed the radius of their private circle, of which she was the revolving center; and she, too, stepped a tiny circumference of her own, in order to accommodate the horse and allow him his maximum scope. She had on a short-skirted costume and a conical straw hat. Her legs were bare and she wore high heels, which probed deep into the loose tanbark and kept her ankles in a state of constant turmoil. The great size and meekness of the horse, the repetitious exercise, the heat of the afternoon, all exerted a hypnotic charm that invited boredom; we spectators were experiencing a languor—we neither expected relief nor felt entitled to any. We had paid a dollar to get into the grounds, to be sure, but we had got our dollar's worth a few minutes before, when the lion tamer's whiplash had got caught around a toe of one of the lions. What more did we want for a dollar?

2   Behind me I heard someone say, "Excuse me, please," in a low voice. She was halfway into the building when I turned and saw her—a girl of sixteen or seventeen, politely threading her way through us onlookers who blocked the entrance. As she emerged in front of us, I saw that she was barefoot, her dirty little feet fighting the uneven ground. In most respects she was like any of two or three dozen showgirls you encounter if you wander about the winter quarters of Mr. John Ringling North's circus, in Sarasota—cleverly proportioned, deeply browned by the sun, dusty, eager, and almost naked. But her grave face and the naturalness of her manner gave her a sort of quick distinction and brought a new note into the gloomy octagonal building where we had all cast our lot for a few moments. As soon as she had squeezed through the crowd, she spoke a word or two to the older woman, whom I took to be her mother, stepped to the ring, and waited while the horse coasted to a stop in front of her. She gave the animal a couple of affectionate swipes on his enormous neck and then swung herself aboard. The horse immediately resumed his rocking canter, the woman goading him on, chanting something that sounded like "Hop! Hop!"

3   In attempting to recapture this mild spectacle, I am merely acting as recording secretary for one of the oldest of societies— the society of those who, at one time or another, have surrendered, without even a show of resistance, to the bedazzlement of a circus rider. As a writing man, or secretary, I have always felt charged with the safekeeping of all unexpected items of worldly or unworldly enchantment, as though I might be held personally responsible if even a small one were to be lost. But it is not easy to communicate anything of this nature. The circus comes as close to being the world in microcosm as anything I know; in a way, it puts all the rest of show business in the shade. Its magic is universal and complex. Out of its wild disorder comes order; from its rank smell rises the good aroma of courage and daring; out of its preliminary shabbiness comes the final splendor. And buried in the familiar boasts of its advance agents lies the modesty of most of its people. For me the circus is at its best before it has been put together. It is at its best at certain moments when it comes to a point, as though a burning glass, in the activity and destiny of a single performer out of so many. One ring is always bigger than three. One rider, one aerialist, is always greater than six. In short, a man has to catch the circus unawares to experience its full impact and share its gaudy dream.

4   The ten-minute ride the girl took achieved—as far as I was concerned, who wasn't looking for it, and quite unbeknownst to her, who wasn't even striving for it—the thing that is sought by performers everywhere, on whatever stage, whether struggling in the tidal currents of Shakespeare or bucking the difficult motion of a horse. I somehow got the idea she was just cadging a ride, improving a shining ten minutes in the diligent way all serious artists seize free moments to hone the blade of their talent and keep themselves in trim. Her brief tour included only elementary postures and tricks, perhaps because they were all she was capable of, perhaps because her warmup at this hour was unscheduled and the ring was not rigged for a real practice session. She swung herself off and on the horse several times, gripping his mane. She did a few knee-stands—or whatever they are called—dropping to her knees and quickly bouncing back up on her feet again. Most of the time she simply rode in a standing position, well aft on the beast, her hands hanging easily at her sides, her head erect, her straw-colored ponytail lightly brushing her shoulders, the blood of exertion showing faintly through the tan of her skin. Twice she

managed a one-foot stance—a sort of ballet pose, with arms outstretched. At one point the neck strap of her bathing suit broke and she went twice around the ring in the classic attitude of a woman making minor repairs to a garment. The fact that she was standing on the back of a moving horse while doing this invested the matter with a clownish significance that perfectly fitted the spirit of the circus—jocund, yet charming. She just rolled the strap into a neat ball and stowed it inside her bodice while the horse rocked and rolled beneath her in dutiful innocence. The bathing suit proved as self-reliant as its owner and stood up well enough without benefit of strap.

5   The richness of the scene was in its plainness, its natural condition—of horse, of ring, of girl, even to the girl's bare feet that gripped the bare back of her proud and ridiculous mount. The enchantment grew not out of anything that happened or was performed but out of something that seemed to go round and around and around with the girl, attending her, a steady gleam in the shape of a circle—a ring of ambition, of happiness, of youth. (And the positive pleasures of equilibrium under difficulties.) In a week or two, all would be changed, all (or almost all) lost: the girl would wear makeup, the horse would wear gold, the ring would be painted, the bark would be clean for the feet of the horse, the girl's feet would be clean for the slippers that she'd wear. All, all would be lost.

6   As I watched with the others, our jaws adroop, our eyes alight, I became painfully conscious of the element of time. Everything in the hideous old building seemed to take the shape of a circle, conforming to the course of the horse. The rider's gaze, as she peered straight ahead, seemed to be circular, as though bent by force of circumstance; then time itself began running in circles, and so the beginning was where the end was, and the two were the same, and one thing ran into the next and time went round and around and got nowhere. The girl wasn't so young that she did not know the delicious satisfaction of having a perfectly behaved body and the fun of using it to do a trick most people can't do, but she was too young to know that time does not really move in a circle at all. I thought: "She will never be as beautiful as this again"—a thought that made me acutely unhappy—and in a flash my mind (which is too much of a busybody to suit me) had projected her twenty five years ahead, and she was now in the center of the ring, on foot, wearing a conical hat and

high-heeled shoes, the image of the older woman, holding the long rein, caught in the treadmill of an afternoon long in the future. "She is at that enviable moment in life [I thought] when she believes she can go once around the ring, make one complete circuit, and at the end be exactly the same age as at the start." Everything in her movements, her expression, told you that for her the ring of time was perfectly formed, changeless, predictable, without beginning or end, like the ring in which she was traveling at this moment with the horse that wallowed under her. And then I slipped back into my trance, and time was circular again—time, pausing quietly with the rest of us, so as not to disturb the balance of a performer.

7   Her ride ended as casually as it had begun. The older woman stopped the horse, and the girl slid to the ground. As she walked toward us to leave, there was a quick, small burst of applause. She smiled broadly, in surprise and pleasure; then her face suddenly regained its gravity and she disappeared through the door.

8   It has been ambitious and plucky of me to attempt to describe what is indescribable, and I have failed, as I knew I would. But I have discharged my duty to my society; and besides, a writer, like an acrobat, must occasionally try a stunt that is too much for him. At any rate, it is worth reporting that long before the circus comes to town, its most notable performances have already been given. Under the bright lights of the finished show, a performer need only reflect the electric candle power that is directed upon him; but in the dark and dirty old training rings and in the makeshift cages, whatever light is generated, whatever excitement, whatever beauty, must come from original sources—from internal fires of professional hunger and delight, from the exuberance and gravity of youth. It is the difference between planetary light and the combustion of stars.

QUESTIONS

Ideas

1. What does White mean by his suggestion in paragraph 3 that the circus is "the world in microcosm"?

2. In what sense is this an essay about the circus, about performance, about time?

3. Has White failed to accomplish what he set out to do (paragraph 8)? What seems to be his purpose in "The Ring of Time"?

4. Twice in the essay White refers to his task and responsibility as a writer. What is his point?

Organization

5. In the opening paragraph White locates and describes the scene. Later, he moves from that initial description to speculation about what he has seen. As you read, or reread, the essay, note which sections are descriptive and which speculative. Explain how the essay as a whole is structured.

6. Try reorganizing the essay by ordering its paragraphs another way: 1, 2, 4, 7, 3, 5, 6, 8. Is there any advantage to reading (and writing) the essay this way? Any disadvantage?

7. What connections exist between the end of the essay and the beginning? Explain why paragraph 8 does or does not sound like a conclusion, an ending.

Sentences

8. The following sentence appears in paragraph 3:

> (1) Out of its wild disorder comes order;
> (2) from its rank smell rises the good aroma of courage and daring;
> (3) out of its preliminary shabbiness comes the final splendor.

Read the sentence aloud as it is written. Then read it aloud as you reorder its three parts. Try a few different combinations (2, 3, 1, 2, 1, 3; 1, 3, 2; 3, 2, 1; 3, 1, 2). Which version(s) do you prefer and why? Besides experimenting with different arrangements of the three major parts of the sentence, you might consider different kinds of word order within each part. The first clause, for example, might be rewritten like this: "Order comes out of its wild disorder"; and the second: "the good aroma of courage and daring rises from its rank smell." How would the third section be rewritten? Which versions of each do you prefer and why?

9. The following sentence, like the sentence discussed in question 8, inverts the regular word order of the English sentence—subject, verb, object. How does the following alteration compare with the sentence as White wrote it?

> *White:* And buried in the familiar boasts of its advance agents lies the modesty of most of its people.

> *Revised:* The modesty of most of its people lies buried in the familiar boasts of its advance agents.

Look at each version in the context in which White's original sentence appears (paragraph 3). Notice what kinds of sentences precede and follow. Then explain which version you prefer.

10. Read paragraph 5 aloud. Mark off the repeated sounds at the level of syllable, phrase, and sentence.

Words

11. Reread the opening paragraph and underline, circle, or list all the words suggesting circularity—all the "circle" words. Why does White include so many of them? And how is the notion of circularity relevant to the ideas and title of the essay?

12. Look through paragraph 6 for echoes and repetitions of the details of the opening paragraph. What is the effect of the repetitions? How are these repetitions of word and phrase related to what White is suggesting about the girl and about time?

13. If paragraph 1 is heavily saturated with "circle" words, primarily nouns, paragraph 2 is noteworthy for its use of precise, vivid verbs. Before you reread the paragraph fill in the blanks in the verb-deleted version below. Compare your choices with White's and with the choices of other students. Discuss the different effects of the various verbs used.

> Behind me I _____ someone _____, "Excuse me, please," in a low voice. She _____ halfway into the building when I turned and _____ her—a girl of sixteen or seventeen, politely _____ her way through us onlookers who _____ the entrance. As she _____ in front of us, I _____ that she _____ barefoot, her dirty little feet _____ the uneven ground. In most respects she _____ like any of two or three dozen showgirls you _____ if you _____ about the winter quarters of Mr. John Ringling North's circus in Sarasota—cleverly proportioned, deeply browned by the sun, dusty, eager, and almost naked. But her grave face and the naturalness of her manner _____ her a sort of quick distinction and _____ a new note into the gloomy octagonal building where we had all _____ our lot for a few moments. As soon as she had _____ through the crowd, she _____ a word or two to the older woman, whom I _____ to be her mother, _____ to the ring, and _____ while the horse _____ to a stop in front of her. She _____ the animal a couple of affectionate swipes on his enormous neck and then _____ herself aboard. The horse immediately _____ his rocking canter, the woman _____ him on, _____ something that sounded like "Hop! Hop!"

14. Paragraph 3 introduces the language of light, which burns so brilliantly in the essay's final sentences. List all the "light" (and "dark")

words you can find in this paragraph. Explain what each of the images means, especially this one: "out of its preliminary shabbiness comes the final splendor."

15. Paragraph 8 contains a number of "light" words. Explain which are literal and which metaphorical. Explain the point of each metaphorical word, especially the following: "whatever light is generated, whatever excitement, whatever beauty, must come from original sources—from internal fires of professional hunger and delight, from the exuberance and gravity of youth. It is the difference between planetary light and the combustion of stars."

Suggestions for Writing

A. Recall an incident in your life which made you feel old, perhaps when something had passed you by, when someone else was moving into the place you once held. You might think, for example, of periods of transition or graduation—from elementary school, from high school, from Little League, Girl Scouts, or something similar. Recreate the scene from your past, its time, place, and tone with concrete details. Weave into your description your insights and speculations on time, change, and age.

B. Write imitations of the sentences discussed in questions 8 and 9.

C. Write an imitation of paragraph 5.

D. Write an analysis of "The Ring of Time." Explain what White is saying in the essay. Discuss his strategy of organization and his use of language. Summarize his main points and paraphrase the essay's most important paragraphs.

Once More to the Lake

August 1941

1   One summer, along about 1904, my father rented a camp on a lake in Maine and took us all there for the month of August. We all got ringworm from some kittens and had to rub Pond's Extract on our arms and legs night and morning, and my father rolled over in a canoe with all his clothes on; but outside of that the vacation was a success and from then on none of us ever thought there was any place in the world like that lake in Maine.

We returned summer after summer—always on August 1 for one month. I have since become a salt-water man, but sometimes in summer there are days when the restlessness of the tides and the fearful cold of the sea water and the incessant wind that blows across the afternoon and into the evening make me wish for the placidity of a lake in the woods. A few weeks ago this feeling got so strong I bought myself a couple of bass hooks and a spinner and returned to the lake where we used to go, for a week's fishing and to revisit old haunts.

2   I took along my son, who had never had any fresh water up his nose and who had seen lily pads only from train windows. On the journey over to the lake I began to wonder what it would be like. I wondered how time would have marred this unique, this holy spot—the coves and streams, the hills that the sun set behind, the camps and the paths behind the camps. I was sure that the tarred road would have found it out, and I wondered in what other ways it would be desolated. It is strange how much you can remember about places like that once you allow your mind to return into the grooves that lead back. You remember one thing, and that suddenly reminds you of another thing. I guess I remembered clearest of all the early mornings, when the lake was cool and motionless, remembered how the bedroom smelled of the lumber it was made of and of the wet woods whose scent entered through the screen. The partitions in the camp were thin and did not extend clear to the top of the rooms, and as I was always the first up I would dress softly so as not to wake the others, and sneak out into the sweet outdoors and start out in the canoe, keeping close along the shore in the long shadows of the pines. I remembered being very careful never to rub my paddle against the gunwale for fear of disturbing the stillness of the cathedral.

3   The lake had never been what you would call a wild lake. There were cottages sprinkled around the shores, and it was in farming country although the shores of the lake were quite heavily wooded. Some of the cottages were owned by nearby farmers, and you would live at the shore and eat your meals at the farmhouse. That's what our family did. But although it wasn't wild, it was a fairly large and undisturbed lake and there were places in it that, to a child at least, seemed infinitely remote and primeval.

4   I was right about the tar: it led to within half a mile of the shore. But when I got back there, with my boy, and we settled into a camp near a farmhouse and into the kind of summertime I had

known, I could tell that it was going to be pretty much the same as
it had been before—I knew it, lying in bed the first morning,
smelling the bedroom and hearing the boy sneak quietly out and
go off along the shore in a boat. I began to sustain the illusion
that he was I, and therefore, by simple transposition, that I was my
father. This sensation persisted, kept cropping up all the time we
were there. It was not an entirely new feeling, but in this setting it
grew much stronger. I seemed to be living a dual existence. I
would be in the middle of some simple act, I would be picking up
a bait box or laying down a table fork, or I would be saying something, and suddenly it would be not I but my father who was saying the words or making the gesture. It gave me a creepy sensation.

5   We went fishing the next morning. I felt the same damp
moss covering the worms in the bait can, and saw the dragonfly
alight on the tip of my rod as it hovered a few inches from the surface of the water. It was the arrival of this fly that convinced me
beyond any doubt that everything was as it always had been, that
the years were a mirage and that there had been no years. The
small waves were the same, chucking the rowboat under the chin
as we fished at anchor, and the boat was the same boat, the same
color green and the ribs broken in the same places, and under
the floorboards the same fresh-water leavings and debris—the
dead helgramite, the wisps of moss, the rusty discarded fishhook,
the dried blood from yesterday's catch. We stared silently at the
tips of our rods, at the dragonflies that came and went. I lowered
the tip of mine into the water, tentatively, pensively dislodging the
fly, which darted two feet away, poised, darted two feet back, and
came to rest again a little farther up the rod. There had been no
years between the ducking of this dragonfly and the other one—
the one that was part of memory. I looked at the boy, who was
silently watching his fly, and it was my hands that held his rod, my
eyes watching. I felt dizzy and didn't know which rod I was at the
end of.

6   We caught two bass, hauling them in briskly as though they
were mackerel, pulling them over the side of the boat in a businesslike manner without any landing net, and stunning them with
a blow on the back of the head. When we got back for a swim
before lunch, the lake was exactly where we had left it, the same
number of inches from the dock, and there was only the merest
suggestion of a breeze. This seemed an utterly enchanted sea, this

lake you could leave to its own devices for a few hours and come
back to, and find that it had not stirred, this constant and trust-
worthy body of water. In the shallows, the dark, water-soaked
sticks and twigs, smooth and old, were undulating in clusters on
the bottom against the clean ribbed sand, and the track of the
mussel was plain. A school of minnows swam by, each minnow
with its small individual shadow, doubling the attendance, so clear
and sharp in the sunlight. Some of the other campers were in
swimming, along the shore, one of them with a cake of soap, and
the water felt thin and clear and unsubstantial. Over the years
there had been this person with the cake of soap, this cultist, and
here he was. There had been no years.

7   Up to the farmhouse to dinner through the teeming, dusty
field, the road under our sneakers was only a two-track road. The
middle track was missing, the one with the marks of the hooves
and the splotches of dried, flaky manure. There had always been
three tracks to choose from in choosing which track to walk in;
now the choice was narrowed down to two. For a moment I
missed terribly the middle alternative. But the way led past the
tennis court, and something about the way it lay there in the sun
reassured me; the tape had loosened along the backline, the
alleys were green with plantains and other weeds, and the net
(installed in June and removed in September) sagged in the dry
noon, and the whole place steamed with midday heat and hunger
and emptiness. There was a choice of pie for dessert, and one was
blueberry and one was apple, and the waitresses were the same
country girls, there having been no passage of time, only the illusion of it as in a dropped curtain—the waitresses were still fifteen;
their hair had been washed, that was the only difference—they
had been to the movies and seen the pretty girls with the clean
hair.

8   Summertime, oh, summertime, pattern of life indelible, the
fadeproof lake, the woods unshatterable, the pasture with the
sweetfern and the juniper forever and ever, summer without end;
this was the background, and the life along the shore was the
design, the cottagers with their innocent and tranquil design,
their tiny docks with the flagpole and the American flag floating
against the white clouds in the blue sky, the little paths over the
roots of the trees leading from camp to camp and the paths leading back to the outhouses and the can of lime for sprinkling, and
at the souvenir counters at the store the miniature birchbark

canoes and the postcards that showed things looking a little better than they looked. This was the American family at play, escaping the city heat, wondering whether the newcomers in the camp at the head of the cove were "common" or "nice," wondering whether it was true that the people who drove up for Sunday dinner at the farmhouse were turned away because there wasn't enough chicken.

9   It seemed to me, as I kept remembering all this, that those times and those summers had been infinitely precious and worth saving. There had been jollity and peace and goodness. The arriving (at the beginning of August) had been so big a business in itself, at the railway station the farm wagon drawn up, the first smell of the pine-laden air, the first glimpse of the smiling farmer, and the great importance of the trunks and your father's enormous authority in such matters, and the feel of the wagon under you for the long ten-mile haul, and at the top of the last long hill catching the first view of the lake after eleven months of not seeing this cherished body of water. The shouts and cries of the other campers when they saw you, and the trunks to be unpacked, to give up their rich burden. (Arriving was less exciting nowadays, when you sneaked up in your car and parked it under a tree near the camp and took out the bags and in five minutes it was all over, no fuss, no loud wonderful fuss about trunks.)

10   Peace and goodness and jollity. The only thing that was wrong now, really, was the sound of the place, an unfamiliar nervous sound of the outboard motors. This was the note that jarred, the one thing that would sometimes break the illusion and set the years moving. In those other summertimes all motors were inboard; and when they were at a little distance, the noise they made was a sedative, an ingredient of summer sleep. They were one-cylinder and two-cylinder engines, and some were make-and-break and some were jump-spark, but they all made a sleepy sound across the lake. The one-lungers throbbed and fluttered, and the twin-cylinder ones purred and purred, and that was a quiet sound, too. But now the campers all had outboards. In the daytime, in the hot mornings, these motors made a petulant, irritable sound; at night, in the still evening when the afterglow lit the water, they whined about one's ears like mosquitoes. My boy loved our rented outboard, and his great desire was to achieve single-handed mastery over it, and authority, and he soon learned the trick of choking it a little (but not too much), and the adjust-

ment of the needle valve. Watching him I would remember the things you could do with the old one-cylinder engine with the heavy flywheel, how you could have it eating out of your hand if you got really close to it spiritually. Motorboats in those days didn't have clutches, and you would make a landing by shutting off the motor at the proper time and coasting in with a dead rudder. But there was a way of reversing them, if you learned the trick, by cutting the switch and putting it on again exactly on the final dying revolution of the flywheel, so that it would kick back against compression and begin reversing. Approaching a dock in a strong following breeze, it was difficult to slow up sufficiently by the ordinary coasting method, and if a boy felt he had complete mastery over his motor, he was tempted to keep it running beyond its time and then reverse it a few feet from the dock. It took a cool nerve, because if you threw the switch a twentieth of a second too soon you would catch the flywheel when it still had speed enough to go up past center, and the boat would leap ahead, charging bull-fashion at the dock.

11   We had a good week at the camp. The bass were biting well and the sun shone endlessly, day after day. We would be tired at night and lie down in the accumulated heat of the little bedrooms after the long hot day and the breeze would stir almost imperceptibly outside and the smell of the swamp drift in through the rusty screens. Sleep would come easily and in the morning the red squirrel would be on the roof, tapping out his gay routine. I kept remembering everything, lying in bed in the mornings—the small steamboat that had a long rounded stern like the lip of a Ubangi, and how quietly she ran on the moonlight sails, when the older boys played their mandolins and the girls sang and we ate doughnuts dipped in sugar, and how sweet the music was on the water in the shining night, and what it had felt like to think about girls then. After breakfast we would go up to the store and the things were in the same place—the minnows in a bottle, the plugs and spinners disarranged and pawed over by the youngsters from the boys' camp, the Fig Newtons and the Beeman's gum. Outside, the road was tarred and cars stood in front of the store. Inside, all was just as it had always been, except there was more Coca-Cola and not so much Moxie and root beer and birch beer and sarsaparilla. We would walk out with the bottle of pop apiece and sometimes the pop would backfire up our noses and hurt. We explored the streams, quietly, where the turtles slid off the sunny logs and dug

their way into the soft bottom; and we lay on the town wharf and fed worms to the tame bass. Everywhere we went I had trouble making out which was I, the one walking at my side, the one walking in my pants.

19 One afternoon while we were there at that lake a thunderstorm came up. It was like the revival of an old melodrama that I had seen long ago with childish awe. The second-act climax of the drama of the electrical disturbance over a lake in America had not changed in any important respect. This was the big scene, still the big scene. The whole thing was so familiar, the first feeling of oppression and heat and a general air around camp of not wanting to go very far away. In midafternoon (it was all the same) a curious darkening of the sky, and a lull in everything that had made life tick; and then the way the boats suddenly swung the other way at their moorings with the coming of a breeze out of the new quarter, and the premonitory rumble. Then the kettle drum, then the snare, then the bass drum and cymbals, then crackling light against the dark, and the gods grinning and licking their chops in the hills. Afterward the calm, the rain steadily rustling in the calm lake, the return of light and hope and spirits, and the campers running out in joy and relief to go swimming in the rain, their bright cries perpetuating the deathless joke about how they were getting simply drenched, and the children screaming with delight at the new sensation of bathing in the rain, and the joke about getting drenched linking the generations in a strong indestructible chain. And the comedian who waded in carrying an umbrella.

13 When the others went swimming, my son said he was going in, too. He pulled his dripping trunks from the line where they had hung all through the shower and wrung them out. Languidly, and with no thought of going in, I watched him, his hard little body, skinny and bare, saw him wince slightly as he pulled up around his vitals the small, soggy, icy garment. As he buckled the swollen belt, suddenly my groin felt the chill of death.

QUESTIONS

Ideas

1. Like "The Ring of Time," "Once More to the Lake" is a lyrical and speculative essay. It is, of course, a reminiscence of a memorable

summer. But it is something more: a meditation on time. What ideas about time does White suggest? Consider especially what he says in paragraphs 4, 5, and 6.

2. Explain what you think White means by the following statements:

    I seemed to be living a dual existence. (4)

    I felt dizzy and didn't know which rod I was at the end of. (5)

    I began to sustain the illusion that he was I, and therefore, by simple transposition, that I was my father. (4)

3. Besides time and change, what is this essay about?

Organization

4. Divide the essay into sections and provide titles for each part. In deciding upon your sections and titles, consider which paragraphs are primarily descriptive and which are speculative.

5. White gains emphasis by positioning his key ideas at the ends of paragraphs. Reread paragraphs 4, 5, and 6, attending to the final sentence of each paragraph. All three build toward the concluding sentence, which completes the idea in a forceful statement or embodies it in a striking image. Find at least one other example of a final effective sentence in a paragraph. Explain how it completes the paragraph.

6. Examine paragraphs 9 and 10 to see how White uses comparison and contrast to elaborate his point about the place. Note all the words and phrases that set up and emphasize the comparisons White makes between the lake in the past and the present.

Sentences

7. A number of White's sentences resonate and reverberate with repeated words and phrases. Read the following sentence aloud, noting its repetitions:

    The small waves were the same, chucking the rowboat under the chin as we fished at anchor, and the boat was the same boat, the same color green and the ribs broken in the same places, and under the floorboards the same fresh-water leavings and débris— the dead helgramite, the wisps of moss, the rusty discarded fishhook, the dried blood from yesterday's catch.

8. Another way White uses repetition in the essay is to employ the same words in different sentences. For example, the following sentences occur in different paragraphs:

There had been jollity and peace and goodness. (9)

Peace and goodness and jollity. (10)

Reread these two sentences in their context. Does the reordering of words affect the meaning? Why might White have altered the word order when he came to repeat the words?

9. In the sentences that follow, White expands his thought and accumulates details toward the end—after a brief direct statement of idea. You might think of the sentence formed this way as a string or a stack of details laid out in a series of parallel clauses or phrases.

> It was the arrival of this fly that convinced me beyond any doubt
>   that everything was as it always had been,
>   that the years were a mirage
>   and that there had been no years.

> We caught two bass,
>   hauling them in briskly as though they were mackerel,
>   pulling them in over the side of the boat in a businesslike
>   manner without any landing net,
>   and stunning them with a blow on the back of the head.

10. Compare the following sentence by White with the alternate form for sound and rhythm.

> *White:* I wondered how time would have marred this unique, this holy spot—the coves and streams, the hills that the sun set behind, the camps and the paths behind the camps.

> *Alternate:* I wondered how time would have marred this unique, holy spot—the coves, streams, hills, camps and paths.

Words

11. What words in paragraphs 1 and 2 describe the lake? What connotations does each possess? What overall impression of the lake is created by the accumulation of these words? How do the final words of paragraph 3 reinforce this impression?

12. "Once More to the Lake" is rich in sensuous detail—in images of sight, sound, smell, taste, and touch. List the visual details of paragraph 7 and the sound and sense details of paragraphs 10, 11, and 12. What is the overall effect of each paragraph?

13. White's diction in this essay and in others combines the high and the low, the common and the unusual, the formally elegant and the colloquially casual. Compare the tone, sound, and rhythm of the following remarks: (1) "the restlessness of the tides"; "the incessant wind that blows across the afternoon"; "the placidity of a lake in the

woods." (2) "A few weeks ago this feeling got so strong I bought myself a couple of bass hooks and a spinner and returned to the lake where we used to go, for a week's fishing and to revisit old haunts." What is different about the second voice? Which words in particular are responsible for its feeling and tone?

14. In this essay and in others White combines factual with emotional details. He extends a literal fact into a metaphoric detail, which carries a charge of meaning and a spark of feeling. Here is an example: "the whole place steamed with midday heat and hunger and emptiness" (7). To obtain the full force of how this literal fact (the heat) is extended to a human fact of feeling (hunger and emptiness) you'll need to read the sentence in context. Try to find another example of White's shading a fact into a metaphor and explain how the literal and metaphorical meanings intersect.

Suggestions for Writing

A. Write an essay about a place you have revisited after a long absence. Try to account for what the place meant to you after the first visit and after the later visit. Give some sense of what you expected and hoped for on the later visit. Try to suggest how the place had changed and how it remained the way you remembered it.

B. Explain, in a short essay, the sources of White's appeal as a writer. Does it have something to do with his subjects? With his ideas? His attitude and tone? His style?

C. In a paragraph or short essay, explain the idea of the following poem. Consider especially the imagery of stanzas 3 and 4. Compare the ideas about time in the poem with the ideas about time in White's essay. (Note especially the last stanza of the poem and the last paragraph of the essay.)

MEN AT FORTY

Men at forty
Learn to close softly
The doors to rooms they will not be
Coming back to.

At rest on a stair landing,
They feel it moving
Beneath them now like the deck of a ship,
Though the swell is gentle.

And deep in mirrors
They rediscover
The face of the boy as he practices tying
His father's tie there in secret

And the face of that father,
Still warm with the mystery of lather.
They are more fathers than sons themselves now.
Something is filling them, something

That is like the twilight sound
Of the crickets, immense,
Filling the woods at the foot of the slope
Behind their mortgaged houses.

—DONALD JUSTICE

D. Write an essay explaining White's ideas in two of his essays. You might compare and contrast his treatment of a similar subject or discuss his treatment of a similar theme using two different subjects.

E. Write imitations of the sentences discussed in questions 7, 9, and 10.

SIXTEEN

Tom Wolfe

(1931–   )

Tom Wolfe is one of the most famous of the New Journalists, a group of writers who imported the techniques of fiction into journalism. Wolfe's account of how he wrote his essay on custom cars, "The Kandy-Kolored Tangerine-Flake Streamline Baby," provides an insight into both his working habits and the new style he was unwittingly developing.

With an abundance of material about his subject and with too little time to organize, write, revise, and edit in the conventional manner, Wolfe began typing his notes in a letter to his editor at *Esquire*, where the piece was to be published. His letter took the form of a long memorandum, Wolfe supposing that somebody at the magazine would be responsible for shaping his rambling notes and writing the story. Wolfe describes the experience of writing the piece this way: "I just recorded it all, and inside a couple of hours, typing along like a madman, I could tell that something was beginning to happen. By midnight this memorandum was . . . twenty pages long and I was still typing like a maniac. . . . about 6:15 A.M. . . . it was 49 pages long." *Esquire* published it as written, inaugurating thereby an alternate writing style that was later named the "New Journalism."

In an introduction to an anthology of new-journalistic essays entitled, appropriately enough, *The New Journalism*, Wolfe singles out four techniques as being especially important for this new style. The basic device, he notes, is "scene-by-scene construction, telling the story by moving from scene to scene and resorting as little as possible to

sheer historical narrative." Another technique is to rely
heavily on dialogue since, as Wolfe has pointed out, "realistic dialogue involves the reader more completely than
any other single device. It also establishes and defines
character more quickly than any other single device." The
third technique involves manipulating the point of view,
the angle of vision, the perspective from which a scene is
presented. New Journalists will interview someone at the
center of a scene, then import into their write-ups the
thoughts and emotions of those interviewed. The purpose
of this strategy, as Wolfe notes, is to "give the reader the
feeling of being inside the character's mind and experiencing the emotional reality of the scene as he experiences it." The fourth technique concerns what Wolfe
describes as "the recording of everyday gestures, habits,
manners, customs . . . looks, glances, poses, styles of
walking and other symbolic details. . . ."

To these can be added what Winston Weathers in
his fine book, *An Alternate Style,* calls the *crot*—an obsolete
word meaning "bit" or "fragment": "an autonomous unit,
characterized by the absence of any transitional devices
. . . in its most intense form . . . by a certain abruptness
in its termination." Crots are something like snapshots,
something like vignettes. Putting them together without
transitions can make for effects of montage, collage, surprise—and sometimes confusion. They challenge readers
and involve them by inviting them to figure out how the
fragments are related to one another. Besides the crot,
about which Wolfe has said, "it will have you making crazy
leaps of logic, leaps you never dreamed of before,"
Weathers singles out other devices frequently used by
Wolfe and his new-journalistic colleagues: the labyrin-
thine sentence, the fragment, and the use of repetitions,
lists, and refrains.

Wolfe began his career as an academic, earning a
doctorate in American Studies at Yale. But his inclination
was more journalistic than academic, and he worked for
The Washington Post as a reporter and then as a magazine
writer for *The New York Herald-Tribune.* Since 1968 he has
been a contributing editor to *New York Magazine.* He has
written articles on trends in American popular culture,
primarily essays that have been published first in magazines and later in books. Following his first collection, *The
Kandy-Kolored Tangerine-Flake Streamline Baby* (1965), came
a series of books with such zany titles as *The Electric Kool-*

Aid Acid Test (1968)—on pot; *The Pump House Gang*
(1968)—on California surfers (among other things);
Radical Chic and Mau-Mauing the Flak Catchers (1970)—on
rich New Yorkers vis-à-vis the Black Panthers; *Mauve
Gloves and Madmen, Clutter and Vine* (1976)—on miscella-
neous subjects; *The Right Stuff* (1979)—on the astronauts;
In Our Time (1980), a collection of satirical pictorial
sketches with brief notes and comments; *From Bauhaus to
Our House* (1981), a critique of modern architecture; and
The Purple Decade (1982), a selection from his earlier
books. His most recent book is a novel, *Bonfire of the
Vanities* (1988).

Wolfe takes great risks in his writing: his style is daring, flamboyant, energetic, humorous, and satirical. Reading him is like listening to a talented raconteur who reen-
acts the scenes and situations he describes, who
comments on them in a free-wheeling style filled with
digressions and associative ramblings, with less concern to
instruct and moralize than to entertain and delight. His
essays tend to be long and steeped in detail. He seems to
need room to present the various facets of his subjects,
time to amass details and space to allow his characters to
reveal, even display themselves. The masses of detail, the
loose structure, the transcriptions of dialogue, the crots,
lists, repetitions, and refrains cumulatively create a sense
of immediacy and authenticity which suggests the reality
of "This is how it is; this is what it's like."

The Right Stuff, Wolfe's longest and most ambitious
work, has drawn wide critical acclaim, as well as becoming
a best seller. Early in the book Wolfe describes just what
the right stuff is that men need to become successful test
pilots and astronauts. His comments relate as much to his
own style and performance as a writer as they do to the
astronauts. The right stuff, Wolfe explains, is "an amal-
gam of stamina, guts, fast neural synapses and old-fashioned hell raising." These elements, along with nerve,
exhilaration, and a satirically edged humor, suggest something of Wolfe's tone and voice.

The essays included here span Wolfe's new-journalistic career. "Las Vegas," from *The Kandy-Kolored Tangerine-
Flake Streamline Baby,* offers a series of impressions about
one of America's most famous places. "Only One Life" is
excerpted from a long essay, "The Me Decade and the
Third Great Awakening," which appeared in *Mauve Gloves
and Madmen, Clutter and Vine.* The essay satirizes the self-

centered manias of people looking out for and looking into themselves. The "Pump House Gang" excerpt combines a tragic narrative about age segregation with the rise of surfing culture. "The Right Stuff" is taken from *The Right Stuff,* a book from which a film was made. The chapter excerpted here shows what it takes to make it as a test pilot, defining the ineffable quality through illustration and description, anecdote and analysis.

Wolfe has been interviewed frequently and has commented extensively on writing. On one occasion he noted that "writing, unlike painting or drawing, is a process in which you *can't* tell right away whether it's successful or not. Some nights you go to bed thinking you've written some brilliant stuff, and you wake up the next morning and you realize it *is* just pure bullshit." And in response to a question about why he writes, Wolfe noted that he doesn't have a ready answer, but that if pressed he thinks that he writes out of a concern for his own glory, with more concern for *how* he handles the materials of his craft than for the issues he writes about. The challenge in writing, thus, for Wolfe, seems to reside in the compositional problem that confronts him. Aesthetic and linguistic challenges excite him more than the subjects he writes about. But this subjective priority of form over content hasn't prevented Wolfe from offering acutely intelligent analyses of contemporary fads, fashions, and mores. He is one of our best cultural critics and one of our most innovative and entertaining writers.

Las Vegas (What?) Las Vegas (Can't hear you! Too noisy) Las Vegas!!!!

---

1   Hernia, hernia, hernia, hernia, hernia, hernia, hernia, hernia, hernia, hernia, hernia, hernia, hernia, HERNia; hernia, HERNia, hernia, hernia, hernia, hernia, HERNia, HERNia, HERNia, hernia, hernia, hernia, hernia, hernia, hernia, hernia, eight is the point, the point is eight; hernia, hernia, HERNia; hernia, hernia, hernia, hernia, all right, hernia, hernia, hernia, her-

nia, hard eight, hernia, hernia, hernia, HERNia, hernia, hernia, hernia, HERNia, hernia, hernia, hernia, HERNia, hernia, hernia, hernia, hernia.

2   "What is all this *hernia hernia* stuff?"

3   This was Raymond talking to the wavy-haired fellow with the stick, the dealer, at the craps table about 3:45 Sunday morning. The stickman had no idea what this big wiseacre was talking about, but he resented the tone. He gave Raymond that patient arch of the eyebrows known as a Red Hook brush-off, which is supposed to convey some such thought as, I am a very tough but cool guy, as you can tell by the way I carry my eyeballs low in the pouches, and if this wasn't such a high-class joint we would take wiseacres like you out back and beat you into jellied madrilene.

4   At this point, however, Raymond was immune to subtle looks.

5   The stickman tried to get the game going again, but every time he would start up his singsong, by easing the words out through the nose, which seems to be the style among craps dealers in Las Vegas—"All right, a new shooter . . . eight is the point, the point is eight" and so on—Raymond would start droning along with him in exactly the same tone of voice, "Hernia, hernia, hernia; hernia, HERNia, HERNia, hernia; hernia, hernia, hernia."

6   Everybody at the craps table was staring in consternation to think that anybody would try to needle a tough, hip, elite *soldat* like a Las Vegas craps dealer. The gold-lamé odalisques of Los Angeles were staring. The Western sports, fifty-eight-year-old men who wear Texas string ties, were staring. The old babes at the slot machines, holding Dixie Cups full of nickels, were staring at the craps tables, but cranking away the whole time.

7   Raymond, who is thirty-four years old and works as an engineer in Phoenix, is big but not terrifying. He has the sort of thatchwork hair that grows so low all along the forehead there is no logical place to part it, but he tries anyway. He has a huge, prognathous jaw, but it is as smooth, soft and round as a melon, so that Raymond's total effect is that of an Episcopal divinity student.

8   The guards were wonderful. They were dressed in cowboy uniforms like Bruce Cabot in *Sundown* and they wore sheriff's stars.

9   "Mister, is there something we can do for you?"

10   "The expression is 'Sir,'" said Raymond. "You said 'Mister.' The expression is 'Sir.' How's your old Cosa Nostra?"

11   Amazingly, the casino guards were easing Raymond out peaceably, without putting a hand on him. I had never seen the fellow before, but possibly because I had been following his progress for the last five minutes, he turned to me and said, "Hey, do you have a car? This wild stuff is starting again."

12   The gist of it was that he had left his car somewhere and he wanted to ride up the Strip to the Stardust, one of the big hotel-casinos. I am describing this big goof Raymond not because he is a typical Las Vegas tourist, although he has some typical symptoms, but because he is a good example of the marvelous impact Las Vegas has on the senses. Raymond's senses were at a high pitch of excitation, the only trouble being that he was going off his nut. He had been up since Thursday afternoon, and it was now about 3:45 A.M. Sunday. He had an envelope full of pep pills—amphetamine—in his left coat pocket and an envelope full of Equanils—meprobamate—in his right pocket, or were the Equanils in the left and the pep pills in the right? He could tell by looking, but he wasn't going to look anymore. He didn't care to see how many were left.

13   He had been rolling up and down the incredible electric-sign gauntlet of Las Vegas' Strip, U.S. Route 91, where the neon and the par lamps—bubbling, spiraling, rocketing, and exploding in sunbursts ten stories high out in the middle of the desert—celebrate one-story casinos. He had been gambling and drinking and eating now and again at the buffet tables the casinos keep heaped with food day and night, but mostly hopping himself up with good old amphetamine, cooling himself down with meprobamate, then hooking down more alcohol, until now, after sixty hours, he was slipping into the symptoms of toxic schizophrenia.

14   He was also enjoying what the prophets of hallucinogen call "consciousness expansion." The man was psychedelic. He was beginning to isolate the components of Las Vegas' unique bombardment of the senses. He was quite right about this *hernia hernia* stuff. Every casino in Las Vegas is, among the other things, a room full of craps tables with dealers who keep up a running singsong that sounds as though they are saying "hernia, hernia, hernia, hernia, hernia" and so on. There they are day and night, easing a running commentary through their nostrils. What they have to say contains next to no useful instruction. Its underlying message is, We are the initiates, riding the crest of chance. That the accumulated sound comes out "hernia" is merely an unfortunate phonet-

ic coincidence. Actually, it is part of something rare and rather grand: a combination of baroque stimuli that brings to mind the bronze gongs, no larger than a blue plate, that Louis XIV, his ruff collars larded with the lint of the foul Old City of Byzantium, personally hunted out in the bazaars of Asia Minor to provide exotic acoustics for his new palace outside Paris.

15   The sounds of the craps dealer will be in, let's say, the middle register. In the lower register will be the sound of the old babes at the slot machines. Men play the slots too, of course, but one of the indelible images of Las Vegas is that of the old babes at the row upon row of slot machines. There they are at six o'clock Sunday morning no less than at three o'clock Tuesday afternoon. Some of them pack their old hummocky shanks into Capri pants, but many of them just put on the old print dress, the same one day after day, and the old hob-heeled shoes, looking like they might be going out to buy eggs in Tupelo, Mississippi. They have a Dixie Cup full of nickels or dimes in the left hand and an Iron Boy work glove on the right hand to keep the callouses from getting sore. Every time they pull the handle, the machine makes a sound much like the sound a cash register makes before the bell rings, then the slot pictures start clattering up from left to right, the oranges, lemons, plums, cherries, bells, bars, buckaroos—the figure of a cowboy riding a bucking bronco. The whole sound keeps churning up over and over again in eccentric series all over the place, like one of those random-sound radio symphonies by John Cage. You can hear it at any hour of the day or night all over Las Vegas. You can walk down Fremont Street at dawn and hear it without even walking in a door, that and the spins of the wheels of fortune, a boring and not very popular sort of simplified roulette, as the tabs flap to a stop. As an overtone, or at times simply as a loud sound, comes the babble of the casino crowds, with an occasional shriek from the craps tables, or, anywhere from 4 P.M. to 6 A.M., the sound of brass instruments or electrified string instruments from the cocktail-lounge shows.

16   The crowd and band sounds are not very extraordinary, of course. But Las Vegas' Muzak is. Muzak pervades Las Vegas from the time you walk into the airport upon landing to the last time you leave the casinos. It is piped out to the swimming pool. It is in the drugstores. It is as if there were a communal fear that someone, somewhere in Las Vegas, was going to be left with a totally vacant minute on his hands.

17   Las Vegas has succeeded in wiring an entire city with this electronic stimulation, day and night, out in the middle of the desert. In the automobile I rented, the radio could not be turned off, no matter which dial you went after. I drove for days in a happy burble of Action Checkpoint News, "Monkey No. 9," "Donna, Donna, the Prima Donna," and picking-and-singing jingles for the Frontier Bank and the Fremont Hotel.

18   One can see the magnitude of the achievement. Las Vegas takes what in other American towns is but a quixotic inflammation of the senses for some poor salary mule in the brief interval between the flagstone rambler and the automatic elevator downtown and magnifies it, foliates it, embellishes it into an institution.

19   For example, Las Vegas is the only town in the world whose skyline is made up neither of buildings, like New York, nor of trees, like Wilbraham, Massachusetts, but signs. One can look at Las Vegas from a mile away on Route 91 and see no buildings, no trees, only signs. But such signs! They tower. They revolve, they oscillate, they soar in shapes before which the existing vocabulary of art history is helpless. I can only attempt to supply names— Boomerang Modern, Palette Curvilinear, Flash Gordon Ming-Alert Spiral, McDonald's Hamburger Parabola, Mint Casino Elliptical, Miami Beach Kidney. Las Vegas' sign makers work so far out beyond the frontiers of conventional studio art that they have no names themselves for the forms they create. Vaughan Cannon, one of those tall, blond Westerners, the builders of places like Las Vegas and Los Angeles, whose eyes seem to have been bleached by the sun, is in the back shop of the Young Electric Sign Company out on East Charleston Boulevard with Herman Boernge, one of his designers, looking at the model they have prepared for the Lucky Strike Casino sign, and Cannon points to where the sign's two great curving faces meet to form a narrow vertical face and says:

20   "Well, here we are again—what do we call that?"

21   "I don't know," says Boernge. "It's sort of a nose effect. Call it a nose."

22   Okay, a nose, but it rises sixteen stories high above a two-story building. In Las Vegas no farseeing entrepreneur buys a sign to fit a building he owns. He rebuilds the building to support the biggest sign he can get up the money for and, if necessary, changes the name. The Lucky Strike Casino today is the Lucky Casino, which fits better when recorded in sixteen stories of

flaming peach and incandescent yellow in the middle of the Mo
jave Desert. In the Young Electric Sign Co. era signs have become
the architecture of Las Vegas, and the most whimsical, Yale-semi-
nar-frenzied devices of the two late geniuses of Baroque Modern,
Frank Lloyd Wright and Eero Saarinen, seem rather stuffy business, like a jest at a faculty meeting, compared to it. Men like
Boernge, Kermit Wayne, Ben Mitchem and Jack Larsen, formerly
an artist for Walt Disney, are the designer-sculptor geniuses of Las
Vegas, but their motifs have been carried faithfully throughout
the town by lesser men, for gasoline stations, motels, funeral par-
lors, churches, public buildings, flophouses and sauna baths.

23   Then there is a stimulus that is both visual and sexual—the
Las Vegas buttocks décolletage. This is a form of sexually provocative dress seen more and more in the United States, but avoided
like Broadway message-embroidered ("Kiss Me, I'm Cold") underwear in the fashion pages, so that the euphemisms have not been
established and I have no choice but clinical terms. To achieve
buttocks décolletage a woman wears bikini-style shorts that cut
across the round fatty masses of the buttocks rather than cupping
them from below, so that the outer-lower edges of these fatty
masses, or "cheeks," are exposed. I am in the cocktail lounge of
the Hacienda Hotel, talking to managing director Dick Taylor
about the great success his place has had in attracting family and
tour groups, and all around me the waitresses are bobbing on
their high heels, bare legs and décolletage-bare backsides, set off
by pelvis-length lingerie of an uncertain denomination. I stare,
but I am new here. At the White Cross Rexall drugstore on the
Strip a pregnant brunette walks in off the street wearing black
shorts with buttocks décolletage aft and illusion-of-cloth nylon lingerie hanging fore, and not even the old mom's-pie pensioners
up near the door are staring. They just crank away at the slot
machines. On the streets of Las Vegas, not only the show girls, of
which the town has about two hundred fifty, bona fide, in residence, but girls of every sort, including, especially, Las Vegas' little high-school buds, who adorn what locals seeking roots in the
sand call "our city of churches and schools," have taken up the
chic of wearing buttocks décolletage step-ins under flesh-tight
slacks, with the outline of the undergarment showing through
fashionably. Others go them one better. They achieve the effect
of having been dipped once, briefly, in Helenca stretch nylon.
More and more they look like those wonderful old girls out of

Flash Gordon who were wrapped just once over in Baghdad pan-
taloons of clear polyethylene with only Flash Gordon between
them and the insane red-eyed assaults of the minions of Ming. It
is as if all the hip young suburban gals of America named Lana,
Deborah and Sandra, who gather wherever the arc lights shine
and the studs steady their coiffures in the plate-glass reflection,
have convened in Las Vegas with their bouffant hair above and
anatomically stretch-pant-swathed little bottoms below, here on
the new American frontier. But exactly!

24   The allure is most irresistible not to the young but the old.
No one in Las Vegas will admit it—it is not the modern, glamorous notion—but Las Vegas is a resort for old people. In those
last years, before the tissue deteriorates and the wires of the cere-
bral cortex hang in the skull like a clump of dried seaweed, they
are seeking liberation.

25   At eight o'clock Sunday morning it is another almost boring-
ly sunny day in the desert, and Clara and Abby, both about sixty,
and their husbands, Earl, sixty-three, and Ernest, sixty-four, come
squinting out of the Mint Casino onto Fremont Street.

26   "I don't know what's wrong with me," Abby says. "Those last
three drinks, I couldn't even feel them. It was just like drinking
fizz. You know what I mean?"

27   "Hey," says Ernest, "how about that place back 'ere? We ain't
been back 'ere. Come on."

28   The others are standing there on the corner, squinting and
looking doubtful. Abby and Clara have both entered old babe-
hood. They have that fleshy, humped-over shape across the back
of the shoulders. Their torsos are hunched up into fat little loaves
supported by bony, atrophied leg stems sticking up into their
hummocky hips. Their hair has been fried and dyed into improbable designs.

29   "You know what I mean? After a while it just gives me gas,"
says Abby. "I don't even feel it."

30   "Did you see me over there?" says Earl. "I was just going
along, nice and easy, not too much, just riding along real nice.
You know? And then, boy, I don't know what happened to me.
First thing I know I'm laying down fifty dollars. . . ."

31   Abby lets out a great belch. Clara giggles.

32   "Gives me gas," Abby says mechanically.

33   "Hey, how about that place back 'ere?" says Ernest.

34   ". . . Just nice and easy as you please. . . ."

35 ". . . get me all fizzed up. . . ."

36 "Aw, come on. . . ."

37 And there at eight o'clock Sunday morning stand four old parties from Albuquerque, New Mexico, up all night, squinting at the sun, belching from a surfeit of tall drinks at eight o'clock Sunday morning, and— marvelous!—there is no one around to snigger at what an old babe with decaying haunches looks like in Capri pants with her heels jacked up on decorated wedgies.

38 "Where do we *come* from?" Clara said to me, speaking for the first time since I approached them on Fremont Street. "He wants to know where we come from. I think it's past your bedtime, swects."

39 "Climb the stairs and go to bed," said Abby.

40 Laughter all around.

41 "Climb the stairs" was Abby's finest line. At present there are almost no stairs to climb in Las Vegas. Avalon homes are soon to go up, advertising "Two-Story Homes!" as though this were an incredibly lavish and exotic concept. As I talked to Clara, Abby, Earl and Ernest, it came out that "climb the stairs" was a phrase they brought along to Albuquerque with them from Marshall-town, Iowa, those many years ago, along with a lot of other baggage, such as the entire cupboard of Protestant taboos against drinking, lusting, gambling, staying out late, getting up late, loafing, idling, lollygagging around the streets and wearing Capri pants—all designed to deny a person short-term pleasures so he will center his energies on bigger, long-term goals.

42 "We was in 'ere"—the Mint—"a couple of hours ago, and that old boy was playing the guitar, you know. 'Walk right in, set right down,' and I kept hearing an old song I haven't heard for twenty years. It has this little boy and his folks keep telling him it's late and he has to go to bed. He keeps saying, 'Don't make me go to bed and I'll be good.' Am I *good*, Earl? Am I *good?*"

43 The liberated cortex in all its glory is none other than the old babes at the slot machines. Some of them are tourists whose husbands said, *Here is fifty bucks, go play the slot machines,* while they themselves went off to more complex pleasures. But most of these old babes are part of the permanent landscape of Las Vegas. In they go to the Golden Nugget or the Mint, with their Social Security check or their pension check from the Ohio telephone company, cash it at the casino cashier's, pull out the Dixie Cup and the Iron Boy work glove, disappear down a row of slots and

get on with it. I remember particularly talking to another Abby—a
widow, sixty-two years old, built short and up from the bottom like
a fire hydrant. After living alone for twelve years in Canton, Ohio,
she had moved out to Las Vegas to live with her daughter and her
husband, who worked for the Army.

44   "They were wonderful about it," she said. "Perfect hyp-
ocrites. She kept saying, you know, 'Mother, we'd be delighted
to have you, only we don't think you'll *like* it. It's practically a fron-
tier town,' she says. 'It's so *ga*rish,' she says. So I said, I told her,
'Well, if you'd rather I didn't come. . . .' 'Oh, no!' she says. I
wish I could have heard what her husband was saying. He calls me
'Mother.' *'Mother,'* he says. Well, once I was here, they figured,
well, I *might* make a good baby-sitter and dishwasher and duster
and mopper. The children are nasty little things. So one day I
was in town for something or other and I just played a slot
machine. It's fun—I can't describe it to you. I suppose I lose. I
lose a little. And *they* have fits about it. 'For God's sake,
Grandmother,' and so forth. They always say *'Grand* mother' when
I am supposed to 'act my age' or crawl through a crack in the
floor. Well, I'll tell you, the slot machines are a *whole lot* better
than sitting in that little house all day. They kind of get you; I
can't explain it."

45   The childlike megalomania of gambling is, of course, from
the same cloth as the megalomania of the town. And, as the children of the liberated cortex, the old guys and babes are running
up and down the Strip around the clock like everybody else. It is
not by chance that much of the entertainment in Las Vegas, especially the second-stringers who perform in the cocktail lounges,
will recall for an aging man what was glamorous twenty-five years
ago when he had neither the money nor the freedom of spirit to
indulge himself in it. In the big theatre-dining room at the Desert
Inn, The Painted Desert Room, Eddie Fisher's act is on and he is
saying cozily to a florid guy at a table right next to the stage,
"Manny, you know you shouldn'a sat this close—you know you're
in for it now, Manny, baby," while Manny beams with fright. But
in the cocktail lounge, where the idea is chiefly just to keep the
razzle-dazzle going, there is Hugh Farr, one of the stars of another
era in the West, composer of two of the five Western songs the
Library of Congress has taped for posterity, "Cool Water" and
"Tumbling Tumbleweed," when he played the violin for the Sons
of the Pioneers. And now around the eyes he looks like an aging

Chinese savant, but he is wearing a white tuxedo and powder-blue leather boots and playing his sad old Western violin with an electric cord plugged in it for a group called The Country Gentlemen. And there is Ben Blue, looking like a waxwork exhibit of vaudeville, doffing his straw skimmer to reveal the sculptural qualities of his skull. And down at the Flamingo cocktail lounge—Ella Fitzgerald is in the main room—there is Harry James, looking old and pudgy in one of those toy Italian-style show-biz suits. And the Ink Spots are at the New Frontier and Louis Prima is at the Sahara, and the old parties are seeing it all, roaring through the dawn into the next day, until the sun seems like a par lamp fading in and out. The casinos, the bars, the liquor stores are open every minute of every day, like a sempiternal wading pool for the childhood ego. ". . . Don't make me go to bed. . . ."

QUESTIONS

Ideas

1. What image of Las Vegas does Wolfe convey? What is his attitude toward what he describes?
2. In what ways can Las Vegas be considered a "frontier," whether new or old? What American cultural values are illustrated in Wolfe's piece?

Organization

3. How is the essay organized? Describe the structure of the selection by dividing it into sections, characterizing them and pointing out their relation to one another.
4. How does Wolfe move from one aspect of his description of Las Vegas to another? What transitions does he use?

Sentences

5. Examine one of Wolfe's long sentences. Explain how Wolfe keeps it going, how he structures it grammatically. Consider the effect of breaking it into three or four shorter sentences.
6. Many of the sentences in paragraphs 12, 13, and 14 begin with pronouns, often "he." Explain how Wolfe achieves variety in these paragraphs.

Words

7. Identify three comparisons, whether similes, metaphors, images, or symbols, and explain their purpose and point. Comment on the effectiveness of each.

8. Explain the following italicized words:

> a *quixotic inflammation* of the senses (18)
> buttocks *décolletage* (23)
> *baroque* stimuli (14)

Suggestions for Writing

A. Imitate the sentences described in questions 5 and 6.
B. Compare Wolfe's portrayal of Las Vegas with Joan Didion's in "Marrying Absurd."
C. Argue with Wolfe by offering a counterview of Las Vegas.
D. Imitate Wolfe by satirically describing a place you know.

Only One Life

---

1   In 1961 a copy writer named Shirley Polykoff was working for the Foote, Cone & Belding advertising agency on the Clairol hair-dye account when she came up with the line: "If I've only one life, let me live it as a blonde!" In a single slogan she had summed up what might be described as the secular side of the Me Decade. "If I've only one life, let me live it as a _____ !" (You have only to fill in the blank.)

2   This formula accounts for much of the popularity of the women's liberation or feminist movement. "What does a woman want?" said Freud. Perhaps there are women who want to humble men or reduce their power or achieve equality or even superiority for themselves and their sisters. But for every one such woman, there are nine who simply want to *fill in the blank* as they see fit. "If I've only one life, let me live it as . . . a free spirit!" (Instead of . . . a house slave: a cleaning woman, a cook, a nursemaid, a station-wagon hacker, and an occasional household sex aid.) But even that may be overstating it, because often the unconscious desire is nothing more than: *Let's talk about Me.* The great unexpected divi-

dend of the feminist movement has been to elevate an ordinary status—woman, housewife—to the level of drama. One's very existence as *a woman* . . . as *Me* . . . becomes something all the world analyzes, agonizes over, draws cosmic conclusions from, or, in any event, takes seriously. Every woman becomes Emma Bovary, Cousin Bette, or Nora . . . or Erica Jong or Consuelo Saah Baehr.

3   Among men the formula becomes: "If I've only one life, let me live it as a . . . Casanova or a Henry VIII!" (instead of a humdrum workadaddy, eternally faithful, except perhaps for a mean little skulking episode here and there, to a woman who now looks old enough to be your aunt and needs a shave or else has electrolysis lines above her upper lip, as well as atrophied calves, and is an embarrassment to be seen with when you take her on trips). The right to shuck overripe wives and take on fresh ones was once seen as the prerogative of kings only, and even then it was scandalous. In the 1950's and 1960's it began to be seen as the prerogative of the rich, the powerful, and the celebrated (Nelson Rockefeller, Henry Ford, and Show Business figures), although it retained the odor of scandal. Wife-shucking damaged Adlai Stevenson's chances of becoming President in 1952 and 1956 and Rockefeller's chances of becoming the Republican nominee in 1964 and 1968. Until the 1970's wife-shucking made it impossible for an astronaut to be chosen to go into space. Today, in the Me Decade, it becomes *normal behavior,* one of the factors that has pushed the divorce rate above 50 percent.

4   When Eugene McCarthy filled in the blank in 1972 and shucked his wife, it was hardly noticed. Likewise in the case of several astronauts. When Wayne Hays filled in the blank in 1976 and shucked his wife of thirty-eight years, it did not hurt his career in the slightest. Copulating with the girl in the office, however, was still regarded as scandalous. (Elizabeth Ray filled in the blank in another popular fashion: If I've only one life, let me live it as a . . . Celebrity!" As did Arthur Bremer, who kept a diary during his stalking of Nixon and, later, George Wallace . . . with an eye toward a book contract. Which he got.) Some wiseacre has remarked, supposedly with levity, that the federal government may in time have to create reservations for women over thirty-five, to take care of the swarms of shucked wives and widows. In fact, women in precisely those categories have begun setting up communes or "extended families" to provide one another support and companionship in a world without

workadaddies. ("If I've only one life, why live it as an anachronism?")

5   Much of what is now known as the "sexual revolution" has consisted of both women and men filling in the blank this way: "If I've only one life, let me live it as . . . a Swinger!" (Instead of a frustrated, bored monogamist.) In "swinging," a husband and wife give each other license to copulate with other people. There are no statistics on the subject that mean anything, but I do know that it pops up in conversation today in the most unexpected corners of the country. It is an odd experience to be in De Kalb, Illinois, in the very corncrib of America, and have some conventional-looking housewife (not *housewife,* damn it!) come up to you and ask: "Is there much tripling going on in New York?"

6   "*Tripling?*"

7   Tripling turns out to be a practice, in De Kalb, anyway, in which a husband and wife invite a third party—male or female, but more often female—over for an evening of whatever, including polymorphous perversity, even the practices written of in the one-hand magazines, such as *Hustler,* all the things involving tubes and hoses and tourniquets and cups and double-jointed sailors.

8   One of the satisfactions of this sort of life, quite in addition to the groin spasms, is talk: *Let's talk about Me.* Sexual adventurers are given to the most relentless and deadly serious talk . . . about Me. They quickly succeed in placing themselves onstage in the sexual drama whose outlines were sketched by Freud and then elaborated by Wilhelm Reich. Men and women of all sorts, not merely swingers, are given just now to the most earnest sort of talk about the Sexual Me. A key drama of our own day is Ingmar Bergman's movie *Scenes from a Marriage.* In it we see a husband and wife who have good jobs and a well-furnished home but who are unable to "communicate"—to cite one of the signature words of the Me Decade. Then they begin to communicate, and thereupon their marriage breaks up and they start divorce proceedings. For the rest of the picture they communicate endlessly, with great candor, but the "relationship"—another signature word—remains doomed. Ironically, the lesson that people seem to draw from this movie has to do with . . . "the need to communicate."

9   *Scenes from a Marriage* is one of those rare works of art, like *The Sun Also Rises,* that not only succeed in capturing a certain mental atmosphere in fictional form . . . but also turn around

and help radiate it throughout real life. I personally know of two instances in which couples, after years of marriage, went to see *Scenes from a Marriage* and came home convinced of the "need to communicate." The discussions began with one of the two saying, Let's try to be completely candid for once. You tell me exactly what you don't like about me, and I'll do the same for you. At this, the starting point, the whole notion is exciting. We're going to talk about *Me!* (And I can take it.) I'm going to find out what he (or she) really thinks about me! (Of course, I have my faults, but they're minor . . . or else exciting.)

10   She says, "Go ahead. What don't you like about me?"

11   They're both under the Bergman spell. Nevertheless, a certain sixth sense tells him that they're on dangerous ground. So he decides to pick something that doesn't seem too terrible.

12   "Well," he says, "one thing that bothers me is that when we meet people for the first time, you never know what to say. Or else you get nervous and start chattering away, and it's all so banal, it makes me look bad."

13   Consciously she's still telling herself, "I can take it." But what he has just said begins to seep through her brain like scalding water. What's he talking about?—makes *him* look bad? *He's saying I'm unsophisticated, a social liability and an embarrassment. All those times we've gone out, he's been ashamed of me!* (And what makes it worse—it's the sort of disease for which there's no cure!) She always knew she was awkward. His crime is: he *noticed!* He's known it, too, all along. He's had *contempt* for me.

14   Out loud she says, "Well, I'm afraid there's nothing I can do about that."

15   He detects the petulant note. "Look," he says, "you're the one who said to be candid."

16   She says, "I know. I *want* you to be."

17   He says, "Well, it's your turn."

18   "Well," she says, "I'll tell *you* something about when we meet people and when we go places. You never clean yourself properly—you don't know how to wipe yourself. Sometimes we're standing there talking to people, and there's . . . a smell. And I'll tell you something else: People can tell it's you."

19   And he's still telling *him*self, "I can take it"—but what inna namea Christ is *this?*

20   He says, "But you've never said anything—about anything like that."

21   She says, "But I *tried* to. How many times have I told you about your dirty drawers when you were taking them off at night?"

22   Somehow this really makes him angry . . . All those times . . . and his mind immediately fastens on Harley Thatcher and his wife, whom he has always wanted to impress . . . From underneath my $350 suits I smelled of *shit!* What infuriates him is that this is a humiliation from which there's no recovery. *How often have they sniggered about it later?—or not invited me places? Is it something people say every time my name comes up?* And all at once he is intensely annoyed with his wife, not because she never told him all these years, but simply because she *knows* about his disgrace—and she was the one who *brought him the bad news!*

23   From that moment on they're ready to get the skewers in. It's only a few minutes before they've begun trying to sting each other with confessions about their little affairs, their little slipping around, their little coitus on the sly—"Remember that time I told you my flight from Buffalo was canceled?"—and at that juncture the ranks of those *who can take it* become very thin indeed. So they communicate with great candor! and break up! and keep on communicating! and they find the relationship hopelessly doomed.

24   One couple went into group therapy. The other went to a marriage counselor. Both types of therapy are very popular forms, currently, of *Let's talk about Me.* This phase of the breakup always provides a rush of exhilaration—for what more exhilarating topic is there than . . . *Me?* Through group therapy, marriage counseling, and other forms of "psychological consultation" they can enjoy that same *Me* euphoria that the very rich have enjoyed for years in psychoanalysis. The cost of the new Me sessions is only $10 to $30 an hour, whereas psychoanalysis runs from $50 to $125. The woman's exhilaration, however, is soon complicated by the fact that she is (in the typical case) near or beyond the cutoff age of thirty-five and will have to retire to the reservation.

25   Well, my dear Mature Moderns . . . Ingmar never promised you a rose garden!

QUESTIONS

Ideas

1. What is Wolfe's subject here? Women's Liberation? Talk Therapy? Selfishness? Something else? And what is the predominant tone of

the essay? How does this tone reveal and carry Wolfe's attitude toward his subject?

2. What is Wolfe's purpose, and who is his implied audience? Consider the literary allusions in paragraph 2, the historical and political allusions in paragraph 3, and the contemporary allusions in paragraph 4.

Organization

3. "Only One Life" falls into two major parts: paragraphs 1–8 and paragraphs 9–23—with paragraphs 24 and 25 as a wrap-up. Identify the subject and point of the two main parts and explain how Wolfe moves, in paragraphs 8 and 9, from the subject of the first part to the subject of the second.

4. Paragraphs 1 and 2 are about women, 3 and 4 about men, and 5–8 about both. What ties all eight paragraphs together?

5. Examine the transitions Wolfe uses to link his first eight paragraphs. How does the first sentence of each paragraph tie it to the preceding paragraph? What specific words and phrases form the links? And why are transitions sparse in paragraphs 9–25?

Sentences

6. Wolfe uses a slogan, which he repeats throughout the first part of the essay: "If I've only one life, let me live it as a *blonde!*" Examine the variations he works on this slogan. What is the point of the variations?

7. He uses another repeated sentence as well, this one without variation: "Let's talk about Me" (paragraphs 2, 8, and 24). What tone is established with this repeated sentence?

8. What are the function and the effect of the parenthetical sentences in paragraphs 1, 2, 4, 9, and 13? Of the ellipses in sentences in paragraphs 2, 3, 4, 5, 8, 9, and 24?

Words

9. Reread the dialogue in paragraphs 9–23. Explain why some words are italicized. What is the effect of this?

10. Wolfe's diction ranges from the colloquial and the familiar to the unusual and the recondite. Find examples of different kinds of words and phrases showing evidence of Wolfe's range and diversity of language.

Suggestions for Writing

A. Write an essay responding to the comments from paragraph 2 that follow:

    1. "The great unexpected dividend of the feminist movement has been to elevate an ordinary status—woman, housewife—to the level of drama."

    2. "One's very existence as *a woman* . . . as *Me* . . . becomes something all the world analyzes, agonizes over, draws cosmic conclusions from, or, in any event, takes seriously."

B. Imitate the second part of this essay by writing a dialogue that includes not only what the speakers say, but also what they think. You will have, then, an inner-outer dialogue, which gains effect by the discrepancy between what is said and what is thought. You may include, as Wolfe does, a narrator to explain the conversation, perhaps to comment on it.

C. Take a popular slogan from advertising or from a contemporary issue. Write an essay examining its implications and ramifications. Explain how the slogan sums up and epitomizes important attitudes, ideals, and values of whoever uses it, believes in it, or lives by it.

The Pump House Gang

---

1   Our boys never hair out. The black panther has black feet. Black feet on the crumbling black panther. Pan-thuh. Mee-dah. Pam Stacy, 16 years old, a cute girl here in La Jolla, California, with a pair of orange bell-bottom hip-huggers on, sits on a step about four steps down the stairway to the beach and she can see a pair of revolting black feet without lifting her head. So she says it out loud, "The black panther."

2   Somebody farther down the stairs, one of the boys with the *major* hair and khaki shorts, says, "The black feet of the black panther."

3   "Mee-dah," says another kid. This happens to be the cry of a, well, *underground* society known as the Mac Meda Destruction Company.

4   "The pan-thuh."

5   "The poon-thuh."

6   All these kids, seventeen of them, members of the Pump House crowd, are lollygagging around the stairs down to

WIndansea Beach, La Jolla, California, about 11 a.m., and they all look at the black feet, which are a woman's pair of black street shoes, out of which stick a pair of old veiny white ankles, which lead up like a senile cone to a fudge of tallowy, edematous flesh, her thighs, squeezing out of her bathing suit, with old faded yellow bruises on them, which she probably got from running eight feet to catch a bus or something. She is standing with her old work-a-hubby, who has on *san*dals: you know, a pair of navy-blue anklet socks and these sandals with big, wide, new-smelling tan straps going this way and that, *for keeps*. Man, they look like orthopedic sandals, if one can imagine that. Obviously, these people come from Tucson or Albuquerque or one of those hincty adobe towns. All these hincty, crumbling black feet come to La Jolla-by-the-sea from the adobe towns for the weekend. They even drive in cars all full of thermos bottles and mayonnaisey sandwiches and some kind of latticework wooden-back support for the old crock who drives and Venetian blinds on the back window.

7   "The black panther."

8   "Pan-thuh."

9   "Poon-thuh."

10   "Mee-dah."

11   Nobody says it to the two old crocks directly. God, they must be practically 50 years old. Naturally, they're carrying every piece of garbage imaginable: the folding aluminum chairs, the newspapers, the lending-library book with the clear plastic wrapper on it, the sunglasses, the sun ointment, about a vat of goo—

12   It is a Mexican standoff. In a Mexican standoff, both parties narrow their eyes and glare but nobody throws a punch. Of course, nobody in the Pump House crowd would ever even jostle these people or say anything right to them; they are too cool for that.

13   Everybody in the Pump House crowd looks over, even Tom Coman, who is a cool person. Tom Coman, 16 years old, got thrown out of his garage last night. He is sitting up on top of the railing, near the stairs, up over the beach, with his legs apart. Some nice long willowy girl in yellow slacks is standing on the sidewalk but leaning into him with her arms around his body, just resting. Neale Jones, 16, a boy with great lank perfect surfer's hair, is standing nearby with a Band-Aid on his upper lip, where the sun has burnt it raw. Little Vicki Ballard is up on the sidewalk. Her older sister, Liz, is down the stairs by the Pump House itself, a concrete block, 15 feet high, full of machinery for the La Jolla

water system. Liz is wearing her great "Liz" styles, a hulking rabbit-fur vest and black-leather boots over her Levis, even though it is about 85 out here and the sun is plugged in up there like God's own dentist lamp and the Pacific is heaving in with some fair-to-middling surf. Kit Tilden is lollygagging around, and Tom Jones, Connie Carter, Roger Johnson, Sharon Sandquist, Mary Beth White, Rupert Fellows, Glenn Jackson, Dan Watson from San Diego, they are all out here, and everybody takes a look at the panthers.

14   The old guy, one means, you know, he must be practically 50 years old, he says to his wife, "Come on, let's go farther up," and he takes her by her fat upper arm as if to wheel her around and aim her away from here.

15   But she says, "No! We have just as much right to be here as they do."

16   "That's *not the point*—"

17   "Are you going to—"

18   "*Mrs. Roberts,*" the work-a-hubby says, calling his own wife by her official married name, as if to say she took a vow once and his word is law, even if he is not testing it with the blond kids here—"farther up, *Mrs. Roberts.*"

19   They start to walk up the sidewalk, but one kid won't move his feet, and, oh, god, her work-a-hubby breaks into a terrible shaking Jello smile as she steps over them, as if to say, Excuse me, sir, I don't mean to make trouble, please, and don't you and your colleagues rise up and jump me, screaming *Gotcha*—

20   Mee-dah!

21   But exactly! This beach *is* verboten for people practically 50 years old. This is a segregated beach. They can look down on Windansea Beach and see nothing but lean tan kids. It is posted "no swimming" (for safety reasons), meaning surfing only. In effect, it is segregated by age. From Los Angeles on down the California coast, this is an era of age segregation. People have always tended to segregate themselves by age, teenagers hanging around with teenagers, old people with old people, like the old men who sit on the benches up near the Bronx Zoo and smoke black cigars. But before, age segregation has gone on within a larger community. Sooner or later during the day everybody has melted back into the old community network that embraces practically everyone, all ages.

22   But in California today surfers, not to mention rock 'n' roll kids and the hot-rodders or Hair Boys, named for their fanciful pompadours—all sorts of sets of kids—they don't merely hang around together. They establish whole little societies for themselves. In some cases they live with one another for months at a time. The "Sunset Strip" on Sunset Boulevard used to be a kind of Times Square for Hollywood hot dogs of all ages, anyone who wanted to promenade in his version of the high life. Today "The Strip" is almost completely the preserve of kids from about 16 to 25. It is lined with go-go clubs. One of them, a place called It's Boss, is set up for people 16 to 25 and won't let in anybody over 25, and there are some terrible I'm-dying-a-thousand-deaths scenes when a girl comes up with her boyfriend and the guy at the door at It's Boss doesn't think she looks under 25 and tells her she will have to produce some identification proving she is young enough to come in here and live The Strip kind of life and—she's *had* it, because she can't get up the I.D. and nothing in the world is going to make a woman look stupider than to stand around trying to argue *I'm younger than I look, I'm younger than I look.* So she practically shrivels up like a Peruvian shrunken head in front of her boyfriend and he trundles her off, looking for some place you can get an old doll like this into. One of the few remaining clubs for "older people," curiously, is the Playboy Club. There are apartment houses for people 20 to 30 only, such as the Sheri Plaza in Hollywood and the E'Questre Inn in Burbank. There are whole suburban housing developments, mostly private developments, where only people over 45 or 50 can buy a house. Whole towns, meantime, have become identified as "young": Venice, Newport Beach, Balboa—or "old": Pasadena, Riverside, Coronado Island.

23   Behind much of it—especially something like a whole nightclub district of a major city, "The Strip," going teenage—is, simply, money. World War II and the prosperity that followed pumped incredible amounts of money into the population, the white population at least, at every class level. All of a sudden here is an area with thousands of people from 16 to 25 who can get their hands on enough money to support a whole nightclub belt and to have the cars to get there and to set up autonomous worlds of their own in a fairly posh resort community like La Jolla—

24   —Tom Coman's garage. Some old bastard took Tom Coman's garage away from him, and that means eight or nine surfers are out of a place to stay.

25   "I went by there this morning, you ought to see the guy," Tom Coman says. Yellow Stretch Pants doesn't move. She has him around the waist. "He was out there painting and he had this brush and about a thousand gallons of ammonia. He was really going to scrub me out of there."

26   "What did he do with the furniture?"

27   "I don't know. He threw it out."

28   "What are you going to do?"

29   "I don't know."

30   "Where are you going to stay?"

31   "I don't know. I'll stay on the beach. It wouldn't be the first time. I haven't had a place to stay for three years, so I'm not going to start worrying now."

32   Everybody thinks that over awhile. Yellow Stretch just hangs on and smiles. Tom Coman, 16 years old, piping fate again. One of the girls says, "You can stay at my place, Tom."

33   "Um. Who's got a cigarette?"

34   Pam Stacy says, "You can have these."

35   Tom Coman lights a cigarette and says, "Let's have a destructo." A destructo is what can happen in a garage after eight or 10 surfers are kicked out of it.

36   "Mee-dah!"

37   "Wouldn't that be bitchen?" says Tom Coman. Bitchen is a surfer's term that means "great," usually.

38   "Bitchen!"

39   "Mee-dah!"

40   It's incredible—that old guy out there trying to scour the whole surfing life out of that garage. He's a pathetic figure. His shoulders are hunched over and he's dousing and scrubbing away and the sun doesn't give him a tan, it gives him these . . . *mottles* on the back of his neck. But never mind! The hell with destructo. One only has a destructo spontaneously, a Dionysian . . . *bursting out,* like those holes through the wall during the Mac Meda Destruction Company Convention at Manhattan Beach—Mee-dah!

41   Something will pan out. It's a magic economy—yes!—all up and down the coast from Los Angeles to Baja California kids can go to one of these beach towns and live the complete surfing life.

They take off from home and get to the beach, and if they need a place to stay, well, somebody rents a garage for twenty bucks a month and everybody moves in, girls and boys. Furniture—it's like, one means, you know, one *appropriates* furniture from here and there. It's like the Volkswagen buses a lot of kids now use as beach wagons instead of woodies. Woodies are old station wagons, usually Fords, with wooden bodies, from back before 1953. One of the great things about a Volkswagen bus is that one can . . . *exchange* motors in about three minutes. A good VW motor exchanger can go up to a parked Volkswagen, and a few ratchets of the old wrench here and it's up and out and he has a new motor. There must be a few nice old black panthers around wondering why their nice hubby-mommy VWs don't run so good anymore—but—then—they—are—probably—puzzled—about—a—lot of things. Yes.

42   Cash—it's practically in the air. Around the beach in La Jolla a guy can walk right out in the street and stand there, stop cars and make the candid move. Mister, I've got a quarter, how about 50 cents so I can get a *large* draft. Or, I need some after-ski boots. And the panthers give one a Jello smile and hand it over. Or a guy who knows how to do it can get $40 from a single night digging clams, and it's nice out there. Or he can go around and take up a collection for a keg party, a keg of beer. Man, anybody who won't kick in a quarter for a keg is a jerk. A couple of good keg collections—that's a trip to Hawaii, which is the surfer's version of a trip to Europe: there is a great surf and great everything there. Neale spent three weeks in Hawaii last year. He got $30 from a girl friend, he scrounged a little here and there and got $70 more and he headed off for Hawaii with $100.02, that being the exact plane fare, and borrowed 25 cents when he got there to . . . blast the place up. He spent the 25 cents in a photo booth, showed the photos to the people on the set of *Hawaii* and got a job in the movie. What's the big orgy about money? It's warm, nobody even wears shoes, nobody is starving.

43   All right, Mother gets worried about all this, but it is limited worry, as John Shine says. Mainly, Mother says, *Sayonara*, you all, and you head off for the beach.

44   The thing is, everybody, practically everybody, comes from a good family. Everyone has been . . . *reared well*, as they say. Everybody is very upper middle, if you want to bring it down to that. It's just that this is a new order. Why hang around in the

hubby-mommy household with everybody getting neurotic hang-ups with each other and slamming doors and saying, Why can't they have some privacy? Or, it doesn't mean anything that I have to work for a living, does it? It doesn't mean a thing to you. All of you just lie around here sitting in the big orange easy chair smoking cigarettes. I'd hate for you to have to smoke standing up, you'd probably get phlebitis from it—Listen to me, Sarah—

45 —why go through all that? It's a good life out here. Nobody is mugging everybody for money and affection. There are a lot of bright people out here, and there are a lot of interesting things. One night there was a toga party in a garage, and everybody dressed in sheets, like togas, boys and girls and they put on the appropriated television set to an old Deanna Durbin movie and turned off the sound and put on Rolling Stones records, and you should have seen Deanna Durbin opening her puckered kumquat mouth with Mick Jagger's voice bawling out, *I ain't got no satisfaction.* Of course, finally everybody started pulling the togas off each other, but that is another thing. And one time they had a keg party down on the beach in Mission Bay and the lights from the amusement park were reflected all over the water and that, the whole design of the thing, those nutty lights, that was part of the party. Liz put out the fire throwing a "sand potion" or something on it. One can laugh at Liz and her potions, her necromancy and everything, but there is a lot of thought going into it, a lot of, well, mysticism.

46 You can even laugh at mysticism if you want to, but there is a kid like Larry Alderson, who spent two years with a monk, and he learned a lot of stuff, and Artie Nelander is going to spend next summer with some Outer Mongolian tribe; he really means to do that. Maybe the "mysterioso" stuff is a lot of garbage, but still, it is interesting. The surfers around the Pump House use that word, mysterioso, quite a lot. It refers to the mystery of the Oh Mighty Hulking Pacific Ocean and everything. Sometimes a guy will stare at the surf and say, "Mysterioso." They keep telling the story of Bob Simmons' wipeout, and somebody will say "mysterioso."

47 Simmons was a fantastic surfer. He was fantastic even though he had a bad leg. He rode the really big waves. One day he got wiped out at Windansea. When a big wave overtakes a surfer, it drives him right to the bottom. The board came in but he never came up and they never found his body. Very mysterioso. The black panthers all talked about what happened to "the Simmons

boy." But the mysterioso thing was how he could have died at all. If he had been one of the old pan-thuhs, hell, sure he could have got killed. But Simmons was, well, one's own age, he was the kind of guy who could have been in the Pump House gang, he was . . . *immune*, he was plugged into the whole pattern, he could feel the whole Oh Mighty Hulking Sea, he didn't have to think it out step by step. But he got wiped out and killed. Very mysterioso.

48   Immune! If one is in the Pump House gang and really keyed in to this whole thing, it's—well, one is . . . *immune*, one is not full of black pan-thuh panic. Two kids, a 14-year-old girl and a 16-year-old boy, go out to Windansea at dawn, in the middle of winter, cold as hell, and take on 12-foot waves all by themselves. The girl, Jackie Haddad, daughter of a certified public accountant, wrote a composition about it, just for herself, called "My Ultimate Journey":

49   "It was six o'clock in the morning, damp, foggy and cold. We could feel the bitter air biting at our cheeks. The night before, my friend Tommy and I had seen one of the greatest surf films, *Surf Classics*. The film had excited us so much we made up our minds to go surfing the following morning. That is what brought us down on the cold, wet, soggy sand of Windansea early on a December morning.

50   "We were the first surfers on the beach. The sets were rolling in at eight to 10, filled with occasional 12-footers. We waxed up and waited for a break in the waves. The break came, neither of us said a word, but instantly grabbed our boards and ran into the water. The paddle out was difficult, not being used to the freezing water.

51   "We barely made it over the first wave of the set, a large set. Suddenly Tommy put on a burst of speed and shot past me. He cleared the biggest wave of the set. It didn't hit me hard as I rolled under it. It dragged me almost 20 yards before exhausting its strength. I climbed on my board gasping for air. I paddled out to where Tommy was resting. He laughed at me for being wet already. I almost hit him but I began laughing, too. We rested a few minutes and then lined up our position with a well known spot on the shore.

52   "I took off first. I bottom-turned hard and started climbing up the wave. A radical cut-back caught me off balance and I fell, barely hanging onto my board. I recovered in time to see Tommy

go straight over the falls on a 10-footer. His board shot nearly 30 feet in the air. Luckily, I could get it before the next set came in, so Tommy didn't have to make the long swim in. I pushed it to him and then laughed. All of a sudden Tommy yelled, 'Outside!'

53   "Both of us paddled furiously. We barely made it up to the last wave, it was a monster. In precision timing we wheeled around and I took off. I cut left in reverse stance, then cut back, driving hard toward the famous Windansea bowl. As I crouched, a huge wall of energy came down over me, covering me up. I moved toward the nose to gain more speed and shot out of the fast-flowing suction just in time to kick out as the wave closed out.

54   "As I turned around I saw Tommy make a beautiful drop-in, then the wave peaked and fell all at once. Miraculously he beat the suction. He cut back and did a spinner, which followed with a reverse kick-up.

55   "Our last wave was the biggest. When we got to shore, we rested, neither of us saying a word, but each lost in his own private world of thoughts. After we had rested, we began to walk home. We were about half way and the rain came pouring down. That night we both had bad colds, but we agreed it was worth having them after the thrill and satisfaction of an extra good day of surfing."

56   John Shine and Artie Nelander are out there right now. They are just "outside," about one fifth of a mile out from the shore, beyond where the waves start breaking. They are straddling their surfboards with their backs to the shore, looking out toward the horizon, waiting for a good set. Their backs look like some kind of salmon-colored porcelain shells, a couple of tiny shells bobbing up and down as the swells roll under them, staring out to sea like Phrygian sacristans looking for a sign.

57   John and Artie! They are—they are what one means when one talks about the surfing life. It's like, you know, one means, they have this life all of their own; it's like a glass-bottom boat, and it floats over the "real" world, or the square world or whatever one wants to call it. They are not exactly off in a world of their own, they are and they aren't. What it is, they float right through the real world, but it can't touch them. They do these things, like the time they went to Malibu, and there was this party in some guy's apartment, and there wasn't enough *legal* parking space for

everybody, and so somebody went out and painted the red curbs white and everybody parked. Then the cops came. Everybody ran out. Artie and John took an airport bus to the Los Angeles Airport, just like they were going to take a plane, in khaki shorts and T-shirts with Mac Meda Destruction Company stenciled on them. Then they took a helicopter to Disneyland. At Disneyland crazy Ditch had his big raincoat on and a lot of flasks strapped onto his body underneath, Scotch, bourbon, all kinds of stuff. He had plastic tubes from the flasks sticking out of the flyfront of his raincoat and everybody was sipping whiskey through the tubes—

58   Ooooo-eeee—Mee-dah! They chant this chant, Mee-dah, in a real fakey deep voice, and it *really bugs people.* They don't know what the hell it is. It is the cry of the Mac Meda Destruction Company. The Mac Meda Destruction Company is . . . an *underground* society that started in La Jolla about three years ago. Nobody can remember exactly how; they have arguments about it. Anyhow, it is mainly something to *bug* people with and organize huge beer orgies with. They have their own complete, bogus phone number in La Jolla. They have Mac Meda Destruction Company decals. They stick them on phone booths, on cars, any place. Some mommy-hubby will come out of the shopping plaza and walk up to his Mustang, which is supposed to make him a hell of a tiger now, and he'll see a sticker on the side of it saying, "Mac Meda Destruction Company," and for about two days or something he'll think the sky is going to fall in.

59   But the big thing is the parties, the "conventions." Anybody can join, any kid, anybody can come, as long as they've heard about it, and they can only hear about it by word of mouth. One was in the Sorrento Valley, in the gulches and arroyos, and the fuzz came, and so the older guys put the young ones and the basket cases, the ones just too stoned out of their gourds, into the tule grass, and the cops shined their searchlights and all they saw was tule grass, while the basket cases moaned scarlet and oozed on their bellies like reptiles and everybody else ran down the arroyos, yelling Mee-dah.

60   The last one was at Manhattan Beach, inside somebody's poor hulking house. The party got *very Dionysian* that night and somebody put a hole through one wall, and everybody else decided to see if they could make it bigger. Everybody was stoned out of their hulking gourds, and it got to be about 3:30 a.m. and

everybody decided to go see the riots. These were the riots in Watts. The Los Angeles *Times* and the San Diego *Union* were all saying, WATTS NO-MAN'S LAND and STAY WAY FROM WATTS YOU GET YO' SE'F KILLED, but naturally nobody believed that. Watts was a blast, and the Pump House gang was immune to the trembling gourd panic rattles of the L.A. *Times* black pan-thuhs. Immune!

61   So John Shine, Artie Nelander and Jerry Sterncorb got in John's VW bus, known as the Hog of Steel, and they went to Watts. Gary Wickham and some other guys ran into an old man at a bar who said he owned a house in Watts and had been driven out by the drunk niggers. So they drove in a car to save the old guy's house from the drunk niggers. Artie and John had a tape recorder and decided they were going to make a record called "Random Sounds from the Watts Riots." They drove right into Watts in the Hog of Steel and there was blood on the streets and roofs blowing off the stores and all these apricot flames and drunk Negroes falling through the busted plate glass of the liquor stores. Artie got a nice recording of a lot of Negroes chanting "Burn, baby, burn." They all got out and talked to some Negro kids in a gang going into a furniture store, and the Negro kids didn't say Kill Whitey or Geed'um or any of that. They just said, Come on, man, it's a party and it's free. After they had been in there for about three hours talking to Negroes and watching drunks collapse in the liquor stores, some cop with a helmet on came roaring up and said, "Get the hell out of here, you kids, we cannot and will not provide protection."

62   Meantime, Gary Wickham and his friends drove in a car with the old guy, and a car full of Negroes *did* stop them and say, Whitey, Geed'um, and all that stuff, but one of the guys in Gary's car just draped a pistol he had out the window and the colored guys drove off. Gary and everybody drove the old guy to his house and they all walked in and had a great raunchy time drinking beer and raising hell. A couple of Negroes, the old guy's neighbors, came over and told the old guy to cut out the racket. There were flames in the sky and ashes coming down with little rims of fire on them, like apricot crescents. The old guy got very cocky about all his "protection" and went out on the front porch about dawn and started yelling at some Negroes across the street, telling them "No more drunk niggers in Watts" and a lot of other unwise slogans. So Gary Wickham got up and everybody left. They were there

about four hours altogether and when they drove out, they had to go through a National Guard checkpoint, and a lieutenant from the San Fernando Valley told them he could not and would not provide protection.

63   But exactly! Watts just happened to be what was going on at the time, as far as the netherworld of La Jolla surfing was concerned, and so one goes there and sees what is happening and comes back and tells everybody about it and laughs at the L.A. *Times.* That is what makes it so weird when all these black pan-thuhs come around to pick up "surfing styles," like the clothing manufacturers. They don't know what any of it means. It's like archaeologists discovering hieroglyphics of something, and they say, god, that's neat—Egypt!—but they don't know what the hell it is. They don't know anything about . . . *The Life.* It's great to think of a lot of old emphysematous pan-thuhs in the Garment District in New York City struggling in off the street against a gummy 15-mile-an-hour wind full of soot and coffee-brown snow and gasping in the elevator to clear their old nicotine-phlegm tubes on the way upstairs to make out the invoices on a lot of surfer stuff for 1966, the big nylon windbreakers with the wide, white horizontal competition stripes, nylon swimming trunks with competition stripes, bell-bottom slacks for girls, the big hairy sleeveless jackets, vests, the blue "tennies," meaning tennis shoes, and the . . . *look,* the Major Hair, all this long lank blond hair, the plain face kind of tanned and bleached out at the same time, but with big eyes. It all starts in a few places, a few strategic groups, the Pump House gang being one of them, and then it moves up the beach, to places like Newport Beach and as far up as Malibu.

64   Well, actually there is a kind of back-and-forth thing with some of the older guys, the old heroes of surfing, like Bruce Brown, John Severson, Hobie Alter and Phil Edwards. Bruce Brown will do one of those incredible surfing movies and he is out in the surf himself filming Phil Edwards coming down a 20-footer in Hawaii, and Phil has on a pair of nylon swimming trunks, which he has had made in Hawaii, because they dry out fast—and it is like a grapevine. Everybody's got to have a pair of nylon swimming trunks, and then the manufacturers move in, and everybody's making nylon swimming trunks, boxer trunk style, and pretty soon every kid in Utica, N.Y., is buying a pair of them, with

the competition stripe and the whole thing, and they never heard
of Phil Edwards. So it works back and forth—but so what? Phil
Edwards is part of it. He may be an old guy, he is 28 years old, but
he and Bruce Brown, who is even older, 30, and John Severson, 32,
and Hobie Alter, 29, never haired out to the square world even
though they make thousands. Hair refers to courage. A guy who
"has a lot of hair" is courageous; a guy who "hairs out" is yellow.

65   Bruce Brown and Severson and Alter are known as the
"surfing millionaires." They are not millionaires, actually, but they
must be among the top businessmen south of Los Angeles. Brown
grossed something around $500,000 in 1965 even before his
movie *Endless Summer* became a hit nationally; and he has only
about three people working for him. He goes out on a surfboard
with a camera encased in a plastic shell and takes his own movies
and edits them himself and goes around showing them himself
and narrating them at places like the Santa Monica Civic
Auditorium, where 24,000 came in eight days once, at $1.50 a per-
son, and all he has to pay is for developing the film and hiring the
hall. John Severson has the big surfing magazine, *Surfer*. Hobie
Alter is the biggest surfboard manufacturer, all hand-made
boards. He made 5,000 boards in 1965 at $140 a board. He also
designed the "Hobie" skate boards and gets 25 cents for every one
sold. He grossed between $900,000 and $1 million in 1964.

66   God, if only everybody could grow up like these guys and
know that crossing the horror dividing line, 25 years old, won't be
the end of everything. One means, keep on living *The Life* and not
get sucked into the ticky-tacky life with some insurance salesman
sitting forward in your stuffed chair on your wall-to-wall telling
you that life is like a football game and you sit there and take that
stuff. The hell with that! Bruce Brown has the money and *The Life*.
He has a great house on a cliff about 60 feet above the beach at
Dana Point. He is married and has two children, but it is not that
hubby-mommy you're-breaking-my-gourd scene. His office is only
two blocks from his house and he doesn't even have to go on the
streets to get there. He gets on his Triumph scrambling motorcycle and cuts straight across a couple of vacant lots and one can see
him . . . *bounding* to work over the vacant lots. The Triumph hits
ruts and hummocks and things and Bruce Brown bounces into
the air with the motor—*thragggggh*—moaning away, and when he
gets to the curbing in front of his office, he just leans back and

pulls up the front wheel and hops it and gets off and walks into the office barefooted. *Barefooted;* why not? He wears the same things now that he did when he was doing nothing but surfing. He has on a faded gray sweatshirt with the sleeves cut off just above the elbows and a pair of faded corduroys. His hair is the lightest corn yellow imaginable, towheaded, practically white, from the sun. Even his eyes seem to be bleached. He has a rain-barrel old-apple-tree Tom-Sawyer little-boy roughneck look about him, like Bobby Kennedy.

67   Sometimes he carries on his business right there at the house. He has a dugout room built into the side of the cliff, about 15 feet down from the level of the house. It is like a big pale green box set into the side of the cliff, and inside is a kind of uphol-stered bench or settee you can lie down on if you want to and look out at the Pacific. The surf is crashing like a maniac on the rocks down below. He has a telephone in there. Sometimes it will ring, and Bruce Brown says hello, and the surf is crashing away down below, roaring like mad, and the guy on the other end, maybe one of the TV networks calling from New York or some movie hair-out from Los Angeles, says:

68   "What is all that noise? It sounds like you're sitting out in the surf."

69   "That's right," says Bruce Brown, "I have my desk out on the beach now. It's nice out here."

70   The guy on the other end doesn't know what to think. He is another Mr. Efficiency who just got back from bloating his colon up at a three-hour executive lunch somewhere and now he is Mr.-Big-Time-Let's-Get-This-Show-on-the-Road.

71   "On the beach?"

72   "Yeah. It's cooler down here. And it's good for you, but it's not so great for the desk. You know what I have now? A warped leg."

73   "A warped leg?"

74   "Yeah, and this is an $800 desk."

75   Those nutball California kids—and he will still be muttering that five days after Bruce Brown delivers his film, on time, and Mr. Efficiency is still going through memo thickets or heaving his way into the bar car to Darien—in the very moment that Bruce Brown and Hobie Alter are both on their motorcycles out on the vacant lot in Dana Point. Hobie Alter left his surfboard plant about two

in the afternoon because the wind was up and it would be good catamaranning and he wanted to go out and see how far he could tip his new catamaran without going over, and he did tip it over, about half a mile out in high swells and it was hell getting the thing right side up again. But he did, and he got back in time to go scrambling on the lot with Bruce Brown. They are out there, roaring over the ruts, bouncing up in the air, and every now and then they roar up the embankment so they can . . . fly, going up in the air about six feet off the ground as they come up off the embankment—*thraaagggggh*—all these people in the houses around there come to the door and look out. These two . . . nuts are at it again. Well, they can only fool around there for 20 minutes, because that is about how long it takes the cops to get there if anybody gets burned up enough and calls, and what efficient business magnate wants to get hauled off by the Dana Point cops for scrambling on his motorcycle in a vacant lot.

76   Bruce Brown has it figured out so no one in the whole rubber-bloated black pan-thuh world can trap him, though. He bought a forest in the Sierras. There is nothing on it but trees. His own wilds: no house, no nothing, just Bruce Brown's forest. Beautiful things happen up there. One day, right after he bought it, he was on the edge of his forest, where the road comes into it, and one of these big rancher king motheroos with the broad belly and the $70 lisle Safari shirt comes tooling up in a Pontiac convertible with a funnel of dust pouring out behind. He gravels it to a great flashy stop and yells:

77   "Hey! You!"

78   Of course, what he sees is some towheaded barefooted kid in a torn-off sweatshirt fooling around the edge of the road.

79   "Hey! You!"

80   "Yeah?" says Bruce Brown.

81   "Don't you know this is private property?"

82   "Yeah," says Bruce Brown.

83   "Well, then, why don't you get your ass off it?"

84   "Because it's mine, it's my private property," says Bruce Brown. "Now you get *yours* off it."

85   And Safari gets a few rays from that old apple-tree rainbarrel don't-cross-that-line look and doesn't say anything and roars off, slipping gravel, the dumb crumbling pan-thuh.

86   But . . . perfect! It is like, one means, you know, poetic justice for all the nights Bruce Brown slept out on the beach at San

Onofre and such places in the old surfing days and would wake up with some old crock's black feet standing beside his head and some phlegmy black rubber voice saying:

87   "All right, kid, don't you know this is private property?"

88   And he would prop his head up and out there would be the Pacific Ocean, a kind of shadowy magenta-mauve, and one thing, *that* was nobody's private property—

89   But how many Bruce Browns can there be? There is a built-in trouble with age segregation. Eventually one *does* reach the horror age of 25, the horror dividing line. Surfing and the surfing life have been going big since 1958, and already there are kids who—well, who aren't kids anymore, they are pushing 30, and they are stagnating on the beach. Pretty soon the California littoral will be littered with these guys, stroked out on the beach like beached white whales, and girls, too, who can't give up the mystique, the mysterioso mystique, Oh Mighty Hulking Sea, who can't *conceive* of living any other life. It is pathetic when they are edged out of groups like the Pump House gang. Already there are some guys who hang around with the older crowd around the Shack who are stagnating on the beach. Some of the older guys, like Gary Wickham, who is 24, are still in *The Life,* they still have it, but even Gary Wickham will be 25 one day and then 26 and then. . . . and then even pan-thuh age. Is one really going to be pan-thuh age one day? Watch those black feet go. And Tom Coman still snuggles with Yellow Slacks, and Liz still roosts moodily in her rabbit fur at the bottom of the Pump House and Pam still sits on the steps contemplating the mysterioso mysteries of Pump House ascension and John and Artie still bob, tiny pink porcelain shells, way out there waiting for godsown bitchen *set,* and godsown sun still turned on like a dentist's lamp and so far—

90   —the panthers scrape on up the sidewalk. They are at just about the point Leonard Anderson and Donna Blanchard got that day, December 6, 1964, when Leonard said, Pipe it, and fired two shots, one at her and one at himself. Leonard was 18 and Donna was 21—21!—god, for a girl in the Pump House gang that is almost the horror line right there. But it was all so mysterioso. Leonard was just lying down on the beach at the foot of the Pump House, near the stairs, just talking to John K. Weldon down there, and then Donna appeared at the top of the stairs and Leonard got up and went up the stairs to meet her, and they didn't say any-

thing, they weren't *angry* over anything, they never had been, although the police said they had, they just turned and went a few feet down the sidewalk, away from the Pump House and—blam blam!—these two shots. Leonard fell dead on the sidewalk and Donna died that afternoon in Scripps Memorial Hospital. Nobody knew what to think. But one thing it seemed like—well, it seemed like Donna and Leonard thought they had lived *The Life* as far as it would go and now it was running out. All that was left to do was—but that is an *insane* idea. It can't be like that, *The Life* can't run out, people can't change all that much just because godsown chronometer runs on and the body packing starts deteriorating and the fudgy tallow shows up at the thighs where they squeeze out of the bathing suit—

91   Tom, boy! John, boy! Gary, boy! Neale, boy! Artie, boy! Pam, Liz, Vicki, Jackie Haddad! After all this—just a pair of bitchen black panther bunions inching down the sidewalk away from the old Pump House stairs?

QUESTIONS

Ideas

1. Can you summarize the point of this piece in a sentence? If not, why do you need more room to explain what Wolfe means here?
2. In part "The Pump House Gang" describes age segregation, especially how the age or generation gap is evidenced in differing styles of language and dress and even more importantly in differing beliefs, attitudes, and values. To what extent is Wolfe's description of such age segregation from an earlier time relevant today?

Organization

3. Is this selection logically organized? Explain. Identify its pattern of organization.
4. Consider the structure of a single paragraph or any group of paragraphs that you consider a unit. Identify the basis of that unity and explain how Wolfe achieves it.

Sentences

5. Many of Wolfe's sentences are interrupted with one or more dashes. Find three examples and comment on the function of the dashes in each.

6. Select one sentence that you find particularly effective and explain why and how it achieves the effects it does.

Words

7. Select one passage in which Wolfe's language captures the temper and flavor of the Pump House Gang, and which shows Wolfe as something of an insider. Identify individual words and phrases that reflect their style of discourse—in short, their talk.
8. Select another passage in which Wolfe seems to look at the Pump House Gang from the outside—as an outside observer. What do you notice about his language here?

Suggestions for Writing

A. Identify what you see as an age gap and write an essay in which you both explain and illustrate the divided age groups.
B. Compare Wolfe's depiction of the world of the sixties with that of Joan Didion in "The White Album." Explain which vision you find more appealing and why.

The Right Stuff

1   A young man might go into military flight training believing that he was entering some sort of technical school in which he was simply going to acquire a certain set of skills. Instead, he found himself all at once enclosed in a fraternity. And in this fraternity, even though it was military, men were not rated by their outward rank as ensigns, lieutenants, commanders, or whatever. No, herein the world was divided into those who had it and those who did not. This quality, this *it*, was never named, however, nor was it talked about in any way.
2   As to just what this ineffable quality was . . . well, it obviously involved bravery. But it was not bravery in the simple sense of being willing to risk your life. The idea seemed to be that any fool could do that, if that was all that was required, just as any fool could throw away his life in the process. No, the idea here (in the all-enclosing fraternity) seemed to be that a man should have the ability to go up in a hurtling piece of machinery and put his hide on the line and then have the moxie, the reflexes, the experience,

the coolness, to pull it back in the last yawning moment—and then to go up again *the next day,* and the next day, and every next day, even if the series should prove infinite—and, ultimately, in its best expression, do so in a cause that means something to thousands, to a people, a nation, to humanity, to God. Nor was there *a test* to show whether or not a pilot had this righteous quality. There was, instead, a seemingly infinite series of tests. A career in flying was like climbing one of those ancient Babylonian pyramids made up of a dizzy progression of steps and ledges, a ziggurat, a pyramid extraordinarily high and steep; and the idea was to prove at every foot of the way up that pyramid that you were one of the elected and anointed ones who had *the right stuff* and could move higher and higher and even—ultimately, God willing, one day— that you might be able to join that special few at the very top, that elite who had the capacity to bring tears to men's eyes, the very Brotherhood of the Right Stuff itself.

3   None of this was to be mentioned, and yet it was acted out in a way that a young man could not fail to understand. When a new flight (i.e., a class) of trainees arrived at Pensacola, they were brought into an auditorium for a little lecture. An officer would tell them: "Take a look at the man on either side of you." Quite a few actually swiveled their heads this way and that, in the interest of appearing diligent. Then the officer would say: "One of the three of you is not going to make it!"—meaning, not get his wings. That was the opening theme, the *motif* of primary training. We already know that one-third of you do not have the right stuff—it only remains to find out who.

4   Furthermore, that was the way it turned out. At every level in one's progress up that staggeringly high pyramid, the world was once more divided into those men who had the right stuff to continue the climb and those who had to be *left behind* in the most obvious way. Some were eliminated in the course of the opening classroom work, as either not smart enough or not hardworking enough, and were left behind. Then came the basic flight instruction, in single-engine, propeller-driven trainers, and a few more— even though the military tried to make this stage easy—were washed out and left behind. Then came more demanding levels, one after the other, formation flying, instrument flying, jet training, all-weather flying, gunnery, and at each level more were washed out and left behind. By this point easily a third of the original candidates had been, indeed, eliminated . . . from the ranks of those who might prove to have the right stuff.

5   In the Navy, in addition to the stages that Air Force trainees went through, the neophyte always had waiting for him, out in the ocean, a certain grim gray slab; namely, the deck of an aircraft carrier; and with it perhaps the most difficult routine in military flying, carrier landings. He was shown films about it, he heard lectures about it, and he knew that carrier landings were hazardous. He first practiced touching down on the shape of a flight deck painted on an airfield. He was instructed to touch down and gun right off. This was safe enough—the shape didn't move, at least—but it could do terrible things to, let us say, the gyroscope of the soul. *That shape!—it's so damned small!* And more candidates were washed out and left behind. Then came the day, without warning, when those who remained were sent out over the ocean for the first of many days of reckoning with the slab. The first day was always a clear day with little wind and a calm sea. The carrier was so steady that it seemed, from up there in the air, to be resting on pilings, and the candidate usually made his first carrier landing successfully, with relief and even *élan*. Many young candidates looked like terrific aviators up to that very point—and it was not until they were actually standing on the carrier deck that they first began to wonder if they had the proper stuff, after all. In the training film the flight deck was a grand piece of gray geometry, perilous, to be sure, but an amazing abstract shape as one looks down upon it on the screen. And yet once the newcomer's two feet were on it . . . *Geometry*—my God, man, this is a . . . skillet! It *heaved*, it moved up and down underneath his feet, it pitched up, it pitched down, it rolled to port (this great beast *rolled!*) and it rolled to starboard, as the ship moved into the wind and, therefore, into the waves, and the wind kept sweeping across, sixty feet up in the air out in the open sea, and there were no railings whatsoever. This was a *skillet!*—a frying pan!—a short-order grill!—not gray but black, smeared with skid marks from one end to the other and glistening with pools of hydraulic fluid and the occasional jet-fuel slick, all of it still hot, sticky, greasy, runny, virulent from God knows what traumas—still ablaze!—consumed in detonations, explosions, flames, combustion, roars, shrieks, whines, blasts, horrible shudders, fracturing impacts, as little men in screaming red and yellow and purple and green shirts with black Mickey Mouse helmets over their ears skittered about on the surface as if for their very lives (you've said it now!), hooking fighter planes onto the catapult shuttles so that they can explode their afterburners and be slung off the deck in a red-mad fury with a

kaboom! that pounds through the entire deck—a procedure that seems absolutely controlled, orderly, sublime, however, compared to what he is about to watch as aircraft return to the ship for what is known in the engineering stoicisms of the military as "recovery and arrest." To say that an F-4 was coming back onto this heaving barbecue from out of the sky at a speed of 135 knots . . . that might have been the truth in the training lecture, but it did not begin to get across the idea of what the newcomer saw from the deck itself, because it created the notion that perhaps the plane was gliding in. On the deck one knew differently! As the aircraft came closer and the carrier heaved on into the waves and the plane's speed did not diminish and the deck did not grow steady—indeed, it pitched up and down five or ten feet per greasy heave—one experienced a neural alarm that no lecture could have prepared him for: This is not an *airplane* coming toward me, it is a brick with some poor sonofabitch riding it *(someone much like myself!)*, and it is not *gliding*, it is *falling*, a fifty-thousand-pound brick, headed not for a stripe on the deck but for *me*—and with a horrible *smash!* it hits the skillet, and with a blur of momentum as big as a freight train's it hurtles toward the far end of the deck—another blinding storm!—another roar as the pilot pushes the throttle up to full military power and another smear of rubber screams out over the skillet—and this is nominal!—quite okay!—for a wire stretched across the deck has grabbed the hook on the end of the plane as it hit the deck tail down, and the smash was the rest of the fifteen-ton brute slamming onto the deck, as it tripped up, so that it is now straining against the wire at full throttle, in case it hadn't held and the plane had "boltered" off the end of the deck and had to struggle up into the air again. And already the Mickey Mouse helmets are running toward the fiery monster . . .

6   And the candidate, looking on, begins to *feel* that great heaving sun-blazing deathboard of a deck wallowing in his own vestibular system—and suddenly he finds himself backed up against his own limits. He ends up going to the flight surgeon with so-called conversion symptoms. Overnight he develops blurred vision or numbness in his hands and feet or sinusitis so severe that he cannot tolerate changes in altitude. On one level the symptom is real. He really cannot see too well or use his fingers or stand the pain. But somewhere in his subconscious he knows it is a plea and a beg-off; he shows not the slightest concern

(the flight surgeon notes) that the condition might be permanent and affect him in whatever life awaits him outside the arena of the right stuff.

7   Those who remained, those who qualified for carrier duty— and even more so those who later on qualified for *night* carrier duty—began to feel a bit like Gideon's warriors. *So many have been left behind!* The young warriors were now treated to a deathly sweet and quite unmentionable sight. They could gaze at length upon the crushed and wilted pariahs who had washed out. They could inspect those who did not have that righteous stuff.

8   The military did not have very merciful instincts. Rather than packing up these poor souls and sending them home, the Navy, like the Air Force and the Marines, would try to make use of them in some other role, such as flight controller. So the washout has to keep taking classes with the rest of his group, even though he can no longer touch an airplane. He sits there in the classes staring at sheets of paper with cataracts of sheer human mortification over his eyes while the rest steal looks at him . . . this man reduced to an ant, this untouchable, this poor sonof-abitch. And in what test had he been found wanting? Why, it seemed to be nothing less than *manhood* itself. Naturally, this was never mentioned, either. Yet there it was. *Manliness, manhood, manly courage* . . . there was something ancient, primordial, irresistible about the challenge of this stuff, no matter what a sophisticated and rational age one might think he lived in.

9   Perhaps because it could not be talked about, the subject began to take on superstitious and even mystical outlines. A man either had it or he didn't! There was no such thing as having *most* of it. Moreover, it could blow at any seam. One day a man would be ascending the pyramid at a terrific clip, and the next— bingo!—he would reach his own limits in the most unexpected way. Conrad and Schirra met an Air Force pilot who had had a great pal at Tyndall Air Force Base in Florida. This man had been the budding ace of the training class; he had flown the hottest fighter-style trainer, the T-38, like a dream; and then he began the routine step of being checked out in the T-33. The T-33 was not nearly as hot an aircraft as the T-38; it was essentially the old P-80 jet fighter. It had an exceedingly small cockpit. The pilot could barely move his shoulders. It was the sort of airplane of which everybody said, "You don't get into it, you *wear* it." Once inside a T-33 cockpit this man, this budding ace, developed claustropho-

bia of the most paralyzing sort. He tried everything to overcome it. He even went to a psychiatrist, which was a serious mistake for a military officer if his superiors learned of it. But nothing worked. He was shifted over to flying jet transports, such as the C-135. Very demanding and necessary aircraft they were, too, and he was still spoken of as an excellent pilot. But as everyone knew—and, again, it was never explained in so many words—only those who were assigned to fighter squadrons, the "fighter jocks," as they called each other with a self-satisfied irony, remained in the true fraternity. Those assigned to transports were not humiliated like washouts—*somebody* had to fly those planes—nevertheless, they, too, had been *left behind* for lack of the right stuff.

10   Or a man could go for a routine physical one fine day, feeling like a million dollars, and be grounded for *fallen arches*. It happened!—just like that! (And try raising them.) Or for breaking his wrist and losing only *part* of its mobility. Or for a minor deterioration of eyesight, or for any of hundreds of reasons that would make no difference to a man in an ordinary occupation. As a result all fighter jocks began looking upon doctors as their natural enemies. Going to see a flight surgeon was a no-gain proposition; a pilot could only hold his own or lose in the doctor's office. To be grounded for a medical reason was no humiliation, looked at objectively. But it was a humiliation, nonetheless!—for it meant you no longer had that indefinable, unutterable, integral stuff. (It could blow at *any* seam.)

11   All the hot young fighter jocks began trying to test the limits themselves in a superstitious way. They were like believing Presbyterians of a century before who used to probe their own experience to see if they were truly among *the elect*. When a fighter pilot was in training, whether in the Navy or the Air Force, his superiors were continually spelling out strict rules for him, about the use of the aircraft and conduct in the sky. They repeatedly forbade so-called hot-dog stunts, such as outside loops, buzzing, flathatting, hedgehopping and flying under bridges. But somehow one got the message that the man who truly *had* it could ignore those rules—not that he should make a point of it, but that he *could*—and that after all there was only one way to find out—and that in some strange unofficial way, peeking through his fingers, his instructor halfway expected him to challenge all the limits. They would give a lecture about how a pilot should never fly without a good solid breakfast—eggs, bacon, toast, and so forth—

because if he tried to fly with his blood-sugar level too low, it could impair his alertness. Naturally, the next day every hot dog in the unit would get up and have a breakfast consisting of one cup of black coffee and take off and go up into a vertical climb until the weight of the ship exactly canceled out the upward pull of the engine and his air speed was zero, and he would hang there for one thick adrenal instant—and then fall like a rock, until one of three things happened: he keeled over nose first and regained his aerodynamics and all was well, he went into a spin and fought his way out of it, or he went into a spin and had to eject or crunch it, which was always supremely possible.

12 Likewise, "hassling"—mock dogfighting was strictly forbidden, and so naturally young fighter jocks could hardly wait to go up in, say, a pair of F-100s and start the duel by making a pass at each other at 800 miles an hour, the winner being the pilot who could slip in behind the other one and get locked in on his tail ("wax his tail"), and it was not uncommon for some eager jock to try too tight an outside turn and have his engine flame out, whereupon, unable to restart it, he has to eject . . . and he shakes his fist at the victor as he floats down by parachute and his half-a-million-dollar aircraft goes *kaboom!* on the palmetto grass or the desert floor, and he starts thinking about how he can get together with the other guy back at the base in time for the two of them to get their stories straight before the investigation: "I don't know what happened, sir. I was pulling up after a target run, and it just flamed out on me." Hassling was forbidden, and hassling that led to the destruction of an aircraft was a serious court-martial offense, and the man's superiors knew that the engine hadn't *just flamed out,* but every unofficial impulse on the base seemed to be saying: "Hell, we wouldn't give you a nickel for a pilot who hasn't done some crazy rat-racing like that. It's all part of the right stuff."

13 The other side of this impulse showed up in the reluctance of the young jocks to admit it when they had maneuvered themselves into a bad corner they couldn't get out of. There were two reasons why a fighter pilot hated to declare an emergency. First, it triggered a complex and very public chain of events at the field: all other incoming flights were held up, including many of one's comrades who were probably low on fuel; the fire trucks came trundling out to the runway like yellow toys (as seen from way up there), the better to illustrate one's hapless state; and the bureaucracy began to crank up the paper monster for the investigation

that always followed. And second, to declare an emergency, one first had to reach that conclusion in his own mind, which to the young pilot was the same as saying: "A minute ago I still *had* it— now I need your help!" To have a bunch of young fighter pilots up in the air thinking this way used to drive flight controllers crazy. They would see a ship beginning to drift off the radar, and they couldn't rouse the pilot on the microphone for anything other than a few meaningless mumbles, and they would know he was probably out there with engine failure at a low altitude, trying to reignite by lowering his auxiliary generator rig, which had a little propeller that was supposed to spin in the slipstream like a child's pinwheel.

14   "Whiskey Kilo Two Eight, do you want to declare an emergency?"

15   *This* would rouse him!—to say: "Negative, negative, Whiskey Kilo Two Eight is not declaring an emergency."

16   Kaboom. Believers in the right stuff would rather crash and burn.

17   One fine day, after he had joined a fighter squadron, it would dawn on the young pilot exactly how the losers in the great fraternal competition were now being left behind. Which is to say, not by instructors or other superiors or by failures at prescribed levels of competence, but by death. At this point the essence of the enterprise would begin to dawn on him. Slowly, step by step, the ante had been raised until he was now involved in what was surely the grimmest and grandest gamble of manhood. Being a fighter pilot—for that matter, simply taking off in a single-engine jet fighter of the Century series, such as an F-102, or any of the military's other marvelous bricks with fins on them—presented a man, on a perfectly sunny day, with more ways to get himself killed than his wife and children could imagine in their wildest fears. If he was barreling down the runway at two hundred miles an hour, completing the takeoff run, and the board started lighting up red, should he (a) abort the takeoff (and try to wrestle with the monster, which was gorged with jet fuel, out in the sand beyond the end of the runway) or (b) eject (and hope that the goddamned human cannonball trick works at zero altitude and he doesn't shatter an elbow or a kneecap on the way out) or (c) continue the takeoff and deal with the problem aloft (knowing full well that the ship may be on fire and therefore seconds away from exploding)? He would have one second to sort out the

options and act, and this kind of little workaday decision came up all the time. Occasionally a man would look coldly at the binary problem he was now confronting every day—Right Stuff/Death— and decide it wasn't worth it and voluntarily shift over to transports or reconnaissance or whatever. And his comrades would wonder, for a day or so, what evil virus had invaded his soul . . . as they left him behind. More often, however, the reverse would happen. Some college graduate would enter Navy aviation through the Reserves, simply as an alternative to the Army draft, fully intending to return to civilian life, to some waiting profession or family business; would become involved in the obsessive business of ascending the ziggurat pyramid of flying; and, at the end of his enlistment, would astound everyone back home and very likely himself as well by signing up for another one. What on earth got into him? He couldn't explain it. After all, the very words for it had been amputated. A Navy study showed that two-thirds of the fighter pilots who were rated in the top rungs of their groups—i.e., the hottest young pilots—reenlisted when the time came, and practically all were college graduates. By this point, a young fighter jock was like the preacher in *Moby Dick* who climbs up into the pulpit on a rope ladder and then pulls the ladder up behind him; except the pilot could not use the words necessary to express the vital lessons. Civilian life, and even home and hearth, now seemed not only far away but far *below,* back down many levels of the pyramid of the right stuff.

18   A fighter pilot soon found he wanted to associate only with other fighter pilots. Who else could understand the nature of the little proposition (right stuff/death) they were all dealing with? And what other subject could compare with it? It was riveting! To talk about it in so many words was forbidden, of course. The very words *death, danger, bravery, fear* were not to be uttered except in the occasional specific instance or for ironic effect. Nevertheless, the subject could be adumbrated in *code* or *by example.* Hence the endless evenings of pilots huddled together talking about flying. On these long and drunken evenings (the bane of their family life) certain theorems would be propounded and demonstrated— and all by *code* and *example.* One theorem was: There are no *accidents* and no fatal flaws in the machines; there are only pilots with the wrong stuff. (I.e., blind Fate can't kill me.) When Bud Jennings crashed and burned in the swamps at Jacksonville, the other pilots in Peter Conrad's squadron said: *How could he have*

been so stupid? It turned out that Jennings had gone up in the SNJ with his cockpit canopy opened in a way that was expressly forbidden in the manual, and carbon monoxide had been sucked in from the exhaust, and he passed out and crashed. All agreed that Bud Jennings was a good guy and a good pilot, but his epitaph on the ziggurat was: *How could he have been so stupid?* This seemed shocking at first, but by the time Conrad had reached the end of that bad string at Pax River, he was capable of his own corollary to the theorem: viz., no single factor ever killed a pilot; there was always a chain of mistakes. But what about Ted Whelan, who fell like a rock from 8,100 feet when his parachute failed? Well, the parachute was merely part of the chain: first, someone should have caught the structural defect that resulted in the hydraulic leak that triggered the emergency; second, Whelan did not check out his seat-parachute rig, and the drogue failed to separate the main parachute from the seat; but even after those two mistakes, Whelan had fifteen or twenty seconds, as he fell, to disengage himself from the seat and open the parachute manually. Why just stare at the scenery coming up to smack you in the face! And everyone nodded. (He failed—but I wouldn't have!) Once the theorem and the corollary were understood, the Navy's statistics about one in every four Navy aviators dying meant nothing. The figures were averages, and averages applied to those with average stuff.

19   A riveting subject, especially if it were one's own hide that was on the line. Every evening at bases all over America, there were military pilots huddled in officers clubs eagerly cutting the right stuff up in coded slices so they could talk about it. What more compelling topic of conversation was there in the world? In the Air Force there were even pilots who would ask the tower for priority landing clearance so that they could make the beer call on time, at 4 P.M. sharp, at the Officers Club. They would come right out and state the reason. The drunken rambles began at four and sometimes went on for ten or twelve hours. Such conversations! They diced that righteous stuff up into little bits, bowed ironically to it, stumbled blindfolded around it, groped, lurched, belched, staggered, bawled, sang, roared, and feinted at it with self-deprecating humor. Nevertheless!—they never mentioned it by name. No, they used the approved codes, such as: "Like a jerk I got myself into a hell of a corner today." They told of how they "lucked out of it." To get across the extreme peril of his exploit,

one would use certain oblique cues. He would say, "I looked over at Robinson"—who would be known to the listeners as a non-com who sometimes rode backseat to read radar—"and he wasn't talking any more, he was just staring at the radar, like this, giving it that *zombie* look. Then I *knew* I was in trouble!" Beautiful! Just right! For it would also be known to the listeners that the non-coms advised one another: "*Never* fly with a lieutenant. *Avoid* captains and majors. Hell, man, do yourself a favor: don't fly with anybody below colonel." Which in turn said: "Those young bucks shoot dice with death!" And yet once in the air the non-com had his own standards. He was determined to remain as outwardly cool as the pilot, so that when the pilot did something that truly petrified him, he would say nothing; instead, he would turn silent, catatonic, like a zombie. Perfect! *Zombie.* There you had it, compressed into a single word all of the foregoing. I'm a hell of a pilot! I shoot dice with death! And now all you fellows know it! And I haven't spoken of that unspoken stuff even once!

20   The talking and drinking began at the beer call, and then the boys would break for dinner and come back afterward and get more wasted and more garrulous or else more quietly fried, drinking good cheap PX booze until 2 a.m. The night was young! Why not get the cars and go out for a little proficiency run? It seemed that every fighter jock thought himself an ace driver, and he would do anything to obtain a hot car, especially a sports car, and the drunker he was, the more convinced he would be about his driving skills, as if the right stuff, being indivisible, carried over into any enterprise whatsoever, under any conditions. A little proficiency run, boys! (There's only one way to find out!) And they would roar off in close formation from, say, Nellis Air Force Base, down Route 15, into Las Vegas, barreling down the highway, rat-racing, sometimes four abreast, jockeying for position, piling into the most listless curve in the desert flats as if they were trying to root each other out of the groove at the Rebel 500—and then bursting into downtown Las Vegas with a rude fraternal roar like the Hell's Angels— and the natives chalked it up to youth and drink and the bad element that the Air Force attracted. They knew nothing about the right stuff, of course.

21   More fighter pilots died in automobiles than in airplanes. Fortunately, there was always some kindly soul up the chain to certify the papers "line of duty," so that the widow could get a better break on the insurance. That was okay and only proper because

somehow the system itself had long ago said *Skol!* and *Quite right!* to the military cycle of Flying & Drinking and Drinking & Driving, as if there were no other way. Every young fighter jock knew the feeling of getting two or three hours' sleep and then waking up at 5:30 a.m. and having a few cups of coffee, a few cigarettes, and then carting his poor quivering liver out to the field for another day of flying. There were those who arrived not merely hungover but still drunk, slapping oxygen tank cones over their faces and trying to burn the alcohol out of their systems, and then going up, remarking later: "I don't *advise* it, you understand, but it *can* be done." (Provided you have the right stuff, you miserable pud-knocker.)

22   Air Force and Navy airfields were usually on barren or marginal stretches of land and would have looked especially bleak and Low Rent to an ordinary individual in the chilly light of dawn. But to a young pilot there was an inexplicable bliss to coming out to the flight line while the sun was just beginning to cook up behind the rim of the horizon, so that the whole field was still in shadow and the ridges in the distance were in silhouette and the flight line was a monochrome of Exhaust Fume Blue, and every little red light on top of the water towers or power stanchions looked dull, shriveled, congealed, and the runway lights, which were still on, looked faded, and even the landing lights on a fighter that had just landed and was taxiing in were no longer dazzling, as they would be at night, and looked instead like shriveled gobs of candlepower out there—and yet it was beautiful, exhilarating!—for he was revved up with adrenalin, anxious to take off before the day broke, to burst up into the sunlight over the ridges before all those thousands of comatose souls down there, still dead to the world, snug in home and hearth, even came to their senses. To take off in an F-100F at dawn and cut on the afterburner and hurtle twenty-five thousand feet up into the sky in thirty seconds, so suddenly that you felt not like a bird but like a trajectory, yet with full control, full control of *four tons* of thrust, all of which flowed from your will and through your fingertips, with the huge engine right beneath you, so close that it was as if you were riding it bareback, until all at once you were supersonic, an event registered on earth by a tremendous cracking boom that shook windows, but up here only by the fact that you now felt utterly free of the earth—to describe it, even to wife, child, near ones and dear ones, seemed impossible. So the pilot kept it to himself,

along with an even more indescribable . . . an even more sinfully inconfessable . . . feeling of superiority, appropriate to him and to his kind, lone bearers of the right stuff.

23   From *up here* at dawn the pilot looked down upon poor hopeless Las Vegas (or Yuma, Corpus Christi, Meridian, San Bernardino, or Dayton) and began to wonder: How can all of them down there, those poor souls who will soon be waking up and trudging out of their minute rectangles and inching along their little noodle highways toward whatever slots and grooves make up their everyday lives—how could they live like that, with such earnestness, if they had the faintest idea of what it was like up here in this righteous zone?

24   But of course! Not only the washed-out, grounded, and dead pilots had been left behind—but also all of those millions of sleepwalking souls who never even attempted the great gamble. The entire world below . . . *left behind*. Only at this point can one begin to understand just how big, how titanic, the ego of the military pilot could be. The world was used to enormous egos in artists, actors, entertainers of all sorts, in politicians, sports figures, and even journalists, because they had such familiar and convenient ways to show them off. But that slim young man over there in uniform, with the enormous watch on his wrist and the withdrawn look on his face, that young officer who is so shy that he can't even open his mouth unless the subject is flying—that young pilot—well, my friends, his ego is even *bigger!*—so big, it's *breathtaking!* Even in the 1950's it was difficult for civilians to comprehend such a thing, but *all* military officers and many enlisted men tended to feel superior to civilians. It was really quite ironic, given the fact that for a good thirty years the rising business classes in the cities had been steering their sons away from the military, as if from a bad smell, and the officer corps had never been held in lower esteem. Well, career officers returned the contempt in trumps. They looked upon themselves as men who lived by higher standards of behavior than civilians, as men who were the bearers and protectors of the most important values of American life, who maintained a sense of discipline while civilians abandoned themselves to hedonism, who maintained a sense of honor while civilians lived by opportunism and greed. Opportunism and greed: there you had your much-vaunted corporate business world. Khrushchev was right about one thing: when it came time to hang the capitalist West, an American businessman would sell

him the rope. When the showdown came—and the showdowns
always came—not all the wealth in the world or all the sophisticated nuclear weapons and radar and missile systems it could buy
would take the place of those who had the uncritical willingness
to face danger, those who, in short, had the right stuff.

25   In fact, the feeling was so righteous, so exalted, it could
become religious. Civilians seldom understood this, either. There
was no one to teach them. It was no longer the fashion for serious
writers to describe the glories of war. Instead, they dwelt upon its
horrors, often with cynicism or disgust. It was left to the occasional pilot with a literary flair to provide a glimpse of the pilot's self-
conception in its heavenly or spiritual aspect. When a pilot named
Robert Scott flew his P-43 over Mount Everest, quite a feat at the
time, he brought his hand up and snapped a salute to his fallen
adversary. He thought he had *defeated* the mountain, surmounting
all the forces of nature that had made it formidable. And why not?
"God is my co-pilot," he said—that became the title of his book—
and he meant it. So did the most gifted of all the pilot authors,
the Frenchman Antoine de Saint-Exupéry. As he gazed down
upon the world . . . from up there . . . during transcontinental
flights, the good Saint-Ex saw civilization as a series of tiny fragile
patches clinging to the otherwise barren rock of Earth. He felt
like a lonely sentinel, a protector of those vulnerable little oases,
ready to lay down his life in their behalf, if necessary; a saint, in
short, true to his name, flying up here at the right hand of God.
The good Saint-Ex! And he was not the only one. He was merely
the one who put it into words most beautifully and anointed himself before the altar of the right stuff.

QUESTIONS

Ideas

1. While recognizing and allowing for differences among individuals,
    Wolfe presents a generalized profile of a military test pilot. He sug-
    gests that to succeed, a test pilot needs "the right stuff." What is "the
    right stuff"? What qualities and attributes are necessary for success
    as a military test pilot?

2. What does Wolfe mean when he says that the men were in "an
    enclosing fraternity"? How does that fact affect their view of them-
    selves and their behavior? Is such isolation necessary?

3. In paragraphs 11 and 12, Wolfe presents two sides of the test pilots—the official and the unofficial. Why is it important for us to see both sides? What effect does Wolfe create with these contrasted views?

4. Paragraphs 22 and 23 are written from the point of view of the pilot. We are taken up with him into the sky, and we enter into and read his thoughts. Can Wolfe legitimately include such details even though he himself never piloted a jet?

5. What point is made at the end of paragraph 21? In paragraphs 24–25? In paragraph 9?

Organization

6. The overall structure of this selection breaks down into something like this: paragraphs 1–4; 5; 6–10; 11–16; 17–25. Explain what unifies the paragraphs in each grouping. And explain how each section is related to the one before. (Why is paragraph 5 a self-contained unit?)

7. Paragraph 5—the odd one in the structure of the whole—is extremely long. Is there a reason for this? What would be the effect of breaking it into two or three or even more parts? What is the purpose of this paragraph?

8. Read the first two paragraphs for coherence. Note how within each paragraph Wolfe joins one sentence to another, and also how he links one paragraph to another.

9. Wolfe doesn't bother with interparagraph transitions in paragraphs 14–17. Why not?

10. What do you notice about the final sentence of each paragraph? Are there any differences among the various repetitions and variations? Consider, for example, the final words of paragraphs 6 and 7.

11. In paragraphs 17 and 18 Wolfe makes different points at the beginning and at the end. Explain how, in each paragraph, Wolfe gets from his opening idea to his concluding one.

Sentences

12. In paragraph 5 Wolfe uses an extraordinarily long sentence beginning "This was a skillet. . . ." What would be lost or gained if this sentence were divided into three or four parts?

13. What is the effect of the two long sentences of paragraph 22? Should these two sentences be converted to a series of shorter ones? Why or why not?

14.   In the last sentence of paragraph 2 Wolfe stacks a series of parallel phrases:

> a dizzy progression of steps
> a ziggurat
> a pyramid

and again:

> that special few
> that elite
> the very Brotherhood

What would be lost if in each of these series there were not three items, but only two? (Or only one?)

15.   Explain which version of the following sentence you prefer.

> *Wolfe:* In the Navy, in addition to the stages that Air Force trainees went through, the neophyte always had waiting for him, out in the ocean, a certain grim gray slab! (5)

> *Revision:* In addition to the stages that Air Force trainees went through, in the Navy the neophyte always had a grim gray slab waiting for him out in the ocean.

16.   Wolfe mixes the lengths of his sentences effectively throughout "The Right Stuff." Look closely at paragraph 2, attending both to the variety of sentence lengths and to the long sentence with its series of parallel pieces:

> the moxie, the reflexes, the experience, the coolness:

and later:

> to go up, to go up again the next day
> and the next day
> and every next day
> in a cause that means something to thousands,
> to a people,
> a nation,
> to humanity,
> to God.

What is the effect of this elaboration and repetition? Why does Wolfe mix in some short sentences as well?

Words

17.   Throughout "The Right Stuff" Wolfe mixes idiomatic, colloquial language with formal, technical diction. Find passages where one or the other predominates.

18. In paragraph 5 Wolfe compares the slab, the aircraft carrier, to a skillet, a frying pan, a short-order grill. Does that comparison in its three variations seem appropriate? Farfetched? What is Wolfe's point in making it? What details does he use to elaborate and extend the analogy?

19. How do the quoted remarks in paragraph 19 help us understand what Wolfe means by "the right stuff"? Why don't the pilots use the words Wolfe uses in paragraph 18: "death," "danger," "bravery," "fear"?

20. Wolfe makes frequent use of triplets—groups of three words, phrases or details. He often uses them at the ends of paragraphs, as in the following examples:

    ancient, primordial, irresistible (8)

    manliness, manhood, manly courage (8)

    indefinable, unutterable, integral (10)

    Find two more examples. Try mentally eliminating one of the three terms from each set, as in this revised version of the triplet from paragraph 8: "ancient and primordial" or "ancient and irresistible." What is different about the triplet?

21. What is the effect of the direct speech, the dialogue, that Wolfe uses in paragraphs 12–15?

22. What is the effect of Wolfe's repetitions and variations of the term "the right stuff"? Why is the term capitalized at the end of paragraph 2?

23. Wolfe frequently italicizes words and phrases. Explain the effect of each of the following:

    it (1)
    the next day; the right stuff; a test (2)
    left behind (4)
    that shape—it's so damned small; heaved; rolled (5)

Suggestions for Writing

A. Write an essay explaining what field you will go into—what kind of work you expect to do, and why. Explain what "the right stuff" is that you think necessary for success in whatever you expect to do.

B. Interview three or four athletes, teachers, musicians, scholars, students, who have what you think of as "the right stuff." Write an essay presenting a composite picture of a _____ with the right stuff.

C. Write imitations of the sentences discussed in questions 13–16.

OTHER VOICES:

Fifteen Writers

Wendell Berry

(1934–   )

Wendell Berry has written novels, short stories, poetry, criticism, and essays; but his great loves are farming
and the Kentucky land where he grew up and has chosen
to live. Since 1977, when he left his last academic position
at the University of Kentucky, Berry has lived as a farmer
and a writer. He farms using organic methods and reject
ing modern machinery, using draft horses instead. Like
his farming, his poetry and prose share themes and techniques that emphasize the interrelationship of humanity
and nature. Ideally, there is mutual communion, but
when the natural order is disrupted, humanity loses: "If
we do not live where we work, and when we work," he
writes, "we are wasting our lives, and our work, too." In
"Feminism, the Body, and the Machine," from his book of
essays *What Are People For?* (1990), Berry deals explicitly
with the issue of work.

Feminism, the Body, and the Machine

1   Some time ago *Harper's* reprinted a short essay of
mine in which I gave some of my reasons for refusing to buy a
computer. Until that time, the vast numbers of people who disagree with my writings had mostly ignored them. An unusual
number of people, however, neglected to ignore my insensitivity
to the wonders of computer enhancement. Some of us, it seems,

would be better off if we would just realize that this is already the best of all possible worlds, and is going to get even better if we will just buy the right equipment.

2   *Harper's* published only five of the letters the editors received in response to my essay, and they published only negative letters. But of the twenty letters received by the *Harper's* editors, who forwarded copies to me, three were favorable. This I look upon as extremely gratifying. If these letters may be taken as a fair sample, then one in seven of *Harper's* readers agreed with me. If I had guessed beforehand, I would have guessed that my supporters would have been fewer than one in a thousand. And so I suppose, after further reflection, that my surprise at the intensity of the attacks on me is mistaken. There are more of us than I thought. Maybe there is even a "significant number" of us.

3   Only one of the negative letters seemed to me to have much intelligence in it. That one was from R. N. Neff of Arlington, Virginia, who scored a direct hit: "Not to be obtuse, but being willing to bare my illiterate soul for all to see, is there indeed a 'work demonstrably better than Dante's' . . . which was written on a Royal standard typewriter?" I like this retort so well that I am tempted to count it a favorable response, raising the total to four. The rest of the negative replies, like the five published ones, were more feeling than intelligent. Some of them, indeed, might be fairly described as exclamatory.

4   One of the letter writers described me as "a fool" and "doubly a fool," but fortunately misspelled my name, leaving me a speck of hope that I am not the "Wendell Barry" he was talking about. Two others accused me of self-righteousness, by which they seem to have meant that they think they are righter than I think I am. And another accused me of being more concerned about my own moral purity than with "any ecological effect," thereby making the sort of razor-sharp philosophical distinction that could cause a person to be elected president.

5   But most of my attackers deal in feelings either feminist or technological, or both. The feelings expressed seem to be representative of what the state of public feeling currently permits to be felt, and of what public rhetoric currently permits to be said. The feelings, that is, are similar enough, from one letter to another, to be thought representative, and as representative letters they have an interest greater than the quarrel that occasioned them.

6   Without exception, the feminist letters accuse me of exploiting my wife, and they do not scruple to allow the most insulting implications of their indictment to fall upon my wife. They fail entirely to see that my essay does not give any support to their accusation—or if they see it, they do not care. My essay, in fact, does not characterize my wife beyond saying that she types my manuscripts and tells me what she thinks about them. It does not say what her motives are, how much work she does, or whether or how she is paid. Aside from saying that she is my wife and that I value the help she gives me with my work, it says nothing about our marriage. It says nothing about our economy.

7   There is no way, then, to escape the conclusion that my wife and I are subjected in these letters to a condemnation by category. My offense is that I am a man who receives some help from his wife; my wife's offense is that she is a woman who does some work for her husband—which work, according to her critics and mine, makes her a drudge, exploited by a conventional subservience. And my detractors have, as I say, no evidence to support any of this. Their accusation rests on a syllogism of the flimsiest sort: my wife helps me in my work, some wives who have helped their husbands in their work have been exploited, therefore my wife is exploited.

8   This, of course, outrages justice to about the same extent that it insults intelligence. Any respectable system of justice exists in part as a protection against such accusations. In a just society nobody is expected to plead guilty to a general indictment, because in a just society nobody can be convicted on a general indictment. What is required for a just conviction is a particular accusation that can be *proved*. My accusers have made no such accusation against me.

9   That feminists or any other advocates of human liberty and dignity should resort to insult and injustice is regrettable. It is equally regrettable that all of the feminist attacks on my essay implicitly deny the validity of two decent and probably necessary possibilities: marriage as a state of mutual help, and the household as an economy.

10   Marriage, in what is evidently its most popular version, is now on the one hand an intimate "relationship" involving (ideally) two successful careerists in the same bed, and on the other

hand a sort of private political system in which rights and interests must be constantly asserted and defended. Marriage, in other words, has now taken the form of divorce: a prolonged and impassioned negotiation as to how things shall be divided. During their understandably temporary association, the "married" couple will typically consume a large quantity of merchandise and a large portion of each other.

11   The modern household is the place where the consumptive couple do their consuming. Nothing productive is done there. Such work as is done there is done at the expense of the resident couple or family, and to the profit of suppliers of energy and household technology. For entertainment, the inmates consume television or purchase other consumable diversion elsewhere.

12   There are, however, still some married couples who understand themselves as belonging to their marriage, to each other, and to their children. What they have they have in common, and so, to them, helping each other does not seem merely to damage their ability to compete against each other. To them, "mine" is not so powerful or necessary a pronoun as "ours."

13   This sort of marriage usually has at its heart a household that is to some extent productive. The couple, that is, makes around itself a household economy that involves the work of both wife and husband, that gives them a measure of economic independence and self-protection, a measure of self-employment, a measure of freedom, as well as a common ground and a common satisfaction. Such a household economy may employ the disciplines and skills of housewifery, of carpentry and other trades of building and maintenance, of gardening and other branches of subsistence agriculture, and even of woodlot management and woodcutting. It may also involve a "cottage industry" of some kind, such as a small literary enterprise.

14   It is obvious how much skill and industry either partner may put into such a household and what a good economic result such work may have, and yet it is a kind of work now frequently held in contempt. Men in general were the first to hold it in contempt as they departed from it for the sake of the professional salary or the hourly wage, and now it is held in contempt by such feminists as those who attacked my essay. Thus farm wives who help to run the kind of household economy that I have described are apt to be asked by feminists, and with great condescension, "But what do you *do*?" By this they invariably mean that there is something bet-

ter to do than to make one's marriage and household, and by better they invariably mean "employment outside the home."

15 I know that I am in dangerous territory, and so I had better be plain: what I have to say about marriage and household I mean to apply to men as much as to women. I do not believe that there is anything better to do than to make one's marriage and household, whether one is a man or a woman. I do not believe that "employment outside the home" is as valuable or important or satisfying as employment at home, for either men or women. It is clear to me from my experience as a teacher, for example, that children need an ordinary daily association with *both* parents. They need to see their parents at work; they need, at first, to play at the work they see their parents doing, and then they need to work with their parents. It does not matter so much that this working together should be what is called "quality time," but it matters a great deal that the work done should have the dignity of economic value.

16 I should say too that I understand how fortunate I have been in being able to do an appreciable part of my work at home. I know that in many marriages both husband and wife are now finding it necessary to work away from home. This issue, of course, is troubled by the question of what is meant by "necessary," but it is true that a family living that not so long ago was ordinarily supplied by one job now routinely requires two or more. My interest is not to quarrel with individuals, men or women, who work away from home, but rather to ask why we should consider this general working away from home to be a desirable state of things, either for people or for marriage, for our society or for our country.

17 If I had written in my essay that my wife worked as a typist and editor for a publisher, doing the same work that she does for me, no feminists, I daresay, would have written to *Harper's* to attack me for exploiting her—even though, for all they knew, I might have forced her to do such work in order to keep me in gambling money. It would have been assumed as a matter of course that if she had a job away from home she was a "liberated woman," possessed of a dignity that no home could confer upon her.

18 As I have said before, I understand that one cannot construct an adequate public defense of a private life. Anything that I might say here about my marriage would be immediately (and

rightly) suspect on the ground that it would be only *my* testimony. But for the sake of argument, let us suppose that whatever work my wife does, as a member of our marriage and household, she does both as a full economic partner and as her own boss, and let us suppose that the economy we have is adequate to our needs. Why, granting that supposition, should anyone assume that my wife would increase her freedom or dignity or satisfaction by becoming the employee of a boss, who would be in turn also a corporate underling and in no sense a partner?

19   Why would any woman who would refuse, properly, to take the marital vow of obedience (on the ground, presumably, that subservience to a mere human being is beneath human dignity) then regard as "liberating" a job that puts her under the authority of a boss (man or woman) whose authority specifically requires and expects obedience? It is easy enough to see why women came to object to the role of Blondie, a mostly decorative custodian of a degraded, consumptive modern household, preoccupied with clothes, shopping, gossip, and outwitting her husband. But are we to assume that one may fittingly cease to be Blondie by becoming Dagwood? Is the life of a corporate underling—even acknowledging that corporate underlings are well paid—an acceptable end to our quest for human dignity and worth? It is clear enough by now that one does not cease to be an underling by reaching "the top." Corporate life is composed only of lower underlings and higher underlings. Bosses are everywhere, and all the bosses are underlings. This is invariably revealed when the time comes for accepting responsibility for something unpleasant, such as the Exxon fiasco in Prince William Sound, for which certain lower underlings are blamed but no higher underling is responsible. The underlings at the top, like telephone operators, have authority and power, but no responsibility.

20   And the oppressiveness of some of this office work defies belief. Edward Mendelson (in the *New Republic,* February 22, 1988) speaks of "the office worker whose computer keystrokes are monitored by the central computer in the personnel office, and who will be fired if the keystrokes-per-minute figure doesn't match the corporate quota." (Mr. Mendelson does not say what form of drudgery this worker is being saved from.) And what are we to say of the diversely skilled country housewife who now bores the same six holes day after day on an assembly line? What higher form of womanhood or humanity is she evolving toward?

21   How, I am asking, can women improve themselves by sub-

mitting to the same specialization, degradation, trivialization, and tyrannization of work that men have submitted to? And that question is made legitimate by another. How have men improved themselves by submitting to it? The answer is that men have not, and women cannot, improve themselves by submitting to it.

22   Women have complained, justly, about the behavior of "macho" men. But despite their he-man pretensions and their captivation by masculine heroes of sports, war, and the Old West, most men are now entirely accustomed to obeying and currying the favor of their bosses. Because of this, of course, they hate their jobs—they mutter, "Thank God it's Friday" and "Pretty good for Monday"—but they do as they are told. They are more compliant than most housewives have been. Their characters combine feudal submissiveness with modern helplessness. They have accepted almost without protest, and often with relief, their dispossession of any usable property and, with that, their loss of economic independence and their consequent subordination to bosses. They have submitted to the destruction of the household economy and thus of the household, to the loss of home employment and self-employment, to the disintegration of their families and communities, to the desecration and pillage of their country, and they have continued abjectly to believe, obey, and vote for the people who have most eagerly abetted this ruin and who have most profited from it. These men, moreover, are helpless to do anything for themselves or anyone else without money, and so for money they do whatever they are told. They know that their ability to be useful is precisely defined by their willingness to be somebody else's tool. Is it any wonder that they talk tough and worship athletes and cowboys? Is it any wonder that some of them are violent?

23   It is clear that women cannot justly be excluded from the daily fracas by which the industrial economy divides the spoils of society and nature, but their inclusion is a poor justice and no reason for applause. The enterprise is as devastating with women in it as it was before. There is no sign that women are exerting a "civilizing influence" upon it. To have an equal part in our juggernaut of national vandalism is to be a vandal. To call this vandalism "liberation" is to prolong, and even ratify, a dangerous confusion that was once principally masculine.

24   A broader, deeper criticism is necessary. The problem is not just the exploitation of women by men. A greater problem is that women and men alike are consenting to an economy that exploits women and men and everything else.

25   Another decent possibility my critics implicitly deny is that of work as a gift. Not one of them supposed that my wife may be a consulting engineer who helps me in her spare time out of the goodness of her heart; instead they suppose that she is "a household drudge." But what appears to infuriate them the most is their supposition that she works for nothing. They assume—and this is the orthodox assumption of the industrial economy—that the only help worth giving is not given at all, but sold. Love, friendship, neighborliness, compassion, duty—what are they? We are realists. We will be most happy to receive your check.

26   The various reductions I have been describing are fairly directly the results of the ongoing revolution of applied science known as "technological progress." This revolution has provided the means by which both the productive and the consumptive capacities of people could be detached from household and community and made to serve other people's purely economic ends. It has provided as well a glamor of newness, ease, and affluence that made it seductive even to those who suffered most from it. In its more recent history especially, this revolution has been successful in putting unheard-of quantities of consumer goods and services within the reach of ordinary people. But the technical means of this popular "affluence" has at the same time made possible the gathering of the real property and the real power of the country into fewer and fewer hands.

27   Some people would like to think that this long sequence of industrial innovations has changed human life and even human nature in fundamental ways. Perhaps it has—but, arguably, almost always for the worse. I know that "technological progress" can be defended, but I observe that the defenses are invariably quantitative—catalogs of statistics on the ownership of automobiles and television sets, for example, or on the increase of life expectancy—and I see that these statistics are always kept carefully apart from the related statistics of soil loss, pollution, social disintegration, and so forth. That is to say, there is never an effort to determine the *net* result of this progress. The voice of its defenders is not that of the responsible bookkeeper, but that of the propagandist or salesman, who says that the net gain is more than 100 percent—that the thing we have bought has perfectly replaced everything it has cost, and added a great deal more: "You just can't lose!" We thus have got rich by spending, just as the advertisers

have told us we would, and the best of all possible worlds is getting better every day.

28   The statistics of life expectancy are favorites of the industrial apologists, because they are perhaps the hardest to argue with. Nevertheless, this emphasis on longevity is an excellent example of the way the isolated aims of the industrial mind reduce and distort human life, and also the way statistics corrupt the truth. A long life has indeed always been thought desirable; everything that is alive apparently wishes to continue to live. But until our own time, that sentence would have been qualified: long life is desirable and everything wishes to live *up to a point*. Past a certain point, and in certain conditions, death becomes preferable to life. Moreover, it was generally agreed that a good life was preferable to one that was merely long, and that the goodness of a life could not be determined by its length. The statisticians of longevity ignore good in both its senses; they do not ask if the prolonged life is virtuous, or if it is satisfactory. If the life is that of a vicious criminal, or if it is inched out in a veritable hell of captivity within the medical industry, no matter—both become statistics to "prove" the good luck of living in our time.

29   But in general, apart from its own highly specialized standards of quantity and efficiency, "technological progress" has produced a social and ecological decline. Industrial war, except by the most fanatically narrow standards, is worse than war used to be. Industrial agriculture, except by the standards of quantity and mechanical efficiency, diminishes everything it affects. Industrial workmanship is certainly worse than traditional workmanship, and is getting shoddier every day. After forty-odd years, the evidence is everywhere that television, far from proving a great tool of education, is a tool of stupefaction and disintegration. Industrial education has abandoned the old duty of passing on the cultural and intellectual inheritance in favor of baby-sitting and career preparation.

30   After several generations of "technological progress," in fact, we have become a people who *cannot* think about anything important. How far down in the natural order do we have to go to find creatures who raise their young as indifferently as industrial humans now do? Even the English sparrows do not let loose into the streets young sparrows who have no notion of their identity or their adult responsibilities. When else in history would you find "educated" people who know more about sports than about the

history of their country, or uneducated people who do not know the stories of their families and communities?

31 To ask a still more obvious question, what is the purpose of this technological progress? What higher aim do we think it is serving? Surely the aim cannot be the integrity or happiness of our families, which we have made subordinate to the education system, the television industry, and the consumer economy. Surely it cannot be the integrity or health of our communities, which we esteem even less than we esteem our families. Surely it cannot be love of our country, for we are far more concerned about the desecration of the flag than we are about the desecration of our land. Surely it cannot be the love of God, which counts for at least as little in the daily order of business as the love of family, community, and country.

32 The higher aims of "technological progress" are money and ease. And this exalted greed for money and ease is disguised and justified by an obscure, cultish faith in "the future." We do as we do, we say, "for the sake of the future" or "to make a better future for our children." How we can hope to make a good future by doing badly in the present, we do not say. We cannot think about the future, of course, for the future does not exist: the existence of the future is an article of faith. We can be assured only that, if there is to be a future, the good of it is already implicit in the good things of the present. We do not need to plan or devise a "world of the future"; if we take care of the world of the present, the future will have received full justice from us. A good future is implicit in the soils, forests, grasslands, marshes, deserts, mountains, rivers, lakes, and oceans that we have now, and in the good things of human culture that we have now; the only valid "futurology" available to us is to take care of those things. We have no need to contrive and dabble at "the future of the human race"; we have the same pressing need that we have always had—to love, care for, and teach our children.

33 And so the question of the desirability of adopting any technological innovation is a question with two possible answers—not one, as has been commonly assumed. If one's motives are money, ease, and haste to arrive in a technologically determined future, then the answer is foregone, and there is, in fact, no question, and no thought. If one's motive is the love of family, community, country, and God, then one will have to think, and one may have to decide that the proposed innovation is undesirable.

34   The question of how to end or reduce dependence on some of the technological innovations already adopted is a baffling one. At least, it baffles me. I have not been able to see, for example, how people living in the country, where there is no public transportation, can give up their automobiles without becoming less useful to each other. And this is because, owing largely to the influence of the automobile, we live too far from each other, and from the things we need, to be able to get about by any other means. Of course, you *could* do without an automobile, but to do so you would have to disconnect yourself from many obligations. Nothing I have so far been able to think about this problem has satisfied me.

35   But if we have paid attention to the influence of the automobile on country communities, we know that the desirability of technological innovation is an issue that requires thinking about, and we should have acquired some ability to think about it. Thus if I am partly a writer, and I am offered an expensive machine to help me write, I ought to ask whether or not such a machine is desirable.

36   I should ask, in the first place, whether or not I wish to purchase a solution to a problem that I do not have. I acknowledge that, as a writer, I need a lot of help. And I have received an abundance of the best of help from my wife, from other members of my family, from friends, from teachers, from editors, and sometimes from readers. These people have helped me out of love or friendship, and perhaps in exchange for some help that I have given them. I suppose I should leave open the possibility that I need more help than I am getting, but I would certainly be ungrateful and greedy to think so.

37   But a computer, I am told, offers a kind of help that you can't get from other humans; a computer will help you to write faster, easier, and more. For a while, it seemed to me that every university professor I met told me this. Do I, then, want to write faster, easier, and more? No. My standards are not speed, ease, and quantity. I have already left behind too much evidence that, writing with a pencil, I have written too fast, too easily, and too much. I would like to be a *better* writer, and for that I need help from other humans, not a machine.

38   The professors who recommended speed, ease, and quantity to me were, of course, quoting the standards of their universities. The chief concern of the industrial system, which is to say the present university system, is to cheapen work by increasing volume.

But implicit in the professors' recommendation was the idea that one needs to be up with the times. The pace-setting academic intellectuals have lately had a great hankering to be up with the times. They don't worry about keeping up with the Joneses: as intellectuals, they know that they are supposed to be Nonconformists and Independent Thinkers living at the Cutting Edge of Human Thought. And so they are all a-dither to keep up with the times—which means adopting the latest technological innovations as soon as the Joneses do.

39   Do I wish to keep up with the times? No.

40   My wish simply is to live my life as fully as I can. In both our work and our leisure, I think, we should be so employed. And in our time this means that we must save ourselves from the products that we are asked to buy in order, ultimately, to replace ourselves.

41   The danger most immediately to be feared in "technological progress" is the degradation and obsolescence of the body. Implicit in the technological revolution from the beginning has been a new version of an old dualism, one always destructive, and now more destructive than ever. For many centuries there have been people who looked upon the body, as upon the natural world, as an encumbrance of the soul, and so have hated the body, as they have hated the natural world, and longed to be free of it. They have seen the body as intolerably imperfect by spiritual standards. More recently, since the beginning of the technological revolution, more and more people have looked upon the body, along with the rest of the natural creation, as intolerably imperfect by mechanical standards. They see the body as an encumbrance of the mind—the mind, that is, as reduced to a set of mechanical ideas that can be implemented in machines—and so they hate it and long to be free of it. The body has limits that the machine does not have; therefore, remove the body from the machine so that the machine can continue as an unlimited idea.

42   It is odd that simply because of its "sexual freedom" our time should be considered extraordinarily physical. In fact, our "sexual revolution" is mostly an industrial phenomenon, in which the body is used as an idea of pleasure or a pleasure machine with the aim of "freeing" natural pleasure from natural consequence. Like any other industrial enterprise, industrial sexuality seeks to conquer nature by exploiting it and ignoring the consequences,

by denying any connection between nature and spirit or body and soul, and by evading social responsibility. The spiritual, physical, and economic costs of this "freedom" are immense, and are characteristically belittled or ignored. The diseases of sexual irresponsibility are regarded as a technological problem and an affront to liberty. Industrial sex, characteristically, establishes its freeness and goodness by an industrial accounting, dutifully toting up numbers of "sexual partners," orgasms, and so on, with the inevitable industrial implication that the body is somehow a limit on the idea of sex, which will be a great deal more abundant as soon as it can be done by robots.

43   This hatred of the body and of the body's life in the natural world, always inherent in the technological revolution (and sometimes explicitly and vengefully so), is of concern to an artist because art, like sexual love, is of the body. Like sexual love, art is of the mind and spirit also, but it is made with the body and it appeals to the senses. To reduce or shortcut the intimacy of the body's involvement in the making of a work of art (that is, of any artifice, anything made by art) inevitably risks reducing the work of art and the art itself. In addition to the reasons I gave previously, which I still believe are good reasons, I am not going to use a computer because I don't want to diminish or distort my bodily involvement in my work. I don't want to deny myself the *pleasure* of bodily involvement in my work, for that pleasure seems to me to be the sign of an indispensable integrity.

44   At first glance, writing may seem not nearly so much an art of the body as, say, dancing or gardening or carpentry. And yet language is the most intimately physical of all the artistic means. We have it palpably in our mouths; it is our *langue,* our tongue. Writing it, we shape it with our hands. Reading aloud what we have written—as we must do, if we are writing carefully—our language passes in at the eyes, out at the mouth, in at the ears; the words are immersed and steeped in the senses of the body before they make sense in the mind. They *cannot* make sense in the mind until they have made sense in the body. Does shaping one's words with one's own hand impart character and quality to them, as does speaking them with one's own tongue to the satisfaction of one's own ear? There is no way to prove that it does. On the other hand, there is no way to prove that it does not, and I believe that it does.

45   The act of writing language down is not so insistently tangible an act as the act of building a house or playing the violin. But

to the extent that it is tangible, I love the tangibility of it. The computer apologists, it seems to me, have greatly underrated the value of the handwritten manuscript as an artifact. I don't mean that a writer should be a fine calligrapher and write for exhibition, but rather that handwriting has a valuable influence on the work so written. I am certainly no calligrapher, but my handwritten pages have a homemade, handmade look to them that both pleases me in itself and suggests the possibility of ready correction. It looks hospitable to improvement. As the longhand is transformed into typescript and then into galley proofs and the printed page, it seems increasingly to resist improvement. More and more spunk is required to mar the clean, final-looking lines of type. I have the notion—again not provable—that the longer I keep a piece of work in longhand, the better it will be.

46   To me, also, there is a significant difference between ready correction and easy correction. Much is made of the ease of correction in computer work, owing to the insubstantiality of the light-image on the screen; one presses a button and the old version disappears, to be replaced by the new. But because of the substantiality of paper and the consequent difficulty involved, one does not handwrite or typewrite a new page every time a correction is made. A handwritten or typewritten page therefore is usually to some degree a palimpsest; it contains parts and relics of its own history—erasures, passages crossed out, interlineations—suggesting that there is something to go back to as well as something to go forward to. The light-text on the computer screen, by contrast, is an artifact typical of what can only be called the industrial present, a present absolute. A computer destroys the sense of historical succession, just as do other forms of mechanization. The well-crafted table or cabinet embodies the memory of (because it embodies respect for) the tree it was made of and the forest in which the tree stood. The work of certain potters embodies the memory that the clay was dug from the earth. Certain farms contain hospitably the remnants and reminders of the forest or prairie that preceded them. It is possible even for towns and cities to remember farms and forests or prairies. All good human work remembers its history. The best writing, even when printed, is full of intimations that it is the present version of earlier versions of itself, and that its maker inherited the work and the ways of earlier makers. It thus keeps, even in print, a suggestion of the quality of the handwritten page; it is a palimpsest.

47   Something of this undoubtedly carries over into industrial products. The plastic Clorox jug has a shape and a loop for the forefinger that recalls the stoneware jug that went before it. But something vital is missing. It embodies no memory of its source or sources in the earth or of any human hand involved in its shaping. Or look at a large factory or a power plant or an airport, and see if you can imagine—even if you know—what was there before. In such things the materials of the world have entered a kind of orphanhood.

48   It would be uncharitable and foolish of me to suggest that nothing good will ever be written on a computer. Some of my best friends have computers. I have only said that a computer cannot help you to write *better*, and I stand by that. (In fact, I know a publisher who says that under the influence of computers—or of the immaculate copy that computers produce—many writers are now writing worse.) But I do say that in using computers writers are flirting with a radical separation of mind and body, the elimination of the work of the body from the work of the mind. The text on the computer screen, and the computer printout too, has a sterile, untouched, factorymade look, like that of a plastic whistle or a new car. The body does not do work like that. The body *characterizes* everything it touches. What it makes it traces over with the marks of its pulses and breathings, its excitements, hesitations, flaws, and mistakes. On its good work, it leaves the marks of skill, care, and love persisting through hesitations, flaws, and mistakes. And to those of us who love and honor the life of the body in this world, these marks are precious things, necessities of life.

49   But writing is of the body in yet another way. It is preeminently a walker's art. It can be done on foot and at large. The beauty of its traditional equipment is simplicity. And cheapness. Going off to the woods, I take a pencil and some paper (*any* paper—a small notebook, an old envelope, a piece of a feed sack), and I am as well equipped for my work as the president of IBM. I am also free, for the time being at least, of everything that IBM is hooked to. My thoughts will not be coming to me from the power structure or the power grid, but from another direction and way entirely. My mind is free to go with my feet.

50   I know that there are some people, perhaps many, to whom you cannot appeal on behalf of the body. To them, disembodiment is a goal, and they long for the realm of pure mind—or pure machine; the difference is negligible. Their departure from

their bodies, obviously, is much to be desired, but the rest of us had better be warned: they are going to cause a lot of dangerous commotion on their way out.

51   Some of my critics were happy to say that my refusal to use a computer would not do any good. I have argued, and am convinced, that it will at least do *me* some good, and that it may involve me in the preservation of some cultural goods. But what they meant was real, practical, public good. They meant that the materials and energy I save by not buying a computer will not be "significant." They meant that no individual's restraint in the use of technology or energy will be "significant." That is true.

52   But each one of us, by "insignificant" individual abuse of the world, contributes to a general abuse that is devastating. And if I were one of thousands or millions of people who could afford a piece of equipment, even one for which they had a conceivable "need," and yet did not buy it, *that* would be "significant." Why, then, should I hesitate for even a moment to be one, even the first one, of that "significant" number? Thoreau gave the definitive reply to the folly of "significant numbers" a long time ago: Why should anybody wait to do what is right until everybody does it? It is not "significant" to love your own children or to eat your own dinner, either. But normal humans will not wait to love or eat until it is mandated by an act of Congress.

53   One of my correspondents asked where one is to draw the line. That question returns me to the bewilderment I mentioned earlier: I am unsure where the line ought to be drawn, or how to draw it. But it is an intelligent question, worth losing some sleep over.

54   I know how to draw the line only where it is easy to draw. It is easy—it is even a luxury—to deny oneself the use of a television set, and I zealously practice that form of self-denial. Every time I see television (at other people's houses), I am more inclined to congratulate myself on my deprivation. I have no doubt, as I have said, that I am better off without a computer. I joyfully deny myself a motorboat, a camping van, an off-road vehicle, and every other kind of recreational machinery. I have, and want, no "second home." I suffer very comfortably the lack of colas, TV dinners, and other counterfeit foods and beverages.

55   I am, however, still in bondage to the automobile industry and the energy companies, which have nothing to recommend

them except our dependence on them. I still fly on airplanes, which have nothing to recommend them but speed; they are inconvenient, uncomfortable, undependable, ugly, stinky, and scary. I still cut my wood with a chainsaw, which has nothing to recommend it but speed, and has all the faults of an airplane, except it does not fly.

56   It is plain to me that the line ought to be drawn without fail wherever it can be drawn easily. And it ought to be easy (though many do not find it so) to refuse to buy what one does not need. If you are already solving your problem with the equipment you have—a pencil, say—why solve it with something more expensive and more damaging? If you don't have a problem, why pay for a solution? If you love the freedom and elegance of simple tools, why encumber yourself with something complicated?

57   And yet, if we are ever again to have a world fit and pleasant for little children, we are surely going to have to draw the line where it is *not* easily drawn. We are going to have to learn to give up things that we have learned (in only a few years, after all) to "need." I am not an optimist; I am afraid that I won't live long enough to escape my bondage to the machines. Nevertheless, on every day left to me I will search my mind and circumstances for the means of escape. And I am not without hope. I knew a man who, in the age of chainsaws, went right on cutting his wood with a handsaw and an axe. He was a healthier and a saner man than I am. I shall let his memory trouble my thoughts.

REFLECTIONS

Wendell Berry has combined two seemingly unrelated topics in this essay: a response to feminists who object to his wife's serving as his secretary and editor, and a response to technology enthusiasts who insist that his writing would be improved by using a computer. Can you detect underlying themes that make this a unified essay? Berry argues that his critics use faulty logic when they assume that his wife is exploited because she works for her husband in their home. Is Berry's refutation logical? Are his suggestions pragmatic? What can you say about his statement that both men and women are exploited in the workplace? Do you agree with his assertion that working at home or writing with a pencil is somehow more natural than the alternatives? How would you define "natural" human behavior?

Gretel Ehrlich

(1946–   )

Gretel Ehrlich has lived in Wyoming since she worked there on a documentary film in 1976. Raised in southern California, Ehrlich attended Bennington College in Vermont, UCLA Film School, and the New School for Social Research in New York. Since she began her full-time career as a writer in 1979, she has published numerous articles in magazines, two collections of poetry, a coedited collection of stories with Edward Hoagland, and the novel *Heart Mountain* (1988). Her first collection of essays, *The Solace of Open Spaces,* from which the following selection is taken, won the Harold B. Vurcell Memorial Award.

Friends, Foes, and Working Animals

I used to walk in my sleep. On clear nights when the seals barked and played in phosphorescent waves, I climbed out the window and slept in a horse stall. Those "wild-child" stories never seemed odd to me; I had the idea that I was one of them, refusing to talk, sleeping only on the floor. Having become a city dweller, the back-to-the-land fad left me cold and I had never thought of moving to Wyoming. But here I am, and unexpectedly, my noctambulist's world has returned. Not in the sense that I still walk in my sleep—such restlessness has left me—but rather, the intimacy with what is animal in me has returned. To live and work on a ranch implicates me in new ways: I have blood on my hands and noises in my throat that aren't human.

2   Animals give us their constant, unjaded faces and we burden them with our bodies and civilized ordeals. We're both humbled by and imperious with them. We're comrades who save each other's lives. The horse we pulled from a boghole this morning bucked someone off later in the day; one stock dog refuses to work sheep, while another brings back a calf we had overlooked while trailing cattle to another pasture; the heifer we doctored for pneumonia backed up to a wash and dropped her newborn calf over the edge; the horse that brings us home safely in the dark kicks us the next day. On and on it goes. What's stubborn, secretive, dumb, and keen in us bumps up against those same qualities in them. Their births and deaths are as jolting and random as ours, and because ranchers are food producers, we give ourselves as wholly to the sacrament of nurturing as to the communion of eating their flesh. What develops in this odd partnership is a stripped-down compassion, one that is made of frankness and respect and rigorously excludes sentimentality.

3   What makes westerners leery of "outsiders"—townspeople and city-slickers—is their patronizing attitude toward animals. "I don't know what in the hell makes those guys think they're smarter than my horse. Nothing I see them do would make me believe it," a cowboy told me. "They may like their steaks, but they sure don't want to help out when it comes to butchering. And their damned back-yard horses are spoiled. They make it hard for a horse to do something right and easy for him to do everything wrong. They're scared to get hot and tired and dirty out here like us; then they don't understand why a horse won't work for them."

4   On a ranch, a mother cow must produce calves, a bull has to perform, a stock dog and working horse should display ambition, savvy, and heart. If they don't, they're sold or shot. But these relationships of mutual dependency can't be dismissed so briskly. An animal's wordlessness takes on the cleansing qualities of space: we freefall through the beguiling operations of our own minds with which we calculate our miseries to responses that are immediate. Animals hold us to what is present: to who we are at the time, not who we've been or how our bank accounts describe us. What is obvious to an animal is not the embellishment that fattens our emotional résumés but what's bedrock and current in us: aggression, fear, insecurity, happiness, or equanimity. Because they have

the ability to read our involuntary tics and scents, we're transparent to them and thus exposed—we're finally ourselves.

5   Living with animals makes us redefine our ideas about intelligence. Horses are as mischievous as they are dependable. Stupid enough to let us use them, they are cunning enough to catch us off guard. We pay for their loyalty: they can be willful, hard to catch, dangerous to shoe, and buck on frosty mornings. In turn, they'll work themselves into a lather cutting cows, not for the praise they'll get but for the simple glory of outdodging a calf or catching up with an errant steer. The outlaws in a horse herd earn their ominous names—the red roan called Bonecrusher, the sorrel gelding referred to as Widowmaker. Others are talented but insist on having things their own way. One horse used only for roping doesn't like to be tied up by the reins. As soon as you jump off he'll rub the headstall over his ears and let the bit drop from his mouth, then just stand there as if he were tied to the post. The horses that sheepherders use become chummy. They'll stick their heads into a wagon when you get the cookies out, and eat the dogfood. One sheepherder I knew, decked out in bedroom slippers and baggy pants, rode his gelding all summer with nothing but bailing string tied around the horse's neck. They picnicked together every day on the lunch the herder had fixed: two sandwiches and a can of beer for each of them.

6   A dog's reception of the jolts and currents of life comes in more clearly than a horse's. Ranchers use special breeds of dogs to work livestock—blue and red heelers, border collies, Australian shepherds, and kelpies. Heelers, favored by cattlemen, are small, muscular dogs with wide heads and short, blue-gray hair. Their wide and deep chests enable them—like the quarter horse—to run fast for a short distance and endow them with extra lung capacity to work at high altitudes. By instinct they move cows, not by barking at them but by nipping their heels. What's uncanny about all these breeds is their responsiveness to human beings: we don't shout commands, we whisper directions, and because of their unshakable desire to please us, they can be called back from chasing a cow instantaneously. Language is not an obstacle to these dogs; they learn words very quickly. I know several dogs who are bilingual: they understand Spanish and English. Others are whizzes with names. On a pack trip my dog learned the names of ten horses and remembered the horse and the sound of his name for years. One friend taught his cowdog to jump onto the saddle

so he could see the herd ahead, wait for a command with his front feet riding the neck of the horse, then leap to the ground and bring a calf back or turn the whole herd.

7   My dog was born under a sheep wagon. He's a blue heeler–kelpie cross with a natural bobbed tail. Kelpies, developed in Australia in the nineteenth century, are also called dingoes, though they're part Scottish sheepdog too. While the instinct to work livestock is apparent from the time they are puppies, they benefit from further instruction, the way anyone with natural talent does. They're not sent to obedience school; these dogs learn from each other. A pup, like mine was, lives at sheep camp and is sent out with an older dog to learn his way around a band of sheep. They learn to turn the herd, to bring back strays, and to stay behind the horse when they're not needed.

8   Dogs who work sheep have to be gentler than cowdogs. Sheep are skittish and have a natural fear of dogs, whereas a mother cow will turn and fight a dog who gets near her calf. If kelpies, border collies, and Australian shepherds cower, they do so from timidness and because they've learned to stay low and out of sight of the sheep. With their pointed ears and handsome, wolfish faces, their resemblance to coyotes is eerie. But their instinct to work sheep is only a refinement of the desire to kill; they lick their chops as they approach the herd.

9   After a two-year apprenticeship at sheep camp, Rusty came home with me. He was carsick all the way, never having ridden in a vehicle, and, once home, there were more firsts: when I flushed the toilet, he ran out the door; he tried to lick the image on the screen of the television; when the phone rang he jumped on my lap, shoving his head under my arm. In April the ewes and lambs were trailed to spring range and Rusty rejoined them. By his second birthday he had walked two hundred miles behind a horse, returning to the mountain top where he had been born.

10   Dogs read minds and also maps. Henry III's greyhound tracked the king's coach from Switzerland to Paris, while another dog found his owner in the trenches during World War I. They anticipate comings and goings and seem to possess a prescient knowledge of danger. The night before a sheep foreman died, his usually well-behaved blue heeler acted strangely. All afternoon he scratched at the windows in an agony of panic, yet refused to go outside. The next day Keith was found dead on the kitchen floor, the dog standing over the man's chest as if shielding the defective heart that had killed his master.

11   While we cherish these personable working animals, we unfairly malign those that live in herds. Konrad Lorenz thinks of the anonymous flock as the first society, not unlike early medieval cities: the flock works as a wall of defense protecting the individual against aggressors. Herds are democratic, nonhierarchical. Wyoming's landscapes are so wide they can accommodate the generality of a herd. A band of fifteen hundred sheep moves across the range like a single body of water. To work them in a corral means opposing them: if you walk back through the middle of the herd, they will flow forward around you as if you were a rock in a stream. Sheep graze up a slope, not down the way cows do, as if they were curds of cream rising.

12   Cows are less herd-smart, less adhesive, less self-governing. On long treks, they travel single file, or in small, ambiguous crowds from which individuals veer off in a variety of directions. That's why cowboying is more arduous than herding sheep. On a long circle, cowboys are assigned positions and work like traffic cops directing the cattle. Those that "ride point" are the front men. They take charge of the herd's course, turning the lead down a draw, up a ridge line, down a creek, galloping ahead to chase off steers or bulls from someone else's herd, then quickly returning to check the speed of the long column. The cowboys at the back "ride drag." They push the cows along and pick up stragglers and defectors, inhaling the sweet and pungent perfume of the animals—a mixture of sage, sweet grass, milk, and hide, along with gulps of dust.

13   What we may miss in human interaction here we make up for by rubbing elbows with wild animals. Their florid, temperamental lives parallel ours, as do their imperfect societies. They fight and bicker, show off, and make love. I watched a Big Horn ram in rut chase a ewe around a tree for an hour. When he caught and mounted her, his horns hit a low branch and he fell off. She ran away with a younger ram in pursuit. The last I saw of them, she was headed for a dense thicket of willows and the old ram was peering through the maze looking for her.

14   When winter comes there is a sudden population drop. Frogs, prairie dogs, rattlesnakes, and rabbits go underground, while the mallards and cinnamon teal, as well as scores of songbirds, fly south because they are smarter than we are. One winter day I saw a coyote take a fawn down on our frozen lake where in summer I row through fragrant flowers. He jumped her, grabbed her hind leg, and hung on as she ran. Halfway across the lake the

fawn fell and the coyote went for her jugular. In a minute she was dead. Delighted with his catch, he dragged her here and there on the ice, then lay down next to her in a loving way and rubbed his silvery ruff in her hair before he ate her.

15   In late spring, which here, at six thousand feet, is June, the cow elk become proud mothers. They bring their day-old calves to a hill just above the ranch so we can see them. They're spotted like fawns but larger, and because they are so young, they wobble and fall when they try to play.

16   Hot summer weather brings the snakes and bugs. It's said that 80 percent of all animal species are insects, including six thousand kinds of ants and ten thousand bugs that sting. Like the wild ducks that use our lake as a flyaway, insects come and go seasonally. Mosquitoes come early and stay late, followed by black flies, gnats, Stendhalian red-and-black ants, then yellow jackets and wasps.

17   I know it does no good to ask historical questions—why so many insects exist—so I content myself with the cold ingenuity of their lives. In winter ants excavate below their hills and live snugly in subterranean chambers. Their heating system is unique. Worker ants go above ground and act as solar collectors, descending frequently to radiate heat below. They know when spring has come because the workers signal the change of seasons with the sudden increase of body heat: it's time to reinhabit the hill.

18   In a drought year rattlesnakes are epidemic. I sharpen my shovel before I irrigate the alfalfa fields and harvest vegetables carrying a shotgun. Rattlesnakes have heat sensors and move toward warm things. I tried nude sunbathing once: I fell asleep and woke just in time to see the grim, flat head of a snake angling toward me. Our new stock dog wasn't as lucky. A pup, he was bitten three times in one summer. After the first bite he staggered across the hayfield toward me, then keeled over, his eyes rolling back and his body shaking. The cure for snakebite is the same for animals as it is for humans: a costly antiserum must be injected as quickly as possible. I had to carry the dog half a mile to my pickup. By the time I had driven the thirty miles to town, his head and neck had swollen to a ghoulish size, but two days later he was heeling cows again.

19   Fall brings the wildlife down from the mountains. Elk and deer migrate through our front yard while in the steep draws above us, mountain lions and black bears settle in for the winter.

Last night, while I was sleeping on the veranda, the sound of clattering dishes turned out to be two buck deer sparring in front of my bed. Later, a porcupine and her baby waddled past: "Meeee . . . meeee . . . meeee," the mother squeaked to keep the young one trundling along. From midnight until dawn I heard the bull elk bugle—a whistling, looping squeal that sounds porpoiselike at first, and then like a charging elephant. The screaming catlike sound that wakes us every few nights is a bobcat crouched in the apple tree.

20   Bobcats are small, weighing only twenty pounds or so, with short tails and long, rabbity back feet. They can nurse two small litters of kittens a year. "She's meaner than a cotton sack full of wildcats," I heard a cowboy say about a woman he'd met in the bar the night before. A famous riverman's boast from the paddlewheel days on the Mississippi goes this way: "I'm all man, save what's wildcat and extra lightning." *Les chats sauvages,* the French call them, but their savagery impresses me much less than their acrobatic skills. Bobcats will kill a doe by falling on her from a tree and riding her shoulders as she runs, reaching around and scratching her face until she falls. But just as I was falling asleep again, I thought I heard the bobcat purring.

REFLECTIONS

Ehrlich's thoughts about animals refer specifically to their lives as friends (helping on the ranch) and foes (as predators and as threats to livestock and people). To what extent do her ruminations apply to other more domesticated scenes? How would you characterize her attitude toward horses and dogs? What qualities of character and what features of mindfulness does she observe in them? What about her image of wild animals? Were you shocked or appalled by her description of forms of animal killing? (Or did you respond in some other way?) How does Ehrlich's image of wolf and bobcat compare with Barry Lopez's portrayal of animals? With Annie Dillard's?

Louise Erdrich

(1954–   )

Louise Erdrich first became known for her poems in *Jacklight* (1984), followed soon by her first novel, *Love Medicine* (1984), which won the National Book Critics Circle Award. In these books and in later novels, *The Beet Queen* (1986) and *Tracks* (1988), Erdrich writes with power and affection about the people of the American West, particularly Native Americans. The Chippewa culture that is part of her heritage is mentioned only tangentially in the foreword to *The Broken Cord* excerpted here, when she alludes to the severity of the alcohol problem on some Indian reservations and to the success of some tribes in overcoming it. As in her poetry and her fiction, Erdrich uses small and specific details in this nonfiction piece to reveal character and relate a powerful (and intensely personal) narrative.

Foreword to *The Broken Cord*

1   The snow fell deep today. February 4, 1988, two days before Michael and I are to leave for our first trip abroad together, ten days before Saint Valentine's holiday, which we will spend in Paris, fifteen days after Adam's twentieth birthday. This is no special day, it marks no breakthrough in Adam's life or in mine, it is a day held in suspension by the depth of snow, the silence, school closing, our seclusion in the country along a steep gravel road which no cars will dare use until the town plow goes through.

2   It is just a day when Adam had a seizure. His grandmother called and said that she could see, from out the window, Adam lying in the snow, having a seizure. He had fallen while shoveling the mailbox clear. Michael was at the door too, but I got out first because I had on sneakers. Jumping into the snow I felt a moment of obscure gratitude to Michael for letting me go to Adam's rescue. Though unacknowledged between us, these are the times when it is easy to be a parent to Adam. His seizures are increasingly grand mal now. And yet, unless he hurts himself in the fall there is nothing to do but be a comforting presence, make sure he's turned on his side, breathing. I ran to Adam and I held him, spoke his name, told him I was there, used my most soothing tone. When he came back to consciousness I rose, propped him against me, and we stood to shake out his sleeves and the neck of his jacket.

3   A lone snowmobiler passed, then circled to make sure we were all right. I suppose we made a picture that could cause mild concern. We stood, propped together, hugging and breathing hard. Adam is taller than me, and usually much stronger. I held him around the waist with both arms and looked past his shoulder. The snow was still coming, drifting through the deep-branched pines. All around us there was such purity, a wet and electric silence. The air was warm and the snow already melting in my shoes.

4   It is easy to give the absolute, dramatic love that a definite physical problem requires, easy to stagger back, slipping, to take off Adam's boots and make sure he gets the right amount of medicine into his system.

5   It is easy to be the occasional, ministering angel. But it is not easy to live day in and day out with a child disabled by Fetal Alcohol Syndrome or Fetal Alcohol Effect. This set of preventable birth defects is manifested in a variety of ways, but caused solely by alcohol in an unborn baby's developing body and brain. The U.S. Surgeon General's report for 1988 warned about the hazards of drinking while pregnant, and many doctors now say that since no level of alcohol has been established as safe for the fetus, the best policy to follow for nine months, longer if a mother nurses, is complete abstinence. As you will read, every woman reacts differently to alcohol, depending on age, diet, and metabolism. However, drinking at the wrong time of development can cause facial and bodily abnormalities, as well as lower intelligence, and may

also impair certain types of judgment, or alter behavior. Adam suffers all the symptoms that I've mentioned, to some degree. It's a lot of fate to play with for the sake of a moment's relaxation.

6   I never intended to be the mother of a child with problems. Who does? But when, after a year of marriage to their father I legally adopted Adam, Sava, and Madeline—the three children *he* had adopted, years before, as a single parent—it simply happened. I've got less than the ordinary amount of patience, and for that reason I save all my admiration for those like Ken Kramberg, Adam's teacher, and others like Faith and Bob Annis, who work day in and day out with disability. I save it for my husband, Michael, who spent months of his life teaching Adam to tie his shoes. Living with Adam touches on my occupation only in the most peripheral ways; this is the first time I've ever written about him. I've never disguised him as a fictional character or consciously drawn on our experience together. It is, in fact, painful for a writer of fiction to write about actual events in one's personal life.

7   I have seen Michael, an anthropologist and novelist, struggle with this manuscript for six years. The work was a journey from the world of professional objectivity to a confusing realm where boundaries could no longer be so easily drawn. It has been wrenching for Michael to relive this story, but in the end, I think he felt compelled to do so after realizing the scope of the problem, after receiving so many desperate and generous stories from other people, and, in the end, out of that most frail of human motives—hope. If one story of FAS could be made accessible and real, it might just stop someone, somewhere, from producing another alcohol-stunted child.

8   Adam does not read with great ease, but he has pressed himself to read this story. He has reacted to it with fascination, and he has agreed to its publication. Although he has no concern about us as professionals, neither pride nor the slightest trace of resentment, Adam takes pleasure when, as a family, our pictures have occasionally appeared in the paper. He sees Michael and me primarily in the roles to which we've assigned ourselves around the house. Michael is the laundryman, I am the cook. And beyond that, most important, we are the people who respond to him. In that way, though an adult, he is at the stage of a very young child who sees the world only as an extension of his or her will. Adam is the world, at least his version of it, and he knows us only as who we are when we enter his purview.

9   Because of this, there are ways Adam knows us better than we know ourselves, though it would be difficult for him to describe this knowledge. He knows our limits, and I, at least, hide my limits from myself, especially when I go beyond them, especially when it comes to anger. Sometimes it seems to me that from the beginning, in living with Adam, anger has been inextricable from love, and I've been as helpless before the one as before the other.

10   We were married, Michael, his three children, and I, on a slightly overcast October day in 1981. Adam was thirteen, and because he had not yet gone through puberty, he was small, about the size of a ten-year-old. He was not, and is not, a charming person, but he is generous, invariably kind-hearted, and therefore lovable. He had then, and still possesses, the gift—which is also a curse, given the realities of the world—of absolute, serene trust. He took our ceremony, in which we exchanged vows, literally. At the end of it we were pronounced husband, wife, and family by the same friend, a local judge, who would later formally petition for me to become the adoptive mother of Adam, Sava, and Madeline; then still later, as we painfully came to terms with certain truths, he helped us set up a lifelong provision for Adam in our wills. As Judge Daschbach pronounced the magic words, Adam turned to me with delight and said, "Mom!" not Louise. Now it was official. I melted. That trust was not to change a whit, until I changed it.

11   Ten months pass. We're at the dinner table. I've eaten, so have our other children. It's a good dinner, one of their favorites. Michael's gone. Adam eats a bite then puts down his fork and sits before his plate. When I ask him to finish, he says, "But, Mom, I don't like this food."

12   "Yes, you do," I tell him. I'm used to a test or two from Adam when Michael is away, and these challenges are wearying, sometimes even maddening. But Adam has to know that I have the same rules as his father. He has to know, over and over and over. And Adam *does* like the food. I made it because he gobbled it down the week before and said he liked it, and I was happy.

13   "You have to eat or else you'll have a seizure in the morning," I tell him. This has proved to be true time and again. I am reasonable, firm, even patient at first, although I've said the same thing many times before. This is normal, Adam's way, just a test. I tell him again to finish.

14   "I don't like this food," he says again.

15   "Adam," I say, "you have to eat or you'll have a seizure."

16   He stares at me. Nothing.

17   Our younger children take their empty dishes to the sink. I wash them. Adam sits. Sava and Madeline go upstairs to play, and Adam sits. I check his forehead, think perhaps he's ill, but he is cool, and rather pleased with himself. He has now turned fourteen years old. But he still doesn't understand that, in addition to his medication, he must absorb so many calories every day or else he'll suffer an attack. The electricity in his brain will lash out, the impulses scattered and random.

18   "Eat up. I'm not kidding."

19   "I did," he says, the plate still full before him.

20   I simply point.

21   "I don't like this food," he says to me again.

22   I walk back to the cupboard. I slap a peanut butter sandwich together. He likes those. Maybe a concession on my part will satisfy him, maybe he'll eat, but when I put it on his plate he just looks at it.

23   I go into the next room. It is eight o'clock and I am in the middle of a book by Bruce Chatwin. There is more to life . . . but I'm responsible. I have to make him see that he's not just driving me crazy.

24   "Eat the sandwich . . ."

25   "I did." The sandwich is untouched.

26   "Eat the dinner . . ."

27   "I don't like this food."

28   "Okay then. Eat half."

29   He won't. He sits there. In his eyes there is an expression of stubborn triumph that boils me with the suddenness of frustration, dammed and suppressed, surfacing all at once.

30   "EAT!" I yell at him.

31   Histrionics, stamping feet, loud voices, usually impress him with the serious nature of our feelings much more than the use of reason. But not this time. There is no ordering, begging, or pleading that will make him eat, even for his own good. And he is thin, so thin. His face is gaunt, his ribs arch out of his sternum, his knees are big, bony, and his calves and thighs straight as sticks. I don't want him to fall, to seize, to hurt himself.

32   "Please . . . for me. Just do it."

33   He looks at me calmly.

34   "Just for me, okay?"

35   "I don't like this food."

36   The lid blows off. Nothing is left. If I can't help him to survive in the simplest way, how can I be his mother?

37   "Don't eat then. And don't call me Mom!"

38   Then I walk away, shaken. I leave him sitting and he does not eat, and the next morning he does have a seizure. He falls next to the aquarium, manages to grasp the table, and as his head bobs and his mouth twists, I hold him, wait it out. It's still two days before Michael will arrive home and I don't believe that I can handle it and I don't know how Michael has, but that is only a momentary surge of panic. Adam finally rights himself. He changes his pants. He goes on with his day. He does not connect the seizure with the lack of food: he won't. But he does connect my words, I begin to notice. He does remember. From that night on he starts calling me Louise, and I don't care. I'm glad of it at first, and think it will blow over when we forgive and grow close again. After all, he forgets most things.

39   But of all that I've told Adam, all the words of love, all the encouragements, the orders that I gave, assurances, explanations, and instructions, the only one he remembers with perfect, fixed, comprehension, even when I try to contradict it, even after months, is "Don't call me Mom."

40   Adam calls me "Mother" or "Mom" now, but it took years of patience, of backsliding, and of self-control, it took Adam's father explaining and me explaining and rewarding with hugs when he made me feel good, to get back to mother and son again. It took a long trip out west, just the two of us. It took a summer of side-by-side work. We planted thirty-five trees and one whole garden and a flower bed. We thinned the strawberries, pruned the lilacs and forsythia. We played tic-tac-toe, then Sorry. We lived together. And I gave up making him eat, or distanced myself enough to put the medicine in his hand and walk away, and realize I can't protect him.

41   That's why I say it takes a certain fiber I don't truly possess to live and work with a person obstinate to the core, yet a victim. Constant, nagging insults to good sense eventually wear on the steel of the soul. Logic that flies in the face of logic can madden one. In the years I've spent with Adam, I have learned more about my limits than I ever wanted to know. And yet, in spite of the ridiculous arguments, the life-and-death battles over medication

and the puny and wearying orders one must give every day, in spite of pulling gloves onto the chapped, frost-bitten hands of a nearly grown man and knowing he will shed them, once out of sight, in the minus-thirty windchill of January, something mysterious has flourished between us, a bond of absolute simplicity, love. That is, unquestionably, the alpha and omega of our relationship, even now that Adam has graduated to a somewhat more independent life.

42   But as I said, that love is inextricable from anger, and in loving Adam, the anger is mostly directed elsewhere, for it is impossible to love the sweetness, the inner light, the qualities that I trust in Adam, without hating the fact that he will always be kept from fully expressing those aspects of himself because of his biological mother's drinking. He is a Fetal Alcohol Effect victim. He'll always, all his life, be a lonely person.

43   I drank hard in my twenties, and eventually got hepatitis. I was lucky. Beyond an occasional glass of wine, I can't tolerate liquor anymore. But from those early days, I understand the urge for alcohol, its physical pull. I had formed an emotional bond with a special configuration of chemicals, and I realize to this day the attraction of the relationship and the immense difficulty in abandoning it.

44   Adam's mother never did let go. She died of alcohol poisoning, and I'd feel sorrier for her, if we didn't have Adam. As it is, I only hope that she died before she had a chance to produce another child with his problems. I can't help but wish, too, that during her pregnancy, if she couldn't be counseled or helped, she had been forced to abstain for those crucial nine months. On some American Indian reservations, due to Reagan-era slashing of alcohol and drug treatment and prenatal care programs, the situation has grown so desperate that a jail internment during pregnancy has been the only answer possible in some cases. Some people, whose views you will read in these pages, have taken more drastic stands and even called for the forced sterilization of women who, after having previously blunted the lives of several children like Adam, refuse to stop drinking while they're pregnant. This will outrage some women, and men, good people who believe that it is the right of individuals to put themselves in harm's way, that drinking is a choice we make, that a person's liberty to court either happiness or despair is sacrosanct. I believed this, too, and yet the poignancy and frustration of Adam's life has fed my doubts, has convinced me that some of my principles were

smug, untested. After all, where is the measure of responsibility here? Where, exactly, is the demarcation between self-harm and child abuse? Gross negligence is nearly equal to intentional wrong, goes a legal maxim. Where do we draw the line?

45   The people who advocate forcing pregnant women to abstain from drinking come from within the communities dealing with a problem of nightmarish proportions. Everyone agrees that the best answer is not to lock up pregnant women, but to treat them. However, this problem is now generations in the making. Women who themselves suffer from Fetal Alcohol Syndrome or Effect are extremely difficult to counsel because one of the most damaging aspects of FAS is the inability to make cause–effect connections, or to "think ahead." In addition, many alcohol and drug treatment programs are closed to pregnant women and, therefore, also to unborn children—the most crucial patients of all. It is obvious that the much-ballyhooed war on drugs is not being won with guns, but requires the concerted efforts of a compassionate society. Alcohol rehabilitation programs should be as easy to get into as liquor stores, and they should be free, paid for by the revenues from state liquor stores in some areas, and liquor taxes in others.

46   Since we the people are the government, we are all in some way to blame for allowing a problem of this magnitude to occur. Still, it is to devalue the worth of the individual not to hold one person, in some measure, responsible for his or her behavior. Once a woman decides to carry a child to term, to produce another human being, has she also the right to inflict on that person Adam's life? And isn't it also a father's responsibility to support and try to ensure an alcohol-free pregnancy? Because his mother drank, Adam is one of the earth's damaged. Did his mother have the right to take away Adam's curiosity, the right to take away the joy he could have felt at receiving a high math score, in reading a book, in wondering at the complexity and quirks of nature? Did she and his absent father have the right to make him an outcast among children, to make him friendless, to make of his sexuality a problem more than a pleasure, to slit his brain, to give him violent seizures?

47   It seems to me, in the end, that no one has the right to inflict such harm, even from the depth of ignorance. Roman Catholicism defines two kinds of ignorance, vincible and invincible. Invincible ignorance is that state in which a person is unex-

posed to certain forms of knowledge. The other type of ignorance, vincible, is willed. It is a conscious turning away from truth.
In either case, I don't think Adam's mother had the right to harm
her, and our, son.

48   Knowing what I know now, I am sure that even when I drank
hard, I would rather have been incarcerated for nine months and
produce a normal child than bear a human being who would, for
the rest of his or her life, be imprisoned by what I had done. I
would certainly go to jail for nine months now if it would make
Adam whole. For those still outraged at this position, those so
sure, so secure in opposition, I say the same thing I say to those
who would not allow a poor woman a safe abortion and yet have
not themselves gone to adoption agencies and taken in the
unplaceable children, the troubled, the unwanted:

49   If you don't agree with me, then please, go and sit beside
the alcohol-affected while they try to learn how to add. My mother, Rita Erdrich, who works with disabled children at the Wahpe-
ton Indian School, does this every day. Dry their frustrated tears.
Fight for them in the society they don't understand. Tell them
every simple thing they must know for survival, one million, two
million, three million times. Hold their heads when they have
unnecessary seizures and wipe the blood from their bitten lips.
Force them to take medicine. Keep the damaged of the earth safe.
Love them. Watch them grow up to sink into the easy mud of
alcoholism. Suffer a crime they won't understand committing. Try
to understand lack of remorse. As taxpayers, you are already paying for their jail terms, and footing the bills for expensive treatment and education. Be a victim yourself, beat your head against
a world of brick, fail constantly. Then go back to the mother, face
to face, and say again: *"It was your right."*

50   When I am angriest, I mentally tear into Adam's mother
because, in the end, it was her hand that lifted the bottle. When I
am saddest, I wish her, exhaustedly . . . but there is nowhere to
wish her worse than the probable hell of her life and death. If I
ever met her, I don't know what I'd do. Perhaps we'd both be
resigned before this enormous lesson. It is almost impossible to
hold another person responsible for so much hurt. Even though I
know our son was half-starved, tied to the bars of his crib,
removed by a welfare agency, I still think it must have been "society's fault." In public, when asked to comment on Native
American issues, I am defensive. Yes, I say, there are terrible prob-

lems. It takes a long, long time to heal communities beaten by waves of conquest and disease. It takes a long time for people to heal themselves. Sometimes, it seems hopeless. Yet in places, it is happening. Tribal communities, most notably the Alkali Lake Band in Canada, are coming together, rejecting alcohol, reembracing their own humanity, their own culture. These are tough people and they teach a valuable lesson: to whatever extent we can, we must take charge of our lives.

51   Yet, in loving Adam, we bow to fate. Few of his problems can be solved or ultimately changed. So instead, Michael and I concentrate on only what we can control—our own reactions. If we can muster grace, joy, happiness in helping him confront and conquer the difficulties life presents . . . then we have received gifts. Adam has been deprived of giving so much else.

52   What I know my husband hopes for, in offering *The Broken Cord*, is a future in which this particular and preventable tragedy will not exist. I feel the same way. I would rather that FAS and FAE were eradicated through enlightenment, through education and a new commitment to treatment. That is the hope in which this book was written. But if that isn't possible, I would eliminate them any way I could.

53   Michael and I have a picture of our son. For some reason, in this photograph, taken on my grandfather's land in the Turtle Mountains of North Dakota, no defect is evident in Adam's stance or face. Although perhaps a knowing doctor could make the fetal alcohol diagnosis from his features, Adam's expression is intelligent and serene. He is smiling, his eyes are brilliant, and his brows are dark, sleek. There is no sign in this portrait that anything is lacking.

54   I look at this picture and think, "Here is the other Adam. The one our son would be if not for alcohol." Sometimes Michael and I imagine that we greet him, that we look into his eyes, and he into ours, for a long time and in that gaze we not only understand our son, but he also understands us. He has grown up to be a colleague, a peer, not a person who needs pity, protection, or special breaks. By the old reservation cabin where my mother was born, in front of the swirled wheat fields and woods of ancestral land, Adam stands expectantly, the full-hearted man he was meant to be. The world opens before him—so many doors, so much light. In this picture, he is ready to go forward with his life.

REFLECTIONS

Louise Erdrich relates a great deal of information about Fetal Alcohol Syndrome in this essay, yet it is given in the form of a personal narrative. What is the effect on the reader of this way of presenting the information? If this were presented as an argument against drinking alcohol while pregnant, would you be convinced? What details strike you as the most effective? Do you think that the argument would have been more convincing if it had been written as an objective, logical argument with no personal references or appeals to emotion? What do you think of the author's suggestion that women should be prevented from drinking alcohol during pregnancy, even to the extent of imprisoning expectant mothers who cannot control their alcohol abuse?

Mary
Gordon
(1949–   )

Mary Gordon was born on Long Island, New York. She grew up in an Irish Catholic family and attended Roman Catholic elementary and high schools, facts that play a dominant role in her fiction, especially her novel *Men and Angels*. She is currently Professor of English at Barnard College, where she earned her B.A. in 1971.

"The Parable of the Cave; or, In Praise of Watercolors" reflects her interest in the writing of women and in painting, particularly the work of Mary Cassatt. In the essay, which appears in a collection of Gordon's nonfiction, *Good Boys and Dead Girls* (1991), she explores various ways women writers suffer prejudice.

The Parable of the Cave; or, In Praise of Watercolors

1   Once, I was told a story by a famous writer. "I will tell you what women writers are like," he said. The year was 1971. The women's movement had made men nervous; it had made a lot of women write. "Women writers are like a female bear who goes into a cave to hibernate. The male bear shoves a pine cone up her ass, because he knows if she shits all winter, she'll stink up the cave. In the spring, the pressure of all that built-up shit makes her expel the pine cone, and she shits a winter's worth all over the walls of the cave."

2   That's what women writers are like, said the famous writer.

3   He told the story with such geniality; he looked as if he were giving me a wonderful gift. I felt I ought to smile; everyone knows there's no bore like a feminist with no sense of humor. I did not write for two months after that. It was the only time in my life I have suffered from writer's block. I should not have smiled. But he was a famous writer and spoke with geniality. And in truth, I did not have the courage for clear rage. There is no seduction like that of being thought a good girl.

4   Theodore Roethke said that women poets were "stamping a tiny foot against God." I have been told by male but not by female critics that my work was "exquisite," "lovely," "like a watercolor." They, of course, were painting in oils. They were doing the important work. Watercolors are cheap and plentiful; oils are costly: their base—oil—must be bought. And the idea is that oil paintings will endure. But what will they endure against? Fire? Flood? Bombs? Earthquake? Their endurance is another illusion: one more foolish bet against nature, or against natural vulnerabilities; one more scheme, like fallout shelters; one more gesture of illusory safety.

5   There are people in the world who derive no small pleasure from the game of "major" and "minor." They think that no major work can be painted in watercolors. They think, too, that Hemingway writing about boys in the woods is major; Mansfield writing about girls in the house is minor. Exquisite, they will hasten to insist, but minor. These people join up with other bad specters, and I have to work to banish them. Let us pretend these specters are two men, two famous poets, saying, "Your experience is an embarrassment; your experience is insignificant."

6   I wanted to be a good girl, so I tried to find out whose experience was not embarrassing. The prototype for a writer who was not embarrassing was Henry James. And you see, the two specters said, proffering hope, he wrote about social relationships, but his distance gave them grandeur.

7   Distance, then, was what I was to strive for. Distance from the body, from the heart, but most of all, distance from the self as writer. I could never understand exactly what they meant or how to do it; it was like trying to follow the directions on a home permanent in 1959.

8   If Henry James had the refined experience, Conrad had the significant one. The important moral issues were his: men pitted against nature in moments of extremity. There are no important

women in Conrad's novels, except for *Victory,* which, the critics tell us, is a romance and an exception. Despite the example of Conrad, it was all right for the young men I knew, according to my specters, to write about the hymens they had broken, the diner waitresses they had seduced. Those experiences were significant. But we were not to write about our broken hearts, about the married men we loved disastrously, about our mothers or our children. Men could write about their fears of dying by exposure in the forest; we could not write about our fears of being suffocated in the kitchen. Our desire to write about these experiences only revealed our shallowness; it was suggested we would, in time, get over it. And write about what? Perhaps we would stop writing.

9   And so, the specters whispered to me, if you want to write well, if you want us to take you seriously, you must be distant, you must be extreme.

10   I suppose the specters were not entirely wrong. Some of the literature that has been written since the inception of the women's movement is lacking in style and moral proportion. But so is the work of Mailer, Miller, Burroughs, Ginsberg. Their lack of style and proportion may be called offensive, but not embarrassing. They may be referred to as off the mark, but they will not be called trivial.

11   And above all I did not wish to be *trivial;* I did not wish to be embarrassing. But I did not want to write like Conrad, and I did not want to write like Henry James. The writers I wanted to imitate were all women: Charlotte Brontë, Woolf, Mansfield, Bowen, Lessing, Olsen. I discovered that what I loved in writing was not distance but radical closeness; not the violence of the bizarre but the complexity of the quotidian.

12   I lost my fear of being trivial, but not my fear of being an embarrassment. And so I wrote my first novel in the third person. No one would publish it. Then a famous woman writer asked why I had written a first-person novel in the third person. She is a woman of abiding common sense, and so I blushed to tell her: "I wanted to sound serious. I didn't want to be embarrassing."

13   Only her wisdom made me write the novel I meant to. I can say it now: I will probably never read Conrad again; what he writes about simply does not interest me. Henry James I will love always, but it is not for his distance that I love him. The notion that style and detachment are necessary blood brothers is crude and bigoted. It is an intellectual embarrassment.

14   And I can say it now: I would rather own a Mary Cassatt watercolor than a Velázquez oil.

15   Here is the good side of being a woman writer: the company of other women writers, dead and living. My writer friends, all women, help me banish the dark specters. So does Katherine Mansfield; so does Christina Rossetti. I feel their closeness to the heart of things; I feel their aptness and their bravery.

16   I think it is lonelier to be a man writer than a woman writer now, because I do not think that men are as good at being friends to one another as women are. Perhaps, since they have not thought they needed each other's protection, as women have known we have needed each other's, they have not learned the knack of helpful, rich concern that centers on a friend's work. They may be worried, since they see themselves as hewers of wood and slayers of animals, about production, about the kind of achievement that sees its success only in terms of another's failure. They may not be as kind to one another; they may not know how. These are the specters that men now must banish. Our specters may be easier to chase. For the moment. They were not always so.

17   To this tale there should be an appendix, an explanation. Why was I so susceptible to the bad advice of men? What made me so ready to listen? Where did I acquire my genius for obedience?

18   I had a charming father. In many crucial ways, he was innocent of sexism, although he may have substituted narcissism in its place. He wanted me to be like him. He was a writer, an unsuccessful writer, and my mother worked as a secretary to support us. Nevertheless, he was a writer; he could think of himself as nothing else. He wanted me to be a writer too. I may have been born to be one, which made things easier. He died when I was seven. But even in those years we had together I learned well that I was his child, not my mother's. His mind was exalted, my mother's common. That she could earn the money to support us was only proof of the ordinariness of her nature, an ordinariness to which I was in no way heir. So I was taught to read at three, taught French at six, and taught to despise the world of women, the domestic. I was a docile child. I brought my father great joy, and I learned the pleasures of being a good girl.

19   And I earned, as a good girl, no mean rewards. Our egos are born delicate. Bestowing pleasure upon a beloved father is much easier than discovering the joys of solitary achievements. It was

easy for me to please my father; and this ease bred in me a desire to please men—a desire for the rewards of a good girl. They are by no means inconsiderable: safety and approval, the warm, incomparable atmosphere created when one pleases a man who has vowed, in his turn, to keep the wolf from the door.

20 But who is the wolf?

21 He is strangers. He is the risk of one's own judgments, one's own work.

22 I have learned in time that I am at least as much my mother's daughter as my father's. Had I been only my mother's daughter, it is very possible that I would never have written: I may not have had the confidence required to embark upon a career so valueless in the eyes of the commonsense world. I did what my father wanted; I became a writer. I grew used to giving him the credit. But now I see that I am the *kind* of writer I am because I am my mother's daughter. My father's tastes ran to the metaphysical. My mother taught me to listen to conversations at the dinner table; she taught me to remember jokes.

23 My subject as a writer has far more to do with family happiness than with the music of the spheres. I don't know what the nature of the universe is, but I have a good ear. What it hears best are daily rhythms, for that is what I value, what I would wish, as a writer, to preserve.

24 My father would have thought this a stubborn predilection for the minor. My mother knows better.

REFLECTIONS

Gordon writes about how she had wanted to be a "good girl" and accept what various male authorities told her—about her own writing and about the limitations of women's writing in general. In the course of explaining why she writes about what she does, she offers a defense that does not adhere to the writerly ideals of "distance" and "objectivity." And she further explains that she is simply not interested in the writings of certain male writers such as Joseph Conrad, who have been deemed "significant." Do you accept her argument against the privileging of male subjects? Do you find yourself sympathetic to her position? And what do you think of her remarks about the differences in bonding and community that exist among male and female writers? Finally, what is Gordon's purpose in bringing her parents into this discussion of her writing?

Edward Hoagland

(1932—   )

Edward Hoagland splits his time between New York City, where he was born and raised, and New England country where he attended college (Harvard) and gets in touch with nature. Though Hoagland is perhaps best known as a nature writer, he is also a novelist and travel writer. Among his books are *African Calliope: A Journey to the Sudan*, a novel, and *The Tugman's Passage*, one of his essay collections. *The Edward Hoagland Reader* offers a sample of Hoagland's writings. The following essay considers the essay as a genre, offering some fruitful insights into why we read and write essays.

What I Think, What I Am

---

1   Our loneliness makes us avid column readers these days. The personalities in the *New York Post, Chicago Daily News, San Francisco Chronicle* constitute our neighbors now, some of them local characters but also the opinionated national stars. And movie reviewers thrive on our need for somebody emotional who is willing to pay attention to us and return week after week, year after year, through all the to-and-fro of other friends to flatter us by pouring out his (her) heart. They are essayists as Elizabeth Hardwick is, James Baldwin was. We sometimes hear that essays are an old-fashioned form, that so-and-so is the "last essayist," but the facts of the marketplace argue quite otherwise. Essays of almost any kind are so much easier for a writer to sell now than short stories, so many more see print, it's odd that though two

fine anthologies remain which publish the year's best stories, no comparable collection exists for essays. Such changes in the reading public's taste aren't always to the good, needless to say. The art of telling stories predated even cave-painting surely; and if we ever find ourselves living in caves again, it (with painting) will be the only art left, after movies, novels, essays, photography, biography and all the rest have gone down the drain—the art to build from.

2   One has the sense with the short story form that while everything may have been done, nothing has been overdone, it has a permanence. Essays, if a comparison is to be made, although they go back 400 years to Montaigne, seem a newfangled mercurial, sometimes hokey sort of affair which has lent itself to many of the excesses of the age, from spurious autobiography to spurious hallucination, as well as the shabby careerism of traditional journalism. It's a greased pig. Essays are associated with the way young writers fashion a name—on plain, crowded newsprint in hybrid vehicles like *The Village Voice, Rolling Stone, The Soho Weekly News* (also *Fiction* magazine), instead of the thick paper stock and thin readership of *Partisan Review.*

3   Essays, however, hang somewhere on a line between two sturdy poles: this is what I think, and this is what I am. Autobiographies which aren't novels are generally extended essays, indeed. A personal essay is like the human voice talking, its order the mind's natural flow, instead of a systematized outline of ideas. Though more wayward or informal than an article or treatise, somewhere it contains a point which is its real center, even if the point couldn't be expressed in fewer words than the essayist has employed. Essays don't usually "boil down" to a summary, as articles do, but on the other hand they have fewer "levels" than first-rate fiction—a flatter surface—because we aren't supposed to argue about their meaning. In the old distinction between teaching versus story-telling—however cleverly the author muddies it up—an essay is intended to convey the same point to each of us.

4   This emphasis upon mind speaking to mind is what makes essays less universal in their appeal than stories. They are addressed to an educated, perhaps a middle-class reader, with certain presuppositions shared, a frame of reference, even a commitment to civility—not the grand and golden empathy inherent in every man which the story-teller has a chance to tap. At the same time, of course, the artful "I" of an essay can be as chameleon as

any narrator in fiction; and essays do tell a story just as often as a short story stakes a claim to a particular viewpoint.

5   Mark Twain's piece called "Corn-pone Opinions," for example, which is about public opinion, begins with a vignette as vivid as any in "Huckleberry Finn." When he was a boy of 15, Twain says, he used to hang out a back window and listen to the sermons preached by a neighbor's slave standing on top of a woodpile. The fellow "imitated the pulpit style of the several clergymen of the village, and did it well and with fine passion and energy. To me he was a wonder. I believed he was the greatest orator in the United States and would some day be heard from. But it did not happen; in the distribution of rewards he was overlooked.

6   "He interrupted his preaching now and then to saw a stick of wood, but the sawing was a pretense—he did it with his mouth, exactly imitating the sound the bucksaw makes in shrieking its way through the wood. But it served its purpose, it kept his master from coming out to see how the work was getting along."

7   The extraordinary flexibility of essays is what has enabled them to ride out rough weather and hybridize into forms to suit the times. And just as one of the first things a fiction writer learns is that he needn't actually be writing fiction to write a short story—he can tell his own history or anyone else's as exactly as he remembers it and it will still be "fiction" if it remains primarily a story—an essayist soon discovers that he doesn't have to tell the whole truth and nothing but the truth; he can shape or shave his memories as long as the purpose is served of elucidating a truthful point. A personal essay frequently is not autobiographical at all, but what it does keep in common with autobiography is that, through its tone and tumbling progression, it conveys the quality of the author's mind. Nothing gets in the way. Because essays are directly concerned with the mind and its idiosyncrasy, the very freedom the mind possesses is bestowed on this branch of literature that does honor to it, and the fascination of the mind is the fascination of the essay.

REFLECTIONS

Throughout this piece, Hoagland makes distinctions. He distinguishes between essay and story, essay and article, essay and autobiography. What does the essay have in common with each of these forms, and how, according to Hoagland, does it differ from each of them? Is it true that, as Hoagland says, "an essay is intended to convey the same point to each of us"? Do you agree with Hoagland that an "emphasis upon mind speaking to mind" is what makes essays less universal in their appeal than stories? And what do you think Hoagland means when he says that essays "hang somewhere on a line between two sturdy poles: This is what I think, and this is what I am"?

Zora Neale Hurston

(1903–1960)

Zora Neale Hurston was born in Eatonville, Florida, and educated at Howard University, Barnard College, from which she received a B.A. in 1928, and Columbia University, where she did graduate work. A folklorist, Hurston collected folklore in Bermuda, Haiti, Honduras, Jamaica, and the American South. Her collection of black folklore, *Mules and Men,* is among her most important works. She also worked as a drama teacher, a staff writer at Paramount, a maid, a freelance writer and journalist, and a librarian at the Library of Congress. She is best known, however, as a prominent figure of the Harlem Renaissance in the 1920s and 1930s. The dignity of her racial heritage and the grace and courage of womanhood are celebrated in her well-known novel, *Their Eyes Were Watching God.*

How It Feels to Be Colored Me

1   I am colored but I offer nothing in the way of extenuating circumstances except the fact that I am the only Negro in the United States whose grandfather on the mother's side was *not* an Indian chief.

2   I remember the very day that I became colored. Up to my thirteenth year I lived in the little Negro town of Eatonville, Florida. It is exclusively a colored town. The only white people I knew passed through the town going to or coming from Orlando. The native whites rode dusty horses, the Northern tourists

chugged down the sandy village road in automobiles. The town knew the Southerners and never stopped cane chewing when they passed. But the Northerners were something else again. They were peered at cautiously from behind curtains by the timid. The more venturesome would come out on the porch to watch them go past and got just as much pleasure out of the tourists as the tourists got out of the village.

3   The front porch might seem a daring place for the rest of the town, but it was a gallery seat for me. My favorite place was atop the gate-post. Proscenium box for a born first-nighter. Not only did I enjoy the show, but I didn't mind the actors knowing that I liked it. I usually spoke to them in passing. I'd wave at them and when they returned my salute, I would say something like this: "Howdy-do-well-I-thank-you-where-you-goin'?" Usually automobile or the horse paused at this, and after a queer exchange of compliments, I would probably "go a piece of the way" with them, as we say in farthest Florida. If one of my family happened to come to the front in time to see me, of course negotiations would be rudely broken off. But even so, it is clear that I was the first "welcome-to-our-state" Floridian, and I hope the Miami Chamber of Commerce will please take notice.

4   During this period, white people differed from colored to me only in that they rode through town and never lived there. They liked to hear me "speak pieces" and sing and wanted to see me dance the parse-me-la, and gave me generously of their small silver for doing these things, which seemed strange to me for I wanted to do them so much that I needed bribing to stop. Only they didn't know it. The colored people gave no dimes. They deplored any joyful tendencies in me, but I was their Zora nevertheless. I belonged to them, to the nearby hotels, to the county— everybody's Zora.

5   But changes came in the family when I was thirteen, and I was sent to school in Jacksonville. I left Eatonville, the town of the oleanders, as Zora. When I disembarked from the river-boat at Jacksonville, she was no more. It seemed that I had suffered a sea change. I was not Zora of Orange County any more, I was now a little colored girl. I found it out in certain ways. In my heart as well as in the mirror, I became a fast brown—warranted not to rub nor run.

6   But I am not tragically colored. There is no great sorrow dammed up in my soul, nor lurking behind my eyes. I do not

mind at all. I do not belong to the sobbing school of Negrohood who hold that nature somehow has given them a lowdown dirty deal and whose feelings are all hurt about it. Even in the helter-skelter skirmish that is my life, I have seen that the world is to the strong regardless of a little pigmentation more or less. No, I do not weep at the world—I am too busy sharpening my oyster knife.

7 Someone is always at my elbow reminding me that I am the granddaughter of slaves. It fails to register depression with me. Slavery is sixty years in the past. The operation was successful and the patient is doing well, thank you. The terrible struggle that made me an American out of a potential slave said "On the line!" The Reconstruction said "Get set!"; and the generation before said "Go!" I am off to a flying start and I must not halt in the stretch to look behind and weep. Slavery is the price I paid for civilization, and the choice was not with me. It is a bully adventure and worth all that I have paid through my ancestors for it. No one on earth ever had a greater chance for glory. The world to be won and nothing to be lost. It is thrilling to think—to know that for any act of mine, I shall get twice as much praise or twice as much blame. It is quite exciting to hold the center of the national stage, with the spectators not knowing whether to laugh or to weep.

8 The position of my white neighbor is much more difficult. No brown specter pulls up a chair beside me when I sit down to eat. No dark ghost thrusts its leg against mine in bed. The game of keeping what one has is never so exciting as the game of getting.

9 I do not always feel colored. Even now I often achieve the unconscious Zora of Eatonville before the Hegira. I feel most colored when I am thrown against a sharp white background.

10 For instance at Barnard. "Beside the waters of the Hudson" I feel my race. Among the thousand white persons, I am a dark rock surged upon, and overswept, but through it all, I remain myself. When covered by the waters, I am; and the ebb but reveals me again.

11 Sometimes it is the other way around. A white person is set down in our midst, but the contrast is just as sharp for me. For instance, when I sit in the drafty basement that is The New World Cabaret with a white person, my color comes. We enter chatting about any little nothing that we have in common and are seated by the jazz waiters. In the abrupt way that jazz orchestras have, this one plunges into a number. It loses no time in circumlocutions, but gets right down to business. It constricts the thorax and splits the heart with its tempo and narcotic harmonies. This orchestra

grows rambunctious, rears on its hind legs and attacks the tonal veil with primitive fury, rending it, clawing it until it breaks through to the jungle beyond. I follow those heathen—follow them exultingly. I dance wildly inside myself; I yell within, I whoop; I shake my assegai above my head, I hurl it true to the mark *yeeeeooww!* I am in the jungle and living in the jungle way. My face is painted red and yellow and my body is painted blue. My pulse is throbbing like a war drum. I want to slaughter something—give pain, give death to what, I do not know. But the piece ends. The men of the orchestra wipe their lips and rest their fingers. I creep back slowly to the veneer we call civilization with the last tone and find the white friend sitting motionless in his seat, smoking calmly.

12   "Good music they have here," he remarks, drumming the table with his fingertips.

13   Music. The great blobs of purple and red emotion have not touched him. He has only heard what I felt. He is far away and I see him but dimly across the ocean and the continent that have fallen between us. He is so pale with his whiteness then and I am *so* colored.

14   At certain times I have no race, I am *me*. When I set my hat at a certain angle and saunter down Seventh Avenue, Harlem City, feeling as snooty as the lions in front of the Forty-Second Street Library, for instance. So far as my feelings are concerned, Peggy Hopkins Joyce on the Boule Mich with her gorgeous raiment, stately carriage, knees knocking together in a most aristocratic manner, has nothing on me. The cosmic Zora emerges. I belong to no race nor time. I am the eternal feminine with its string of beads.

15   I have no separate feeling about being an American citizen and colored. I am merely a fragment of the Great Soul that surges within the boundaries. My country, right or wrong.

16   Sometimes, I feel discriminated against, but it does not make me angry. It merely astonishes me. How *can* any deny themselves the pleasure of my company? It's beyond me.

17   But in the main, I feel like a brown bag of miscellany propped against a wall. Against a wall in company with other bags, white, red and yellow. Pour out the contents, and there is discovered a jumble of small things priceless and worthless. A first-water diamond, an empty spool, bits of broken glass, lengths of string, a

key to a door long since crumbled away, a rusty knife-blade, old shoes saved for a road that never was and never will be, a nail bent under the weight of things too heavy for any nail, a dried flower or two still a little fragrant. In your hand is the brown bag. On the ground before you is the jumble it held—so much like the jumble in the bags, could they be emptied, that all might be dumped in a single heap and the bags refilled without altering the content of any greatly. A bit of colored glass more or less would not matter. Perhaps that is how the Great Stuffer of Bags filled them in the first place—who knows?

REFLECTIONS

Zora Neale Hurston writes about herself as a young black woman. How does she see herself? How does she characterize the differences between the worlds of blacks and whites? To what extent do you find her argument convincing? To what extent do you think her experience represents that of other members of minorities? You might also consider the various metaphors and images Hurston uses to present her vision of experience.

Martin Luther King, Jr.

(1929–1968)

Martin Luther King, Jr., was born in Atlanta, Georgia, in 1929, the son of a Baptist minister. King grew up and attended school and church in Atlanta, where he was exposed to a strong and deep religious influence. At seventeen King became assistant pastor at his father's church. After graduating from Morehouse College at nineteen, he went on to study for a B.A. in divinity at Crozer Seminary and then to Boston University for a Ph.D. in theology. King is best known for his work of peaceful or nonviolent protest against racism, having been influenced by the nonviolent philosophy of Mahatma Gandhi. The selection that follows is a speech that King delivered at the Lincoln Memorial before a quarter of a million people who had gathered for the March on Washington August 28, 1963. Five years later Martin Luther King, Jr., was assassinated.

I Have a Dream

1   I am happy to join with you today in what will go down in history as the greatest demonstration for freedom in the history of our nation.

2   Fivescore years ago, a great American, in whose symbolic shadow we stand today, signed the Emancipation Proclamation. This momentous decree came as a great beacon light of hope to millions of Negro slaves who had been seared in the flames of withering injustice. It came as a joyous daybreak to end the long night of their captivity.

3   But one hundred years later, the Negro still is not free; one hundred years later, the life of the Negro is still sadly crippled by the manacles of segregation and the chains of discrimination; one hundred years later, the Negro lives on a lonely island of poverty in the midst of a vast ocean of material prosperity; one hundred years later, the Negro is still languished in the corners of American society and finds himself in exile in his own land.

4   So we've come here today to dramatize a shameful condition. In a sense we've come to our nation's capital to cash a check. When the architects of our republic wrote the magnificent words of the Constitution and the Declaration of Independence, they were signing a promissory note to which every American was to fall heir. This note was the promise that all men, yes, black men as well as white men, would be guaranteed the unalienable rights of life, liberty, and the pursuit of happiness.

5   It is obvious today that America has defaulted on this promissory note in so far as her citizens of color are concerned. Instead of honoring this sacred obligation, America has given the Negro people a bad check; a check which has come back marked "insufficient funds." We refuse to believe that there are insufficient funds in the great vaults of opportunity of this nation. And so we've come to cash this check, a check that will give us upon demand the riches of freedom and the security of justice.

6   We have also come to this hallowed spot to remind America of the fierce urgency of now. This is no time to engage in the luxury of cooling off or to take the tranquilizing drug of gradualism. Now is the time to make real the promises of democracy; now is the time to rise from the dark and desolate valley of segregation to the sunlit path of racial justice; now is the time to lift our nation from the quicksands of racial injustice to the solid rock of brotherhood; now is the time to make justice a reality for all God's children. It would be fatal for the nation to overlook the urgency of the moment. This sweltering summer of the Negro's legitimate discontent will not pass until there is an invigorating autumn of freedom and equality.

7   Nineteen sixty-three is not an end, but a beginning. And those who hope that the Negro needed to blow off steam and will now be content, will have a rude awakening if the nation returns to business as usual.

8   There will be neither rest nor tranquility in America until the Negro is granted his citizenship rights. The whirlwinds of

revolt will continue to shake the foundations of our nation until the bright day of justice emerges.

9 But there is something that I must say to my people who stand on the warm threshold which leads into the palace of justice. In the process of gaining our rightful place we must not be guilty of wrongful deeds.

10 Let us not seek to satisfy our thirst for freedom by drinking from the cup of bitterness and hatred. We must forever conduct our struggle on the high plane of dignity and discipline. We must not allow our creative protest to degenerate into physical violence. Again and again we must rise to the majestic heights of meeting physical force with soul force.

11 The marvelous new militancy which has engulfed the Negro community must not lead us to a distrust of all white people, for many of our white brothers, as evidenced by their presence here today, have come to realize that their destiny is tied up with our destiny and they have come to realize that their freedom is inextricably bound to our freedom. This offense we share mounted to storm the battlements of injustice must be carried forth by a biracial army. We cannot walk alone.

12 And as we walk, we must make the pledge that we shall always march ahead. We cannot turn back. There are those who are asking the devotees of civil rights, "When will you be satisfied?" We can never be satisfied as long as the Negro is the victim of the unspeakable horrors of police brutality.

13 We can never be satisfied as long as our bodies, heavy with fatigue of travel, cannot gain lodging in the motels of the highways and the hotels of the cities. We cannot be satisfied as long as the Negro's basic mobility is from a smaller ghetto to a larger one.

14 We can never be satisfied as long as our children are stripped of their selfhood and robbed of their dignity by signs stating "for whites only." We cannot be satisfied as long as a Negro in Mississippi cannot vote and a Negro in New York believes he has nothing for which to vote. No, we are not satisfied, and we will not be satisfied until justice rolls down like waters and righteousness like a mighty stream.

15 I am not unmindful that some of you have come here out of excessive trials and tribulation. Some of you have come fresh from narrow jail cells. Some of you have come from areas where your quest for freedom left you battered by the storms of persecution

and staggered by the winds of police brutality. You have been the veterans of creative suffering. Continue to work with the faith that unearned suffering is redemptive.

16   Go back to Mississippi; go back to Alabama; go back to South Carolina; go back to Georgia; go back to Louisiana; go back to the slums and ghettos of the northern cities, knowing that somehow this situation can, and will be changed. Let us not wallow in the valley of despair.

17   So I say to you, my friends, that even though we must face the difficulties of today and tomorrow, I still have a dream. It is a dream deeply rooted in the American dream that one day this nation will rise up and live out the true meaning of its creed—we hold these truths to be self-evident, that all men are created equal.

18   I have a dream that one day on the red hills of Georgia, sons of former slaves and sons of former slave-owners will be able to sit down together at the table of brotherhood.

19   I have a dream that one day, even the state of Mississippi, a state sweltering with the heat of injustice, sweltering with the heat of oppression, will be transformed into an oasis of freedom and justice.

20   I have a dream my four little children will one day live in a nation where they will not be judged by the color of their skin but by the content of their character. I have a dream today!

21   I have a dream that one day, down in Alabama, with its vicious racists, with its governor having his lips dripping with the words of interposition and nullification, that one day, right there in Alabama, little black boys and black girls will be able to join hands with little white boys and white girls as sisters and brothers. I have a dream today!

22   I have a dream that one day every valley shall be exalted, every hill and mountain shall be made low, the rough places shall be made plain, and the crooked places shall be made straight and the glory of the Lord will be revealed and all flesh shall see it together.

23   This is our hope. This is the faith that I go back to the South with.

24   With this faith we will be able to hear out of the mountain of despair a stone of hope. With this faith we will be able to transform the jangling discords of our nation into a beautiful symphony of brotherhood.

25   With this faith we will be able to work together, to pray together, to struggle together, to go to jail together, to stand up for freedom together, knowing that we will be free one day. This will be the day when all of God's children will be able to sing with new meaning—"my country 'tis of thee; sweet land of liberty; of thee I sing; land where my fathers died, land of the pilgrim's pride; from every mountainside, let freedom ring"—and if America is to be a great nation, this must become true.

So let freedom ring from the prodigious hilltops of New Hampshire.
Let freedom ring from the mighty mountains of New York.
Let freedom ring from the heightening Alleghenies of Pennsylvania.
Let freedom ring from the snow-capped Rockies of Colorado.
Let freedom ring from the curvaceous slopes of California.
But not only that.
Let freedom ring from Stone Mountain of Georgia.
Let freedom ring from Lookout Mountain of Tennessee.
Let freedom ring from every hill and molehill of Mississippi, from every mountainside, let freedom ring.

26   And when we allow freedom to ring, when we let it ring from every village and hamlet, from every state and city, we will be able to speed up that day when all of God's children—black men and white men, Jews and Gentiles, Catholics and Protestants—will be able to join hands and to sing in the words of the old Negro spiritual, "Free at last, free at last; thank God Almighty, we are free at last!"

REFLECTIONS

King's piece is very much a speech. It was written to be read, recited, preached. Look through and identify places that seem particularly oratorical. Find others that seem especially suited to a sermon. Ideally you should read or listen to this piece read aloud. Identify and consider the effectiveness of King's uses of repetition as well as his figures of speech, especially images and metaphors. Consider also the relevance and rhetorical effectiveness of his allusions to literary, historical, and biblical documents. And finally, consider why this piece has become the best known and best loved of King's works.

Norman Mailer

(1923–   )

Norman Mailer refuses to conform to traditional notions of what is normal. He resists harmony and peace, and cultivates a violent and erratic persona for himself. Since his first novel, *The Naked and the Dead*, which incorporates his own experiences during World War II, Mailer has written both fiction and nonfiction; and it is not always easy to determine which is which. Mailer deliberately positions himself as an active character in both history and fiction, often with the purpose of altering history and affecting the consciousness of his time. *The Armies of the Night*, usually classified as nonfiction, is subtitled *History as a Novel, the Novel as History*. He continues this history in which he plays the part of the fictional protagonist in *Miami and the Siege of Chicago*, a study of the political events of 1968, which is excerpted here. A winner of two Pulitzer Prizes (one for *The Executioner's Song*, a novel based on a true story, and the other for *Armies of the Night*), Norman Mailer continues to challenge the boundaries between fact and fiction in *Harlot's Ghost* (1991), a novel about the CIA, which took seven years to research and write and which *Rolling Stone* characterizes as "nothing less than a history of America in our times."

The Siege of Chicago

1   Meanwhile, a mass meeting was taking place about the bandshell in Grant Park, perhaps a quarter of a mile east of Michigan Avenue and the Conrad Hilton. The meeting was under the auspices of the Mobilization, and a crowd of ten or fifteen

thousand appeared. The Mayor had granted a permit to assemble, but had refused to allow a march. Since the Mobilization had announced that it would attempt, no matter how, the march to the Amphitheatre that was the first purpose of their visit to Chicago, the police were out in force to surround the meeting.

2   An episode occurred during the speeches. Three demonstrators climbed a flag pole to cut down the American flag and put up a rebel flag. A squad of police charged to beat them up, but got into trouble themselves, for when they threw tear gas, the demonstrators lobbed the canisters back, and the police, choking on their own gas, had to fight their way clear through a barrage of rocks. Then came a much larger force of police charging the area, overturning benches, busting up members of the audience, then heading for Rennie Davis at the bullhorn. He was one of the coordinators of the Mobilization, his face was known, he had been fingered and fingered again by plainclothesmen. Now urging the crowd to sit down and be calm, he was attacked from behind by the police, his head laid open in a three-inch cut, and he was unconscious for a period. Furious at the attack, Tom Hayden, who had been in disguise these last two days to avoid any more arrests for himself, spoke to the crowd, said he was leaving to perform certain special tasks, and suggested that others break up into small groups and go out into the streets of the Loop "to do what they have to do." A few left with him; the majority remained. While it was a People's Army and therefore utterly unorganized by uniform or unity, it had a variety of special troops and regular troops; everything from a few qualified Kamikaze who were ready to charge police lines in a Japanese snake dance and dare on the consequence, some vicious beatings, to various kinds of small saboteurs, rock-throwers, gauntlet-runners—some of the speediest of the kids were adept at taunting cops while keeping barely out of range of their clubs—not altogether aline to running the bulls at Pamplona. Many of those who remained, however, were still nominally pacifists, protesters, Gandhians—they believed in non-violence, in the mystical interposition of their body to the attack, as if the violence of the enemy might be drained by the spiritual act of passive resistance over the years, over the thousands, tens of thousands, hundreds of thousands of beatings over the years. So Allen Ginsberg was speaking now to them.

3   The police looking through the plexiglass face shields they had flipped down from their helmets were then obliged to watch

the poet with his bald head, soft eyes magnified by horn-rimmed eyeglasses, and massive dark beard, utter his words in a croaking speech. He had been gassed Monday night and Tuesday night, and had gone to the bench at dawn to read Hindu Tantras to some of the Yippies, the combination of the chants and the gassings had all but burned out his voice, his beautiful speaking voice, one of the most powerful and hypnotic instruments of the Western world was down to the scrapings of the throat now, raw as flesh after a curettage.

4   "The best strategy for you," said Ginsberg, "in cases of hysteria, overexcitement or fear, is still to chant 'OM' together. It helps to quell flutterings of butterflies in the belly. Join me now as I try to lead you."

5   The crowd chanted with Ginsberg. They were of a generation which would try every idea, every drug, every action—it was even possible a few of them had made out with freaky kicks on tear gas these last few days—so they would chant OM. There were Hindu fanatics in the crowd, children who loved India and scorned everything in the West; there were cynics who thought the best thing to be said for a country which allowed its excess population to die by the millions in famine-ridden fields was that it would not be ready soon to try to dominate the rest of the world. There were also militants who were ready to march. And the police there to prevent them, busy now in communication with other detachments of police, by way of radios whose aerials were attached to their helmets, thereby giving them the look of giant insects.

6   A confused hour began. Lincoln Park was irregular in shape with curving foot walks; but Grant Park was indeed not so much a park as a set of belts of greenery cut into files by major parallel avenues between Michigan Avenue and Lake Michigan half a mile away. Since there were also cross streets cutting the belts of green perpendicularly, a variety of bridges and pedestrian overpasses gave egress to the city. The park was in this sense an alternation of lawn with superhighways. So the police were able to pen the crowd. But not completely. There were too many bridges, too many choices, in effect, for the police to anticipate. To this confusion was added the fact that every confrontation of demonstrators with police, now buttressed by the National Guard, attracted hundreds of newsmen, and hence began a set of attempted negotiations between spokesmen for the demonstrators and troops, the

demonstrators finally tried to force a bridge and get back to the city. Repelled by tear gas, they went to other bridges, still other bridges, finally found a bridge lightly guarded, broke through a passage and were loose in the city at six-thirty in the evening. They milled about in the Loop for a few minutes, only to encounter the mules and three wagons of the Poor People's Campaign. City officials, afraid of provoking the Negroes on the South Side, had given a permit to the Reverend Abernathy, and he was going to march the mules and wagons down Michigan Avenue and over to the convention. An impromptu march of the demonstrators formed behind the wagons immediately on encountering them and ranks of marchers, sixty, eighty, a hundred in line across the width of Michigan Avenue began to move forward in the gray early twilight of 7 P.M.; Michigan Avenue was now suddenly jammed with people in the march, perhaps so many as four or five thousand people, including onlookers on the sidewalk who jumped in. The streets of the Loop were also reeking with tear gas—the wind had blown some of the gas west over Michigan Avenue from the drops on the bridges, some gas still was penetrated into the clothing of the marchers. In broken ranks, half a march, half a happy mob, eyes red from gas, faces excited by the tension of the afternoon, and the excitement of the escape from Grant Park, now pushing down Michigan Avenue toward the Hilton Hotel with dreams of a march on to the Amphitheatre four miles beyond, and in the full pleasure of being led by the wagons of the Poor People's March, the demonstrators shouted to everyone on the sidewalk, "Join us, join us, join us," and the sidewalk kept disgorging more people ready to march.

7   But at Balbo Avenue, just before Michigan Avenue reached the Hilton, the marchers were halted by the police. It was a long halt. Perhaps thirty minutes. Time for people who had been walking on the sidewalk to join the march, proceed for a few steps, halt with the others, wait, get bored, and leave. It was time for someone in command of the hundreds of police in the neighborhood to communicate with his headquarters, explain the problem, time for the dilemma to be relayed, alternatives examined, and orders conceivably sent back to attack and disperse the crowd. If so, a trap was first set. The mules were allowed to cross Balbo Avenue, then were separated by a line of police from the marchers, who now, several thousand compressed in this one place, filled the intersection of Michigan Avenue and Balbo.

There, dammed by police on three sides, and cut off from the wagons of the Poor People's March, there, right beneath the windows of the Hilton which looked down on Grant Park and Michigan Avenue, the stationary march was abruptly attacked. The police attacked with tear gas, with mace, and with clubs, they attacked like a chain saw cutting into wood, the teeth of the saw the edge of their clubs, they attacked like a scythe through grass, lines of twenty and thirty policemen striking out in an arc, their clubs beating, demonstrators fleeing. Seen from overhead, from the nineteenth floor, it was like a wind blowing dust, or the edge of waves riding foam on the shore.

8   The police cut through the crowd one way, then cut through them another. They chased people into the park, ran them down, beat them up; they cut through the intersection at Michigan and Balbo like a razor cutting a channel through a head of hair, and then drove columns of new police into the channel who in turn pushed out, clubs flailing, on each side, to cut new channels, and new ones again. As demonstrators ran, they reformed in new groups only to be chased by the police again. The action went on for ten minutes, fifteen minutes, with the absolute ferocity of a tropical storm, and watching it from a window on the nineteenth floor, there was something of the detachment of studying a storm at evening through a glass, the light was a lovely gray-blue, the police had uniforms of sky-blue, even the ferocity had an abstract elemental play of forces of nature at battle with other forces, as if sheets of tropical rain were driving across the street in patterns, in curving patterns which curved upon each other again. Police cars rolled up, prisoners were beaten, shoved into wagons, driven away. The rain of police, maddened by the uncoiling of their own storm, pushed against their own barricades of tourists pressed on the street against the Hilton Hotel, then pressed them so hard—but here is a quotation from J. Anthony Lukas in *The New York Times:*

> Even elderly bystanders were caught in the police onslaught. At one point, the police turned on several dozen persons standing quietly behind police barriers in front of the Conrad Hilton Hotel watching the demonstrators across the street.
>
> For no reason that could be immediately determined, the blue-helmeted policemen charged the barriers, crushing the spectators against the windows of the Haymarket Inn, a restaurant in the hotel. Finally the window gave way, sending screaming middle-

aged women and children backward through the broken shards of glass.

The police then ran into the restaurant and beat some of the victims who had fallen through the windows and arrested them.

9   Now another quote from Steve Lerner in *The Village Voice:*

When the charge came, there was a stampede toward the sidelines. People piled into each other, humped over each other's bodies like coupling dogs. To fall down in the crush was just as terrifying as facing the police. Suddenly I realized my feet weren't touching the ground as the crowd pushed up onto the sidewalk. I was grabbing at the army jacket of the boy in front of me; the girl behind me had a stranglehold on my neck and was screaming incoherently in my ear.

10   Now, a longer quotation from Jack Newfield in *The Village Voice.* (The accounts in *The Voice* of September 5 were superior to any others encountered that week.)

At the southwest entrance to the Hilton, a skinny, long-haired kid of about seventeen skidded down on the sidewalk, and four overweight cops leaped on him, chopping strokes on his head. His hair flew from the force of the blows. A dozen small rivulets of blood began to cascade down the kid's temple and onto the sidewalk. He was not crying or screaming, but crawling in a stupor toward the gutter. When he saw a photographer take a picture, he made a V sign with his fingers.

A doctor in a white uniform and Red Cross arm band began to run toward the kid, but two other cops caught him from behind and knocked him down. One of them jammed his knee into the doctor's throat and began clubbing his rib cage. The doctor squirmed away, but the cops followed him, swinging hard, sometimes missing.

A few feet away a phalanx of police charged into a group of women, reporters, and young McCarthy activists standing idly against the window of the Hilton Hotel's Haymarket Inn. The terrified people began to go down under the unexpected police charge when the plate glass window shattered, and the people tumbled backward through the glass. The police then climbed through the broken window and began to beat people, some of whom had been drinking quietly in the hotel bar.

At the side entrance of the Hilton Hotel four cops were chasing one frightened kid of about seventeen. Suddenly, Fred Dutton, a former aide to Robert Kennedy, moved out from under the marquee and interposed his body between the kid and the police.

"He's my guest in this hotel," Dutton told the cops.

The police started to club the kid.

Dutton screamed for the first cop's name and badge number. The cop grabbed Dutton and began to arrest him, until a Washington *Post* reporter identified Dutton as a former RFK aide.

Demonstrators, reporters, McCarthy workers, doctors, all began to stagger into the Hilton lobby, blood streaming from face and head wounds. The lobby smelled from tear gas, and stink bombs dropped by the Yippies. A few people began to direct the wounded to a makeshift hospital on the fifteenth floor, the McCarthy staff headquarters.

Fred Dutton was screaming at the police, and at the journalists to report all the "sadism and brutality." Richard Goodwin, the ashen nub of a cigar sticking out of his fatigued face, mumbled, "This is just the beginning. There'll be four years of this."

The defiant kids began a slow, orderly retreat back up Michigan Avenue. They did not run. They did not panic. They did not fight back. As they fell back they helped pick up fallen comrades who were beaten or gassed. Suddenly, a plainclothesman dressed as a soldier moved out of the shadows and knocked one kid down with an overhand punch. The kid squatted on the pavement of Michigan Avenue, trying to cover his face, while the Chicago plainclothesman punched him with savage accuracy. Thud, thud, thud. Blotches of blood spread over the kid's face. Two photographers moved in. Several police formed a closed circle around the beating to prevent pictures. One of the policemen then squirted Chemical Mace at the photographers, who dispersed. The plainclothesman melted into the line of police.

11   Let us escape to the street. The reporter, watching in safety from the nineteenth floor, could understand now how Mussolini's son-in-law had once been able to find the bombs he dropped from his airplane beautiful as they burst, yes, children, and youths, and middle-aged men and women were being pounded and clubbed and gassed and beaten, hunted and driven, sent scattering in all directions by teams of policemen who had exploded out of their restraints like the bursting of a boil, and nonetheless he felt a sense of calm and beauty, void even of the desire to be down there, as if in years to come there would be beatings enough, some chosen, some from nowhere, but it was as if the war had finally begun, and this was therefore a great and solemn

moment, as if indeed even the gods of history had come together
from each side to choose the very front of the Hilton Hotel before
the television cameras of the world and the eyes of the campaign
workers and the delegates' wives, yes, there before the eyes of half
the principals at the convention was this drama played, as if the
military spine of a great liberal party had finally separated itself
from the skin, as if, no metaphor large enough to suffice, the
Democratic Party had here broken in two before the eyes of a
nation like Melville's whale charging right out of the sea.

12   A great stillness rose up from the street through all the small
noise of clubbing and cries, small sirens, sigh of loaded arrest vans
as off they pulled, shouts of police as they wheeled in larger circles, the intersection clearing further, then further, a stillness rose
through the steel and stone of the hotel, congregating in the
shocked centers of every room where delegates and wives and
Press and campaign workers innocent until now of the intimate
working of social force, looked down now into the murderous
paradigm of Vietnam there beneath them at this huge intersection of this great city. Look—a boy was running through the park,
and a cop was chasing. There he caught him on the back of the
neck with his club! There! The cop is returning to his own! And
the boy stumbling to his feet is helped off the ground by a girl
who has come running up.

13   Yes, it could only have happened in a meeting of the Gods,
that history for once should take place not on some back street,
or some inaccessible grand room, not in some laboratory indistinguishable from others, or in the sly undiscoverable hypocrisies of
a committee of experts, but rather on the center of the stage, as if
each side had said, "Here we will have our battle. Here we will
win."

14   The demonstrators were afterward delighted to have been
manhandled before the public eye, delighted to have pushed and
prodded, antagonized and provoked the cops over these days with
rocks and bottles and cries of "Pig" to the point where police had
charged in a blind rage and made a stage at the one place in the
city (besides the Amphitheatre) where audience, actors, and cameras could all convene, yes, the rebels thought they had had a
great victory, and perhaps they did; but the reporter wondered,
even as he saw it, if the police in that half hour of waiting had not
had time to receive instructions from the power of the city, perhaps the power of the land, and the power had decided, "No, do

not let them march another ten blocks and there disperse them on some quiet street, no, let it happen before all the land, let everybody see that their dissent will soon be equal to their own blood; let them realize that the power is implacable, and will beat and crush and imprison and yet kill before it will ever relinquish the power. So let them see before their own eyes what it will cost to continue to mock us, defy us, and resist. There are more millions behind us than behind them, more millions who wish to weed out, poison, gas, and obliterate every flower whose power they do not comprehend than heroes for their side who will view our brute determination and still be ready to resist. There are more cowards alive than the brave. Otherwise we would not be where we are," said the Prince of Greed.

15   Who knew. One could thank the city of Chicago where drama was still a property of the open stage. It was quiet now, there was nothing to stare down on but the mules, and the police guarding them. The mules had not moved through the entire fray. Isolated from the battle, they had stood there in harness waiting to be told to go on. Only once in a while did they turn their heads. Their role as actors in the Poor People's March was to wait and to serve. Finally they moved on. The night had come. It was dark. The intersection was now empty. Shoes, ladies' handbags, and pieces of clothing lay on the street outside the hotel.

REFLECTIONS

Some critics fault Norman Mailer for his long, complex sentences and his "associative rambling." Mailer, however, has made a conscious artistic choice to do just that. What effect does this style have when he is presenting events that actually happened? Find examples of long sentences and explain their effect and how Mailer keeps them going without losing the reader along the way. From what point of view is the scene in Chicago in 1968 presented? Why does Mailer include quotations from news accounts? Do you think these reports are a representative cross section of the reporting that went on? How might you verify this?

Nancy Mairs

(1943–   )

Nancy Mairs was born in California and raised in New England. She was educated at the University of Arizona, from which she earned a Ph.D. She has worked as a technical editor at the Smithsonian Astrophysical Observatory, the MIT Press, and the Harvard Law School. Her books include an award-winning volume of poems, *In All the Rooms of the Yellow House*, a memoir, *In the Churnel House*, and a collection of essays, *Plaintext*, from which "On Being a Cripple" was taken.

On Being a Cripple

> *To escape is nothing. Not to escape is nothing.*
> —LOUISE BOGAN

1   The other day I was thinking of writing an essay on being a cripple. I was thinking hard in one of the stalls of the women's room in my office building, as I was shoving my shirt into my jeans and tugging up my zipper. Preoccupied, I flushed, picked up my book bag, took my cane down from the hook, and unlatched the door. So many movements unbalanced me, and as I pulled the door open I fell over backward, landing fully clothed on the toilet seat with my legs splayed in front of me: the old beetle-on-its-back routine. Saturday afternoon, the building deserted, I was free to laugh aloud as I wriggled back to my feet, my voice bouncing off the yellowish tiles from all directions. Had anyone

been there with me, I'd have been still and faint and hot with chagrin. I decided that it was high time to write the essay.

2   First, the matter of semantics. I am a cripple. I choose this
word to name me. I choose from among several possibilities, the
most common of which are "handicapped" and "disabled." I
made the choice a number of years ago, without thinking,
unaware of my motives for doing so. Even now, I'm not sure what
those motives are, but I recognize that they are complex and not
entirely flattering. People—crippled or not—wince at the word
"cripple," as they do not at "handicapped" or "disabled." Perhaps
I want them to wince. I want them to see me as a tough customer,
one to whom the fates/gods/viruses have not been kind, but who
can face the brutal truth of her existence squarely. As a cripple, I
swagger.

3   But, to be fair to myself, a certain amount of honesty underlies my choice. "Cripple" seems to me a clean word, straightforward and precise. It has an honorable history, having made its
first appearance in the Lindisfarne Gospel in the tenth century.
As a lover of words, I like the accuracy with which it describes my
condition: I have lost the full use of my limbs. "Disabled," by contrast, suggests any incapacity, physical or mental. And I certainly
don't like "handicapped," which implies that I have deliberately
been put at a disadvantage, by whom I can't imagine (my God is
not a Handicapper General), in order to equalize chances in the
great race of life. These words seem to me to be moving away
from my condition, to be widening the gap between word and
reality. Most remote is the recently coined euphemism "differently abled," which partakes of the same semantic hopefulness that
transformed countries from "undeveloped" to "underdeveloped,"
then to "less developed," and finally to "developing" nations.
People have continued to starve in those countries during the
shift. Some realities do not obey the dictates of language.

4   Mine is one of them. Whatever you call me, I remain crippled. But I don't care what you call me, so long as it isn't "differently abled," which strikes me as pure verbal garbage designed, by
its ability to describe anyone, to describe no one. I subscribe to
George Orwell's thesis that "the slovenliness of our language
makes it easier for us to have foolish thoughts." And I refuse to
participate in the degeneration of the language to the extent that
I deny that I have lost anything in the course of this calamitous
disease; I refuse to pretend that the only differences between you
and me are the various ordinary ones that distinguish any one

person from another. But call me "disabled" or "handicapped" if you like. I have long since grown accustomed to them; and if they are vague, at least they hint at the truth. Moreover, I use them myself. Society is no readier to accept crippledness than to accept death, war, sex, sweat, or wrinkles. I would never refer to another person as a cripple. It is the word I use to name only myself.

5   I haven't always been crippled, a fact for which I am soundly grateful. To be whole of limb is, I know from experience, infinitely more pleasant and useful than to be crippled; and if that knowledge leaves me open to bitterness at my loss, the physical soundness I once enjoyed (though I did not enjoy it half enough) is well worth the occasional stab of regret. Though never any good at sports, I was a normally active child and young adult. I climbed trees, played hopscotch, jumped rope, skated, swam, rode my bicycle, sailed. I despised team sports, spending some of the wretchedest afternoons of my life, sweaty and humiliated, behind a field-hockey stick and under a basketball hoop. I tramped alone for miles along the bridle paths that webbed the woods behind the house I grew up in. I swayed through countless dim hours in the arms of one man or another under the scattered shot of light from mirrored balls, and gyrated through countless more as Tab Hunter and Johnny Mathis gave way to the Rolling Stones, Creedence Clearwater Revival, Cream. I walked down the aisle. I pushed baby carriages, changed tires in the rain, marched for peace.

6   When I was twenty-eight I started to trip and drop things. What at first seemed my natural clumsiness soon became too pronounced to shrug off. I consulted a neurologist, who told me that I had a brain tumor. A battery of tests, increasingly disagreeable, revealed no tumor. About a year and a half later I developed a blurred spot in one eye. I had, at last, the episodes "disseminated in space and time" requisite for a diagnosis: multiple sclerosis. I have never been sorry for the doctor's initial misdiagnosis, however. For almost a week, until the negative results of the tests were in, I thought that I was going to die right away. Every day for the past nearly ten years, then, has been a kind of gift. I accept all gifts.

7   Multiple sclerosis is a chronic degenerative disease of the central nervous system, in which the myelin that sheathes the nerves is somehow eaten away and scar tissue forms in its place, interrupting the nerves' signals. During its course, which is unpredictable and uncontrollable, one may lose vision, hearing, speech,

the ability to walk, control of bladder and/or bowels, strength in any or all extremities, sensitivity to touch, vibration, and/or pain, potency, coordination of movements—the list of possibilities is lengthy and, yes, horrifying. One may also lose one's sense of humor. That's the easiest to lose and the hardest to survive without.

8   In the past ten years, I have sustained some of these losses. Characteristic of MS are sudden attacks, called exacerbations, followed by remissions, and these I have not had. Instead, my disease has been slowly progressive. My left leg is now so weak that I walk with the aid of a brace and a cane; and for distances I use an Amigo, a variation on the electric wheelchair that looks rather like an electrified kiddie car. I no longer have much use of my left hand. Now my right side is weakening as well. I still have the blurred spot in my right eye. Overall, though, I've been lucky so far. My world has, of necessity, been circumscribed by my losses, but the terrain left me has been ample enough for me to continue many of the activities that absorb me: writing, teaching, raising children and cats and plants and snakes, reading, speaking publicly about MS and depression, even playing bridge with people patient and honorable enough to let me scatter cards every which way without sneaking a peek.

9   Lest I begin to sound like Pollyanna, however, let me say that I don't like having MS. I hate it. My life holds realities—harsh ones, some of them—that no right-minded human being ought to accept without grumbling. One of them is fatigue. I know of no one with MS who does not complain of bone-weariness; in a disease that presents an astonishing variety of symptoms, fatigue seems to be a common factor. I wake up in the morning feeling the way most people do at the end of a bad day, and I take it from there. As a result, I spend a lot of time *in extremis* and, impatient with limitation, I tend to ignore my fatigue until my body breaks down in some way and forces rest. Then I miss picnics, dinner parties, poetry readings, the brief visits of old friends from out of town. The offspring of a puritanical tradition of exceptional venerability, I cannot view these lapses without shame. My life often seems a series of small failures to do as I ought.

10   I lead, on the whole, an ordinary life, probably rather like the one I would have led had I not had MS. I am lucky that my predilections were already solitary, sedentary, and bookish— unlike the world-famous French cellist I have read about, or the young woman I talked with one long afternoon who wanted only

to be a jockey. I had just begun graduate school when I found out something was wrong with me, and I have remained, interminably, a graduate student. Perhaps I would not have if I'd thought I had the stamina to return to a full-time job as a technical editor; but I've enjoyed my studies.

11   In addition to studying, I teach writing courses. I also teach medical students how to give neurological examinations. I pick up freelance editing jobs here and there. I have raised a foster son and sent him into the world, where he has made me two grandbabies, and I am still escorting my daughter and son through adolescence. I go to Mass every Saturday. I am a superb, if messy, cook. I am also an enthusiastic laundress, capable of sorting a hamper full of clothes into five subtly differentiated piles, but a terrible housekeeper. I can do italic writing and, in an emergency, bathe an oil-soaked cat. I play a fiendish game of Scrabble. When I have the time and the money, I like to sit on my front steps with my husband, drinking Amaretto and smoking a cigar, as we imagine our counterparts in Leningrad and make sure that the sun gets down once more behind the sharp childish scrawl of the Tucson Mountains.

12   This lively plenty has its bleak complement, of course, in all the things I can no longer do. I will never run again, except in dreams, and one day I may have to write that I will never walk again. I like to go camping, but I can't follow George and the children along the trails that wander out of a campsite through the desert or into the mountains. In fact, even on the level I've learned never to check the weather or try to hold a coherent conversation: I need all my attention for my wayward feet. Of late, I have begun to catch myself wondering how people can propel themselves without canes. With only one usable hand, I have to select my clothing with care not so much for style as for ease of ingress and egress, and even so, dressing can be laborious. I can no longer do fine stitchery, pick up babies, play the piano, braid my hair. I am immobilized by acute attacks of depression, which may or may not be physiologically related to MS but are certainly its logical concomitant.

13   These two elements, the plenty and the privation, are never pure, nor are the delight and wretchedness that accompany them. Almost every pickle that I get into as a result of my weakness and clumsiness—and I get into plenty—is funny as well as maddening and sometimes painful. I recall one May afternoon when a friend

and I were going out for a drink after finishing up at school. As we were climbing into opposite sides of my car, chatting, I tripped and fell, flat and hard, onto the asphalt parking lot, my abrupt departure interrupting him in mid-sentence. "Where'd you go?" he called as he came around the back of the car to find me hauling myself up by the door frame. "Are you all right?" Yes, I told him, I was fine, just a bit rattly, and we drove off to find a shady patio and some beer. When I got home an hour or so later, my daughter greeted me with "What have you done to yourself?" I looked down. One elbow of my white turtleneck with the green froggies, one knee of my white trousers, one white kneesock were blood-soaked. We peeled off the clothes and inspected the damage, which was nasty enough but not alarming. That part wasn't funny: The abrasions took a long time to heal, and one got a little infected. Even so, when I think of my friend talking earnestly, suddenly, to the hot thin air while I dropped from his view as though through a trap door, I find the image as silly as something from a Marx Brothers movie.

14   I may find it easier than other cripples to amuse myself because I live propped by the acceptance and the assistance and, sometimes, the amusement of those around me. Grocery clerks tear my checks out of my checkbook for me, and sales clerks find chairs to put into dressing rooms when I want to try on clothes. The people I work with make sure I teach at times when I am least likely to be fatigued, in places I can get to, with the materials I need. My students, with one anonymous exception (in an end-of-the-semester evaluation), have been unperturbed by my disability. Some even like it. One was immensely cheered by the information that I paint my own fingernails; she decided, she told me, that if I could go to such trouble over fine details, she could keep on writing essays. I suppose I became some sort of bright-fingered muse. She wrote good essays, too.

15   The most important struts in the framework of my existence, of course, are my husband and children. Dismayingly few marriages survive the MS test, and why should they? Most twenty-two- and nineteen-year-olds, like George and me, can vow in clear conscience, after a childhood of chickenpox and summer colds, to keep one another in sickness and in health so long as they both shall live. Not many are equipped for catastrophe: the dismay, the depression, the extra work, the boredom that a degenerative disease can insinuate into a relationship. And our society, with its

emphasis on fun and its association of fun with physical performance, offers little encouragement for a whole spouse to stay with a crippled partner. Children experience similar stresses when faced with a crippled parent, and they are more helpless, since parents and children can't usually get divorced. They hate, of course, to be different from their peers, and the child whose mother is tacking down the aisle of a school auditorium packed with proud parents like a Cape Cod dinghy in a stiff breeze jolly well stands out in a crowd. Deprived of legal divorce, the child can at least deny the mother's disability, even her existence, forgetting to tell her about recitals and PTA meetings, refusing to accompany her to stores or church or the movies, never inviting friends to the house. Many do.

16   But I've been limping along for ten years now, and so far George and the children are still at my left elbow, holding tight. Anne and Matthew vacuum floors and dust furniture and haul trash and rake up dog droppings and button my cuffs and bake lasagne and Toll House cookies with just enough grumbling so I know that they don't have brain fever. And far from hiding me, they're forever dragging me by racks of fancy clothes or through teeming school corridors, or welcoming gaggles of friends while I'm wandering through the house in Anne's filmy pink babydoll pajamas. George generally calls before he brings someone home, but he does just as many dumb thankless chores as the children. And they all yell at me, laugh at some of my jokes, write me funny letters when we're apart—in short, treat me as an ordinary human being for whom they have some use. I think they like me. Unless they're faking. . . .

17   Faking. There's the rub. Tugging at the fringes of my consciousness always is the terror that people are kind to me only because I'm a cripple. My mother almost shattered me once, with that instinct mothers have—blind, I think, in this case, but unerring nonetheless—for striking blows along the fault-lines of their children's hearts, by telling me, in an attack on my selfishness, "We all have to make allowances for you, of course, because of the way you are." From the distance of a couple of years, I have to admit that I haven't any idea just what she meant, and I'm not sure that she knew either. She was awfully angry. But at the time, as the words thudded home, I felt my worst fear, suddenly realized. I could bear being called selfish: I am. But I couldn't bear the corroboration that those around me were doing in fact what

I'd always suspected them of doing, professing fondness while silently putting up with me because of the way I am. A cripple. I've been a little cracked ever since.

18   Along with this fear that people are secretly accepting shoddy goods comes a relentless pressure to please—to prove myself worth the burdens I impose, I guess, or to build a substantial account of goodwill against which I may write drafts in times of need. Part of the pressure arises from social expectations. In our society, anyone who deviates from the norm had better find some way to compensate. Like fat people, who are expected to be jolly, cripples must bear their lot meekly and cheerfully. A grumpy cripple isn't playing by the rules. And much of the pressure is self-generated. Early on I vowed that, if I had to have MS, by God I was going to do it well. This is a class act, ladies and gentlemen. No tears, no recriminations, no faint-heartedness.

19   One way and another, then, I wind up feeling like Tiny Tim, peering over the edge of the table at the Christmas goose, waving my crutch, piping down God's blessing on us all. Only sometimes I don't want to play Tiny Tim. I'd rather be Caliban, a most scurvy monster. Fortunately, at home no one much cares whether I'm a good cripple or a bad cripple as long as I make vichyssoise with fair regularity. One evening several years ago, Anne was reading at the dining-room table while I cooked dinner. As I opened a can of tomatoes, the can slipped in my left hand and juice spattered me and the counter with bloody spots. Fatigued and infuriated, I bellowed, "I'm so sick of being crippled!" Anne glanced at me over the top of her book. "There now," she said, "do you feel better?" "Yes," I said, "yes, I do." She went back to her reading. I felt better. That's about all the attention my scurviness ever gets.

20   Because I hate being crippled, I sometimes hate myself for being a cripple. Over the years I have come to expect—even accept—attacks of violent self-loathing. Luckily, in general our society no longer connects deformity and disease directly with evil (though a charismatic once told me that I have MS because a devil is in me) and so I'm allowed to move largely at will, even among small children. But I'm not sure that this revision of attitude has been particularly helpful. Physical imperfection, even freed of moral disapprobation, still defies and violates the ideal, especially for women, whose confinement in their bodies as objects of desire is far from over. Each age, of course, has its ideal, and I doubt that ours is any better or worse than any other. Today's ideal woman, who lives on the glossy pages of dozens of

magazines, seems to be between the ages of eighteen and twenty-five; her hair has body, her teeth flash white, her breath smells minty, her underarms are dry; she has a career but is still a fabulous cook, especially of meals that take less than twenty minutes to prepare; she does not ordinarily appear to have a husband or children; she is trim and deeply tanned; she jogs, swims, plays tennis, rides a bicycle, sails, but does not bowl; she travels widely, even to out-of-the-way places like Finland and Samoa, always in the company of the ideal man, who possesses a nearly identical set of characteristics. There are a few exceptions. Though usually white and often blonde, she may be black, Hispanic, Asian, or Native American, so long as she is unusually sleek. She may be old, provided she is selling a laxative or is Lauren Bacall. If she is selling a detergent, she may be married and have a flock of strikingly messy children. But she is never a cripple.

21   Like many women I know, I have always had an uneasy relationship with my body. I was not a popular child, largely, I think now, because I was peculiar: intelligent, intense, moody, shy, given to unexpected actions and inexplicable notions and emotions. But as I entered adolescence, I believed myself unpopular because I was homely: my breasts too flat, my mouth too wide, my hips too narrow, my clothing never quite right in fit or style. I was not, in fact, particularly ugly, old photographs inform me, though I was well off the ideal; but I carried this sense of self-alienation with me into adulthood, where it regenerated in response to the depredations of MS. Even with my brace I walk with a limp so pronounced that, seeing myself on the videotape of a television program on the disabled, I couldn't believe that anything but an inchworm could make progress humping along like that. My shoulders droop and my pelvis thrusts forward as I try to balance myself upright, throwing my frame into a bony S. As a result of contractures, one shoulder is higher than the other and I carry one arm bent in front of me, the fingers curled into a claw. My left arm and leg have wasted into pipe-stems, and I try always to keep them covered. When I think about how my body must look to others, especially to men, to whom I have been trained to display myself, I feel ludicrous, even loathsome.

22   At my age, however, I don't spend much time thinking about my appearance. The burning egocentricity of adolescence, which assures one that all the world is looking all the time, has passed, thank God, and I'm generally too caught up in what I'm doing to step back, as I used to, and watch myself as though upon

a stage. I'm also too old to believe in the accuracy of self-image. I know that I'm not a hideous crone, that in fact, when I'm rested, well dressed, and well made up, I look fine. The self-loathing I feel is neither physically nor intellectually substantial. What I hate is not me but a disease.

23   I am not a disease.

24   And a disease is not—at least not singlehandedly—going to determine who I am, though at first it seemed to be going to. Adjusting to a chronic incurable illness, I have moved through a process similar to that outlined by Elizabeth Kübler-Ross in *On Death and Dying.* The major difference—and it is far more significant than most people recognize—is that I can't be sure of the outcome, as the terminally ill cancer patient can. Research studies indicate that, with proper medical care, I may achieve a "normal" life span. And in our society, with its vision of death as the ultimate evil, worse even than decrepitude, the response to such news is, "Oh well, at least you're not going to *die.*" Are there worse things than dying? I think that there may be.

25   I think of two women I know, both with MS, both enough older than I to have served me as models. One took to her bed several years ago and has been there ever since. Although she can sit in a high-backed wheelchair, because she is incontinent she refuses to go out at all, even though incontinence pants, which are readily available at any pharmacy, could protect her from embarrassment. Instead, she stays at home and insists that her husband, a small quiet man, a retired civil servant, stay there with her except for a quick weekly foray to the supermarket. The other woman, whose illness was diagnosed when she was eighteen, a nursing student engaged to a young doctor, finished her training, married her doctor, accompanied him to Germany when he was in the service, bore three sons and a daughter, now grown and gone. When she can, she travels with her husband; she plays bridge, embroiders, swims regularly; she works, like me, as a symptomatic-patient instructor of medical students in neurology. Guess which woman I hope to be.

26   At the beginning, I thought about having MS almost incessantly. And because of the unpredictable course of the disease, my thoughts were always terrified. Each night I'd get into bed wondering whether I'd get out again the next morning, whether I'd be able to see, to speak, to hold a pen between my fingers. Knowing that the day might come when I'd be physically incapable of killing myself, I thought perhaps I ought to do so right

away, while I still had the strength. Gradually I came to understand that the Nancy who might one day lie inert under a bedsheet, arms and legs paralyzed, unable to feed or bathe herself, unable to reach out for a gun, a bottle of pills, was not the Nancy I was at present, and that I could not presume to make decisions for that future Nancy, who might well not want in the least to die. Now the only provision I've made for the future Nancy is that when the time comes—and it is likely to come in the form of pneumonia, friend to the weak and the old—I am not to be treated with machines and medications. If she is unable to communicate by then, I hope she will be satisfied with these terms.

27   Thinking all the time about having MS grew tiresome and intrusive, especially in the large and tragic mode in which I was accustomed to considering my plight. Months and even years went by without catastrophe (at least without one related to MS), and really I was awfully busy, what with George and children and snakes and students and poems, and I hadn't the time, let alone the inclination, to devote myself to being a disease. Too, the richer my life became, the funnier it seemed, as though there were some connection between largesse and laughter, and so my tragic stance began to waver until, even with the aid of a brace and a cane, I couldn't hold it for very long at a time.

28   After several years I was satisfied with my adjustment. I had suffered my grief and fury and terror, I thought, but now I was at ease with my lot. Then one summer day I set out with George and the children across the desert for a vacation in California. Part way to Yuma I became aware that my right leg felt funny. "I think I've had an exacerbation," I told George. "What shall we do?" he asked. "I think we'd better get the hell to California," I said, "because I don't know whether I'll ever make it again." So we went on to San Diego and then to Orange, up the Pacific Coast Highway to Santa Cruz, across to Yosemite, down to Sequoia and Joshua Tree, and so back over the desert to home. It was a fine two-week trip, filled with friends and fair weather, and I wouldn't have missed it for the world, though I did in fact make it back to California two years later. Nor would there have been any point in missing it, since in MS, once the symptoms have appeared, the neurological damage has been done, and there's no way to predict or prevent that damage.

29   The incident spoiled my self-satisfaction, however. It renewed my grief and fury and terror, and I learned that one never finishes adjusting to MS. I don't know now why I thought one

would. One does not, after all, finish adjusting to life, and MS is simply a fact of my life—not my favorite fact, of course—but as ordinary as my nose and my tropical fish and my yellow Mazda station wagon. It may at any time get worse, but no amount of worry or anticipation can prepare me for a new loss. My life is a lesson in losses. I learn one at a time.

30   And I had best be patient in the learning, since I'll have to do it like it or not. As any rock fan knows, you can't always get what you want. Particularly when you have MS. You can't for example, get cured. In recent years researchers and the organizations that fund research have started to pay MS some attention even though it isn't fatal; perhaps they have begun to see that life is something other than a quantitative phenomenon, that one may be very much alive for a very long time in a life that isn't worth living. The researchers have made some progress toward understanding the mechanism of the disease: It may well be an autoimmune reaction triggered by a slow-acting virus. But they are nowhere near its prevention, control, or cure. And most of us want to be cured. Some, unable to accept incurability, grasp at one treatment after another, no matter how bizarre: megavitamin therapy, gluten-free diet, injections of cobra venom, hypothermal suits, lymphocytopharesis, hyperbaric chambers. Many treatments are probably harmless enough, but none are curative.

31   The absence of a cure often makes MS patients bitter toward their doctors. Doctors are, after all, the priests of modern society, the new shamans, whose business is to heal, and many an MS patient roves from one to another, searching for the "good" doctor who will make him well. Doctors too think of themselves as healers, and for this reason many have trouble dealing with MS patients, whose disease in its intransigence defeats their aims and mocks their skills. Too few doctors, it is true, treat their patients as whole human beings, but the reverse is also true. I have always tried to be gentle with my doctors, who often have more at stake in terms of ego than I do. I may be frustrated, maddened, depressed by the incurability of my disease, but I am not diminished by it, and they are. When I push myself up from my seat in the waiting room and stumble toward them, I incarnate the limitation of their powers. The least I can do is refuse to press on their tenderest spots.

32   This gentleness is part of the reason that I'm not sorry to be a cripple. I didn't have it before. Perhaps I'd have developed it

anyway—how could I know such a thing?—and I wish I had more of it, but I'm glad of what I have. It has opened and enriched my life enormously, this sense that my frailty and need must be mirrored in others, that in searching for and shaping a stable core in a life wrenched by change and loss, change and loss, I must recognize the same process, under individual conditions, in the lives around me. I do not deprecate such knowledge, however I've come by it.

33   All the same, if a cure were found, would I take it? In a minute. I may be a cripple, but I'm only occasionally a loony and never a saint. Anyway, in my brand of theology God doesn't give bonus points for a limp. I'd take a cure; I just don't need one. A friend who also has MS startled me once by asking, "Do you ever say to yourself, 'Why me, Lord?'" "No, Michael, I don't," I told him, "because whenever I try, the only response I can think of is 'Why not?'" If I could make a cosmic deal, who would I put in my place? What in my life would I give up in exchange for sound limbs and a thrilling rush of energy? No one. Nothing. I might as well do the job myself. Now that I'm getting the hang of it.

REFLECTIONS

A good part of Mairs's essay is concerned with the words we use to name those who are differently abled—or as Mairs describes them, "handicapped" or "crippled." Consider the different connotations of the words Mairs introduces into this part of her discussion. And consider also why she prefers the word "cripple" to define herself. Also investigate the way Mairs's multiple sclerosis has affected her life as a woman and a writer.

Maile Meloy

(1972–   )

Maile Meloy was born and raised in Montana. She currently lives in Helena, Montana, and attends Harvard University where she is concentrating in English. She has a modest résumé in theatre and film, teaches swimming, skis, and hopes she won't have to make any future plans just yet.

The Voice of the Looking-Glass

A woman must continually watch herself. She is almost continually accompanied by her own image of herself. Men look at women. Women watch themselves being looked at.
John Berger
Ways of Seeing

The girl was ugly. I was bored during the whole journey.
Casanova
History of My Life

1   From the moment I became conscious of cause and effect I have been conscious of the importance of my own appearance. Little girls (and little boys) learn early that the way women are treated is determined by the way they appear. John Berger, in *Ways of Seeing*, has gotten it right. It is a woman's ever-present task to monitor her image, not to survey a situation to determine the appropriate action, as a man does, but to survey herself and define by her presentation the way she wishes others to act toward her.

645

2   I have a photograph of myself at graduation, with my hair down and fuschia and plumeria leis piled around my neck. I am laughing, with my mouth open, head tilted, and eyes cast to the side, at something the photographer has said. The picture is not posed; I am caught in a spontaneous, joyful moment by the gaze of the camera.

3   I have looked at that picture a lot. It is the way I want to be seen in everyday, spontaneous moments, when soft studio lights are not at my rescue and I am vulnerable: I am pleased with the image. When I am asked for the photograph, my instinctive response is, "But it's the only copy I have," which I blurt out before I realize how narcissistic I sound. We are not to let on that we monitor ourselves so closely. We are to be head-tossing and laughing-eyed without being conscious of our beauty.

4   Why do I need pictures of myself? Because I like them. They are interesting to me. I like to see myself in relation to other people, to see myself how other people see me. I study photographs of myself intently, critically—always appraising, always analyzing, carefully assessing what I see there.

5   I take other opportunities to survey and assess. Most women do. I have mastered a swift glance over my right shoulder at mirrors and windows as I walk by, careful not to linger and let voyeurs behind the glass see my interest in my own image. The left profile is less reassuring, and with scarcely a conscious thought I place people to my right. This self-observation is not vanity. It is a play for approval, and a request to be treated well, with respect and admiration. It says, "I don't want to bore you during the entire journey."

6   The result of the demand for women to be beautiful, combined with a woman's need for approval, according to Berger, is that a woman's "own sense of being in herself is supplanted by a sense of being appreciated by another." Laura Riding's epigraph to the first chapter of Sandra M. Gilbert and Susan Gubar's *The Madwoman in the Attic* addresses this replacement of a woman's self-image with a male's-eye view:

> And the lady of the house was seen only as she appeared in each room, according to the nature of the lord of the room. None saw the whole of her, none but herself. For the light which she was was both her mirror and her body. None could tell the whole of her, none but herself.

7   The chapter, entitled "The Queen's Looking Glass," makes some important observations about "images of women," especially as portrayed in the Grimm brothers' fairy tale, "Little Snow White." They note that "female bonding is extraordinarily difficult in patriarchy: women almost inevitably turn against women because the voice of the looking-glass sets them against each other" (38). Thus we are set up as rivals for each other by the male voice of the looking glass, and Gilbert and Gubar see little hope for female solidarity. They share Anne Sexton's view that Snow White must inevitably become the wicked Queen. Having escaped from one display case (the glass coffin), she has traded it for another, the mirror (41–42). The Prince's home itself is a prison, the same one her mother encountered, where she appears "according to the nature of the lord of the room." To escape her new prison she must become the witch. She must become assertive and therefore monstrous and misogynistic to destroy the "angel woman" Galatea in herself (42).

8   That the perfect Snow White should become the evil Queen is horrifying to me, although Gilbert and Gubar endorse the witch's actions and sympathize with her. It rings true, however, and it turns me to look at my relationship with my own mother. She despises the appearance-oriented environment in which women live, and she fears that I have bought into it. She has sometimes lamented that I was not born unattractive; she is afraid I will have everything given to me, that I'll never know what it is to really earn rewards. She too has bought into the system, however, and perhaps it is that which she laments. Five feet two, beautiful and blonde, a southern-Californian ex-Homecoming Queen, she has been handed a lot on the tarnished silver platter of prettiness. And while carefully maintaining that prettiness, she has despised it. She has always wanted to be tall, dark-haired and magnificent so people would take her seriously. My mother, trapped in her surfer-girl image and unable to transform her appearance, instead majored in microbiology, which she hated, in an attempt to earn the respect she craved.

9   She has since abandoned microbiology and her model-loveliness is beginning to abandon her. It makes me nervous. Old pictures of her from college and early marriage are breathtaking, with her tousled hair, her smooth tan skin, her perfect cheekbones, and her brilliant Homecoming Queen smile. (Holly Near,

singing of her own Queen experience, has observed, "That's what Homecoming Queens do, is smile.") These images, however, are disconcerting. They are reminders for me of the death and disappearance of youth and of what is culturally defined as desirable. I wish I could look forward to such changes, to rejoice in the inner richness that replaces outward worth, but I shudder with the vanity of youth and dread the wrinkles and sagging flesh of age. I delight with Snow White that I am still "the fairest of them all."

10   Because of my dread of becoming what my mother is, and what other older women are, I expect intimidation and jealousy. And because I watch other women, measuring myself against them and judging myself accordingly, I experience intimidation and jealousy. The dynamics of this watching myself/watching you watching me phenomenon create what Margaret Atwood has dubbed "that pale-mauve hostility that you often find among women." It is a shared secret, that we watch ourselves so carefully while feigning nonchalance. We appraise other women as a man would, appraise ourselves as a man would, and weigh the results. It is strangely comforting to find the other wanting. I think most women hate this trap, and hate the pale-mauve hostility. But we learn it as we learn to walk and to wear our hair in pigtails the way daddy likes it. It is our way of surviving in the world we are born into: One in which, like it or not, we must continually impress men.

11   We are taught our meticulous self-observation; it is a learned activity. At the onset of puberty, among the other ridiculously sexist boy-catching hints we receive, girls are often instructed to "learn how to take a compliment." We are expected to accept another person's sense of us as they have expressed it, and to consider it a reward. By accepting it we add it to our expectations of ourself—our checklist as we glance into the mirrors of shop windows, listen to ourselves speak, or choose our clothes, opinions, and other accessories.

12   When a girl "takes a compliment," she accepts the reward and accepts, as well, the requirement that earned her the compliment. Both become internalized. She now needs to be able to earn that other person's sense of her from herself. She practices her "disarming smile" in mirrors, concentrates on "poise," and makes sure she's being "a good listener." Not all compliments are "taken," of course, although they may be acknowledged with a

polite "thank you." Some are discarded because they do not fit her image as the watcher in her sees it, and these rejects can be disconcerting as they suggest discrepancy between the internal surveyor and the external one, but true compliments, the ones that congratulate a girl's or woman's mutable, monitored perception of herself, are internalized and added to the checklist.

13   Sometimes the internal surveyor goes out of control. I have been haunted for several days by the image of one of the homeless people in the city. She sits huddled in a doorstep in a beige coat with a scarf tied around her head, and she clutches a large white plastic bag. The first time I saw her I found myself staring, wondering at her face, which was colored a deep pink. As I neared her, I could make out the cakey texture of makeup and I caught the sweet chemical smell of the pink powder that covered her entire face: forehead, wrinkled cheeks, lips, eyes, eyebrows, and ears, and that was smeared across the lapels of her coat and mixed with the pattern of her headwrap. I fixed my eyes back on the sidewalk, which was covered with white face-powder, and braced for the inevitable request for money. It didn't come. She didn't even notice me; her eyes were riveted to a spot in the corner of the doorstep. I glanced back at that spot as I passed, expecting to see a mirror into which she was staring so intently. There was nothing there. Only the concrete wall stared back at her.

14   Later in the day she was gone, and only a white outline of her seated form remained in the scattered face powder on the sidewalk, along with a sandwich in a baggie that someone must have given her, abandoned there with one bite taken. Disconcerted, I sought my own reflection in a shop window, to replace that of the trembling, staring, cariacature of female vanity I had seen that morning. Even as I caught my own eye, I saw the irony in my means of escape. This poor, ill woman, to whom her own made-up self is more important than food, exists at the outer edge of the obsession with appearance that women learn from childhood.

15   I do not want to be John Berger's pathetically trapped woman, to merely "appear," and to be a composite of other people's perceptions of me. I do not want to value appearance over action, but I cannot escape the habit of constantly having one eye on my own image. In mirrors and windows, in photographs, in other people's glances, and in my own mind I am haunted by images of

myself. I am continually critiquing my appearance, my reactions, my gestures, and my speech. I am already caught in the queen's looking glass, already in conspiracy with the made-up old woman in the street.

16   A Stephen Sondheim character sings of his mistress, "Look at her looking, forever in that mirror. What does she see?" He need not ask, for she sees through his eyes. She sees herself as lover, as desirable object, and as rival before she sees herself as a woman. She sees herself in relation to him and in light of his expectations, and she sees her imperfections in that light. She sees Snow White fading and growing old and yet she clings to the façade. It is what she knows.

REFLECTIONS

One of the most striking aspects of this essay is the way Maile Meloy has brought together a wide range of texts and experiences and shaped them into a cohesive and increasingly complex network of ideas about women's obsession with beauty and appearance. Look back through the piece and identify these fragments out of which the writer has formed a unified whole. Consider what each contributes to her idea. Consider also to what extent Meloy's ideas about women's concern with their beauty are reflected, promoted, endorsed, or questioned in popular music, in television and film, in political and social life.

N. Scott Momaday
(1934–   )

N. Scott Momaday was born in Oklahoma and educated at New Mexico University and at Stanford University, where he earned a Ph.D. and now teaches. Momaday won the 1969 Pulitzer Prize for his novel, *House Made of Dawn*. He is also the author of a children's book, *Owl in the Cedar Tree*, two volumes of poetry, and an autobiography, *The Way to Rainy Mountain*, from which the following selection is excerpted.

From *The Way to Rainy Mountain*

1   A single knoll rises out of the plain in Oklahoma, north and west of the Wichita range. For my people, the Kiowas, it is an old landmark, and they gave it the name Rainy Mountain. The hardest weather in the world is there. Winter brings blizzards, hot tornadic winds arise in the spring, and in summer the prairie is an anvil's edge. The grass turns brittle and brown, and it cracks beneath your feet. There are green belts along the rivers and creeks, linear groves of hickory and pecan, willow and witch hazel. At a distance in July or August the steaming foliage seems almost to writhe in fire. Great green and yellow grasshoppers are everywhere in the tall grass, popping up like corn to sting the flesh, and tortoises crawl about on the red earth, going nowhere in the plenty of time. Loneliness is an aspect of the land. All things in the plain are isolate; there is no confusion of objects in the eye,

but *one* hill or *one* tree or *one* man. To look upon that landscape in the early morning, with the sun at your back, is to lose the sense of proportion. Your imagination comes to life, and this, you think, is where Creation was begun.

2   I returned to Rainy Mountain in July. My grandmother had died in the spring, and I wanted to be at her grave. She had lived to be very old and at last infirm. Her only living daughter was with her when she died, and I was told that in death her face was that of a child.

3   I like to think of her as a child. When she was born, the Kiowas were living the last great moment of their history. For more than a hundred years they had controlled the open range from the Smoky Hill River to the Red, from the headwaters of the Canadian to the fork of the Arkansas and Cimarron. In alliance with the Comanches, they had ruled the whole of the Southern Plains. War was their sacred business, and they were the finest horsemen the world has ever known. But warfare for the Kiowas was preeminently a matter of disposition rather than of survival, and they never understood the grim, unrelenting advance of the U.S. Cavalry. When at last, divided and ill provisioned, they were driven onto the Staked Plains in the cold of autumn, they fell into panic. In Palo Duro Canyon they abandoned their crucial stores to pillage and had nothing then but their lives. In order to save themselves, they surrendered to the soldiers at Fort Sill and were imprisoned in the old stone corral that now stands as a military museum. My grandmother was spared the humiliation of those high gray walls by eight or ten years, but she must have known from birth the affliction of defeat, the dark brooding of old warriors.

4   Her name was Aho, and she belonged to the last culture to evolve in North America. Her forebears came down from the high country in western Montana nearly three centuries ago. They were a mountain people, a mysterious tribe of hunters whose language has never been classified in any major group. In the late seventeenth century they began a long migration to the south and east. It was a journey toward the dawn, and it led to a golden age. Along the way the Kiowas were befriended by the Crows, who gave them the culture and religion of the Plains. They acquired horses, and their ancient nomadic spirit was suddenly free of the ground.

They acquired Tai-me, the sacred sun-dance doll, from that moment the object and symbol of their worship, and so shared in the divinity of the sun. Not least, they acquired the sense of destiny, therefore courage and pride. When they entered upon the Southern Plains they had been transformed. No longer were they slaves to the simple necessity of survival; they were a lordly and dangerous society of fighters and thieves, hunters and priests of the sun. According to their origin myth, they entered the world through a hollow log. From one point of view, their migration was the fruit of an old prophecy, for indeed they emerged from a sunless world.

5   Though my grandmother lived out her long life in the shadow of Rainy Mountain, the immense landscape of the continental interior lay like memory in her blood. She could tell of the Crows, whom she had never seen, and of the Black Hills, where she had never been. I wanted to see in reality what she had seen more perfectly in the mind's eye, and drove fifteen hundred miles to begin my pilgrimage.

6   A dark mist lay over the Black Hills, and the land was like iron. At the top of a ridge I caught sight of Devil's Tower upthrust against the gray sky as if in the birth of time the core of the earth had broken through its crust and the motion of the world was begun. There are things in nature that engender an awful quiet in the heart of man; Devil's Tower is one of them. Two centuries ago, because of their need to explain it, the Kiowas made a legend at the base of the rock. My grandmother said:

7   "Eight children were there at play, seven sisters and their brother. Suddenly the boy was struck dumb; he trembled and began to run upon his hands and feet. His fingers became claws, and his body was covered with fur. There was a bear where the boy had been. The sisters were terrified; they ran, and the bear after them. They came to the stump of a great tree, and the tree spoke to them. It bade them climb upon it, and as they did so, it began to rise into the air. The bear came to kill them, but they were just beyond its reach. It reared against the tree and scored the bark all around with its claws. The seven sisters were borne into the sky, and they became the stars of the Big Dipper." From that moment, and so long as the legend lives, the Kiowas have kinsmen in the night sky. Whatever they were in the mountains,

they could be no more. However tenuous their well-being, however much they had suffered and would suffer again, they had
found a way out of the wilderness.

8   My grandmother had a reverence for the sun, a holy regard
that now is all but gone out of mankind. There was a wariness in
her, and an ancient awe. She was a Christian in her later years,
but she had come a long way about, and she never forgot her
birthright. As a child she had been to the sun dances; she had
taken part in that annual rite, and by it she had learned the
restoration of her people in the presence of Tai-me. She was
about seven when the last Kiowa sun dance was held in 1887 on
the Washita River above Rainy Mountain Creek. The buffalo were
gone. In order to consummate the ancient sacrifice—to impale
the head of a buffalo bull upon the Tai-me tree—a delegation of
old men journeyed into Texas, there to beg and barter for an animal from the Goodnight herd. She was ten when the Kiowas came
together for the last time as a living sun-dance culture. They could
find no buffalo; they had to hang an old hide from the sacred
tree. Before the dance could begin, a company of soldiers rode
out from Fort Sill under orders to disperse the tribe. Forbidden
without cause the essential act of their faith, having seen the wild
herds slaughtered and left to rot upon the ground, the Kiowas
backed away forever from the tree. That was July 20, 1890, at the
great bend of the Washita. My grandmother was there. Without
bitterness, and for as long as she lived, she bore a vision of dei-
cide.

9   Now that I can have her only in memory, I see my grandmother in the several postures that were peculiar to her: standing
at the wood stove on a winter morning and turning meat in a
great iron skillet; sitting at the south window, bent above her
beadwork, and afterwards, when her vision failed, looking down
for a long time into the fold of her hands; going out upon a cane,
very slowly as she did when the weight of age came upon her;
praying. I remember her most often at prayer. She made long,
rambling prayers out of suffering and hope, having seen many
things. I was never sure that I had the right to hear, so exclusive
were they of all mere custom and company. The last time I saw
her she prayed standing by the side of her bed at night, naked to
the waist, the light of a kerosene lamp moving upon her dark
skin. Her long black hair, always drawn and braided in the day, lay
upon her shoulders and against her breasts like a shawl. I do not

speak Kiowa, and I never understood her prayers, but there was something inherently sad in the sound, some merest hesitation upon the syllables of sorrow. She began in a high and descending pitch, exhausting her breath to silence; then again and again— and always the same intensity of effort, of something that is, and is not, like urgency in the human voice. Transported so in the dancing light among the shadows of her room, she seemed beyond the reach of time. But that was illusion; I think I knew then that I should not see her again.

10   Houses are like sentinels in the plain, old keepers of the weather watch. There, in a very little while, wood takes on the appearance of great age. All colors wear soon away in the wind and rain, and then the wood is burned gray and the grain appears and the nails turn red with rust. The window panes are black and opaque; you imagine there is nothing within, and indeed there are many ghosts, bones given up to the land. They stand here and there against the sky, and you approach them for a longer time than you expect. They belong in the distance; it is their domain.

11   Once there was a lot of sound in my grandmother's house, a lot of coming and going, feasting and talk. The summers there were full of excitement and reunion. The Kiowas are a summer people; they abide the cold and keep to themselves, but when the season turns and the land becomes warm and vital they cannot hold still; an old love of going returns upon them. The aged visitors who came to my grandmother's house when I was a child were made of lean and leather, and they bore themselves upright. They wore great black hats and bright ample shirts that shook in the wind. They rubbed fat upon their hair and wound their braids with strips of colored cloth. Some of them painted their faces and carried the scars of old and cherished enmities. They were an old council of warlords, come to remind and be reminded of who they were. Their wives and daughters served them well. The women might indulge themselves; gossip was at once the mark and compensation of their servitude. They made loud and elaborate talk among themselves, full of jest and gesture, fright and false alarm. They went abroad in fringed and flowered shawls, bright beadwork and German silver. They were at home in the kitchen, and they prepared meals that were banquets.

12   There were frequent prayer meetings, and nocturnal feasts. When I was a child I played with my cousins outside, where the lamplight fell upon the ground and the singing of the old people

rose up around us and carried away into the darkness. There were a lot of good things to eat, a lot of laughter and surprise. And afterwards, when the quiet returned, I lay down with my grand-mother and could hear the frogs away by the river and feel the motion of the air.

13   Now there is a funereal silence in the rooms, the endless wake of some final word. The walls have closed in upon my grand-mother's house. When I returned to it in mourning, I saw for the first time in my life how small it was. It was late at night, and there was a white moon, nearly full. I sat for a long time on the stone steps by the kitchen door. From there I could see out across the land; I could see the long row of trees by the creek, the low light upon the rolling plains, and the stars of the Big Dipper. Once I looked at the moon and caught sight of a strange thing. A cricket had perched upon the handrail, only a few inches away. My line of vision was such that the creature filled the moon like a fossil. It had gone there, I thought, to live and die, for there, of all places, was its small definition made whole and eternal. A warm wind rose up and purled like the longing within me.

14   The next morning, I awoke at dawn and went out on the dirt road to Rainy Mountain. It was already hot, and the grasshoppers began to fill the air. Still, it was early in the morning, and birds sang out of the shadows. The long yellow grass on the mountain shone in the bright light, and a scissortail hied above the land. There, where it ought to be, at the end of a long and legendary way, was my grandmother's grave. She had at last succeeded to that holy ground. Here and there on the dark stones were ances-tral names. Looking back once, I saw the mountain and came away.

REFLECTIONS

N. Scott Momaday recollects his childhood in Oklahoma by focusing on memories of his grandmother. He situates her in her physical and cultur-al environment and reveals toward her an attitude of tenderness and rev-erence. What specific values of her world does Momaday identify and what is his attitude toward those values? To what extent does he partici-pate in those shared values? To what extent does he live in a different cultural environment? What image of the Kiowas and related tribes does Momaday inscribe in this piece? Why does he write it in the first place?

Joyce Carol Oates

(1938–   )

Joyce Carol Oates is a versatile and active writer whose works since 1963 have included numerous novels, short stories, poems, plays, essays, and critical articles and reviews. Her earliest work includes a trilogy of novels the last of which, *them* (1969), won a National Book Award. A later novel, *You Must Remember This* (1987), is set in the early fifties and required a great deal of research which, according to Oates, brought back previously forgotten memories. One of the novel's characters is a boxer, and Oates watched old films and tapes of boxing matches that reawakened an interest in boxing that began when she watched matches as a child with her father. The research led to a books of essays, *On Boxing*, and an anthology of writings on boxing, *Reading the Fights*. We have included an excerpt from *On Boxing* in which Oates explores boxing as a peculiarly masculine activity.

"Macho Time"

1   A fairy-tale proposition: the heavyweight champion is the most dangerous man on earth: the most feared, the most manly. His proper mate is very likely the fairy-tale princess whom the mirrors declare the fairest woman on earth.

657

2   Boxing is a purely masculine activity and it inhabits a purely masculine world. Which is not to suggest that most men are defined by it: clearly, most men are not. And though there are female boxers—a fact that seems to surprise, alarm, amuse— women's role in the sport has always been extremely marginal. (At the time of this writing the most famous American woman boxer is the black champion Lady Tyger Trimiar with her shaved head and theatrical tiger-striped attire.) At boxing matches women's role is limited to that of card girl and occasional National Anthem singer: stereotypical functions usually per- formed in stereotypically zestful feminine ways—for women have no natural place in the spectacle otherwise. The card girls in their bathing suits and spike heels, glamour girls of the 1950s, comple- ment the boxers in their trunks and gym shoes but are not to be taken seriously: their public exhibition of themselves involves no risk and is purely decorative. Boxing is for men, and is about men, and *is* men. A celebration of the lost religion of masculinity all the more trenchant for its being lost.

3   In this world, strength of a certain kind—matched of course with intelligence and tirelessly developed skills—determines mas- culinity. Just as a boxer is his body, a man's masculinity is his use of his body. But it is also his triumph over another's use of his body. The Opponent is always male, the Opponent is the rival for one's own masculinity, most fully and combatively realized. Sugar Ray Leonard speaks of coming out of retirement to fight one man, Marvin Hagler: "I want Hagler. I need that man." Thomas Hearns, decisively beaten by Hagler, speaks of having been obsessed with him: "I want the rematch badly . . . there hasn't been a minute or an hour in any day that I haven't thought about it." Hence women's characteristic repugnance for boxing per se coupled with an intense interest in and curiosity about men's fas- cination with it. Men fighting men to determine worth (i.e., mas- culinity) excludes women as completely as the female experience of childbirth excludes men. And is there, perhaps, some connec- tion?

4   In any case, raw aggression is thought to be the peculiar province of men, as nurturing is the peculiar province of women. (The female boxer violates this stereotype and cannot be taken seriously—she is parody, she is cartoon, she is monstrous. Had she an ideology, she is likely to be a feminist.) The psychologist Erik Erikson discovered that, while little girls playing with blocks gen-

erally create pleasant interior spaces and attractive entrances, little boys are inclined to pile up the blocks as high as they can and then watch them fall down: "the contemplation of ruins," Erikson observes, "is a masculine specialty." No matter the mesmerizing grace and beauty of a great boxing match, it is the catastrophic finale for which everyone waits, and hopes: the blocks piled as high as they can possibly be piled, then brought spectacularly down. Women, watching a boxing match, are likely to identify with the losing, or hurt, boxer; men are likely to identify with the winning boxer. There is a point at which male spectators are able to identify with the fight itself as, it might be said, a Platonic experience abstracted from its particulars; if they have favored one boxer over the other, and that boxer is losing, they can shift their loyalty to the winner—or, rather, "loyalty" shifts, apart from conscious volition. In that way the ritual of fighting is always honored. The high worth of combat is always affirmed.

5   Boxing's very vocabulary suggests a patriarchal world taken over by adolescents. This world is young. Its focus is youth. Its focus is of course *macho*—*machismo* raised beyond parody. To enter the claustrophobic world of professional boxing even as a spectator is to enter what appears to be a distillation of the masculine world, empty now of women, its fantasies, hopes, and stratagems magnified as in a distorting mirror, or a dream.

6   Here, we find ourselves through the looking-glass. Values are reversed, evaginated: a boxer is valued not for his humanity but for being a "killer," a "mauler," a "hitman," an "animal," for being "savage," "merciless," "devastating," "ferocious," "vicious," "murderous." Opponents are not merely defeated as in a game but are "decked," "stiffed," "starched," "iced," "destroyed," "annihilated." Even the veteran sportswriters of so respectable a publication as *The Ring* are likely to be pitiless toward a boxer who has been beaten. Much of the appeal of Roberto Durán for intellectual boxing *aficionados* no less than for those whom one might suppose his natural constituency was that he seemed truly to want to kill his opponents: in his prime he was the "baby-faced assassin" with the "dead eyes" and "deadpan" expression who once said, having knocked out an opponent named Ray Lampkin, that he hadn't trained for the fight—next time he would kill the man. (According to legend Durán once felled a horse with a single blow.) Sonny Liston was another champion lauded for his menace, so different in spirit from Floyd Patterson as to seem to

belong to another subspecies; to watch Liston overcome Patterson in tapes of their fights in the early 1960s is to watch the defeat of "civilization" by something so elemental and primitive it cannot be named. Masculinity in these terms is strictly hierarchical—two men cannot occupy the same space at the same time.

7   At the present time twenty-year-old Mike Tyson, Cus D'Amato's much-vaunted protégé, is being groomed as the most dangerous man in the heavyweight division. He is spoken of with awe as a "young bull"; his strength is prodigious, at least as demonstrated against fairly hapless, stationary opponents; he enters the arena robeless—"I feel more like a warrior"—and gleaming with sweat. He does not even wear socks. His boxing model is not Muhammad Ali, the most brilliant heavyweight of modern times, but Rocky Marciano, graceless, heavy-footed, indomitable, the man with the massive right-hand punch who was willing to absorb five blows in the hope of landing one. It was after having broken Jesse Ferguson's nose in a recent match that Tyson told reporters that it was his strategy to try to drive the bone back into the brain . . .

8   The names of boxers! *Machismo* as sheer poetry.

9   Though we had, in another era, "Gentleman Jim" Corbett (world heavyweight champion, 1892–97); and the first black heavyweight champion, Jack Johnson (1908–15) called himself "Li'l Arthur" as a way of commenting playfully on his powerful physique and savage ring style. (Johnson was a white man's nightmare: the black man who mocked his white opponents as he humiliated them with his fists.) In more recent times we had "Sugar Ray" Robinson and his younger namesake "Sugar Ray" Leonard. And Tyrone Crawley, a thinking man's boxer, calls himself "The Butterfly." But for the most part a boxer's ring name is chosen to suggest something more ferocious: Jack Dempsey of Manassa, Colorado, was "The Manassa Mauler"; the formidable Harry Greb was "The Human Windmill"; Joe Louis was, of course, "The Brown Bomber"; Rocky Marciano, "The Brockton Blockbuster"; Jake LaMotta, "The Bronx Bull"; Tommy Jackson, "Hurricane" Jackson; Roberto Durán, "Hands of Stone" and "The Little Killer" variously. More recent are Ray "Boom-Boom" Mancini, Thomas "Hit-Man" Hearns, James "Hard Rock" Green, Al "Earthquake" Carter, Frank "The Animal" Fletcher, Donald "The Cobra" Curry, Aaron "The Hawk" Pryor, "Terrible" Tim

Witherspoon, "Bonecrusher" Smith, Johnny "Bump City" Bumphus, Lonnie "Lightning" Smith, Barry "The Clones Cyclone" McGuigan, Gene "Mad Dog" Hatcher, Livingstone "Pit Bull" Bramble, Hector "Macho Man" Camacho. "Marvelous" Marvin Hagler changed his name legally to Marvelous Marvin Hagler before his fight with Thomas Hearns brought him to national prominence.

10　　It was once said by José Torres that the *machismo* of boxing is a condition of poverty. But it is not, surely, a condition uniquely of poverty? Or even of adolescence? I think of it as the obverse of the feminine, the denial of the feminine-in-man that has its ambiguous attractions for all men, however "civilized." It is a remnant of another, earlier era when the physical being was primary and the warrior's masculinity its highest expression.

REFLECTIONS

Joyce Carol Oates compares "men fighting to determine worth" as analogous to women engaged in childbirth in its exclusiveness to one sex, and later she says that in professional boxing "values are reversed, evaginated." What do you think of this assertion that boxing taps into an essential difference between men and women, or that it represents "a denial of the feminine-in-man" that all men can relate to in some way? Notice how Oates uses general statements and specific details to present her argument that boxing is purely masculine. What is the rhetorical effect of the long list of ring names placed just before the concluding paragraph?

Richard Rodriquez

(1944–   )

Richard Rodriquez was born in San Francisco, the son of Mexican-American immigrants. He was educated in a Catholic grammar school en route to earning a B.A. from Stanford University and an M.A. from Columbia University. He has been awarded a Fulbright Fellowship and has attended the Warburg Institute in London. The story of his assimilation into the American social and educational scene is described in *Hunger of Memory* (1982) from which "Complexion" has been taken.

Complexion

1   Complexion. My first conscious experience of sexual excitement concerns my complexion. One summer weekend, when I was around seven years old, I was at a public swimming pool with the whole family. I remember sitting on the damp pavement next to the pool and seeing my mother, in the spectators' bleachers, holding my younger sister on her lap. My mother, I noticed, was watching my father as he stood on a diving board, waving to her. I watched her wave back. Then saw her radiant, bashful, astonishing smile. In that second I sensed that my mother and father had a relationship I knew nothing about. A nervous excitement encircled my stomach as I saw my mother's eyes follow my father's figure curving into the water. A second or two later, he emerged. I heard him call out. Smiling, his voice sounded, buoyant, calling me to swim to him. But turning to see him, I caught my mother's eye. I heard her shout over to me. In Spanish

663

she called through the crowd: 'Put a towel on over your shoulders.' In public, she didn't want to say why. I knew.

2   That incident anticipates the shame and sexual inferiority I was to feel in later years because of my dark complexion. I was to grow up an ugly child. Or one who thought himself ugly. *(Feo.)* One night when I was eleven or twelve years old, I locked myself in the bathroom and carefully regarded my reflection in the mirror over the sink. Without any pleasure I studied my skin. I turned on the faucet. (In my mind I heard the swirling voices of aunts, and even my mother's voice, whispering, whispering incessantly about lemon juice solutions and dark, *feo* children.) With a bar of soap, I fashioned a thick ball of lather. I began soaping my arms. I took my father's straight razor out of the medicine cabinet. Slowly, with steady deliberateness, I put the blade against my flesh, pressed it as close as I could without cutting, and moved it up and down across my skin to see if I could get out, somehow lessen, the dark. All I succeeded in doing, however, was in shaving my arms bare of their hair. For as I noted with disappointment, the dark would not come out. It remained. Trapped. Deep in the cells of my skin.

3   Throughout adolescence, I felt myself mysteriously marked. Nothing else about my appearance would concern me so much as the fact that my complexion was dark. My mother would say how sorry she was that there was not money enough to get braces to straighten my teeth. But I never bothered about my teeth. In three-way mirrors at department stores, I'd see my profile dramatically defined by a long nose, but it was really only the color of my skin that caught my attention.

4   I wasn't afraid that I would become a menial laborer because of my skin. Nor did my complexion make me feel especially vulnerable to racial abuse. (I didn't really consider my dark skin to be a racial characteristic. I would have been only too happy to look as Mexican as my light-skinned older brother.) Simply, I judged myself ugly. And, since the women in my family had been the ones who discussed it in such worried tones, I felt my dark skin made me unattractive to women.

5   Thirteen years old. Fourteen. In a grammar school art class, when the assignment was to draw a self-portrait, I tried and tried but could not bring myself to shade in the face on the paper to anything like my actual tone. With disgust then I would come face to face with myself in mirrors. With disappointment I located

myself in class photographs— my dark face undefined by the camera which had clearly described the white faces of classmates. Or I'd see my dark wrist against my long-sleeved white shirt.

6   I grew divorced from my body. Insecure, overweight, listless. On hot summer days when my rubber-soled shoes soaked up the heat from the sidewalk, I kept my head down. Or walked in the shade. My mother didn't need anymore to tell me to watch out for the sun. I denied myself a sensational life. The normal, extraordinary, animal excitement of feeling my body alive—riding shirtless on a bicycle in the warm wind created by furious self-propelled motion—the sensations that first had excited in me a sense of my maleness, I denied. I was too ashamed of my body. I wanted to forget that I had a body because I had a brown body. I was grateful that none of my classmates ever mentioned the fact.

7   I continued to see the *braceros,* those men I resembled in one way and, in another way, didn't resemble at all. On the watery horizon of a Valley afternoon, I'd see them. And though I feared looking like them, it was with silent envy that I regarded them still. I envied them their physical lives, their freedom to violate the taboo of the sun. Closer to home I would notice the shirtless construction workers, the roofers, the sweating men tarring the street in front of the house. And I'd see the Mexican gardeners. I was unwilling to admit the attraction of their lives. I tried to deny it by looking away. But what was denied became strongly desired.

8   In high school physical education classes, I withdrew, in the regular company of five or six classmates, to a distant corner of a football field where we smoked and talked. Our company was composed of bodies too short or too tall, all graceless and all—except mine—pale. Our conversation was usually witty. (In fact we were intelligent.) If we referred to the athletic contests around us, it was with sarcasm. With savage scorn I'd refer to the 'animals' playing football or baseball. It would have been important for me to have joined them. Or for me to have taken off my shirt, to have let the sun burn dark on my skin, and to have run barefoot on the warm wet grass. It would have been very important. Too important. It would have been too telling a gesture—to admit the desire for sensation, the body, my body.

9   Fifteen, sixteen. I was a teenager shy in the presence of girls. Never dated. Barely could talk to a girl without stammering. In high school I went to several dances, but I never managed to ask a girl to dance. So I stopped going. I cannot remember high school

years now with the parade of typical images: bright drive-ins or gliding blue shadows of a Junior Prom. At home most weekend nights, I would pass evenings reading. Like those hidden, precocious adolescents who have no real-life sexual experiences, I read a great deal of romantic fiction. 'You won't find it in your books,' my brother would playfully taunt me as he prepared to go to a party by freezing the crest of the wave in his hair with sticky pomade. Through my reading, however, I developed a fabulous and sophisticated sexual imagination. At seventeen, I may not have known how to engage a girl in small talk, but I had read *Lady Chatterley's Lover.*

10   It annoyed me to hear my father's teasing: that I would never know what 'real work' is; that my hands were so soft. I think I knew it was his way of admitting pleasure and pride in my academic success. But I didn't smile. My mother said she was glad her children were getting their educations and would not be pushed around like *los pobres.* I heard the remark ironically as a reminder of my separation from *los braceros.* At such times I suspected that education was making me effeminate. The odd thing, however, was that I did not judge my classmates so harshly. Nor did I consider my male teachers in high school effeminate. It was only myself I judged against some shadowy, mythical Mexican laborer—dark like me, yet very different.

11   Language was crucial. I knew that I had violated the ideal of the *macho* by becoming such a dedicated student of language and literature. *Machismo* was a word never exactly defined by the persons who used it. (It was best described in the 'proper' behavior of men.) Women at home, nevertheless, would repeat the old Mexican dictum that a man should be *feo, fuerte, y formal.* 'The three *F's,'* my mother called them, smiling slyly. *Feo* I took to mean not literally ugly so much as ruggedly handsome. (When my mother and her sisters spent a loud, laughing afternoon determining ideal male good looks, they finally settled on the actor Gilbert Roland, who was neither too pretty nor ugly but had looks 'like a man.') *Fuerte,* 'strong,' seemed to mean not physical strength as much as inner strength, character. A dependable man is *fuerte. Fuerte* for that reason was a characteristic subsumed by the last of the three qualities, and the one I most often considered—*formal.* To be *formal* is to be steady. A man of responsibility, a good provider. Someone *formal* is also constant. A person to

be relied upon in adversity. A sober man, a man of high seriousness.

12   I learned a great deal about being *formal* just by listening to
the way my father and other male relatives of his generation
spoke. A man was not silent necessarily. Nor was he limited in the
tones he could sound. For example, he could tell a long, involved,
humorous story and laugh at his own humor with high-pitched
giggling. But a man was not talkative the way a woman could be. It
was permitted a woman to be gossipy and chatty. (When one
heard many voices in a room, it was usually women who were talking.) Men spoke much less rapidly. And often men spoke in
monologues. (When one voice sounded in a crowded room, it was
most often a man's voice one heard.) More important than any of
this was the fact that a man never verbally revealed his emotions.
Men did not speak about their unease in moments of crisis or
danger. It was the woman who worried aloud when her husband
got laid off from work. At times of illness or death in the family, a
man was usually quiet, even silent. Women spoke up to voice
prayers. In distress, women always sounded quick ejaculations to
God or the Virgin; women prayed in clearly audible voices at a
wake held in a funeral parlor. And on the subject of love, a
woman was verbally expansive. She spoke of her yearning and
delight. A married man, if he spoke publicly about love, usually
did so with playful, mischievous irony. Younger, unmarried men
more often were quiet. (The *macho* is a silent suitor. *Formal.*)

13   At home I was quiet, so perhaps I seemed *formal* to my relations and other Spanish-speaking visitors to the house. But outside the house—my God!—I talked. Particularly in class or alone
with my teachers, I chattered. (Talking seemed to make teachers
think I was bright.) I often was proud of my way with words.
Though, on other occasions, for example, when I would hear my
mother busily speaking to women, it would occur to me that my
attachment to words made me like her. Her son. Not *formal* like
my father. At such times I even suspected that my nostalgia for
sounds—the noisy, intimate Spanish sounds of my past—was
nothing more than effeminate yearning.

14   High school English teachers encouraged me to describe
very personal feelings in words. Poems and short stories I wrote,
expressing sorrow and loneliness, were awarded high grades. In
my bedroom were books by poets and novelists—books that I
loved—in which male writers published feelings the men in my

family never revealed or acknowledged in words. And it seemed to me that there was something unmanly about my attachment to literature. Even today, when so much about the myth of the *macho* no longer concerns me, I cannot altogether evade such notions. Writing these pages, admitting my embarrassment or my guilt, admitting my sexual anxieties and my physical insecurity, I have not been able to forget that I am not being *formal.*

15   So be it.

REFLECTIONS

To what extent is Rodriquez's piece about self-image and to what extent about his cultural inheritance? He describes his "complexion" as being dark-skinned, his features as being "ugly," and his body as "brown." How does his image of himself affect his behavior, his relation to his cultural past, and his idea of the masculine ideal? What effect does Rodriquez achieve by including Spanish words such as *machismo, feo, fuerto,* and *los braceros?*

Philip Roth

(1933–   )

Philip Roth was born and raised in Newark, New Jersey, graduated from Bucknell University and received an M.A. from the University of Chicago in 1955. Roth has written highly praised novels and short stories, including the trilogy *Zuckerman Bound* (1985). He is still most widely associated with the controversial novel *Portnoy's Complaint* (1969), which was both condemned as pornography and praised as an audacious and brilliant work of a virtuoso. Like *Portnoy's Complaint*, the nonfiction selection "Safe at Home," from Roth's autobiographical *The Facts* (1988), focuses on themes and experiences of growing up Jewish in an America still filled with subtle and overt biases toward minorities.

Safe at Home

1   The greatest menace while I was growing up came from abroad, from the Germans and the Japanese, our enemies because we were American. I still remember my terror as a nine-year-old when, running in from playing on the street after school, I saw the banner headline CORREGIDOR FALLS on the evening paper in our doorway and understood that the United States actually could lose the war it had entered only months before. At home the biggest threat came from the Americans who opposed or resisted us—or condescended to us or rigorously excluded us—because we were Jews. Though I knew that we were tolerated and accepted as well—in publicized individual cases, even specially

esteemed—and though I never doubted that this country was mine (and New Jersey and Newark as well), I was not unaware of the power to intimidate that emanated from the highest and lowest reaches of gentile America.

2   At the top were the gentile executives who ran my father's company, the Metropolitan Life, from the home office at Number One Madison Avenue (the first Manhattan street address I ever knew). When I was a small boy, my father, then in his early thirties, was still a new Metropolitan agent, working a six-day week, including most evenings, and grateful for the steady, if modest, living this job provided, even during the Depression; a family shoe store he'd opened after marrying my mother had gone bankrupt some years before, and in between he'd had to take a variety of low-paying, unpromising jobs. He proudly explained to his sons that the Metropolitan was "the largest financial institution in the world" and that as an agent he provided Metropolitan Life policyholders with "an umbrella for a rainy day." The company put out dozens of pamphlets to educate its policyholders about health and disease; I collected a new batch off the racks in the waiting room on Saturday mornings when he took me along with him to the narrow downtown street where the Essex district office of Newark occupied nearly a whole floor of a commercial office building. I read up on "Tuberculosis," "Pregnancy," and "Diabetes," while he labored over his ledger entries and his paperwork. Sometimes at his desk, impressing myself by sitting in his swivel chair, I practiced my penmanship on Metropolitan stationery; in one corner of the paper was my father's name and in the other a picture of the home-office tower, topped with the beacon that he described to me, in the Metropolitan's own phrase, as the light that never failed.

3   In our apartment a framed replica of the Declaration of Independence hung above the telephone table on the hallway wall—it had been awarded by the Metropolitan to the men of my father's district for a successful year in the field, and seeing it there daily during my first school years forged an association between the venerated champions of equality who signed that cherished document and our benefactors, the corporate fathers at Number One Madison Avenue, where the reigning president was, fortuitously, a Mr. Lincoln. If that wasn't enough, the home-office executive whom my father would trek from New Jersey to see when his star began to rise slightly in the company was the super-

intendent of agencies, a Mr. Wright, whose good opinion my father valued inordinately all his life and whose height and imposing good looks he admired nearly as much as he did the man's easygoing diplomacy. As my father's son I felt no less respectful toward these awesomely named gentiles than he did, but I, like him, knew that they had to be the very officials who openly and guiltlessly conspired to prevent more than a few token Jews from assuming positions of anything approaching importance within the largest financial institution in the world.

4   One reason my father so admired the Jewish manager of his own district, Sam Peterfreund—aside, of course, from the devotion that Peterfreund inspired by recognizing my father's drive early on and making him an assistant manager—was that Peterfreund had climbed to the leadership of such a large, productive office despite the company's deep-rooted reluctance to allow a Jew to rise too high. When Mr. Peterfreund was to make one of his rare visits for dinner, the green felt protective pads came out of the hall closet and were laid by my brother and me on the dining room table, it was spread with a fresh linen cloth and linen napkins, water goblets appeared, and we ate off "the good dishes" in the dining room, where there hung a large oil painting of a floral arrangement, copied skillfully from the Louvre by my mother's brother, Mickey; on the sideboard were framed photographic portraits of the two dead men for whom I'd been named, my mother's father, Philip, and my father's younger brother, Milton. We ate in the dining room only on religious holidays, on special family occasions, and when Mr. Peterfreund came—and we all called him Mr. Peterfreund, even when he wasn't there; my father also addressed him directly as "Boss." "Want a drink, Boss?" Before dinner we sat unnaturally, like guests in our own living room, while Mr. Peterfreund sipped his schnapps and I was encouraged to listen to his wisdom. The esteem he inspired was a tribute to a gentile-sanctioned Jew managing a big Metropolitan office as much as to an immediate supervisor whose goodwill determined my father's occupational well-being and our family fate. A large, bald-headed man with a gold chain across his vest and a slightly mysterious German accent, whose family lived (in high style, I imagined) in New York (*and* on Long Island) while (no less glamorously to me) he slept during the week in a Newark hotel, the Boss was our family's Bernard Baruch.

5   Opposition more frightening than corporate discrimination came from the lowest reaches of the gentile world, from the gangs of *lumpen* kids who, one summer, swarmed out of Neptune, a ramshackle little town on the Jersey shore, and stampeded along the boardwalk into Bradley Beach, hollering "Kikes! Dirty Jews!" and beating up whoever hadn't run for cover. Bradley Beach, a couple of miles south of Asbury Park on the mid-Jersey coast, was the very modest little vacation resort where we and hundreds of other lower-middle-class Jews from humid, mosquito-ridden north Jersey cities rented rooms or shared small bungalows for several weeks during the summer. It was paradise for me, even though we lived three in a room, and four when my father drove down the old Cheesequake highway to see us on weekends or to stay for his two-week vacation. In all of my intensely secure and protected childhood, I don't believe I ever felt more exuberantly snug than I did in those mildly anarchic rooming houses, where—inevitably with more strain than valor—some ten or twelve women tried to share the shelves of a single large icebox, and to cook side by side, in a crowded communal kitchen, for children, visiting husbands, and elderly parents. Meals were eaten in the unruly, kibbutzlike atmosphere—so unlike the ambiance in my own orderly home—of the underventilated dining room.

6   The hot, unhomelike, homey hubbub of the Bradley Beach rooming house was somberly contrasted, in the early forties, by reminders all along the shore that the country was fighting in an enormous war: bleak, barbwired Coast Guard bunkers dotted the beaches, and scores of lonely, very young sailors played the amusement machines in the arcades at Asbury Park; the lights were blacked out along the boardwalk at night and the blackout shades on the rooming-house windows made it stifling indoors after dinner; there was even tarry refuse, alleged to be from torpedoed ships, that washed up and littered the beach—I sometimes had fears of wading gleefully with my friends into the surf and bumping against the body of someone killed at sea. Also—and most peculiarly, since we were all supposed to be pulling together to beat the Axis Powers—there were these "race riots," as we children called the hostile nighttime invasions by the boys from Neptune: violence directed against the Jews by youngsters who, as everyone said, could only have learned their hatred from what they heard at home.

7   Though the riots occurred just twice, for much of one July and August it was deemed unwise for a Jewish child to venture out

after supper alone, or even with friends, though nighttime freedom in shorts and sandals was one of Bradley's greatest pleasures for a ten-year-old on vacation from homework and the school year's bedtime hours. The morning after the first riot, a story spread among the kids collecting Popsicle sticks and playing ring-a-lievo on the Lorraine Avenue beach; it was about somebody (whom nobody seemed to know personally) who had been caught before he could get away: the anti-Semites had held him down and pulled his face back and forth across the splintery surface of the boardwalk's weathered planks. This particular horrific detail, whether apocryphal or not—and it needn't necessarily have been—impressed upon me how barbaric was this irrational hatred of families who, as anyone could see, were simply finding in Bradley Beach a little inexpensive relief from the city heat, people just trying to have a quiet good time, bothering no one, except occasionally each other, as when one of the women purportedly expropriated from the icebox, for her family's corn on the cob, somebody else's quarter of a pound of salt butter. If that was as much harm as any of us could do, why make a bloody pulp of a Jewish child's face?

8   The home-office gentiles in executive positions at Number One Madison Avenue were hardly comparable to the kids swarming into Bradley screaming "Kike!"; and yet when I thought about it, I saw that they were no more reasonable or fair: they too were against Jews for no good reason. Small wonder that at twelve, when I was advised to begin to think seriously about what I would do when I grew up, I decided to oppose the injustices wreaked by the violent and the privileged by becoming a lawyer for the underdog.

9   When I entered high school, the menace shifted to School Stadium, then the only large football grounds in Newark, situated on alien Bloomfield Avenue, a forty-minute bus ride from Weequahic High. On Saturdays in the fall, four of the city's seven high schools would meet in a doubleheader, as many as two thousand kids pouring in for the first game, which began around noon, and then emptying en masse into the surrounding streets when the second game had ended in the falling shadows. It was inevitable after a hard-fought game that intense school rivalries would culminate in a brawl somewhere in the stands and that, in an industrial city of strongly divergent ethnic backgrounds and subtle, though pronounced, class gradations, fights would break out among volatile teenagers from four very different neighbor-

hoods. Yet the violence provoked by the presence of a Weequahic crowd—particularly after a rare Weequahic victory—was unlike any other.

10   I remember being in the stands with my friends in my sophomore year, rooting uninhibitedly for the "Indians," as our Weequahic teams were known in the Newark sports pages; after never having beaten Barringer High in the fourteen years of Weequahic's existence, our team was leading them 6–0 in the waning minutes of the Columbus Day game. The Barringer backfield was Berry, Peloso, Short, and Thompson; in the Weequahic backfield were Weissman, Weiss, Gold, and fullback Fred Rosenberg, who'd led a sustained march down the field at the end of the first half and then, on a two-yard plunge, had scored what Fred, now a PR consultant in New Jersey, recently wrote to tell me was "one of the only touchdowns notched by the Indians that entire season, on a run that probably was one of the longer runs from scrimmage in 1947."

11   As the miraculous game was nearing its end—as Barringer, tied with Central for first place in the City League, was about to be upset by the weakest high school team in Newark—I suddenly noticed that the rival fans on the other side of the stadium bowl had begun to stream down the aisles, making their way around the far ends of the stadium toward us. Instead of waiting for the referee's final whistle, I bolted for an exit and, along with nearly everyone else who understood what was happening, ran down the stadium ramp in the direction of the buses waiting to take us back to our neighborhood. Though there were a number of policemen around, it was easy to see that once the rampage was under way, unless you were clinging to a cop with both arms and both legs, his protection wouldn't be much help; should you be caught on your own by a gang from one of the other three schools waiting to get their hands on a Weequahic Jew—our school was almost entirely Jewish—it was unlikely that you'd emerge from the stadium without serious injury.

12   The nearest bus was already almost full when I made it on board; as soon as the last few kids shoved their way in, the uniformed Public Service driver, fearful for his own safety as a transporter of Weequahic kids, drew the front door shut. By then there were easily ten or fifteen of the enemy, aged twelve to twenty, surrounding the bus and hammering their fists against its sides. Fred Rosenberg contends that "every able-bodied man from north

Newark, his brother, and their offspring got into the act." When one of them, having worked his hands through a crevice under the window beside my seat, started forcing the window up with his fingers, I grabbed it from the top and brought it down as hard as I could. He howled and somebody took a swing at the window with a baseball bat, breaking the frame but miraculously not the glass. Before the others could join together to tear back the door, board the bus, and go straight for me—who would have been hard put to explain that the reprisal had been uncharacteristic and intended only in self-defense—the driver had pulled out from the curb and we were safely away from the postgame pogrom, which, for our adversaries, constituted perhaps the most enjoyable part of the day's entertainment.

13   That evening I fled again, not only because I was a fourteen-year-old weighing only a little over a hundred pounds but because I was never to be one of the few who stayed behind for a fight but always among the many whose impulse is to run to avoid it. A boy in our neighborhood might be expected to protect himself in a schoolyard confrontation with another boy his age and size, but no stigma attached to taking flight from a violent melee—by and large it was considered both shameful and stupid for a bright Jewish child to get caught up in something so dangerous to his physical safety, and so repugnant to Jewish instincts. The collective memory of Polish and Russian pogroms had fostered in most of our families the idea that our worth as human beings, even perhaps our distinction as a people, was embodied in the *incapacity* to perpetrate the sort of bloodletting visited upon our ancestors.

14   For a while during my adolescence I studiously followed prizefighting, could recite the names and weights of all the champions and contenders, and even subscribed briefly to *Ring*, Nat Fleischer's colorful boxing magazine. As kids my brother and I had been taken by our father to the local boxing arena, where invariably we all had a good time. From my father and his friends I heard about the prowess of Benny Leonard, Barney Ross, Max Baer, and the clownishly nicknamed Slapsie Maxie Rosenbloom. And yet Jewish boxers and boxing aficionados remained, like boxing itself, "sport" in the bizarre sense, a strange deviation from the norm and interesting largely for that reason: in the world whose values first formed me, unrestrained physical aggression was considered contemptible everywhere else. I could no more smash a nose with a fist than fire a pistol into someone's heart. And what

imposed this restraint, if not on Slapsie Maxie Rosenbloom, then
on me, was my being Jewish. In my scheme of things, Slapsie
Maxie was a more miraculous Jewish phenomenon by far than Dr.
Albert Einstein.

15   The evening following our escape from School Stadium the
ritual victory bonfire was held on the dirt playing field on Chancellor Avenue, across from Syd's, a popular Weequahic hangout
where my brother and I each did part-time stints selling hot dogs
and french fries. I'd virtually evolved as a boy on that playing
field; it was two blocks from my house and bordered on the grade
school—"Chancellor Avenue"—that I'd attended for eight years,
which itself stood next to Weequahic High. It was the field where
I'd played pickup football and baseball, where my brother had
competed in school track meets, where I'd shagged flies for hours
with anybody who would fungo the ball out to me, where my
friends and I hung around on Sunday mornings, watching with
amusement as the local fathers—the plumbers, the electricians,
the produce merchants—kibitzed their way through their weekly
softball game. If ever I had been called on to express my love for
my neighborhood in a single reverential act, I couldn't have done
better than to get down on my hands and knees and kiss the
ground behind home plate.

16   Yet upon this, the sacred heart of my inviolate homeland,
our stadium attackers launched a nighttime raid, the conclusion
to the violence begun that afternoon, their mopping-up exercise.
A few hours after the big fire had been lit, as we happily sauntered
around the dark field, joking among ourselves and looking for
girls to impress, while in the distance the cartwheeling cheerlead-
ers led the chant of the crowd encircling the fire—"And when
you're up against Weequahic you're upside down!"—the cars
pulled up swiftly on Chancellor Avenue, and the same guys who'd
been pounding on the sides of my bus (or so I quickly assumed)
were racing onto the field, some of them waving baseball bats.
The field was set into the slope of the Chancellor Avenue hill; I
ran through the dark to the nearest wall, jumped some six feet
down into Hobson Street, and then just kept going, through alley-
ways, between garages, and over backyard fences, until I'd made it
safely home in less than five minutes. One of my Leslie Street
friends, the football team water boy, who'd been standing in the
full glare of the fire wearing his Weequahic varsity jacket, was not
so quick or lucky; his assailants—identified in the neighborhood

the next day as "Italians"—picked him up and threw him bodily toward the flames. He landed just at the fire's edge and, though he wasn't burned, spent days in the hospital recovering from internal injuries.

17   But this was a unique calamity. Our lower-middle-class neighborhood of houses and shops—a few square miles of tree-lined streets at the corner of the city bordering on residential Hillside and semi-industrial Irvington—was as safe and peaceful a haven for me as his rural community would have been for an Indiana farm boy. Ordinarily nobody more disquieting ever appeared there than the bearded old Jew who sometimes tapped on our door around dinnertime; to me an unnerving specter from the harsh and distant European past, he stood silently in the dim hallway while I went to get a quarter to drop into his collection can for the Jewish National Fund (a name that never sank all the way in: the only nation for Jews, as I saw it, was the democracy to which I was so loyally—and lyrically—bound, regardless of the unjust bias of the so-called best and the violent hatred of some of the worst). Shapiro, the immigrant tailor who also did dry cleaning, had two thumbs on one hand, and that made bringing our clothes to him a little eerie for me when I was still small. And there was LeRoy "the moron," a somewhat gruesome but innocuous neighborhood dimwit who gave me the creeps when he sat down on the front stoop to listen to a bunch of us talking after school. On our street he was rarely teased but just sat looking at us stupidly with his hollow eyes and rhythmically tapping one foot—and that was about as frightening as things ever got.

18   A typical memory is of five or six of us energetically traversing the whole length of the neighborhood Friday nights on our way back from a double feature at the Roosevelt Theater. We would stop off at the Watson Bagel Company on Clinton Place to buy, for a few pennies each, a load of the first warm bagels out of the oven—and this was four decades before the bagel became a breakfast staple at Burger King. Devouring three and four apiece, we'd circuitously walk one another home, howling with laughter at our jokes and imitating our favorite baritones. When the weather was good we'd sometimes wind up back of Chancellor Avenue School, on the wooden bleachers along the sidelines of the asphalt playground adjacent to the big dirt playing field. Stretched on our backs in the open night air, we were as carefree as any kids anywhere in postwar America, and certainly we felt

ourselves no less American. Discussions about Jewishness and being Jewish, which I was to hear so often among intellectual Jews once I was an adult in Chicago and New York, were altogether unknown; we talked about being misunderstood by our families, about movies and radio programs and sex and sports, we even argued about politics, though this was rare since our fathers were all ardent New Dealers and there was no disagreement among us about the sanctity of F.D.R. and the Democratic Party. About being Jewish there was nothing more to say than there was about having two arms and two legs. It would have seemed to us strange *not* to be Jewish—stranger still, to hear someone announce that he wished he weren't a Jew or that he intended not to be in the future.

19   Yet, simultaneously, this intense adolescent camaraderie was the primary means by which we were deepening our *Americanness.* Our parents were, with few exceptions, the first-generation off-spring of poor turn-of-the-century immigrants from Galicia and Polish Russia, raised in predominantly Yiddish-speaking Newark households where religious Orthodoxy was only just beginning to be seriously eroded by American life. However unaccented and American-sounding their speech, however secularized their own beliefs, and adept and convincing their American style of lower-middle-class existence, they were influenced still by their child-hood training and by strong parental ties to what often seemed to us antiquated, socially useless old-country mores and perceptions.

20   My larger boyhood society cohered around the most inher-ently American phenomenon at hand—the game of baseball, whose mystique was encapsulated in three relatively inexpensive fetishes that you could have always at your side in your room, not only while you did your homework but in bed with you while you slept if you were a worshiper as primitive as I was at ten and eleven: they were a ball, a bat, and a glove. The solace that my Orthodox grandfather doubtless took in the familiar leathery odor of the flesh-worn straps of the old phylacteries in which he wrapped himself each morning, I derived from the smell of my mitt, which I ritualistically donned every day to work a little on my pocket. I was an average playground player, and the mitt's enchantment had to do less with foolish dreams of becoming a major leaguer, or even a high school star, than with the bestowal of membership in a great secular nationalistic church from which nobody had ever seemed to suggest that Jews should be excluded.

(The blacks were another story, until 1947.) The softball and hardball teams we organized and reorganized obsessively throughout our grade school years—teams we called by unarguably native names like the Seabees and the Mohawks and described as "social and athletic clubs"—aside from the opportunity they afforded to compete against one another in a game we loved, also operated as secret societies that separated us from the faint, residual foreignness still clinging to some of our parents' attitudes and that validated our own spotless credentials as American kids. Paradoxically, our remotely recent old-country Jewish origins may well have been a source of our especially intense devotion to a sport that, unlike boxing or even football, had nothing to do with the menace of brute force unleashed against flesh and bones.

21   The Weequahic neighborhood for over two decades now has been part of the vast black Newark slum. Visiting my father in Elizabeth, I'll occasionally take a roundabout route off the parkway into my old Newark and, to give myself an emotional workout, drive through the streets still entirely familiar to me despite the boarded-up shops and badly decaying houses, and the knowledge that my white face is not at all welcome. Recently, snaking back and forth in my car along the one-way streets of the Weequahic section, I began to imagine house plaques commemorating the achievements of the boys who'd once lived there, markers of the kind you see in London and Paris on the residences of the historically renowned. What I inscribed on those plaques, along with my friends' names and their years of birth and of local residence, wasn't the professional status they had attained in later life but the position each had played on those neighborhood teams of ours in the 1940s. I thought that if you knew that in this four-family Hobson Street house there once lived the third baseman Seymour Feldman and that down a few doors had lived Ronnie Rubin, who in his boyhood had been our catcher, you'd understand how and where the Feldman and the Rubin families had been naturalized irrevocably by their young sons.

22   In 1982, while I was visiting my widowed father in Miami Beach during his first season there on his own, I got him one night to walk over with me to Meyer Lansky's old base of operations, the Hotel Singapore on Collins Avenue; earlier in the day he'd told me that wintering at the Singapore were some of the last of his generation from our neighborhood—the ones, he mordantly added, "still aboveground." Among the faces I recognized in

the lobby, where the elderly residents met to socialize each evening after dinner, was the mother of one of the boys who also used to play ball incessantly "up the field" and who hung around on the playground bleachers after dark back when we were Seabees together. As we sat talking at the edge of a gin-rummy game, she suddenly took hold of my hand and, smiling at me with deeply emotional eyes—with that special heart-filled look that *all* our mothers had—she said, "Phil, the feeling there was among you boys—I've never seen anything like it again." I told her, altogether truthfully, that I haven't either.

REFLECTIONS

Although Roth narrates examples of intolerance, he doesn't seem bitter or even angry. Is this your reading of his tone? Accounts of one's childhood are often overly sentimental and nostalgic. Do you feel Roth is giving the reader a balanced account of his youth? How can you explain Roth's last sentence? What in your own youth might elicit such an observation?

Susan Sontag
(1933–   )

Susan Sontag has functioned as a provocative and controversial intellectual figure since the publication in the late 1960s of *Against Interpretation and Other Essays* and *Styles of Radical Will.* Her critical writings on a wide range of subjects, including art, film, history, literature, philosophy, and photography, as well as social and political issues, challenge readers to examine their language and assumptions about current events and ideas. In *AIDS and Its Metaphors,* published in 1989, Sontag continues to explore the cultural impact of the language we use to discuss specific diseases and the people who are diagnosed as having them—an exploration she began in *Illness as Metaphor* in response to her own cancer diagnosis in 1977. In this excerpt, Sontag argues that the words we use and the stories we tell about a specific disease may profoundly affect our treatment of those who have it, then shows how diseases themselves come to stand as metaphors for perceived dangers or evils.

On AIDS

1   "Plague" is the principal metaphor by which the AIDS epidemic is understood. And because of AIDS, the popular misidentification of cancer as an epidemic, even a plague, seems to be receding: AIDS has banalized cancer.

2   Plague, from the Latin *plaga* (stroke, wound), has long been used metaphorically as the highest standard of collective calamity,

evil, scourge—Procopius, in his masterpiece of calumny, *The Secret History,* called the Emperor Justinian worse than the plague ("fewer escaped")—as well as being a general name for many frightening diseases. Although the disease to which the word is permanently affixed produced the most lethal of recorded epidemics, being experienced as a pitiless slayer is not necessary for a disease to be regarded as plague-like. Leprosy, very rarely fatal now, was not much more so when at its greatest epidemic strength, between about 1050 and 1350. And syphilis has been regarded as a plague—Blake speaks of "the youthful Harlot's curse" that "blights with plagues the Marriage hearse"—not because it killed often, but because it was disgracing, disempowering, disgusting.

3   It is usually epidemics that are thought of as plagues. And these mass incidences of illness are understood as inflicted, not just endured. Considering illness as a punishment is the oldest idea of what causes illness, and an idea opposed by all attention to the ill that deserves the noble name of medicine. Hippocrates, who wrote several treatises on epidemics, specifically ruled out "the wrath of God" as a cause of bubonic plague. But the illnesses interpreted in antiquity as punishments, like the plague in *Oedipus,* were not thought to be shameful, as leprosy and subsequently syphilis were to be. Diseases, insofar as they acquired meaning, were collective calamities, and judgments on a community. Only injuries and disabilities, not diseases, were thought of as individually merited. For an analogy in the literature of antiquity to the modern sense of a shaming, isolating disease, one would have to turn to Philoctetes and his stinking wound.

4   The most feared diseases, those that are not simply fatal but transform the body into something alienating, like leprosy and syphilis and cholera and (in the imagination of many) cancer, are the ones that seem particularly susceptible to promotion to "plague." Leprosy and syphilis were the first illnesses to be consistently described as repulsive. It was syphilis that, in the earliest descriptions by doctors at the end of the fifteenth century, generated a version of the metaphors that flourish around AIDS: of a disease that was not only repulsive and retributive but collectively invasive. Although Erasmus, the most influential European pedagogue of the early sixteenth century, described syphilis as "nothing but a kind of leprosy" (by 1529 he called it "something worse than leprosy"), it had already been understood as something dif-

ferent, because sexually transmitted. Paracelsus speaks (in
Donne's paraphrase) of "that foule contagious disease which then
had invaded mankind in a few places, and since overflowes in all,
that for punishment of generall licentiousnes God first inflicted
that disease." Thinking of syphilis as a punishment for an individual's transgression was for a long time, virtually until the disease
became easily curable, not really distinct from regarding it as
retribution for the licentiousness of a community—as with AIDS
now, in the rich industrial countries. In contrast to cancer, understood in a modern way as a disease incurred by (and revealing of)
individuals, AIDS is understood in a premodern way, as a disease
incurred by people both as individuals and as members of a "risk
group"—that neutral-sounding, bureaucratic category which also
revives the archaic idea of a tainted community that illness has
judged.

•

5   Not every account of plague or plague-like diseases, of
course, is a vehicle for lurid stereotypes about illness and the ill.
The effort to think critically, historically, about illness (about disaster generally) was attempted throughout the eighteenth century: say, from Defoe's *A Journal of the Plague Year* (1722) to
Alessandro Manzoni's *The Betrothed* (1827). Defoe's historical fiction, purporting to be an eyewitness account of bubonic plague in
London in 1665, does not further any understanding of the
plague as punishment or, a later part of the script, as a transform-
ing experience. And Manzoni, in his lengthy account of the passage of plague through the duchy of Milan in 1630, is avowedly
committed to presenting a more accurate, less reductive view than
his historical sources. But even these two complex narratives reinforce some of the perennial, simplifying ideas about plague.
6   One feature of the usual script for plague: the disease invariably comes from somewhere else. The names for syphilis, when it
began its epidemic sweep through Europe in the last decade of
the fifteenth century, are an exemplary illustration of the need to
make a dreaded disease foreign. It was the "French pox" to the
English, *morbus Germanicus* to the Parisians, the Naples sickness to
the Florentines, the Chinese disease to the Japanese. But what
may seem like a joke about the inevitability of chauvinism reveals
a more important truth: that there is a link between imagining

disease and imagining foreignness. It lies perhaps in the very concept of wrong, which is archaically identical with the non-us, the
alien. A polluting person is always wrong, as Mary Douglas has
observed. The inverse is also true: a person judged to be wrong is
regarded as, at least potentially, a source of pollution.

7   The foreign place of origin of important illnesses, as of drastic changes in the weather, may be no more remote than a neighboring country. Illness is a species of invasion, and indeed is often
carried by soldiers. Manzoni's account of the plague of 1630
begins:

> The plague which the Tribunal of Health had feared might enter
> the Milanese provinces with the German troops had in fact en-
> tered, as is well known; and it is also well known that it did not stop
> there, but went on to invade and depopulate a large part of Italy.

8   Defoe's chronicle of the plague of 1665 begins similarly,
with a flurry of ostentatiously scrupulous speculation about its foreign origin:

> It was about the beginning of September, 1664, that I, among the
> rest of my neighbours, heard in ordinary discourse that the plague
> was returned again in Holland; for it had been very violent there,
> and particularly at Amsterdam and Rotterdam, in the year 1663,
> whither, they say, it was brought, some said from Italy, others from
> the Levant, among some goods which were brought home by their
> Turkey fleet; others said it was brought from Candia; others from
> Cyprus. It mattered not from whence it came; but all agreed it was
> come into Holland again.

9   The bubonic plague that reappeared in London in the
1720s had arrived from Marseilles, which was where plague in the
eighteenth century was usually thought to enter Western Europe:
brought by seamen, then transported by soldiers and merchants.
By the nineteenth century the foreign origin was usually more
exotic, the means of transport less specifically imagined, and the
illness itself had become phantasmagorical, symbolic.

10   At the end of *Crime and Punishment* Raskolnikov dreams of
plague: "He dreamt that the whole world was condemned to a terrible new strange plague that had come to Europe from the
depths of Asia." At the beginning of the sentence it is "the whole
world," which turns out by the end of the sentence to be

"Europe," afflicted by a lethal visitation from Asia. Dostoevsky's model is undoubtedly cholera, called Asiatic cholera, long endemic in Bengal, which had rapidly become and remained through most of the nineteenth century a worldwide epidemic disease. Part of the centuries-old conception of Europe as a privileged cultural entity is that it is a place which is colonized by lethal diseases coming from elsewhere. Europe is assumed to be by rights free of disease. (And Europeans have been astoundingly callous about the far more devastating extent to which they—as invaders, as colonists—have introduced *their* lethal diseases to the exotic, "primitive" world: think of the ravages of smallpox, influenza, and cholera on the aboriginal populations of the Americas and Australia.) The tenacity of the connection of exotic origin with dreaded disease is one reason why cholera, of which there were four great outbreaks in Europe in the nineteenth century, each with a lower death toll than the preceding one, has continued to be more memorable than smallpox, whose ravages increased as the century went on (half a million died in the European smallpox pandemic of the early 1870s) but which could not be construed as, plague-like, a disease with a non-European origin.

11   Plagues are no longer "sent," as in Biblical and Greek antiquity, for the question of agency has blurred. Instead, peoples are "visited" by plagues. And the visitations recur, as is taken for granted in the subtitle of Defoe's narrative, which explains that it is about that "which happened in London during the Last Great Visitation in 1665." Even for non-Europeans, lethal disease may be called a visitation. But a visitation on "them" is invariably described as different from one on "us." "I believe that about one half of the whole people was carried off by this visitation," wrote the English traveler Alexander Kinglake, reaching Cairo at a time of the bubonic plague (sometimes called "oriental plague"). "The Orientals, however, have more quiet fortitude than Europeans under afflictions of this sort." Kinglake's influential book *Eothen* (1844)—suggestively subtitled "Traces of Travel Brought Home from the East"—illustrates many of the enduring Eurocentric presumptions about others, starting from the fantasy that peoples with little reason to expect exemption from misfortune have a lessened capacity to *feel* misfortune. Thus it is believed that Asians (or the poor, or blacks, or Africans, or Muslims) don't suffer or don't grieve as Europeans (or whites) do. The fact that illness is associated with the poor—who are, from the perspective of the

privileged, aliens in one's midst—reinforces the association of illness with the foreign: with an exotic, often primitive place.

12   Thus, illustrating the classic script for plague, AIDS is thought to have started in the "dark continent," then spread to Haiti, then to the United States and to Europe, then . . . . It is understood as a tropical disease: another infestation from the so-called Third World, which is after all where most people in the world live, as well as a scourge of the *tristes tropiques*. Africans who detect racist stereotypes in much of the speculation about the geographical origin of AIDS are not wrong. (Nor are they wrong in thinking that depictions of Africa as the cradle of AIDS must feed anti-African prejudices in Europe and Asia.) The subliminal connection made to notions about a primitive past and the many hypotheses that have been fielded about possible transmission from animals (a disease of green monkeys? African swine fever?) cannot help but activate a familiar set of stereotypes about animality, sexual license, and blacks. In Zaire and other countries in Central Africa where AIDS is killing tens of thousands, the counterreaction has begun. Many doctors, academics, journalists, government officials, and other educated people believe that the virus was sent to Africa from the United States, an act of bacteriological warfare (whose aim was to decrease the African birth rate) which got out of hand and has returned to afflict its perpetrators. A common African version of this belief about the disease's provenance has the virus fabricated in a CIA–Army laboratory in Maryland, sent from there to Africa, and brought back to its country of origin by American homosexual missionaries returning from Africa to Maryland.

13   At first it was assumed that AIDS must become widespread elsewhere in the same catastrophic form in which it has emerged in Africa, and those who still think this will eventually happen invariably invoke the Black Death. The plague metaphor is an essential vehicle of the most pessimistic reading of the epidemiological prospects. From classic fiction to the latest journalism, the standard plague story is of inexorability, inescapability. The unprepared are taken by surprise; those observing the recommended precautions are struck down as well. *All* succumb when the story is told by an omniscient narrator, as in Poe's parable "The Masque of the Red Death" (1842), inspired by an account of a ball held in Paris during the cholera epidemic of 1832. Almost

all—if the story is told from the point of view of a traumatized witness, who will be a benumbed survivor, as in Jean Giono's
Stendhalian novel *Horseman on the Roof* (1951), in which a young
Italian nobleman in exile wanders through cholera-stricken southern France in the 1830s.

•

14   Plagues are invariably regarded as judgments on society, and
the metaphoric inflation of AIDS into such a judgment also accus-
toms people to the inevitability of global spread. This is a traditional use of sexually transmitted diseases: to be described as punishments not just of individuals but of a group ("generall
licentiousnes"). Not only venereal diseases have been used in this
way, to identify transgressing or vicious populations. Interpreting
any catastrophic epidemic as a sign of moral laxity or political
decline was as common until the later part of the last century as
associating dreaded diseases with foreignness. (Or with despised
and feared minorities.) And the assignment of fault is not contra-
dicted by cases that do not fit. The Methodist preachers in
England who connected the cholera epidemic of 1832 with
drunkenness (the temperance movement was just starting) were
not understood to be claiming that *everybody* who got cholera was
a drunkard: there is always room for "innocent victims" (children,
young women). Tuberculosis, in its identity as a disease of the
poor (rather than of the "sensitive"), was also linked by late-nine-
teenth-century reformers to alcoholism. Responses to illnesses
associated with sinners and the poor invariably recommended the
adoption of middle-class values: the regular habits, productivity,
and emotional self-control to which drunkenness was thought the
chief impediment. Health itself was eventually identified with
these values, which were religious as well as mercantile, health
being evidence of virtue as disease was of depravity. The dictum
that cleanliness is next to godliness is to be taken quite literally.
The succession of cholera epidemics in the nineteenth century
shows a steady waning of religious interpretations of the disease;
more precisely, these increasingly coexisted with other explanations. Although, by the time of the epidemic of 1866, cholera was
commonly understood not simply as a divine punishment but as
the consequence of remediable defects of sanitation, it was still

regarded as the scourge of the sinful. A writer in *The New York Times* declared (April 22, 1866): "Cholera is especially the punishment of neglect of sanitary laws; it is the curse of the dirty, the intemperate, and the degraded."

15   That it now seems unimaginable for cholera or a similar disease to be regarded in this way signifies not a lessened capacity to moralize about diseases but only a change in the kind of illnesses that are used didactically. Cholera was perhaps the last major epidemic disease fully qualifying for plague status for almost a century. (I mean cholera as a European and American, therefore a nineteenth-century, disease; until 1817 there had never been a cholera epidemic outside the Far East.) Influenza, which would seem more plague-like than any other epidemic in this century if loss of life were the main criterion, and which struck as suddenly as cholera and killed as quickly, usually in a few days, was never viewed metaphorically as a plague. Nor was a more recent epidemic, polio. One reason why plague notions were not invoked is that these epidemics did not have enough of the attributes perennially ascribed to plagues. (For instance, polio was construed as typically a disease of children—of the innocent.) The more important reason is that there has been a shift in the focus of the moralistic exploitation of illness. This shift, to diseases that can be interpreted as judgments on the individual, makes it harder to use epidemic disease as such. For a long time cancer was the illness that best fitted this secular culture's need to blame and punish and censor through the imagery of disease. Cancer was a disease of an individual, and understood as the result not of an action but rather of a failure to act (to be prudent, to exert proper self-control, or to be properly expressive). In the twentieth century it has become almost impossible to moralize about epidemics—except those which are transmitted sexually.

16   The persistence of the belief that illness reveals, and is a punishment for, moral laxity or turpitude can be seen in another way, by noting the persistence of descriptions of disorder or corruption as a disease. So indispensable has been the plague metaphor in bringing summary judgments about social crisis that its use hardly abated during the era when collective diseases were no longer treated so moralistically—the time between the influenza and encephalitis pandemics of the early and mid-1920s and the acknowledgment of a new, mysterious epidemic illness in the early 1980s—and when great infectious epidemics were so often

and confidently proclaimed a thing of the past. The plague metaphor was common in the 1930s as a synonym for social and psychic catastrophe. Evocations of plague of this type usually go with rant, with antiliberal attitudes: think of Artaud on theatre and plague, of Wilhelm Reich on "emotional plague." And such a generic "diagnosis" necessarily promotes antihistorical thinking. A theodicy as well as a demonology, it not only stipulates something emblematic of evil but makes this the bearer of a rough, terrible justice. In Karel Čapek's *The White Plague* (1937), the loathsome pestilence that has appeared in a state where fascism has come to power afflicts only those over the age of forty, those who could be held morally responsible.

17   Written on the eve of the Nazi takeover of Czechoslovakia, Čapek's allegorical play is something of an anomaly—the use of the plague metaphor to convey the menace of what is defined as barbaric by a mainstream European liberal. The play's mysterious, grisly malady is something like leprosy, a rapid, invariably fatal leprosy that is supposed to have come, of course, from Asia. But Čapek is not interested in identifying political evil with the incursion of the foreign. He scores his didactic points by focusing not on the disease itself but on the management of information about it by scientists, journalists, and politicians. The most famous specialist in the disease harangues a reporter ("The disease of the hour, you might say. A good five million have died of it to date, twenty million have it and at least three times as many are going about their business, blithely unaware of the marble-like, marble-sized spots on their bodies"); chides a fellow doctor for using the popular terms, "the white plague" and "Peking leprosy," instead of the scientific name, "the Cheng Syndrome"; fantasizes about how his clinic's work on identifying the new virus and finding a cure ("every clinic in the world has an intensive research program") will add to the prestige of science and win a Nobel Prize for its discoverer; revels in hyperbole when it is thought a cure has been found ("it was the most dangerous disease in all history, worse than the bubonic plague"); and outlines plans for sending those with symptoms to well-guarded detention camps ("Given that every carrier of the disease is a potential spreader of the disease, we *must* protect the uncontaminated from the contaminated. All sentimentality in this regard is fatal and therefore criminal"). However cartoonish Čapek's ironies may seem, they are a not improbable sketch of catastrophe (medical, ecological) as a

managed public event in modern mass society. And however conventionally he deploys the plague metaphor, as an agency of retribution (in the end the plague strikes down the dictator himself), Čapek's feel for public relations leads him to make explicit in the play the understanding of disease *as* a metaphor. The eminent doctor declares the accomplishments of science to be as nothing compared with the merits of the dictator, about to launch a war, "who has averted a far worse scourge: the scourge of anarchy, the leprosy of corruption, the epidemic of barbaric liberty, the plague of social disintegration fatally sapping the organism of our nation."

18   Camus's *The Plague,* which appeared a decade later, is a far less literal use of plague by another great European liberal, as subtle as Čapek's *The White Plague* is schematic. Camus's novel is not, as is sometimes said, a political allegory in which the outbreak of bubonic plague in a Mediterranean port city represents the Nazi occupation. This plague is not retributive. Camus is not protesting anything, not corruption or tyranny, not even mortality. The plague is no more or less than an exemplary event, the irruption of death that gives life its seriousness. His use of plague, more epitome than metaphor, is detached, stoic, aware—it is not about bringing judgment. But, as in Čapek's play, characters in Camus's novel declare how unthinkable it is to have a plague in the twentieth century . . . as if the belief that such a calamity could not happen, could not happen *anymore,* means that it must.

REFLECTIONS

Drawing parallels between AIDS and earlier "plagues," Susan Sontag speaks of metaphors that characterize such illnesses as "not only repulsive and retributive but collectively invasive." Explore the connotations of these adjectives and their possible effect on attitudes toward people who have AIDS. In current discussions of AIDS, what rumors have you encountered? Most U.S. newspapers did not reprint stories from Europe and Africa that the AIDS virus was developed in an Army–CIA lab in Maryland, even though they related other unlikely rumors of origin. What reasons might explain this omission? Can public reactions and proposed solutions to AIDS be explained in terms of the physical disease itself, or has AIDS become a metaphor for something else?

Acknowledgments